THE BOOK OF
POSITIVE
QUOTATIONS

SECOND EDITION

Compiled and Arranged
by John Cook

Edited by Steve Deger & Leslie Ann Gibson

Fairview Press
Minneapolis

Fairview Press is a division of Fairview Health Services, a community-focused health system, affiliated with the University of Minnesota, providing a complete range of services, from the prevention of illness and injury to care for the most complex medical conditions.

Library of Congress Cataloging-in-Publication Data

The book of positive quotations / compiled and arranged by John Cook ; edited by Steve Deger & Leslie Ann Gibson.—2nd ed.
    p. cm.
  Rev. ed. of: The Rubicon dictionary of positive, motivational, life-affirming & inspirational quotations.
  Includes index.
  ISBN 978-1-57749-169-9 (pbk. : alk. paper)
  1. Quotations, English. 2. Motivation (Psychology)—Quotations, maxims, etc.
3. Inspiration—Quotations, maxims, etc. I. Cook, John, 1939- II. Deger, Steve, 1966- III. Gibson, Leslie Ann, 1956- IV. Cook, John, 1939- Rubicon dictionary of positive, motivational, life-affirming & inspirational quotations.
  PN6081.R83 2007
  082—dc22

                        2007025696

Printed in the United States of America
First printing of second edition: October 2007
12 11 10 09   7 6 5 4 3

Cover design: Laurie Ingram

for Freddi, Blake, Brian, and Timmy

Contents

Introduction   *ix*

PART 1: PEACE OF MIND

Peace of Mind   2
Happiness   5
Acceptance   44
Forgiveness   59
Counting Our Blessings   67
The Grass Is Always Greener
    on the Other Side of the Fence   88
Helping Other People   100
Friendship   122
Our Higher Power, or God   153
Faith and Belief   161
Prayer   174
Self-Knowledge   214
Self-Acceptance   222
Self-Control   234
Self-Confidence   240
Self-Reliance   249
Simplicity   262

PART 2: LIVING ONE DAY AT A TIME

One Day   270
Yesterday: The Past   291
Today: The Present   301
This Moment   311

Mornings   *314*

Evenings   *320*

Tomorrow: The Future   *323*

Average, "Boring" Days   *328*

Difficult Days   *332*

PART 3: PREPARING FOR SUCCESS

Positive Thinking and Self-Fulfilling
    Prophesies and Actions   *340*

Enthusiasm   *364*

Hope   *372*

Visualization   *381*

Role Models   *385*

PART 4: KNOWING WHAT TO DO

Change   *390*

Decisions   *406*

Instincts   *417*

Doing What's Right for Us   *424*

Motivation   *440*

Realistic Expectations   *448*

Goals   *457*

PART 5: OVERCOMING NEGATIVES
AND UNCERTAINTIES

Fear   *476*

Worry   *494*

Doubts and Uncertainties   *501*

Security   *507*

Risks   *510*

Courage   *521*

Ignorance   *542*

Getting Going   *546*

PART 6: MAKING DREAMS COME TRUE

Success   *560*

Luck   *584*

Opportunity   *592*

Commitment   *597*

Concentration   *604*

Work   608

Perfection   619

Just Do the Footwork, Then Let It Go   623

Take One Step at a Time   631

Perseverance   639

Problems   655

Failures and Mistakes   659

The Advantages of Adversity   675

Reacting to Events   691

Self-Pity   701

Index   705

Introduction

There are many excellent collections of quotations. My hope is that this volume may prove a worthy companion to them, in two main ways.

First, in its size and scope. *The Book of Positive Quotations* is the largest collection of its kind, containing over 10,300 quotations on 62 subjects. And, within those subjects, the quotations are arranged according to 703 concepts. (Similar, if less comprehensive, collections include Frank S. Mead's *Encyclopedia of Religious Quotations,* Margaret Pepper's *The Harper Religious and Inspirational Quotation Companion,* and Albert M. Well, Jr.'s *Inspiring Quotations, Contemporary and Classical,* all of which are wonderful resources.)

Second, in its practicality and ease of use. Special steps have been taken to make this dictionary as friendly to users as possible.

To begin with, the quotations are arranged not just by individual subjects or concepts—such as "Acceptance" or "Self-Reliance"—but by specific aspects of, or approaches to, these concepts.

For example, the chapter "Acceptance" consists of sixteen sections, such as "Acceptance Isn't Resignation" (eleven quotes), "Tension, Trouble, and Adversity Are Normal Parts of Life" (twenty-three quotes), and "Paradox: Acceptance Can Lead to Change" (seven quotes). And "Self-Reliance" features eleven sections, such as "We Must Rely on What's Inside Us" (twenty-four quotes), "We're Responsible for Our Own Happiness" (thirty-two quotes), and "Accepting Responsibility for Our Errors and Mistakes" (fifteen quotes).

And, to provide readers with a wide selection of styles and tones, the collection includes many different ways of expressing each concept. Including many expressions of a concept lends that concept more credibility. Further, it shows how smart, sensitive men and women throughout history have agreed about certain basic approaches to life. They have expressed these ideas in very different ways, of course. But whether expressed in the language of the schools or the language of the streets, there must be truth in concepts that so many different people have believed in and lived by—and, in some cases, died for.

The Book of Positive Quotations is one of the few, if not the only, collection to include the same quotation in more than one category; this brings the total number of entries to more than 11,500. One reason for this approach is that, because of their subject matter, insight, or eloquence, many quotations and concepts virtually demand to appear in more than one category. (Does it not make sense to include the twenty-four quotations in the section entitled "Doing Our Duty and Pursuing Goals Leads to Happiness" in two chapters, "Goals" and "Happiness"? And shouldn't the thirty-nine quotations found in "Having Realistic Expectations of Ourselves" be included in the chapters on "Realistic Expectations" and "Self-Acceptance"?)

Equally important, however, making each chapter self-sufficient gives readers—quickly and easily, with minimal cross-checking of other chapters—the greatest range of quotations about a particular topic. (It's a shame to miss a wonderful quotation because it doesn't appear exactly where one is looking.)

• • •

Numerous questions and concerns about accuracy confront anyone who compiles quotations. Take, for example, differences in the spelling of sources' names. The same famous Russian novelist has had his name spelled "Dostoevski," "Dostoievski," and "Dostoyevsky."

The formality required to identify sources is another issue. The Spanish Jesuit writer Baltasar Gracian Y Morales, for example, is more commonly referred to as "Baltasar Gracian," or simply "Gracian." And some sources are almost universally referred to by only one name, usually in the interest of brevity, and because it would be difficult to confuse them with anyone else. "Crebillion," for example, is used for Prosper Jolyot de Crebillion, the French dramatic poet.

And, of course, through the years many exact quotations—and even more that are very similar—have been attributed to more than one source.

I have made every effort to present each quotation as accurately as possible, and to recognize and honor the appropriate source. In particularly demanding situations, the language and sources cited are those most often used by other compilers and editors. Where it was impossible to verify the accuracy or source of a quotation, I have included it anyway if I believed that the usefulness of the quotation outweighed the demands of scholarly rigor.

• • •

This book originated as a selection of life-affirming quotations I compiled for my nephews and niece for Christmas 1989.

Because I was concerned that one of them was too young for it, I wrote in a letter that accompanied the collection, "just put it away in a safe place until you're ready for it." To address the question of how someone would know they were "ready," I wrote:

"You'll be ready the first time things don't go the way you want them to, the first time you doubt your ability to do something, the first time you're tempted to quit or give up, the first time you actually fail at something.

"You'll be ready the first time you doubt a friend, or think you can't trust anyone.

"You'll be ready the first time you have to make an important decision, or choice.

"You'll be ready the first time you're afraid of something, or worried.

"You'll know when you're ready. When you are, these thoughts should give you the courage and confidence and spirit you need . . . and they'll remind you of the wonder and the joy of life, regardless of how dark things seem at the moment.

"I know they will. . . . They always have for me."

So, in addition to being a resource for researchers, writers, students, and professionals, I hope this collection will provide comfort and inspiration for the casual browser or reader.

PART I

Peace of Mind

Peace of Mind

WE ALL SEEK PEACE OF MIND

I take it that what all men are really after is some form of, perhaps only some formula of, peace.
—James Conrad

The mind is never right but when it is at peace within itself.
—Seneca

I am searching for that which every man seeks—peace and rest.
—Dante Alighieri

PRIMARY SOURCES OF PEACE OF MIND

It is a peaceful thing to be the one succeeding.
—Gertrude Stein

[In] back of tranquility lies always conquered unhappiness.
—David Grayson

Order your soul; reduce your wants; live in charity; associate in Christian community; obey the laws; trust in Providence.
—Saint Augustine

Thinking about interior peace destroys interior peace. The patient who constantly feels his pulse is not getting any better.
—Hubert van Zeller

To be glad of life, because it gives you the chance to love and to work and to play and to look up at the stars; to be satisfied with your possessions, but not contented with yourself until you have made the best of them; to despise nothing in the world except falsehood and meanness, and to fear nothing except cowardice; to be governed by your admirations rather than by your disgusts; to covet nothing that is your neighbor's except his kindness of heart and gentleness of manners; to think seldom of your enemies, often of your friends, and every day of Christ; and to spend as much time as you can, with body and with spirit, in God's out-of-doors—these are little guideposts on the footpath to peace.
—Henry Van Dyke

Forgiving those who hurt us is the key to personal peace.
—G. Weatherly

The first rule is to keep an untroubled spirit. The second is to look things in the face and know them for what they are. —Marcus Aurelius

It takes time, love, and support to find peace with the restless one.
—Deidra Sarault

The only peace, the only security, is in fulfillment. —Henry Miller

Peace of mind is that mental condition in which you have accepted the worst. —Lin Yutang

In truth, to attain to interior peace, one must be willing to pass through the contrary to peace.
—Swami Brahmananda

When at night you cannot sleep, talk to the Shepherd and stop counting sheep. —Anon.

WE MUST FIND PEACE WITHIN OURSELVES

When we are unable to find tranquility within ourselves, it is useless to seek it elsewhere.
—Francois de La Rochefoucauld

If you do not find peace in yourself, you will never find it anywhere else.
—Paula A. Bendry

If there is to be any peace it will come through being, not having.
—Henry Miller

Nowhere can man find a quieter or more untroubled retreat than in his own soul. —Marcus Aurelius

Peace does not dwell in outward things, but within the soul; we may preserve it in the midst of the bitterest pain, if our will remains firm and submissive. Peace in this life springs from acquiescence to, not in an exemption from, suffering.
—Francois de Fenelon

Nothing can bring you peace but yourself. —Ralph Waldo Emerson

PEACE AND A HIGHER POWER

In a world filled with causes for worry and anxiety . . . we need the peace of God standing guard over our hearts and minds.
—Jerry W. McCant

Peace is not the absence of conflict, but the presence of God no matter what the conflict. —Anon.

There may be those on earth who dress better or eat better, but those who enjoy the peace of God sleep better. —L. Thomas Holdcroft

This is a sane, wholesome, practical, working faith: That it is a man's business to do the will of God; second, that God himself takes on the care of that man; and third, that therefore that man ought never to be afraid of anything. —George MacDonald

When we believe that God is Father, we also believe that such a father's hand will never cause his child a needless tear. We may not understand life any better, but we will not resent life any longer. —William Barclay

The peace is won by accompanying
God into the battle.
—Eivind Josef Berggrav

GENERAL QUOTATIONS ABOUT PEACE OF MIND

I do not want the peace which passeth understanding, I want the understanding which bringeth peace.
—Helen Keller

It takes more distress and poison to
kill someone who has peace of mind
and loves life.
—Bernie S. Siegel, M.D.

She could not separate success from
peace of mind. The two must go
together.   —Daphne du Maurier

Happiness

The Importance of Happiness

When a man has lost all happiness, he's not alive. Call him a breathing corpse.   —Sophocles

Whether you are talking about education, career, or service, you are talking about life. And life must really have joy. It's supposed to be fun.
—Barbara Bush

Why is it that people who cannot show feeling presume that that is a strength and not a weakness?
—May Sarton

Happiness is the meaning and the purpose of life, the whole aim and end of human existence   —Aristotle

Happiness is the only sanction in life; where happiness fails, existence remains a mad and lamentable experiment.   —George Santayana

The pursuit of happiness ... is the greatest feat man has to accomplish.
—Robert Henri

Make us happy and you make us good.   —Robert Browning

A good laugh makes any interview, or any conversation, so much better.
—Barbara Walters

The joyfulness of a man prolongeth his days.   —Proverbs 10:27

I love myself when I am laughing.
—Zora Neale Hurston

Everyone, without exception, is searching for happiness.
—Blaise Pascal

Living Fully and Enjoying Life

I will not be just a tourist in the world of images, just watching images passing by which I cannot live in, make love to, possess as permanent sources of joy and ecstasy.
—Anaïs Nin

Celebrate the happiness that friends are always giving, make every day a holiday and celebrate just living!
—Amanda Bradley

Live all you can; it's a mistake not to.
It doesn't so much matter what you
do in particular, so long as you have
your life. If you haven't had that,
what have you had?   —Henry James

Is life worth living?
Aye, with the best of us,
Heights of us, depths of us—
Life is the test of us!
            —Corinne Roosevelt Robinson

The general rule is that people who
enjoy life also enjoy marriage.
                    —Phyllis Battelle

It is only by expressing all that is
inside that purer and purer streams
come.   —Brenda Ueland

Age does not protect you from love
but love to some extent protects you
from age.   —Jeanne Moreau

There is no cure for birth and death
save to enjoy the interval.
            —George Santayana

I don't want to get to the end of
my life and find that I lived just the
length of it. I want to have lived the
width of it as well.
            —Diane Ackerman

Men are made for happiness, and
anyone who is completely happy has
a right to say to himself: "I am doing
God's will on earth."
            —Anton Chekhov

To live is so startling it leaves little
time for anything else.
            —Emily Dickinson

Living well and beautifully and justly
are all one thing.   —Socrates

Without pleasure man would live like
a fool and soon die.
            —Pierre de Beaumarchais

Life has got to be lived—that's all
that there is to it.
            —Eleanor Roosevelt

All animals except man know that
the principle business of life is to
enjoy it.   —Samuel Butler

Everything holds its breath except
spring. She bursts through as strong
as ever.   —B.M. Bower

To live as fully, as completely as possible, to be happy . . . is the true aim
and end to life.   —Llewelyn Powers

This is life! It can harden and it can
exalt!   —Henrik Ibsen

All I can say about life is, Oh God,
enjoy it!   —Bob Newhart

It is in his pleasure that a man really
lives.   —Agnes Repplier

Happiness hates the timid!
            —Eugene O'Neill

I have smelt all the aromas there
are in the fragrant kitchen they call
Earth; and what we can enjoy in this
life, I surely have enjoyed just like a
lord!   —Heinrich Heine

Man is that he might have joy.
            —Joseph Smith

It is better to be happy for a moment
and be burned up with beauty than
to live a long time and be bored all
the while.   —Don Marquis

If you want to die happily, learn to live; if you would live happily, learn to die. —Celio Calcagnini

Happiness comes more from loving than being loved; and often when our affection seems wounded it is only our vanity bleeding. To love, and to be hurt often, and to love again—this is the brave and happy life.
—J.E. Buchrose

The true object of all human life is play. —G.K. Chesterton

The right to happiness is fundamental. —Anna Pavlova

LOVE AND HAPPINESS

Love lights more fires than hate extinguishes,
And men grow better as the world grows old. —Ella Wheeler Wilcox

The Eskimos had fifty-two names for snow because it was important to them; there ought to be as many for love. —Margaret Atwood

Not all of us have to possess earth-shaking talent. Just common sense and love will do. —Myrtle Auvil

The secret of a happy marriage is finding the right person. You know they're right if you love to be with them all of the time. —Julia Child

We can sometimes love what we do not understand, but it is impossible completely to understand what we do not love. —Anna Jameson

To serve thy generation, this thy fate: "Written in water," swiftly fades thy name;
But he who loves his kind does, first or late,
A work too great for fame.
—Mary Clemmer

Love and respect are the most important aspects of parenting, and of all relationships. —Jodie Foster

Perhaps the best function of parenthood is to teach the young creature to love with safety, so that it may be able to venture unafraid when later emotion comes; the thwarting of the instinct to love is the root of all sorrow and not sex only but divinity itself is insulted when it is repressed. To disapprove, to condemn—the human soul shrivels under barren righteousness. —Freya Stark

Love, I find, is like singing. Everybody can do enough to satisfy themselves, though it may not impress the neighbors as being very much. —Zora Neale Hurston

Love is the same as like except you feel sexier. —Judith Viorst

Love is the only thing we can carry with us when we go, and it makes the end so easy. —Louisa May Alcott

Love, by its very nature, is unworldly, and it is for this reason rather than its rarity that it is not only apolitical but anti-political, perhaps the most powerful of all anti-political human forces. —Hannah Arendt

I love, and the world is mine!
—Florence Earle Coates

When love is out of your life, you're
through in a way. Because while it
is there it's like a motor that's going,
you have such vitality to do things,
big things, because love is goosing
you all the time.   —Fanny Brice

A caress is better than a career.
                    —Elizabeth Marbury

I don't want to live—I want to love
first, and live incidentally.
                    —Zelda Fitzgerald

What is it that love does to a
woman? Without it, she only sleeps;
with it alone, she lives.   —Ouida

What a richly colored strong warm
coat is woven when love is the warp
and work is the woof.
                    —Marge Piercy

We cannot really love anybody with
whom we never laugh.
                    —Agnes Repplier

There is only one happiness in life, to
love and be loved.   —George Sand

When you come right down to it, the
secret of having it all is loving it all.
                    —Dr. Joyce Brothers

Where there is great love, there are
always wishes.   —Willa Cather

The cure for all ills and wrongs, the
cares, the sorrows and the crimes
of humanity, all lie in the one word
'love.' It is the divine vitality that
everywhere produces and restores
life.   —Lydia M. Child

To love is to receive a glimpse of
heaven.   —Karen Sunde

Love is a force more formidable than
any other. It is invisible—it cannot
be seen or measured, yet it is powerful enough to transform you in a
moment, and offer you more joy than
any material possession could.
                    —Barbara De Angelis

Love is the only effective counter to
death.   —Maureen Duffy

There are only two things that are
absolute realities, love and knowledge, and you can't escape them.
                    —Olive Schreiner

There is nothing ridiculous in love.
                    —Olive Schreiner

Our society allows people to be
absolutely neurotic and totally out of
touch with their feelings and everyone else's feelings, and yet be very
respectable.   —Ntozake Shange

From the moment we walk out the
door until we come back home our
sensibilities are so assaulted by the
world that we have to soak up as
much love as we can get, simply to
arm ourselves.   —Patty Duke

Infatuation is when you think that
he's as sexy as Robert Redford, as
smart as Henry Kissinger, as noble
as Ralph Nader, as funny as Woody
Allen, and as athletic as Jimmy
Conners. Love is when you realize
that he's as sexy as Woody Allen, as
smart as Jimmy Conners, as funny
as Ralph Nader, as athletic as Henry
Kissinger, and nothing like Robert
Redford—but you'll take him anyway.   —Judith Viorst

I was in love with the whole world
and all that lived in its rainy arms.
—Louise Erdrich

'Tis what I love determines how I love.
—George Eliot

WE HAVE A DUTY TO BE HAPPY

Not only is there a right to be happy,
there is a duty to be happy. So much
sadness exists in the world that we
are all under obligation to contribute
as much joy as lies within our powers. —John Sutherland Bonnell

There is no duty so much underrated
as the duty of being happy.
—Robert Louis Stevenson

Pleasure is the object, duty and the
goal of all rational creatures.
—Voltaire

THERE ARE DIFFERENT FORMS OF HAPPINESS FOR DIFFERENT PEOPLE

Different men seek . . . happiness
in different ways and by different
means. —Aristotle

What's joy to one is a nightmare to
the other. —Bertolt Brecht

People genuinely happy in their
choices seem less often tempted to
force them on other people than
those who feel martyred and broken
by their lives. —Jane Rule

Happiness . . . leads none of us by the
same route. —Charles Caleb Colton

Even the lowliest, provided he is
whole, can be happy, and in his own
way, perfect. —Johann von Goethe

Happiness, to some, is elation; to
others it is mere stagnation.
—Amy Lowell

No sooner is it a little calmer with
me than it is almost too calm, as
though I have the true feeling of
myself only when I am unbearably
unhappy —Franz Kafka

Your readiest desire is your path to
joy . . . even if it destroys you.
—Holbrook Jackson

All men have happiness as their
object: there are no exceptions.
However different the means they
employ, they aim at the same end.
—Blaise Pascal

We all live with the objective of being
happy; our lives are all different and
yet the same. —Anne Frank

The world is so full of a number of
things, I'm sure we should all be as
happy as kings.
—Robert Louis Stevenson

THE BEAUTY OF HAPPINESS

There is no cosmetic for beauty like
happiness.
—Lady Marguerite Blessington

Love is a great beautifier.
—Louisa May Alcott

Taking joy in life is a woman's best
cosmetic. —Rosalind Russell

Beauty is a radiance that originates from within and comes from inner security and strong character.
—Jane Seymour

BEWARE FALSE HAPPINESS

Real happiness is cheap enough, yet how dearly we pay for its counterfeit.
—Hosea Ballou

False happiness renders men stern and proud, and that happiness is never communicated. True happiness renders kind and sensible, and that happiness is always shared.
—Charles de Montesquieu

Don't mistake pleasures for happiness. They are a different breed of dog.
—Josh Billings

Mirth is better than fun, and happiness is better than mirth.
—William Blake

Amusement is the happiness of those who cannot think. —Alexander Pope

Happiness is a small and unworthy goal for something as big and fancy as a whole lifetime, and should be taken in small doses. —Russell Baker

False happiness is like false money; it passes for a long time as well as the true, and serves some ordinary occasions; but when it is brought to the touch, we find the lightness and alloy, and feel the loss. —Alexander Pope

There is more to life than just existing and having a pleasant time.
—J.C.F. von Schiller

The test of enjoyment is the remembrance which it leaves behind.
—Logan Pearsall Smith

WE'RE RESPONSIBLE FOR OUR OWN HAPPINESS

When I have been unhappy, I have heard an opera . . . and it seemed the shrieking of winds; when I am happy, a sparrow's chirp is delicious to me. But it is not the chirp that makes me happy, but I that make it sweet.
—John Ruskin

Happiness depends upon ourselves.
—Aristotle

The U.S. Constitution doesn't guarantee happiness, only the pursuit of it. Your have to catch up with it yourself. —Benjamin Franklin

Happiness belongs to those who are sufficient unto themselves. For all external sources of happiness and pleasure are, by their very nature, highly uncertain, precarious, ephemeral and subject to chance.
—Arthur Schopenhauer

Most folks are about as happy as they make up their minds to be.
—Abraham Lincoln

One is happy as a result of one's own efforts—once one knows the necessary ingredients of happiness—simple tastes, a certain degree of courage, self-denial to a point, love of work, and, above all, a clear conscience.
—George Sand

Nothing can bring you peace but yourself. —Ralph Waldo Emerson

Discontent is want of self-reliance; it is infirmity of will.
—Ralph Waldo Emerson

I'm happier. . . . I guess I made up my mind to be that way.
—Merle Haggard

The essence of philosophy is that a man should so live that his happiness shall depend as little as possible on external things.   —Epictetus

No one gives joy or sorrow. . . . We gather the consequences of our own deeds.   —Garuda Purana

Happiness, happiness . . . the flavor is with you—with you alone, and you can make it as intoxicating as you please.   —Joseph Conrad

Few are they who have never had the chance to achieve happiness . . . and fewer those who have taken that chance.   —André Maurois

To win one's joy through struggle is better than to yield to melancholy.
—André Gide

Life is a romantic business, but you have to make the romance.
—Oliver Wendell Holmes

To be obliged to beg our daily happiness from others bespeaks a more lamentable poverty than that of him who begs his daily bread.
—Charles Caleb Colton

Some pursue happiness, others create it.   —Anon.

Man is the artificer of his own happiness.   —Henry David Thoreau

The man who makes everything that leads to happiness depend upon himself, and not upon other men, has adopted the very best plan for living happily.   —Plato

It is not the level of prosperity that makes for happiness but the kinship of heart to heart and the way we look at the world. Both attitudes are within our power, so that a man is happy so long as he chooses to be happy, and no one can stop him.
—Aleksandr Solzhenitsyn

Happy is he that chastens himself.
—Anon.

How unhappy is he who cannot forgive himself.   —Publilius Syrus

WE CAN LEARN HOW TO BE HAPPY

There is always something left to love. And if you ain't learned that, you ain't learned nothing.
—Lorraine Hansbury

Like swimming, riding, writing or playing golf, happiness can be learned.   —Dr. Boris Sokoloff

Being happy is something you have to learn. I often surprise myself by saying, "Wow, this is it. I guess I'm happy. I've got a home that I love. A career that I love. I'm even feeling more and more at peace with myself." If there's something else to happiness, let me know. I'm ambitious for that, too.   —Harrison Ford

Learn how to feel joy.   —Seneca

Prescriptions for Total Happiness

Someone once asked me what I regarded as the three most important requirements for happiness. My answer was: "A feeling that you have been honest with yourself and those around you; a feeling that you have done the best you could both in your personal life and in your work; and the ability to love others."
　　　　　　　—Eleanor Roosevelt

Nine requisites for contented living: Health enough to make work a pleasure. Wealth enough to support your needs. Strength to battle with difficulties and overcome them. Grace enough to confess your sins and forsake them. Patience enough to toil until some good is accomplished. Charity enough to see some good in your neighbor. Love enough to move you to be useful and helpful to others. Faith enough to make real the things of God. Hope enough to remove all anxious fears concerning the future.　　—Johann von Goethe

Happiness comes of the capacity to feel deeply, to enjoy simply, to think freely, to risk life, to be needed.
　　　　　　　—Storm Jameson

Do not worry; eat three square meals a day; say your prayers; be courteous to your creditors; keep your digestion good; exercise; go slow and easy. Maybe there are other things your special case requires to make you happy; but, my friend, these I reckon will give you a good lift.
　　　　　　　—Abraham Lincoln

To love deeply in one direction makes us more loving in all others.
　　　　　　　—Anne-Sophie Swetchine

Have a variety of interests. . . . These interests relax the mind and lessen tension on the nervous system. People with many interests live, not only longest, but happiest.
　　　　　　　—George Matthew Allen

Build a little fence of trust
Around today;
Fill the space with loving work,
And therein stay.
　　　　　　　—Mary Frances Butts

This is wisdom: to love wine, beauty, and the heavenly spring. That's sufficient—the rest is worthless.
　　　　　　　—Theodore De Banville

If a man has important work, and enough leisure and income to enable him to do it properly, he is in possession of as much happiness as is good for any of the children of Adam.
　　　　　　　—R.H. Tawney

The secret of happiness . . . is to be in harmony with existence, to be always calm, always lucid, always willing "to be joined to the universe without being more conscious of it than an idiot," to let each wave of life wash us a little farther up the shore.
　　　　　　　—Cyril Connolly

Good friends, good books and a sleepy conscience: this is the ideal life.
　　　　　　　—Mark Twain

The grand essentials to happiness in this life are something to do, something to love and something to hope for.　　　　—Joseph Addison

The best philosophy is to do one's duties, to take the world as it comes, submit respectfully to one's lot, and bless the goodness that has given us so much happiness with it, whatever it is. —Horace Walpole

One is happy as a result of one's own efforts—once one knows the necessary ingredients of happiness—simple tastes, a certain degree of courage, self-denial to a point, love of work, and, above all, a clear conscience. —George Sand

In order to be utterly happy the only thing necessary is to refrain from comparing this moment with other moments in the past, which I often did not fully enjoy because I was comparing them with other moments of the future. —André Gide

From birth to age eighteen, a girl needs good parents. From eighteen to thirty-five, she needs good looks. From thirty-five to fifty-five, she needs a good personality. From fifty-five on, she needs good cash. —Sophie Tucker

To make a man happy, fill his hands with work, his heart with affection, his mind with purpose, his memory with useful knowledge, his future with hope, and his stomach with food. —Frederick E. Crane

For me, happiness came from prayer to a kindly God, faith in a kindly God, love for my fellow man, and doing the very best I could every day of my life. I had looked for happiness in fast living, but it was not there. I tried to find it in money, but it was not there, either. But when I placed myself in tune with what I believe to be fundamental truths of life, when I began to develop my limited ability, to rid my mind of all kinds of tangled thoughts and fill it with zeal and courage and love, when I gave myself a chance by treating myself decently and sensibly, I began to feel the stimulating, warm glow of happiness. —Edward Young

There are three ingredients in the good life: learning, earning and yearning. —Christopher Morley

Work and love—these are the basics. Without them there is neurosis. —Theodor Reik

If thou workest at that which is before thee . . . expecting nothing, fearing nothing, but satisfied with thy present activity according to Nature, and with heroic truth in every word and sound which thou utterest, thou wilt live happy. And there is no man who is able to prevent this. —Marcus Aurelius

Our greatest happiness does not depend on the condition of life in which chance has placed us, but is always the result of a good conscience, good health, occupation and freedom in all just pursuits. —Thomas Jefferson

I believe the recipe for happiness to be just enough money to pay the monthly bills you acquire, a little surplus to give you confidence, a little too much work each day, enthusiasm for your work, a substantial share of good health, a couple of real friends and a wife and children to share life's beauty with you. —J. Kenfield Morley

If we could learn how to balance rest against effort, calmness against strain, quiet against turmoil, we would assure ourselves of joy in living and psychological health for life.
—Josephine Rathbone

Five great enemies to peace inhabit us: avarice, ambition, envy, anger and pride. If those enemies were to be banished, we should infallibly enjoy perpetual peace.
—Ralph Waldo Emerson

True happiness . . . arises, in the first place, from the enjoyment of one's self, and in the next, from the friendship and conversation of a few select companions. —Joseph Addison

May you have warmth in your igloo, oil in your lamp, and peace in your heart. —Eskimo proverb

What can be added to the happiness of man who is in health, out of debt, and has a clear conscience?
—Adam Smith

To do the useful thing, to say the courageous thing, to contemplate the beautiful thing: that is enough for one man's life. —T.S. Eliot

Let your boat of life be light, packed only with what you need—a homely home and simple pleasures, one or two friends worth the name, someone to love and to love you, a cat, a dog, enough to eat and enough to wear, and a little more than enough to drink, for thirst is a dangerous thing.
—Jerome K. Jerome

To be glad of life, because it gives you the chance to love and to work and to play and to look up at the stars; to be satisfied with your possessions, but not contented with yourself until you have made the best of them; to despise nothing in the world except falsehood and meanness, and to fear nothing except cowardice; to be governed by your admirations rather than by your disgusts; to covet nothing that is your neighbor's except his kindness of heart and gentleness of manners; to think seldom of your enemies, often of your friends, and every day of Christ; and to spend as much time as you can, with body and with spirit, in God's out-of-doors— these are little guideposts on the footpath to peace. —Henry Van Dyke

Order your soul; reduce your wants; live in charity; associate in Christian community; obey the laws; trust in Providence. —Saint Augustine

Simplicity, clarity, singleness: these are the attributes that give our lives power and vividness and joy.
—Richard Halloway

To live content with small means; to seek elegance rather than luxury, and refinement rather than fashion; to be worthy, not respectable, and wealthy, not rich; to study hard, think quietly, talk gently, act frankly; to listen to the stars and birds, to babes and sages, with open heart; to bear on cheerfully, do all bravely, awaiting occasions, worry never; in a word to, like the spiritual, unbidden and unconscious, grow up through the common. —William Ellery Channing

The attributes of a great lady may still be found in the rule of the four S's: Sincerity, Simplicity, Sympathy, and Serenity. —Emily Post

Manifest plainness,
Embrace simplicity,
Reduce selfishness,
Have few desires. —Lao-tzu

Do you prefer that you be right, or that you be happy?
—*A Course in Miracles*

Happiness comes of the capacity to feel deeply, to enjoy simply, to think freely, to risk life, to be needed.
—Storm Jameson

Fear less, hope more; eat less, chew more; whine less, breathe more; talk less, say more; love more, and all good things will be yours.
—Swedish proverb

Practice easing your way along. Don't get het up or in a dither. Do your best; take it as it comes. You can handle anything if you think you can. Just keep your cool and your sense of humor. —Smiley Blanton

To live and let live, without clamor for distinction or recognition; to wait on divine Love; to write truth first on the tablet of one's own heart—this is the sanity and perfection of living, and my human ideal.
—Mary Baker Eddy

Do all the good you can,
By all the means you can,
In all the ways you can,
In all the places you can,
At all the times you can. —Anon.

Go placidly amid the noise and the haste, and remember what peace there may be in silence. As far as possible without surrender, be on good terms with all persons. Speak your truth quietly and clearly, and listen to others, even the dull and ignorant; they too have their story. . . . Be yourself. Especially do not feign affection. Neither be cynical about love; for in the face of all aridity and disenchantment it is as perennial as the grass. Take kindly the counsel of the years, gracefully surrendering the things of youth. Nurture strength of spirit to shield you in sudden misfortune. But do not distress yourself with imaginings. Many fears are born of fatigue and loneliness. Beyond a wholesome discipline, be gentle with yourself. You are a child of the universe no less than the trees and the stars; you have a right to be here. And whether or not it is clear to you, no doubt the universe is unfolding as it should. Therefore be at peace with God, whatever you conceive Him to be, and whatever your labours and aspirations, in the noisy confusion of life keep peace with your soul. With all its sham, drudgery and broken dreams, it is still a beautiful world.
—Max Ehrmann

Accept the pain, cherish the joys, resolve the regrets; then can come the best of benedictions—"If I had my life to live over, I'd do it all the same." —Joan McIntosh

The way of a superior man is threefold: Virtuous, he is free from anxieties; wise, he is free from perplexities; bold, he is free from fear.
—Confucius

The first rule is to keep an untroubled spirit. The second is to look things in the face and know them for what they are.   —Marcus Aurelius

Happiness Comes from Who and What We Are, and Our Inner Life

It is not easy to find happiness in ourselves, and it is not possible to find it elsewhere.   —Agnes Repplier

Joy is the feeling of grinning on the inside.   —Dr. Melba Colgrove

It is those who have a deep and real inner life who are best able to deal with the irritating details of outer life.
—Evelyn Underhill

To live happily is an inward power of the soul.   —Marcus Aurelius

The secret of staying young is to live honestly, eat slowly, and lie about your age.   —Lucille Ball

Virtue, like a dowerless beauty, has more admirers than followers.
—Lady Marguerite Blessington

We can build upon foundations anywhere, if they are well and truly laid.
—Ivy Compton-Burnett

Though language forms the preacher, 'Tis "good works" make the man.
—Eliza Cook

All times are beautiful for those who maintain joy within them; but there is no happy or favorable time for those with disconsolate or orphaned souls.
—Rosalia Castro

When you're in your nineties and looking back, it's not going to be how much money you made or how many awards you've won. It's really what did you stand for. Did you make a positive difference for people?
—Elizabeth Dole

For attractive lips, speak words of kindness.
For lovely eyes, seek out the good in people.
For a slim figure, share your food with the hungry.
For beautiful hair, let a child run his or her fingers through it once a day.
For poise, walk with the knowledge you'll never walk alone.
—Audrey Hepburn

What you become is what counts.
—Liz Smith

If an Arab in the desert were suddenly to discover a spring in his tent, and so would always be able to have water in abundance, how fortunate he would consider himself; so too, when a man who . . . is always turned toward the outside, thinking that his happiness lies outside him, finally turns inward and discovers that the source is within him.
—Søren Kierkegaard

Happiness is not in our circumstances, but in ourselves. It is not something we see, like a rainbow, or feel, like the heat of a fire. Happiness is something we are.
—John B. Sheerin

Seek not outside yourself, heaven is within.   —Mary Lou Cook

If we have not peace within ourselves, it is in vain to seek it from outward sources.
—Francois de La Rochefoucauld

Most true happiness comes from one's inner life, from the disposition of the mind and soul. Admittedly, a good inner life is difficult to achieve, especially in these trying times. It takes reflection and contemplation and self-discipline.   —W.L. Shirer

It's what you do that makes your soul, not the other way around.
—Barbara Kingsolver

The happiest people seem to be those who have no particular cause for being happy except that they are so.
—William Ralph Inge

I think the inner person is the most important. . . . I would like to see an invention that keeps the mind alert. That's what is important.
—Julia Child

I don't think that . . . one gets a flash of happiness once, and never again; it is there within you, and it will come as certainly as death.   —Isak Dinesen

There is no other solution to man's progress but the day's honest work, the day's honest decisions, the day's generous utterances, and the day's good deed.   —Clare Boothe Luce

You have much more power when you are working for the right thing than when you are working for the wrong thing.   —Peace Pilgrim

I am convinced that we must train not only the head, but the heart and hand as well.
—Madame Chiang Kai-Shek

Live virtuously, and you cannot die too soon, or live too long.
—Lady R. Russell

A happy life is one which is in accordance with its own nature.
—Marcus Annaeus Seneca

IF WE ARE OPEN TO HAPPINESS, IT WILL REVEAL ITSELF

People see God every day, they just don't recognize Him.   —Pearl Bailey

We hear voices in solitude, we never hear in the hurry and turmoil of life; we receive counsels and comforts we get under no other condition.
—Amelia Barr

We are new every day.
—Irene Claremont de Castillego

IT DOESN'T PAY TO SEEK HAPPINESS DIRECTLY

Happiness is not a possession to be prized, it is a quality of thought, a state of mind.   —Daphne du Maurier

Happiness is a butterfly which, when pursued, is always beyond our grasp, but, if you will sit down quietly, may alight upon you.
—Nathaniel Hawthorne

Happiness is something that comes into our lives through doors we don't even remember leaving open.
—Rose Wilder Lane

To seek after beauty as an end, is a wild goose chase, a will-o'-the-wisp, because it is to misunderstand the very nature of beauty, which is the normal condition of a thing being as it should be. —Ada Bethune

Perfect happiness is the absence of striving for happiness. —Chuang-tzu

This will be triumph! This will be happiness! Yea, that very thing, happiness, which I have been pursuing all my life, and have never yet overtaken. —Joanna Baillie

I don't sit around thinking that I'd like to have another husband; only another man would make me think that way. —Lauren Bacall

Pleasure is very seldom found where it is sought. Our brightest blazes are commonly kindled by unexpected sparks. —Samuel Johnson

A sure way to lose happiness, I found, is to want it at the expense of everything else. —Bette Davis

Those who seek happiness miss it, and those who discuss it, lack it.
—Holbrook Jackson

Inspiration never arrived when you were searching for it. —Lisa Alther

Nothing is more hopeless than a scheme of merriment.
—Samuel Johnson

Now and then it's good to pause in our pursuit of happiness and just be happy. —*The Cockle Bur*

Happiness is never stopping to think if you are. —Palmer Sondreal

It is the paradox of life that the way to miss pleasure is to seek it first. The very first condition of lasting happiness is that a life should be full of purpose, aiming at something outside self. —Hugh Black

If you pursue happiness you'll never find it. —C.P. Snow

Some of us might find happiness if we quit struggling so desperately for it. —William Feather

Seek not happiness too greedily, and be not fearful of unhappiness.
—Lao-tzu

The man of pleasure, by a vain attempt to be more happy than any man can be, is often more miserable than most men.
—Charles Caleb Colton

The bird of paradise alights only on the hand that does not grasp.
—John Berry

The only way to happiness is never to give happiness a thought.
—Elton Trueblood

Everyone chases after happiness, not noticing that happiness is at their heels. —Bertolt Brecht

Seek to do good, and you will find that happiness will run after you.
—James Freeman Clarke

Deliberately to pursue happiness is not the surest way of achieving it. Seek it for its own sake and I doubt whether you will find it.
—Robert J. McCracken

Happiness must not be sought for; when what disturbs passes away, happiness comes of itself.
—*The Gospel According to Zen*

Enjoyment is not a goal, it is a feeling that accompanies important ongoing activity.
—Paul Goodman

If only we'd stop trying to be happy we'd have a pretty good time.
—Edith Wharton

Most men pursue pleasure with such breathless haste that they hurry past it.
—Søren Kierkegaard

Happiness comes most to persons who seek it least, and think least about it. It is not an object to be sought, it is a state to be induced. It must follow and not lead. It must overtake you, and not you overtake it.
—John Burroughs

Happiness sneaks in through a door you didn't know you left open.
—John Barrymore

Happiness is like a cat. If you try to coax it or call it, it will avoid you. It will never come. But if you pay no attention to it and go about your business, you'll find it rubbing against your legs and jumping into your lap.
—William Bennett

One must never look for happiness: one meets it by the way.
—Isabelle Eberhardt

They seemed to come suddenly upon happiness as if they had surprised a butterfly in the winter woods.
—Edith Wharton

Happiness in this world, when it comes, comes incidentally. Make it the object of pursuit, and it leads us on a wild-goose chase, and is never attained. Follow some other object, and very possibly we may find that we have caught happiness without dreaming of it.
—Nathaniel Hawthorne

Happiness and beauty are by-products. Folly is the direct pursuit of happiness and beauty.
—George Bernard Shaw

It is the very pursuit of happiness that thwarts happiness.
—Viktor Frankel

If you ever find happiness by hunting for it, you will find it, as the old woman did her lost spectacles, safe on her nose all the time.
—Josh Billings

Happiness is not a goal, it is a by-product.
—Eleanor Roosevelt

Happiness is mostly a by-product of doing what makes us feel fulfilled.
—Dr. Benjamin Spock

Happiness is something you get as a by-product in the process of making something else.
—Aldous Huxley

Happiness is not a horse, you cannot harness it.
—Chinese proverb

TO BE HAPPY, WE MUST BE TRUE TO OURSELVES

The attainment of justice is the highest human endeavor.
—Florence Ellinwood Allen

Conscience, as I understand it, is the impulse to do the right thing because it is right, regardless of personal ends, and has nothing whatever to do with the ability to distinguish between right and wrong.
—Margaret Collier Graham

I cannot and will not cut my conscience to fit this year's fashions.
—Lillian Hellman

The principles we live by, in business and in social life, are the most important part of happiness.
—Harry Harrison

If you aren't good at loving yourself, you will have a difficult time loving anyone, since you'll resent the time and energy you give another person that you aren't even giving to yourself.
—Barbara De Angelis

Happiness is when what you think, what you say, and what you do are in harmony.
—Mahatma Gandhi

A good message will always find a messenger.
—Amelia Barr

It's no good saying one thing and doing another.
—Catherine Cookson

There can be no happiness if the things we believe in are different from the things we do.
—Freya Stark

Let how you live your life stand for something, no matter how small and incidental it may seem.
—Jodie Foster

Happy is the man who ventures boldly to defend what he holds dear.
—Ovid

It is necessary to the happiness of man that he be mentally faithful to himself.
—Thomas Paine

Happiness is that state of consciousness which proceeds from the achievement of one's values.
—Ayn Rand

It is the chiefest point of happiness that a man is willing to be what he is.
—Erasmus

Resolve to be thyself; and know that who finds himself, loses his misery.
—Matthew Arnold

There is only one history of any importance, and it is the history of what you once believed in, and the history of what you came to believe in.
—Kay Boyle

The needle of our conscience is as good a compass as any.
—Ruth Wolff

But what is happiness except the simple harmony between a man and the life he leads?
—Albert Camus

That kind of life is most happy which affords us most opportunities of gaining our own esteem.
—Samuel Johnson

KEEPING BUSY IS A KEY TO HAPPINESS

Happiness is not something you get, but something you do.
—Marcelene Cox

Happiness is action.
—David Thomas

I am enjoying to a full that period of reflection which is the happiest conclusion to a life of action.
—Willa Cather

Action may not always bring happiness, but there is no happiness without action. —William James

I want a busy life, a just mind, and a timely death. —Zora Neale Hurston

Happiness is often the result of being too busy to be miserable. —Anon.

Painting's not important. The important thing is keeping busy.
—Grandma Moses

To attain happiness in another world we need only to believe something; to secure it in this world, we must do something.
—Charlotte P. Gilman

To fill the hour, and leave no crevice . . . that is happiness.
—Ralph Waldo Emerson

If you observe a really happy man, you will find . . . that he is happy in the course of living life twenty-four crowded hours of each day.
—W. Beran Wolfe

I find my joy of living in the fierce and ruthless battles of life.
—August Strindberg

Happiness is an expression of the soul in considered actions.
—Aristotle

We must be doing something to be happy. —William Hazlitt

Happiness lies in the fulfillment of the spirit through the body.
—Cyril Connolly

We must not seek happiness in peace, but in conflict. —Paul Claudel

Happiness walks on busy feet.
—Kitte Turmell

Our actions are the springs of our happiness or misery. —Philip Skelton

The formula for complete happiness is to be very busy.
—A. Edward Newton

The busiest man is the happiest man.
—Sir Theodore Martin

To be busy is man's only happiness.
—Mark Twain

The only way to avoid being miserable is not to have enough leisure to wonder whether you are happy or not. —George Bernard Shaw

The happiest people are those who are too busy to notice whether they are or not. —William Feather

Accepting the Inevitable Is Critical to Our Happiness

In great moments life seems neither right nor wrong, but something greater: it seems inevitable.
—Margaret Sherwood

Happiness . . . can exist only in acceptance.
—Denis De Rougemont

Knowledge of what is possible is the beginning of happiness.
—George Santayana

There is only one way to happiness, and that is to cease worrying about things which are beyond the power of our will.
—Epictetus

Happiness comes from . . . some curious adjustment to life.
—Hugh Walpole

Happy is he who learns to bear what he cannot change!
—J.C.F. von Schiller

The secret of happiness is not in doing what one likes, but in liking what one has to do.
—Sir James M. Barrie

He is happy whose circumstances suit his temper; but he is more excellent who suits his temper to any circumstances.
—David Hume

Happiness is experienced when your life gives you what you are willing to accept.
—Ken Keyes, Jr.

Peace of mind is that mental condition in which you have accepted the worst.
—Lin Yutang

Life is not always what one wants it to be, but to make the best of it as it is, is the only way of being happy.
—Jennie Jerome Churchill

We deem those happy who from the experience of life have learned to bear its ills, without being overcome by them.
—Juvenal

Doing Our Duty and Pursuing Goals Leads to Happiness

This is true joy of life—being used for a purpose that is recognized by yourself as a mighty one . . . instead of being a feverish, selfish little clod of ailments and grievances, complaining that the world will not devote itself to making you happy.
—George Bernard Shaw

Never mind your happiness; do your duty.
—Will Durant

Human happiness and moral duty are inseparably connected.
—George Washington

When we . . . devote ourselves to the strict and unsparing performance of duty, then happiness comes of itself.
—Wilhelm von Humboldt

Seek happiness for its own sake, and you will not find it; seek for duty, and happiness will follow as the shadow comes with the sunshine.
—Tyron Edwards

True happiness . . . is not attained through self-gratification, but through fidelity to a worthy purpose.
—Helen Keller

The only true happiness comes from squandering ourselves for a purpose.
—William Cowper

Happiness is the natural flower of duty.
—Phillips Brooks

The happiest excitement in life is to be convinced that one is fighting for all one is worth on behalf of some clearly seen and deeply felt good.
—Ruth Benedict

True happiness, we are told, consists in getting out of one's self. But the point is not only to get out, you must stay out. And to stay out, you must have some absorbing errand.
—Henry James

The secret of living is to find . . . the pivot of a concept on which you can make your stand. —Luigi Pirandello

A man's happiness: to do the things proper to man. —Marcus Aurelius

Happy [is] the man who knows his duties!
—Christian Furchtegott Gellert

The only ones among you who will be really happy are those who will have sought and found how to serve.
—Albert Schweitzer

He who never sacrificed a present to a future good, or a personal to a general one, can speak of happiness only as the blind speak of color.
—Horace Mann

There is no happiness except in the realization that we have accomplished something. —Henry Ford

I believe half the unhappiness in life comes from people being afraid to go straight at things. —William J. Locke

The full-grown modern human being . . . is conscious of touching the highest pinnacle of fulfillment . . . when he is consumed in the service of an idea, in the conquest of the goal pursued.
—R. Briffault

Happiness is essentially a state of going somewhere, wholeheartedly, one-directionally, without regret or reservation. —William H. Sheldon

Happiness is the overcoming of not unknown obstacles toward a known goal. —L. Ron Hubbard

Give a man health and a course to steer, and he'll never stop to trouble about whether he's happy or not.
—George Bernard Shaw

Having a goal is a state of happiness.
—E.J. Bartek

Happiness lies in the joy of achievement and the thrill of creative effort.
—Franklin Delano Roosevelt

Without duty, life is soft and boneless. —Joseph Joubert

TRUE HAPPINESS COMES FROM LITTLE THINGS—NOT BIG ONES

It is always the simple that produces the marvelous. —Amelia Barr

Happiness consists not in having much, but in being content with little.
—Lady Marguerite Blessington

23

Man is meant for happiness and this happiness is in him, in the satisfaction of the daily needs of his existence.
—Leo Tolstoy

I have had more than half a century of such happiness. A great deal of worry and sorrow, too, but never a worry or a sorrow that was not offset by a purple iris, a lark, a bluebird, or a dewy morning glory.
—Mary McLeod Bethune

A multitude of small delights constitute happiness. —Charles Baudelaire

The happiness of life is made up of minute fractions—the little, soon-forgotten charities of a kiss or smile, a kind look, a heart-felt compliment, and the countless infinitesimals of pleasurable and genial feeling.
—Samuel Taylor Coleridge

For me it is sufficient to have a corner by my hearth, a book and a friend, and a nap undisturbed by creditors or grief.
—Fernandez de Andrada

A happy life is made up of little things . . . a gift sent, a letter written, a call made, a recommendation given, transportation provided, a cake made, a book lent, a check sent.
—Carol Holmes

Yes, there is a Nirvanah; it is in leading your sheep to a green pasture, and in putting your child to sleep, and in writing the last line of your poem.
—Kahlil Gibran

First health, then wealth, then pleasure, and do not owe anything to anybody. —Catherine the Great

I know well that happiness is in little things. —John Ruskin

Sooner or later we all discover that the important moments in life are not the advertised ones, not the birthdays, the graduations, the weddings, not the great goals achieved. The real milestones are less prepossessing. They come to the door of memory.
—Susan B. Anthony

There is nothing like staying at home for real comfort. —Jane Austen

I don't think about whether people will remember me or not. I've been an okay person. I've learned a lot. I've taught people a thing or two. That's what's important.
—Julia Child

What would life be without art? Science prolongs life. To consist of what—eating, drinking, and sleeping? What is the good of living longer if it is only a matter of satisfying the requirements that sustain life? All this is nothing without the charm of art.
—Sarah Bernhardt

It is by studying little things that we attain the great knowledge of having as little misery and as much happiness as possible. —Samuel Johnson

The happiest people I have known in this world have been the Saints—and, after these, the men and women who get immediate and conscious enjoyment from little things.
—Hugh Walpole

The little things are infinitely the most important.
—Sir Arthur Conan Doyle

We women ought to put first things first. Why should we mind if men have their faces on the money, as long as we get our hands on it?
—Ivy Baker Priest

Eating is not merely a material pleasure. Eating well gives a spectacular joy to life and contributes immensely to goodwill and happy companionship. It is of great importance to the morale.   —Elsa Schiapirelli

I am beginning to learn that it is the sweet, simple things of life which are the real ones after all.
—Laura Ingalls Wilder

Happiness consists more in small conveniences or pleasures that occur every day, than in great pieces of good fortune that happen but seldom.   —Benjamin Franklin

The happiness of most people is not ruined by great catastrophes or fatal errors, but by the repetition of slowly destructive little things.
—Ernest Dimnet

Enjoy the little things, for one day you may look back and realize they were the big things.   —Robert Brault

Why not learn to enjoy the little things—there are so many of them.
—Anon.

Anyone who's a great kisser I'm always interested in.   —Cher

Moderation. Small helpings. Sample a little bit of everything. These are the secrets of happiness and good health.
—Julia Child

The best things are nearest: breath in your nostrils, light in your eyes, flowers at your feet, duties at your hand, the path of God just before you. Then do not grasp at the stars, but do life's plain, common work as it comes, certain that daily duties and daily bread are the sweetest things of life.   —Robert Louis Stevenson

In violent and chaotic times such as these, our only chance for survival lies in creating our own little islands of sanity and order, in making little havens of our homes.
—Susan Kaufman

Small kindnesses, small courtesies, small considerations, habitually practiced in our social intercourse, give a greater charm to the character than the display of great talents and accomplishments. —Mary Ann Kelty

For most of life, nothing wonderful happens. If you don't enjoy getting up and working and finishing your work and sitting down to a meal with family or friends, then the chances are you're not going to be very happy. If someone bases his happiness or unhappiness on major events like a great new job, huge amounts of money, a flawlessly happy marriage or a trip to Paris, that person isn't going to be happy much of the time. If, on the other hand, happiness depends on a good breakfast, flowers in the yard, a drink or a nap, then we are more likely to live with quite a bit of happiness.
—Andy Rooney

The mere sense of living is joy enough.
—Emily Dickinson

Our Happiness Increases When We Help Other People

The true way to soften one's troubles is to solace those of others.
—Madame De Maintenon

To complain that life has no joys while there is a single creature whom we can relieve by our bounty, assist by our counsels or enliven by our presence, is . . . just as rational as to die of thirst with the cup in our hands.
—Thomas Fitzosborne

We learn the inner secret of happiness when we learn to direct our inner drives, our interest, and our attention to something besides ourselves.
—Ethel Percy Andrus

Little deeds of kindness, little words of love,
Help to make earth happy like the heaven up above.
—Julia A. Fletcher Carney

In about the same degree as you are helpful, you will be happy.
—Karl Reiland

Hire the best. Pay them fairly. Communicate frequently. Provide challenges and rewards. Believe in them. Get out of their way and they'll knock your socks off.
—Mary Ann Allison

Treat a horse like a woman and a woman like a horse. And they'll both win for you.   —Elizabeth Arden

Invest in the human soul. Who knows, it might be a diamond in the rough.
—Mary McLeod Bethune

All the goodness, beauty, and perfection of a human being belong to the one who knows how to recognize these qualities.   —Georgette Leblanc

You cannot always have happiness, but you can always give happiness.
—Anon.

The nice thing about teamwork is that you always have others on your side.   —Margaret Carty

No one can sincerely try to help another without helping himself.
—Charles Dudley Warner

Happiness is a by-product of helping others.   —Denny Miller

The most exquisite pleasure is giving pleasure to others.
—Jean de La Bruyère

No man can live happily who regards himself alone, who turns everything to his own advantage. Thou must live for another if thou wishest to live for thyself.   —Marcus Annaeus Seneca

Scatter seeds of kindness everywhere you go;
Scatter bits of courtesy—watch them grow and grow.
Gather buds of friendship, keep them till full-blown;
You will find more happiness than you have ever known.
—Amy R. Raabe

If all our happiness is bound up entirely in our personal circumstances, it is difficult not to demand of life more than it has to give.
—Bertrand Russell

No man is more cheated than the selfish man.   —Henry Ward Beecher

The habit of being uniformly considerate toward others will bring increased happiness to you.
—Grenville Kleiser

If you have not often felt the joy of doing a kind act, you have neglected much, and most of all yourself.
—A. Neilen

We cannot hold a torch to light another's path without brightening our own.   —Ben Sweetland

Life becomes harder for us when we live for others, but it also becomes richer and happier.
—Albert Schweitzer

Happiness . . . consists in giving, and in serving others.
—Henry Drummond

Pleasure is a reciprocal; no one feels it who does not at the same time give it. To be pleased, one must please.
—Lord Chesterfield

He that despiseth his neighbor sinneth; but he that hath mercy on the poor, happy is he.   —Proverbs 14:21

Instinct teaches us to look for happiness outside ourselves.
—Blaise Pascal

A bit of fragrance always clings to the hand that gives you roses.
—Chinese proverb

When you dig another out of their troubles, you find a place to bury your own.   —Anon.

One thing I know: the only ones among you who will be really happy are those who will have sought and found how to serve.
—Albert Schweitzer

Caring about others, running the risk of feeling, and leaving an impact on people, brings happiness.
—Rabbi Harold Kushner

The entire sum of existence is the magic of being needed by just one person.   —Vi Putnam

One of the things I keep learning is that the secret of being happy is doing things for other people.
—Dick Gregory

Make one person happy each day and in forty years you will have made 14,600 human beings happy for a little time, at least.   —Charley Willey

The most satisfying thing in life is to have been able to give a large part of oneself to others.
—Pierre Teilhard de Chardin

To be kind to all, to like many and love a few, to be needed and wanted by those we love, is certainly the nearest we can come to happiness.
—Mary Roberts Rinehart

Seldom can the heart be lonely,
If it seeks a lonelier still;
Self-forgetting, seeking only
Emptier cups of love to fill.
—Frances Ridley Havergal

The older you get, the more you realize that kindness is synonymous with happiness.   —Lionel Barrymore

There is no happiness in having or in getting, but only in giving.
—Henry Drummond

Make happy those who are near, and those who are far will come.
—Chinese proverb

True happiness consists in making others happy. —Hindu proverb

HAPPINESS IS MEANT TO BE SHARED

All who would win joy, must share it; happiness was born a twin.
—Lord Byron

Happiness is not so much in having as sharing. We make a living by what we get, but we make a life by what we give. —Norman MacEwan

Happiness quite unshared can scarcely be called happiness; it has no taste.
—Charlotte Brontë

Happiness is a sunbeam which may pass through a thousand bosoms without losing a particle of its original ray; nay, when it strikes on a kindred heart, like the converged light on a mirror, it reflects itself with redoubled brightness. It is not perfected till it is shared. —Jane Porter

The tourist may complain of other tourists, but he would be lost without them. —Agnes Repplier

Unshared joy is an unlighted candle.
—Spanish proverb

A joy that's shared is a joy made double. —English proverb

The human heart, at whatever age, opens only to the heart that opens in return. —Maria Edgeworth

Happiness is the cheapest thing in the world . . . when we buy it for someone else. —Paul Flemming

To get the full value of a joy you must have somebody to divide it with.
—Mark Twain

We have no more right to consume happiness without producing it than to consume wealth without producing it. —George Bernard Shaw

When someone does something good, applaud! You will make two people happy. —Samuel Goldwyn

Happiness is not perfected until it is shared. —Jane Porter

Happiness . . . is achieved only by making others happy.
—Stuart Cloete

OUR THOUGHTS DETERMINE OUR HAPPINESS

High above hate I dwell,
O storms! Farewell.
—Louise Imogen Guiney

The happiness of your life depends upon the quality of your thoughts.
—Marcus Aurelius

I am happy and content because I think I am. —Alain-Rene Lesage

All happiness is in the mind.
—Anon.

Happiness is not a matter of events; it depends upon the tides of the mind.
—Alice Meynell

A happy life consists in tranquility of mind. —Cicero

The real winners in life are the people who look at every situation with an expectation that they can make it work or make it better.
—Barbara Pletcher

A man's as miserable as he thinks he is.
—Marcus Annaeus Seneca

The happiest person is the person who thinks the most interesting thoughts. —William Lyon Phelps

Unhappiness indicates wrong thinking, just as ill health indicates a bad regimen. —Paul Bourge

He is happy that knoweth not himself to be otherwise. —Thomas Fuller

The greater part of our happiness or misery depends on our dispositions, and not our circumstances.
—Martha Washington

Happiness does not depend on outward things, but on the way we see them. —Leo Tolstoy

Happiness will never be any greater than the idea we have of it.
—Maurice Maeterlinck

We are never so happy or so unhappy as we think.
—Francois de La Rochefoucauld

Misery is almost always the result of thinking. —Joseph Joubert

A great obstacle to happiness is to expect too much happiness.
—Bernard de Fontenelle

It isn't our position, but our disposition, that makes us happy. —Anon.

A man's happiness or unhappiness depends as much on his temperament as on his destiny.
—Francois de La Rochefoucauld

WORK IS ESSENTIAL TO MOST PEOPLE'S HAPPINESS

I went back to being an amateur, in the sense of somebody who loves what she is doing. If a professional loses the love of work, routine sets in, and that's the death of work and life.
—Ada Bethune

The high prize of life, the crowning fortune of man, is to be born with a bias to some pursuit which finds him in employment and happiness.
—Ralph Waldo Emerson

The medals don't mean anything and the glory doesn't last. It's all about your happiness. The rewards are going to come, but my happiness is just loving the sport and having fun performing. —Jackie Joyner-Kersee

The road to happiness lies in two simple principles: find what it is that interests you and that you can do well, and when you find it put your whole soul into it—every bit of energy and ambition and natural ability you have. —John D. Rockefeller III

They are happy men whose natures sort with their vocations.
—Francis Bacon

Happiness consists in the full employment of our faculties in some pursuit.
—Harriet Martineau

The happy people are those who are producing something.
—William Ralph Inge

Congenial labor is the secret of happiness. —Arthur Christopher Benson

To find out what one is fitted to do, and to secure an opportunity to do it, is the key to happiness.
—John Dewey

If I were to suggest a general rule for happiness, I would say "Work a little harder; Work a little longer; Work!"
—Frederick H. Ecker

To make a man happy, fill his hands with work. —Frederick E. Crane

Work is the true elixir of life. The busiest man is the happiest man.
—Sir Theodore Martin

Happiness . . . loves to see men work. She loves sweat, weariness, self-sacrifice. She will not be found in the palaces, but lurking in cornfields and factories, and hovering over littered desks. —David Grayson

Every job has drudgery. . . . The first secret of happiness is the recognition of this fundamental fact.
—M.C. McIntosh

All happiness depends on courage and work. —Honore de Balzac

There is work that is work and there is play that is play; there is play that is work and work that is play. And in only one of these lie happiness.
—Gelett Burgess

Employment . . . is so essential to human happiness that indolence is justly considered the mother of misery.
—Robert Burton

Happiness comes only when we push our brains and hearts to the farthest reaches of which we are capable.
—Leo C. Rosten

A man is relieved and gay when he has put his heart into his work and done his best.
—Ralph Waldo Emerson

There is certainly no greater happiness than to be able to look back on a life usefully and virtuously employed, to trace our own progress in existence by such tokens as excite neither shame nor sorrow.
—Samuel Johnson

Continuity of purpose is one of the most essential ingredients of happiness in the long run, and for most men this comes chiefly through their work.
—Bertrand Russell

Blessed is he who has found his work; let him ask no other blessedness. He has a work, a life-purpose. . . . Get your happiness out of your work or you will never know what real happiness is. . . . Even in the meanest sorts of labor, the whole soul of a man is composed into a kind of real harmony the instant he sets himself to work.
—Thomas Carlyle

Man is happy only as he finds a work
worth doing—and does it well.
—E. Merrill Root

Life without absorbing occupation
is hell.   —Elbert Hubbard

Few persons realize how much of their
happiness, such as it is, is dependent
upon their work.   —John Burroughs

Joy is the will which labours, which
overcomes obstacles, which knows
triumph.   —William Butler Yeats

Get happiness out of your work
or you may never know what
happiness is.   —Elbert Hubbard

When men are rightly occupied, their
amusement grows out of their work,
as the color-petals out of a fruitful
flower.   —John Ruskin

HOME AND FAMILY LIFE CAN BE A PRIME SOURCE OF HAPPINESS

Parents, however old they and we may
grow to be, serve among other things
to shield us from a sense of our doom.
As long as they are around, we can
avoid the fact of our mortality; we can
still be innocent children.
—Jane Howard

You leave home to seek your fortune
and, when you get it, you go home
and share it with your family.
—Anita Baker

Sometimes the strength of mother-
hood is greater than natural laws.
—Barbara Kingsolver

He is happiest, be he king or peasant,
who finds peace in his home.
—Johann von Goethe

My child looked at me and I looked
back at him in the delivery room, and
I realized that out of a sea of infinite
possibilities it had come down to
this: a specific person, born on the
hottest day of the year, conceived on
a Christmas Eve, made by his father
and me miraculously from scratch.
—Anna Quindlen

And when our baby stirs and struggles to be born it compels humility:
what we began is now its own.
—Anne Ridler

What families have in common the
world around is that they are the
place where people learn who they
are and how to be that way.
—Jean Illsley Clarke

Family life is the source of the greatest human happiness.
—Robert J. Havighurst

Where thou art, that is home.
—Emily Dickinson

Parenting, at its best, comes as
naturally as laughter. It is automatic,
involuntary, unconditional love.
—Sally James

If this world affords true happiness,
it is to be found in a home where
love and confidence increase with
the years, where the necessities of life
come without severe strain, where
luxuries enter only after their cost has
been carefully considered.
—A. Edward Newton

There are four things a child needs: plenty of love, nourishing food, regular sleep, and lots of soap and water. —Ivy Baker Priest

Family jokes, though rightly cursed by strangers, are the bond that keeps most families alive. —Stella Benson

The secret of a happy marriage is finding the right person. You know they're right if you love to be with them all of the time. —Julia Child

An easygoing husband is the one indispensable comfort of life. —Ouida

My father got me strong and straight
    and slim
And I give thanks to him.
My mother bore me glad and sound
    and sweet,
I kiss her feet.
            —Marguerite Wilkinson

A house is not a home unless it contains food and fire for the mind as well as the body. —Margaret Fuller

No music is so pleasant to my ears as that word—father. —Lydia M. Child

He who leaves his house in search of happiness pursues a shadow. —Anon.

If solid happiness we prize,
within our breast this jewel lies,
And they are fools who roam;
the world has nothing to bestow,
From our own selves our bliss must
    flow,
And that dear hut—our home.
            —Nathaniel Cotton

Happiness grows at our own firesides, and is not to be picked in strangers' gardens. —Douglas Jerrold

A mother's arms are more comforting than anyone else's. —Diana, Princess of Wales

He who would be happy should stay at home. —Greek proverb

Every family is a "normal" family— no matter whether it has one parent, two, or no children at all. —Shere Hite

Within our family there was no such thing as a person who did not matter. Second cousins thrice removed mattered. —Shirley Abbott

All the wealth of the world cannot be compared with the happiness of living together happily united. —Saint Mary Margaret d'Youville

There's a thread that binds all of us together, pull one end of the thread, the strain is felt all down the line. —Rosamond Marshall

Love from one being to another can only be that two solitudes come nearer, recognize and protect and comfort each other. —Han Suyin

HAPPINESS AND HEALTH

Happiness is good health and a bad memory. —Ingrid Bergman

Where there is laughter there is always more health than sickness. —Phyllis Bottome

In the Orient people believed that the basis of all disease was unhappiness. Thus to make a patient happy again was to restore him to health.
—Donald Law

Loving, like prayer, is a power as well as a process. It's curative. It is creative. —Zona Gale

The simple truth is that happy people generally don't get sick.
—Bernie S. Siegel, M.D.

Laughter is by definition healthy.
—Doris Lessing

Laughter is the best medicine.
—Anon.

Love is the great miracle cure. Loving ourselves works miracles in our lives.
—Louise L. Hay

Happiness is not being pained in body nor troubled in mind.
—Thomas Jefferson

One of the quickest ways to become exhausted is by suppressing your feelings. —Sue Patton Thoele

Being asked one day what was the surest way of remaining happy in this world, the Emperor Sigismund of Germany replied: "Only do in health what you have promised to do when you were sick." —Anon.

HAPPINESS AND MONEY AND SUCCESS

The best things in life aren't things.
—Ann Landers

Money, or even power, can never yield happiness unless it be accompanied by the goodwill of others.
—B.C. Forbes

To fulfill a dream, to be allowed to sweat over lonely labor, to be given the chance to create, is the meat and potatoes of life. The money is the gravy.
—Bette Davis

I have now reigned above fifty years in victory or peace, beloved by my subjects, dreaded by my enemies, respected by my allies. Riches and honors, power and pleasure, have awaited my call, nor does any earthly blessing seem to have been wanting . . . I have diligently numbered the days of pure and genuine happiness that have fallen to my lot; they amount to fourteen.
—Abd al-Rahman

I don't want to make money. I just want to be wonderful.
—Marilyn Monroe

It's pretty hard to tell what does bring happiness; poverty and wealth have both failed. —Kin Hubbard

It is neither wealth nor splendor, but tranquility and occupation, which give happiness. —Thomas Jefferson

Joy has nothing to do with material things, or with a man's outward circumstance . . . a man living in the lap of luxury can be wretched, and a man in the depths of poverty can overflow with joy.
—William Barclay

Hope costs nothing. —Colette

Getting what you go after is success; but liking it while you are getting it is happiness. —Bertha Damon

Success can also cause misery. The trick is not to be surprised when you discover it doesn't bring you all the happiness and answers you thought it would. —Prince

No social system will bring us happiness, health and prosperity unless it is inspired by something greater than materialism. —Clement R. Attlee

The essence of philosophy is that a man should so live that his happiness shall depend as little as possible on external things. —Epictetus

Happiness depends, as Nature shows, less on exterior things than most suppose. —William Cowper

There are two things to aim at in life: first, to get what you want; and, after that, to enjoy it. Only the wisest of mankind achieve the second.
—Logan Pearsall Smith

In this world there are only two tragedies. One is not getting what one wants, and the other is getting it.
—Oscar Wilde

A life of frustration is inevitable for any coach whose main enjoyment is winning. —Chuck Noll

Money is human happiness in the abstract; he, then, who is no longer capable of enjoying human happiness in the concrete devotes himself utterly to money. —Arthur Schopenhauer

Happiness seems to require a modicum of external prosperity.
—Aristotle

Those who have easy, cheerful attitudes tend to be happier than those with less pleasant temperaments regardless of money, "making it" or success. —Dr. Joyce Brothers

Money, or even power, can never yield happiness unless it be accompanied by the goodwill of others.
—B.C. Forbes

The secret of happiness is to admire without desiring. —F.H. Bradley

Few rich men own their own property. Their property owns them.
—Robert G. Ingersoll

HAPPINESS AND WISDOM

We can be wise from goodness and good from wisdom.
—Marie von Ebner-Eschenbach

She knew what all smart women knew: Laughter made you live better and longer. —Gail Parent

An Arabian proverb says there are four sorts of men:
He who knows not and knows not he knows not: he is a fool—shun him.
He who knows not and knows he knows not: he is simple—teach him.
He who knows and knows not he knows: he is asleep—wake him.
He who knows and knows he knows: he is wise—follow him.
—Lady Isabel Burton

34

There are only two things that are absolute realities, love and knowledge, and you can't escape them.
—Olive Schreiner

Wisdom is the most important part of happiness. —Sophocles

Knowledge is the prime need of the hour. —Mary McLeod Bethune

Better be happy than wise. —Anon.

Be happy. It's one way of being wise.
—Colette

With happiness comes intelligence to the heart. —Chinese proverb

Joy is the holy fire that keeps our purpose warm and our intelligence aglow.
—Helen Keller

Our happiness depends on wisdom all the way. —Sophocles

The genius of happiness is still so rare, is indeed on the whole the rarest genius. To possess it means to approach life with the humility of a beggar, but to treat it with the proud generosity of a prince; to bring to its totality the deep understanding of a great poet and to each of its moments the abandonment and ingenuousness of a child. —Ellen Key

What matters most is that we learn from living. —Doris Lessing

Best trust the happy moments. . . .
The days that make us happy make us wise. —John Masefield

OTHER SOURCES OF HAPPINESS

It is an aspect of all happiness to suppose that we deserve it.
—Joseph Joubert

A garden isn't meant to be useful. It's for joy. —Rumer Godden

A reasonable man needs only to practice moderation to find happiness.
—Johann von Goethe

To forget oneself is to be happy.
—Robert Louis Stevenson

Happiness is a resultant of the relative strengths of positive and negative feelings rather than an absolute amount of one or the other.
—Norman Bradburn

The first recipe for happiness is: Avoid too lengthy meditations on the past.
—André Maurois

Man needs, for his happiness, not only the enjoyment of this or that, but hope and enterprise and change.
—Bertrand Russell

Happy is the man who can do only one thing; in doing it, he fulfills his destiny. —Joseph Joubert

And may I live the remainder of my life . . . for myself; may there be plenty of books and many years' store of the fruits of the earth! —Horace

Behold, we count them happy which endure. —James 5:11

The will of man is his happiness.
—J.C.F. von Schiller

Happiness to a dog is what lies on the other side of the door.
—Charlton Ogburn, Jr.

The supreme happiness of life is the conviction that we are loved.
—Victor Hugo

The happiness of a man in this life does not consist in the absence, but in the mastery, of his passions.
—Alfred, Lord Tennyson

It is comparison that makes men happy or miserable. —Anon.

Let him that would be happy for a day, go to the barber; for a week, marry a wife; for a month, buy him a new horse; for a year, build him a new house; for all his lifetime, be an honest man. —Anon.

Who will present pleasure refrain, shall in time to come the more pleasure obtain. —Anon.

A happy life must be to a great extent a quiet life, for it is only in an atmosphere of quiet that true joy can live.
—Bertrand Russell

It is in virtue that happiness consists, for virtue is the state of mind which tends to make the whole of life harmonious. —Zeno

To live we must conquer incessantly, we must have the courage to be happy.
—Henri Frederic Amiel

Happiness has many roots, but none more important than security.
—E.R. Stettinius, Jr.

No man can be merry unless he is serious. —G.K. Chesterton

Happy [is] the man who has learned the cause of things and has put under his feet all fear, inexorable fate, and the noisy strife of the hell of greed.
—Virgil

The happiest man is he who learns from nature the lesson of worship.
—Ralph Waldo Emerson

It takes great wit and interest and energy to be happy. The pursuit of happiness is a great activity. One must be open and alive. It is the greatest feat man has to accomplish.
—Robert Henri

Talk happiness. The world is sad enough without your woe. No path is wholly rough. —Ella Wheeler Wilcox

We act as though comfort and luxury were the chief requirements of life, when all that we need to make us really happy is something to be enthusiastic about. —Charles Kingsley

What we call happiness is what we do not know. —Anatole France

For the happiest life, days should be rigorously planned, nights left open to chance. —Mignon McLaughlin

Happy people plan actions, they don't plan results. —Dennis Wholey

If you want others to be happy, practice compassion. If you want to be happy, practice compassion.
—The Dalai Lama

It is neither wealth nor splendor, but tranquility and occupation, which give happiness.   —Thomas Jefferson

The best way for a person to have happy thoughts is to count his blessings and not his cash.   —Anon.

All happiness depends on a leisurely breakfast.   —John Gunther

Happy is he who still loves something he loved in the nursery: He has not been broken in two by time; he is not two men, but one, and he has saved not only his soul, but his life.
   —G.K. Chesterton

To be happy means to be free, not from pain or fear, but from care or anxiety.   —W.H. Auden

The Sources of Our Happiness Change

The art of living does not consist in preserving and clinging to a particular mode of happiness, but in allowing happiness to change its form without being disappointed by the change; happiness, like a child, must be allowed to grow up.
   —Charles L. Morgan

Just as a cautious businessman avoids investing all his capital in one concern, so wisdom would probably admonish us also not to anticipate all our happiness from one quarter alone.   —Sigmund Freud

Growth itself contains the germ of happiness.   —Pearl S. Buck

When one door of happiness closes, another opens; but often we look so long at the closed door that we do not see the one which has been opened for us.   —Helen Keller

We live in an ascending scale when we live happily, one thing leading to another in an endless series.
   —Robert Louis Stevenson

Happiness Is a Journey

Happiness is not a station to arrive at, but a manner of traveling.
   —Margaret Lee Runbeck

Everyone only goes around the track once in life, and if you don't enjoy that trip, it's pretty pathetic.
   —Gary Rogers

I believe that a worthwhile life is defined by a kind of spiritual journey and a sense of obligation.
   —Hillary Rodham Clinton

The really happy man is one who can enjoy the scenery on a detour.
   —Anon.

Happiness is to be found along the way, not at the end of the road, for then the journey is over and it is too late.   —Robert R. Updegraff

Spiritual life is like a moving sidewalk. Whether you go with it or spend your whole life running against it, you're still going to be taken along.
   —Bernadette Roberts

Happiness is a way station between too little and too much.
   —Channing Pollock

DON'T EXAMINE HAPPINESS ... JUST ENJOY IT

Enjoy your happiness while you have it, and while you have it do not too closely scrutinize its foundation.
—Joseph Farrall

Suspicion of happiness is in our blood.
—E.V. Lucas

Love is like a beautiful flower which I may not touch, but whose fragrance makes the garden a place of delight just the same.
—Helen Keller

My advice to you is not to inquire why or whither, but just enjoy your ice cream while it's on your plate.
—Thornton Wilder

Most people ask for happiness on condition. Happiness can only be felt if you don't set any condition.
—Arthur Rubinstein

Ask yourself whether you are happy, and you will cease to be so.
—John Stuart Mill

Best to live lightly, unthinkingly.
—Sophocles

The secret of being miserable is to have leisure to bother about whether you are happy or not.
—George Bernard Shaw

To describe happiness is to diminish it.
—Stendhal

My life has no purpose, no direction, no aim, no meaning, and yet I'm happy. I can't figure it out. What am I doing right?
—Charles M. Schulz

DON'T POSTPONE HAPPINESS

People who postpone happiness are like children who try chasing rainbows in an effort to find the pot of gold at the rainbow's end. . . . Your life will never be fulfilled until you are happy here and now.
—Ken Keyes, Jr.

Happiness consists of living each day as if it were the first day of your honeymoon and the last day of your vacation.
—Anon.

For a long time it seemed to me that real life was about to begin, but there was always some obstacle in the way. Something had to be got through first, some unfinished business; time still to be served, a debt to be paid. Then life would begin. At last it dawned on me that these obstacles were my life.
—Bette Howland

Every minute your mouth is turned down you lose sixty seconds of happiness.
—Tom Walsh

Why not seize the pleasure at once? How often is happiness destroyed by preparation, foolish preparation?
—Jane Austen

Enjoy yourself. These are the "good old days" you're going to miss in the years ahead.
—Anon.

UNHAPPINESS

Is anyone in all the world safe from unhappiness?
—Sophocles

Unhappiness is the ultimate form of self-indulgence.
—Tom Robbins

Unhappiness indicates wrong thinking, just as ill health indicates a bad regimen.   .—Paul Bourge

Unhappiness is best defined as the difference between our talents and our expectations.
                    —Dr. Edward De Bono

By becoming more unhappy, we sometimes learn how to be less so.
                    —Madame Swetchine

Men are the only animals that devote themselves, day in and day out, to making one another unhappy.
                    —H.L. Mencken

The worst sin—perhaps the only sin—passion can commit is to be joyless.
                    —Dorothy L. Sayers

Those who are unhappy have no need for anything in this world but people capable of giving them their attention.   —Simone Weil

Irresolution on the schemes of life which offer themselves to our choice, and inconstancy in pursuing them, are the greatest causes of all unhappiness.   —Joseph Addison

O Lord! Unhappy is the man whom man can make unhappy.
                    —Ralph Waldo Emerson

Unhappiness is not knowing what we want and killing ourselves to get it.
                    —Don Herold

All mankind's unhappiness derives from one thing: his inability to know how to remain in repose in one room.
                    —Blaise Pascal

None think the great unhappy but the great.   —Edward Young

The primary cause of unhappiness in the world today is . . . lack of faith.
                    —Carl Jung

Sadness is a state of sin.
                    —André Gide

Fate often puts all the material for happiness and prosperity into a man's hands just to see how miserable he can make himself with them.
                    —Don Marquis

Whenever one finds oneself inclined to bitterness, it is a sign of emotional failure.   —Bertrand Russell

CHEERFULNESS

Steady as a clock, busy as a bee, and cheerful as a cricket.
                    —Martha Washington

I'm not happy, I'm cheerful. There's a difference. A happy woman has no cares at all. A cheerful woman has cares but has learned how to deal with them.   —Beverly Sills

The clearest sign of wisdom is continued cheerfulness.
                    —Michel de Montaigne

Cheerfulness is as natural to the heart of man in strong health as color to his cheek; and wherever there is habitual gloom there must be either bad air, unwholesome food, improperly severe labor or erring habits of life.
                    —John Ruskin

Cheerfulness prepares a glorious mind for all the noblest acts.
—Elizabeth Ann Seton

A man of gladness seldom falls into madness.　　　　—Anon.

Always let them think of you as singing and dancing.　—Anita Brookner

Developing a cheerful disposition can permit an atmosphere wherein one's spirit can be nurtured and encouraged to blossom and bear fruit. Being pessimistic and negative about our experiences will not enhance the quality of our lives.
—Barbara W. Winder

Gaiety alone, as it were, is the hard cash of happiness; everything else is just a promissory note.
—Arthur Schopenhauer

Happiness Can Come From Unhappiness

No pleasure without pain.　—Anon.

But here's what I've learned in this war, in this country, in this city: to love the miracle of having been born.
—Oriana Fallaci

Pleasure is not pleasant unless it cost dear.　　　　　　　　—Anon.

The sweetest joy, the wildest woe is love.　　　　　—Pearl Bailey

So they speak soothingly about progress and the greatest possible happiness, forgetting that happiness is itself poisoned if the measure of suffering has not been fulfilled.　—Carl Jung

Life begins on the other side of despair.
—Jean-Paul Sartre

Sadness and gladness succeed each other.　　　　　　—Anon.

The Happiness of Not Needing Happiness

The greatest happiness you can have is knowing that you do not necessarily require happiness.
—William Saroyan

Happiness comes fleetingly now and then to those who have learned to do without it, and to them only.
—Don Marquis

Unquestionably, it is possible to do without happiness; it is done involuntarily by nineteen-twentieths of mankind.　　　　—John Stuart Mill

Perfect happiness is the absence of striving for happiness.　—Chuang-tzu

We're Happier than We Think

Happiness lies in the consciousness we have of it.　　　—George Sand

There are men who are happy without knowing it.　　　—Vauvenargues

Eden is that old-fashioned house we dwell in every day without suspecting our abode until we drive away.
—Emily Dickinson

Why is it that so many people are afraid to admit that they are happy?
—William Lyon Phelps

Man's real life is happy, chiefly because he is ever expecting that it soon will be so.   —Edgar Allan Poe

What a wonderful life I've had! I only wish I'd realized it sooner.
                                    —Colette

Those who are the most happy appear to know it the least; happiness is something that for the most part seems to mainly consist in not knowing it.
                        —Dr. Joyce Brothers

We are all happy, if we only knew it.
                        —Fyodor Dostoyevsky

Eden is that old-fashioned house we dwell in every day Without suspecting our abode until we drive away.
                        —Emily Dickinson

Happiness is a Swedish sunset; it is there for all, but most of us look the other way and lose it. —Mark Twain

Paradise is exactly like where you are right now . . . only much, much better.
                        —Laurie Anderson

Time is compressed like the fist I close on my knee . . . I hold inside it the clues and solutions and the power for what I must do now.
                        —Margaret Atwood

The major job was getting people to understand that they had something within their power that they could use.
                        —Ella Baker

Each moment in time we have it all, even when we think we don't.
                        —Melody Beattie

Happiness always looks small while you hold it in your hands, but let it go, and you learn at once how big and precious it is.   —Maxim Gorky

HAPPINESS AND CONTENTMENT

Contentment is not happiness. An oyster may be contented. Happiness is compounded of richer elements.
                        —Christian Bovee

Everything has its wonders, even darkness and silence, and I learn, whatever state I may be in, therein to be content.
                        —Helen Keller

The world is full of people looking for spectacular happiness while they snub contentment.   —Doug Larson

Happiness is a rare plant that seldom takes root on earth—few ever enjoyed it, except for a brief period; the search after it is rarely rewarded by the discovery, but there is an admirable substitute for it . . . a contented spirit.
                        —Lady Marguerite Blessington

If all were gentle and contented as sheep, all would be as feeble and helpless.   —John Lancaster Spalding

GENERAL QUOTATIONS ABOUT HAPPINESS

The world of those who are happy is different from the world of those who are not. —Ludwig Wittgenstein

My heart is like a singing bird.
                        —Christina Georgina Tossetti

I don't think being an athlete is unfeminine. I think of it as a kind of grace. —Jackie Joyner-Kersee

If happiness truly consisted in physical ease and freedom from care, then the happiest individual . . . would be, I think, an American cow. —William Lyon Phelps

My happiness is not the means to any end. It is the end. It is its own goal. It is its own purpose. —Ayn Rand

When unhappy, one doubts everything; when happy, one doubts nothing. —Joseph Roux

The more the heart is sated with joy, the more it becomes insatiable. —Gabrielle Roy

There is a courage of happiness as well as a courage of sorrow. —Maurice Maeterlinck

The truth is, laughter always sounds more perfect than weeping. Laughter flows in a violent riff and is effortlessly melodic. Weeping is often fought, choked, half strangled, or surrendered to with humiliation. —Anne Rice

No man is happy unless he believes he is. —Publilius Syrus

Who is the happiest of men? He who values the merits of others, And in their pleasure takes joy, even as though t'were his own. —Johann von Goethe

Only man clogs his happiness with care, destroying what is, with thoughts of what may be. —John Dryden

If you obey all the rules you miss all the fun. —Katharine Hepburn

We never enjoy perfect happiness; our most fortunate successes are mingled with sadness; some anxieties always perplex the reality of our satisfaction. —Pierre Corneille

Happiness is not the end of life; character is. —Henry Ward Beecher

Human life is basically a comedy. Even its tragedies often seem comic to the spectator, and not infrequently they actually have comic touches to the victim. Happiness probably consists largely in the capacity to detect and relish them. —H.L. Mencken

We may fail of our happiness, strive we ever so bravely; but we are less likely to fail if we measure with judgement our chances and our capabilities. —Agnes Repplier

We always have enough to be happy if we are enjoying what we do have— and not worrying about what we don't have. .—Ken Keyes, Jr.

That sanguine expectation of happiness which is happiness itself. —Jane Austen

A great obstacle to happiness is to expect too much happiness. —Bernard de Fontenelle

If you always do what interests you, at least one person is pleased. —Katharine Hepburn

Suffering is not a prerequisite for happiness. —Judy Tatelbaum

He is happy that knoweth not himself
to be otherwise.   —Thomas Fuller

That man is happiest who lives from
day to day and asks no more, garnering the simple goodness of a life.
                              —Euripides

Change is an easy panacea. It takes
character to stay in one place and be
happy there.
                —Elizabeth Clarke Dunn

Such is the state of life that none
are happy but by the anticipation of
change. The change itself is nothing;
when we have made it the next wish
is to change again.
                        —Samuel Johnson

Life delights in life.   —William Blake

I look at what I have not and think
myself unhappy; others look at what
I have and think me happy.
                              —Joseph Roux

Part of the happiness of life consists
not in fighting battles, but in avoiding them. A masterly retreat is in
itself a victory.
                      —Norman Vincent Peale

Acceptance

ACCEPTANCE ISN'T RESIGNATION

Some people confuse acceptance with apathy, but there's all the difference in the world. Apathy fails to distinguish between what can and what cannot be helped; acceptance makes that distinction. Apathy paralyzes the will-to-action; acceptance frees it by relieving it of impossible burdens.
—Arthur Gordon

Acceptance says, "True, this is my situation at the moment. I'll look unblinkingly at the reality of it. But I'll also open my hands to accept willingly whatever a loving Father sends me."   —Catharine Marshall

It's not a very big step from contentment to complacency.
—Simone de Beauvoir

The minute you settle for less than you deserve, you get even less than you settled for.   —Maureen Dowd

"Good enough never is" has become the motto of this company.
—Debbi Fields

God, grant me the serenity to accept the things I cannot change, the courage to change the things I can, and the wisdom to know the difference.
—Reinhold Niebuhr

We must accept finite disappointment, but we must never lose infinite hope.
—Martin Luther King, Jr.

Acceptance is not submission; it is acknowledgement of the facts of a situation. Then deciding what you're going to do about it.
—Kathleen Casey Theisen

Self-complacency is fatal to progress.
—Margaret Elizabeth Sangster

You have to take it as it happens, but you should try to make it happen the way you want to take it.
—Old German proverb

Never deny a diagnosis, but do deny the negative verdict that may go with it.   —Norman Cousins

TENSION, TROUBLE, AND ADVERSITY ARE NORMAL PARTS OF LIFE

All that is necessary is to accept the impossible, do without the indispensable, and bear the intolerable.
—Kathleen Norris

The happy and efficient people in this world are those who accept trouble as a normal detail of human life and resolve to capitalize it when it comes along.   —H. Bertram Lewis

For those who live neither with religious consolations about death nor with a sense of death (or of anything else) as natural, death is the obscene mystery, the ultimate affront, the thing that cannot be controlled. It can only be denied.   —Susan Sontag

Who except the gods can live without any pain?   —Aeschylus

Misfortune comes to all men.
—Chinese proverb

The real world is not easy to live in. It is rough; it is slippery. Without the most clear-eyed adjustments we fall and get crushed.   —Clarence Day

Life has no smooth road for any of us; and in the bracing atmosphere of a high aim the very roughness stimulates the climber to steadier steps 'til the legend, "over steep ways to the stars," fulfills self.
—W. C. Doane

Maturity is achieved when a person accepts life as full of tension.
—Joshua L. Liebman

Yet man is born unto trouble, as the sparks fly upward.   —Job 5:7

Into each life some rain must fall, some days must be dark and dreary.
—Henry Wadsworth Longfellow

There is no man in this world without some manner of tribulation or anguish, though he be king or pope.
—Thomas à Kempis

There is no armor against fate; death lays his icy hands on kings.
—James Shirley

There is no easy path leading out of life, and few are the easy ones that lie within it.   —Walter Savage Landor

A man shares his days with hunger, thirst, and cold, with the good times and the bad, and the first part of being a man is to understand that.
—Louis L'Amour

It is arrogance to expect that life will always be music. . . . Harmony, like a following breeze at sea, is the exception. In a world where most things wind up broken or lost, our lot is to tack and tune.   .—Harvey Oxenhorn

One cannot get through life without pain. . . . What we can do is choose how to use the pain life presents to us.
—Bernie S. Siegel, M.D.

The mass of men lead lives of quiet desperation. —Henry David Thoreau

If you have arthritis, calmly say, I was always complaining about the ruts in the road until I realized that the ruts are the road.   —Anon.

"Okay, I have arthritis, and this is the way arthritis is." Take pain as it comes and you can better master it.
—Charles Clifford Peale

It is right it should be so,
Man was made for joy and woe;
And when this we rightly know,
Through the world we safely go.
—William Blake

Anyone who proposes to do good must not expect people to roll stones out of his way, but must accept his lot calmly, even if they roll a few more upon it.   —Albert Schweitzer

Free man is by necessity insecure; thinking man by necessity uncertain.
—Erich Fromm

You have come into a hard world. I know of only one easy place in it, and that is the grave.
—Henry Ward Beecher

ACCEPTANCE AND NECESSITY

Against necessity, against its strength, no one can fight and win.
—Aeschylus

A wise man never refuses anything to necessity.   —Publilius Syrus

When necessity speaks, it demands.
—Russian proverb

How base a thing it is when a man will struggle with necessity! We have to die.   —Euripides

ACCEPTING THIS WORLD

Whatever is—is best.
—Ella Wheeler Wilcox

Anything in life that we don't accept will simply make trouble for us until we make peace with it.
—Shakti Gawain

The reasonable man adapts himself to the world; the unreasonable one persists in trying to adapt the world to himself.   —George Bernard Shaw

Much sheer effort goes into avoiding the truth; left to itself, it sweeps in like the tide.   —Fay Weldon

We win half the battle when we make up our minds to take the world as we find it, including the thorns.
—Orison Swett Marden

A man must live in the world and make the best of it, such as it is.
—Michel de Montaigne

There are some people that you cannot change, you must either swallow them whole or leave them alone.
—Margot Asquith

The world is not to be put in order, the world is order incarnate. It is for us to put ourselves in unison with this order.   —Henry Miller

God asks no man whether he will accept life. This is not the choice. You must take it. The only question is how.   —Henry Ward Beecher

There is no cure for birth or death save to enjoy the interval.
—George Santayana

No man can have society upon his own terms.
—Ralph Waldo Emerson

The most popular persons are those who take the world as it is, who find the least fault.
—Charles Dudley Warner

GOING WITH THE FLOW

If you bear the cross unwillingly, you make it a burden, and load yourself more heavily; but you must bear it.
—Thomas à Kempis

There are two ways of meeting difficulties: you alter the difficulties, or you alter yourself to meet them.
—Phyllis Bottome

I find that it is not the circumstances in which we are placed, but the spirit in which we face them, that constitutes our comfort.
—Elizabeth T. King

It is almost more important how a person takes his fate than what it is.
—Wilhelm von Humboldt

The individual who is best prepared for any occupation is the one . . . able to adapt himself to any situation.
—Mortimer Smith

To act with common sense, according to the moment, is the best wisdom; and the best philosophy is to do one's duties, to take the world as it comes, submit respectfully to one's lot, and bless the goodness that has given us so much happiness with it, whatever it is.
—Horace Walpole

The art of life lies in a constant readjustment to our surroundings.
—Okakura Kakuzo

To repel one's cross is to make it heavier.   —Henri Frederic Amiel

Ask not that events should happen as you will, but let your will be that events should happen as they do, and you shall have peace.   —Epictetus

The survival of the fittest is the ageless law of nature, but the fittest are rarely the strong. The fittest are those endowed with the qualifications for adaptation, the ability to accept the inevitable and conform to the unavoidable, to harmonize with existing or changing conditions.
—Dave E. Smalley

The ideal man bears the accidents of life with dignity and grace, making the best of circumstances.
—Aristotle

He is happy whose circumstances suit his temper; but he is more excellent who can suit his temper to any circumstances.   —David Hume

Life is 10 percent what you make it, and 90 percent how you take it.
—Irving Berlin

A mountain man tries to live with the country instead of against it.
—Louis L'Amour

Vex not thy spirit at the course of things; they heed not thy vexation. How ludicrous and outlandish is astonishment at anything that may happen in life.   —Marcus Aurelius

If you can't fight, and you can't flee, flow. —Robert Eliot

Today I know that I cannot control the ocean tides. I can only go with the flow. . . . When I struggle and try to organize the Atlantic to my specifications, I sink. If I flail and thrash and growl and grumble, I go under. But if I let go and float, I am borne aloft. —Marie Stilkind

One learns to adapt to the land in which one lives. —Louis L'Amour

She had believed the land was her enemy, and she struggled against it, but you could not make war against a land any more than you could against the sea. One had to learn to live with it, to belong to it, to fit into its seasons and its ways.
—Louis L'Amour

Flow with whatever may happen and let your mind be free. Stay centered by accepting whatever you are doing. This is the ultimate. —Chuang-tzu

When you have got an elephant by the hind legs and he is trying to run away, it is best to let him run.
—Abraham Lincoln

Learn to drink the cup of life as it comes. —Agnes Turnbull

Arrange whatever pieces come your way. —Virginia Woolf

Everything in life that we really accept undergoes a change. So suffering must become love. That is the mystery.
—Katherine Mansfield

You can't fight the desert . . . you have to ride with it.
—Louis L'Amour

All I can do is play the game the way the cards fall.
—James A. Michener

Don't be sad, don't be angry, if life deceives you! Submit to your grief; your time for joy will come, believe me. —Aleksandr Pushkin

When we see ourselves in a situation which must be endured and gone through, it is best to meet it with firmness, and accommodate everything to it in the best way practicable. This lessens the evil, while fretting and fuming only increase your own torments.
—Thomas Jefferson

Always fall in with what you're asked to accept. . . . My aim in life has always been to hold my own with whatever's going. Not against: with.
—Robert Frost

There is no quality of human nature so nearly royal as the ability to yield gracefully. —Charles Conrad

The best thing we can do is to make wherever we're lost look as much like home as we can. —Christopher Fry

Make a virtue of necessity.
—Geoffrey Chaucer

Cooperation is doing with a smile what you have to do anyhow.
—Anon.

We must make the best of those ills which cannot be avoided.
—Alexander Hamilton

For so must it be, and help me do
my part.   —A Tibetan master

ADAPTING TO NEW CONDITIONS

There are no conditions to which a
man cannot become accustomed.
                    —Leo Tolstoy

A private railroad car is not an
acquired taste. One takes to it immediately.   —Eleanor R. Belmont

Man adapts himself to everything, to
the best and the worst.
            —José Ortega y Gasset

Being unready and ill-equipped is
what you have to expect in life. It is
the universal predicament. It is your
lot as a human being to lack what
it takes. Circumstances are seldom
right. You never have the capacities,
the strength, the wisdom, the virtue
you ought to have. You must always
do with less than you need in a situation vastly different from what you
would have chosen as appropriate for
your special endowments.
              —Charlton Ogburn, Jr.

In the face of an obstacle which is
impossible to overcome, stubbornness
is stupid.   —Simone de Beauvoir

Very few live by choice. Every man
is placed in his present condition
by causes which acted without his
foresight, and with which he did not
always willingly cooperate; and therefore you will rarely meet one who
does not think the lot of his neighbor
better than his own.
                —Samuel Johnson

To exist is to adapt, and if one could
not adapt, one died and made room
for those who could.
                —Louis L'Amour

ACCEPTING THE SPREAD BETWEEN WISHES AND REALITIES

Happy the man who early learns
the wide chasm that lies between his
wishes and his powers.
              —Johann von Goethe

Real life is, to most men . . . a perpetual compromise between the ideal
and the possible.   —Bertrand Russell

People are lucky and unlucky . . .
according to the ratio between what
they get and what they have been led
to expect.   —Samuel Butler

He who cannot do what he wants
must make do with what he can.
                    —Terence

What has always made a hell on
earth has been that man has tried to
make it his heaven.
              —Friedrich Holderlin

Good is not good, where better is
expected.   —Thomas Fuller

Nobody has things just as he would
like them. The thing to do is to make
a success with what material I have.
It is a sheer waste of time and soul-
power to imagine what I would do
if things were different. They are not
different.   —Dr. Frank Crane

We must like what we have when we
don't have what we like.
                —Bussy-Rabutin

Better is the enemy of the good.
—Voltaire

If you aspire to the highest place, it is no disgrace to stop at the second, or even the third, place.   —Cicero

Genius does what it must, talent does what it can.
—Edward Bulwer-Lytton

Nature is what you may do. There is much you may not do.
—Ralph Waldo Emerson

Results are what you expect; consequences are what you get.   —Anon.

To expect life to be tailored to our specifications is to invite frustration.
—Anon.

The resistance to the unpleasant situation is the root of suffering.
—Ram Dass and Paul Gorman

The chief pang of most trials is not so much the actual suffering itself as our own spirit of resistance to it.
—Jean Nicholas Grou

Each of us does, in effect, strike a series of "deals" or compromises between the wants and longings of the inner self, and an outer environment that offers certain possibilities and sets certain limitations.
—Maggie Scarf

Man is the only animal that laughs and weeps; for he is the only animal that is struck with the difference between what things are and what they might have been.
—William Hazlitt

Every creator painfully experiences the chasm between his inner vision and its ultimate expression. The chasm is never completely bridged. We all have the conviction, perhaps illusory, that we have much more to say than appears on the paper.
—Isaac Bashevis Singer

The greatest and most important problems in life are all in a certain sense insoluble. They can never be solved, but only outgrown.
—Carl Jung

We do not write as we want, but as we can.   —W. Somerset Maugham

The art of living lies less in eliminating our troubles than in growing with them.   —Bernard M. Baruch

A body shouldn't heed what might be. He's got to do with what is.
—Louis L'Amour

The greatest evil which fortune can inflict on men is to endow them with small talents and great ambitions.
—Vauvenargues

We may fail of our happiness, strive we ever so bravely; but we are less likely to fail if we measure with judgment our chances and our capabilities.
—Agnes Repplier

One of the signs of maturity is a healthy respect for reality—a respect that manifests itself in the level of one's aspirations and in the accuracy of one's assessment of the difficulties which separate the facts of today from the bright hopes of tomorrow.
—Robert H. Davies

Is life so wretched? Isn't it rather your hands which are too small, your vision which is muddled? You are the one who must grow up.
—Dag Hammarskjold

Nothing you write, if you hope to be any good, will ever come out as you first hoped.   —Lillian Hellman

Unhappiness is best defined as the difference between our talents and our expectations.
—Dr. Edward De Bono

Anxiety is that range of distress which attends willing what cannot be willed.
—Leslie H. Farber

There is a mortal breed most full of futility. In contempt of what is at hand, they strain into the future, hunting impossibilities on the wings of ineffectual hopes.   —Pindar

A life of frustration is inevitable for any coach whose man enjoyment is winning.   —Chuck Noll

No traveler e'er reached that blest abode who found not thorns and briers in his road.   —William Cowper

The trouble with most people is that they think with their hopes or fears or wishes rather than with their minds.
—Will Durant

It is a common observation that those who dwell continually upon their expectations are apt to become oblivious to the requirements of their actual situation.   —Charles Sanders Peirce

A hero is a man who does what he can.   —Romain Rolland

Life's under no obligation to give us what we expect.
—Margaret Mitchell

Buddha's doctrine: Man suffers because of his craving to possess and keep forever things which are essentially impermanent . . . this frustration of the desire to possess is the immediate cause of suffering.   —Alan Watts

IT IS WISE TO SEEK OUT THE BEST THINGS IN WHATEVER WE MUST ACCEPT

The point . . . is to dwell upon the brightest parts in every prospect, to call off the thoughts when turning upon disagreeable objects, and strive to be pleased with the present circumstances.   —Abraham Tucker

Everything has its wonders, even darkness and silence, and I learn, whatever state I may be in, therein to be content.
—Helen Keller

Life is not always what one wants it to be, but to make the best of it, as it is, is the only way of being happy.
—Jennie Jerome Churchill

The English know how to make the best of things. Their so-called muddling through is simply skill at dealing with the inevitable.
—Sir Winston Churchill

I make the most of all that comes and the least of all that goes.
—Sara Teasdale

It's Best to Accept Things Enthusiastically

We cannot conquer fate and necessity, yet we can yield to them in such a manner as to be greater than if we could. —Walter Savage Landor

The idea came to me that I was, am, and will be, but perhaps will not become. This did not scare me. There was for me in being an intensity I did not feel in becoming.
—Nina Berberova

Here is a rule to remember when anything tempts you to feel bitter: not, "This is a misfortune," but "To bear this worthily is good fortune."
—Marcus Aurelius

There is no good in arguing with the inevitable. The only argument available with an east wind is to put on your overcoat.
—James Russell Lowell

Trouble will come soon enough, and when he does come receive him as pleasantly as possible . . . the more amiably you greet him, the sooner he will go away. —Artemus Ward

Adapt yourself to the things among which your lot has been cast and love sincerely the fellow creatures with whom destiny has ordained that you shall live. —Marcus Aurelius

When we accept tough jobs as a challenge to our ability and wade into them with joy and enthusiasm, miracles can happen.
—Arland Gilbert

Love only what befalls you and is spun for you by fate.
—Marcus Aurelius

What you can't get out of, get into wholeheartedly.
—Mignon McLaughlin

Let us train our minds to desire what the situation demands.
—Marcus Annaeus Seneca

Ride the horse in the direction that it's going. —Werner Erhard

If one has to submit, it is wasteful not to do so with the best grace possible.
—Sir Winston Churchill

Since God has been pleased to give us the Papacy, let us enjoy it.
—Pope Leo X

It is no use to grumble and complain;
It's just as cheap and easy to rejoice;
When God sorts out the weather and sends rain—Why, rain's my choice.
—James Whitcomb Riley

When a dog runs at you, whistle for him. —Henry David Thoreau

Nature Shows That It's Better to Bend Than to Break

An oak and a reed were arguing about their strength. When a strong wind came up, the reed avoided being uprooted by bending and leaning with the gusts of wind. But the oak stood firm and was torn up by the roots.
—Aesop

The grass must bend when the wind blows across it. —Confucius

He who attempts to resist the wave is swept away, but he who bends before it abides.　—Genesis Rabbah 44:15

Adapt or perish, now as ever, is nature's inexorable imperative.
—H.G. Wells

One does not have to stand again the gale.
One yields and becomes part of the wind.
—Emmanuel

I like trees because they seem more resigned to the way they have to live than other things do.
—Willa Cather

Nature magically suits a man to his fortunes, by making them the fruit of his character.
—Ralph Waldo Emerson

Better bend than break.
—Scottish proverb

ACCEPTANCE AND HAPPINESS

The secret of success is to be in harmony with existence, to be always calm ... to let each wave of life wash us a little farther up the shore.
—Cyril Connolly

There is only one way to happiness, and that is to cease worrying about things which are beyond the power of our will.　—Epictetus

The truth does not change according to our ability to stomach it emotionally.
—Flannery O'Connor

Happiness . . . can exist only in acceptance.　—Denis De Rougemont

Happiness comes from within a man, from some curious adjustment to life.
—Hugh Walpole

Happy he who learns to bear what he cannot change!　—J.C.F. von Schiller

Contentment, and indeed usefulness, comes as the infallible result of great acceptances, great humilities—of not trying to conform to some dramatized version of ourselves.
—David Grayson

My advice to you is not to inquire why or whither, but just enjoy your ice cream while it's on your plate.
—Thornton Wilder

It is not necessarily those lands which are the most fertile or most favored in climate that seem to me the happiest, but those in which a long struggle of adaptation between man and his environment has brought out the best qualities of both.　—T.S. Eliot

Life is not always what one wants it to be, but to make the best of it, as it is, is the only way of being happy.
—Jennie Jerome Churchill

Everything has its wonders, even darkness and silence, and I learn, whatever state I may be in, therein to be content.
—Helen Keller

I accept life unconditionally. . . . Most people ask for happiness on condition. Happiness can only be felt if you don't set any condition.
—Arthur Rubenstein

Happiness is a function of accepting what is. —Werner Erhard

ACCEPTANCE AND WISDOM

One's first step in wisdom is to question everything; one's last is to come to terms with everything.
—Georg Christoph Lichtenberg

If you are wise, live as you can; if you cannot, live as you would.
—Baltasar Gracian

Wisdom never kicks at the iron walls it can't bring down.
—Olive Schreiner

For this is wisdom: to live, to take what fate, or the Gods, may give.
—Laurence Hope

Acceptance and Work
If you have a job without aggravations, you don't have a job.
—Malcolm Forbes

When I decided to go into politics I weighed the costs. I would get criticism. But I went ahead. So when virulent criticism came I wasn't surprised. I was better able to handle it.
—Herbert Hoover

Every job has drudgery. . . . The first secret of happiness is the recognition of this fundamental fact.
—M.C. McIntosh

The fishermen know that the sea is dangerous and the storm terrible, but they have never found these dangers sufficient reason for remaining ashore. —Vincent van Gogh

ACCEPTANCE AND THE SOUL

He who doesn't accept the conditions of life sells his soul.
—Charles Baudelaire

Greatness of soul consists not so much in soaring high and in pressing forward, as in knowing how to adapt and limit oneself.
—Michel de Montaigne

The beauty of the soul shines out when a man bears with composure one heavy mischance after another, not because he does not feel them, but because he is a man of high and heroic temper. —Aristotle

The great soul surrenders itself to fate.
—Marcus Annaeus Seneca

THE BENEFITS OF ACCEPTING THE INEVITABLE

The mind which renounces, once and forever, a futile hope, has its compensations in ever-growing calm.
—George R. Gissing

I not only bow to the inevitable, I am fortified by it. —Thornton Wilder

I have accepted all and I am free. The inner chains are broken, as well as those outside. —C.F. Ramuz

The most beautiful thing is inevitability of events, and the most ugly thing is trying to resist inevitability.
—Katherine Butler Hathaway

Peace of mind is that mental condition in which you have accepted the worst.
—Lin Yutang

If we can recognize that change and uncertainty are basic principles, we can greet the future and the transformation we are undergoing with the understanding that we do not know enough to be pessimistic.
—Hazel Henderson

We cannot change anything unless we accept it.
—Carl Jung

Acceptance of what has happened is the first step to overcoming the consequence of any misfortune.
—William James

Almost any event will put on a new face when received with cheerful acceptance.
—Henry S. Haskins

What it is forbidden to be put right becomes lighter by acceptance.
—Horace

One completely overcomes only what one assimilates.
—André Gide

If you cast away one cross, you will certainly find another, and perhaps a heavier.
—Thomas à Kempis

To repel one's cross is to make it heavier.
—Henri Frederic Amiel

Science says: "We must live," and seeks the means of prolonging, increasing, facilitating and amplifying life, of making it tolerable and acceptable; wisdom says: "We must die," and seeks how to make us die well.
—Miguel de Unamuno

True freedom lies in the realization and calm acceptance of the fact that there may very well be no perfect answer.
—Allen Reid McGinnis

As the soft yield of water cleaves obstinate stone,
So to yield with life solves the insolvable:
To yield, I have learned, is to come back again.
—Lao-tzu

Things turn out best for people who make the best of the way things turn out.
—Anon.

And acceptance is the answer to all my problems today. . . . I can find no serenity until I accept that person, place, thing, or situation as being exactly the way it is supposed to be at this moment.
—Alcoholics Anonymous

Resistance causes pain and lethargy. It is when we practice acceptance that new possibilities appear.
—Anon.

To oppose something is to maintain it.
—Ursula K. LeGuin

No life is so hard that you can't make it easier by the way you take it.
—Ellen Glasgow

Anything in life that we don't accept will simply make trouble for us until we make peace with it.
—Shakti Gawain

Often the prudent, far from making their destinies, succumb to them.
—Voltaire

Things past redress are now with me past care.
—William Shakespeare

What we call reality is an agreement that people have arrived at to make life more livable.
—Louise Nevelson

He who has calmly reconciled his life to fate . . . can look fortune in the face.
　　　　　　　　　　　—Boethius

To Get What We Want, We Must Accept Some Things We Don't Want

No rose without a thorn.
　　　　　　　　　—French proverb

Life leaps like a geyser for those who drill through the rock of inertia.
　　　　　　　　　—Dr. Alexis Carrel

If you want a place in the sun, you've got to put up with a few blisters.
　　　　　　　　　—Abigail Van Buren

Those who aim at great deeds must also suffer greatly.　　　—Plutarch

Paradox: Acceptance Can Lead to Change

Nature, to be commanded, must be obeyed.　　　　—Francis Bacon

The first step toward change is acceptance. Once you accept yourself, you open the door to change. That's all you have to do. Change is not something you do, it's something you allow.
　　—Will Garcia, person with AIDS

Keep doing what you're doing and you'll keep getting what you're getting.
　　　　　　　　　　　—Anon.

Everything in life that we really accept undergoes a change. So suffering must become love. That is the mystery.
　　　　　　　—Katherine Mansfield

Our very first problem is to accept our present circumstances as they are, ourselves as we are, and the people about us as they are. This is to adopt a realistic humility without which no genuine advance can even begin. . . . Provided we strenuously avoid turning these realistic surveys of the facts of life into unrealistic alibis for apathy or defeatism, they can be the sure foundation upon which increased emotional health and therefore spiritual progress can be built.
　　　　　　　　　—As Bill Sees It

We cannot change anything unless we accept it. Condemnation does not liberate, it oppresses.　　—Carl Jung

When you make your peace with authority, you become authority.
　　　　　　　　　—Jim Morrison

General Quotations about Acceptance

Ours must be the first age whose great goal, on a nonmaterial plane, is not fulfillment but adjustment.
　　　　　　　—Louis Kronenberger

Woman must not accept; she must challenge.　　—Margaret Sanger

We have fought this fight as long, and as well, as we know how. We have been defeated. There is now but one course to pursue. We must accept the situation.　　—Robert E. Lee

Competition is about passion for perfection, and passion for other people who join in this impossible quest.
　　　　　　—Mariah Burton Nelson

It is so. It cannot be otherwise.
—Cathedral inscription, Amsterdam

Teach me neither to cry for the moon
nor over spilt milk.
—On the library wall of
George V of England

Better to accept whatever happens.
—Horace

If we cannot do what we will, we
must will what we can.
—Yiddish proverb

Every man must be content with that
glory which he may have at home.
—Boethius

Every new adjustment is a crisis in
self-esteem.   —Eric Hoffer

What cannot be avoided, t'were
childish weakness to lament or fear.
—William Shakespeare

I will not meddle with that which I
cannot mend.   —Thomas Fuller

I have learned to live with it all ...
whatever happens ... all of it.
—Edelgard

There is no such thing as pure pleasure; some anxiety always goes with it.
—Ovid

If a ship has been sunk, I can't bring
it up. If it is going to be sunk, I can't
stop it. I can use my time much better
working on tomorrow's problem than
by fretting about yesterday's. Besides,
if I let those things get me, I wouldn't
last long.   —Admiral Ernest J. King

One of the many lessons that one
learns in prison is that things are
what they are and will be what they
will be.   —Oscar Wilde

Part of the happiness of life consists
not in fighting battles, but in avoiding them. A masterly retreat is in
itself a victory.
—Norman Vincent Peale

A flower falls even though we love it.
A weed grows even though we don't
love it.   —Dogen

Acceptance says, True, this is my situation at the moment. I'll look unblinkingly at the reality of it. But I'll also
open my hands to accept willingly
whatever a loving Father sends me.
—Catharine Marshall

Man is a pliant animal, a being who
gets accustomed to anything.
—Fyodor Dostoyevsky

The unknown is what it is. And to
be frightened of it is what sends
everybody scurrying around chasing
dreams, illusions, wars, peace, love,
hate, all that. Unknown is what it
is. Accept that it's unknown, and it's
plain sailing.   —John Lennon

Happiness is experienced when your
life gives you what you are willing to
accept.   —Ken Keyes, Jr.

Acceptance is the truest kinship with
humanity.   —G.K. Chesterton

What must be shall be; and that
which is a necessity to him that struggles, is little more than choice to him
that is willing.
—Marcus Annaeus Seneca

Acceptance makes any event put on a new face. —Henry S. Haskins

There is no sense in the struggle, but there is no choice but to struggle.
—Ernie Pyle

Boys, this is only a game. But it's like life in that you will be dealt some bad hands. Take each hand, good or bad, and don't whine and complain, but play it out. If you're men enough to do that, God will help and you will come out well.
—Dwight D. Eisenhower's mother

Practice easing your way along. Don't get het up or in a dither. Do your best; take it as it comes. You can handle anything if you think you can. Just keep your cool and your sense of humor. —Smiley Blanton, M.D.

Accept that all of us can be hurt, that all of us can—and surely will at times—fail. Other vulnerabilities, like being embarrassed or risking love, can be terrifying too. I think we should follow a simple rule: if we can take the worst, take the risk.
—Dr. Joyce Brothers

Do not weep; do not wax indignant. Understand. —Baruch Spinoza

We must learn to accept life and to accept ourselves . . . with a shrug and a smile . . . because it's all we've got.
—Harvey Mindess

I have accepted fear as a part of life —specifically the fear of change . . . I have gone ahead despite the pounding in the heart that says: turn back. . . .
—Erica Jong

There are things I can't force. I must adjust. —C.M. Ward

Let a man accept his destiny. No pity and no tears. —Euripides

Wood may remain ten years in the water, but it will never become a crocodile. —Congolese proverb

No matter how much you feed a wolf, he will always return to the forest.
—Russian proverb

Can the Ethiopian change his skin, or the leopard his spots?
—Jeremiah 13:23

Forgiveness

FORGIVING AND FORGETTING—REALLY LETTING GO

How we remember, what we remember, and why we remember form the most personal map of our individuality.
—Christina Baldwin

Reconciliation is more beautiful than victory.
—Violeta Barrios de Chamorro

The stupid neither forgive nor forget; the naive forgive and forget; the wise forgive, but do not forget.
—Thomas Szasz

Forgetting is the cost of living cheerfully.
—Zoë Akins

Forgiveness is the key to action and freedom.
—Hannah Arendt

"I can forgive, but I cannot forget" is only another way of saying, "I will not forgive." Forgiveness ought to be like a canceled note—torn in two and burned up so that it never can be shown against one.
—Henry Ward Beecher

Life appears to me too short to be spent in nursing animosity or registering wrong.
—Charlotte Brontë

Anger repressed can poison a relationship as surely as the cruelest words.
—Dr. Joyce Brothers

Forgiveness means letting go of the past.
—Gerald Jampolsky

I know now that patriotism is not enough; I must have no hatred and bitterness toward anyone.
—Edith Cavell

Stretch out your hand! Let no human soul wait for a benediction.
—Marie Corelli

Nobody ever forgets where he buried a hatchet.
—Kin Hubbard

Anger as soon as fed is dead, 'tis starving makes it fat.
—Emily Dickinson

Once a woman has forgiven a man, she must not reheat his sins for breakfast.
—Marlene Dietrich

There's no point in burying a hatchet if you're going to put up a marker on the site. —Sydney J. Harris

As long as you don't forgive, who and whatever it is will occupy a rent-free space in your mind.
—Isabelle Holland

Courage and clemency are equal virtues. —Mary Delarivière Manley

One may have been a fool, but there's no foolishness like being bitter.
—Kathleen Norris

Not the power to remember, but its very opposite, the power to forget, is a necessary condition for our existence. —Sholem Asch

Once a woman has forgiven a man, she must not reheat his sins for breakfast. —Marlene Dietrich

Keeping score of old scores and scars, getting even and one-upping, always make you less than you are.
—Malcolm Forbes

Forgiveness is all-powerful. Forgiveness heals all ills.
—Catherine Ponder

The forgiving state of mind is a magnetic power for attracting good.
—Catherine Porter

Forgiveness is an act of the will, and the will can function regardless of the temperature of the heart.
—Corrie ten Boom

To be wronged is nothing unless you continue to remember it.
—Confucius

Who understands much, forgives much. —Madame de Staël

Forgiveness is the act of admitting we are like other people.
—Christina Baldwin

Grace fills empty spaces, but it can only enter where there is a void to receive it, and it is grace itself which makes this void. —Simone Weil

WE RARELY KNOW EVERYTHING ABOUT A SITUATION

Know all and you will pardon all.
—Thomas à Kempis

People are more than the worst thing they have ever done in their lives.
—Helen Prejean

The secret of forgiving everything is to understand nothing.
—George Bernard Shaw

Speak not against anyone whose burden you have not weighed yourself.
—Marion Zimmer Bradley

Nothing's easier than believing we understand experiences we've never had. —Gwen Bristow

The heart has always the pardoning power. —Anne-Sophie Swetchine

To understand is to forgive, even oneself. —Alexander Chase

To what extent is any given man morally responsible for any given act? We do not know.
—Dr. Alexis Carrel

ONLY THE STRONG CAN FORGIVE

The weak can never forgive.
Forgiveness is the attribute of the
strong.   —Mahatma Ghandi

Only the brave know how to forgive.
. . . A coward never forgave; it is not
in his nature.   —Laurence Sterne

Any man can seek revenge; it takes a
king or prince to grant a pardon.
          —Arthur J. Rehrat

To be angry about trifles is mean
and childish; to rage and be furious
is brutish; and to maintain perpetual
wrath is akin to the practice and
temper of devils; but to prevent and
suppress rising resentment is wise and
glorious, is manly and divine.
          —Isaac Watts

RESENTMENTS AND HATRED

Hatred is a death wish for the hated,
not a life wish for anything else.
          —Audre Lorde

Hatred is a passion requiring one hundred times the energy of love. Keep it
for a cause, not an individual. Keep it
for intolerance, injustice, stupidity. For
hatred is the strength of the sensitive.
Its power and its greatness depend on
the selflessness of its use.
          —Olive Moore

Resentment is the "number one"
offender. It destroys more alcoholics
than anything else. From it stem all
forms of spiritual disease, for we have
been not only mentally and physically
ill, we have been spiritually sick.
          —Alcoholics Anonymous

To oppose something is to maintain it.
          —Ursula K. LeGuin

Dwelling on the negative simply contributes to its power.
          —Shirley MacLaine

To carry a grudge is like being stung
to death by one bee.
          —William H. Walton

Resentments are burdens we don't
need to carry.   —Anon.

The enslaver is enslaved, the hater,
harmed.   —Marianne Moore

By putting his hand around my neck,
he slowly strangled himself.
          —Minako Ohba

The one who deals the mortal blow
receives the mortal wound.
          —Maude Parker

Without forgiveness life is governed
. . . by an endless cycle of resentment
and retaliation.   —Robert Assaglioli

Malice drinks one-half of its own
poison.   —Marcus Annaeus Seneca

I tell you, there is no such thing as
creative hate!   —Willa Cather

Reject hatred without hating.
          —Mary Baker Eddy

Hate would destroy him who hated.
          —Louis L'Amour

In hatred as in love, we grow like
the thing we brood upon. What we
loathe, we graft into our very soul.
          —Mary Renault

Resentment is weak and lowers your
self-esteem.   —Barbara Sher

Hate is a prolonged form of suicide.
          —Douglas V. Steere

Hatred is like fire—it makes even
light rubbish deadly.   —George Eliot

You cannot shake hands with a
clenched fist.   —Indira Gandhi

Hate is all a lie, there is no truth in
hate.   —Kathleen Norris

Hate is not a good counselor.
          —Victoria Wolff

Bitterness imprisons life; love
releases it. —Harry Emerson Fosdick

If the will remains in protest, it stays
dependent on that which it is protest-
ing against.   —Rollo May

Hate smolders and eventually
destroys, not the hated but the hater.
          —Dorothy Thompson

It is almost impossible to throw dirt
on someone without getting a little
on yourself.   —Abigail Van Buren

If you hate a person, you hate something in him that is part of yourself.
          —Herman Hesse

Fire destroys that which feeds it.
          —Simone Weil

You cannot hate other people without hating yourself. —Oprah Winfrey

Whom they have injured, they also
hate.   —Marcus Annaeus Seneca

Rage and bitterness do not foster
femininity. They harden the heart and
make the body sick.
          —Marion Woodman

ANGER

I used to store my anger and it affected my play. Now I get it out. I'm never
rude to my playing partner. I'm very
focused on the ball. Then it's over.
          —Helen Alfredsson

Anger is a short madness.   —Horace

My mother used to say, "He who
angers you conquers you."
          —Elizabeth Kenny

The angry people are those people
who are most afraid.
          —Dr. Robert Anthony

Anger as soon as fed is dead, 'tis
starving makes it fat.
          —Emily Dickinson

Anger dwells only in the bosom of
fools.   —Albert Einstein

Anger and worry are the enemies of
clear thought.   —Madeleine Brent

Holding on to anger is like grasping
a hot coal with the intent of throwing
it at someone else; you are the one
who gets burned.   —Buddha

Anger is a killing thing: it kills the
man who angers, for each rage leaves
him less than he had been before—it
takes something from him.
          —Louis L'Amour

REVENGE

Something of vengeance I had tasted for the first time; as aromatic wine it seemed, on swallowing, warm and racy; its after-flavor, metallic and corroding, gave me a sensation as if I had been poisoned.
—Charlotte Brontë

Revenge could steal a man's life until there was nothing left but emptiness.
—Louis L'Amour

Revenge may not be a particularly high consciousness-oriented activity.
—Carrie Fisher

The human heart in its perversity finds it hard to escape hatred and revenge.
—Moses Luzzatto

A man can lose sight of everything else when he's bent on revenge, and it ain't worth it.
—Louis L'Amour

The whole human race loses by every act of personal vengeance.
—Rae Foley

Forgiveness is the sweetest revenge.
—Isaac Friedmann

FORGIVENESS AND LOVE

One forgives to the degree that one loves.
—Francois de La Rochefoucauld

One is as one is, and the love that can't encompass both is a poor sort of love.
—Marya Mannes

Forgiveness is the final form of love.
—Reinhold Niebuhr

The days are too short even for love; how can there be enough time for quarreling?
—Margaret Gatty

Forgiveness is the most tender part of love.
—John Sheffield

The best proof of love is trust.
—Dr. Joyce Brothers

Love is an act of endless forgiveness, a tender look which becomes a habit.
—Peter Ustinov

We are told that people stay in love because of chemistry, or because they remain intrigued with each other, because of many kindnesses, because of luck. . . . But part of it has got to be forgiveness and gratefulness.
—Ellen Goodman

For me it's not possible to forget, and I don't understand people who, when the love is ended, can bury the other person in hatred or oblivion. For me, a man I have loved becomes a kind of brother.
—Jeanne Moreau

Today I forgive all those who have ever offended me. I give my love to all thirsty hearts, both to those who love me and to those who do not love me.
—Paramahansa Yogananda

Experience is how life catches up with us and teaches us to love and forgive each other.
—Judy Collins

FORGIVENESS AND GOD

We never ask God to forgive anybody except when we haven't.
—Elbert Hubbard

Forgiveness is God's command.
—Martin Luther

God will forgive me, that is His
business.   —Heinrich Heine

God will forgive me the foolish
remarks I have made about Him just
as I will forgive my opponents the
foolish things they have written about
me, even though they are spiritually as
inferior to me as I to thee, O God!
—Heinrich Heine

Let all bitterness, and wrath, and
anger, and clamour, and evil speaking, be put away from you, with
all malice; and be ye kind to one
another, tenderhearted, forgiving one
another, even as God, for Christ's
sake, hath forgiven you.
—Ephesians 4:31–32

I have looked on a lot of women with
lust. I've committed adultery in my
heart many times. God recognizes I
will do this and forgives me.
—Jimmy Carter

How Forgiveness Helps Us
Forgiveness is the answer to the
child's dream of a miracle by which
what is broken is made whole again,
what is soiled is again made clean.
—Dag Hammarskjold

Forgiveness is all-powerful. Forgiveness heals all ills.
—Catherine Ponder

Those who are free of resentful
thoughts surely find peace. —Buddha

I can have peace of mind only when I
forgive rather than judge.
—Gerald Jampolsky

The forgiving state of mind is a magnetic power for attracting good.
—Catherine Ponder

Judge not, that ye be not judged.
—Matthew 7:1

It is in pardoning that we are pardoned.   —Saint Francis of Assisi

Forgiving those who hurt us is the
key to personal peace.
—G. Weatherly

Forgive all who have offended you,
not for them, but for yourself.
—Harriet Uts Nelson

To forgive is the highest, most beautiful form of love. In return, you will
receive untold peace and happiness.
—Robert Muller

Forgiveness is the key to action and
freedom.   —Hannah Arendt

Forgiveness is the way to true health
and happiness.   —Gerald Jampolsky

Humanity is never so beautiful as
when praying for forgiveness, or else
forgiving another.
—Jean Paul Richter

Those who can't forget are worse off
than those who can't remember.
—Anon.

Forgiveness is the remission of sins.
For it is by this that what has been
lost, and was found, is saved from
being lost again.   —Saint Augustine

We Must Forgive Ourselves, Too

I can pardon everybody's mistakes except my own.
—Marcus Porcius Cato "the Elder"

If you haven't forgiven yourself something, how can you forgive others?
—Dolores Huerta

The moment an individual can accept and forgive himself, even a little, is the moment in which he becomes to some degree lovable.
—Eugene Kennedy

They may not deserve forgiveness, but I do. —Anon.

I forgive myself for having believed for so long that . . . I was never good enough to have, get, be what I wanted.
—Ceanne DeRohan

How unhappy is he who cannot forgive himself. —Publilius Syrus

I learned that true forgiveness includes total self-acceptance. And out of acceptance wounds are healed and happiness is possible again.
—Catharine Marshall

Every man treats himself as society treats the criminal.
—Harvey Fergusson

To understand is to forgive, even oneself. —Alexander Chase

Give us this day our daily bread. And forgive us our debts, as we forgive our debtors.
—Matthew 6:11–12

He that cannot forgive others breaks the bridge over which he must pass himself; for every man has need to be forgiven. —Thomas Fuller

Forgiveness Doesn't Always Please Those We Forgive

Always forgive your enemies; nothing annoys them so much.
—Oscar Wilde

Forgiveness is the noblest vengeance.
—H.G. Bohn

There is no revenge so complete as forgiveness. —Josh Billings

Many promising reconciliations have broken down because while both parties came prepared to forgive, neither party came prepared to be forgiven.
—Charles William

General Quotations about Forgiveness

Forgiveness is man's deepest need and highest achievement.
—Horace Bushnell

Abandon your animosities and make your sons Americans!
—Robert E. Lee

Her breasts and arms ached with the beauty of her own forgiveness.
—Meridel Le Sueur

Life is an adventure in forgiveness.
—Norman Cousins

The cut worm forgives the plow.
—William Blake

Forgiveness is the highest and most difficult of all moral lessons.
— Joseph Jacobs

The fragrance of the violet sheds on the heel that has crushed it.
— Mark Twain

How shall I love the sin, yet keep the
    sense,
And love the offender, yet detest the
    offence?
— Alexander Pope

Forgiveness is the giving, and so the receiving, of life.
— George MacDonald

Dream of your brother's kindnesses instead of dwelling in your dreams on his mistakes. Select his thoughtfulness to dream about instead of counting up the hurts he gave.
— *A Course in Miracles*

Who would care to question the ground of forgiveness or compassion?
— Joseph Conrad

O friends, I pray tonight,
Keep not your kisses for my dead
    cold brow.
The way is lonely; let me feel them
    now.
Think gently of me; I am travel-worn,
My faltering feet are pierced with
    many a   thorn.
Forgive! O hearts estranged, forgive,
    I plead!
When ceaseless bliss is mine I shall
    not need
The tenderness for which I long
    tonight.
— Belle Eugenia Smith

Let us forget and forgive injuries.
— Miguel de Cervantes

Even a stopped clock is right twice a day.
— Marie von Ebner-Eschenbach

It is easier to forgive an enemy than a friend.
— Madame Dorothee Deluzy

It is very easy to forgive others their mistakes; it takes more grit and gumption to forgive them for having witnessed your own.
— Jessamyn West

When you pray for anyone you tend to modify your personal attitude toward him.
— Norman Vincent Peale

Forgiving means to pardon the unpardonable, faith means believing the unbelievable, and hoping means to hope when things are hopeless.
— G.K. Chesterton

To err is human; to forgive, divine.
— Alexander Pope

Counting Our Blessings

WE SHOULD BE AWARE OF THE BLESSINGS OF OUR EVERYDAY LIVES

Normal day, let me be aware of the treasure you are. Let me learn from you, love you, bless you before you depart. Let me not pass you by in quest of some rare and perfect tomorrow. Let me hold you while I may, for it may not always be so. One day I shall dig my nails into the earth, or bury my face in the pillow, or stretch myself taut, or raise my hands to the sky and want, more than all the world, your return.
—Mary Jean Iron

The unthankful heart . . . discovers no mercies; but let the thankful heart sweep through the day and, as the magnet finds the iron, so it will find, in every hour, some heavenly blessings!
—Henry Ward Beecher

Joy is what happens to us when we allow ourselves to recognize how good things really are.
—Marianne Williamson

Good heavens, of what uncostly material is our earthly happiness composed . . . if we only knew it. What incomes have we not had from a flower, and how unfailing are the dividends of the seasons.
—James Russell Lowell

Be on the lookout for mercies. The more we look for them, the more of them we will see. . . . Better to loose count while naming your blessings than to lose your blessings to counting your troubles.
—Maltbie D. Babcock

The man who thinks his wife, his baby, his house, his horse, his dog, and himself severely unequalled, is almost sure to be a good-humored person.
—Oliver Wendell Holmes

Every dog has its day, but it's not every dog that knows when he's having it.
—Winifred Gordon

We must give ourselves more earnestly and intelligently and generously than we have to the happy duty of appreciation.
—Mariana Griswold Van Rensselaer

There is nothing so bitter that a patient mind cannot find some solace for it. —Marcus Annaeus Seneca

I thank You God for this most amazing day; for the leaping greenly spirits of trees and a blue true dream of sky; and for everything which is natural which is infinite which is yes.
                    —e.e. cummings

My private measure of success is daily. If this were to be the last day of my life would I be content with it? To live in a harmonious balance of commitments and pleasures is what I strive for.   —Jane Rule

Yes, there is a Nirvanah: it is in leading your sheep to a green pasture, and in putting your child to sleep, and in writing the last line of your poem.
                    —Kahlil Gibran

Blessed are those who can give without remembering and take without forgetting.
                —Elizabeth Asquith Bibesco

That daily life is really good one appreciates when one wakes from a horrible dream, or when one takes the first outing after a sickness. Why not realize it now?
                —William Lyon Phelps

Thank God every morning when you get up that you have something to do which must be done, whether you like it or not.   —Charles Kingsley

When I first open my eyes upon the morning meadows and look out upon the beautiful world, I thank God I am alive.   —Ralph Waldo Emerson

Each day comes bearing its own gifts. Untie the ribbons.
                —Ruth Ann Schabacker

We can be thankful to a friend for a few acres or a little money; and yet for the freedom and command of the whole earth, and for the great benefits of our being, our life, health, and reason, we look upon ourselves as under no obligation.
                —Marcus Annaeus Seneca

When something does not insist on being noticed, when we aren't grabbed by the collar or struck on the skull by a presence or an event, we take for granted the very things that most deserve our gratitude.
                —Cynthia Ozick

Why do some people always see beautiful skies and grass and lovely flowers and incredible human beings, while others are hard-pressed to find anything or any place that is beautiful?
                —Leo Buscaglia

Most human beings have an almost infinite capacity for taking things for granted.   —Aldous Huxley

My country . . . gave me schooling, independence of action and opportunity for service. . . . I am indebted to my country beyond any human power to repay.   —Herbert Hoover

Dwell upon the brightest parts in every prospect . . . and strive to be pleased with the present circumstances.
                —Abraham Tucker

We are never either so wretched or so happy as we say we are.
                —Honore de Balzac

The best things are nearest: breath in your nostrils, light in your eyes, flowers at your feet, duties at your hand, the path of God just before you. Then do not grasp at the stars, but do life's plain, common work as it comes, certain that daily duties and daily bread are the sweetest things of life.
—Robert Louis Stevenson

Is life so wretched? Isn't it rather your hands which are too small, your vision which is muddled? You are the one who must grow up.
—Dag Hammarskjold

Looking for Silver Linings
Our real blessings often appear to us in the shape of pains, losses and disappointments. —Joseph Addison

Most of my major disappointments have turned out to be blessings in disguise. So whenever anything bad does happen to me, I kind of sit back and feel, well, if I give this enough time, it'll turn out that this was good, so I shan't worry about it too much.
—William Gaines

Sometimes the best deals are the ones you don't make. —Bill Veeck

The advantages of a losing team: (1) There is everything to hope for and nothing to fear. (2) Defeats do not disturb one's sleep. (3) An occasional victory is a surprise and a delight. (4) There is no danger of any club passing you. (5) You are not asked fifty times a day, "What was the score?"; people take it for granted that you lost.
—Elmer E. Bates

That which does not kill me makes me stronger. —Friedrich Nietzsche

Not being beautiful was the true blessing. . . . Not being beautiful forced me to develop my inner resources. The pretty girl has a handicap to overcome.
—Golda Meir

The difficulties, hardships and trials of life, the obstacles ... are positive blessings. They knit the muscles more firmly, and teach self-reliance.
—William Matthews

Many a man curses the rain that falls upon his head, and knows not that it brings abundance to drive away hunger. —Saint Basil

Trouble is only opportunity in work clothes. —Henry J. Kaiser

Adversity has the same effect on a man that severe training has on the pugilist: it reduces him to his fighting weight. —Josh Billings

You will never be the person you can be if pressure, tension and discipline are taken out of your life.
—Dr. James G. Bilkey

God brings men into deep waters not to drown them, but to cleanse them.
—Aughey

Some troubles, like a protested note of a solvent debtor, bear interest.
—Honore de Balzac

Failure changes for the better, success for the worse.
—Marcus Annaeus Seneca

The basis of optimism is sheer terror.
—Oscar Wilde

No evil is without its compensation
. . . it is not the loss itself, but the
estimate of the loss, that troubles us.
—Marcus Annaeus Seneca

Let me embrace thee, sour adversity, for wise men say it is the wisest
course.   —William Shakespeare

Give thanks for sorrow that teaches
you pity; for pain that teaches you
courage—and give exceeding thanks
for the mystery which remains a
mystery still—the veil that hides you
from the infinite, which makes it possible for you to believe in what you
cannot see.   —Robert Nathan

A Christian could even give thanks for
Hell, because Hell was a threat and a
warning to keep him in the right way.
—Anon.

To every disadvantage there is a corresponding advantage.
—W. Clement Stone

Too many people miss the silver lining because they're expecting gold.
—Maurice Setter

If you count all your assets, you
always show a profit.
—Robert Quillen

Too happy would you be, did ye but
know your own advantages! —Virgil

Much unhappiness results from our
inability to remember the nice things
that happen to us.   —W.N. Rieger

If we go down into ourselves, we
find that we possess exactly what we
desire.   —Simone Weil

LIFE ITSELF IS A BLESSING

Be grateful for yourself . . . be thankful.
—William Saroyan

Keep a grateful journal. Every night,
list five things that you are grateful
for. What it will begin to do is change
your perspective of your day and
your life.   —Oprah Winfrey

There is no wealth but life.
—John Ruskin

Just to be is a blessing. Just to live is
holy.   —Abraham Heschel

Life may be hard, but it's also wonderful.   —Small Change

I like living. I have sometimes been
wildly, despairingly, acutely miserable, racked with sorrow, but through
it all I still know quite certainly that
just to be alive is a grand thing.
—Agatha Christie

Be glad of life because it gives you
the chance to love, and to work, and
to play and to look up at the stars.
—Henry Van Dyke

To be alive, to be able to see, to walk
. . . it's all a miracle. I have adapted
the technique of living life from miracle to miracle.   —Arthur Rubinstein

This is another day! Are its eyes
    blurred
With maudlin grief for any wasted
    past?
A thousand thousand failures shall
    not daunt!
Let dust clasp dust, death, death; I
    am alive!

—Don Marquis

The mere sense of living is joy enough.
—Emily Dickinson

However mean your life is, meet it and live it; do not shun it and call it hard names. It is not so bad as you are. It looks poorest when you are richest. The fault-finder will find faults even in Paradise. Love your life.
—Henry David Thoreau

Life is the first gift, love is the second, and understanding the third.
—Marge Piercy

THE SIMPLEST THINGS ARE BLESSINGS

To have a full stomach and fixed income are no small things .
—Elbert Hubbard

For one mother, joy is the quiet pleasure found in gently rubbing shampoo into her young child's hair. For another woman it's taking a long walk alone, while for yet another it's reveling in a much-anticipated vacation.
—Eileen Stukane

How can they say my life is not a success? Have I not for more than sixty years gotten enough to eat and escaped being eaten?
—Logan Pearsall Smith

Sunshine is delicious, rain is refreshing, wind braces us up, snow is exhilarating; there is really no such thing as bad weather, only different kinds of good weather. —John Ruskin

Only a stomach that rarely feels hungry scorns common things.
—Horace

My gratitude for good writing is unbounded; I'm grateful for it the way I'm grateful for the ocean.
—Anne Lamott

Is it so small a thing to have enjoyed the sun, to have lived light in the spring, to have loved, to have thought, to have done?
—Matthew Arnold

When something does not insist on being noticed, when we aren't grabbed by the collar or struck on the skull by a presence or an event, we take for granted the very things that most deserve our gratitude.
—Cynthia Ozick

You say grace before meals. All right. But I say grace before the concert and the opera, and grace before the play and pantomime, and grace before I open a book, and grace before sketching, painting, swimming, fencing, boxing, walking, playing, dancing and grace before I dip the pen in the ink. —G.K. Chesterton

Thank God for dirty dishes; they
	have a tale to tell.
While other folks go hungry, we're
	eating pretty well.
With home, and health, and happiness, we shouldn't want to fuss;
For by this stack of evidence, God's
	very good to us.
—Anon.

It is strange what a contempt men have for the joys that are offered them freely. —Georges Duhamel

Grateful for the blessing lent of simple tastes and mind content!
—Oliver Wendell Holmes

An easy thing, O Power Divine,
To thank thee for these gifts of Thine,
For summer's sunshine, winter's
    snow,
For hearts that kindle, thoughts that
    glow;
But when shall I attain to this—
To thank Thee for the things I miss?
        —Thomas W. Higginson

I thank Thee, Lord, for blessings, big
    and small;
For spring's warm glow and song-
    bird's welcome call;
For autumn's hue and winter's white
    snow shawl.
I thank Thee for the harvest rich with
    grain;
For tall trees and the quiet shadowed
    lane;
For rushing stream, for birds that
    love to fly;
My country's land, the mountains
    and the plain.
I thank Thee for each sunset in the
    sky.
For sleepy nights, the bed in which I
    lie;
A life of truth and peace; a woman's
    hand,
Her hand in mine until the day I die.
I thank Thee, Lord for all these
    things above;
But most of all I thank Thee for Thy
    Love.
    —Ralph Gaither (written while a
        pow POW in North Vietnam)

People call me an optimist, but I'm
really an appreciator . . . years ago, I
was cured of a badly infected finger
with antibiotics when once my doctor
could have recommended only a hot
water soak or, eventually, surgery. . . .
When I was six years old and had
scarlet fever, the first of the miracle
drugs, sulfanilamide, saved my life.
I'm grateful for computers and pho-
tocopiers . . . I appreciate where we've
come from.   —Julian Simon

If only the people who worry about
their liabilities would think about the
riches they do possess, they would
stop worrying. Would you sell both
your eyes for a million dollars . . . or
your two legs . . . or your hands . . .
or your hearing? Add up what you
do have, and you'll find that you
won't sell them for all the gold in
the world. The best things in life are
yours, if you can appreciate yourself.
        —Dale Carnegie

Most of us miss out on life's big prizes. The Pulitzer. The Nobel. Oscars.
Tonys. Emmys. But we're all eligible
for life's small pleasures. A pat on the
back. A kiss behind the ear. A four-
pound bass. A full moon. An empty
parking space. A crackling fire. A
great meal. A glorious sunset. Hot
soup. Cold beer. Don't fret about copping life's grand awards. Enjoy its tiny
delights. There are plenty for all of us.
    —United Technologies Corporation
                    advertisement

We can be thankful to a friend for a
few acres or a little money; and yet
for the freedom and command of
the whole earth, and for the great
benefits of our being, our life, health,
and reason, we look upon ourselves
as under no obligation.
        —Marcus Annaeus Seneca

HEALTH IS A GIFT

Health is . . . a blessing that money
cannot buy.   —Izaak Walton

Happiness lies, first of all, in health.
—George William Curtis

A sound mind in a sound body is a short but full description of a happy state in this world.　　—John Locke

Health is the vital principle of bliss.
—James Thomson

THINK OF ALL THE PROBLEMS WE'VE BEEN SPARED, OF HOW MUCH TOUGHER THINGS COULD BE

If you can't be thankful for what you receive, be thankful for what you escape.　　—Anon.

Even though we can't have all we want, we ought to be thankful we don't get all we deserve.　　—Anon.

Happy the man who can count his sufferings.　　—Ovid

Happiness is composed of misfortunes avoided.　　—Alphonse Karr

Considering the fortune you might have lost, you'll have to admit you're rich already.　　—John Rothchild

I thank Thee first because I was never robbed before; second, because although they took my purse they did not take my life; third, because although they took my all, it was not much; and fourth because it was I who was robbed, and not I who robbed.
—Matthew Henry

Think of the ills from which you are exempt.　　—Joseph Joubert

A man should always consider . . . how much more unhappy he might be than he is.　　—Joseph Addison

The happiness of any given life is to be measured not by its joys and pleasures, but by the extent to which it has been free from suffering, from positive evil.
—Arthur Schopenhauer

Better to suffer than to die.
—Jean de La Fontaine

For grief unsuffered, tears unshed, for
　　clouds that scattered overhead;
For pestilence that came not high, for
　　dangers great that passed me by;
For sharp suspicion smoothed,
　　allayed, for doubt dispelled that
　　made afraid;
For fierce temptation well withstood,
　　for evil plot that brought forth
　　good;
For weakened links in friendship's
　　chain that, sorely tested, stood the
　　strain;
For harmless blows with malice dealt,
　　for base ingratitude unfelt;
For hatred's sharp unuttered word,
　　for bitter jest unknown, unheard;
For every evil turned away, unmea-
　　sured thanks I give today.
　　　　　　　　　　　—Anon.

Better a little fire to warm us than a great one to burn us.
—Thomas Fuller

It isn't important to come out on top. What matters is to come out alive.
—Bertolt Brecht

He who limps still walks.
—Stanislaw Lec

I have gout, asthma, and seven other maladies, but am otherwise very well.
—Sydney Smith

THE ABSENCE OF PAIN IS A BLESSING

Luckily, I never feel at one time more than half my pains.
—Joseph Joubert

Pain is no longer pain when it is past.
—Margaret Junkin Preston

We are content to forgo joy when pain is also lost. —Latin proverb

The happiest is he who suffers the least pain; the most miserable, he who enjoys the least pleasure.
—Jean-Jacques Rousseau

Happiness is not being pained in body, or troubled in mind.
—Thomas Jefferson

The end of pain we take as happiness.
—Giacomo Leopardi

You can be happy indeed if you have breathing space from pain.
—Giacomo Leopardi

The summit of pleasure is the elimination of all that gives pain.
—Epicurus

I seek the utmost pleasure and the least pain. —Plautus

WE SHOULD BE THANKFUL FOR WHAT WE'VE GOT, NOT UNHAPPY OVER WHAT WE DON'T HAVE

A prudent man will think more important what fate has conceded to him, than what it has denied.
—Baltasar Gracian

It is better to be looked over than overlooked. —Mae West

Blessed are those who can give without remembering and take without forgetting.
—Elizabeth Asquith Bibesco

He is a man of sense who does not grieve for what he has not, but rejoices in what he has. —Epictetus

Enjoy the successes that you have, and don't be too hard on yourself when you don't do well. Too many times we beat up on ourselves. Just relax and enjoy it. —Patty Sheehan

For everything you have missed, you have gained something else.
—Ralph Waldo Emerson

Few love what they may have.
—Ovid

The knowledge that something remains yet unenjoyed impairs our enjoyment of the good before us.
—Samuel Johnson

May we never let the things we can't have, or don't have, spoil our enjoyment of the things we do have and can have. —Richard L. Evans

It is not customary to love what one has. —Anatole France

The talent for being happy is appreciating and liking what you have, instead of what you don't have.
—Woody Allen

Happy thou art not; for what thou hast not, still thou striv'est to get; and what thou hast, forget'est.
—William Shakespeare

Men . . . always think that something they are going to get is better than what they have got.
—John Oliver Hobbes

When we cannot get what we love, we must love what is within our reach.
—French proverb

Take full account of the excellencies which you possess, and in gratitude remember how you would hanker after them, if you had them not.
—Marcus Aurelius

A wise man cares not for what he cannot have.
—Anon.

A man can refrain from wanting what he has not, and cheerfully make the best of a bird in the hand.
—Marcus Annaeus Seneca

Long only for what you have.
—André Gide

The tulip is, among flowers, what the peacock is among birds. A tulip lacks scent, a peacock has an unpleasant voice. The one takes pride in its garb, the other in its tail.
—French proverb

Slight not what is near though aiming at what is far.
—Euripides

Greediness of getting more, deprives . . . the enjoyment of what it had got.
—Thomas Sprat

There is a mortal breed most full of futility. In contempt of what is at hand, they strain into the future, hunting impossibilities on the wings of ineffectual hopes.
—Pindar

What you really value is what you miss, not what you have.
—Jorge Luis Borges

While you fear missing a meal, you aren't fully aware of the meals you do eat.
—Dan Millman

To be upset over what you don't have is to waste what you do have.
—Ken Keyes, Jr.

If there's no bread, cakes are very good.
—Spanish proverb

Not what we have, but what we enjoy, constitutes our abundance.
—J. Petit-Senn

Not what we have, but what we use, not what we see, but what we choose—these are the things that mar or bless human happiness.
—Joseph Fort Newton

The happiness which is lacking makes one think even the happiness one has unbearable.
—Joseph Roux

We always have enough to be happy if we are enjoying what we do have— and not worrying about what we don't have.
—Ken Keyes, Jr.

Welcome everything that comes to you, but do not long for anything else. —André Gide

The superiority of the distant over the present is only due to the mass and variety of the pleasures that can be suggested, compared with the poverty of those that can at any time be felt. —George Santayana

If there is a sin against life, it consists perhaps not so much in despairing of life as in hoping for another, and in eluding the implacable grandeur of this life. —Albert Camus

WE OFTEN DON'T VALUE THINGS AFTER WE GET THEM

Mankind, by the perverse depravity of their nature, esteem that which they have most desired as of no value the moment it is possessed, and torment themselves with fruitless wishes for that which is beyond their reach. —Francois de Fenelon

All your youth you want to have your greatness taken for granted; when you find it taken for granted, you are unnerved. —Elizabeth Bowen

Do not spoil what you have by desiring what you have not; remember that what you now have was once among the things only hoped for. —Epicurus

It ain't so much trouble to get rich as it is to tell when we have got rich. —Josh Billings

What you have become is the price you paid to get what you used to want. —Mignon McLaughlin

No man can be satisfied with his attainment, although he may be satisfied with his circumstances. —Frank Swinnerton

Life is a progress from want to want, not from enjoyment to enjoyment. —Samuel Johnson

We spend our time searching for security and hate it when we get it. —John Steinbeck

There must be more to life than having everything. —Maurice Sendak

Is there no end to this escalation of desire? —Marya Mannes

Ambition has its disappointments to sour us, but never the good fortune to satisfy us. —Benjamin Franklin

There is no banquet but some dislike something in it. —Thomas Fuller

If we get everything that we want, we will soon want nothing that we get. —Vernon Luchies

It matters very little whether a man is discontented in the name of pessimism or progress, if his discontent does in fact paralyse his power of appreciating what he has got. —G.K. Chesterton

We Often Don't Appreciate What We Have Until We Lose It

So long as we can lose any happiness, we possess some. —Booth Tarkington

Happiness always looks small while you hold it in your hands, but let it go, and you learn at once how big and precious it is. —Maxim Gorky

After my mother's death, I began to see her as she had really been. . . . It was less like losing someone than discovering someone. —Nancy Hale

We never know the worth of water till the well is dry. —English proverb

The way to love anything is to realize that it may be lost.
—G.K. Chesterton

Jesus, please teach me to appreciate what I have before time forces me to appreciate what I had.
—Susan L. Lenzkes

Eden is that old-fashioned house we dwell in every day
Without suspecting our abode, until we drive away. —Emily Dickinson

Generally the man with a good wife, or the woman with a good husband, or the children with good parents discover too late the goodness they overlooked while it was in full bloom.
—James Douglas

Jesus, please teach me to appreciate what I have, before time forces me to appreciate what I had.
—Susan L. Lenzkes

The best things in life are appreciated most after they have been lost.
—Roy L. Smith

Only with a new ruler do you realize the value of the old.
—Burmese proverb

I remember those happy days and often wish I could speak into the ears of the dead the gratitude which was due to them in life and so ill-returned.
—Gwyn Thomas

You can't appreciate home until you've left it, money till it's spent, your wife till she's joined a woman's club, nor Old Glory till you see it hanging on a broomstick on the shanty of a consul in a foreign town.
—O. Henry

What Counts Is What's Left

Birds sing after a storm; why shouldn't people feel as free to delight in whatever remains to them?
—Rose Fitzgerald Kennedy

Think of all the beauty still left around you and be happy.
—Anne Frank

Oh, my friend, it's not what they take away from you that counts—it's what you do with what you have left.
—Hubert H. Humphrey, after cancer surgery

Giving Thanks

God gave you a gift of 86,400 seconds today. Have you used one to say "thank you"? —William A. Ward

The Pilgrims made seven times more graves than huts. No Americans have been more impoverished than these who, nevertheless, set aside a day of thanksgiving. —H.U. Westermayer

The greatest saint in the world is not he who prays most or fasts most; it is not he who gives alms, or is most eminent for temperance, chastity or justice. It is he who is most thankful to God. —William Law

Not what we say about our blessings, but how we use them, is the true measure of our thanksgiving. —W.T. Purkiser

The unthankful heart . . . discovers no mercies; but the thankful heart . . . will find, in every hour, some heavenly blessings. —Henry Ward Beecher

Thanksgiving is a sure index of spiritual health. —Maurice Dametz

If the only prayer you say in your whole life is "Thank you," that would suffice. —Meister Eckhart

Who does not thank for little will not thank for much. —Estonian proverb

The beginning of men's rebellion against God was, and is, the lack of a thankful heart. —Francis Schaeffer

A thankful heart is not only the greatest virtue, but the parent of all other virtues. —Cicero

Seeds of discouragement will not grow in the thankful heart. —Anon.

The private and personal blessings we enjoy—the blessings of immunity, safeguard, liberty and integrity— deserve the thanksgiving of a whole life. —Jeremy Taylor

One of life's gifts is that each of us, no matter how tired and downtrodden, finds reasons for thankfulness. —J. Robert Maskin

GRATITUDE

Joy is the simplest form of gratitude. —Karl Barth

He who receives a benefit with gratitude repays the first installment on his debt. —Marcus Annaeus Seneca

Gratitude unlocks the fullness of life. It turns what we have into enough, and more. It turns denial into acceptance, chaos to order, confusion to clarity. It can turn a meal into a feast, a house into a home, a stranger into a friend. Gratitude makes sense of our past, brings peace for today, and creates a vision for tomorrow. —Melody Beattie

Remember that not to be happy is not to be grateful. —Elizabeth Carter

Gratitude weighs heavy on us only when we no longer feel it. —Comtesse Diane

Appreciation is yeast, lifting ordinary to extraordinary. —Mary-Ann Petro

Gratitude is the memory of the heart. —Jean Baptiste Massieu

One can never pay in gratitude; one can only pay "in kind" somewhere else in life.
—Anne Morrow Lindbergh

Silent gratitude isn't much use to anyone.　—Gladys Browyn Stern

Happiness is itself a kind of gratitude.　—Joseph Wood Krutch

What Is Enough?

One cannot collect all the beautiful shells on the beach.
—Anne Morrow Lindbergh

A man who accustoms himself to buy superfluities is often in want of necessities.　—Hannah Farnham Lee

What is the proper limit for wealth? It is, first, to have what is necessary; and, second, to have what is enough.
—Marcus Annaeus Seneca

He has enough who is contented with little.　—Anon.

There is a great difference between satisfaction and satiation.
—Mary Jane Sherfey

More than enough is too much.
—Anon.

It's a grand thing to be able to take your money in your hand and to think no more of it when it slips away from you than you would a trout that would slip back into the stream.
—Augusta Gregory

Let him who has enough wish for nothing more.　—Horace

Nothing is enough to the man for whom enough is too little.
—Epicurus

Sufficiency's enough for men of sense.
—Euripides

You never know what is enough unless you know what is more than enough.　—William Blake

Enough is as good as a feast.
—John Heywood

There is satiety in all things, in sleep, and love-making, in the loveliness of singing and the innocent dance.
—Homer

The average man is rich enough when he has a little more than he has got.
—William Ralph Inge

A wise man will desire no more than what he may get justly, use soberly, distribute cheerfully, and leave contently.　—Benjamin Franklin

Money and time are the heaviest burdens of life, and the unhappiest of all mortals are those who have more of either than they know how to use.
—Samuel Johnson

Whoever is not in his coffin and the dark grave, let him know he has enough.　—Walt Whitman

Too much is unwholesome.
—Georg Christoph Lichtenberg

This only grant me, that my means may lie too low for envy, for contempt too high.　—Abraham Cowley

Moderation is the key to lasting enjoyment.   —Hosea Ballou

Nothing in excess.   —Solon

Ask the gods nothing excessive.
            —Aeschylus

Avarice is as destitute of what it has as poverty is of what it has not.
            —Publilius Syrus

Philosophy . . . should not pretend to increase our present stock, but make us economists of what we are possessed of.   —Oliver Goldsmith

The use we make of our fortune determines as to its sufficiency. A little is enough if used wisely, and too much is not enough if expended foolishly.
            —Christian Bovee

It is possible to own too much. A man with one watch knows what time it is; a man with two watches is never quite sure.   —Lee Segall

Happiness is a way station between too much and too little.
            —Channing Pollock

GREED

He who is greedy is always in want.
            —Horace

No gain satisfies a greedy mind.
            —Latin proverb

Ambition if it feeds at all, does so on the ambition of others.
            —Susan Sontag

You can stand tall without standing on someone. You can be a victor without having victims.
            —Harriet Woods

Greed lessens what is gathered.
            —Arab proverb

We risk all in being too greedy.
            —Jean de La Fontaine

Greed is a bottomless pit which exhausts the person in an endless effort to satisfy the need without ever reaching satisfaction.
            —Erich Fromm

Greed, like the love of comfort, is a kind of fear.   —Cyril Connolly

Pillars are fallen at thy feet
Fanes quiver in the air
A prostrate city is thy seat
And thou alone art there.
            —Lydia M. Child

On what strange stuff Ambition feeds!
            —Eliza Cook

The greedy man is incontent with a whole world set before him.
            —Sa'di

For greed, all nature is too little.
            —Marcus Annaeus Seneca

Greed's worst point is its ingratitude.
            —Marcus Annaeus Seneca

CONTROLLING WANTS

To be able to dispense with good things is tantamount to possessing them.   —Jean Francois Regnard

We don't need to increase our goods nearly as much as we need to scale down our wants. Not wanting something is as good as possessing it.
—Donald Horban

The hardest thing is to take less when you can get more.　—Kin Hubbard

Whoever does not regard what he has as most ample wealth is unhappy, though he is master of the world.
—Epicurus

I have learned to seek my happiness by limiting my desires, rather than in attempting to satisfy them.
—John Stuart Mill

How few are our real wants, and how easy is it to satisfy them! Our imaginary ones are boundless and insatiable.　—Julius Charles Hare

Of all the people in the world, those who want the most are those who have the most.　—David Grayson

Who covets more is evermore a slave.
—Robert Herrick

If you desire many things, many things will seem but a few.
—Benjamin Franklin

The heart is great which shows moderation in the midst of prosperity.
—Marcus Annaeus Seneca

Want is a growing giant whom the coat of Have was never large enough to cover.　—Ralph Waldo Emerson

Freedom is not procured by a full enjoyment of what is desired, but by controlling the desire.　—Epictetus

How many things there are which I do not want.　　　—Socrates

Moderate desires constitute a character fitted to acquire all the good which the world can yield. He who has this character is prepared, in whatever situation he is, therewith to be content and has learned the science of being happy.
—Timothy Dwight

Were a man to order his life by the rules of true reason, a frugal substance joined to a contented mind is for him great riches.　—Lucretius

One is never fortunate or as unfortunate as one imagines.
—Francois de La Rochefoucauld

Man needs so little . . . yet he begins wanting so much.　—Louis L'Amour

Man never has what he wants, because what he wants is everything.
—C.F. Ramuz

If your desires be endless, your cares and fears will be so, too.
—Thomas Fuller

We are no longer happy so soon as we wish to be happier.
—Walter Savage Landor

He is not rich that possesses much, but he that covets no more; and he is not poor that enjoys little, but he that wants too much. —Francis Beaumont

Independence may be found in comparative as well as in absolute abundance; I mean where a person contracts his desires within the limits of his fortune.　—William Shenstone

There Are Always Others Worse Off Than Us

One never hugs one's good luck so affectionately as when listening to the relation of some horrible misfortunes which has overtaken others.
—Alexander Smith

If you would but exchange places with the other fellow, how much more you could appreciate your own position.
—Victor E. Gardner

We should learn, by reflection on the misfortunes of others, that there is nothing singular in those which befall ourselves. —Thomas Fitzosborne

Double—no, triple—our troubles and we'd still be better off than any other people on earth. —Ronald Reagan

I wept because I had no shoes, until I saw a man who had no feet.
—Ancient Persian saying

When life's problems seem over-whelming, look around and see what other people are coping with. You may consider yourself fortunate.
—Ann Landers

If all misfortunes were laid in one common heap whence everyone must take an equal portion, most people would be contented to take their own and depart. —Socrates

Who Is Really Poor?

Not he who has little, but he who wishes more, is poor.
—Marcus Annaeus Seneca

The covetous man is always poor.
—Claudian

He is not poor that hath not much, but he that craves much.
—Thomas Fuller

He is poor who does not feel content.
—Japanese proverb

Who Is Really Rich?

I have no riches but my thoughts. Yet these are wealth enough for me.
—Sara Teasdale

He who curbs his desires will always be rich enough. —French proverb

There is a gigantic difference between earning a great deal of money and being rich. —Marlene Dietrich

That man is richest whose pleasures are the cheapest.
—Henry David Thoreau

If you want an accounting of your worth, count your friends.
—Merry Browne

I've had an exciting life; I married for love and got a little money along with it.
—Rose Fitzgerald Kennedy

True affluence is not needing anything.
—Gary Snyder

There are many excuses for the person who made the mistake of con-founding money and wealth. Like many others they mistook the sign for the thing signified.
—Millicent Garrett Fawcett

Friends are the thermometer by which we may judge the temperature of our fortunes.
    —Lady Marguerite Blessington

To be satisfied with what one has; that is wealth. As long as one sorely needs a certain additional amount, that man isn't rich.   —Mark Twain

I have the greatest of all riches: that of not desiring them.
    —Eleonora Duse

My friends are my estate.
    —Emily Dickinson

A man is rich in proportion to the things he can afford to let alone.
    —Henry David Thoreau

There are people who have money and people who are rich.
    —Coco Chanel

He is rich that is satisfied.
    —Thomas Fuller

Nor need we power or splendor, wide hall or lordly dome; the good, the true, the tender—these form the wealth of home.
    —Sarah Josepha Hale

He is well paid that is well satisfied.
    —William Shakespeare

He who is content in his poverty is wonderfully rich.   —Anon.

He who is contented is rich.
    —Lao-tzu

A BMW can't take you as far as a diploma.   —Joyce A. Myers

All fortune belongs to him who has a contented mind. —The Panchatantra

Poor and content is rich, and rich enough.   —William Shakespeare

The greatest wealth is contentment with a little.   —Anon.

No one has yet had the courage to memorialize his wealth on his tombstone. A dollar mark would not look well there.   —Corra May Harris

So many of us define ourselves by what we have, what we wear, what kind of house we live in, and what kind of car we drive . . . if you think of yourself as the woman in the Cartier watch and the Hermes scarf, a house fire will destroy not only your possessions but your self.
    —Linda Henley

The externals are simply so many props; everything we need is within us.
    —Etty Hillesum

He is not rich that possesses much, but he that is content with what he has.
    —Anon.

Being Thankful for Our Abilities and Talents

One well-cultivated talent, deepened and enlarged, is worth one hundred shallow faculties.
    —William Matthews

If only every man would make proper use of his strength and do his utmost, he need never regret his limited ability.
    —Cicero

I knew I had no lyrical quality, a small vocabulary, little gift of metaphor. The original and striking simile never occurred to me. Poetic flights . . . were beyond my powers. On the other hand, I had an acute power of observation, and it seemed to me that I could see a great many things that other people missed. I could put down in clear terms what I saw. . . . I knew that I should never write as well as I could wish, but I thought, with pains, that I could arrive at writing as well as my natural defects allowed.
—W. Somerset Maugham

Anyone is to be pitied who has just sense enough to perceive his deficiencies. —William Hazlitt

What strange perversity is it that induces a man to set his heart on doing those things which he has not succeeded in, and makes him slight those in which his achievement has been respectable.
—Gamaliel Bradford

I may not amount to much, but at least I am unique.
—Jean-Jacques Rousseau

Happy is the man who can do only one thing: in doing it, he fulfills his destiny. —Joseph Joubert

The real tragedy of life is not being limited to one talent, but in failing to use that one talent.
—Edgar Watson Howe

Too many people overvalue what they are not and undervalue what they are. —Malcolm Forbes

CONTENTMENT

Nothing will content him who is not content with a little.
—Greek proverb

Contentment is worth more than riches. —German proverb

I figure if I have my health, can pay the rent and I have my friends, I call it "content." —Lauren Bacall

Be content with what thou hast received, and smooth thy frowning forehead. —Hafez

He is poor who does not feel content.
—Japanese proverb

If thou covetest riches, ask not but for contentment, which is an immense treasure. —Sa'di

Who is content with nothing possesses all things. —Nicolas Boileau

My crown is called content, a crown that seldom kings enjoy.
—William Shakespeare

It is right to be contented with what we have, never with what we are.
—Mackintosh

Be content with your lot; one cannot be first in everything. —Aesop

Content may dwell in all stations. To be low, but above contempt, may be high enough to be happy.
—Sir Thomas Browne

He is not rich that possesses much, but he that is content with what he has. —Anon.

True contentment . . . is the power of getting out of any situation all that there is in it. It is arduous, and it is rare. —G.K. Chesterton

Poor and content is rich, and rich enough. —William Shakespeare

The greatest wealth is contentment with a little. —Anon.

And be content with such things as ye have. —Hebrews 13:5

Everything has its wonders, even darkness and silence, and I learn, whatever state I may be in, therein to be content. —Helen Keller

Try to live the life of the good man who is more than content with what is allocated to him.
—Marcus Aurelius

The world is full of people looking for spectacular happiness while they snub contentment. —Doug Larson

We are never content with our lot.
—Jean de La Fontaine

Until you make peace with who you are, you'll never be content with what you have. —Doris Mortman

True contentment depends not upon what we have; a tub was large enough for Diogenes, but a world was too little for Alexander.
—Charles Caleb Colton

To be content with little is difficult; to be content with much, impossible.
—Anon.

HAPPINESS

To be without some of the things you want is an indispensable part of happiness. —Bertrand Russell

Man is fond of counting his troubles, but he does not count his joys. If he counted them up as he ought to, he would see that every lot has enough happiness provided for it.
—Fyodor Dostoyevsky

Happiness is itself a kind of gratitude.
—Joseph Wood Krutch

I am happy and content because I think I am. —Alain-Rene Lesage

Unhappy is the man, though he rule the world, who doesn't consider himself supremely blessed.
—Marcus Annaeus Seneca

The happiness which is lacking makes one think even the happiness one has unbearable. —Joseph Roux

Happiness is a result of the relative strengths of positive and negative feelings, rather than an absolute amount of one or the other.
—Norman Bradburn

The best way for a person to have happy thoughts is to count his blessings and not his cash. —Anon.

Surfeits of happiness are fatal.
—Baltasar Gracian

If thou wouldst be happy . . . have an indifference for more than what is sufficient. —William Penn

You will live wisely if you are happy in your lot. —Horace

We always have enough to be happy if we are enjoying what we do have—and not worrying about what we don't have. —Ken Keyes, Jr.

Talk happiness. The world is sad enough without your woe. No path is wholly rough. —Ella Wheeler Wilcox

Count Today's Blessings, Rather Than Longing for Yesterday's

Reflect upon your present blessings, of which every man has many; not on your past misfortunes, of which all men have some. —Charles Dickens

No longer forward nor behind
I look in hope or fear;
But, grateful, take the good I find,
The best of now and here.
—John Greenleaf Whittier

We're Better Off, and Happier, Than We Realize or Admit

What a wonderful life I've had! I only wish I'd realized it sooner. —Colette

Was it always my nature to take a bad time and block out the good times, until any success became an accident and failure seemed the only truth? —Lillian Hellman

Most human beings have an almost infinite capacity for taking things for granted. —Aldous Huxley

There are men who are happy without knowing it. —Vauvenargues

We are all of us richer than we think we are. —Michel de Montaigne

What a miserable thing life is: you're living in clover, only the clover isn't good enough. —Bertolt Brecht

I am convinced, the longer I live, that life and its blessings are not so entirely unjustly distributed as when we are suffering greatly we are inclined to suppose. —Mary Todd Lincoln

General Quotations about Our Blessings

Life is hard. Next to what? —Anon.

Over a period of time it's been driven home to me that I'm not going to be the most popular writer in the world, so I'm always happy when anything in any way is accepted. —Stephen Sondheim

It made me gladsome to be getting some education, it being like a big window opening. —Mary Webb

Too much of a good thing can be wonderful. —Mae West

We give thanks for unknown blessings already on their way. —Sacred ritual chant

A man with ambition and love for his blessings here on earth is ever so alive. Having been alive, it won't be so hard in the end to lie down and rest. —Pearl Bailey

In the country of the blind, the one-
eyed man is king.
—Michael Apostolius

Be satisfied, and pleased with what
    thou art,
Act cheerfully and well thou allotted
    part;
Enjoy the present hour, be thankful
    for the past,
And neither fear, nor wish, the
    approaches of the last.
—Martial

No one is satisfied with his fortune,
or dissatisfied with his intellect.
—Antoinette Deshouliere

'Tis better to have loved and lost
than never to have loved at all.
—Alfred, Lord Tennyson

The Grass Is Always Greener on the Other Side of the Fence

You always admire what you really don't understand.
—Eleanor Roosevelt

What you can't get is just what suits you.   —French proverb

The dream is real, my friends. The failure to realize it is the only reality.
—Toni Cade Bambara

The true exercise of freedom is—cannily and wisely and with grace—to move inside what space confines—and not seek to know what lies beyond and cannot be touched or tasted.
—A.S. Byatt

Death and taxes and childbirth! There's never any convenient time for any of them!   —Margaret Mitchell

No one is content with his own lot.
—Horace

Let us accept truth, even when it surprises us and alters our views.
—George Sand

To have ideals is not the same as to have impracticable ideals.
—L. Susan Stebbing

There has never been an age that did not applaud the past and lament the present.   —Lillian Eichler Watson

Every stage of life has its troubles, and no man is content with his own age.
—Ausonius

We love in others what we lack ourselves, and would be everything but what we are.   —R.H. Stoddard

There is less in this than meets the eye.
—Tallulah Bankhead

When you don't have any money, the problem is food. When you have money, it's sex. When you have both, it's health. If everything is simply jake, then you're frightened of death.
—J.P. Donleavy

Diogenes was asked what wine
he liked best, and he answered,
"Somebody else's."
　　　　　—Michel de Montaigne

The apples on the other side of the
wall are the sweetest.　　　—Anon.

Nothing is so good as it seems
beforehand.　　　—George Eliot

Happiness is . . . usually attributed by
adults to children, and by children to
adults.　　　—Thomas Szasz

Acorns were good till bread was
found.　　　—Anon.

None of us is ever satisfied with what
we are.　　　—Terence

We always long for forbidden things,
and desire what is denied us.
　　　　　—Francois Rabelais

Man's heart is never satisfied; the
snake would swallow the elephant.
　　　　　—Chinese proverb

We all envy other people's luck.
　　　　　—Latin proverb

When every blessed thing you have is
made of silver, or of gold, you long
for simple pewter.　　—W.S. Gilbert

I'd rather have written "Cheers" than
anything I've written.
　　　　　—Kurt Vonnegut

When a man's busy, leisure strikes
him as a wonderful pleasure; and at
leisure once is he? Straightway he
wants to be busy.
　　　　　—Robert Browning

To most of us the real life is the life
we do not lead.　　　—Oscar Wilde

Happiness to a dog is what lies on
the other side of the door.
　　　　　—Charlton Ogburn, Jr.

Man would be otherwise. That is the
essence of the specifically human.
　　　　　—Antonio Machado

He who would be happy should stay
at home.　　　—Greek proverb

He who leaves his house in search of
happiness pursues a shadow.
　　　　　—Anon.

DISTANT PLACES AND THINGS

It is not irritating to be where one
is. It is only irritating to think one
would like to be somewhere else.
　　　　　—John Cage

Pioneers may be picturesque figures,
but they are often rather lonely ones.
　　　　　—Nancy Astor

He that is discontented in one place
will seldom be happy in another.
　　　　　—Aesop

We are under the spell always of
what is distant from us. It is not in
our nature to desire passionately
what is near at hand.　—Alec Waugh

In all climates, under all skies, man's
happiness is always somewhere else.
　　　　　—Giacomo Leopardi

In Rome you long for the country. In
the country you praise to the skies
the distant town.　　　—Horace

He who would be happy should stay at home. —Greek proverb

Life is a hospital in which every patient is possessed by the desire of changing his bed. One would prefer to suffer near the fire, and another is certain he would get well if he were by the window.
—Charles Baudelaire

It is common to overlook what is near by keeping the eye fixed on something remote. —Samuel Johnson

There are three wants which can never be satisfied: that of the rich, who want something more; that of the sick, who want something different; and that of the traveler, who says, "Anywhere but here."
—Ralph Waldo Emerson

Happiness grows at our firesides, and is not to be picked in strangers' gardens. —Douglas Jerrold

Men run away to other countries because they are not good in their own, and run back to their own because they pass for nothing in the new places. —Ralph Waldo Emerson

The proper means of increasing the love we bear our native country is to reside some time in a foreign one.
—William Shenstone

If solid happiness we prize, within
  our breast this jewel lies,
And they are fools who roam; the
  world has nothing to bestow,
From our own selves our bliss must
  flow,
And that dear hut—our home.
—Nathaniel Cotton

A child on a farm sees a plane fly overhead and dreams of a faraway place. A traveler on the plane sees the farmhouse and dreams of home.
—Carl Burns

Everyone Has Problems and Difficulties

Life has no smooth road for any of us; and in the bracing atmosphere of a high aim the very roughness stimulates the climber to steadier steps till the legend, "over steep ways to the stars," fulfills itself. —W.C. Doane

The only normal people are the ones you don't know very well.
—Foe Ancis

Before we set our hearts too much upon anything, let us examine how happy they are who already possess it.
—Francois de La Rochefoucauld

What makes us discontented with our condition is the absurdly exaggerated idea we have of the happiness of others. —Anon.

Nobody's problem is ideal. Nobody has things just as he would like them.
—Dr. Frank Crane

Everybody in the world ought to be sorry for everybody else. We all have our little private hell.
—Bettina von Hutton

We are convinced that happiness is never to be found, and each believes it possessed by others, to keep alive the hope of obtaining it for himself.
—Samuel Johnson

Men would be angels; angels would
be gods.   —Alexander Pope

If every man's internal care
Were written on his brow,
How many would our pity share
Who raise our envy now?
          —Pietro Metastasio

Misfortunes come to all men.
          —Chinese proverb

You have no idea how big the other
fellow's troubles are.   —B.C. Forbes

THE POWERFUL, FAMOUS AND RICH ALL HAVE THEIR TROUBLES

I have now reigned above fifty years
in victory or peace, beloved by my
subjects, dreaded by my enemies,
respected by my allies. Riches and
honors, power and pleasure, have
awaited my call, nor does any earthly
blessing seem to have been wanting.
. . . I have diligently numbered the
days of pure and genuine happiness that have fallen to my lot; they
amount to fourteen.
          —Abd al-Rahman

I have been very happy, very rich,
very beautiful, much adulated, very
famous and very unhappy.
          —Brigitte Bardot

I feel successful when the writing
goes well. This lasts five minutes.
Once, when I was on the bestseller
list, I also felt successful. That lasted
three minutes.   —Jacqueline Briskin

Great and small suffer the same mishaps.   —Blaise Pascal

None think the great unhappy but
the great.   —Edward Young

I thought I had reached a point in life
where everything would be smooth.
But it is not. It just gets more jagged
and pitted and filled with turns that
take you into the dark recesses of
your mind. It never seems to get easy.
          —Sylvester Stallone

If I were given a change of life, I'd
like to see how it would be to live as
a mere six-footer.
          —Wilt Chamberlain

I just want to be an ordinary girl.
          —Princess Stephanie of Monaco

Money is another pressure. I'm not
complaining, I'm just saying that
there's a certain luxury in having no
money. I spent ten years in New York
not having it, not worrying about
it. Suddenly you have it, then you
worry, where is it going? Am I doing
the right thing with it?
          —Dustin Hoffman

On the outside one is a star. But
in reality, one is completely alone,
doubting everything. To experience
this loneliness of soul is the hardest
thing in the world.   —Brigitte Bardot

There is no man in this world without some manner of tribulation or
anguish, though he be king or pope.
          —Thomas à Kempis

The only incurable troubles of the
rich are the troubles that money can't
cure.   —Ogden Nash

There is no man in any rank who is always at liberty to act as he would incline; in some quarter or other he is limited by circumstances.

—Bonnie Blair

None of us can be free of conflict and woe. Even the greatest men have had to accept disappointments as their daily bread. . . . The art of living lies less in eliminating our troubles than in growing with them.

—Bernard M. Baruch

Renown is a source of toil and sorrow; obscurity is a source of happiness.

—Johann L. von Mosheim

My crown is called content; a crown it is that seldom kings enjoy.

—William Shakespeare

If I had my life to live over, I wish I could be a great pianist or something.

—Woody Allen

There is no armour against fate; death lays his icy hands on kings.

—James Shirley

Pale death with impartial tread beats at the poor man's cottage door and at the palaces of kings.   —Horace

I want to be able to live without a crowded calendar. I want to be able to read a book without feeling guilty, or go to a concert when I like.

—Golda Meir

I'd like to be a truck driver. I think you could run your life that way. It wouldn't be such a bad way of doing it. It would offer a chance to be alone.

—Princess Anne of England

There is as much confusion in the world of the gods as in ours.

—Euripides

Pray the gods do not envy your happiness!   —Euripides

The suffering of the rich is among the sweetest pleasures of the poor.

—R.M. Huber

Oh God, don't envy me, I have my own pains.   —Barbra Streisand

SUCCESS ISN'T ALWAYS THE ANSWER

Success is counted sweetest by those who never succeed.

—Emily Dickinson

I have known no man of genius who had not to pay, in some affliction or defect either physical or spiritual, for what the gods had given him.

—Max Beerbohm

I have been very happy, very rich, very beautiful, much adulated, very famous and very unhappy.

—Brigitte Bardot

I feel successful when the writing goes well. This lasts five minutes. Once, when I was on the bestseller list, I also felt successful. That lasted three minutes.   —Jacqueline Briskin

Men are all the same. They always think that something they are going to get is better than what they have got.

—John Oliver Hobbes

Not all speed is movement.

—Toni Cade

Success is not greedy, as people think, but insignificant. That's why it satisfies nobody.
—Marcus Annaeus Seneca

Oh, I wish that God had not given me what I prayed for! It was not so good as I thought. —Johanna Spyri

Beggars do not envy millionaires, though of course they will envy other beggars who are more successful.
—Bertrand Russell

Ambition, having reached the summit, longs to descend.
—Pierre Corneille

What we call progress is the exchange of one nuisance for another nuisance. —Henry Havelock Ellis

The superpowers often behave like two heavily armed blind men feeling their way around a room, each believing himself in mortal peril from the other, who he assumes to have perfect vision. —Henry Kissinger

Wanting to change, to improve, a person's situation means offering him, for difficulties in which he is practiced and experienced, other difficulties that will find him perhaps even more bewildered.
—Rainer Maria Rilke

BEING YOUNGER OR BETTER LOOKING WOULDN'T SOLVE OUR PROBLEMS

Being considered beautiful at a young age sends confusing signals. You think people only like you because of your beauty. —Priscilla Presley

Youth is not a question of years: one is young or old from birth.
—Natalie Clifford Barney

When I was fourteen, I was the oldest I ever was. . . . I've been getting younger ever since.
—Shirley Temple Black

A child's world is fresh and new and beautiful, full of wonder and excitement. It is our misfortune that for most of us that clear-eyed vision, that true instinct for what is beautiful and awe-inspiring, is dimmed and even lost before we reach adulthood.
—Rachel Carson

Sure, I'm for helping the elderly. I'm going to be old myself someday.
—Lillian Carter

Youth is something very new: twenty years ago no one mentioned it.
—Coco Chanel

A comfortable old age is the reward of a well-spent youth. Instead of its bringing sad and melancholy prospects of decay, it would give us hopes of eternal youth in a better world.
—Lydia M. Child

We turn not older with years, but newer every day. —Emily Dickinson

Old age is when the liver spots show through your gloves. —Phyllis Diller

The middle years, caught between children and parents, free of neither: the past stretches back too densely, it is too thickly populated, the future has not yet thinned out.
—Margaret Drabble

It is not how old you are, but how you are old. —Marie Dressler

One of the many things nobody ever tells you about middle age is that it's such a nice change from being young. —Dorothy Canfield Fisher

When you become 100, life changes completely. —Lady Willie Forbus

This is a youth-oriented society, and the joke is on them because youth is a disease from which we all recover. —Dorothy Fuldheim

Old age, believe me, is a good and pleasant thing. It is true you are gently shouldered off the stage, but then you are given such a comfortable front stall as spectator. —Jane Harrison

I look forward to growing old and wise and audacious. —Glenda Jackson

It is so comical to hear oneself called old, even at ninety I suppose! —Alice James

I enjoy my wrinkles and regard them as badges of distinction—I've worked hard for them! —Maggie Kuhn

Time—our youth—it never really goes, does it? It is all held in our minds. —Helen Hoover Santmyer

Even I don't wake up looking like Cindy Crawford. —Cindy Crawford

We all lose our looks eventually, better develop your character and interest in life. —Jacqueline Bisset

The lovely thing about being forty is that you can appreciate twenty-five-year-old men more. —Colleen McCullough

The only thing that makes one place more attractive to me than another is the quantity of heart I find in it. —Jane Welsh Carlyle

A woman may develop wrinkles and cellulite, lose her waistline, her bustline, her ability to bear a child, even her sense of humor, but none of that implies a loss of her sexuality, her femininity. —Barbara Gordon

Old age is like a plane flying through a storm. Once you are aboard there is nothing you can do. —Golda Meir

In youth the days are short and the years are long. In old age the years are short and day's long. —Nikita Ivanovich Panin

How long can you be cute? —Goldie Hawn

Being pretty on the inside means you don't hit your brother and you eat all your peas—that's what my grandma taught me. —Elizabeth Heller

Beauty is in the eye of the beholder. —Margaret Wolfe Hungerford

When you're fifty, you start thinking about things you haven't thought about before. I used to think getting old was about vanity—but actually it's about losing people you love. Getting wrinkles is trivial. —Joyce Carol Oates

I am desperate and vulnerable. . . . I
am always terrified. . . . Beauty can
sometimes be so very troublesome.
—Faye Dunaway

I hate myself on the screen. I want to
die . . . my voice is either too high or
too gravelly. I want to dive under the
carpet. . . . I'd love to be tall and wil-
lowy . . . I'm short.
—Elizabeth Taylor

After a certain number of years, our
faces become our biographies.
—Cynthia Ozick

I don't like my voice. I don't like
the way I look. I don't like the way
I move. I don't like the way I act. I
mean, period. So, you know, I don't
like myself.   —Elizabeth Taylor

Not always the fanciest cake that's
there
Is the best to eat!
—Margaret Elizabeth Sangster

No, Doctor, I don't want to grow
young again. I just want to keep on
growing old.
—Madame de Rothschild

It is quite wrong to think of old age
as a downward slope. On the contrary, one climbs higher and higher
with the advancing years, and that,
too, with surprising strides.
—George Sand

I look forward to being older, when
what you look like becomes less and
less an issue and what you are is the
point.   —Susan Sarandon

When you've got the personality, you
don't need the nudity.   —Mae West

The only real elegance is in the mind;
if you've got that, the rest really
comes from it.   —Diana Vreeland

Beauty can get a woman what she
wants: love and money. But when
beauty leaves you, so can the things it
brought.   —Paulina Porizkova

If you're considered a beauty, it's
hard to be accepted doing anything
but standing around.
—Cybil Shepherd

Just because you're beautiful, they
think you can't act.... I've got a lot
more to prove.   —Carol Alt

I intimidate men. . . . People look a lot,
but there's no line outside my door.
—Joan Severance

People see you as an object, not as
a person, and they project a set of
expectations onto you. People who
don't have it think beauty is a blessing, but actually it sets you apart.
—Candice Bergen

I can count the number of dates I've
had on one hand. I wish that guys
would approach me, but they don't.
—LaToya Jackson

When you step on the first tee it
doesn't matter what you look like. . . .
It doesn't help your 5-iron if you're
pretty.   —Laura Baugh

For years I stopped reading beauty
magazines because I couldn't look
at one without wanting to blow my
brains out. How can those women
look so good?   —Jamie Lee Curtis

Each time I get off a plane in Hollywood, I don't think I'm pretty enough.
—Christine Lahti

Frankly, I like the fact that I no longer fit the young beauty type—people take me more seriously now.
—Cybil Shepherd

You know how many stunning women told me they can't stand a good-looking man? . . . Women feel secure with an ugly guy because a man in bad shape isn't gonna cheat.
—Jackie Mason

Outstanding beauty, like outstanding gifts of any kind, tends to get in the way of normal emotional development, and thus of that particular success in life which we call happiness.
—Milton R. Sapirstein

A full bosom is actually a millstone around a woman's neck. . . . [Breasts] are not parts of a person but lures slung around her neck, to be kneaded and twisted like magic putty, or mumbled and mouthed like lolly ices.
—Germaine Greer

Plain women know more about men than beautiful ones do.
—Katharine Hepburn

People are crying up the rich and variegated plumage of the peacock, and he is himself blushing at the sight of his ugly feet.
—Sa'di

I'm walking insecurity. Without all this makeup, I look like a refugee when I get up in the morning. . . .
I generally look like one major bow-wow. I mean arf.   —Connie Chung

You start out happy that you have no hips or boobs. All of a sudden you get them, and it feels sloppy. Then just when you start liking them, they start dropping.   —Cindy Crawford

The problem with beauty is that it's like being born rich and getting poorer.
—Joan Collins

Guys think that if a girl is pretty, she's automatically going to say no. Most of the guy's I've gone out with, I've had to make it completely obvious that I'd like them to ask me out. Or, I've had to ask them.
—Brooke Shields

I think if I weren't so beautiful, maybe I'd have more character.
—Jerry Hall

Not many people ask me out.
—Marina Sirtis

BE CAREFUL IN MAKING COMPARISONS

The striking point about our model family is not simply the compete-compete, consume-consume style of life it urges us to follow. The striking point, in the face of all the propaganda, is how few Americans actually live this way.   —Louise Kapp Howe

Instead of comparing our lot with that of those who are more fortunate than we are, we should compare it with the lot of the great majority of our fellow men. It then appears that we are among the privileged.
—Helen Keller

I murmured because I had no shoes, until I met man who had no feet.
—Persian proverb

Comparison, more than reality, makes men happy or wretched.
—Thomas Fuller

The man with a toothache thinks everyone happy whose teeth are sound. The poverty-stricken man makes the same mistake about the rich man.   —George Bernard Shaw

If you compare yourself with others, you may become vain or bitter, for always there will be greater and lesser persons than yourself.
—Max Ehrmann

I look at what I have not and think myself unhappy; others look at what I have and think me happy.
—Joseph Roux

Enjoy your own life without comparing it with that of another.
—*The Condorcet*

If we only wanted to be happy it would be easy; but we want to be happier than other people, which is almost always difficult, since we think them happier than they are.
—Charles de Montesquieu

I never admired another's fortune so much that I became dissatisfied with my own.   —Cicero

Every horse thinks his own pack heaviest.   —Thomas Fuller

Comparisons of one's lot with others' teaches us nothing and enfeebles the will.   —Thornton Wilder

To think well of every other man's condition, and to dislike our own, is one of the misfortunes of human nature.   —Robert Burton

Other people's eggs have two yolks.
—Hungarian proverb

No story ever looks as bad as the story you've just bought; no story ever looks as good as the story the other fellow just bought.
—Irving Thalberg

If all our misfortunes were laid in one common heap, whence every one must take an equal portion, most people would be content to take their own and depart.   —Solon

Money, it turned out, was exactly like sex; you thought of nothing else if you didn't have it and thought of other things if you did.
—James Baldwin

WE CAN'T LET OURSELVES BE WARPED BY JEALOUSY AND ENVY

Envy is an insult to oneself.
—Yevgeny Yevtushenko

Jealousy is no more than feeling alone against smiling enemies.
—Elizabeth Bowen

Envy has the ugliness of a trapped rat that has gnawed its own foot in its effort to escape.   —Angus Wilson

Jealousy is never satisfied with anything short of omniscience that would detect the subtlest fold in the heart.
—George Eliot

Envy eats nothing but its own heart.
—German proverb

Jealousy would be far less torturous if we understood that love is a passion entirely unrelated to our merits.
—Paul Eldridges

In jealousy there is more of self-love than love.
—Francois de La Rochefoucauld

Jealousy is an inner consciousness of one's own inferiority. It is a mental cancer.
—B.C. Forbes

Jealousy, that dragon which slays love under the pretense of keeping it alive.
—Havelock Ellis

There is no greater glory than love, nor any greater punishment than jealousy.
—Lope de Vega

As a moth gnaws a garment, so doth envy consume a man.
—Saint John Chrysostom

Envy is the most stupid of vices, for there is no single advantage to be gained from it.
—Honore de Balzac

The jealous are troublesome to others, but torment to themselves.
—William Penn

Envy and fear are the only passions to which no pleasure is attached.
—John Churton Collins

If malice or envy were tangible and had a shape, it would be the shape of a boomerang.
—Charley Reese

Jealousy is all the fun you think they had.
—Erica Jong

Envy is a kind of praise.
—John Gay

Envy, among other ingredients, has a mixture of the love of justice in it. We are more angry at undeserved than at deserved good fortune.
—William Hazlitt

Envy comes from people's ignorance of, or lack of belief in, their own gifts.
—Jean Vanier

To cure jealousy is to see it for what it is, a dissatisfaction with self.
—Joan Didion

If envy were a fever, all the world would be ill.
—Danish proverb

Jealousy is not a barometer by which the depth of love can be read. It merely records the degree of the lover's insecurity.
—Margaret Mead

The heaven of the envied is hell for the envious.
—Baltasar Gracian

You can't be envious and happy at the same time.
—Frank Tyger

BEING CONSIDERATE OF OTHERS

The whole art of life is knowing the right time to say things.
—Maeve Binchy

It is not until you become a mother that your judgment slowly turns to compassion and understanding.
—Erma Bombeck

If we would build on a sure foundation in friendship, we must love friends for their sake rather than for our own.   —Charlotte Brontë

Friendship, which is of its nature a delicate thing, fastidious, slow of growth, is easily checked, will hesitate, demur, recoil where love, good old blustering love, bowls ahead and blunders through every obstacle.
                    —Colette

It is all right to say exactly what you think if you have learned to think exactly.   —Marcelene Cox

Silence sweeter is than speech.
    —Dinah Maria Mulock Craik

When we get to wishing a great deal for ourselves, whatever we get soon turns into mere limitation and exclusion.   —George Eliot

The opposite of talking isn't listening. The opposite of talking is waiting.
                    —Fran Lebowitz

Listening is not merely not talking, though even that is beyond most of our powers; it means taking a vigorous, human interest in what is being told us.   —Alice Duer Miller

Why is it that people who cannot show feeling presume that that is a strength and not a weakness?
                    —May Sarton

True love grows by sacrifice and the more thoroughly the soul rejects natural satisfaction the stronger and more detached its tenderness becomes.   —Thérèse of Lisieux

The nice thing about teamwork is that you always have others on your side.
                    —Margaret Carty

Helping Other People

WE CAN'T LIVE JUST FOR OURSELVES

Let everyone who has the grace of intelligence fear that, because of it, he will be judged more heavily if he is negligent. —Saint Bridget of Sweden

Service to others is the rent you pay for living on this planet.
—Marian Wright Edelman

To be a revolutionary you have to be a human being. You have to care about people who have no power.
—Jane Fonda

Never reach out your hand unless you're willing to extend an arm.
—Elizabeth Fuller

It is not who you attend school with but who controls the school you attend. —Nikki Giovanni

What is buried in the past of one generation falls to the next to claim.
—Susan Griffin

Everyone needs help from everyone.
—Bertolt Brecht

We've got to work to save our children and do it with full respect for the fact that if we do not, no one else is going to do it. —Dorothy Height

The entire population of the universe, with one trifling exception, is composed of others.
—John Andrew Holmes

The woman who does not choose to love should cut the matter short at once, by holding out no hopes to her suitor. —Marguerite de Valois

No matter what accomplishments you make, somebody helped you.
—Althea Gibson

Much misconstruction and bitterness are spared to him who thinks naturally upon what he owes to others, rather than on what he ought to expect from them.
—Elizabeth de Meulan Guizot

No matter how lofty you are in your department, the responsibility for what your lowliest assistant is doing is yours. —Bessie Rowland James

Until the great mass of the people shall be filled with the sense of responsibility for each other's welfare, social justice can never be attained.
—Helen Keller

The oppressed never free themselves—they do not have the necessary strengths.   —Clare Boothe Luce

I shall not pass this way again:
Then let me now relieve some pain,
Remove some barrier from the road,
Or brighten some one's heavy load.
—Eva Rose Park

I think if I were dying and I heard of an act of injustice, it would start me up to a moment's life again.
—Olive Schreiner

If you bungle raising your children, I don't think whatever else you do matters very much.
—Jacqueline Kennedy Onassis

My satisfaction comes from my commitment to advancing a better world.
—Faye Wattleton

You don't live in a world all your own. Your brothers are here, too.
—Albert Schweitzer

What do we live for if not to make life less difficult for each other?
—George Eliot

It is human nature that rules the world, not governments and regimes.
—Svetlana Alliluyeva

Injustice is a sixth sense, and rouses all the others.   —Amelia Barr

The service we render others is the rent we pay for our room on earth.
—Wilfred Grenfell

A man is called selfish not for pursuing his own good, but for neglecting his neighbor's.   —Richard Whately

In this world we must help one another.   —Jean de La Fontaine

Man absolutely cannot live by himself.
—Erich Fromm

We cannot live only for ourselves. A thousand fibers connect us with our fellow men.   —Herman Melville

We have no more right to consume happiness without producing it than to consume wealth without producing it.   —George Bernard Shaw

In the time we have it is surely our duty to do all the good we can to all the people we can in all the ways we can.   —William Barclay

There ain't nothing but one thing wrong with every one of us, and that's selfishness.   —Will Rogers

He who lives only for himself is truly dead to others.   —Publilius Syrus

Provision for others is a fundamental responsibility of human life.
—Woodrow Wilson

Everything that lives, lives not alone, nor for itself.   —William Blake

A man wrapped up in himself makes a very small bundle.
—Benjamin Franklin

Maturity begins to grow when you can sense your concern for others outweighing your concern for yourself.
—John MacNaughton

Nothing Is More Important Than Kindness

I see their souls, and I hold them in my hands, and because I love them they weigh nothing.   —Pearl Bailey

Three things in human life are important: The first is to be kind. The second is to be kind. And the third is to be kind.   —Henry James

I'm not a competitive person, and I think women like me because they don't think I'm competitive, just nice.
—Barbara Bush

As perfume to the flower, so is kindness to speech.   —Katherine Francke

To be told we are loved is not enough. We must feel loved.
—Lauren Hutton

It's never what you say, but how you make it sound sincere.
—Marya Mannes

I never fight, except against difficulties.
—Helen Keller

Nothing has happened today except kindness.   —Gertrude Stein

In a great romance, each person plays a part the other really likes.
—Elizabeth Ashley

Etiquette—a fancy word for simple kindness.   —Elsa Maxwell

If I can stop one heart from breaking,
I shall not live in vain;
If I can ease one life the aching,
Or cool one pain,
Or help one fainting robin
Unto his nest again,
I shall not live in vain.
—Emily Dickinson

The legacy I want to leave is a child-care system that says no kid is going to be left alone or left unsafe.
—Marian Wright Edelman

I think women need kindness more than love. When one human being is kind to another, it's a very deep matter.
—Alice Childress

Life is just a short walk from the cradle to the grave—and it sure behooves us to be kind to one another along the way.   —Alice Childress

I'm a competitive person, but I have never understood people's competitiveness at the expense of their colleagues.   —Geraldine Ferraro

You know, we're all going in the same direction, or at least trying to. So we need to live together, get along together, and give each other enough space to be comfortable on that road.
—Lillian Gideon

The demand for equal rights in every vocation of life is just and fair; but, after all, the most vital right is the right to love and be loved.
—Emma Goldman

Good manners are the techniques of expressing consideration for the feelings of others   —Alice Duer Miller

Moments of kindness and reconciliation are worth having, even if the parting has to come sooner or later.
—Alice Munro

A happy life is made up of little things—a gift sent, a letter written, a call made, a recommendation given, transportation provided, a cake made, a book lent, a check sent.
—Carol Holmes

If a man is pictured chopping off a woman's breast, it only gets an R rating, but if, God forbid, a man is pictured kissing a woman's breast, it gets an X rating. Why is violence more acceptable than tenderness?
—Sally Struthers

If I didn't start painting, I would have raised chickens.   —Grandma Moses

Be kind, for everyone you meet is fighting a hard battle.   —Plato

One's life has value so long as one attributes value to the life of others, by means of love, friendship, indignation, and compassion.
—Simone de Beauvoir

Kindness in words creates confidence. Kindness in thinking creates profoundness. Kindness in giving creates love.
—Lao-tzu

I'd like people to think of me as someone who cares about them.
—Diana, Princess of Wales

Tenderness is greater proof of love than the most passionate of vows.
—Marlene Dietrich

Kindness is the language which the deaf can hear and the blind can see.
—Mark Twain

One of the most valuable things we can do to heal one another is listen to each other's stories.   —Rebecca Falls

It's a rare thing, graciousness. The shape of it can be acquired, but not, I think, the substance.
—Gertrude Schweitzer

Wherever there is a human being, there is an opportunity for a kindness.
—Marcus Annaeus Seneca

Oh! may each youthful bosom, catch the sacred fire.   —Ann Plato

Kindness is the golden chain by which society is bound together.
—Johann von Goethe

The best index to a person's character is (a) how he treats people who can't do him any good, and (b) how he treats people who can't fight back.
—Abigail Van Buren

To nourish children and raise them against odds is in any time, any place, more valuable than to fix bolts in cars or design nuclear weapons.
—Marilyn French

Sympathy is the charm of human life.
—Grace Aguilar

I expect to pass through life but once. If, therefore, there be any kindness I can show, or any good thing I can do for any fellow being, let me do it now . . . as I shall not pass this way again.
—William Penn

We bear the world and we make it. . . . There was never a great man who had not a great mother—it is hardly an exaggeration.   —Olive Schreiner

I wonder why it is that we are not all kinder to each other. . . . How much the world needs it! How easily it is done!   —Henry Drummond

Miss no single opportunity of making some small sacrifice, here by a smiling look, there by a kindly word; always doing the smallest right and doing it all for love.
    —Thérèse of Lisieux

After the verb "to Love," "to Help" is the most beautiful verb in the world.
    —Bertha von Suttner

We are made kind by being kind.
    —Eric Hoffer

Kindness causes us to learn, and to forget, many things.
    —Madame Swetchine

There is nothing in life but refraining from hurting others, and comforting those that are sad.   —Olive Schreiner

Without kindness, there can be no true joy.   —Thomas Carlyle

Wise sayings often fall on barren ground, but a kind word is never thrown away.   —Sir Arthur Helps

A word of kindness is seldom spoken in vain, while witty sayings are as easily lost as the pearls slipping from a broken string.   —George Prentice

A kind word is like a Spring day.
    —Russian proverb

Kindness is in our power, even when fondness is not.   —Samuel Johnson

Kindness affects more than severity.
    —Aesop

Always be a little kinder than necessary.   —Sir James M. Barrie

Kindness is the ability to love people more than they deserve.   —Anon.

The sense that someone else cares always helps because it is the sense of love.   —George E. Woodberry

Today I bent the truth to be kind, and I have no regret, for I am far surer of what is kind that I am of what is true.   —Robert Brault

Kindness, I've discovered, is everything in life.   —Isaac Bashevis Singer

What wisdom can you find that is greater than kindness?
    —Jean-Jacques Rousseau

Have you had a kindness shown?
Pass it on!
'Twas not given for thee alone,
Pass it on!
Let it travel down the years,
Let it wipe another's tears,
Till in Heaven the deed appears—
Pass it on!
    —Henry Burton

Goodwill . . . is an immeasurable and tremendous energy, the atomic energy of the spirit.   —Eleanor B. Stock

Goodwill is the mightiest practical force in the universe.
    —Charles F. Dole

Knowing sorrow well, I learn to
succor the distressed.   —Virgil

Compassion is the basis of all morality.
     —Arthur Schopenhauer

Success has nothing to do with what
you gain in life or accomplish for
yourself. It's what you do for others.
     —Danny Thomas

Right Now Is the Time to Be Kind
You cannot do a kindness too soon,
for you never know how soon it will
be too late. —Ralph Waldo Emerson

There's no use in doing a kindness if
you do it a day too late.
     —Charles Kingsley

He who sees a need and waits to be
asked for help is as unkind as if he
had refused it.   —Dante Alighieri

The golden rule is of no use whatsoever unless you realize that it is your
move.   —Dr. Frank Crane

He gives twice who gives promptly.
     —Publilius Syrus

We Mustn't Judge
Before We Help

Tact is the ability to describe others
as they see themselves.
     —Mary Pettibone Poole

Instead of getting hard ourselves and
trying to compete, women should try
to give their best qualities to men—
bring them softness, teach them how
to cry.   —Joan Baez

Youth condemns; maturity condones.
     —Josephine Preston Peabody

It is unfair to hold people responsible
for our illusions of them.
     —Comtesse Diane

The deadliest feeling that can be
offered to a woman is pity.
     —Vicki Baum

People who won't help others in
trouble "because they got into trouble through their own fault" would
probably not throw a lifeline to a
drowning man until they learned
whether he fell in through his own
fault or not.   —Sydney J. Harris

If you judge people, you have no time
to love them.   —Mother Teresa

Justice and judgment lie often a
world apart.   —Emmeline Pankhurst

With compassion, we see benevolent-
ly our own human condition and the
condition of our fellow beings. We
drop prejudice. We withhold judgment.   —Christina Baldwin

A few observations and much reasoning lead to error; many observations
and a little reasoning to truth.
     —Dr. Alexis Carrel

Nobody who is somebody looks
down on anybody.
     —Margaret Deland

Really listening and suspending one's
own judgment is necessary in order
to understand other people on their
own terms. As we have noted, this
is a process that requires trust and
builds trust.   —Mary Field Belenky

Reform is born of need, not pity.
—Rebecca Harding Davis

I am convinced that any feeling of exaltation because we have people under us should be conquered, for I am sure that if we enjoy being over people, there will be something in our manner which will make them dislike being under us.
—Mary Parker Follett

"Honesty" without compassion and understanding is not honesty, but subtle hostility.
—Rose N. Franzblau

Theories and goals of education don't matter a whit if you do not consider your students to be human beings.
—Lou Ann Walker

It's compassion that makes gods of us.
—Dorothy Gilman

We Help When We Liberate

When God made up this world of
    ours,
He made it long and wide,
And meant that it should shelter all,
And none should be denied.
—Carrie Jacobs Bond

I've always thought that people need to feel good about themselves and I see my role as offering support to them, to provide some light along the way.   —Diana, Princess of Wales

The finest inheritance you can give a child is to allow it to make its own way, completely on its own feet.
—Isadora Duncan

Let our girls feel that we expect something more of them than that they merely look pretty and appear well in society. Teach them that there is a race with special needs which they and only they can help; that the world needs and is already asking for their trained and efficient forces.
—Anna Julia Cooper

A child is a temporarily disabled and stunted version of a larger person, whom you will someday know. Your job is to help them overcome the disabilities associated with their size and inexperience so that they get on with being that larger person.
—Barbara Ehrenreich

We have to improve life, not just for those who have the most skills and those who know how to manipulate the system. But also for and with those who often have so much to give but never get the opportunity.
—Dorothy Height

The most notable fact that culture imprints on women is the sense of our limits. The most important thing one woman can do for another is to illuminate and expand her sense of actual possibilities.   —Adrienne Rich

First, teach a person to develop to the point of his limitations and then— pfft!—break the limitations.
—Viola Spolin

If you want a baby, have a new one. Don't baby the old one.
—Jessamyn West

When anything gets freed, a zest goes round the world.
—Hortense Calisher

If we can't turn the world around we can at least bolster the victims.
—Liz Carpenter

If We Want to Help Someone, We Should Give Them Practical Help

If a child is too keep alive his inborn sense of wonder . . . he needs the companionship of at least one adult who can share it, rediscovering with him the joy, excitement, and mystery of the world we live in.
—Rachel Carson

We ought to be doing all we can to make it possible for every child to fulfill his or her God-given potential.
—Hillary Rodham Clinton

You cannot create genius. All you can do is nurture it.   —Ninette de Valois

Most convicted felons are just people who were not taken to museums or Broadway musicals as children.
—Libby Gelman-Waxner

No one has yet realized the wealth of sympathy, the kindness and generosity hidden in the soul of a child. The effort of every true education should be to unlock that treasure.
—Emma Goldman

I'm not an American hero. I'm a person who loves children.
—Clara McBride Hale

When a person is down in the world, an ounce of help is better than a pound of preaching.
—Edward Bulwer-Lytton

The greatest gift is the passion for reading. It is cheap, it consoles, it distracts, it excites, it gives you knowledge of the world and experience of a wide kind. It is a moral illumination.
—Elizabeth Hardwick

A little help is worth a great deal of pity.   —Anon.

Don't give advice unless you're asked.
—Amy Alcott

Generosity gives assistance, rather than advice.   —Vauvenargues

Our worth is determined by the good deeds we do, rather than by the fine emotions we feel.   —Elias L. Magoon

Nagging is the repetition of unpalatable truths.
—Baroness Edith Summerskill

Orthodox criticism . . . is a murderer of talent. And because the most modest and sensitive people are the most talented, having the most imagination and sympathy, these are the first ones to get killed off.   —Brenda Ueland

With every deed you are sowing a seed, though the harvest you may not see.   —Ella Wheeler Wilcox

Giving kids clothes and food is one thing, but it's much more important to teach them that other people besides themselves are important and that the best thing they can do with their lives is to use them in the service of other people.   —Dolores Huerta

What its children become, that will the community become.
—Suzannea LaFollette

107

A child is fed with milk and praise.
—Mary Lamb

Children are forced to live very rapidly in order to live at all. They are given only a few years in which to learn hundreds of thousands of things about life and the planet and themselves.   —Phyllis McGinley

Live and let live is not enough; live and help live is not too much.
—Orison Swett Marden

To give pleasure to a single heart by a single kind act is better than a thousand head-bowings in prayer.
—Sa'di

Establishing lasting peace is the work of education; all politics can do is keep us out of war.
—Maria Montessori

Pity costs nothing and ain't worth nothing.   —Josh Billings

The greatness of the human personality begins at the hour of birth. From this almost mystic affirmation there comes what may seem a strange conclusion: that education must start from birth.   —Maria Montessori

To feel sorry for the needy is not the mark of a Christian—to help them is.
—Frank A. Clark

What we remember from childhood we remember forever—permanent ghosts, stamped, imprinted, eternally seen.   —Cynthia Ozick

I don't believe civilization can do a lot more than educate a person's senses.   —Grace Paley

'Tis not enough to help the feeble up, but to support him after.
—William Shakespeare

Where our bread is concerned, it is a material matter. Where our neighbor's bread is concerned, it is a spiritual matter.   —I.D. Douglas

A good education is that which prepares us for our future sphere of action and makes us contented with that situation in life in which God, in his infinite mercy, has seen fit to place us, to be perfectly resigned to our lot in life, whatever it may be.
—Ann Plato

Teaching was the hardest work I had ever done, and it remains the hardest work I have done to date.
—Ann Richards

To me education is a leading out of what is already there in the pupil's soul.   —Muriel Spark

To throw obstacles in the way of a complete education is like putting out the eyes.   —Elizabeth Cady Stanton

No other job in the world could possibly dispossess one so completely as this job of teaching. You could stand all day in a laundry, for instance, still in possession of your mind. But this teaching utterly obliterates you. It cuts right into your being: essentially, it takes over your spirit.
—Sylvia Ashton-Warner

It made me gladsome to be getting some education, it being like a big window opening.   —Mary Webb

Teaching is the royal road to learning.
—Jessamyn West

Teaching was the best way to learn.
—Edna Gardner Whyte

Teaching is the greatest act of optimism.
—Colleen Wilcox

I think education is power. I think that being able to communicate with people is power. One of my main goals on the planet is to encourage people to empower themselves.
—Oprah Winfrey

Helping Others to Help Themselves

If you feed a man a meal, you only feed him for a day—but if you teach a man to grow food, you feed him for a lifetime.
—Peace Pilgrim

People will support that which they help to create.
—Mary Kay Ash

The greatest good you can do for another is not just to share your riches, but to reveal to him his own.
—Benjamin Disraeli

Listen long enough and the person will generally come up with an adequate solution.
—Mary Kay Ash

The truest help we can render an afflicted man is not to take his burden from him, but to call out his best energy, that he may be able to bear the burden.
—Phillips Brooks

A mother is not a person to lean on but a person to make leaning unnecessary.
—Dorothy Canfield Fisher

A wise parent humors the desire for independent action, so as to become the friend and advisor when his absolute rule shall cease.
—Elizabeth Gaskell

Time and money spent in helping men to do more for themselves is far better than mere giving.
—Henry Ford

I don't give advice. I can't tell anybody what to do. Instead I say this is what we know about this problem at this time. And here are the consequences of these actions.
—Dr. Joyce Brothers

Hold up to him his better self, his real self that can dare and do and win out. . . . People radiate what is in their minds and in their hearts.
—Eleanor H. Porter

The manager cannot share his power with division superintendent or foreman or workman, but he can give them opportunities for developing their power.
—Mary Parker Follett

Once you wake up thought in a man, you can never put it to sleep again.
—Zora Neale Hurston

Never help a child with a task at which he feels he can succeed.
—Maria Montessori

We Help When We Give Respect

To know one's self is wisdom, but to know one's neighbor is genius.
—Minna Antrim

Gossip is a sort of smoke that comes from the dirty tobacco-pipes of those who diffuse it; it proves nothing but the bad taste of the smoker.
—George Eliot

I know that everyone brings to the work his or her own experiences and background and may interpret the piece like a Rorschach, in their own way.   —Ida Applebroog

There are no little events in life, those we think of no consequence may be full of fate, and it is at our own risk if we neglect the acquaintances and opportunities that seem to be casually offered, and of small importance.
—Amelia Barr

I believe every person has the ability to achieve something important, and with that in mind I regard everyone as special.   —Mary Kay Ash

The fact that we are human beings is infinitely more important than all the peculiarities that distinguish human beings from one another.
—Simone de Beauvoir

The sexes in each species of beings . . . are always true equivalents—equals but not identicals.
—Antoinette Brown Blackwell

To understand another human being you must gain some insight into the conditions which made him what he is.
—Margaret Bourke-White

Like snowflakes, the human pattern is never cast twice. We are uncommonly and marvelously intricate in thought and action.
—Alice Childress

Everyone needs to be valued. Everyone has the potential to give something back.
—Diana, Princess of Wales

Every human being is trying to say something to others. Trying to cry out I am alive, notice me! Speak to me! Confirm that I am important, that I matter!   —Marion D. Hanks

The Christian tradition was passed on to me as a great rich mixture, a bouillabaisse of human imagination and wonder brewed from the richness of individual lives.   —Mary Bateson

Connected knowers do not measure other people's words by some impersonal standard. Their purpose is not to judge but to understand.
—Mary Field Belenky

Tyranny and anarchy are alike incompatible with freedom, security, and the enjoyment of opportunity.
—Jeane Kirkpatrick

Unless one's philosophy is all-inclusive, nothing can be understood.
—Mary Ritter Beard

Nature is just enough; but men and women must comprehend and accept her suggestions.
—Antoinette Brown Blackwell

The motto should not be: Forgive one another; rather understand one another.   —Emma Goldman

Someone has said that it requires less mental effort to condemn than to think.   —Emma Goldman

We cannot safely assume that other people's minds work on the same principles as our own. All too often, others with whom we come in contact do not reason as we reason, or do not value the things we value, or are not interested in what interests us.
—Isabel Briggs Myers

To have one's individuality completely ignored is like being pushed quite out of life. Like being blown out as one blows out a light. —Evelyn Scott

It's funny how your initial approach to a person can determine your feelings toward them, no matter what facts develop later on.
—Dorothy Uhnak

Nobody really knows Indians who cheat them and treat them badly.
—Sarah Winnemucca

[Tolerance] is the greatest gift of the mind; it requires the same effort of the brain that it takes to balance oneself on a bicycle. —Helen Keller

Africa has her mysteries, and even a wise man cannot understand them. But a wise man respects them.
—Miriam Makeba

To argue over who is the more noble is nothing more than to dispute whether dirt is better for making bricks or for making mortar.
—Teresa of Avila

What women want is what men want. They want respect.
—Marilyn vos Savant

All sweeping assertions are erroneous.
—L.E. Landon

Truth has never been, can never be, contained in any one creed or system.
—Mary Augusta Ward

HELP CREATES LASTING BONDS

Sons branch out, but one woman leads to another.
—Margaret Atwood

It's really important that, as women, we tell our stories. That is what helps seed our imaginations.
—Ann Bancroft

Female friendships that work are relationships in which women help each other belong to themselves.
—Louise Bernikow

SHARING

Women's propensity to share confidences is universal. We confirm our reality by sharing.
—Barbara Grizzuti Harrison

Sharing is sometimes more demanding than giving. —Mary Bateson

If my hands are fully occupied in holding on to something, I can neither give nor receive.
—Dorothy Sölle

We are rich only through what we give, and poor only through what we refuse. —Anne-Sophie Swetchine

Find out how much God has given you and from it take what you need; the remainder is needed by others.
—Saint Augustine

111

[Our children] had the privilege of growing up where they'd raised a lot of food. They were never hungry. They could share their food with people. And so, you share your lives with people. —Ella Baker

For we must share, if we would keep, that blessing from above;
Ceasing to give, we cease to have; such is the law of love.
—Richard C. Trench

An unshared life is not living. He who shares does not lessen, but greatens, his life. —Stephen S. Wise

Sharing what you have is more important than what you have.
—Albert M. Wells, Jr.

GIVING

You cannot always have happiness, but you can always give happiness.
—Anon.

That's what I consider true generosity. You give your all and yet you always feel as if it costs you nothing.
—Simone de Beauvoir

A cup that is already full cannot have more added to it. In order to receive the further good to which we are entitled, we must give of that which we have. —Margaret Becker

The fragrance always stays in the hand that gives the rose.
—Heda Bejar

You can give without loving, but you cannot love without giving.
—Amy Carmichael

Measure thy life by loss instead of gain,
Not by the wine drunk, but by the wine poured forth.
—Harriet King

Be charitable and indulgent to every one but thyself. —Joseph Joubert

Be pretty if you can, be witty if you must, but be gracious if it kills you.
—Elsie de Wolfe

Real unselfishness consists in sharing the interests of others.
—George Santayana

Purposeful giving is not as apt to deplete one's resources; it belongs to that natural order of giving that seems to renew itself even in the act of depletion.
—Anne Morrow Lindbergh

If my hands are fully occupied in holding on to something, I can neither give nor receive.
—Dorothy Sölle

Whoever in trouble and sorrow needs your help, give it to him. Whoever in anxiety or fear needs your friendship, give it to him. It isn't important whether he likes you. It isn't important whether you approve of his conduct. It isn't important what his creed or nationality may be. —E.N. West

I was hungered, and ye gave me meat: I was thirsty, and ye gave me drink: I was a stranger, and ye took me in: I was naked, and ye clothed me: I was sick, and ye visited me: I was in prison, and ye came unto me.
—Anon.

Generosity with strings is not generosity: it is a deal.   —Marya Mannes

To give and then not feel that one has given is the very best of all ways of giving.   —Max Beerbohm

To have and not to give is often worse than to steal.
—Marie von Ebner-Eschenbach

It is more blessed to give than to receive.   —Acts 20:35

God loveth a cheerful giver.
—2 Corinthians 9:7

CHARITY

Almsgiving leaves a man just where he was before. Aid restores him to society as an individual worthy of all respect and not as a man with a grievance.   —Eva Perón

In necessary things, unity; in doubtful things, liberty; in all things, charity.
—Richard Baxter

Real charity and a real ability never to condemn—the one real virtue—is so often the result of a waking experience that gives a glimpse of what lies beneath things.
—Ivy Compton-Burnett

We must give alms. Charity wins souls and draws them to virtue.
—Angela Merici

Did universal charity prevail, earth would be a heaven, and hell a fable.
—Charles Caleb Colton

The results of philanthropy are always beyond calculation.
—Miriam Beard

I have as little fear that God will damn a man that has charity as I hope that the priests can save one who has not.
—Alexander Pope

Charity. To love human beings in so far as they are nothing. That is to love them as God does.
—Simone Weil

An institution or reform movement that is not selfish, must originate in the recognition of some evil that is adding to the sum of human suffering, or diminishing the sum of happiness. I suppose it is a philanthropic movement to try to reverse the process.
—Clara Barton

In faith and hope the world will disagree, but all mankind's concern is charity.   —Alexander Pope

There is no real religious experience that does not express itself in charity.
—C.H. Dodd

Charity begins at home, and usually stays there.   —Elbert Hubbard

Charity begins at home, but should not end there.   —Thomas Fuller

Sow good services; sweet remembrances will grow from them.
—Madame de Staël

Charity looks at the need, not at the cause.   —German proverb

Make the world better.   —Lucy Stone

He is rich who hath enough to be charitable. —Sir Thomas Browne

He that has no charity deserves no mercy. —English proverb

WE NEEDN'T BE CONCERNED THAT WE CAN'T GIVE "ENOUGH"

Give what you have. To someone else it may be better than you dare to think.
—Henry Wadsworth Longfellow

Discipline is a symbol of caring to a child. He needs guidance. If there is love, there is no such thing as being too tough with a child.
—Bette Davis

Even if it's a little thing, do something for those who have need of help, something for which you get no pay but the privilege of doing it.
—Albert Schweitzer

Give, if thou can, an alms; if not, a sweet and gentle word.
—Robert Herrick

Two thirds of help is to give courage.
—Irish proverb

It was only a sunny smile,
And little it cost in the giving.
But like morning light, it scattered the night,
And made the day worth living.
—Anon.

WE SHOULDN'T BE CONCERNED THAT WE MIGHT GIVE "TOO MUCH"

The principle was right there—you couldn't miss it. The more you did for your customers, the more they did for us. —Debbi Fields

What boundary ever set limits to the service of mankind? —Claudian

Kindness consists in loving people more than they deserve.
—Jacqueline Schiff

I hate the giving of the hand unless the whole man accompanies it.
—Ralph Waldo Emerson

You can never expect too much of yourself in the matter of giving yourself to others. —Theodore C. Speers

Isn't it better to have men be ungrateful, than to miss a chance to do good? —Denis Diderot

Better to expose ourselves to ingratitude than fail in assisting the unfortunate. —Du Coeur

THE BEST GIFT IS OURSELVES

Behold! I do not give lectures on a little charity. When I give, I give myself.
—Walt Whitman

To be one woman, truly, wholly, is to be all women. Tend one garden and you will birth worlds.
—Kate Braverman

One filled with joy preaches without preaching. —Mother Teresa

Simply give others a bit of yourself; a thoughtful act, a helpful idea, a word of appreciation, a lift over a rough spot, a sense of understanding, a timely suggestion. You take something out of your mind, garnished in kindness out of your heart, and put it into the other fellow's mind and heart.
—Charles H. Burr

The only gift is a portion of thyself.
—Ralph Waldo Emerson

Blessed influence of one truly loving soul on another! —George Eliot

When one is frank, one's very presence is a compliment.
—Marianne Moore

There is no greater loan than a sympathetic ear. —Frank Tyger

Do not inflict your will. Just give love. The soul will take that love and put it where it can best be used.
—Emmanuel

You give but little when you give of your possessions. It is when you give of yourself that you truly give.
—Kahlil Gibran

WHAT NOT HELPING OTHERS INDICATES

A hurtful act is the transference to others of the degradation which we bear in ourselves. —Simone Weil

We are cold to others only when we are dull in ourselves.
—William Hazlitt

As long as you keep a person down, some part of you has to be down there to hold him down, so it means you cannot soar as you otherwise might.
—Marian Anderson

Cruelty is the only sin.
—Ellen Glasgow

Violence is a symptom of impotence.
—Anaïs Nin

The mortal sickness of a mind too unhappy to be kind.
—A.E. Housman

Where there is no capacity to affirm another as a person in his own right, there is no love. There is only masked fear. —Bonaro Overstreet

WHAT'S IN IT FOR US

In real love you want the other person's good. —Margaret Anderson

It is only in the giving of oneself to others that we truly live.
—Ethel Percy Andrus

One cannot make oneself, but one can sometimes help a little in the making of somebody else.
—Dinah Maria Mulock Craik

Giving presents is a talent; to know what a person wants, to know when and how to get it, to give it lovingly and well. —Pamela Glenconner

The habit of being uniformly considerate toward others will bring increased happiness to you.
—Grenville Kleiser

There are times when sympathy is as necessary as the air we breathe.
—Rose Pastor Stokes

He who does not live in some degree for others, hardly lives for himself.
—Michel de Montaigne

It is no good to think that other people are out to serve our interests.
—Ivy Compton-Burnett

Love is a choice—not simply, or necessarily, a rational choice, but rather a willingness to be present to others without pretense or guile.
—Carter Heyward

I wish that every child could have growing space because I think children are a little like plants. If they grow too close together, they become thin and sickly and never obtain maximum growth. We need room to grow.
—Peace Pilgrim

We cannot hold a torch to light another's path without brightening our own.   —Ben Sweetland

What I spent, is gone; what I kept, I
    lost;
but what I gave away will be mine
    forever.
—Ethel Percy Andrus

In helping others, we shall help ourselves, for whatever good we give out completes the circle and comes back to us.   —Flora Edwards

An act of goodness is of itself an act of happiness.
—Maurice Maeterlinck

My happiness derives from knowing the people I love are happy.
—Holly Ketchel

There is nothing to make you like other human beings so much as doing things for them.
—Zora Neale Hurston

Happiness . . . is achieved only by making others happy.
—Stuart Cloete

The most infectiously joyous men and women are those who forget themselves in thinking about others and serving others.
—Robert J. McCracken

Giving opens the way for receiving.
—Florence Scovel Shinn

Fill the cup of happiness for others, and there will be enough overflowing to fill yours to the brim.
—Rose Pastor Stokes

Nothing liberates our greatness like the desire to help, the desire to serve.
—Marianne Williamson

He that will not permit his wealth to do any good for others . . . cuts himself off from the truest pleasure here and the highest happiness later.
—Charles Caleb Colton

The closer I'm bound in love to you, the closer I am to free.
—Indigo Girls

True religion . . . is giving and finding one's happiness by bringing happiness into the lives of others.
—William J.H. Boetcker

Power is the ability to do good things for others. —Brooke Astor

If you give your life as a wholehearted response to love, then love will wholeheartedly respond to you.
—Marianne Williamson

Pleasure is a reciprocal; no one feels it who does not at the same time give it. To be pleased, one must please.
—Lord Chesterfield

When their children flourish, almost all mothers have a sense of well-being. —Sara Ruddick

If we had no regard for others' feelings or fortune, we would grow cold and indifferent to life itself.
—George Matthew Adams

To devote a portion of one's leisure to doing something for someone else is one of the highest forms of recreation.
—Gerald B. Fitzgerald

Live for thy neighbor if thou wouldst live for thyself.
—Marcus Annaeus Seneca

The true way to soften one's troubles is to solace those of others.
—Madame Dde Maintenon

Anything done for another is done for oneself. —Boniface VIII

What we frankly give, forever is our own. —George Granville

Every charitable act is a stepping stone toward heaven.
—Henry Ward Beecher

The human being who lives only for himself finally reaps nothing but unhappiness. Selfishness corrodes. Unselfishness ennobles, satisfies. Don't put off the joy derivable from doing helpful, kindly things for others.
—B.C. Forbes

There is no exercise better for the heart than reaching down and lifting people up. —John Andrew Holmes

Goodness is the only investment that never fails. —Henry David Thoreau

Help your brother's boat across, and your own will reach the shore.
—Hindu proverb

Be unselfish. . . . If you think of yourself only, you cannot develop because you are choking the source of development, which is spiritual expansion through thought for others.
—Charles W. Eliot

An effort made for the happiness of others lifts us above ourselves.
—Lydia M. Child

Happiness . . . consists in giving, and in serving others.
—Henry Drummond

Try to forget yourself in the service of others. For when we think too much of ourselves and our own interests, we easily become despondent. But when we work for others, our efforts return to bless us. —Sidney Powell

Doing good is the only certainly happy action of a man's life.
—Sir Philip Sidney

The greatest happiness in the world is to make others happy.
—Luther Burbank

We make a living by what we get, but we make a life by what we give.
—Norman MacEwan

You may not have saved a lot of money in your life, but if you have saved a lot of heartaches for other folks, you are a pretty rich man.
—Seth Parker

Only a life lived for others is a life worth while.　—Albert Einstein

Unless we give part of ourselves away, unless we can live with other people and understand them and help them, we are missing the most essential part of our own lives.
—Harold Taylor

To complain that life has no joys while there is a single creature whom we can relieve by our bounty, assist by our counsels or enliven by our presence, is to lament the loss of that which we possess, and is just as rational as to die of thirst with the cup in our hands.　—Thomas Fitzosborne

The world has cares enough to plague us; but he who meditates on others' woes shall, in that meditation, lose his own.　—Cumberland

If you have not often felt the joy of doing a kind act, you have neglected much, and most of all yourself.
—A. Neilen

As the purse is emptied, the heart is filled.　—Victor Hugo

Goodwill to others . . . helps build you up. It is good for your body. It makes your blood purer, your muscles stronger, and your whole form more symmetrical in shape. It is the real elixir of life.　—Prentice Mulford

Set about doing good to somebody. Put on your hat and go and visit the sick and poor of your neighborhood; inquire into their circumstances and minister to their wants. Seek out the desolate and afflicted and oppressed . . . I have often tried this method, and have always found it the best medicine for a heavy heart.
—Anon.

We grow by love . . . others are our nutriment.
—William Ellery Channing

When you learn to live for others, they will live for you.
—Paramahansa Yogananda

No man is more cheated than the selfish man.　—Henry Ward Beecher

In about the same degree as you are helpful, you will be happy.
—Karl Reiland

He that despiseth his neighbor sinneth; but he that hath mercy on the poor, happy is he.　—Proverbs 14:21

The most exquisite pleasure is giving pleasure to others.
—Jean de La Bruyère

Happiness is a by-product of an effort to make someone else happy.
—Gretta Brooker Palmer

The fragrance of what you give away
stays with you.   —Earl Allen

Life becomes harder for us when we
live for others, but it also becomes
richer and happier.
                    —Albert Schweitzer

Sow good services; sweet remembrances will grow from them.
                    —Madame de Staël

We all of us need assistance. Those
who sustain others themselves want
to be sustained.   —Maurice Hulst

When you cease to make a contribu-
tion, you begin to die.
                    —Eleanor Roosevelt

To help all created things, that is the
measure of our responsibility; to be
helped by all, that is the measure of
our hope.   —Gerald Vann

Those who bring sunshine to the lives
of others cannot keep it from themselves.   —Sir James M. Barrie

When one's own problems are
unsolvable and all best efforts are
frustrated, it is lifesaving to listen to
other people's problems.
                    —Suzanne Massie

The best way to cheer yourself is to
try to cheer somebody else up.
                    —Mark Twain

There is no happiness in having or in
getting, but only in giving.
                    —Henry Drummond

Do things for others and you'll find
your self-consciousness evaporating
like morning dew.   —Dale Carnegie

There remain times when one can
only endure. One lives on, one
doesn't die, and the only thing that
one can do, is to fill one's mind and
time as far as possible with the concerns of other people. It doesn't bring
immediate peace, but it brings the
dawn nearer.
                    —Arthur Christopher Benson

Avarice hoards itself poor; charity
gives itself rich.   —German proverb

ASKING FOR AND ACCEPTING
HELP FROM OTHERS

The hearts that never lean must fall.
                    —Emily Dickinson

Be brave enough to accept the help of
others.
     —Dr. Melba Colgrove, Harold H.
        Bloomfield, Peter McWilliams

The people you need to help you
make your dream come true are
everywhere, and within your reach.
                    —Marcia Wieder

Like the body that is made up of different limbs and organs, all mortal
creatures exist depending upon one
another.   —Hindu proverb

We not only need to be willing to
give, but also to be open to receiving
from others.   —On Hope

It seems sometimes as if one were
powerless to do any more from
within to overcome troubles, and that
help must come from without.
                    —Arthur Christopher Benson

The smartest thing I ever said was, "Help Me!"   —Anon.

The healthy and strong individual is the one who asks for help when he needs it. Whether he's got an abscess on his knee, or in his soul.
                    —Rona Barrett

The healthy, the strong individual, is the one who asks for help when he needs it. Whether he has an abscess on his knee or in his soul.
                    —Rona Barrett

My only advice is to stay aware, listen carefully and yell for help if you need it.   —Judy Blume

Silence is not certain token
That no secret grief is there;
Sorrow which is never spoken
Is the heaviest load to bear.
                    —Frances Ridley Havergal

It is true that no one can harm the person who wears armor. But no one can help him either.   —Kristin Hunter

We can't help everyone, but everyone can help someone.
                    —Dr. Loretta Scott

Trouble is part of your life, and if you don't share it, you don't give the person who loves you a chance to love you enough.   —Dinah Shore

Get the knack of getting people to help you and also pitch in yourself.
                    —Ruth Gordon

I've discovered I'm a strong and capable person. I can handle almost anything except being alone with this.
                    —Keith Gann, person with AIDS

You really can change the world if you care enough.
                    —Marian Wright Edelman

Service is the rent we pay for the privilege of living on this earth.
                    —Shirley Chisholm

We want to create an atmosphere in which creation is possible.
                    —Marie Rambert

All altruism springs from putting yourself in the other person's place.
                    —Harry Emerson Fosdick

A helping word to one in trouble is often like a switch on a railroad track . . . an inch between wreck and smooth, rolling prosperity.
                    —Henry Ward Beecher

Often we can help each other most by leaving each other alone; at other times we need the hand-grasp and the word of cheer.   —Elbert Hubbard

If I can stop one heart from breaking, I shall not live in vain.
                    —Emily Dickinson

It takes wisdom and discernment to minister to people in need. We must look beyond the apparent and seek to meet the needs of the whole person.
                    —Richard C. Chewning

If I am not for myself, who will be for me? If I am not for others, who am I for? And if not now, when?
                    —Talmud

Believe, when you are most unhappy, that there is something for you to do in the world. So long as you can sweeten another's pain, life is not in vain. —Helen Keller

Much misconstruction and bitterness are spared to him who thinks naturally upon what he owes to others, rather than on what he ought to expect from them.
—Elizabeth de Meulan Guizot

If we could all hear one another's prayers, God might be relieved of some of his burden.
—Ashleigh Brilliant

I know some good marriages—marriages where both people are just trying to get through their days by helping each other, being good to each other. —Erica Jong

The entire sum of existence is the magic of being needed by just one person. —Vi Putnam

Happiness is the cheapest thing in the world when we buy it for someone else. —Paul Flemming

Who is the happiest of men? He who values the merits of others, and in their pleasure takes joy, even as though it were his own.
—Johann von Goethe

The race of mankind would perish did they cease to aid each other. We cannot exist without mutual help. All therefore that need aid have a right to ask it from their fellow man; and no one who has the power of granting can refuse it without guilt.
—Sir Walter Scott

It is the individual who is not interested in his fellow men who has the greatest difficulties in life and provides the greatest injury to others. It is from among such individuals that all human failures spring.
—Alfred Adler

Make yourself necessary to somebody.
—Ralph Waldo Emerson

It is enough that I am of value to somebody today. —Hugh Prather

And they said one to another, We are verily guilty concerning our brother, in that we saw the anguish of his soul, when he besought us, and we would not hear. —Genesis 42:21

Friendship

FRIENDSHIP IS ONE OF THE MOST IMPORTANT THINGS IN LIFE

And we find at the end of a perfect
  day,
The soul of a friend we've made.
    —Carrie Jacobs Bond

Love is like the wild-rose briar;
Friendship is like the holly-tree.
The holly is dark when the rose briar
  blooms,
But which will bloom most constantly?
    —Emily Brontë

Life without a friend is death without
a witness.   —Spanish proverb

Without friends no one would choose
to live, though he had all other
goods.   —Aristotle

We call that person who has lost his
father, an orphan; and a widower,
that man who has lost his wife.
But that man who has known that
immense unhappiness of losing a
friend, by what name do we call him?
Here every language holds its peace
in impotence.   —Joseph Roux

The great difference between voyages
rests not in ships but in the people
you meet on them.   —Amelia Burr

Only solitary men know the full joys
of friendship. Others have their family; but to a solitary and an exile his
friends are everything.
    —Willa Cather

It seems to me that trying to live
without friends is like milking a bear
to get cream for your morning coffee.
It is a whole lot of trouble, and then
not worth much after you get it.
    —Zora Neale Hurston

Friendship is the bread of the heart.
    —Mary Russell Mitford

There is no hope or joy except in
human relations.
    —Antoine de Saint-Exupery

I feel the need of relations and friendship, of affection, of friendly intercourse. . . . I cannot miss these things
without feeling, as does any other
intelligent man, a void and a deep
need.   —Vincent van Gogh

Your wealth is where your friends are.
                                    —Plautus

Today a man discovered gold and
    fame,
Another flew the stormy seas;
Another set an unarmed world
    aflame,
One found the germ of a disease.
But what high fates my path attend
for I—today—I found a friend.
                        —Helen Barker Parker

Though Love be deeper, Friendship is
more wide.
                —Corinne Roosevelt Robinson

That is the best—to laugh with
someone because you think the same
things are funny.
                        —Gloria Vanderbilt

Can you understand how cruelly
I feel the lack of friends who will
believe in me a bit?
                        —D.H. Lawrence

To have a good friend is one of the
highest delights of life; to be a good
friend is one of the noblest and most
difficult undertakings.   —Anon.

The two most important things in life
are good friends and a strong bull pen.
                        —Bob Lemon

There is no wilderness like a life
without friends; friendship multiplies
blessings and minimizes misfortunes;
it is a unique remedy against adversity, and it soothes the soul.
                        —Baltasar Gracian

There is nothing on this earth more
to be prized than true friendship.
                —Saint Thomas Aquinas

Man's best support is a very dear
friend.   —Cicero

A cheer, then, for the noblest breast
That fears not danger's post;
And like the lifeboat, proves a friend,
When friends are wanted most.
                        —Eliza Cook

I know what things are good: friendship and work and conversation.
                        —Rupert Brooke

Friendship is the source of the greatest pleasures, and without friends
even the most agreeable pursuits
become tedious.
                —Saint Thomas Aquinas

No medicine is more valuable, none
more efficacious, none better suited
to the cure of all our temporal ills
than a friend to whom we may turn
for consolation in time of trouble,
and with whom we may share our
happiness in time of joy.
                —Saint Alfred of Rievaulx

My only sketch, profile, of heaven is
a large blue sky, and larger than the
biggest I have seen in June—and in it
are my friends—every one of them.
                        —Emily Dickinson

If I don't have friends, then I ain't
nothing.   —Billie Holiday

Brotherhood is the very price and
condition of man's survival.
                        —Carlos P. Romulo

One thing everybody in the world
wants and needs is friendliness.
                        —William E. Holler

A man cannot be said to succeed in this life who does not satisfy one friend. —Henry David Thoreau

We take care of our health, we lay up money, we make our roof tight and our clothing sufficient, but who provides wisely that he shall not be wanting in the best property of all—friends. —Ralph Waldo Emerson

There is no physician like a true friend. —Anon.

There is nothing meritorious but virtue and friendship. —Alexander Pope

The bird, a nest; the spider, a web; man, friendship. —William Blake

True happiness . . . arises, in the first place, from the enjoyment of one's self, and in the next from the friendship and conversation of a few select companions. —Joseph Addison

It was such a joy to see thee. I wish I could tell how much thee is to my life. I always turn to thee as a sort of rest. —Lady Henry Somerset

Today a man discovered gold and
   fame,
Another flew the stormy seas;
Another set an unarmed world
   aflame,
One found the germ of a disease.
But what high fates my path attend:
For I—today—I found a friend.
—Helen Barker Parker

Good friends, good books and a sleepy conscience: this is the ideal life. —Mark Twain

Man is a knot, a web, a mesh into which relationships are tied. Only those relationships matter. —Antoine de Saint-Exupery

Friendship is the only cement that will ever hold the world together. —Woodrow Wilson

Friends are an aid to the young, to guard them from error; to the elderly, to attend to their wants and to supplement their failing power of action; to those in the prime of life, to assist them to noble deeds. —Aristotle

Friendship is the allay of our sorrows, the ease of our passions, the discharge of our oppression, the sanctuary of our calamities, the counselor of our doubts, the clarity of our minds, the emission of our thoughts, the exercise and improvement of what we dedicate. —Jeremy Taylor

Of all the things which wisdom provides to make life entirely happy, much the greatest is the possession of friendship. —Epicurus

There's nothing worth the wear of winning but laughter, and the love of friends. —Hilaire Belloc

Each friend represents a world in us, a world possibly not born until they arrive, and it is only by this meeting that a new world is born. —Anaïs Nin

The feeling of friendship is like that of being comfortably filled with roast beef, love, like being enlivened with champagne. —Samuel Johnson

One is taught by experience to put a premium on those few people who can appreciate you for what you are.
—Gail Godwin

Oh Dear! How unfortunate I am not to have anyone to weep with!
—Marie de Rabutin-Chantal

The worst solitude is to be destitute of sincere friendship.
—Francis Bacon

If you want an accounting of your worth, count your friends.
—Merry Browne

A man with few friends is only half-developed; there are whole sides of his nature which are locked up and have never been expressed. He cannot unlock them himself, he cannot even discover them; friends alone can stimulate him and open him.
—Randolph Bourne

'Tis the human touch in the world
　　that counts—the touch of your
　　hand and mine—
Which means far more to the sink-
　　ing heart than shelter or bread or
　　wine
For shelter is gone when the night is
　　o'er, and bread lasts only a day
But the touch of the hand and the
　　sound of the voice
Live on in the soul always.
—Spencer M. Free

Good company and good discourse are the very sinews of virtue.
—Izaak Walton

Friends are the sunshine of life.
—John Hay

My friends have made the story of my life. In a thousand ways they have turned my limitations into beautiful privileges, and enabled me to walk serene and happy in the shadow cast by my deprivation.　　—Helen Keller

The support of one's personality is friends. A part of one's self and a real foundation and existence.
—Katharine Butler Hathaway

No greater burden can be born by an individual than to know none who cares or understands.
—Arthur H. Stainback

My life seems to have become suddenly hollow, and I do not know what is hanging over me. I cannot even put the shadow that has fallen on me into words. At least into written words. I would give a great deal for a friend's voice.
—John Addington Symonds

A true friend is the best possession.
—Anon.

It is not so much our friends' help that helps us, as the confidence of their help.　　—Epicurus

FRIENDS MAKE LIFE BEARABLE

But I have certainty enough,
For I am sure of you.　—Amelia Burr

Best friend, my well-spring in the wilderness!　　—George Eliot

Plant a seed of friendship; reap a bouquet of happiness.
—Lois L. Kaufman

Our happiness in this world depends on the affections we are able to inspire. —Duchess Prazlin

Some people go to priests; others to poetry; I to my friends.
—Virginia Woolf

FAMILY MEMBERS ARE OFTEN OUR BEST FRIENDS

The family. We are a strange little band of characters trudging through life sharing diseases and toothpaste, coveting one another's desserts, hiding shampoo, locking each other out of our rooms, inflicting pain and kissing to heal it in the same instant, loving, laughing, defending, and trying to figure out the common thread that bound us all together.
—Erma Bombeck

You hear a lot of dialogue on the death of the American family. Families aren't dying. They're merging into big conglomerates.
—Erma Bombeck

If ever two were one, then surely we. If ever man were loved by wife, then thee. —Anne Bradstreet

Friends are the family we choose for ourselves. —Edna Buchanan

I think togetherness is a very important ingredient to family life. It's a cliche and we use it too much but I think for a husband and wife, the way to stay close is to do things together and share. —Barbara Bush

Jimmy and I were always partners.
—Rosalynn Carter

He [Winston Churchill] has a future and I have a past, so we should be all right. —Jennie Jerome Churchill

Parents are friends that life gives us; friends are parents that the heart chooses. —Comtesse Diane

[My father] was generous with his affection, given to great, awkward, engulfing hugs, and I can remember so clearly the smell of his hugs, all starched shirt, tobacco, Old Spice, and Cutty Sark. Sometimes I think I've never been properly hugged since.
—Linda Ellerbee

Both within the family and without, our sisters hold up our mirrors: our images of who we are and of who we can dare to become.
—Elizabeth Fishel

Sisters define their rivalry in terms of competition for the gold cup of parental love. It is never perceived as a cup which runneth over, rather a finite vessel from which the more one sister drinks, the less is left over for the others. —Elizabeth Fishel

The desire to be and have a sister is a primitive and profound one that may have everything or nothing to do with the family a woman is born to. It is a desire to know and be known by someone who shares blood and body, history and dreams.
—Elizabeth Fishel

Where there is lasting love, there is a family. —Shere Hite

Is solace anywhere more comforting than in the arms of sisters?
—Alice Walker

126

Call it a clan, call it a network, call it
a tribe, call it a family: Whatever you
call it, whoever you are, you need one.
                    —Jane Howard

Old as she was, she still missed her
daddy sometimes.   —Gloria Naylor

[Families] are made to make you
forget yourself occasionally, so that
the beautiful balance of life is not
destroyed.   —Anaïs Nin

The family unit plays a critical role in
our society and in the training of the
generation to come.
                —Sandra Day O'Connor

Families will not be broken. Curse
and expel them, send their children
wandering, drown them in floods
and fires, and old women will make
songs of all these sorrows and sit in
the porches and sing them on mild
evenings.   —Marilynne Robinson

The family is the building block for
whatever solidarity there is in society.
                    —Jill Ruckelshaus

Who ran to help me when I fell
And would some pretty story tell
Or kiss the place to make it well?
My mother.   —Jane Taylor

All love that has not friendship for its
    base,
Is like a mansion built upon the sand.
                —Ella Wheeler Wilcox

How We Can Be a Better Friend

One can find traces of every life in
each life.   —Susan Griffin

Friendship is an art, and very few
persons are born with a natural gift
for it.   —Kathleen Norris

The art of friendship has been little
cultivated in our society.
                —Robert J. Havighurst

We flatter those we scarcely know,
We please the fleeting guest,
And deal full many a thoughtless
    blow
To those who love us best.
                —Ella Wheeler Wilcox

Good friendships are fragile things
and require as much care as any
other fragile and precious thing.
                —Randolph Bourne

Remember that you are all people
and that all people are you.
                    —Joy Harjo

Human beings are born into this little
span of life of which the best thing
is its friendships and intimacies . . .
and yet they leave their friendships
and intimacies with no cultivation,
to grow as they will by the roadside,
expecting them to "keep" by force of
mere inertia.   —William James

The only way to have a friend is to
be one.   —Ralph Waldo Emerson

Friendships, like marriages, are dependent on avoiding the unforgivable.
                —John D. MacDonald

Beware of the danger signals that flag
problems: silence, secretiveness, or
sudden outburst.
                —Eleanor H. Porter

To accept a favor from a friend is to confer one.   —John Churton Collins

There is a magnet in your heart that will attract true friends. That magnet is unselfishness, thinking of others first ... when you learn to live for others, they will live for you.
—Paramahansa Yogananda

Blessed are they who have the gift of making friends, for it is one of God's best gifts. It involves many things, but above all, the power of getting out of one's self, and appreciating whatever is noble and loving in another.   —Thomas Hughes

Don't ask of your friends what you yourself can do.   —Quintus Ennius

Half the secret of getting along with people is consideration of their values; the other half is tolerance in one's own views.   —Daniel Frohman

A true friend unbosoms freely, advises justly, assists readily, adventures boldly, takes all patiently, defends courageously, and continues a friend unchangeably.   —William Penn

Confidence is the foundation of friendship. If we give it, we will receive it.
—Harry E. Humphreys, Jr.

There is a definite process by which one made people into friends, and it involved talking to them and listening to them for hours at a time.
—Rebecca West

Actions, not words, are the true criterion of the attachment of friends.
—George Washington

One who knows how to show and to accept kindness will be a friend better than any possession.   —Sophocles

Any man will usually get from other men what he is expecting from them. If he is looking for friendship, he will likely receive it. If his attitude is that of indifference, it will beget indifference. And if a man is looking for a fight, he will in all likelihood be accommodated in that.
—John Richelsen

There is nothing we like to see so much as the gleam of pleasure in a person's eye when he feels that we have sympathized with him, understood him, interested ourself in his welfare. At these moments something fine and spiritual passes between two friends. These moments are the moments worth living.
—Don Marquis

He does good to himself who does good to his friend.   —Erasmus

A sense of duty is useful in work, but offensive in personal relations. People wish to be liked, not endured with patient resignation.
—Bertrand Russell

When a friend is in trouble, don't annoy him by asking if there is anything you can do. Think up something appropriate and do it.
—Edgar Watson Howe

Loyalty is what we seek in friendship.
—Cicero

True friendship comes when silence between two people is comfortable.
—Dave Tyson Gentry

If two friends ask you to judge a dispute, don't accept, because you will lose one friend; on the other hand, if two strangers come with the same request, accept, because you will gain one friend. —Saint Augustine

Perhaps the most delightful friendships are those in which there is much agreement, much disputation, and yet more personal liking.
—George Eliot

There can be no friendship when there is no freedom. Friendship loves the free air, and will not be fenced up in straight and narrow enclosures.
—William Penn

You will find yourself refreshed by the presence of cheerful people. Why not make earnest effort to confer that pleasure on others?...Half the battle is gained if you never allow yourself to say anything gloomy.
—Lydia M. Child

Wear a smile and have friends; wear a scowl and have wrinkles.
—George Eliot

Lead the life that will make you kindly and friendly to everyone about you, and you will be surprised what a happy life you will live.
—Charles M. Schwab

Those who cannot give friendship will rarely receive it, and never hold it.
—Dagobert D. Runes

It is not the services we render them, but the services they render us, that attaches people to us.
—Labiche et Martin

We cherish our friends not for their ability to amuse us, but for ours to amuse them. —Evelyn Waugh

It is foolish to make experiments upon the constancy of a friend, as upon the chastity of a wife.
—Samuel Johnson

Give and take makes good friends.
—Scottish proverb

A quarrel between friends, when made up, adds a new tie to friendship, as . . . the callosity formed 'round a broken bone makes it stronger than before.
—Saint Francis de Sales

No real friendship is ever made without an initial clashing which discloses the metal of each to each.
—David Grayson

Nothing wounds a friend like a want of confidence.
—Jean Baptiste LaCordaire

The first thing to learn in intercourse with others is non-interference with their own peculiar ways of being happy, provided those ways do not assume to interfere with ours.
—William James

No man can have society upon his own terms. If he seeks it, he must serve it too. —Ralph Waldo Emerson

We cannot tell the precise moment when friendship is formed. As in filling a vessel drop by drop, there is at last a drop which makes it run over. So in a series of kindnesses there is, at last, one which makes the heart run over. —James Boswell

Friendship is a plant which must be often watered. —Anon.

A friend should bear his friend's infirmities. —William Shakespeare

No man is much pleased with a companion who does not increase, in some respect, his fondness of himself. —Samuel Johnson

You win the victory when you yield to friends. —Sophocles

The condition which high friendship demands is the ability to do without it. —Ralph Waldo Emerson

Women can form a friendship with a man very well; but to preserve it, a slight physical antipathy most probably helps. —Friedrich Nietzsche

Love your friends as if they would some day hate you. —R.D. Hicks

Friendship is a strong and habitual inclination in two persons to promote the good and happiness of one another. —Eustace Budgell

Friendship is the pleasing game of interchanging praise. —Oliver Wendell Holmes

The hardest of all is learning to be a well of affection, and not a fountain, to show them that we love them, not when we feel like it, but when they do. —Nan Fairbrother

If you want to be listened to, you should put in time listening. —Marge Piercy

"Stay" is a charming word in a friend's vocabulary. —Louisa May Alcott

The only service a friend can really render is to keep up your courage by holding up to you a mirror in which you can see a noble image of yourself. —George Bernard Shaw

The way to make a true friend is to be one. Friendship implies loyalty, esteem, cordiality, sympathy, affection, readiness to aid, to help, to stick, to fight for, if need be.... Radiate friendship and it will return sevenfold. —B.C. Forbes

The most called-upon prerequisite of a friend is an accessible ear. —Maya Angelou

A loyal friend laughs at your jokes when they're not so good, and sympathizes with your problems when they're not so bad. —Arnold Glasow

Politeness is an inexpensive way of making friends. —William Feather

The secret of success in society is a certain heartiness and sympathy. —Ralph Waldo Emerson

Sometimes we owe a friend to the lucky circumstance that we give him no cause for envy. —Friedrich Nietzsche

Friendship requires great communication. —Saint Francis de Sales

Friendship requires more time than poor busy men can usually command. —Ralph Waldo Emerson

We should behave to our friends as we would wish our friends to behave to us. —Aristotle

You can make more friends in two months by becoming more interested in other people than you can in two years by trying to get people interested in you. —Anon.

We secure our friends not by accepting favors but by doing them. —Thucydides

Friendship multiplies the good of life and divides the evil. 'Tis the sole remedy against misfortune, the very ventilation of the soul. —Baltasar Gracian

FREQUENCY OF INTERACTION

It is easier to visit friends than to live with them. —Chinese proverb

The loneliness you get by the sea is personal and alive. It doesn't subdue you and make you feel abject. It's stimulating loneliness. —Anne Morrow Lindbergh

The chain of friendship, however bright, does not stand the attrition of constant close contact. —Sir Walter Scott

Fond as we are of our loved ones, there comes at times during their absence an unexplained peace. —Ann Shaw

Friendship increases in visiting friends, but not in visiting them too often. —Anon.

Go oft to the house of thy friend, for weeds choke the unused path. —Ralph Waldo Emerson

I am quite sure that no friendship yields its true pleasure and nobility of nature without frequent communication, sympathy and service. —George E. Woodberry

I am learning to live close to the lives of my friends without ever seeing them. No miles of any measurement can separate your soul from mine. —John Muir

The most beautiful discovery true friends make is that they can grow separately without growing apart. —Elizabeth Foley

Friends are lost by calling often and calling seldom. —Scottish proverb

A hedge between keeps friendships green. —Anon.

Solitude is one thing and loneliness is another. —May Sarton

WE MUST MAKE ALLOWANCES FOR OUR FRIENDS, AND OVERLOOK THEIR LITTLE FAILINGS

My friend and I have built a wall
Between us thick and wide:
The stones of it are laid in scorn
And plastered high with pride. —Elizabeth Cutter Morrow

When my friends lack an eye, I look at them in profile. —Joseph Joubert

You can always tell a real friend; when you've made a fool of yourself he doesn't feel you've done a permanent job. —Laurence J. Peter

A friend is one who withholds judgment no matter how long you have his unanswered letter.
—Sophie Irene Loeb

The best rule of friendship is to keep your heart a little softer than your head. —Anon.

Who seeks a faultless friend remains friendless. —Turkish proverb

Unless you bear with the faults of a friend you betray your own.
—Publilius Syrus

Probably no man ever had a friend he did not dislike a little; we are all so constituted by nature that no one can possibly entirely approve of us.
—Edgar Watson Howe

Love your friend with his fault.
—Anon.

It is well, when judging a friend, to remember that he is judging you with the same godlike and superior impartiality. —Arnold Bennett

Two persons cannot long be friends if they cannot forgive each other's little failings. —Jean de La Bruyère

To find a friend one must close one eye. To keep him . . . two.
—Norman Douglas

It is easier to forgive an enemy than a friend.
—Madame Dorothee Deluzy

Sooner or later you've heard all your best friends have to say. Then comes the tolerance of real love.
—Ned Rorem

We shall never have friends if we expect to find them without fault.
—Thomas Fuller

It is well there is no one without fault; for he would not have a friend in the world. He would seem to belong to a different species.
—William Hazlitt

The essence of true friendship is to make allowance for another's little lapses. —David Storey

To be social is to be forgiving.
—Robert Frost

It is more shameful to distrust our friends than to be deceived by them.
—Francois de La Rochefoucauld

It is better to be deceived by one's friends than to deceive them.
—Johann von Goethe

The man who trusts other men will make fewer mistakes than he who distrusts them. —Camillo Di Cavour

It should be part of our private ritual to devote a quarter of an hour every day to the enumeration of the good qualities of our friends. When we are not active we fall back idly upon defects, even of those whom we most love. —Mark Rutherford

Friendship admits of difference of character, as love does that of sex.
—Joseph Roux

Between friends there is no need of justice. —Aristotle

What I cannot love, I overlook. —Anaïs Nin

Treat your fiends as you do your picture, and place them in their best light. —Jennie Jerome Churchill

Friendships aren't perfect and yet they are very precious. For me, not expecting perfection all in one place was a great release. —Letty Cottin Pogrebin

A friend who cannot at a pinch remember a thing or two that never happened is as bad as one who does not know how to forget. —Samuel Butler

Courtesy and Friendship

Being considerate of others will take you and your children further in life than any college or professional degree. —Marian Wright Edelman

Nothing is ever lost by courtesy. It is the cheapest of pleasures, costs nothing, and conveys much. It pleases him who gives and receives and thus, like mercy, is twice blessed. —Erastus Wiman

Truth is a rough, honest, helter-skelter terrier, that none like to see brought into their drawing rooms. —Ouida

Friendship cannot live with ceremony, nor without civility. —Lord Halifax

Don't flatter yourself that friendship authorizes you to say disagreeable things to your intimates. The nearer you come into relation with a person, the more necessary do tact and courtesy become. —Oliver Wendell Holmes

There are limits to the indulgence which friendship allows. —Cicero
The truth is the kindest thing we can give folks in the end. —Harriet Beecher Stowe

Friends are like a pleasant park where you wish to go; while you may enjoy the flowers, you may not eat them. —Edgar Watson Howe

Friendship is honey, but don't eat it all. —Moroccan proverb

Candor about Friends

Except in cases of necessity, which are rare, leave your friend to learn unpleasant things from his enemies; they are ready enough to tell him. —Oliver Wendell Holmes

It's important to our friends to believe that we are unreservedly frank with them, and important to our friendship that we are not. —Mignon McLaughlin

Don't tell your friends their social faults; they will cure the fault and never forgive you. —Logan Pearsall Smith

There are worse words than cuss words; there are words that hurt. —Tillie Olsen

Nobody likes having salt rubbed into their wounds, even if it is the salt of the earth.   —Rebecca West

Flattery makes friends, truth enemies.
          —Spanish proverb

Before a secret is told, one can often feel the weight of it in the atmosphere.
          —Susan Griffin

A cruel story runs on wheels, and every hand oils the wheels as they run.
          —Ouida

It is terrible to destroy a person's picture of himself in the interests of truth or some other abstraction.
          —Doris Lessing

If we all told what we know of one another, there would not be four friends in the world   —Blaise Pascal

We all need somebody to talk to. It would be good if we talked . . . not just pitter-patter, but real talk. We shouldn't be so afraid, because most people really like this contact; that you show you are vulnerable makes them free to be vulnerable.
          —Liv Ullmann

If we were all given by magic the power to read each other's thoughts, I suppose the first effect would be to dissolve all friendships.   —Anon.

The truth that is suppressed by friends is the readiest weapon of the enemy.   —Robert Louis Stevenson

So often the truth is told with hate, and lies are told with love.
          —Rita Mae Brown

Give me the avowed, the erect and manly foe,
Bold I can meet, perhaps may turn the blow;
But of all plagues, good Heaven, thy wrath can send,
Save, oh save me from the candid friend!   —George Canning

A good friend can tell you what is the matter with you in a minute. He may not seem such a good friend after telling.   —Arthur Brisbane

Do not remove a fly from your friend's forehead with a hatchet.
          —Chinese proverb

Friendship will not stand the strain of very much good advice for very long.
          —Robert Lynd

There is not so good an understanding between any two, but the exposure by the one of a serious fault in the other will produce a misunderstanding in proportion to its heinousness.
          —Henry David Thoreau

A friend should be a master at guessing and keeping still.
          —Friedrich Nietzsche

A cheerful friend is like a sunny day, which sheds its brightness on all around.   —John Lubbock

The more we love our friends, the less we flatter them; it is by excusing nothing that pure love shows itself.
          —Moliere

It is the weak and confused who worship the pseudo-simplicities of brutal directness.   —Marshall McLuhan

What a wonderful thing it is to have a good friend. He identifies your innermost desires, and spares you the embarrassment of disclosing them to him yourself.   —Jean de La Fontaine

I always felt that the great high privilege, relief and comfort of friendship was that one had to explain nothing.
—Katherine Mansfield

Nobody who is afraid of laughing, and heartily too, at his friend can be said to have a true and thorough love for him.   —Julius Charles Hare

Don't believe your friends when they ask you to be honest with them. All they really want is to be maintained in the good opinion they have of themselves.   —Albert Camus

Only friends will tell you the truths you need to hear to make . . . your life bearable. —Francine Du Plessix Gray

Keep the other person's well-being in mind when you feel an attack of soul-purging truth coming on.
—Betty White

If it's very painful for you to criticize your friends—you're safe in doing it. But if you take the slightest pleasure in it, that's the time to hold your tongue.   —Alice Duer Miller

Flatterers look like friends, as wolves like dogs.   —George Chapman

Friendship may sometimes step a few paces in advance of truth.
—Walter Savage Landor

CANDOR ABOUT OURSELVES

A friend is a person with whom I may be sincere. Before him, I may think aloud.
—Ralph Waldo Emerson

Oh, the comfort, the inexpressible comfort of feeling safe with a person, having neither to weigh thoughts nor measure words, but pouring them all out, just as they are, chaff and grain together, certain that a faithful hand will take and sift them, keep what is worth keeping, and with a breath of kindness blow the rest away.
—Dinah Maria Mulock Craik

One's friends are that part of the human race with which one can be human.   —George Santayana

I should like to tell you again of my bitter troubles so that mutually, by recounting our grief, we can lighten each other's sorrow.
—The Kanteletar

There are only two people who can tell you the truth about yourself—an enemy who has lost his temper and a friend who loves you dearly.
—Antisthenes

Since we are mortal, friendships are best kept to a moderate level, rather than sharing the very depths of our souls.   —Hippolytus

Forget your woes when you see your friend.   —Priscian

Those that lack friends to open themselves unto are cannibals of their own hearts.   —Francis Bacon

But We Must Not Over-Burden Our Friends with Our Troubles

Laugh, and the world laughs with you; weep and you weep alone.
—Ella Wheeler Wilcox

When good cheer is lacking, our friends will be packing. —Anon.

We have no more right to put our discordant states of mind into the lives of those around us and rob them of their sunshine and brightness than we have to enter their houses and steal their silverware.
—Julia Seton

'Tis the privilege of friendship to talk nonsense, and have her nonsense respected. —Charles Lamb

Friends and Money

The richest man in the world is not the one who still has the first dollar he ever earned. It's the man who still has his best friend. —Martha Mason

It is better not to say "lend." There is only giving. —Pearl S. Buck

They are rich who have true friends.
—Thomas Fuller

Friendship is like money, easier made than kept. —Samuel Butler

The rich know not who is his friend.
—Anon.

Prosperity makes few friends.
—Vauvenargues

It is a good thing to be rich, it is a good thing to be strong, but it is a better thing to be beloved of many friends. —Euripides

Better the friend we can see than the money we cannot. —Greek proverb

Never have a friend that's poorer than yourself. —Douglas Jerrold

It is better in times of need to have a friend rather than money.
—Greek proverb

The richer your friends, the more they will cost you.
—Elizabeth Marbury

Wealth maketh many friends.
—Proverbs 17:4

Friendship in Bad Times

It's the friends you can call up at 4 a.m. that matter. —Marlene Dietrich

True friendship is never serene.
—Marie de Rabutin-Chantal

In time of great anxiety we can draw power from our friends. We should at such times, however, avoid friends who sympathize too deeply, who give us pity rather than strength.
—D. Lupton

The firmest friendships have been formed in mutual adversity, as iron is most strongly united by the fiercest flame. —Charles Caleb Colton

A friend in need is a friend indeed.
—Susan Ferrier

Adversity not only draws people together, but brings forth that beautiful inward friendship.
—Søren Kierkegaard

A friend in need is a friend indeed.
—Richard Graves

In times of difficulty friendship is on trial. —Greek proverb

A friend is never known till a man has need. —Anon.

As the yellow gold is tried in fire, so the faith of friendship must be seen in adversity. —Ovid

Friendship, of itself a holy tie, is made more sacred by adversity.
—John Dryden

He who endures penance and hardships for another delights in that person's company.
—Malik Muhammad Jayasi

A cheer, then, for the noble breast
    that fears not danger's post;
And like the lifeboat, proves a friend,
When friends are wanted most.
—Eliza Cook

There are moments in life when all that we can bear is the sense that our friend is near us; our wounds would wince at consoling words that would reveal the depths of our pain.
—Honore de Balzac

FRIENDSHIP IN GOOD TIMES —
AND BAD TIMES

Prosperity makes friends, adversity tries them. —Publilius Syrus

That's the risk you take if you change: that people you've been involved with won't like the new you. But other people who do will come along.
—Lisa Alther

Friendship has splendors that love knows not. It grows stronger when crossed, whereas obstacles kill love. Friendship resists time, which wearies and severs couples. It has heights unknown to love. —Mariama Bâ

True friends are those who really know you but love you anyway.
—Edna Buchanan

Grief can take care of itself, but to get the full value of a joy you must have somebody to divide it with.
—Mark Twain

There is nothing better than the encouragement of a good friend.
—Katherine Butler Hathaway

A friend is someone you can be alone with and have nothing to do and not be able to think of anything to say and be comfortable in the silence.
—Sheryl Condie

It's the friends you can call up at 4:00 a.m. that matter. —Marlene Dietrich

Perhaps the most delightful friendships are those in which there is much agreement, much disputation, and yet more personal liking.
—George Eliot

Prosperity is not just scale; adversity is the only balance to weigh friends.
—Plutarch

There is no man that imparteth his joys to his friends, but he joyeth the more; and no man that imparteth his griefs to his friends, but he grieveth the less. —Francis Bacon

I am treating you as my friend, asking you to share my present minuses in the hope I can ask you to share my future pluses. —Katherine Mansfield

The most beautiful discovery true friends make is that they can grow separately without growing apart. —Elizabeth Foley

Trouble is a sieve through which we sift our acquaintances. Those too big to pass through are our friends. —Arlene Francis

I have come to esteem history as a component of friendships. In my case at least friendships are not igneous but sedimentary. —Jane Howard

No man can be happy without a friend, nor be sure of his friend till he is unhappy. —Thomas Fuller

Friendship makes prosperity more brilliant, and lightens adversity by dividing and sharing it. —Cicero

The friend of my adversity I shall always cherish most. I can better trust those who helped to relieve the gloom of my dark hours than those who are so ready to enjoy with me the sunshine of my prosperity. —Ulysses S. Grant

The growth of true friendship may be a lifelong affair. —Sarah Orne Jewett

Constant use had not worn ragged the fabric of their friendship. —Dorothy Parker

Even where the affections are not strongly moved by any superior excellence, the companions of our childhood always possess a certain power over our minds which hardly any later friend can obtain. —Mary Wollstonecraft Shelley

In prosperity our friends know us; in adversity we know our friends. —John Churton Collins

O summer friendship, whose flattering leaves shadowed us in our prosperity,
With the least gust, drop off in the autumn of adversity. —Philip Massinger

I loathe a friend . . . who takes his friend's prosperity but will not voyage with him in his grief. —Euripides

In prosperity friends do not leave you unless desired, whereas in adversity they stay away of their own accord. —Demetrius

There's no friend like someone who has known you since you were five. —Anne Stevenson

Lots of people want to ride with you in the limo, but what you want is someone who will take the bus with you when the limo breaks down. —Oprah Winfrey

I have lost friends, some by death . . . others by sheer inability to cross the street. —Virginia Woolf

Friendship was given by nature to be an assistant to virtue, not a companion in vice.   —Cicero

We are fonder of visiting our friends in health than in sickness. We judge less favorably of their characters when any misfortune happens to them; and a lucky hit, either in business or reputation, improves even their personal appearance in our eyes.
—William Hazlitt

Women rely on friends. . . . That's where we draw sustenance and find safety. We can count on our women friends when we need a good laugh or a good cry.   —Cokie Roberts

The shifts of fortune test the reliability of friends.   —Cicero

Never befriend the oppressed unless you are prepared to take on the oppressor.   —Ogden Nash

Trouble shared is trouble halved.
—Dorothy L. Sayers

Real friendship is shown in times of trouble; prosperity is full of friends.
—Euripides

FRIENDS AND FAMILY

I figure if I have my health, can pay the rent and I have my friends, I call it "content."   —Lauren Bacall

You leave home to seek your fortune and, when you get it, you go home and share it with your family.
—Anita Baker

If you have a good name, if you are right more often than you are wrong, if your children respect you, if your grandchildren are glad to see you, if your friends can count on you and you can count on them in time of trouble, if you can face your God and say "I have done my best," then you are a success.   —Ann Landers

Is there any stab as deep as wondering where and how much you failed those you loved?
—Florida Scott-Maxwell

My darling little girl-child, after such a long and troublesome waiting I now have you in my arms. I am alone no more, I have my baby.
—Martha Martin

A sympathetic friend can be quite dear as a brother.   —Homer

There's a time when you have to explain to your children why they were born, and it's a marvelous thing if you know the reason by then.
—Hazel Scott

Disorder in the society is the result of disorder in the family.
—Elizabeth Ann Seton

To nourish children and raise them against odds is in any time, any place, more valuable than to fix bolts in cars or design nuclear weapons.
—Marilyn French

I believe that we are always attracted to what we need most, an instinct leading us towards the persons who are to open new vistas in our lives and fill them with new knowledge.
—Helene Iswolsky

If you bungle raising your children, I don't think whatever else you do matters very much.
— Jacqueline Kennedy Onassis

Friends are relatives you make for yourself. — Eustache Deschamps

The darn trouble with cleaning the house is it gets dirty the next day anyway, so skip a week if you have to. The children are the most important thing. — Barbara Bush

The presidency is temporary—but the family is permanent.
— Yvonne de Gaulle

Chance makes our parents, but choice makes our friends.
— Jacques Delille

God gave us our relatives; thank God we can choose our friends.
— Ethel Watts Mumford

A good friend is my nearest relation.
— Thomas Fuller

It seems to me that since I've had children, I've grown richer and deeper. They may have slowed down my writing for a while, but when I did write, I had more of a self to speak from. — Anne Tyler

All love that has not friendship for its base is like a mansion built upon the sand. — Ella Wheeler Wilcox

One loyal friend is worth ten thousand relatives. — Euripides

Biology is the least of what makes someone a mother. — Oprah Winfrey

ENEMIES

Instead of loving your enemies, treat your friends a little better.
— Edgar Watson Howe

One enemy is too many; a hundred friends too few. — Anon.

Faithful are the wounds of a friend, but the kisses of an enemy are deceitful. — Proverbs 27:6

Friends come and go, enemies linger.
— Anon.

SOMETIMES A FRIEND WILL SUPPORT US EVEN WHEN WE'RE WRONG

The proper office of a friend is to side with you when you are in the wrong. Nearly everybody will side with you when you are in the right.
— Mark Twain

It isn't easy to be the person who sometimes has to try to preserve your happiness at the expense of your fun.
— Margaret Culkin Banning

I like a highland friend who will stand by me not only when I am in the right, but when I am a little in the wrong. — Sir Walter Scott

I don't care a damn for your loyal service when you think I am right; when I really want it most is when you think I am wrong.
— General Sir John Monash

We Need Several Kinds of Friends

Nature has been for me, for as long as I remember, a source of solace, inspiration, adventure, and delight; a home, a teacher, a companion.
—Lorraine Anderson

However deep our devotion may be to parents or to children, it is our contemporaries alone with whom understanding is instinctive and entire.
—Vera Brittain

Writers seldom choose as friends those self-contained characters who are never in trouble, never unhappy or ill, never make mistakes, and always count their change when it is handed to them.
—Catherine Drinker Bowen

Fortify yourself with a flock of friends! You can select them at random, write to one, dine with one, visit one, or take your problems to one. There is always at least one who will understand, inspire, and give you the lift you may need at the time.
—George Matthew Adams

Many a person has held close, throughout their entire lives, two friends that always remained strange to one another, because one of them attracted by virtue of similarity, the other by difference. —Emil Ludwig

Nothing is more limiting than a closed circle of acquaintanceship where every avenue of conversation has been explored and social exchanges are fixed in a known routine.
—A.J. Cronin

A man with few friends is only half-developed; there are whole sides of his nature which are locked up and have never been expressed. He cannot unlock them himself, he cannot even discover them; friends alone can stimulate him and open him.
—Randolph Bourne

Friendship is mutual blackmail elevated to the level of love.
—Robin Morgan

Scratch a lover, and find a foe.
—Dorothy Parker

We need old friends to help us grow old and new friends to help us stay young. —Letty Cottin Pogrebin

Friendship is almost always the union of a part of one mind with a part of another; people are friends in spots.
—George Santayana

It's the folks that depend on us for this and for the other that we most do miss. —Mary Webb

Time's passage through the memory is like molten glass that can be opaque or crystallize at any given moment at will: a thousand days are melted into one conversation, one glance, one hurt, and one hurt can be shattered and sprinkled over a thousand.
—Gloria Naylor

Kind words can be short and easy to speak, but their echoes are truly endless. —Mother Teresa

The wise man's . . . friendship is capable of going to extremes with many people, evoked as it is by many qualities. —Charles Dudley Warner

Now and then one sees a face which has kept its smile pure and undefiled. Such a smile transfigures; such a smile, if the artful but know it, is the greatest weapon a face can have.
　　　　　—Helen Hunt Jackson

I cannot concentrate all my friendship on any single one of my friends because no one is complete enough in himself.　　　　　—Anaïs Nin

We need two kinds of acquaintances, one to complain to, while we boast to the others. —Logan Pearsall Smith
No one person can possibly combine all the elements supposed to make up what everyone means by friendship.
　　　　　—Francis Marion Crawford

Every organism requires an environment of friends, partly to shield it from violent changes, and partly to supply it with its wants.
　　　　　—Alfred North Whitehead

Without wearing any mask we are conscious of, we have a special face for each friend.
　　　　　—Oliver Wendell Holmes

SOME THOUGHTS ABOUT OLD FRIENDS

An old friend never can be found, and nature has provided that he cannot easily be lost. —Samuel Johnson

Years and years of happiness only make us realize how lucky we are to have friends that have shared and made that happiness a reality.
　　　　　—Robert E. Frederick

To those who know thee not, no words can paint! And those who know thee, know all words are faint!
　　　　　—Hannah Moore

It is one of the blessings of old friends that you can afford to be stupid with them.
　　　　　—Ralph Waldo Emerson

Old friends are the great blessing of one's later years. . . . They have a memory of the same events and have the same mode of thinking.
　　　　　—Horace Walpole

As in the case of wines that improve with age, the oldest friendships ought to be the most delightful.　　—Cicero

There is a magic in the memory of a schoolboy friendship. It softens the heart, and even affects the nervous system of those who have no heart.
　　　　　—Benjamin Disraeli

It is great to have friends when one is young, but indeed it is still more so when you are getting old. When we are young, friends are, like everything else, a matter of course. In the old days we know what it means to have them.　　　　—Edvard Grieg

When you are young and without success, you have only a few friends. Then, later on, when you are rich and famous, you still have a few . . . if you are lucky.　　—Pablo Picasso

Old friends, we say, are best, when some sudden disillusionment shakes our faith in a new comrade.
　　　　　—Gelett Burgess

Friends and wine should be old.
                                —Spanish proverb

Forsake not an old friend, for the new is not comparable to him; a new friend is as new wine.
                                —Ecclesiastes 9:14

To be capable of steady friendship or lasting love are the two greatest proofs, not only of goodness of heart, but of strength of mind.
                                —William Hazlitt

Ah, how good it feels! The hand of an old friend.
                                —Henry Wadsworth Longfellow

The best mirror is an old friend.
                                —Anon.

WE MUST NOT LOSE OR DISCARD OUR FRIENDS

You can keep your friends by not giving them away.
                                —Mary Pettibone Poole

I keep my friends as misers do their treasure because, of all the things granted us by wisdom, none is greater or better than friendship.
                                —Pietro Aretino

There is only one thing better than making a new friend, and that is keeping an old one.
                                —Elmer G. Letterman

The only way not to break a friendship is not to drop it.   —Julie Holz

To throw away an honest friend is, as it were, to throw your life away.
                                —Sophocles

Hold a true friend with both your hands.   —Nigerian proverb

None is so rich as to throw away a friend.   —Turkish proverb

Those friends thou hast, and their adoption tried, grapple them to thy soul with hoops of steel.
                                —William Shakespeare

True friendship is like sound health; the value of it is seldom known until it be lost.   —Charles Caleb Colton

We die as often as we lose a friend.
                                —Publilius Syrus

Affinities are rare. They come but a few times in a life. It is awful to risk losing one when it arrives.
                                —Florence H. Winterburn

Rather throw away that which is dearest to you, your own life, than turn away a good friend.
                                —Sophocles

Thine own friend, and thy father's friend, forsake not. —Proverbs 27:10

The best way to keep your friends is not to give them away.
                                —Wilson Mizner

SOME THOUGHTS ABOUT NEW FRIENDS

I never enter a new company without the hope that I may discover a friend, perhaps the friend, sitting there with an expectant smile. That hope survives a thousand disappointments.
                                —Arthur Christopher Benson

Since there is nothing so well worth having as friends, never lose a chance to make them.
—Francesco Guicciardini

If a man does not make new acquaintances as he advances through life, he will soon find himself left alone.
—Samuel Johnson

A man's growth is seen in the successive choirs of his friends.
—Ralph Waldo Emerson

Every man passes his life in the search after friendship.
—Ralph Waldo Emerson

What causes us to like new acquaintances is not so much weariness of our old ones, or the pleasure of change, as disgust at not being sufficiently admired by those who know us too well, and the hope of being admired more by those who do not know so much about us.
—Francois de La Rochefoucauld

A new acquaintance is like a new book. I prefer it, even if bad, to a classic.
—Benjamin Disraeli

To cement a new friendship, especially between foreigners or persons of a different social world, a spark with which both were secretly charged must fly from person to person, and cut across the accidents of place and time.
—George Santayana

A new friend is like new wine; when it has aged you will drink it with pleasure.
—Apocrypha

He alone has lost the art to live who cannot win new friends.
—S. Weir Mitchell

Five years from now you will be pretty much the same as you are today except for two things: the books you read and the people you get close to.
—Charles Jones

I want no men around me who have not the knack of making friends.
—Frank A. Vanderlip

Yes'm, old friends is always best, 'less you can catch a new one that's fit to make an old one out of.
—Sarah Orne Jewett

Many a friendship—long, loyal, and self-sacrificing—rested at first upon no thicker a foundation than a kind word.
—Frederick W. Faber

A home-made friend wears longer than one you buy in the market.
—Austin O'Malley

The best time to make friends is before you need them.
—Ethel Barrymore

Accident counts for much in companionship, as in marriage.
—Henry Adams

We need new friends. Some of us are cannibals who have eaten their old friends up; others must have ever-renewed audiences before whom to re-enact an ideal version of their lives.
—Logan Pearsall Smith

We Should Be Careful in Making New Friends

In a world that holds books and babies and canyon trails, why should one condemn oneself to live day in, day out with people one does not like, and sell oneself to chaperone and correct them?   —Ruth Benedict

A true friend is the greatest of all blessings, and that which we take the least care of all to acquire.
              —Francois de La Rochefoucauld

A man must eat a peck of salt with his friend before he knows him.
              —Miguel de Cervantes

Have but few friends, though many acquaintances.   —Anon.

One who's our friend is fond of us; one who's fond of us isn't necessarily our friend.
              —Marcus Annaeus Seneca

Make all good men your well-wishers, and then, in the years' steady sifting, some of them will turn into friends.   —John Hay

Distrust all those who love you extremely upon a very slight acquaintance and without any viable reason.
              —Lord Chesterfield

We often choose a friend as we do a mistress, for no particular excellence in themselves, but merely from some circumstance that flatters our self-love.
              —William Hazlitt

How casually and unobservedly we make all our most valued acquaintances.   —Ralph Waldo Emerson

Be courteous to all, but intimate with few; and let those few be well-tried before you give them your confidence.
              —George Washington

Be slow to fall into friendship; but when thou art in, continue firm and constant.   —Socrates

How often we find ourselves turning our backs on our actual friends, that we may go and meet their ideal cousins.   —Henry David Thoreau

Let him have the key of thy heart, who hath the lock of his own.
              —Sir Thomas Browne

Books and friends should be few but good.   —Anon.

Sudden friendship, sure repentance.
              —Anon.

As there are some flowers which you should smell but slightly to extract all that is pleasant in them . . . so there are some men with whom a slight acquaintance is quite sufficient to draw out all that is agreeable; a more intimate one would be unsafe and unsatisfactory.
              —Walter Savage Landor

Acquaintance I would have, but when it depends not on the number, but the choice of friends.
              —Abraham Cowley

Always set high value on spontaneous kindness. He whose inclination prompts him to cultivate your friendship of his own accord will love you more than one whom you have been at pains to attach to you.
              —Samuel Johnson

Friendship that flames goes out in a flash. —Thomas Fuller

Trouble is a sieve through which we sift our acquaintances. Those too big to pass through are our friends.
—Arlene Francis

Wishing to be friends is quick work, but friendship is a slow-ripening fruit.
—Aristotle

Be slow in choosing a friend, slower in changing. —Benjamin Franklin

WHO WE ASSOCIATE WITH IS CRITICAL, BECAUSE WE MAY BECOME LIKE THEM

Every man is like the company he is wont to keep. —Euripides

Treat your friends as you do your picture, and place them in their best light. —Jennie Jerome Churchill

Character builds slowly, but it can be torn down with incredible swiftness.
—Faith Baldwin

He that lies down with dogs shall rise up with fleas. —Anon.

If I wanted to become a tramp, I would seek information and advice from the most successful tramp I could find. If I wanted to become a failure, I would seek advice from men who have never succeeded. If I wanted to succeed in all things, I would look around me for those who are succeeding, and do as they have done.
—Joseph Marshall Wade

Better fare hard with good men than feast with bad. —Thomas Fuller

By associating with good and evil persons a man acquires the virtues and vices which they possess, even as the wind blowing over different places takes along good and bad odors.
—The Panchatantra

I would prefer as a friend a good man who is ignorant than one more clever who is evil, too. —Euripides

Tell me whom you frequent, and I will tell you who you are.
—French proverb

Associate yourself with men of good quality if you esteem your own reputation, for 'tis better to be alone than in bad company.
—George Washington

Go to the place where the thing you wish to know is native; your best teacher is there. . . . You acquire a language most readily in the country where it is spoken, you study mineralogy best among miners, and so with everything else.
—Johann von Goethe

Tell me thy company, and I'll tell thee what thou art.
—Miguel de Cervantes

Who friendship with a knave hath made, is judged a partner in the trade.
—John Gay

The lion is ashamed, it's true, when he hunts with the fox.
—Gotthold Ephraim Lessing

He that walketh with wise men shall be wise. —Solomon

Life is partly what we make it, and partly what it is made by the friends we choose. —Tehyi Hsieh

If you always live with those who are lame, you will yourself learn to limp. —Latin proverb

Keep good men company, and you shall be of their number. —Anon.

A man becomes like those whose society he loves. —Hindu proverb

A wise man associating with the vicious becomes an idiot; a dog traveling with good men becomes a rational being. —Arab proverb

It is better to weep with wise men than to laugh with fools. —Spanish proverb

A wise man may look ridiculous in the company of fools. —Thomas Fuller

Ill company is like a dog, who dirts those most whom he loves best. —Jonathan Swift

Satan's friendship reaches to the prison door. —Turkish proverb

Have no friends not equal to yourself. —Confucius

Friendship is seldom lasting but between equals, or where the superiority on one side is reduced by some equivalent advantage on the other. —Samuel Johnson

Friendship neither finds nor makes equals. —Publilius Syrus

You cannot be friends upon any other terms than upon the terms of equality. —Woodrow Wilson

A man is known by the company he keeps. —Anon.

THE IMPORTANCE OF SIMILAR VALUES AND INTERESTS

Friendship is nothing else than an accord in all things, human and divine, conjoined with mutual good-will and affection. —Cicero

Friendship is a union of spirits, a marriage of hearts, and the bond there of virtue. —Samuel Johnson

To associate with other like-minded people in small purposeful groups is for the great majority of men and women a source of profound psychological satisfaction. —Aldous Huxley

Shared joys make a friend, not shared sufferings. —Friedrich Nietzsche

Seek those who find your road agreeable, your personality and mind stimulating, your philosophy acceptable, and your experiences helpful. Let those who do not, seek their own kind. —Jean-Henri Fabre

To like and dislike the same things, this is what makes a solid friendship. —Sallust

Friendship is only a reciprocal conciliation of interests. —Francois de La Rochefoucauld

Friendship needs a certain parallelism of life, a community of thought, a rivalry of aim. —Henry Adams

True friends . . . face in the same direction, toward common projects, interests, goals. —C.S. Lewis

That friendship may be at once fond and lasting, there must not only be equal virtue on each part, but virtue of the same kind; not only the same end must be proposed, but the same means must be approved by both. —Samuel Johnson

It is characteristic of spontaneous friendship to take on, without enquiry and almost at first sight, the unseen doings and unspoken sentiments of our friends; the part known gives us evidence enough that the unknown part cannot be much amiss. —George Santayana

Men only become friends by community of pleasures. —Samuel Johnson

We Should Have No Ulterior Motive in Making Friends

If we would build on a sure foundation in friendship, we must love friends for their sake rather than for our own. —Charlotte Brontë

The reward of friendship is itself. The man who hopes for anything else does not understand what true friendship is. —Saint Alfred of Rievaulx

That friendship will not continue to the end which is begun for an end. —Francis Quarles

The friendships which last are those wherein each friend respects the other's dignity to the point of not really wanting anything from him. —Cyril Connolly

My best friend is the man who in wishing me well wishes it for my sake. —Aristotle

I have friends in overalls whose friendship I would not swap for the favor of the kings of the world. —Thomas A. Edison

I have always differentiated between two types of friends; those who want proofs of friendship, and those who do not. One kind loves me for myself, and the others for themselves. —Gerard de Nerval

Friendship, like credit, is highest where it is not used. —Elbert Hubbard

Friendship without self-interest is one of the rare and beautiful things of life. —James F. Byrnes

I have learned that to have a good friend is the purest of all God's gifts, for it is a love that has no exchange of payment. —Frances Farmer

If you press me to say why I loved him, I can say no more than because he was he, and I was I. —Michel de Montaigne

He who looks for advantage out of friendship strips it all of its nobility. —Marcus Annaeus Seneca

Friendship is always a sweet responsibility, never an opportunity.
—Kahlil Gibran

Ourselves as Friends

Friendship with oneself is all-important, because without it one cannot be friends with anyone else.
—Eleanor Roosevelt

In a friend you find a second self.
—Isabelle Norto

Of my friends, I am the only one I have left.
—Terence

I desire so to conduct the affairs of this administration that if at the end ...I have lost every other friend on earth, I shall at least have one friend left, and that friend shall be down inside of me.
—Abraham Lincoln

Be a friend to thyself, and others will be so too.
—Thomas Fuller

Other Definitions of Friendship

Friendship is neither a formality nor a mode: it is rather a life.
—David Grayson

Friendship is one mind in two bodies.
—Menclus

Friendship's a noble name, 'tis love refined.
—Susannah Centlivre

A friend is, as it were, a second self.
—Cicero

Friend: One who knows all about you and loves you just the same.
—Elbert Hubbard

A friend is like a poem.
—Persian proverb

A friend is a present you give to yourself.
—Robert Louis Stevenson

A friend is someone you can do nothing with, and enjoy it.
—*The Optimist*

Friendship needs no words—it is solitude delivered from the anguish of loneliness.
—Dag Hammarskjold

A friend may well be reckoned the masterpiece of nature.
—Ralph Waldo Emerson

Two friends—two bodies with one soul inspired.
—Homer

In poverty and other misfortunes of life, true friends are a sure refuge.
—Aristotle

Friendship is a single soul dwelling in two bodies.
—Aristotle

A faithful friend is the medicine of life.
—Apocrypha

Friends are a second existence.
—Baltasar Gracian

A real friend helps us think our best thoughts, do our noblest deeds, be our finest selves.
—Anon.

Friendship is a furrow in the sand.
—Tongan proverb

Friendship is love without his wings!
—Lord Byron

True friendship is self-love at second hand. —William Hazlitt

The real friend is he or she who can share all our sorrow and double our joys. —B.C. Forbes

GENERAL QUOTATIONS ABOUT FRIENDSHIP

Friendship is a word the very sight of which in print makes the heart warm.
—Augustine Birrell

Most men's friendships are too inarticulate. —William James

My philosophy is: anyone or anything that gives you knowledge inspires you. —Gabrielle Reece

The feeling of friendship is like that of being comfortably filled with roast beef. —Samuel Johnson

The easiest kind of relationship for me is with ten thousand people. The hardest is with one. —Joan Baez

It is easier to forgive an enemy than it is a friend.
—Madame Dorothee Deluzy

To act the part of a true friend requires more conscientious feeling than to fill with credit and complacency any other station or capacity in social life. —Sarah Ellis

Friendship is an art, and very few persons are born with a natural gift for it. —Kathleen Norris

Female friendships that work are relationships in which women help each other belong to themselves.
—Louise Bernikow

The language of friendship is not words, but meanings.
—Henry David Thoreau

I can trust my friends. . . . These people force me to examine myself, encourage me to grow. —Cher

We challenge one another to be funnier and smarter. . . . It's the way friends make love to one another.
—Annie Gottlieb

If I made it, it's half because I was game enough to take a lot of punishment along the way and half because there were a lot of people who cared enough to help me. —Althea Gibson

Iron sharpeneth iron; so a man sharpeneth the countenance of his friend.
—Proverbs 27:17

A friend can tell you things you don't want to tell yourself.
—Frances Ward Weller

I suppose there is one friend in the life of each of us who seems not a separate person, however dear and beloved, but an expansion, an interpretation, of one's self.
—Edith Wharton

Love demands infinitely less than friendship. —George Jean Nathan

Good company upon the road is the shortest cut. —Anon.

The particular human chain we're a part of is central to our individual identity. —Elizabeth Stone

No person is your friend who demands your silence, or denies your right to grow. —Alice Walker

The best preservative to keep the mind in health is the faithful admonition of a friend. —Francis Bacon

What is thine is mine, and all mine is thine. —Plautus

Do not protect yourself by a fence, but rather by your friends. —Czech proverb

If our friends' idealizations of us need the corrective of our own experience, it may be true also that our own sordid view of our lives needs the corrective of our friends' idealizations. —Oscar W. Firkins

In meeting again after a separation, acquaintances ask after our outward life, friends after our inner life. —Marie von Ebner-Eschenbach

In real friendship the judgment, the genius, the prudence of each party become the common property of both. —Maria Edgeworth

The thicker one gets with some people, the thinner they become. —Puzant Thomain

When our friends are alive, we see the good qualities they lack; dead, we remember only those they possessed. —J. Petit-Senn

The company makes the feast. —Anon.

When one friend washes another, both become clean. —Dutch proverb

I observed once to Goethe . . . that when a friend is with us we do not think the same of him as when he is away. He replied, "Yes! because the absent friend is yourself, and he exists only in your head; whereas the friend who is present has an individuality of his own, and moves according to laws of his own, which cannot always be in accordance with those which you form for yourself." —Arthur Schopenhauer

In reality, we are still children. We want to find a playmate for our thoughts and feelings. —Dr. Wilhelm Stekhel

Love me, please; I love you; I can bear to be your friend. So ask of me anything . . . I am not a tentative person. Whatever I do, I give up my whole self to it. —Edna Saint Vincent Millay

Most of our misfortunes are comments of our friends upon them. —Charles Caleb Colton

Greater love hath no man than this, that a man lay down his life for his friends. —John 15:13

Animals are such agreeable friends— they ask no questions, they pass no criticisms. —George Eliot

Great friendship is never without anxiety. —Marie de Rabutin-Chantal

It is good to have friends, even in hell.
                    —Spanish proverb

One of the signs of passing youth is
the birth of a sense of fellowship with
other human beings as we take our
place among them.   —Virginia Woolf

Silences make the real conversations
between friends.
                    —Margaret Lee Runbeck

Live so that your friends can defend
you, but never have to.
                    —Arnold Glasow

Friendship ought to be a gratuitous
joy, like the joys afforded by art.
                    —Simone Weil

Intimacies between women often go
backwards, beginning in revelations
and ending in small talk.
                    —Elizabeth Bowen

There is space within sisterhood for
likeness and difference, for the subtle
differences that challenge and delight;
there is space for disappointment—
and surprise.   —Christine Downing

We challenge one another to be funnier and smarter. . . . It's the way
friends make love to one another.
                    —Annie Gottlieb

Four be the things I am wiser to
know: Idleness, sorrow, a friend and
a foe.   —Anon.

If a man is worth knowing at all, he
is worth knowing well.
                    —Alexander Smith

Our Higher Power, or God

WE CAN'T, DON'T NEED, AND AREN'T EXPECTED TO UNDERSTAND GOD

We know only that we are living in these bodies and have a vague idea, because we have heard it, and because our faith tells us so, that we possess souls. As to what good qualities there may be in our souls, or who dwells within them, or how precious they are, those are things which we seldom consider and so we trouble little about carefully preserving the soul's beauty. —Teresa of Avila

I believe in the incomprehensibility of God. —Honore de Balzac

Every conjecture we can form with regard to the works of God has as little probability as the conjectures of a child with regard to the works of a man. —Thomas Reid

God is incorporeal, divine, supreme, infinite. Mind, Spirit, Soul, Principle, Life, Truth, Love.
—Mary Baker Eddy

No statement about God is simply, literally true. God is far more than can be measured, described, defined in ordinary language, or pinned down to any particular happening.
—David Jenkins

Who fathoms the Eternal Thought?
Who talks of scheme and plan?
The Lord is God! He needeth not
The poor device of man.
—John Greenleaf Whittier

Some people want to see God with their eyes as they see a cow, and to love Him as they love their cow—for the milk and cheese and profit it brings them. This is how it is with people who love God for the sake of outward wealth or inward comfort.
—Meister Eckhart

Your mind cannot possibly understand God. Your heart already knows. Minds were designed for carrying out the orders of the heart.
—Emmanuel

A comprehended God is no God at all.
—Gerhard Tersteegen

"What do you think of God," the teacher asked. After a pause, the young pupil replied, "He's not a think, he's a feel." —Paul Frost

To them that ask, where have you seen the Gods, or how do you know for certain there are Gods, that you are so devout in their worship? I answer: Neither have I ever seen my own soul, and yet I respect and honor it.
—Marcus Aurelius

It is the heart which experiences God, not the reason. —Blaise Pascal

GOD MAY BE DIFFERENT TO EACH OF US

I always say my God will take care of me. If it's my time I'll go, and if it's not I won't. I feel that He really has a lot of important things for me to do. And He's going to make sure that I'm here to do them. —Joycelyn Elders

God is like a mirror. The mirror never changes, but everybody who looks at it sees something different.
—Rabbi Harold Kushner

God is to me that creative Force, behind and in the universe, who manifests Himself as energy, as life, as order, as beauty, as thought, as conscience, as love.
—Henry Sloane Coffin

God is incorporeal, divine, supreme, infinite. Mind, Spirit, Soul, Principle, Life, Truth, Love.
—Mary Baker Eddy

God, that dumping ground of our dreams. —Jean Rostand

The God of many men is little more than their court of appeal against the damnatory judgement passed on their failures by the opinion of the world.
—William James

God, to be God, must transcend what is. He must be the maker of what ought to be. —Rufus M. Jones

God is an unutterable sigh, planted in the depths of the soul.
—Jean Paul Richter

God is a verb, not a noun.
—R. Buckminster Fuller

The most beautiful of all emblems is that of God, whom Timaeus of Locris describes under the image of "A circle whose centre is everywhere and whose circumference is nowhere."
—Voltaire

God is what man finds that is divine in himself. God is the best way man can behave in the ordinary occasions of life, and the farthest point to which man can stretch himself.
—Max Lerner

The deep emotional conviction of the presence of a superior reasoning power, which is revealed in the incomprehensible universe, forms my idea of God. —Albert Einstein

God has many names, though He is only one Being. —Aristotle

There is but one ultimate Power. This Power is to each one what he is to it.
—Ernest Holmes

HOW TO FIND AND REACH GOD

It is impossible to fulfill the law concerning love for Me, God eternal, apart from the law concerning love for your neighbors.
—Saint Catherine of Siena

When we lose God, it is not God who is lost.
—Anon.

If we're not growing, we must feel guilty, because we are not fulfilling Christ's demand.
—Eva Burrows

The soul can split the sky in two, and let the face of God shine through.
—Edna Saint Vincent Millay

God enters by a private door into every individual.
—Ralph Waldo Emerson

The best thing must be to flee from all to the All.
—Teresa of Avila

A humble knowledge of oneself is a surer road to God than a deep searching of the sciences.
—Thomas à Kempis

By learning to contact, listen to, and act on our intuition, we can directly connect to the higher power of the universe and allow it to become our guiding force.
—Shakti Gawain

When a man takes one step toward God, God takes more steps toward that man than there are sands in the worlds of time.
—*The Work of the Chariot*

It's only by forgetting yourself that you draw near to God.
—Henry David Thoreau

Some people talk about finding God, as if He could get lost.
—Anon.

Hunting God is a great adventure.
—Marie DeFloris

In the faces of men and women I see God.
—Walt Whitman

To Be is to live with God.
—Ralph Waldo Emerson

Nothing hath separated us from God but our own will, or rather our own will is our separation from God.
—William Law

The kingdom of God is within you.
—Luke 17:21

Not only then has each man his individual relation to God, but each man has his peculiar relation to God.
—George MacDonald

Because you cannot see him, God is everywhere.
—Yasunari Kawabata

All who call on God in true faith, earnestly from the heart, will certainly be heard, and will receive what they have asked and desired.
—Martin Luther

The light of God surrounds me,
The love of God enfolds me,
The power of God protects me,
The Presence of God watches over
   me,
Wherever I am, God is.
—Prayer Card

To think you are separate from God is to remain separate from your own being.
—D.M. Street

God knows no distance.
—Charleszetta Waddles

We Find Divinity When We Are Open to It

So great was my joy in God that I took no heed of looking at the angels and the saints, because all their goodness and all their beauty was from Him and in Him.
—Saint Angela of Foligno

Our condition is most noble, being so beloved of the Most High God that He was willing to die for our sake—which He would not have done if man had not been a most noble creature and of great worth.
—Saint Angela of Foligno

Our perfection certainly consists in knowing God and ourselves.
—Saint Angela of Foligno

In every out-thrust headland, in every curving beach, in every grain of sand, there is the story of the earth.
—Rachel Carson

To those leaning on the sustaining infinite, today is big with blessings.
—Mary Baker Eddy

Oh, if everyone knew how beautiful Jesus is, how amiable He is! They would all die from love.
—Gemma Galagani

He loves, He hopes, He waits. Our Lord prefers to wait Himself for the sinner for years rather than keep us waiting an instant. —Maria Goretti

The Creator and Lord of all so loved the world, that He sent His Son for its salvation, the Prince and Savior of the faithful, who washed and dried our wounds, and from Him also came that most sweet medicine, from which all the good things of salvation flow.
—Hildegard of Bingen

Sometimes I try my hand at turning out small profundities and uncertain short stories, but I always end up with just one single word: God.
—Etty Hillesum

Eventually I lost interest in trying to control my life, to make things happen in a way that I thought I wanted them to be. I began to practice surrendering to the universe and finding out what "it" wanted me to do.
—Shakti Gawain

God Will Help Us

I would rather walk with God in the dark than go alone in the light.
—Mary Gardiner Brainard

Without the assistance of the Divine Being . . . I cannot succeed. With that assistance, I cannot fail.
—Abraham Lincoln

For the rest of my life I'm going to trust that God is always at work in all things, and give Him thanks long before my simplest prayers are answered. —Nancy Parker Brummett

Divine love always has met and always will meet every human need.
—Mary Baker Eddy

Jesus makes the bitterest mouthful taste sweet.   —Thérèse of Lisieux

The best remedy for those who are afraid, lonely, or unhappy is to go outside, somewhere where they can be quiet, alone with the heavens, nature, and God. Because only then does one feel that all is as it should be and that God wishes to see people happy, amidst the simple beauty of nature. As long as this exists, and it certainly always will, I know that then there will always be comfort for every sorrow, whatever the circumstances may be. And I firmly believe that nature brings solace in all troubles.
                              —Anne Frank

Whoever falls from God's right hand is caught into His left.
                         —Edwin Markham

If I saw the gates of hell open and I stood on the brink of the abyss, I would not despair, I would not lose hope of mercy, because I would trust in You, my God.   —Gemma Galgani

The accidents of life separate us from our dearest friends, but let us not despair. God is like a looking glass in which souls see each other. The more we are united to Him by love, the nearer we are to those who belong to Him.
                    —Elizabeth Ann Seton

In God We Trust.
              —Motto of the United States,
             adopted by Congress for use
            on coins and one-dollar bills

The things which are impossible with men are possible with God.
                            —Luke 18:27

I will not fear, for you are ever with me, and you will never leave me to face my perils alone.
                        —Thomas Merton

Pardon, not wrath, is God's best attribute.   —Bayard Taylor

Walk boldly and wisely. . . . There is a hand above that will help you on.
                    —Philip James Bailey

For the multitude of worldly friends profiteth not, nor may strong helpers anything avail, nor wise counselors give profitable counsel, nor the cunning of doctors give consolation, nor riches deliver in time of need, nor a secret place to defend, if Thou, Lord, do not assist, help, comfort, counsel, inform, and defend.
                      —Thomas à Kempis

Some Ways That God Makes Wishes Known to Us

The Blessed Virgin used me like a broom, and then put me back in my place.   —Bernadette Soubirous

Many a humble soul will be amazed to find that the seed it sowed in weakness, in the dust of daily life, has blossomed into immortal flowers under the eye of the Lord.
                  —Harriet Beecher Stowe

Trust in the Lord with all thine heart, and lean not unto thine own understanding. In all thy ways acknowledge Him, and He shall direct thy paths.   —Proverbs 3:5–6

God speaks to all individuals through what happens to them moment by moment. —J.P. DeCaussade

God uses lust to impel men to marry, ambition to office, avarice to earning, and fear to faith. God led me like an old blind goat. —Martin Luther

An act of God was defined as "something which no reasonable man could have expected." —A.P. Herbert

GOD AND LOVE

Let God love you through others and let God love others through you. —D.M. Street

My debt to you, Beloved,
Is one I cannot pay
In any coin of any realm
On any reckoning day.
—Jessie Rittenhouse

One unquestioned text we read,
All doubt beyond, all fear above;
Nor crackling pile nor cursing creed
Can burn or blot it: God is Love.
—Oliver Wendell Holmes

A true love of God must begin with a delight in his holiness.
—Jonathan Edwards

As to the aridity you are suffering from, it seems to me our Lord is treating you like someone He considers strong: He wants to test you and see if you love Him as much at times of aridity as when He sends you consolations. I think this is a very great favor for God to show you.
—Teresa of Avila

The first condition of human goodness is something to love; the second, something to revere. —George Eliot

No man hates God without first hating himself. —Fulton J. Sheen

GENERAL QUOTATIONS ABOUT A HIGHER POWER, OR GOD

How is it, Lord, that we are cowards in everything save in opposing thee?
—Teresa of Avila

I have never understood why it should be considered derogatory to the Creator to suppose that He has a sense of humor. —William Ralph Inge

Every law of matter or the body, supposed to govern man, is rendered null and void by the law of Life, God.
—Mary Baker Eddy

Whom the heart of man shuts out,
Sometimes the heart of God takes in.
—James Russell Lowell

I need nothing but God, and to lose myself in the heart of God.
—Saint Margaret Mary Alacoque

To love one that is great, is almost to be great one's self. —Madame Necker

I would rather walk with God in the dark than go alone in the light.
—Mary Gardiner Brainard

What we are is God's gift to us. What we become is our gift to God.
—Anon.

Gawd knows, and 'E won't split on a pal. —Rudyard Kipling

Holy church—that mother who is also a queen because she is a king's bride. —Teresa of Avila

"You are accepted!" . . . accepted by that which is greater than you and the name of which you do not know. Do not ask the name now, perhaps you will know it later. Do not try to do anything, perhaps later you will do much. Do not seek for anything, do not perform anything, do not intend anything. Simply accept the fact that you are accepted. —Paul Tillich

As in heaven Your will is punctually performed, so may it be done on earth by all creatures, particularly in me and by me. —Saint Elizabeth of Hungary

Christ has made my soul beautiful with the jewels of grace and virtue. —Saint Agnes

God delays, but doesn't forget. —Spanish proverb

How is it, Lord, that we are cowards in everything save in opposing Thee? —Teresa of Avila

God is clever, but not dishonest. —Albert Einstein

Yet, in the maddening maze of things, And tossed by storm and flood, To one fixed trust my spirit clings; I know that God is good! —John Greenleaf Whittier

I could be whatever I wanted to be if I trusted that music, that song, that vibration of God that was inside of me. —Shirley MacLaine

The million little things that drop into your hands The small opportunities each day brings He leaves us free to use or abuse And goes unchanging along His silent way. —Helen Keller

The Father most tender, Father of all, my immense God—I His atom. —Elizabeth Ann Seton

What is there in man so worthy of honor and reverence as this, that he is capable of contemplating something higher than his own reason, more sublime than the whole universe—that Spirit which alone is self-subsistent, from which all truth proceeds, without which there is no truth? —Friedrich Jacobi

I thank the goodness and the grace Which on my birth have smiled, And made me, in these Christian days, A happy Christian child. —Jane Taylor

A consciousness of God releases the greatest power of all. —Ernest Holmes

Above all am I convinced of the need, irrevocable and inescapable, of every human heart, for God. No matter how we try to escape, to lose ourselves in restless seeking, we cannot separate ourselves from our divine source. There is no substitute for God. —A.J. Cronin

Talking about God is not at all the same thing as experiencing God, or acting out God through our lives. —Phillip Hewett

The person who has a firm trust in the Supreme Being is powerful in his power, wise by his wisdom, happy by his happiness. —Joseph Addison

God has not promised skies always
   blue,
flower-strewn pathways all our lives
   through;
God has not promised sun without
   rain,
joy without sorrow, peace without
   pain.
But God has promised strength for
   the day,
rest for the labor, light for the way,
Grace for the trials, help from above,
   unfailing sympathy, undying love.
        —Annie Johnson Flint

Courage is not afraid to weep, and she is not afraid to pray, even when she is not sure who she is praying to. —J. Ruth Gendler

God is no enemy to you. He asks no more than that He hear you call Him "Friend." —A Course in Miracles

Deep down in every man, woman and child, is the fundamental idea of God. It may be obscured by calamity, by pomp, by worship of other things, but in some form or other it is there. For faith in a Power greater than ourselves, and miraculous demonstrations of that power in human lives, are facts as old as man himself. —Alcoholics Anonymous

Our human resources, as marshalled by the will, were not sufficient; they failed utterly. . . . Every day is a day when we must carry the vision of God's will into all our activities. —Alcoholics Anonymous

Then comes the insight that All is God. One still realizes that the world is as it was, but it does not matter, it does not affect one's faith. —Abraham Heschel

The experience of God, or in any case the possibility of experiencing God, is innate. —Alice Walker

Before me, even as behind, God is, and all is well. —John Greenleaf Whittier

Forgetfulness of self is remembrance of God. —Bayazid Al-Bistami

Every morning I spend fifteen minutes filling my mind full of God, and so there's no room left for worry thoughts. —Howard Chandler Christy

Darkness is strong, and so is Sin,
But surely God endures forever!
        —James Russell Lowell

I need nothing but God, and to lose myself in the heart of God. —Saint Margaret Mary Alacoque

It is not my ability, but my response to God's ability, that counts. —Corrie ten Boom

He is more within us than we are ourselves. —Elizabeth Ann Seton

We have grasped the mystery of the atom and rejected the Sermon on the Mount. —General Omar N. Bradley

Faith and Belief

We Must Have Faith in What We Can't See

Spirit is the real and eternal; matter is the unreal and the temporal.
—Mary Baker Eddy

Faith sees the invisible, believes the unbelievable, and receives the impossible.   —Corrie ten Boom

I believe in the sun even if it isn't shining. I believe in love even when I am alone. I believe in God even when He is silent.   —World War II refugee

For the facts that make up the world need the non-factual as a vantage point from which to be perceived.
—Ingeborg Bachmann

Faith is nothing at all tangible. . . . It is simply believing God; and like sight, it is nothing apart from its object. You might as well shut your eyes and look inside, and see whether you have sight, as to look inside to discover whether you have faith.
—Hannah Whitall Smith

Faith is the daring of the soul to go farther than it can see.
—William Newton Clark

Spirituality leaps where science cannot yet follow, because science must always test and measure, and much of reality and human experience is immeasurable.   —Starhawk

Faith is the substance of things hoped for, the evidence of things not seen.
—Hebrews 11:1

All I have seen teaches me to trust the Creator for all I have not seen.
—Ralph Waldo Emerson

Some things have to be believed to be seen.   —Ralph Hodgson

Faith is like radar that sees through the fog—the reality of things at a distance that the human eye cannot see.
—Corrie ten Boom

Faith sees the invisible, believes the incredible and receives the impossible.
—Anon.

A believer, a mind whose faith is consciousness, is never disturbed because
other persons do not yet see the fact
which he sees.
　　　　　　—Ralph Waldo Emerson

We walk by faith, not by sight.
　　　　　　—2 Corinthians 5:7

Faith is to believe what we do not
see; the reward of this faith is to see
what we believe.　—Saint Augustine

Because you cannot see him, God is
everywhere.　—Yasunari Kawabata

Sorrow looks back, worry looks
around, faith looks up.
　　　　　　—*Guideposts*

You have to believe in gods to see
them.　　　—Hopi Indian saying

Faith declares what the senses do
not see, but not the contrary of what
they see.　　　　—Blaise Pascal

Faith has to do with things that are
not seen, and hope with things that
are not in hand.
　　　　—Saint Thomas Aquinas

Faith is the capacity of the soul to
perceive the abiding . . . the invisible
in the visible.　　　—Leo Baeck

FAITH AND UNITY

I knew without a glimmer of doubt
that all things in the universe were
connected by a living truth that
would not relent its continuing search
for wholeness until every form of life
was united.　　—Lynn V. Andrews

Unity, not uniformity, must be our
aim. We attain unity only through
variety. Differences must be integrat-
ed, not annihilated, not absorbed.
　　　　　—Mary Parker Follett

By virtue of love is the lover transformed in the beloved and the
beloved transformed in the lover.
　　　　—Saint Angela of Foligno

Spiritual love is a position of standing
with one hand extended into the universe and one hand extended into the
world, letting ourselves be a conduit
for passing energy.
　　　　　　—Christina Baldwin

One's life has value so long as one
attributes value to the life of others,
by means of love, friendship, indignation and compassion.
　　　　　　—Simone de Beauvoir

Patience with others is Love, Patience
with self is Hope, Patience with God
is Faith.　　　　—Adel Bestavros

God is universal; confined to no spot,
defined by no dogma, appropriated
by no sect.　　　—Mary Baker Eddy

Trying to do good to people without
God's help is no easier than making
the sun shine at midnight. You discover that you've got to abandon all your
own preferences, your own bright
ideas, and guide souls along the road
our Lord has marked out for them.
You mustn't coerce them into some
path of your own choosing.
　　　　　　—Thérèse of Lisieux

We Must Have Faith in Other People

We must have infinite faith in each other. —Henry David Thoreau

What loneliness is more lonely than distrust? —George Eliot

As contagion of sickness makes sickness, contagion of trust can make trust. —Marianne Moore

Faith in our associates is part of our faith in God.
—Charles Horton Cooley

Those who trust us educate us.
—George Eliot

He who has no faith in others shall find no faith in them. —Lao-tzu

Don't lose faith in humanity: think of all the people in the United States who have never played you a single nasty trick. —Elbert Hubbard

You can't leave humanity out. If you didn't have humanity, you wouldn't have anything. —Alice Neel

We Must Have Faith in Ourselves

I plunged into the job of creating something from nothing. . . . Though I hadn't a penny left, I considered cash money as the smallest part of my resources. I had faith in a living God, faith in myself, and a desire to serve.
—Mary McLeod Bethune

Faith in oneself . . . is the best and safest course. —Michelangelo

All our acts have sacramental possibilities. —Freya Stark

Only the person who has faith in himself is able to be faithful to others.
—Erich Fromm

Faith is Selfless

I never really look for anything. What God throws my way comes. I wake up in the morning and whichever way God turns my feet, I go.
—Pearl Bailey

In order to experience everyday spirituality, we need to remember that we are spiritual beings spending some time in a human body.
—Barbara De Angelis

We must move from asking God to take care of the things that are breaking our hearts, to praying about the things that are breaking His heart.
—Margaret Gibb

Peace . . . was contingent upon a certain disposition of the soul, a disposition to receive the gift that only detachment from self made possible.
—Elizabeth Goudge

You must never lose the awareness that in yourself you are nothing, you are only an instrument. An instrument is nothing until it is lifted.
—Katheryn Hulme

It's very reassuring and spiritual to be connected with something larger than yourself and the inside of your own head. —Joan Osborne

With all this wide and beautiful creation before me, the restless soul longs to enjoy its liberty and rest beyond its bound.   —Teresa of Avila

The country in which I live is not my native country, that lies elsewhere, and it must always be the center of my longings.   —Thérèse of Lisieux

The great majority of men use their own short-sighted ideas as a yard-stick for measuring the divine omnip-otence.   —Thérèse of Lisieux

Faith is the centerpiece of a con-nected life. It allows us to live by the grace of invisible strands. It is a belief in a wisdom superior to our own. Faith becomes a teacher in the absence of fact.
—Terry Tempest Williams

FAITH OR BELIEF: REASON, KNOWLEDGE, AND UNDERSTANDING

Faith is not a series of gilt-edged propositions that you sit down to figure out, and if you follow all the logic and accept all the conclusions, then you have it. It is crumpling and throwing away everything, proposi-tion by proposition, until nothing is left, and then writing a new proposi-tion, your very own, to throw in the teeth of despair.   —Mary Jean Irion

Faith doesn't wait until it under-stands; in that case it wouldn't be faith.   —Vance Havner

Your faith is what you believe, not what you know.
—John Lancaster Spalding

That's the thing about faith. If you don't have it you can't understand it. And if you do, no explanation is nec-essary.   —Major Kira Nerys

Our body is not made of iron. Our strength is not that of stone. Live and hope in the Lord, and let your service be according to reason.
—Saint Clare of Assisi

No, I don't understand my husband's theory of relativity, but I know my husband, and I know he can be trusted.   —Elsa Einstein

It is faith, and not reason, which impels men to action. . . . Intelligence is content to point out the road, but never drives us along it.
—Dr. Alexis Carrel

Faith consists, not in ignorance, but in knowledge, and that, not only of God, but also of the divine will.
—John Calvin

Faith is an excitement and an enthu-siasm, a state of intellectual magnifi-cence which we must not squander on our way through life.
—George Sand

All the scholastic scaffolding falls, as a ruined edifice, before a single word: faith.   —Napoleon Bonaparte

Some like to understand what they believe in. Others like to believe in what they understand.
—Jerzy Lec Stanislaw

Seek not to understand that thou mayest believe, but believe that thou mayest understand.
—Saint Augustine

Faith is a sounder guide than reason. Reason can go only so far, but faith has no limits.   —Blaise Pascal

Logic is the key to an all-inclusive spiritual well-being.
                    —Marlene Dietrich

It is the heart which experiences God, and not the reason.   —Blaise Pascal

There is no object that we see; no action that we do; no good that we enjoy; no evil that we feel, or fear, but we may make some spiritual advantage of all: and he that makes such improvement is wise, as well as pious.
                    —Anne Bradstreet

Faith is the continuation of reason.
                    —William Adams

If we were logical, the future would be bleak indeed. But we are more than logical. We are human beings, and we have faith, and we have hope.
                    —Jacques Cousteau

Faith is the art of holding on to things your reason has once accepted, in spite of your changing moods.
                    —C.S. Lewis

Reason is the triumph of the intellect, faith of the heart.   —James Schouler

Reason is our soul's left hand, Faith her right. By this we reach divinity.
                    —John Donne

It is as absurd to argue men, as to torture them, into believing.
                    —John Henry Cardinal Newman

Reason's voice and God's, Nature's and Duty's, never are at odds.
                    —John Greenleaf Whittier

The way to see by Faith is to shut the eye of Reason.   —Benjamin Franklin

Faith is believing what we cannot prove.   —Alfred, Lord Tennyson

Faith is to believe what you do not yet see; the reward for this faith is to see what you believe.
                    —Saint Augustine

Faith is believing when it is beyond the power of reason to believe.
                    —Voltaire

Faith is a higher faculty than reason.
                    —Henry Christopher Bailey

Faith is reason grown courageous.
                    —Sherwood Eddy

Faith is the result of the act of the will, following upon a conviction that to believe is a duty.
                    —John Henry Cardinal Newman

So often we have a kind of vague, wistful longing that the promises of Jesus should be true. The only way really to enter into them is to believe them with the clutching intensity of a drowning man.   —William Barclay

Man makes holy what he believes, as he makes beautiful what he loves.
                    —Ernest Renan

If life is a comedy to him who thinks, and a tragedy to him who feels, it is a victory to him who believes.
                    —Anon.

You're not free until you've been made captive by supreme belief.
—Marianne Moore

It is by believing in roses that one brings them to bloom.
—French proverb

If you wish to strive for peace of soul and pleasure, then believe.
—Heinrich Heine

Loving is half of believing.
—Victor Hugo

A faith that sets bounds to itself, that will believe so much and no more, that will trust so far and no further, is none.   —Julius Charles Hare

FAITH AND DOUBT

Doubt is a pain too lonely to know that faith is his twin brother.
—Kahlil Gibran

Doubt is a necessity of the mind, faith of the heart.   —Comtesse Diane

For the truly faithful, no miracle is necessary. For those who doubt, no miracle is sufficient.   —Nancy Gibbs

My faith has wavered but has saved me.   —Helen Hayes

Faith which does not doubt is dead faith.   —Miguel de Unamuno

To believe with certainty, we must begin with doubting.   —Stanislaus I

O thou of little faith, why didst thou doubt?   —Matthew 14:31

In the midst of your doubts, don't forget how many of the important questions God does answer.
—Verne Becker

The only limit to our realization of tomorrow will be our doubts of today. Let us move forward with strong and active faith.
—Franklin Delano Roosevelt

It is impossible on reasonable grounds to disbelieve miracles.
—Blaise Pascal

FAITH AND FEAR

Deep faith eliminates fear.
—Lech Walesa

A red-hot belief in eternal glory is probably the best antidote to human panic that there is.
—Phyllis Bottome

Our faith triumphant o'er our fears.
—Henry Wadsworth Longfellow

Let nothing disturb you, nothing frighten you; all things are passing; God never changes.
—Teresa of Avila

Fear imprisons, faith liberates; fear paralyzes, faith empowers; fear disheartens, faith encourages; fear sickens, faith heals; fear makes useless, faith makes serviceable.
—Harry Emerson Fosdick

Fear knocked at the door. Faith answered. And lo, no one was there.
—Anon.

166

TRUSTING AND DARING

How desperately we wish to maintain our trust in those we love! In the face of everything, we try to find reasons to trust. Because losing faith is worse than falling out of love.
—Sonia Johnson

Faith is kind of like jumping out of an airplane at ten thousand feet. If God doesn't catch you, you splatter. But how do you know whether or not He is going to catch you unless you jump out?   —Ann Kiemel

Faith . . . acts promptly and boldly on the occasion, on slender evidence.
—John Henry Cardinal Newman

The will of God will not take you where the grace of God cannot keep you.   —Anon.

Without risk, faith is an impossibility.
—Søren Kierkegaard

If it wasn't for faith, there would be no living in this world; we couldn't even eat hash with any safety.
—Josh Billings

Living is a form of not being sure, not knowing what next, or how. The moment you know how, you begin to die a little. The artist never entirely knows. We guess. We may be wrong, but we take leap after leap in the dark.
—Agnes de Mille

Let us move on, and step out boldly, though it be into the night, and we can scarcely see the way. A Higher Intelligence than the mortal sees the road before us.
—Charles B. Newcomb

Faith is an assent of the mind and a consent of the heart, consisting mainly of belief and trust.   —E.T. Hiscox

WE EACH HAVE OUR OWN FAITH

The relation of faith between subject and object is unique in every case. Hundreds may believe, but each has to believe by himself. —W.H. Auden

Whether we name divine presence synchronicity, serendipity, or graced moment matters little. What matters is the reality that our hearts have been understood. Nothing is as real as a healthy dose of magic which restores our spirits.   —Nancy Long

Maybe the tragedy of the human race was that we had forgotten that we are each divine. —Shirley MacLaine

We cannot hand our faith to one another. . . . Even in the Middle Ages, when faith was theoretically uniform, it was always practically individual.
—John Jay Chapman

HOW TO DEVELOP FAITH

Every human being is born without faith. Faith comes only through the process of making decisions to change before we can be sure it's the right move.
—Dr. Robert H. Schuller

I believe devoutly in the Word. The Word can save all, destroy all, stop the inevitable, and express the inexpressible.   —Nina Voronel

To believe in God is to yearn for His existence, and furthermore, it is to act as if He did exist.

—Miguel de Unamuno

The principle part of faith is patience.

—George MacDonald

FAITH REQUIRES
WORK AND EFFORT

I've been readen th Bible an a hunten God fer a long while—off an on— but it ain't so easy as picken up a nickel off the floor.

—Harriette Arnow

In prayer one must hold fast and never let go, because the one who gives up loses all. If it seems that no one is listening to you, then cry out even louder. If you are driven out of one door, go back in by the other.

—Jane Frances de Chantal

Faith is not belief. Belief is passive. Faith is active.   —Edith Hamilton

Can a faith that does nothing be called sincere?   —Jean Racine

Faith without works is dead.

—James 2:26

He does not believe who does not live according to his belief.

—Thomas Fuller

I pray hard, work hard, and leave the rest to God.

—Florence Griffith Joyner

All effort is in the last analysis sustained by faith that it is worth making.

—Ordway Tweed

It is for us to pray not for tasks equal to our powers, but for powers equal to our tasks, to go forward with a great desire forever beating at the door of our hearts as we travel towards our distant goal.

—Helen Keller

I have fought a good fight, I have finished my course, I have kept the faith.   —2 Timothy 4:7

Faith is not something to grasp, it is a state to grow into.

—Mahatma Gandhi

Possessing faith is not convenient. You still have to live it.

—Françoise Mallet-Joris

Faith is a curious thing, It must be renewed; it has its own spring.

—Gladys Taber

However much we do to avoid them, we shall never lack crosses in this life if we are in the ranks of the Crucified.   —Teresa of Avila

To disbelieve is easy; to scoff is simple; to have faith is harder.

—Louis L'Amour

No faith is our own that we have not arduously won.   —Havelock Ellis

OTHER DEFINITIONS OF
FAITH AND BELIEF

Faith is a living and unshakable confidence, a belief in the grace of God so assured that a man would die a thousand deaths for its sake.

—Martin Luther

It is only mercenaries who expect to be paid by the day. —Teresa of Avila

Spirit is the real and eternal; matter is the unreal and the temporal.
—Mary Baker Eddy

Faith, to my mind, is a stiffening process, a sort of mental starch.
—E.M. Forster

Faith is love taking the form of aspiration.
—William Ellery Channing

Faith is hidden household capital.
—Johann von Goethe

Faith is the soul riding at anchor.
—Josh Billings

Faith is . . . knowing with your heart.
—N. Richard Nash

Faith is an attitude of the person. It means you are prepared to stake yourself on something being so.
—Arthur M. Ramsey

Faith, as an intellectual state, is self-reliance. —Oliver Wendell Holmes

Faith is the subtle chain which binds us to the infinite.
—Elizabeth O. Smith

Faith is nothing but obedience and piety. —Baruch Spinoza

Faith is a theological virtue that inclines the mind, under the influence of the will and grace, to yield firm assent to revealed truths, because of the authority of God.
—Adolphe Tanqueray

Faith is the only known cure for fear.
—Lena K. Sadler

What's up is faith, what's down is heresy. —Alfred, Lord Tennyson

Faith is spiritualized imagination.
—Henry Ward Beecher

Faith is the final triumph over incongruity, the final assertion of the meaningfulness of existence.
—Reinhold Niebuhr

Faith is an encounter in which God takes and keeps the initiative.
—Eugene Joly

Faith is that which is woven of conviction and set with the sharp mordant of experience.
—James Russell Lowell

Faith is a practical attitude of the will.
—John MacMurray

Faith is a total attitude of the self.
—John Macquarrie

Faith is nothing else than trust in the divine mercy promised in Christ.
—Philipp Melanchthon

Faith is the divine evidence whereby the spiritual man discerneth God, and the things of God. —John Wesley

Faith is a passionate intuition.
—William Wordsworth

Faith is a bridge across the gulf of death. —Edward Young

Faith is verification by the heart; confession by the tongue; action by the limbs. —Anon.

Faith is a certitude without proofs ... a sentiment, for it is a hope; it is an instinct, for it precedes all outward instruction.   —Henri Frederic Amiel

Faith is the proper name of religious experience.   —John Baillie

Faith is an outward and visible sign of an inward and spiritual grace.
          —*Book of Common Prayer*

Faith is the soul's adventure.
          —William Bridges

Faith is obedience, nothing else.
          —Emil Brunner

Faith is the response of our spirits to beckonings of the eternal.
          —George A. Buttrick

Faith is a knowledge of the benevolence of God toward us, and a certain persuasion of His veracity.
          —John Calvin

Faith is loyalty to some inspired teacher, some spiritual hero.
          —Thomas Carlyle

Faith is God's work within us.
          —Saint Thomas Aquinas

To me, faith means not worrying.
          —John Dewey

Faith is building on what you know is here, so you can reach what you know is there.   —Cullen Hightower

Faith is a gift of God which man can neither give nor take away by promise of rewards, or menaces of torture.
          —Thomas Hobbes

Faith is primarily a process of identification; the process by which the individual ceases to be himself and becomes part of something eternal.
          —Eric Hoffer

Faith is the function of the heart.
          —Mahatma Gandhi

Faith implies the disbelief of a lesser fact in favor of a greater.
          —Oliver Wendell Holmes

The great act of faith is when a man decides that he is not God.
          —Oliver Wendell Holmes

Faith is the little night-light that burns in a sick-room; as long as it is there, the obscurity is not complete, we turn towards it and await the daylight.
          —Abbé Henri Huvelin

Faith is the summit of the Torah.
          —Solomon Ibn Gabirol

Faith is an act of self-consecration, in which the will, the intellect, and the affections all have their place.
          —William Ralph Inge

Faith is courage; it is creative, while despair is always destructive.
          —David S. Muzzey

Faith is to believe in something not yet proved and to underwrite it with our lives: it is the only way we can leave the future open.
          —Lillian Smith

Faith begins as an experiment and ends as an experience.
          —William Ralph Inge

Faith is an act of a finite being who is grasped by, and turned to, the infinite.
　　　　　　　　　　—Paul Tillich

Faith is not a storm cellar to which men and women can flee for refuge from the storms of life. It is, instead, an inner force that gives them the strength to face those storms and their consequences with serenity of spirit.
　　　　　　　　—Sam J. Ervin, Jr.

Faith is putting all your eggs in God's basket, then counting your blessings before they hatch.
　　　　　　　　—Ramona C. Carroll

Faith is the force of life.
　　　　　　　　　　—Leo Tolstoy

Faith is a kind of betting, or speculation.　　　　—Samuel Butler

GENERAL QUOTATIONS ABOUT FAITH AND BELIEF

Without faith, nothing is possible. With it, nothing is impossible.
　　　　　—Mary McLeod Bethune

Not truth, but faith it is that keeps the world alive.
　　　　—Edna Saint Vincent Millay

Truth is simply whatever you can bring yourself to believe.
　　　　　　　—Alice Childress

You can do very little with faith, but you can do nothing without it.
　　　　　　　—Samuel Butler

I believe in the immortality of the soul because I have within me immortal longings.　　—Helen Keller

The opposite of having faith is having self-pity.　　　—Og Guinness

Out of the chill and the shadow,
Into the thrill and the shine;
Out of the dearth and the famine,
Into the fullness divine.
　　　—Margaret Elizabeth Sangster

Faith is necessary to victory.
　　　　　　—William Hazlitt

Faith is that quality or power by which the things desired become the things possessed.
　　　　　　—Kathryn Kuhlman

Every tomorrow has two handles. We can take hold of it by the handle of anxiety, or by the handle of faith.
　　　　　　　　　—Anon.

Father! Blessed word.
　　　　　—Maria S. Cummins

Faith assuages, guides, restores.
　　　　　　—Arthur Rimbaud

Far graver is it to corrupt the faith that is the life of the soul than to counterfeit the money that sustains temporal life.
　　　　—Saint Thomas Aquinas

I would rather live in a world where my life is surrounded by mystery than live in a world so small that my mind could comprehend it.
　　　　—Harry Emerson Fosdick

We do not believe until we want a thing and feel that we shall die if it is not granted to us, and then we kneel and believe.
　　　—Frances Hodgson Burnett

Writing a novel without being asked seems a bit like having a baby when you have nowhere to live.
—Lucy Ellman

I am living on hope and faith . . . a pretty good diet when the mind will receive them.
—Edwin Arlington Robinson

Faith is the sturdiest, the most manly of the virtues. It lies behind our pluckiest . . . strivings. It is the virtue of the storm, just as happiness is the virtue of the sunshine.
—Ruth Benedict

There is one inevitable criterion of judgment touching religious faith . . . Can you reduce it to practice? If not, have none of it.   —Hosea Ballou

Strike from mankind the principle of faith, and men would have no more history than a flock of sheep.
—Edward Bulwer-Lytton

Be thou faithful unto death.
—Revelation 2:10

Faith is one of the forces by which men live; the total absence of it means collapse.   —William James

Pity the human being who is not able to connect faith within himself with the infinite. . . . He who has faith has . . . an inward reservoir of courage, hope, confidence, calmness, and assuring trust that all will come out well—even though to the world it may appear to come out most badly.
—B.C. Forbes

Faith is a gift of God. —Blaise Pascal

Through the dark and stormy night
Faith beholds a feeble light
Up the blackness streaking;
Knowing God's own time is best,
In a patient hope I rest
For the full day-breaking!
—John Greenleaf Whittier

To win true peace, a man needs to feel himself directed, pardoned and sustained by a supreme power, to feel himself in the right road, at the point where God would have him be—in order with God and the universe. This faith gives strength and calm.
—Henri Frederic Amiel

Faith may be relied upon to produce sustained action and, more rarely, sustained contemplation.
—Aldous Huxley

The person who has a firm trust in the Supreme Being is powerful in his power, wise by his wisdom, happy by his happiness.   —Joseph Addison

The disease with which the human mind now labors is want of faith.
—Ralph Waldo Emerson

As your faith is strengthened you will find that there is no longer the need to have a sense of control, that things will flow as they will, and that you will flow with them, to your great delight and benefit.   —Emmanuel

The historic glory of America lies in the fact that it is the one nation that was founded like a church. That is, it was founded on a faith that was not merely summed up after it had exited, but was defined before it existed.
—G.K. Chesterton

The only faith that wears well and holds its color in all weather is that which is woven of conviction.
—James Russell Lowell

The primary cause of unhappiness in the world today is . . . lack of faith.
—Carl Jung

You do build in darkness if you have faith. When the light returns you have made of yourself a fortress which is impregnable to certain kinds of trouble; you may even find your-self needed and sought by others as a beacon in their dark.
—Olga Rosmanith

It is by faith that poetry, as well as devotion, soars above this dull earth; that imagination breaks through its clouds, breathes a purer air, and lives in a softer light.   —Henry Giles

Religious faith, indeed, relates to that which is above us, but it must arise from that which is within us.
—Josiah Royce

Faith enables persons to be persons because it lets God be God.
—Carter Lindberg

Faith makes the discords of the pres-ent the harmonies of the future.
—Robert Collyer

A person consists of his faith. What-ever is his faith, even so is he.
—Hindu proverb

In Israel, in order to be a realist, you must believe in miracles.
—David Ben-Gurion

For the believer, there is no question; for the non-believer, there is no answer.   —Anon.

Life without faith in something is too narrow a space in which to live.
—George Lancaster Spalding

Something will turn up.
—Benjamin Disraeli

Prayer

Why Pray

I pray on the principle that wine knocks the cork out of a bottle. There is an inward fermentation, and there must be a vent.
—Henry Ward Beecher

They who have steeped their soul in prayer can every anguish calmly bear.
—Richard M. Milnes

Unless I had the spirit of prayer, I could do nothing.
—Charles G. Finney

Prayer is an end to isolation. It is living our daily life with someone; with him who alone can deliver us from solitude.
—Georges Lefevre

Prayer moves the hand that moves the world.
—John Aikman Wallace

Prayer changes things.
—Anon.

Prayer does not change God, but it changes him who prays.
—Søren Kierkegaard

There is no hope but in prayer.
—Andrew Bonar

We can do nothing without prayer. All things can be done by importunate prayer. It surmounts or removes all obstacles, overcomes every resisting force and gains its ends in the face of invincible hindrances.
—E.M. Bounds

By prayer we couple the powers of heaven to our helplessness, the powers which can capture strongholds and make the impossible possible.
—O. Hallesby

Faith, and hope, and patience and all the strong, beautiful, vital forces of piety are withered and dead in a prayerless life. The life of the individual believer, his personal salvation, and personal Christian graces have their being, bloom, and fruitage in prayer.
—E.M. Bounds

Every chain that spirits wear crumbles in the breadth of prayer.
—John Greenleaf Whittier

Though we cannot by our prayers give God any information, yet we must by our prayers give him honor.
—Matthew Henry

In the war upon the powers of darkness, prayer is the primary and mightiest weapon, both in aggressive war upon them and their works; in the deliverance of men from their power; and against them as a hierarchy of powers opposed to Christ and His Church.   —Jessie Penn-Lewis

God shapes the world by prayer. Prayers are deathless. They outlive the lives of those who uttered them.
—E.M. Bounds

Men of God are always men of prayer.
—Henry T. Mahan

Religion is no more possible without prayer than poetry without language or music without atmosphere.
—James Martineau

All who have walked with God have viewed prayer as the main business of their lives.   —Delma Jackson

To have a curable illness and to leave it untreated except for prayer is like sticking your hand in a fire and asking God to remove the flame.
—Sandra L. Douglas

Oh, what a cause of thankfulness it is that we have a gracious God to go to on all occasions! Use and enjoy this privilege and you can never be miserable. Oh, what an unspeakable privilege is prayer!   —Lady Maxwell

What is the life of a Christian but a life of prayer!   —David Brown

Even if no command to pray had existed, our very weakness would have suggested it.
—Francois de Fenelon

He who ceases to pray ceases to prosper.
—Sir William Gurney Benham

By prayer, the ability is secured to feel the law of love, to speak according to the law of love, and to do everything in harmony with the law of love.
—E.M. Bounds

Time spent on the knees in prayer will do more to remedy heart strain and nerve worry than anything else.
—George David Stewart

The one concern of the devil is to keep Christians from praying. He fears nothing from prayerless studies, prayerless work, and prayerless religion. He laughs at our toil, mocks at our wisdom, but trembles when we pray.   —Samuel Chadwick

No heart thrives without much secret converse with God and nothing will make amends for the want of it.
—John Berridge

No one is a firmer believer in the power of prayer than the devil; not that he practices it, but he suffers from it.   —Guy H. King

A man's state before God may always be measured by his prayers.
—J.C. Ryle

Trouble and perplexity drive me to prayer and prayer drives away perplexity and trouble.
—Philipp Melanchthon

Prayer covers the whole of man's life. There is no thought, feeling, yearning, or desire, however low, trifling, or vulgar we may deem it, which, if it affects our real interest or happiness, we may not lay before God and be sure of sympathy. His nature is such that our often coming does not tire him. The whole burden of the whole life of every man may be rolled on to God and not weary him, though it has wearied the man.
—Henry Ward Beecher

The first purpose of prayer is to know God.   —Charles L. Allen

We, one and all of us, have an instinct to pray; and this fact constitutes an invitation from God to pray.
—Charles Sanders Peirce

Teach us to pray that we may cause
The enemy to flee,
That we his evil power may bind,
His prisoners to free.
—Watchman Nee

No matter what may be the test,
God will take care of you;
Lean, weary one, upon His breast,
God will take care of you.
—C.D. Martin

He who has learned to pray has learned the greatest secret of a holy and a happy life.   —William Law

Non-praying is lawlessness, discord, anarchy.   —E.M. Bounds

We look upon prayer as a means of getting things for ourselves; The Bible idea of prayer is that we may get to know God Himself.
—Oswald Chambers

Prayer is the great engine to overthrow and rout my spiritual enemies, the great means to procure the graces of which I stand in hourly need.
—John Newton

Pray, always pray; when sickness wastes thy frame, Prayer brings the healing power of Jesus' name.
—A.B. Simpson

Prayer is of transcendent importance. Prayer is the mightiest agent to advance God's work. Praying hearts and hands only can do God's work. Prayer succeeds when all else fails.
—E.M. Bounds

The goal of prayer is the ear of God, a goal that can only be reached by patient and continued and continuous waiting upon Him, pouring out our heart to Him and permitting Him to speak to us. Only by so doing can we expect to know Him, and as we come to know Him better we shall spend more time in His presence and find that presence a constant and ever-increasing delight.   —E.M. Bounds

Prayer honors God, acknowledges His being, exalts His power, adores His providence, secures His aid.
—E.M. Bounds

The whole meaning of prayer is that we may know God.
—Oswald Chambers

Prayer crowns God with the honor and glory due to His name, and God crowns prayer with assurance and comfort. The most praying souls are the most assured souls.
—Thomas B. Brooks

The purpose of prayer is to reveal the presence of God equally present, all the time, in every condition.
—Oswald Chambers

The value of consistent prayer is not that He will hear us, but that we will hear Him.   —William McGill

PRAYER IS PRACTICAL

The influence of prayer on the human mind and body . . . can be measured in terms of increased physical buoyancy, greater intellectual vigor, moral stamina, and a deeper understanding of the realities underlying human relationships.   —Dr. Alexis Carrel

Prayer is the force as real as terrestrial gravity. As a physician, I have seen men, after all other therapy had failed, lifted out of disease and melancholy by the serene effort of prayer. Only in prayer do we achieve that complete and harmonious assembly of body, mind and spirit which gives the frail human reed its unshakable strength.   —Dr. Alexis Carrel

Prayer is not an old woman's idle amusement. Properly understood and applied, it is the most potent instrument of action.   —Mahatma Gandhi

Today any successful and competent businessman will employ the latest and best-tested methods in production, distribution, and administration, and many are discovering that one of the greatest of all efficiency methods is prayer power.
—Norman Vincent Peale

To have a curable illness and to leave it untreated except for prayer is like sticking your hand in a fire and asking God to remove the flame.
—Sandra L. Douglas

PRAYER CHANGES US

One night alone in prayer might make us new men, changed from poverty of soul to spiritual wealth, from trembling to triumphing.
—Charles Haddon Spurgeon

Every time we pray our horizon is altered, our attitude to things is altered, not sometimes but every time, and the amazing thing is that we don't pray more.
—Oswald Chambers

It is not so true that "prayer changes things" as that prayer changes me and I change things. God has so constituted things that prayer on the basis of Redemption alters the way in which a man looks at things. Prayer is not a question of altering things externally, but of working wonders in a man's disposition.
—Oswald Chambers

Prayer may not change things for you, but it for sure changes you for things.   —Samuel M. Shoemaker

HOW TO PRAY

The main lesson about prayer is just this: Do it! Do it! Do it! You want to be taught to pray? My answer is: pray.   —John Laidlaw

Praying is learned by praying.
—L.A.T. van Dooren

The only way to pray is to pray, and the way to pray well is to pray much.
—Anon.

The less I pray, the harder it gets; the more I pray, the better it goes.
—Martin Luther

It has been well said that almost the only scoffers at prayer are those who never tried it enough.
—*Twelve Steps and Twelve Traditions*

Prayer is a trade to be learned. We must be apprentices and serve our time at it. Painstaking care, much thought, practice and labour are required to be a skillful tradesman in praying. Practice in this, as well as in all other trades, makes perfect.
—E.M. Bounds

If we are willing to spend hours on end to learn to play the piano, operate a computer, or fly an airplane, it is sheer nonsense for us to imagine that we can learn the high art of getting guidance through communion with the Lord without being willing to set aside time for it. —Paul Rees

The great thing in prayer is to feel that we are putting our supplications into the bosom of omnipotent love.
—Andrew Murray

All the prayers in the Scripture you will find to be reasoning with God, not a multitude of words heaped together. —Stephen Charnock

Scream at God if that's the only thing that will get results.
—Brendan Francis

You need not cry very loud; he is nearer to us than we think.
—Brother Lawrence

Rejoice always, pray constantly, and in all circumstances give thanks.
—The Desert Fathers

God tells us to burden him with whatever burdens us. —Anon.

Do I want to pray or only to think about my human problems? Do I want to pray or simply kneel there contemplating my sorrow? Do I want to direct my prayer toward God or let it direct itself towards me?
—Hubert Van Zeller

O thou, by whom we come to God,
The Life, the Truth, the Way,
The path of prayer Thyself hast trod—
Lord teach us how to pray.
—James Montgomery

Dealing in generalities is the death of prayer. —J.H. Evans

Don't try to reach God with your understanding; that is impossible. Reach him in love; that is possible.
—Carlo Carretto

The right way to pray, then, is any way that allows us to communicate with God.
—Colleen Townsend Evans

Grant us grace, Almighty Father, so to pray as to deserve to be heard.
—Jane Austen

178

He prayeth well, who loveth well
Both man and bird and beast.
He prayeth best, who loveth best
All things both great and small;
For the dear God who loveth us,
He made and loveth all.
—Samuel Taylor Coleridge

Confess your faults one to another,
and pray one for another, that ye
may be healed. The effectual, fervent
prayer of a righteous man availeth
much.   —James 5:16

He that will learn to pray, let him to
sea.   —George Herbert

Incense is prayer
That drives no bargain.
Child, learn from incense
How best to pray.
—Alfred Barrett

When we go to our meeting with
God, we should go like a patient
to his doctor, first to be thoroughly
examined and afterwards to be treated for our ailment. Then something
will happen when you pray.
—O. Hallesby

Natural ability and educational
advantages do not figure as factors in
this matter of prayer; but a capacity
for faith, the power of a thorough
consecration, the ability of self-
littleness, an absolute losing of one's
self in God's glory and an ever present and insatiable yearning and seeking after all the fullness of God.
—E.M. Bounds

We have to pray with our eyes on
God, not on the difficulties.
—Oswald Chambers

If our petitions are in accordance
with His will, and if we seek His
glory in the asking, the answers will
come in ways that will astonish us
and fill our hearts with songs of
thanksgiving.   —J.K. Maclean

Pray if thou canst with hope, but ever
pray, though hope be weak or sick
with long delay; pray in the darkness
if there be no light; and if for any
wish thou dare not pray, then pray to
God to cast that wish away. —Anon.

Prayer can assume very different
forms, from quiet, blessed contemplation of God, in which eye meets eye
in restful meditation, to deep sighs or
sudden exclamations of wonder, joy,
gratitude or adoration.
—O. Hallesby

To pray is nothing more involved
than to open the door, giving Jesus
access to our needs and permitting
Him to exercise His own power in
dealing with them.   —O. Hallesby

He prays best who does not know
that he is praying.
—Saint Anthony of Padua

When you cannot pray as you would,
pray as you can.
—Edward M. Goulburn

If you can't pray as you want to,
pray as you can. God knows what
you mean.   —Vance Havner

Pray till you pray.   —D.M. McIntyre

Daily Prayer

A day without prayer is a boast against God.   —Owen Carr

Prayer should be the key of the day and the lock of the night.
          —Thomas Fuller

I care not what black spiritual crisis we may come through or what delightful spiritual Canaan we may enter, no blessing of the Christian life becomes continually possessed unless we are men and women of regular, daily, unhurried, secret lingerings in prayer.   —J. Sidlow Baxter

In the morning, prayer is the key that opens to us the treasures of God's mercies and blessings; in the evening, it is the key that shuts us up under His protection and safeguard.
          —Anon.

Prayer is a kind of calling home every day. And there can come to you a serenity, a feeling of at-homeness in God's universe, a peace that the world can neither give nor disturb, a fresh courage, a new insight, a holy boldness that you'll never, never get any other way.   —Earl G. Hunt, Jr.

O God, if in the day of battle I forget Thee, do not Thou forget me.
          —Anon.

Seven days without prayer makes one weak.   —Allen E. Bartlett

Lord, you know how busy I must be this day. If I forget you, do not you forget me.   —Jacob Astley

We read of preaching the Word out of season, but we do not read of praying out of season, for that is never out of season.
          —Matthew Henry

Let prayer be the key of the morning and the bolt at night. —Philip Henry

Evening, and morning, and at noon, will I pray.   —Psalms 55:17

Prayer should be the means by which I, at all times, receive all that I need, and, for this reason, be my daily refuge, my daily consolation, my daily joy, my source of rich and inexhaustible joy in life.
          —Saint John Chrysostom

Continual Prayer

As impossible as it is for us to take a breath in the morning large enough to last us until noon, so impossible is it to pray in the morning in such a way as to last us until noon. Let your prayers ascend to Him constantly, audibly or silently, as circumstances throughout the day permit.
          —O. Hallesby

To God your every Want
In instant Prayer display,
Pray always; Pray, and never faint;
Pray, without ceasing, Pray.
          —Charles Wesley

Constant prayer quickly straightens out our thoughts.
          —The Desert Fathers

Teach us to pray often, that we may pray oftener.   —Jeremy Taylor

180

Abiding fully means praying much.
                    —Andrew Murray

Pray, always pray; beneath sins
    heaviest load,
Prayer claims the blood from Jesus'
    side that flowed.
Pray, always pray; though weary,
    faint, and lone,
Prayer nestles by the Father's shelter-
    ing throne.   —A.B. Simpson

When the knees are not often bent,
the feet soon slide.   —Anon.

The more praying there is in the
world, the better the world will be;
the mightier the forces against evil
everywhere.   —E.M. Bounds

Those who always pray are necessary
to those who never pray.
                    —Victor Hugo

We Must Make Time to Pray

Tomorrow I plan to work, work,
from early until late. In fact I have so
much to do that I shall spend the first
three hours in prayer.
                    —Martin Luther

Begin to realize more and more that
prayer is the most important thing
you do. You can use your time to no
better advantage than to pray whenever you have an opportunity to do
so, either alone or with others; while
at work, while at rest, or while walking down the street. Anywhere!
                    —O. Hallesby

It is impossible to conduct your life
as a disciple without definite times of
secret prayer.   —Oswald Chambers

Sometimes we think we are too busy
to pray. That is a great mistake, for
praying is a saving of time.
                    —Charles Haddon Spurgeon

Prayer time must be kept up as duly
as meal-time.   —Matthew Henry

The minds of people are so cluttered
up with every-day living these days
that they don't, or won't, take time
out for a little prayer—for mental
cleansing, just as they take a bath for
physical, outer cleansing. Both are
necessary.   —Jo Ann Carlson

The Christian will find his paren-
theses for prayer even in the busiest
hours of life.   —Richard Cecil

Time spent in prayer is never wasted.
                    —Francois de Fenelon

No time is so well spent in every day
as that which we spend upon our
knees.   —J.C. Ryle

Other duties become pressing and
absorbing and crowd our prayer.
"Choked to death" would be the cor-
oner's verdict in many cases of dead
praying if an inquest could be secured
on this dire, spiritual calamity.
                    —E.M. Bounds

When it becomes clear to us that
prayer is a part of our daily program
of work, it will also become clear to
us that we must arrange our daily
program in such a way that there is
time also for this work, just as we set
aside time for other necessary things,
such as eating and dressing.
                    —O. Hallesby

I have to hurry all day to get time to pray. —Martin Luther

While others still slept, He went away to pray and to renew His strength in communion with His Father. He had need of this, otherwise He would not have been ready for the new day. The holy work of delivering souls demands constant renewal through fellowship with God. —Andrew Murray

And in the morning, rising up a great while before day, he went out, and departed into a solitary place, and there prayed. —Mark 1:35

Get into the habit of dealing with God about everything. Unless in the first waking moment of the day you learn to fling the door wide back and let God in, you will work on a wrong level all day; but swing the door wide open and pray to your Father in secret, and every public thing will be stamped with the presence of God. —Oswald Chambers

It is by no haphazard chance that in every age men have risen early to pray. The first thing that marks decline in spiritual life is our relationship to the early morning. —Oswald Chambers

The entire day receives order and discipline when it acquires unity. This unity must be sought and found in morning prayer. The morning prayer determines the day. —Dietrich Bonhoeffer

Cause me to hear thy loving kindness in the morning. —Psalms 143:8

In the morning will I direct my prayer unto thee. —Psalms 5:3

If you have ever prayed in the dawn you will ask yourself why you were so foolish as not to do it always: it is difficult to get into communion with God in the midst of the hurly-burly of the day. —Oswald Chambers

I feel it is far better to begin with God, to see His face first, to get my soul near Him before it is near another. In general it is best to have at least one hour alone with God before engaging in anything else. —E.M. Bounds

Lord, if any have to die this day, let it be me, for I am ready. —Billy Bray

Temptations which accompany the working day will be conquered on the basis of the morning breakthrough to God. Decisions, demanded by work, become easier and simpler where they are made not in the fear of men, but only in the sight of God. He wants to give us today the power which we need for our work. —Dietrich Bonhoeffer

The man who says his prayers in the evening is a captain posting his sentries. After that, he can sleep. —Charles Baudelaire

When at night you cannot sleep, talk to the Shepherd and stop counting sheep. —Anon.

182

I did this night promise my wife
never to go to bed without calling
upon God, upon my knees, in prayer.
—Samuel Pepys

PRAYING WHEN WE BOTTOM OUT

I have been driven many times to my
knees by the overwhelming conviction that I had nowhere else to go. My
own wisdom and that of all about me
seemed insufficient for the day.
—Abraham Lincoln

There are no atheists on turbulent
airplanes.   —Erica Jong

Ordinarily when a man in difficulty
turns to prayer, he has already tried
every other means of escape.
—Austin O'Malley

When life knocks you to your knees,
and it will, why, get up! If it knocks
you to your knees again, as it will,
well, isn't that the best position from
which to pray?   —Ethel Barrymore

Now I am past all comforts here, but
prayer.   —William Shakespeare

Prayer begins where human capacity
ends.   —Marian Anderson

"Oh, God, if I were sure I were to
die tonight I would repent at once."
It is the commonest prayer in all lan-
guages.   —Sir James M. Barrie

If you are swept off your feet, it's
time to get on your knees.
—Fred Beck

When I am weak, then am I strong.
—2 Corinthians 12:10

To pray is to open the door unto
Jesus and admit Him into your distress. Your helplessness is the very
thing which opens wide the door
unto Him and gives Him access to all
your needs.   —O. Hallesby

My helpless friend, your helplessness
is the most powerful plea which rises
up to the tender father-heart of God.
You think that everything is closed
to you because you cannot pray. My
friend, your helplessness is the very
essence of prayer.   —O. Hallesby

Listen, my friend! Your helplessness
is your best prayer. It calls from your
heart to the heart of God with greater
effect than all your uttered pleas. He
hears it from the very moment that
you are seized with helplessness, and
He becomes actively engaged at once
in hearing and answering the prayer
of your helplessness.   —O. Hallesby

Helplessness is unquestionably the
first and the surest indication of a
praying heart. . . . Prayer and helplessness are inseparable. Only he who is
helpless can truly pray.
—O. Hallesby

When we pray for the Spirit's help
. . . we will simply fall down at the
Lord's feet in our weakness. There we
will find the victory and power that
comes from His love.
—Andrew Murray

The more helpless you are, the better
you are fitted to pray, and the more
answers to prayer you will experience.
—O. Hallesby

Being in an agony, he prayed more
earnestly.   —Luke 22:44

When a man is at his wits' end it is not a cowardly thing to pray, it is the only way he can get in touch with Reality.   —Oswald Chambers

When my soul fainted within me . . . my prayer came in unto thee.
                              —Jonah 2:7

He will regard the prayer of the destitute.   —Psalms 102:17

My strength is made perfect in weakness.   —2 Corinthians 12:9

God listens to our weeping when the occasion itself is beyond our knowledge, but still within His love and power.   —Daniel A. Poling

Trouble and prayer are closely related. . . . Trouble often drives men to God in prayer, while prayer is but the voice of men in trouble.   —E.M. Bounds

Trouble and perplexity drive me to prayer and prayer drives away perplexity and trouble.
                    —Philipp Melanchthon

But We Can't Pray Just When We're in Trouble

An agnostic found himself in trouble, and a friend suggested he pray. "How can I pray when I do not know whether or not there is a God?" he asked. "If you are lost in the forest," his friend replied, "you do not wait until you find someone before shouting for help."   —Dan Plies

Many people pray as if God were a big aspirin pill; they come only when they hurt.   —B. Graham Dienert

You pray in your distress and in your need; would that you might also pray in the fullness of your joy and in your days of abundance.   —Kahlil Gibran

Don't pray when it rains if you don't pray when the sun shines.
                              —Satchel Paige

He who cannot pray when the sun is shining will not know how to pray when the clouds come.   —Anon.

All those football coaches who hold dressing-room prayers before a game should be forced to attend church once a week.   —Duffy Daugherty

Prayer is not merely an occasional impulse to which we respond when we are in trouble: prayer is a life attitude.   —Walter A. Mueller

A Special Place for Prayer

Do not have as your motive the desire to be known as a praying man. Get an inner chamber in which to pray where no one knows you are praying, shut the door, and talk to God in secret.   —Oswald Chambers

Nowhere can we get to know the holiness of God, and come under His influence and power, except in the inner chamber. It has been well said: "No man can expect to make progress in holiness who is not often and long alone with God."
                              —Andrew Murray

Private place and plenty of time are the life of prayer.   —E.M. Bounds

But thou, when thou prayest, enter into thy room, and when thou hast shut thy door, pray to thy Father who is in secret; and thy Father who seeth in secret, shall reward thee openly.
—Matthew 6:6

When you enter your secret chamber, take plenty of time before you begin to speak. Let quietude wield its influence upon you. Let the fact that you are alone assert itself. Give your soul time to get released from the many outward things. Give God time to play the prelude to prayer for the benefit of your distracted soul.
—O. Hallesby

There is no need to get to a place of prayer; pray wherever you are.
—Oswald Chambers

Of all things, guard against neglecting God in the secret place of prayer.
—William Wilberforce

Our Prayers Should Be Sincere, and Jibe With How We Live Day to Day

Prayer, to the patriarchs and prophets, was more than the recital of well-known and well-worn phrases—it was the outpouring of the heart.
—Herbert Lockyer

Without the incense of heartfelt prayer, even the greatest of cathedrals is dead.
—Anon.

Follow your own way of speaking to our Lord sincerely, lovingly, confidently, and simply, as your heart dictates.
—Jane Frances de Chantal

Sincerity is the prime requisite in every approach to the God who . . . hates all hypocrisy, falsehood, and deceit.
—Geoffrey B. Wilson

The Lord's Prayer may be committed to memory quickly, but it is slowly learnt by heart.
—Frederick Denison Maurice

God hears no more than the heart speaks; and if the heart be dumb, God will certainly be dumb.
—Thomas B. Brooks

Deep down in me I knowed it was a lie, and He knowed it. You can't pray a lie—I found that out.
—Mark Twain

Prayers not felt by us are seldom heard by God.
—Philip Henry

Many pray with their lips for that for which their hearts have no desire.
—Jonathan Edwards

God may turn his ears from prattling prayers, or preaching prayers, but never from penitent, believing prayers.
—William S. Plumer

Two went to pray? Better to say one went to brag, the other to pray.
—Richard Crashaw

I pray like a robber asking alms at the door of a farmhouse to which he is ready to set fire.
—Leon Bloy

God's ear lies close to the believer's lip.
—Anon.

Heaven is never deaf but when man's heart is dumb.
—Francis Quarles

Do not pray by heart, but with the heart. —Anon.

Our prayers must mean something to us if they are to mean anything to God. —Maltbie D. Babcock

Our prayers must spring from the indigenous soil of our own personal confrontation with the Spirit of God in our lives. —Malcolm Boyd

God eagerly awaits the chance to bless the person whose heart is turned toward Him. —Anon.

We must lay before him what is in us, not what ought to be in us. —C.S. Lewis

In prayer the lips ne'er act the winning part, without the sweet concurrence of the heart. —Robert Herrick

The cry of a young raven is nothing but the natural cry of a creature, but your cry, if it be sincere, is the result of a work of grace in your heart. —Charles Haddon Spurgeon

Every time you pray, if your prayer is sincere, there will be new feeling and new meaning in it which will give you fresh courage, and you will understand that prayer is an education. —Fyodor Dostoyevsky

When you pray, rather let your heart be without words than your words without heart. —John Bunyan

He offered a prayer so deeply devout that he seemed kneeling and praying at the bottom of the sea. —Herman Melville

Prayer is a serious thing. We may be taken at our words. —Dwight L. Moody

Prayer at its best is the expression of the total life, for all things else being equal, our prayers are only as powerful as our lives —A.W. Tozer

And help us, this and every day, to live more nearly as we pray. —John Keble

My words fly up, my thoughts remain below; Words without thoughts never to heaven go. —William Shakespeare

It is not well for a man to pray cream and live skim milk. —Henry Ward Beecher

She heard the snuffle of hypocrisy in her prayer. She had to cease to pray. —George Meredith

None can pray well but he that lives well. —Thomas Fuller

Straight praying is never born of crooked conduct. —E.M. Bounds

A wicked man in prayer may lift up his hands, but he cannot lift up his face. —Thomas Watson

He who prays as he ought, will endeavor to live as he prays. —John Owen

We pray pious blether, our will is not in it, and then we say God does not answer; we never asked Him for anything. Asking means that our wills are in what we ask. —Oswald Chambers

It is good for us to keep some account of our prayers, that we may not unsay them in our practice.
—Matthew Henry

Praying which does not result in pure conduct is a delusion. We have missed the whole office and virtue of praying if it does not rectify conduct. It is in the very nature of things that we must quit praying, or quit bad conduct.
—E.M. Bounds

Our praying, to be strong, must be buttressed by holy living. The life of faith perfects the prayer of faith.
—E.M. Bounds

Search me, O God, and know my heart: try me, and know my thoughts: and see if there be any wicked way in me.   —Psalms 139:23–24

When our will wholeheartedly enters into the prayer of Christ, then we pray correctly.   —Dietrich Bonhoeffer

We cannot talk to God strongly when we have not lived for God strongly. The closet cannot be made holy to God when the life has not been holy to God.   —E.M. Bounds

If we would have God in the closet, God must have us out of the closet. There is no way of praying to God, but by living to God. —E.M. Bounds

Men would pray better if they lived better. They would get more from God if they lived more obedient and well-pleasing to God.
—E.M. Bounds

Be not hot in prayer and cold in praise.
—Anon.

Though smooth be the heartless prayer, no ear in heaven will mind it; And the finest phrase falls dead, if there is no feeling behind it.
—Ella Wheeler Wilcox

Prayer is the soul's sincere desire.
—James Montgomery

OUR PRAYERS NEEDN'T BE ELOQUENT

Prayer is not eloquence, but earnestness; not the definition of helplessness, but the feeling of it; not figures of speech, but earnestness of soul.
—Hannah More

Prayer is something deeper than words. It is present in the soul before it has been formulated in words. And it abides in the soul after the last words of prayer have passed over our lips.
—O. Hallesby

If we rely on the Holy Spirit, we shall find that our prayers become more and more inarticulate; and when they are inarticulate, reverence grows deeper and deeper.
—Oswald Chambers

God prefers bad verses recited with a pure heart to the finest verses chanted by the wicked.   —Voltaire

We cannot all argue, but we can all pray; we cannot all be leaders, but we can all be pleaders; we cannot all be mighty in rhetoric, but we can all be prevalent in prayer.
—Charles Haddon Spurgeon

The best prayers have often more groans than words. —John Bunyan

In prayer it is better to have a heart without words than words without a heart. —John Bunyan

We ought to act with God in the greatest simplicity, speak to Him frankly and plainly, and implore His assistance in our affairs.
—Brother Lawrence

Prayer is not artful monologue
Of voice uplifted from the son;
It is Love's tender dialogue
Between the soul and God.
—John Richard Moreland

They tell about a fifteen-year-old boy in an orphans' home who had an incurable stutter. One Sunday the minister was detained and the boy volunteered to say the prayer in his stead. He did it perfectly, too, without a single stutter. Later he explained, "I don't stutter when I talk to God. He loves me."
—Bennett Cerf

Our groanings, which cannot be uttered, rise to Him and tell Him better than words how dependent we are upon Him. —O. Hallesby

When prayer is a struggle, do not worry about the prayers that you cannot pray. You yourself are a prayer to God at that moment. All that is within you cries out to Him. And He hears all the pleas that your suffering soul and body are making to Him with groanings which cannot be uttered. —O. Hallesby

God can pick sense out of a confused prayer. —Richard Sibbes

Prayer requires more of the heart than of the tongue. —Adam Clarke

Productive prayer requires earnestness, not eloquence. —Anon.

Just pray for a tough hide and a tender heart. —Ruth Graham

Prayer is a fine, delicate instrument. To use it right is a great art, a holy art. There is perhaps no greater art than the art of prayer. Yet the least gifted, the uneducated and the poor can cultivate the holy art of prayer.
—O. Hallesby

THE BEST PRAYERS ARE OFTEN BRIEF

With God there is no need for long speeches. —Jane Frances de Chantal

The fewer the words, the better the prayer. —Martin Luther

In prayer, more is accomplished by listening than by talking.
—Jane Frances de Chantal

Prayer should be short, without giving God Almighty reasons why He should grant this or that; He knows best what is good for us.
—John Selden

God is in heaven, and thou upon earth: therefore let thy words be few.
—Ecclesiastes 5:2

Many words do not a good prayer make; what counts is the heartfelt desire to commune with God, and the faith to back it up.   —Anon.

A little lifting of the heart suffices; a little remembrance of God, one act of inward worship are prayers which, however short, are nevertheless acceptable to God.
—Brother Lawrence

There come times when I have nothing more to tell God. If I were to continue to pray in words, I would have to repeat what I have already said. At such times it is wonderful to say to God, "May I be in Thy presence, Lord? I have nothing more to say to Thee, but I do love to be in Thy presence."   —O. Hallesby

Short prayers pierceth Heaven.
—*The Cloud of Unknowing*

ASKING FOR THINGS THROUGH PRAYER

You are coming to a King,
Large petitions with you bring
For his grace and power are such
None can ever ask too much.
—John Newton

There is no sinner in the world, however much at enmity with God, who cannot recover God's grace by recourse to Mary, and by asking her assistance.   —Saint Bridget of Sweden

Most Christians expect little from God, ask little, and therefore receive little and are content with little.
—A.W. Pink

Ye have not, because ye ask not.
—James 4:2

Ye ask, and receive not, because ye ask amiss.   —James 4:3

Ask, and it shall be given you; seek, and ye shall find; knock, and it shall be opened unto you.   —Matthew 7:7

Whether we like it or not, asking is the rule of the Kingdom.
—Charles Haddon Spurgeon

The simple heart that freely asks in love, obtains.
—John Greenleaf Whittier

Our immediate temptation will be to ask for specific solutions to specific problems, and for the ability to help other people as we have already thought they should be helped. In that case, we are asking God to do it our way.   —Bill W.

It is the will of our heavenly Father that we should come to Him freely and confidently and make known our desires to Him, just as we would have our children come freely and of their own accord and speak to us about the things they would like to have.
—O. Hallesby

My praying friend, continue to make known your desires to God in all things. ... Let Him decide whether you are to receive what you ask for or not.
—O. Hallesby

Let your requests be made known unto God.   —Philippians 4:6

Pray for whatsoever you will. In the name of Jesus you have permission, not only to stand in the presence of God, but also to pray for everything you need. —O. Hallesby

And whatever ye shall ask in my name, that will I do. —John 14:13

We should not be afraid, when praying to God, to give expression to a definite desire, even though we are in doubt at the time we are praying whether it is really the right thing to pray for or not. —O. Hallesby

We can never know God as it is our privilege to know Him by brief repetitions that are requests for personal favors, and nothing more. —E.M. Bounds

Prayer is not only asking, it is an attitude of heart that produces an atmosphere in which asking is perfectly natural, and Jesus says, "every one that asketh receiveth." —Oswald Chambers

Helplessness becomes prayer the moment that you go to Jesus and speak candidly and confidently with him about your needs. This is to believe. —O. Hallesby

The clue is not to ask in a miserly way—the key is to ask in a grand manner. —Ann Wigmore

To avail yourself of His certain wisdom, ask of Him whatever questions you have. But do not entreat Him, for that will never be necessary. —Hugh Prather

O Lord, attend unto my cry. —Psalms 61:1

We pray pious blether, our will is not in it, and then we say God does not answer; we never asked Him for anything. Asking means that our wills are in what we ask. —Oswald Chambers

Ask the gods nothing excessive. —Aeschylus

When praying for healing, ask great things of God and expect great things from God. But let us seek for that healing that really matters, the healing of the heart, enabling us to trust God simply, face God honestly, and live triumphantly. —Arlo F. Newell

Most people do not pray; they only beg. —George Bernard Shaw

Prayer is not asking. It is a longing of the soul. —Mahatma Gandhi

Prayer in the sense of petition, asking for things, is a small part of it; confession and penitence are its threshold, adoration its sanctuary, the presence and vision and enjoyment of God its bread and wine. —C.S. Lewis

God never denied that soul anything that went as far as heaven to ask it. —John Trapp

Ask in faith. —James 1:6

Selfishness and Prayer

If your prayer is selfish, the answer will be something that will rebuke your selfishness. You may not recognize it as having come at all, but it is sure to be there.   —William Temple

Selfishness is never so exquisitely selfish as when it is on its knees. . . . Self turns what would otherwise be a pure and powerful prayer into a weak and ineffective one.
                        —A.W. Tozer

I seldom made an errand to God for another but I got something for myself.   —Samuel Rutherford

When we make self the end of prayer, it is not worship but self-seeking.
                  —Thomas Manton

We look upon prayer as a means of getting things for ourselves; The Bible idea of prayer is that we may get to know God Himself.
                 —Oswald Chambers

We Should Pray for Others

Pray for one another.   —James 5:16

Intercessory prayer for one who is sinning prevails. God says so! The will of the man prayed for does not come into question at all, he is connected with God by prayer, and prayer on the basis of the Redemption sets the connection working and God gives life.   —Oswald Chambers

He who prays for his neighbors will be heard for himself.   —Talmud

We should say to God as we mingle with our dear ones each day, "God, give them each Thy blessing. They need it, because they live with me, and I am very selfish and unwilling to sacrifice very much for them, although I do love them."
                        —O. Hallesby

See to it, night and day, that you pray for your children. Then you will leave them a great legacy of answers to prayer, which will follow them all the days of their life. Then you may calmly and with a good conscience depart from them, even though you may not leave them a great deal of material wealth.   —O. Hallesby

Religion without humanity is a poor human stuff.   —Sojourner Truth

God bless all those that I love; God bless all those that love me; God bless all those that love those that I love and all those that love those that love me.   —New England Sampler

No one who has had a unique experience with prayer has a right to withhold it from others.
                  —Soong Mei-ling

Gratitude

Thou who has given so much to me, give one thing more: a grateful heart.
                  —George Herbert

If the only prayer you say in your whole life is "Thank you," that would suffice.   —Meister Eckhart

Pray without ceasing. In everything give thanks.   —1 Thessalonians 5:17

Fear of trouble, present and future, often blinds us to the numerous small blessings we enjoy, silencing our prayers of praise and thanksgiving.
—Anon.

For food, for raiment, for life and opportunity, for sun and rain, for water and the portage trails, we give you thanks, O Lord.
—Prayer from the North Woods

God deserves far more praise than any of us could ever give Him.
—Anon.

Our Father, let the spirit of gratitude so prevail in our hearts that we may manifest thy Spirit in our lives.
—W.B. Slack

A sensible thanksgiving for mercies received is a mighty prayer in the Spirit of God. It prevails with Him unspeakably.   —John Bunyan

God receives little thanks, even for his greatest gifts.   —Anon.

It is not only blessed to give thanks; it is also of vital importance to our prayer life in general. If we have noted the Lord's answers to our prayers and thanked Him for what we have received of Him, then it becomes easier for us, and we get more courage, to pray for more.
—O. Hallesby

To stand on one leg and prove God's existence is a very different thing from going down on one's knees and thanking him.   —Søren Kierkegaard

Our thanks to God should always precede our requests.   —Anon.

Jesus is moved to happiness every time He sees that you appreciate what He has done for you. Grip His pierced hand and say to Him, "I thank Thee, Savior, because Thou hast died for me." Thank Him likewise for all the other blessings He has showered upon you from day to day. It brings joy to Jesus.
—O. Hallesby

The idea of thanking staff should mean giving them something that they would never buy for themselves.
—Jayne Crook

Let us thank God heartily as often as we pray that we have His Spirit in us to teach us to pray. Thanksgiving will draw our hearts out to God and keep us engaged with Him; it will take our attention from ourselves and give the Spirit room in our hearts.
—Andrew Murray

Let us come before his presence with thanksgiving.   —Psalms 95:2

When we succeed in truly thanking God, we feel good at heart. The reason is that we have been created to give glory to God, now and forevermore. And every time we do so, we feel that we are in harmony with His plans and purposes for our lives. Then we are truly in our element. That is why it is so blessed.
—O. Hallesby

ENTHUSIASTIC PRAYING

Don't be timid when you pray; rather, batter the very gates of heaven with storms of prayer.   —Anon.

Let him never cease from prayer who has once begun it, be his life ever so wicked, for prayer is the way to amend it, and without prayer such amendment will be much more difficult.
—Teresa of Avila

How those holy men of old could storm the battlements above! When there was no way to look but up, they lifted up their eyes to God who made the hills, with unshakable confidence. —Herbert Lockyer

Cold prayers shall never have any warm answers. —Thomas B. Brooks

We must wrestle earnestly in prayer, like men contending with a deadly enemy for life. —J.C. Ryle

We may as well not pray at all as offer our prayers in a lifeless manner.
—William S. Plumer

There is neither encouragement nor room in Bible religion for feeble desires, listless efforts, lazy attitudes; all must be strenuous, urgent, ardent. Flamed desires, impassioned, unwearied insistence delight heaven. God would have His children incorrigibly in earnest and persistently bold in their efforts. Heaven is too busy to listen to half-hearted prayers or to respond to pop-calls. Our whole being must be in our praying.
—E.M. Bounds

It is only when the whole heart is gripped with the passion of prayer that the life-giving fire descends, for none but the earnest man gets access to the ear of God. —E.M. Bounds

To say prayers in a decent, delicate way is not heavy work. But to pray really, to pray till hell feels the ponderous stroke, to pray till the iron gates of difficulty are opened, till the mountains of obstacles are removed, till the mists are exhaled and the clouds are lifted, and the sunshine of a cloudless day brightens—this is hard work, but it is God's work, and man's best labor. —E.M. Bounds

Importunity is a condition of prayer. We are to press the matter, not with vain repetitions, but with urgent repetitions. We repeat, not to count the times, but to gain the prayer. We cannot quit praying because heart and soul are in it. We pray "with all perseverance." We hang to our prayers because by them we live. We press our pleas because we must have them, or die. —E.M. Bounds

The effectual, fervent prayer of a righteous man availeth much.
—James 5:16

From silly devotions and from sour-faced saints, good Lord, deliver us.
—Teresa of Avila

Let me burn out for God . . . prayer is the great thing. Oh, that I may be a man of prayer! —Henry Martyn

Look, as a painted man is no man, and as painted fire is no fire, so a cold prayer is no prayer.
—Thomas B. Brooks

There must be fired affections before our prayers will go up.
—William Jenkyn

Bear up the hands that hang down,
by faith and prayer; support the
tottering knees. Storm the throne
of grace and persevere therein, and
mercy will come down.
—John Wesley

Do not work so hard for Christ that
you have no strength to pray, for
prayer requires strength.
—J. Hudson Taylor

In Fellowship; alone
To God, with Faith, draw near,
Approach His Courts, besiege His
    Throne
With all the power of Prayer.
—Charles Wesley

Productive prayer requires earnestness, not eloquence.   —Anon.

Jesus taught that perseverance is
the essential element of prayer. Men
must be in earnest when they kneel
at God's footstool. Too often we get
faint-hearted and quit praying at
the point where we ought to begin.
We let go at the very point where
we should hold on strongest. Our
prayers are weak because they are
not impassioned by an unfailing and
resistless will.   —E.M. Bounds

THINGS TO PRAY FOR

We must move from asking God to
take care of the things that are breaking our hearts, to praying about the
things that are breaking His heart.
—Margaret Gibb

We cannot ask in behalf of Christ
what Christ would not ask Himself if
He were praying.   —A.B. Simpson

Thou who has given so much to me,
give one thing more: a grateful heart.
—George Herbert

We do pray for mercy, and that same
prayer doth teach us all to render the
deeds of mercy.
—William Shakespeare

Our prayers should be for blessings
in general, for God knows best what
is good for us.   —Socrates

Lord, take my lips and speak through
them; take my mind and think
through it; take my heart and set it
on fire.   —W.H. Aitken

Not what we wish, but what we
    need,
Oh! let your grace supply,
The good unasked, in mercy grant;
The ill, though asked, deny.
—James Merrick

We should pray for a sane mind in a
sound body.   —Juvenal

If we are to pray aright, perhaps it is
quite necessary that we pray contrary
to our own heart. Not what we want
to pray is important, but what God
wants us to pray. The richness of the
Word of God ought to determine our
prayer, not the poverty of our heart.
—Dietrich Bonhoeffer

O Lord, help me not to despise or
oppose what I do not understand.
—William Penn

We are going home to many who
cannot read. So, Lord, make us to be
Bibles so that those who cannot read
the Book can read it in us.
—Anonymous Chinese woman

God's promises are to be our pleas in prayer. —Matthew Henry

Help me to work and pray,
Help me to live each day,
That all I do may say,
Thy kingdom come.
—A.B. Simpson

We must pray for more prayer, for it is the world's mightiest healing force.
—Frank C. Laubach

O Lord, let me not live to be useless!
—Bishop John de Stratford

Humbly asked Him to remove our shortcomings. —*Twelve Steps and Twelve Traditions*

God give me work, till my life shall end
And life, till my work is done.
—Winifred Holtby's epitaph

The whole meaning of prayer is that we may know God.
—Oswald Chambers

Watch your motive before God; have no other motive in prayer than to know Him. —Oswald Chambers

For we know not what we should pray for. —Romans 8:26

Pray a little each day in a childlike way for the Spirit of prayer. If you feel that you know, as yet, very little concerning the deep things of prayer and what prayer really is, then pray for the Spirit of prayer. There is nothing He would rather do than unveil to you the grace of prayer.
—O. Hallesby

God does not exist to answer our prayers, but by our prayers we come to discern the mind of God.
—Oswald Chambers

I sit beside my lonely fire and pray for wisdom yet: for calmness to remember or courage to forget.
—Charles Hamilton Aide

The first petition that we are to make to Almighty God is for a good conscience, the next for health of mind, and then of body. —Seneca

Give us Lord, a bit o'sun,
A bit o'work, and a bit o'fun;
Give us all, in the struggle and sputter
Our daily bread and a bit o'butter.
—On an old inn,
Lancaster, England

When we in prayer seek only the glorification of the name of God, then we are in complete harmony with the spirit of prayer. Then our hearts are at rest both while we pray and after we have prayed. Then we can wait for the Lord. —O. Hallesby

Grant that we may not so much seek to be understood as to understand.
—Saint Francis of Assisi

Grant me the courage not to give up, even though I think it is hopeless.
—Admiral Chester W. Nimitz

Prayer for worldly goods is worse than fruitless, but prayer for strength of soul is that passion of the soul which catches the gift it seeks.
—George Meredith

Just pray for a tough hide and a tender heart.   —Ruth Graham

WE SHOULD PRAY TO
DO GOD'S WILL

The purpose of prayer is not to inform God of our needs, but to invite Him to rule our lives.
          —Clarence Bauman

[P]raying only for knowledge of His will for us and the power to carry that out.   —*Twelve Steps and Twelve Traditions*

Don't pray to escape trouble. Don't pray to be comfortable in your emotions. Pray to do the will of God in every situation. Nothing else is worth praying for.
          —Samuel M. Shoemaker

O Lord, forgive what I have been, sanctify what I am, and order what I shall be.   —Anon.

We had not even prayed rightly. We had always said, "Grant me my wishes" instead of "Thy will be done."
          —*Twelve Steps and Twelve Traditions*

O Lord, you know what is best for me. Let this or that be done, as you please. Give what you will, how much you will, and when you will.
          —Thomas à Kempis

Spread out your petition before God, and then say, "Thy will, not mine, be done." The sweetest lesson I have learned in God's school is to let the Lord choose for me.
          —Dwight L. Moody

Show me your ways, O Lord, teach me your paths; guide me in your truth and teach me, for you are God my Savior, and my hope is in you all day long.   —Psalms 25:4-5

The possibilities of prayer are found in its allying itself with the purposes of God, for God's purposes and man's praying are the combination of all potent and omnipotent forces.
          —E.M. Bounds

If we ask anything according to his will, he heareth us.   —1 John 5:14

I would have no desire other than to accomplish thy will. Teach me to pray; pray thyself in me.
          —Francois de Fenelon

True prayer brings a person's will into accordance with God's will, not the other way around.   —Anon.

Do not forget that prayer is ordained for the purpose of glorifying the name of God. Therefore, whether you pray for big things or for little things, say to God, "If it will glorify Thy name, then grant my prayer and help me."
          —O. Hallesby

It is only when we pray for something according to the will of God that we have the promise of being heard and answered.   —O. Hallesby

I used to pray that God would do this or that; now I pray that God will make His will known to me.
          —Madame Chiang Kai-Shek

PRAYING FOR HELP IN BECOMING BETTER PEOPLE

How many of us will ever sit . . . bow our heads, and pray "Lord, show me where I'm wrong"? —Anon.

Women don't have halos built in.
　　　　　　　　　—Lorraine Hine

A Chinese Christian prayed every day . . . . "Lord, reform Thy world, beginning with me."
　　　—Franklin Delano Roosevelt

Create in me a clean heart, O God.
　　　　　　　　　—Psalms 51:10

WE SHOULDN'T PRAY FOR THE END OF PROBLEMS, BUT FOR THE ABILITY TO HANDLE THEM

Do not pray for easy lives, pray to be stronger men. Do not pray for tasks equal to your powers, pray for powers equal to your tasks.
　　　　　　　　　—Phillips Brooks

The wise man in the storm prays God not for safety from danger, but for deliverance from fear.
　　　　　—Ralph Waldo Emerson

It is quite useless knocking at the door of heaven for earthly comfort. It's not the sort of comfort they supply there. 　　　　　—C.S. Lewis

Pray not for lighter burdens, but for stronger backs.
　　　　　　—Theodore Roosevelt

TURNING THINGS OVER THROUGH PRAYER

Prayer covers the whole of man's life. There is no thought, feeling, yearning, or desire, however low, trifling, or vulgar we may deem it, which if it affects our real interest or happiness, we may not lay before God and be sure of sympathy. His nature is such that our often coming does not tire him. The whole burden of the whole life of every man may be rolled on to God and not weary him, though it has wearied man.
　　　　　　—Henry Ward Beecher

What a friend we have in Jesus,
All our sins and griefs to bear!
What a privilege to carry
Everything to God in Prayer!

Have we trials and temptations?
Is there trouble anywhere?
We should never be discouraged,
Take it to the Lord in prayer.

Are we weak and heavy laden,
Cumbered with a load of care?
Precious Savior, still our refuge,
Take it to the Lord in prayer.

O what peace we often forfeit,
O what needless pain we bear,
All because we do not carry
Everything to God in prayer!
　　　　　　　　—Joseph Scriven

Take my will, and make it Thine,
It shall be no longer mine;
Take my heart, it is Thine own;
It shall be Thy royal throne.
　　　　　—Frances Ridley Havergal

197

And since He bids me seek His face,
Believe His word and trust His grace,
I'll cast on Him my every care,
And wait for thee, sweet hour of
    prayer.   —W.W. Walford

We lie to God in prayer if we do not
rely on him afterwards.
        —Robert Leighton

Prayer puts God's work in his
hands—and keeps it there.
        —E.M. Bounds

I know not by what methods rare,
But this I know: God answers prayer.
I know not if the blessing sought
Will come in just the guise I thought.
I leave my prayer to Him alone
Whose will is wiser than my own.
        —Eliza M. Hickok

Do what you can and pray for what
you cannot yet do. —Saint Augustine

Do not want things to turn out as
they seem best to you, but as God
pleases. Then you will be free from
confusion, and thankful in prayer.
        —The Desert Fathers

O Lord, you know what is best for
me. Let this or that be done, as you
please. Give what you will, how
much you will, and when you will.
        —Thomas à Kempis

Spread out your petition before God,
and then say, "Thy will, not mine,
be done." The sweetest lesson I have
learned in God's school is to let the
Lord choose for me.
        —Dwight L. Moody

Casting all your care upon Him; for
he careth for you.   —1 Peter 5:7

Do not strive in your own strength;
cast yourself at the feet of the Lord
Jesus, and wait upon Him in the sure
confidence that He is with you, and
works in you. Strive in prayer; let
faith fill your heart—so will you be
strong in the Lord, and in the power
of His might.   —Andrew Murray

A humble and contrite heart knows
that it can merit nothing before God,
and that all that is necessary is to be
reconciled to one's helplessness and
let our holy and almighty God care
for us, just as an infant surrenders
himself to his mother's care.
        —O. Hallesby

Cast thy burden upon the Lord, and
he shall sustain thee. —Psalms 55:22

The only prayer which a well-meaning man can pray is, O ye gods, give
me whatever is fitting unto me!
        —Appollonius of Tyana

Our prayer life will become restful
when it really dawns upon us that we
have done all we are supposed to do
when we have spoken to Him about
it. From the moment we have left it
with Him, it is His responsi-bility.
        —O. Hallesby

God tells us to burden him with
whatever burdens us.   —Anon.

This is what I found out about religion: It gives you courage to make
decisions you must make in a crisis,
and then the confidence to leave
the result to a Higher Power. Only
by trust in God can a man carrying
responsibility find repose.
        —Dwight D. Eisenhower

Before we can pray, "Lord, Thy Kingdom come," we must be willing to pray, "My Kingdom go."
—Alan Redpath

We need to learn to know Him so well that we feel safe when we have left our difficulties with Him. To know Jesus in that way is a prerequisite of all true prayer. —O. Hallesby

Prayer and Forgiveness

No prayers can be heard which do not come from a forgiving heart.
—J.C. Ryle

I firmly believe a great many prayers are not answered because we are not willing to forgive someone.
—Dwight L. Moody

When you pray for anyone, you tend to modify your personal attitude toward him.
—Norman Vincent Peale

When my children do wrong, I ache to hear their stumbling requests for forgiveness. I'm sure our heavenly Father aches even more deeply to hear from us. —Anon.

There is nothing that makes us love a man so much as praying for him.
—William Law

We Must Pray, but We Must also Work, and Help Ourselves

Ask God's blessing on your work, but don't ask him to do it for you.
—Dame Flora Robson

Prayer indeed is good, but while calling on the gods, a man should himself lend a hand. —Hippocrates

Prayer, among sane people, has never superseded practical efforts to secure the desired end. —George Santayana

It is vain to expect our prayers to be heard if we do not strive as well as pray. —Aesop

He who labors as he prays lifts his heart to God with his hands.
—Bernard of Clairvaux

Pray as if everything depended on God, and work as if everything depended upon man.
—Archbishop Francis J. Spellman

Work as if everything depended upon work and pray as if everything depended upon prayer.
—William Booth

Help yourself and heaven will help you. —Jean de La Fontaine

Work as if you were to live one hundred years; pray as if you were to die tomorrow. —Benjamin Franklin

God helps those who help themselves.
—German proverb

God help those who do not help themselves. —Wilson Mizner

God gives the nuts, but he does not crack them. —German proverb

God gives every bird its food, but he does not throw it into the nest.
—Josiah G. Holland

Pray devoutly, but hammer stoutly.
—Sir William Gurney Benham

The Ancient Mariner said to Neptune during a great storm, "O God, you will save me if you wish, but I am going to go on holding my tiller straight."   —Michel de Montaigne

Pray to God, but keep rowing to shore.
—Russian proverb

Call on God, but row away from the rocks.   —Indian proverb

To the man who himself strives earnestly, God also lends a helping hand.
—Aeschylus

Trust in Allah, but tie your camel first.   —Arab proverb

It is vain to ask of the gods what man is capable of supplying for himself.
—Epicurus

Heaven ne'er helps the men who will not act.   —Sophocles

To give pleasure to a single heart by a single kind act is better than a thousand head-bowings in prayer.
—Sa'di

Always look for ways to act upon the faith you display in your prayers.
—Anon.

You can do more than pray after you have prayed, but you cannot do more than pray until you have prayed.
—A.J. Gordon

Visualize, "prayerize," "actionize," and your wishes will come true.
—Charles L. Allen

There is a time for all things; a time to preach and a time to pray, but those times have passed away; there is a time to fight, and that time has come!
—General Peter Muhlenberg

Prayer is often a temptation to bank on a miracle of God instead of on a moral issue, i.e., it is much easier to ask God to do my work than it is to do it myself. Until we are disciplined properly, we will always be inclined to bank on God's miracles and refuse to do the moral thing ourselves. It is our job, and it will never be done unless we do it. —Oswald Chambers

SOME RESPONSES TO, AND
REWARDS OF, PRAYING

Some people think that prayer just means asking for things, and if they fail to receive exactly what they asked for, they think the whole thing is a fraud.   —Gerald Vann

Poverty, chastity, and obedience are extremely difficult. But there are always the graces if you will pray for them.   —Katheryn Hulme

Real prayer seeks an audience and an answer.   —William S. Plumer

There are three answers to prayer: yes, no, and wait awhile. It must be recognized that no is an answer.
—Ruth Stafford Peale

There are four ways God answers prayer: No, not yet; No, I love you too much; Yes, I thought you'd never ask; Yes, and here's more.
—Anne Lewis

No answer to prayer is an indication of our merit; every answer to prayer is an indication of God's mercy.
—John Blanchard

God answers all true prayer, either in kind or in kindness.
—Adoniram Judson

God is not a cosmic bellboy for whom we can press a button to get things.
—Harry Emerson Fosdick

More things are wrought by prayer than this world dreams of.
—Alfred, Lord Tennyson

When I have a problem I pray about it, and what comes to mind and stays there I assume to be my answer. And this has been right so often that I know it is God's answer.
—J.L. Kraft

Whenever the insistence is on the point that God answers prayer, we are off the track. The meaning of prayer is that we get hold of God, not of the answer.
—Oswald Chambers

I think Christians fail so often to get answers to their prayers because they do not wait long enough on God. They just drop down and say a few words, and then jump up and forget it and expect God to answer them. Such praying always reminds me of the small boy ringing his neighbor's door-bell, and then running away as fast as he can go.   —E.M. Bounds

When I pray, coincidences happen, and when I don't, they don't.
—William Temple

Our understanding of God is the answer to prayer; getting things from God is God's indulgence of us. When God stops giving us things, He brings us into the place where we can begin to understand Him.
—Oswald Chambers

If God sees that my spiritual life will be furthered by giving the things for which I ask, then He will give them, but that is not the end of prayer. The end of prayer is that I come to know God Himself.   —Oswald Chambers

You say, "But He has not answered." He has, He is so near to you that His silence is the answer. His silence is big with terrific meaning that you cannot understand yet, but presently you will.   —Oswald Chambers

When we pray "in the Name of Jesus" the answers are in accordance with His nature, and if we think our prayers are unanswered it is because we are not interpreting the answer along this line.   —Oswald Chambers

God's silences are His answers. If we only take as answers those that are visible to our senses, we are in a very elementary condition of grace.
—Oswald Chambers

Who rises from prayer a better man, his prayer is answered.
—George Meredith

God has editing rights over our prayers. He will . . . edit them, correct them, bring them in line with His will and then hand them back to us to be resubmitted.   —Stephen Crotts

The great tragedy of life is not unanswered prayer, but unoffered prayer.
—F.B. Meyer

My prayers, my God, flow from what I am not; I think Thy answers make me what I am. —George MacDonald

The greatest blessing of prayer is not receiving the answer, but being the kind of person God can trust with His answer. —Anon.

God answers prayer with certainty. Wish fulfillment is something else.
—Anon.

God delays, but doesn't forget.
—Spanish proverb

A generous prayer is never presented in vain; the petition may be refused, but the petitioner is always, I believe, rewarded by some gracious visitation.
—Robert Louis Stevenson

I tremble for my country when I reflect that God is just.
—Thomas Jefferson

The answer of our prayers is secured by the fact that in rejecting them God would in a certain sense deny His own nature. —John Calvin

There are two main pitfalls on the road to mastery of the art of prayer. If a person gets what he asks for, his humility is in danger. If he fails to get what he asks for, he is apt to lose confidence. Indeed, no matter whether prayer seems to be succeeding or failing, humility and confidence are two virtues which are absolutely essential. —A Trappist monk

If we be empty and poor, it is not because God's hand is straitened, but ours is not opened.
—Thomas Manton

I firmly believe a great many prayers are not answered because we are not willing to forgive someone.
—Dwight L. Moody

I know not by what methods rare,
But this I know: God answers prayer.
I know not if the blessing sought
Will come in just the guise I thought.
I leave my prayer to Him alone
Whose will is wiser than my own.
—Eliza M. Hickok

Our prayers are often filled with selfish "wants"; God always answers with what we need. —Anon.

We ought not to tolerate for a minute the ghastly and grievous thought that God will not answer prayer.
—Charles Haddon Spurgeon

Though I am weak, yet God, when prayed,
Cannot withhold his conquering aid.
—Ralph Waldo Emerson

Beyond our utmost wants
His love and power can bless;
To praying souls he always grants
More than they can express.
—John Newton

Whatever things ye desire, when ye pray, believe that you receive them, and ye shall have them.
—Mark 11:24

The firmament of the Bible is ablaze with answers to prayer.
—T.L. Cuyler

Never was a faithful prayer lost. Some prayers have a longer voyage than others, but then they return with their richer lading at last, so that the praying soul is a gainer by waiting for an answer.   —William Gurnall

In Gethsemane the holiest of all petitioners prayed three times that a certain cup might pass from Him. It did not. After that the idea that prayer is recommended to us as a sort of infallible gimmick may be dismissed.
                              —C.S. Lewis

Sometimes . . . God answers our prayers in the way our parents do, who reply to the pleas of their children with "Not just now" or "I'll have to think about that for a little while."
                              —Roy M. Pearson

Answered prayers cover the field of providential history as flowers cover western prairies.   —T.L. Cuyler

In seasons of distress and grief,
My soul has often found relief,
And oft escaped the tempter's snare,
By thy return, sweet hour of prayer.
                              —W.W. Walford

God answers sharp and sudden on
    some prayers,
And thrusts the thing we have prayed
    for in our face.
A gauntlet with a gift in't.
          —Elizabeth Barrett Browning

Our prayers run along one road and God's answers by another, and by and by they meet.
                              —Adoniram Judson

God's chief gift to those who seek him is Himself.   —E.B. Pusey

Asking for anything is allowed with the understanding that God's answers come from God's perspective. They are not always in harmony with our expectations, for only He knows the whole story.   —Anon.

May the Lord answer you when you are in distress; May the name of the God of Jacob protect you, May he send you help from the sanctuary and grant you support from Zion.
                              —Psalms 20:1–2

Just when I need Him, He is my all,
Answering when upon Him I call;
Tenderly watching lest I should fall.
                              —William Poole

The king shall joy in thy strength, O Lord; and in thy salvation how greatly shall he rejoice! Thou hast given him his heart's desire, and hast not withheld the request of his lips.
                              —Psalms 21:1–2

Those who trade with heaven by prayer grow rich by quick returns.
                              —William S. Plumer

The great thing in prayer is to feel that we are putting our supplications into the bosom of omnipotent love.
                              —Andrew Murray

When you go to your knees, God will help you stand up to anything.
                              —Anon.

Prayer has marked the trees across the wilderness of a skeptical world to direct the traveler in distress, and all paths lead to a single light.
                              —Douglas Meador

Amazing things start happening when we start praying! —Anon.

Prayer enlarges the heart until it is capable of containing God's gift of Himself. —Mother Teresa

The man who prays grows, and the muscles of the soul swell from this whipcord to iron bands. —F.B. Meyer

Prayer opens our eyes that we may see ourselves and others as God sees us. —Clara Palmer

It is impossible to lose your footing while on your knees. —Anon.

The exercise of prayer, in those who habitually exert it, must be regarded by us doctors as the most adequate and normal of all the pacifiers of the mind and calmers of the nerves. —William James

The influence of prayer on the human mind and body . . . can be measured in terms of increased physical buoyancy, greater intellectual vigor, moral stamina, and a deeper understanding of the realities underlying human relationships. —Dr. Alexis Carrel

The essence of prayer, even of a mystical experience, is the way we are altered to see everything from its life-filled dimension. —Matthew Fox

Prayer puts God's work in His hands—and keeps it there. —E.M. Bounds

It is hard to wait and press and pray, and hear no voice, but stay till God answers. —E.M. Bounds

Prayer is a kind of calling home every day. And there can come to you a serenity, a feeling of at-homeness in God's universe, a peace that the world can neither give nor disturb, a fresh courage, a new insight, a holy boldness that you'll never, never get any other way. —Earl G. Hunt, Jr.

Pray because you have a Father, not because it quietens you, and give Him time to answer. —Oswald Chambers

Perhaps one of the greatest rewards of meditation and prayer is the sense of belonging that comes to us. —Bill W.

We impoverish God in our minds when we say there must be answers to our prayers on the material plane; the biggest answers to our prayers are in the realm of the unseen. —Oswald Chambers

Our Lord never referred to unanswered prayer; he taught that prayers are always answered. He ever implied that prayers were answered rightly because of the Heavenly Father's wisdom. —Oswald Chambers

As white snow flakes fall quietly and thickly on a winter day, answers to prayer will settle down upon you at every step you take, even to your dying day. The story of your life will be the story of prayer and answers to prayer. —O. Hallesby

God is a rich and bountiful Father, and He does not forget His children, nor withhold from them anything which it would be to their advantage to receive. —J.K. Maclean

Just as an earthly father knows what is best for his children's welfare, so does God take into consideration the particular needs of His human family, and meets them out of His wonderful storehouse. —J.K. Maclean

Prayer brings a good spirit in our homes. For God hears prayer. Heaven itself would come down to our homes. And even though we who constitute the home all have our imperfections and our failings, our home would, through God's answer to prayer, become a little paradise.
—O. Hallesby

God's willingness to answer our prayers exceeds our willingness to give good and necessary things to our children, just as far as God's ability, goodness and perfection exceed our infirmities and evil. —E.M. Bounds

The greatest answer to prayer is that I am brought into a perfect understanding with God, and that alters my view of actual things.
—Oswald Chambers

God's "nothings" are His most positive answers. We have to stay on God and wait. Never try to help God to fulfill His word. —Oswald Chambers

The shower of answers to your prayers will continue to your dying hour. Nor will it cease then. When you pass out from beneath the shower, your dear ones will step into it. Every prayer and every sigh which you have uttered for them and their future welfare will, in God's time, descend upon them as a gentle rain of answers to prayer. —O. Hallesby

If a door slams shut it means that God is pointing to an open door further on down. —Anna Delaney Peale

We, ignorant of ourselves, beg often our own harms, which the wise powers deny us for our good.
—William Shakespeare

Prayer is the easiest and hardest of all things; the simplest and the sublimest; the weakest and the most powerful; its results lie outside the range of human possibilities—they are limited only by the omnipotence of God.
—E.M. Bounds

Prayer, like faith, obtains promises, enlarges their operation, and adds to the measure of their results.
—E.M. Bounds

If we will make use of prayer to call down upon ourselves and others those things which will glorify the name of God, then we shall see the strongest and boldest promises of the Bible about prayer fulfilled. Then we shall see such answers to prayer as we had never thought were possible.
—O. Hallesby

Let it be your business every day, in the secrecy of the inner chamber, to meet the holy God. You will be repaid for the trouble it may cost you. The reward will be sure and rich.
—Andrew Murray

One great effect of prayer is that it enables the soul to command the body. By obedience I make my body submissive to my soul, but prayer puts my soul in command of my body.
—Oswald Chambers

If we pray for anything according to the will of God, we already have what we pray for the moment we ask it. We do not know exactly when it will arrive; but we have learned to know God through the Spirit of God, and have learned to leave this in His hands, and to live just as happily whether the answer arrives immediately or later.   —O. Hallesby

It is God's will not only to hear our prayer, but to give us the best and the richest answer which He, the almighty and omniscient God, can devise. He will send us the answer when it will benefit us and His cause the most.
                              —O. Hallesby

If God does not give you something you ask for, wait on Him. He will speak with you tenderly and sympathetically about the matter until you yourself understand that He cannot grant your prayer.   —O. Hallesby

The potency of prayer hath subdued the strength of fire; it hath bridled the rage of lions, hushed anarchy to rest, extinguished wars, appeased the elements, expelled demons, burst the chains of death, expanded the gates of heaven, assuaged diseases, repelled frauds, rescued cities from destruction, stayed the sun in its course, and arrested the progress of the thunderbolt.
                —Saint John Chrysostom

Be sure to remember that nothing in your daily life is so insignificant and so inconsequential that the Lord will not help you by answering your prayer.   —O. Hallesby

It's Often a Blessing That We Don't Get What We Pray For

More tears are shed over answered prayers than unanswered ones.
                              —Teresa of Avila

True prayer always receives what it asks for—or something better.
                              —Bryon Edwards

Be thankful that God's answers are wiser than your answers.
                              —William Culbertson

God punishes us mildly by ignoring our prayers, and severely by answering them.   —Richard J. Needham

When the gods wish to punish us, they answer our prayers.
                              —Oscar Wilde

God alone fully understands what each one of us needs; we make mistakes continually and pray for things which would be harmful to us if we received them. Afterwards we see our mistakes and realize that God is good and wise in not giving us these things, even though we plead ever so earnestly for them.   —O. Hallesby

When the gods are angry with a man, they give him what he asks for.
                              —Greek proverb

I have lived to thank God that all my prayers have not been answered.
                              —Jean Ingelow

Prayer and Faith

Prayer is the supreme activity of all that is noblest in our personality, and the essential nature of prayer is faith.
—Oswald Chambers

Prayer is the voice of faith.
—William Van Horne

The prayer that is faithless is fruitless.
—Thomas Watson

A saint is to put forth his faith in prayer, and afterwards follow his prayer with faith.   —Vavasor Powell

The prayer of faith is the only power in the universe to which the great Jehovah yields.   —Robert Hall

Prayers are heard in heaven very much in proportion to your faith. Little faith will get very great mercies, but great faith still greater.
—Charles Haddon Spurgeon

The beginning of anxiety is the end of faith, and the beginning of true faith is the end of anxiety.
—George Mueller

Teach me, O God, not to torture myself, not to make a martyr out of myself through stifling reflection, but rather teach me to breathe deeply in faith.   —Søren Kierkegaard

Faith is the fountain of prayer, and prayer should be nothing else but faith exercised.   —Thomas Manton

Without faith it is impossible to please God, for he that cometh to God must believe that He is.
—Hebrews 11:6

Connecting to God through Prayer

When we pray we link ourselves with an inexhaustible motive power.
—Dr. Alexis Carrel

Jesus Christ is a God whom we approach without pride, and before whom we humble ourselves without despair.   —Blaise Pascal

Granting that we are always in the presence of God, yet it seems to me that those who pray are in His presence in a very different sense; for they, as it were, see that He is looking upon them, while others may go for days on end without even once recollecting that God sees them.
—Teresa of Avila

Why is it when we talk to God we're said to be praying, but when God talks to us we're schizophrenic?
—Lily Tomlin

It is in recognizing the actual presence of God that we find prayer no longer a chore, but a supreme delight.
—Gordon Lindsay

Essentially prayer is based on a relationship. We don't converse freely with someone we don't know. We bare our souls and disclose our hidden secrets only to someone we trust.
—Dean Register

I who still pray at morning and at eve
Thrice in my life perhaps have truly prayed,
Thrice stirred below conscious self
Have felt that perfect disenthrallment which is God.
—James Russell Lowell

207

Because God is the living God, he can hear; because he is a loving God, he will hear; because he is our covenant God, he has bound himself to hear.
—Charles Haddon Spurgeon

Nothing is so blessed as quiet, unbroken communication with our Lord. The sense of the Lord's nearness, which then fills our souls, is greater than any other peace, joy, inner satisfaction, or security which we have known.   —O. Hallesby

We look upon prayer as a means of getting things for ourselves; The Bible idea of prayer is that we may get to know God Himself.
—Oswald Chambers

A person must recognize his need for God before he can request divine aid and give God due thanks.   —Anon.

MEDITATION

Prayer is more than meditation. In meditation the source of strength is one's self. When one prays he goes to a source of strength greater than his own.
—Madame Chiang Kai-Shek

Prayer is when you talk to God; meditation is when you listen to God.
—Diana Robinson

When one devotes oneself to meditation, mental burdens, unnecessary worries, and wandering thoughts drop off one by one; life seems to run smoothly and pleasantly.
—Nyogen Senzaki

But first of all we shall want sunlight; nothing much can grow in the dark. Meditation is our step out into the sun.   —As Bill Sees It

You are used to listening to the buzz of the world, but now is the time to develop the inner ear that listens to the inner world. It is time to have a foot in each world, and it can be done.   —Saint Bartholomew

Meditation is a mental discipline that enables us to do one thing at a time.
—Max Picard

The very best and utmost of attainment in this life is to remain still and let God act and speak in thee.
—Meister Eckhart

All the troubles of life come upon us because we refuse to sit quietly for awhile each day in our rooms.
—Blaise Pascal

It is necessary for us to withdraw at regular intervals and enable our souls to attain that quietude and inward composure which are essential if we would hear the voice of God.
—O. Hallesby

We must hear Jesus speak if we expect him to hear us speak.
—Charles Haddon Spurgeon

The quiet hour of prayer is one of the most favorable opportunities He has in which to speak to us seriously. In quietude and solitude before the face of God our souls can hear better than at any other time.   —O. Hallesby

OTHER DEFINITIONS OF PRAYER

Prayer is man's greatest means of trapping the infinite resources of God. —J. Edgar Hoover

Prayer is the simplest form of speech
That infant lips can try;
Prayer the sublimest strains that
    reach
The Majesty on high.
            —James Montgomery

Prayer is the heavenly telephone that brings the distant near, till heaven to earth comes down. —A.B. Simpson

Prayer is the soul's sincere desire,
Uttered, or unexpressed;
The motion of a hidden fire
That trembles in the breast.
            —James Montgomery

Prayer is conversation with God.
            —Clement of Alexandria

Prayer is invoking the impossible.
            —Jack W. Hayford

Prayer is the golden key that opens heaven. —Thomas Watson

Prayer is the key that opens the door to all that is good in life. —Anon.

Prayer is and remains always a native and deepest impulse of the soul of man. —Thomas Carlyle

Prayer is essentially man standing before his God in wonder, awe, and humility; man, made in the image of God, responding to his maker.
            —George Appleton

Prayer is the language of a man burdened with a sense of need.
            —E.M. Bounds

Prayer is the incense of a holy heart
Rising to God from bruised and broken things,
When kindled by the Spirit's burning breath
And upward borne by faith's ascending wings. —A.B. Simpson

Prayer is a strong wall and fortress of the church; it is a goodly Christian's weapon. —Martin Luther

Prayer is the sovereign remedy.
            —Robert Hall

Prayer is a sincere, sensible, affectionate pouring out of the soul to God, through Christ, in the strength and assistance of the Spirit, for such things as God has promised.
            —John Bunyan

For prayer is not a ritual; it is the soul's inherent response to a relationship with a loving Father.
            —Colleen Townsend Evans

Prayer, even more than sheer thought, is the firmest anchor.
            —Jeremiah A. Denton, Jr.

Prayer is our humble answer to the inconceivable surprise of living.
            —Abraham Heschel

Prayer is not conquering God's reluctance, but taking hold of God's willingness. —Phillips Brooks

Prayers are the leeches of care.
            —Anon.

Prayer is the soul's breathing itself into the bosom of its heavenly Father.
—Thomas Watson

Prayer is a shield to the soul, a sacrifice to God, and a scourge for Satan.
—John Bunyan

Prayer is the spiritual gymnasium in which we exercise and practice godliness.
—V.L. Crawford

Prayer is exhaling the spirit of man and inhaling the spirit of God.
—Edwin Keith

Prayer is the acid test of devotion.
—Samuel Chadwick

Prayer is communion with God, usually comprising petition, adoration, praise, confession, and thanksgiving.
—*International Standard Bible Encyclopedia*

Prayer serves as an edge and border to preserve the web of life from unraveling.
—Robert Hall

Prayer is the ascending vapor which supplies
The showers of blessing, and the stream that flows
Through earth's dry places, till on every side
"The wilderness shall blossom as the rose."
—A.B. Simpson

Prayer is a rising up and a drawing near to God in mind and in heart, and in spirit.
—Alexander Whyte

Prayer means that we have come boldly into the throne room and we are standing in His presence.
—E.W. Kenyon

Prayer is the contemplation of the facts of life from the highest point of view.
—Ralph Waldo Emerson

Prayer does not mean simply to pour out one's heart. It means rather to find the way to God and to speak with him, whether the heart is full or empty.
—Dietrich Bonhoeffer

Prayer is not an exercise, it is the life.
—Oswald Chambers

Prayer is our most formidable weapon, the thing which makes all else we do efficient.
—E.M. Bounds

Prayer is not logical, it is a mysterious moral working of the Holy Spirit.
—Oswald Chambers

Prayer should be the means by which I, at all times, receive all that I need, and, for this reason, be my daily refuge, my daily consolation, my daily joy, my source of rich and inexhaustible joy in life.
—Saint John Chrysostom

Prayer is the spirit speaking truth to Truth.
—Philip James Bailey

Prayer is a cry of distress, a demand for help, a hymn of love.
—Dr. Alexis Carrel

Prayer, in its simplest definition, is merely a wish turned God-ward.
—Phillips Brooks

Prayer is the evidence that I am spiritually concentrated on God.
—Oswald Chambers

Prayer is the pillow of religion.
—Arab proverb

Prayer is God's answer to our poverty, not a power we exercise to obtain an answer.   —Oswald Chambers

Prayer is a condition of mind, an attitude of heart, which God recognizes as prayer whether it manifests itself in quiet thinking, in sighing or in audible words.   —O. Hallesby

Prayer is an all-efficient panoply, a treasure undiminished, a mine which is never exhausted, a sky unobscured by clouds, a heaven unruffled by the storm. It is the root, the fountain, the mother of a thousand blessings.
        —Saint John Chrysostom

To labor is to pray.
        —Motto of the Benedictine Order

General Quotations about Prayer

Some pray to marry the man they love, my prayer will somewhat vary; I humbly pray to Heaven above that I love the man I marry.
        —Rose Pastor Stokes

The prayers of the Christian are secret, but their effect cannot be hidden.   —Howard Chandler Robbins

Man is the only creature which rises by bowing, for he finds elevation in his subjection to his Maker.   —Anon.

Lord, till I reach that blissful shore,
No privilege so dear shall be
As thus my inmost soul to pour
In prayer to thee.   —Charlotte Elliott

Revival fires flame where hearts are praying.   —Dick Eastman

If we could all hear one another's prayers, God might be relieved of some of his burden.
        —Ashleigh Brilliant

What I dislike least in my former self are the moments of prayer.
        —André Gide

Our rages, daughters of despair, creep and squirm like worms. Prayer is the only form of revolt which remains upright.   —Georges Bernanos

Prayer reaches out in love to a dying world and says, "I care."
        —Dick Eastman

To pray together, in whatever tongue or ritual, is the most tender brotherhood of hope and sympathy that man can contract in this life.
        —Madame de Staël

The deepest wishes of the heart find expression in secret prayer.
        —George E. Rees

We are never more like Christ than in prayers of intercession.
        —Austin Phelps

The spirit of prayer is the fruit and token of the Spirit of adoption.
        —John Newton

If we do not love one another, we certainly shall not have much power with God in prayer.
        —Dwight L. Moody

Keep us, Lord, so awake in the duties of our calling that we may sleep in thy peace and wake in thy glory.
        —John Donne

I find in the Psalms much the same range of mood and expression as I perceive within my own life of prayer.
—Malcolm Boyd

I am used to praying when I am alone, thank God. But when I come together with other people, when I need more than ever to pray, I still cannot get used to it.   —Leo Tolstoy

Nothing is discussed more and practiced less than prayer.   —Anon.

I always love to begin a journey on Sundays, because I shall have the prayers of the church to preserve all that travel by land, or by water.
—Jonathan Swift

Nor it is an objection to say that we must understand a prayer if it is to have its true effect. That simply is not the case. Who understands the wisdom of a flower? Yet we can take pleasure in it.   —Rudolph Steiner

I would rather stand against the cannons of the wicked than against the prayers of the righteous.
—Thomas Lye

Restraining prayer, we cease to fight;
Prayer keeps the Christian's armor
    bright;
And Satan trembles when he sees
The weakest saint upon his knees.
—William Cowper

God dwells where we let God in.
—Menachem Mendel

Courage is not afraid to weep, and she is not afraid to pray, even when she is not sure who she is praying to.
—J. Ruth Gendler

Saints of the early church reaped great harvests in the field of prayer and found the mercy seat to be a mine of untold treasures.
—Charles Haddon Spurgeon

At church, with meek and unaffected
    grace,
His looks adorn'd the venerable
    place;
Truth from his lips prevail'd with
    double sway,
And fools who came to scoff,
    remain'd to pray.
—Oliver Goldsmith

The wings of prayer carry high and far.   —Anon.

In the calm of sweet communion
Let thy daily work be done;
In the peace of soul-outpouring
Care be banished, patience won;
And if earth with its enchantments
Seek thy spirit to enthrall,
Ere thou listen, ere thou answer,
Turn to Jesus, tell Him all.
—G.M. Taylor

God warms his hands at man's heart when he prays.   —Masefield

Turn your doubts to question; turn your question to prayers; turn your prayers to God.   —Mark R. Litteton

Prayer, like radium, is a luminous and self-generating form of energy.
—Dr. Alexis Carrel

Whatever you do in revenge against your brother will appear all at once in your heart at the time of payer.
—The Desert Fathers

Any concern too small to be turned
into a prayer is too small to be made
into a burden.   —Corrie ten Boom

Never say you will pray about a
thing; pray about it.
                    —Oswald Chambers

Doubt not but God who sits on high,
Thy secret prayers can hear;
When a dead wall thus cunningly
Conveys soft whispers to the ear.
                              —Anon.

The granting of prayer, when offered
in the name of Jesus, reveals the
Father's love to him, and the honor
which he has put upon him.
            —Charles Haddon Spurgeon

Self-Knowledge

The Importance of Knowing Ourselves

To pursue yourself is an interesting and absorbing thing to do. Once you have caught the scent of a hidden being, your own hidden being, you won't readily be deflected from the tracking down of it.
—Cynthia Propper Seton

Ninety percent of the world's woe comes from people not knowing themselves, their abilities, their frailties, and even their real virtues. Most of us go almost all the way through life as complete strangers to ourselves.
—Sydney J. Harris

If I could know me, I could know the universe.
—Shirley MacLlaine

A man who knows he is a fool is not a great fool.
—Chuang-tzu

I believe that in our constant search for security we can never gain any peace of mind until we are secure in our own soul.
—Margaret Chase Smith

We should know what our convictions are, and stand for them. Upon one's own philosophy, conscious or unconscious, depends one's ultimate interpretation of facts. Therefore it is wise to be as clear as possible about one's subjective principles. As the man is, so will be his ultimate truth.
—Carl Jung

Femininity appears to be one of those pivotal qualities that is so important no one can define it.
—Caroline Bird

I knew what my job was; it was to go out and meet the people and love them.
—Diana, Princess of Wales

People who concentrate on giving good service always get more personal satisfaction as well as better business. How can we get better service? One way is by trying to see ourselves as others do.
—Patricia Fripp

Resolve to be thyself; and know that he who finds himself, loses his misery.
—Matthew Arnold

Let us remember that within us there is a palace of immense magnificence.
—Teresa of Avila

Many men go fishing all of their lives without knowing that it is not fish they are after.
—Henry David Thoreau

It is the individual who knows how little he knows about himself who stands a reasonable chance of finding out something about himself.
—S.I. Hayakawa

Only when one is connected to one's own core is one connected to others. ... And, for me, the core, the inner spring, can best be refound through solitude.
—Anne Morrow Lindbergh

Freedom is knowing who you really are.
—Linda Thomson

If you do not tell the truth about yourself you cannot tell it about other people.
—Virginia Woolf

To understand is to forgive, even oneself.
—Alexander Chase

Knowing others is wisdom, knowing yourself is Enlightenment.
—Lao-tzu

I think self-awareness is probably the most important thing towards becoming a champion.
—Billie Jean King

The life which is unexamined is not worth living.
—Plato

WE MUST SEEK TO IMPROVE AND GROW

The deeper interior you have the more you have in your library.
—Jacqueline Bisset

Follow your interests, get the best available education and training, set your sights high, be persistent, be flexible, keep your options open, accept help when offered, and be prepared to help others.
—Mildred Spiewak Dresselhaus

It's all to do with the training: you can do a lot if you're properly trained.
—Queen Elizabeth II

As it turns out, social scientists have established only one fact about single women's mental health: employment improves it.
—Susan Faludi

Saying "yes" to yourself means acknowledging what you have that's good and working on the things that aren't.
—Patricia Fripp

There is no good reason why we should not develop and change until the last day we live.
—Karen Horney

We can't take any credit for our talents. It's how we use them that counts.
—Madeleine L'Engle

As simple as it sounds, we all must try to be the best person we can: by making the best choices, by making the most of the talents we've been given.
—Mary Lou Retton

What is most beautiful in virile men is something feminine; what is most beautiful in feminine women is something masculine.　—Susan Sontag

You must love and care for yourself, because that's when the best comes out.　—Tina Turner

We Can't Start to Improve Until We Know Who We Are

Show me a sensible person who likes himself or herself! I know myself too well to like what I see. I know but too well that I'm not what I'd like to be.
　—Golda Meir

Until we can understand the assumptions in which we are drenched we cannot know ourselves.
　—Adrienne Rich

Experience isn't interesting till it begins to repeat itself—in fact, till it does that, it hardly is experience.
　—Elizabeth Bowen

Self-knowledge is the beginning of self-improvement.
　—Spanish proverb

We are the same people as we were at three, six, ten or twenty years old. More noticeably so, perhaps, at six or seven, because we were not pretending so much then.
　—Agatha Christie

Until we see what we are, we cannot take steps to become what we should be.　—Charlotte P. Gilman

When a man begins to understand himself, he begins to live.
　—Norvin G. McGranahan

A humble knowledge of oneself is a surer road to God than a deep searching of the sciences.
　—Thomas à Kempis

If you do not ask yourself what it is you know, you will go on listening to others and change will not come because you will not hear your own truth.　—Saint Bartholomew

No man remains quite what he was when he recognizes himself.
　—Thomas Mann

Sometimes a person has to go back, really back—to have a sense, an understanding of all that's gone to make them—before they can go forward.　—Paule Marshall

Awakening begins when a man realizes that he is going nowhere and does not know where to go.
　—Georges Gurdjieff

Self-searching is the means by which we bring new vision, action, and grace to bear upon the dark and negative side of our natures. With it comes the development of that kind of humility that makes it possible for us to receive God's help. . . . We find that bit by bit we can discard the old life—the one that did not work—for a new life that can and does work under conditions whatever.
　—As Bill Sees It

It's Not Easy to Know Ourselves

The most difficult thing in life is to know yourself.   —Thales

You never find yourself until you face the truth.   —Pearl Bailey

It is not only the most difficult thing to know oneself, but the most inconvenient, too.   —Josh Billings

Long ago I understood that it wasn't merely my being a woman that was preventing my being welcomed into the world of what I long thought of as my peers. It was that I had succeeded in an undertaking few men have even attempted: I have become myself.   —Alice Koller

He knows the universe and does not know himself.
          —Jean de La Fontaine

There are chapters in every life which are seldom read and certainly not aloud.   —Carol Shields

No man ever understands quite his own artful dodges to escape from the grim shadow of self-knowledge.
          —Joseph Conrad

Nothing is easier than self-deceit.
          —Demosthenes

Sometimes it takes years to really grasp what has happened to your life.
          —Wilma Rudolph

One may understand the cosmos, but never the ego; the self is more distant than any star.   —G.K. Chesterton

You can live a lifetime and, at the end of it, know more about other people than you know about yourself.
          —Beryl Markham

We Must Know Both Our Possibilities and Our Limitations

Learn what you are, and be such.
          —Pindar

Long tresses down to the floor can be beautiful, if you have that, but learn to love what you have.
          —Anita Baker

I am no longer what I was. I will remain what I have become.
          —Coco Chanel

I always introduce myself as an encyclopedia of defects which I do not deny. Why should I? It took me a whole life to build myself as I am.
          —Oriana Fallaci

The happy man is he who knows his limitations, yet bows to no false gods.
          —Robert W. Service

I shall be an autocrat, that's my trade; and the good Lord will forgive me, that's his.
          —Catherine the Great

Sometimes it is more important to discover what one cannot do, than what one can.   —Lin Yutang

Somehow we learn who we really are and then live with that decision.
          —Eleanor Roosevelt

Self-understanding rather than self-condemnation is the way to inner peace and mature conscience.
—Joshua L. Liebman

To say something nice about themselves, this is the hardest thing in the world for people to do.
—Nancy Friday

After my screen test, the director clapped his hands gleefully and yelled, "She can't talk! She can't act! She's sensational!"
—Ava Gardner

Whenever I dwell for any length of time on my own shortcomings, they gradually begin to seem mild, harmless, rather engaging little things, not at all like the staring defects in other people's characters.
—Margaret Halsey

It's not our disadvantages or shortcomings that are ridiculous, but rather the studious way we try to hide them, and our desire to act as if they did not exist.
—Giacomo Leopardi

Of all the idiots I have met in my life, and the Lord knows that they have not been few or little, I think that I have been the biggest.
—Isak Dinesen

A woman of mystique is fully aware of her flaws and weaknesses, yet she is strong enough to admit them and not be embarrassed by them.
—Jean Lush

Learning too soon our limitations, we never learn our powers.
—Mignon McLaughlin

Your thorns are the best part of you.
—Marianne Moore

Oh, I'm so inadequate. And I love myself!
—Meg Ryan

I am simple, complex, generous, selfish, unattractive, beautiful, lazy, and driven.
—Barbra Streisand

If your head tells you one thing and your heart tells you another, before you do anything, you should first decide whether you have a better head or a better heart.
—Marilyn vos Savant

I did not lose myself all at once. I rubbed out my face over the years washing away my pain, the same way carvings on stone are worn down by water.
—Amy Tan

The precept, "Know yourself," was not solely intended to obviate the pride of mankind; but likewise that we might understand our own worth.
—Cicero

I believe that dreams transport us through the underside of our days, and that if we wish to become acquainted with the dark side of what we are, the signposts are there, waiting for us to translate them.
—Gail Godwin

It is a purely relative matter where one draws the plimsoll-line of condemnation, and . . . if you find the whole of humanity falls below it you have simply made a mistake and drawn it too high. And you are probably below it yourself.
—Frances Partridge

I'm a salami writer. I try to write good salami, but salami is salami.
—Stephen King

Only by pursuing the extremes in one's nature, with all its contradictions, appetites, aversions, rages, can one hope to understand a little . . . oh, I admit only a very little . . . of what life is about. —Françoise Sagan

The basic experience of everyone is the experience of human limitation.
—Flannery O'Connor

We do not make beams from the hollow, decaying trunk of the fallen oak. We use the upsoaring tree in the full vigor of its sap. —Sylvia Pankhurst

We must use what we have to invent what we desire. —Adrienne Rich

WOMEN HAVE UNIQUE STRENGTHS

Whatever glory belongs to the race for a development unprecedented in history for the given length of time, a full share belongs to the womanhood of the race.
—Mary McLeod Bethune

There is a potential heroine in every woman. —Jean Shinoda Bolen

We are volcanoes. When we women offer our experience as our truth, as human truth, all the maps change. There are new mountains.
—Ursula K. LeGuin

I hear the singing of the lives of women. The clear mystery, the offering, the pride. —Muriel Rukeyser

The sexes in each species of beings . . . are always true equivalents—equals but not identicals.
—Antoinette Brown Blackwell

For women there are, undoubtedly, great difficulties in the path, but so much the more to overcome. First no woman would say "I am but a woman!" But a woman! What more can you ask to be? —Maria Mitchell

Ability is sexless.
—Christabel Pankhurst

We bear the world and we make it.... There was never a great man who had not a great mother—it is hardly an exaggeration. —Olive Schreiner

Remember, Ginger Rogers did everything Fred Astaire did, but she did it backwards and in high heels.
—Faith Whittlesey

FIND THINGS IN YOURSELF TO BE PROUD OF

There may be ways in which we can work for change. We don't have to do dramatic things or devote our entire lives to it. We can lead normal lives but at the same time try hard not to be bystanders.
—Helen Bamber

Some people give time, some money, some their skills and connections, some literally give their life's blood . . . but everyone has something to give.
—Barbara Bush

Though I have no productive worth, I have a certain value as an indestructible quantity. —Alice James

I was once the typical daughter, then the easily recognizable wife, and then the quintessential mother. I seem always to have reminded people of someone in their family. Perhaps I am just the triumph of Plain Jane.
—Helen Hayes

God wastes nothing.   —Jan Karon

To be a housewife is . . . a difficult, a wrenching, sometimes ungrateful job if it's looked on as only a job. Regarded as a profession, it is the noblest as it is the most ancient of the catalogue. Let none persuade us differently, or the world will be lost indeed.   —Phyllis McGinley

It's this no-nonsense side of women that is pleasant to deal with. They are the real sportsmen.
—Phyllis McGinley

Not being beautiful was the true blessing. . . . Not being beautiful forced me to develop my inner resources. The pretty girl has a handicap to overcome.   —Golda Meir

There is not one big cosmic meaning for all, there is only the meaning we each give to our life, an individual meaning, an individual plot, like an individual novel, a book for each person.   —Anaïs Nin

I see myself as Rhoda, not Mary Tyler Moore.   —Rosie O'Donnell

The surest sign of fitness is success.
—Olive Schreiner

From the first, I made my learning, what little it was, useful every way I could.   —Mary McLeod Bethune

I was not a classic mother. But my kids were never palmed off to boarding school. So, I didn't bake cookies. You can buy cookies, but you can't buy love.   —Raquel Welch

I am an ordinary person, but carried to extremes.   —Fay Weldon

General Quotations about Self-Knowledge

I am not a glutton—I am an explorer of food.   —Erma Bombeck

I'm just a person trapped inside a woman's body.   —Elayne Boosler

To know oneself, one should assert oneself.   —Albert Camus

I am because my little dog knows me.
—Gertrude Stein

There is a solitude which each and every one of us has always carried within. More inaccessible than the ice-cold mountains, more profound than the midnight sea: the solitude of self.   —Elizabeth Cady Stanton

Whether it was work, marriage, or family, I've always been a late bloomer.   —Sigourney Weaver

Rebellion against your handicaps gets you nowhere. Self-pity gets you nowhere. One must have the adventurous daring to accept oneself as a bundle of possibilities and undertake the most interesting game in the world—making the most of one's best.   —Harry Emerson Fosdick

I want, by understanding myself, to understand others. I want to be all that I am capable of becoming.
—Katherine Mansfield

Real apprenticeship is ultimately always to the self. —Cynthia Ozick

The delights of self-discovery are always available. —Gail Sheehy

Whether there are innately female leadership styles . . . is not really the right question. It is more important to ask why there has been so little attention paid to women leaders over the years as well as why the styles of leading more often exhibited by women are particularly useful at this critical moment in history.
—Charlotte Bunch

In other living creatures the ignorance of themselves is nature, but in men it is a vice. —Boethius

Once, power was considered a masculine attribute. In fact, power has no sex. —Katherine Graham

It is doubtless a vice to turn one's eyes inward too much, but I am my own comedy and tragedy.
—Ralph Waldo Emerson

I write entirely to find out what I'm thinking, what I'm looking at, what I see and what it means, what I want, and what I fear. —Joan Didion

Many people today don't want honest answers insofar as honest means unpleasant or disturbing. They want a soft answer that turneth away anxiety.
—Louis Kronenberger

A single event can awaken within us a stranger totally unknown to us.
—Antoine de Saint-Exupery

No one can figure out your worth but you. —Pearl Bailey

There is no disappointment we endure one-half so great as what we are to ourselves.
—Philip James Bailey

Self-Acceptance

I care not so much what I am to others as what I am to myself. I will be rich by myself, and not by borrowing.
—Michel de Montaigne

You can succeed if nobody else believes it, but you will never succeed if you don't believe in yourself.
—William J.H. Boetcker

Cautious, careful people, always casting about to preserve their reputation and social standing, never can bring about a reform.   —Susan B. Anthony

Everybody wants to do something to help, but nobody wants to be first.
—Pearl Bailey

It is not easy to be a pioneer—but oh, it is fascinating! I would not trade one moment, even the worst moment, for all the riches in the world.
—Elizabeth Blackwell

Do not attempt to do a thing unless you are sure of yourself, but do not relinquish it simply because someone else is not sure of you.
—Stewart E. White

No one can make you feel inferior without your consent.
—Eleanor Roosevelt

Every man stamps his value on himself ... man is made great or small by his own will.   —J.C.F. von Schiller

The decision to speak out is the vocation and lifelong peril by which the intellectual must live.   —Kay Boyle

Let us not forget that among [women's] rights is the right to speak freely.
—Hillary Rodham Clinton

Let a man's talents or virtues be what they may, he will only feel satisfaction as he is satisfied in himself.
—William Hazlitt

I've always tried to go a step past wherever people expected me to end up.   —Beverly Sills

The widening of woman's sphere is to improve her lot. Let us do it, and if the world scoff, let it scoff—if it sneer, let it sneer. —Lucy Stone

It's just like magic. When you live by yourself, all your annoying habits are gone! —Merrill Markoe

When people say: she's got everything, I've only one answer: I haven't had tomorrow. —Elizabeth Taylor

Cuteness in children is totally an adult perspective. The children themselves are unaware that the quality exists, let alone its desirability, until the reactions of grown-ups inform them. —Leontine Young

It is not the eyes of others that I am wary of, but my own. —Noel Coward

Do not let your peace depend on the hearts of men; whatever they say about you, good or bad, you are not because of it another man, for as you are, you are. —Thomas à Kempis

In my business, you measure your respect by the enemies you make. —Theo E. Colborn

Not knowing when the dawn will come, I open every door. —Emily Dickinson

We would worry less about what others think of us if we realized how seldom they do. —Ethel Barrett

A man cannot be comfortable without his own approval. —Mark Twain

I have come to believe over and over again that what is most important to me must be spoken, made verbal and shared, even at the risk of having it bruised or misunderstood. —Audre Lorde

The worst loneliness is not to be comfortable with yourself. —Mark Twain

Perhaps the most important thing we can undertake toward the reduction of fear is to make it easier for people to accept themselves, to like themselves. —Bonaro Overstreet

I have had more trouble with myself than with any other man. —Dwight L. Moody

What you think about yourself is much more important than what others think of you. —Marcus Annaeus Seneca

What a man thinks of himself, that is what determines, or rather indicates, his fate. —Henry David Thoreau

As soon as you trust yourself, you will know how to live. —Johann von Goethe

WE ARE OUR OWN MOST IMPORTANT SOURCE OF RECOGNITION AND APPRECIATION

He who seeks for applause only from without has all his happiness in another's keeping. —Oliver Goldsmith

From self alone expect applause. —Marion L. Burton

Confronted by an absolutely infuriating review, it is sometimes helpful for the victim to do a little personal research on the critic. Is there any truth to the rumor that he had no formal education beyond the age of eleven? In any event, is he able to construct a simple English sentence? Do his participles dangle? When moved to lyricism, does he write "I had a fun time"? Was he ever arrested for burglary? I don't know that you will prove anything this way, but it is perfectly harmless and quite soothing.   —Jean Kerr

You can enjoy encouragement coming from outside, but you cannot need for it to come from outside.
    —Vladimir Zworykin

Next to God we are indebted to women, first for life itself, and then for making it worth living.
    —Mary McLeod Bethune

I am not belittling the brave pioneer men but the sunbonnet as well as the sombrero has helped to settle this glorious land of ours. —Edna Ferber

The older women were Sunbeams and I guess we were Cherubs or Lambs, but our mothers were Nightingales.   —Janet Flanner

Do not look for approval except for the consciousness of doing your best.
    —Bernard M. Baruch

I exist as I am, that is enough,
If no other in the world be aware, I
    sit content,
And if each and all be aware, I sit
    content.   —Walt Whitman

Nobody can be exactly like me. Sometimes even I have trouble doing it.   —Tallulah Bankhead

No matter how lonely you get or how many birth announcements you receive, the trick is not to get frightened. There's nothing wrong with being alone.   —Wendy Wasserstein

I was always willing to take a great deal of the burden of getting along in life on my own shoulders, but I wasn't willing to give myself a pat on the back. I was always looking to somebody else to give me that. . . . That was all wrong. —Raquel Welch

She lacks confidence, she craves admiration insatiably. She lives on the reflections of herself in the eyes of others. She does not dare to be herself.   —Anaïs Nin

Blessed is he who expects no gratitude, for he shall not be disappointed.
    —William Bennett

When you know you are doing your very best within the circumstances of your existence, applaud yourself!
    —Rusty Berkus

To accept ourselves as we are means to value our imperfections as much as our perfections.   —Sandra Bierig

I've learned to take time for myself and to treat myself with a great deal of love and respect 'cause I like me. . . . I think I'm kind of cool.
    —Whoopi Goldberg

Spirituality is . . . the awareness that survival is the savage fight between you and yourself.   —Anon.

I am the only real truth I know.
—Jean Rhys

Not in the shouts and plaudits of the throng, but in ourselves, are triumph and defeat.
—Henry Wadsworth Longfellow

If there are two hundred people in a room and one of them doesn't like me, I've got to get out.
—Marlon Brando

No man is defeated without until he has first been defeated within.
—Eleanor Roosevelt

To make the choice for independent survival, the great man's wife has to become convinced of her own intrinsic worth.
—Joanna T. Steichen

I care not what others think of what I do, but I care very much about what I think of what I do. That is character!
—Theodore Roosevelt

I am somebody. I am me. I like being me. And I need nobody to make me somebody.
—Louis L'Amour

Life, I fancy, would very often be insupportable, but for the luxury of self-compassion. —George R. Gissing

The work praises the man.
—Irish proverb

Of all afflictions, the worst is self-contempt.
—Berthold Auerbach

If you must love your neighbor as yourself, it is at least as fair to love yourself as your neighbor.
—Nicolas de Chamfort

Believing in our hearts that who we are is enough is the key to a more satisfying and balanced life.
—Ellen Sue Stern

I . . . know what I do, and am unmoved by men's blame, or their praise either.   —Robert Browning

Trusting In Our Own Genius

My unreality is chiefly this: I have never felt much like a human being. It's a splendid feeling.
—Margaret Anderson

The mind can store an estimated 100 trillion bits of information—compared with which a computer's mere billions are virtually amnesiac.
—Sharon Begley

The mind's cross-indexing puts the best librarian to shame.
—Sharon Begley

If school results were the key to power, girls would be running the world.   —Sarah Boseley

There is no balking genius. Only death can silence it or hinder.
—Ella Wheeler Wilcox

An artist can show things that other people are terrified of expressing.
—Louise Bourgeois

True genius doesn't fulfill expectations, it shatters them.
—Arlene Croce

Next to genius is the power of feeling where true genius lies.
—Sarah Josepha Hale

If I had influence with the good fairy who is supposed to preside over the christening of all children, I should ask that her gift to each child in the world be a sense of wonder so indestructible that it would last throughout life as an unfailing antidote against the boredom and disenchantments of later years, the sterile preoccupation with things that are artificial, the alienation from the sources of our strength.   —Rachel Carson

You are unique, and if that is not fulfilled then something has been lost.
—Martha Graham

The thing that makes you exceptional, if you are at all, is inevitably that which must also make you lonely.
—Lorraine Hansbury

Everybody is talented, original, and has something important to say.
—Brenda Ueland

Cherish forever what makes you unique, 'cuz you're really a yawn if it goes!   —Bette Midler

I didn't belong as a kid, and that always bothered me. If only I'd known that one day my differentness would be an asset, then my early life would have been much easier.
—Bette Midler

Genius is expansive, irresistible, and irresistibly expansive. If it is in you, no cords can confine it.
—Gail Hamilton

Since you are like no other being ever created since the beginning of time, you are incomparable.
—Brenda Ueland

Genius is the talent for seeing things straight. It is seeing things in a straight line without any bend or break or aberration of sight, seeing them as they are, without any warping of vision. Flawless mental sight! That is genius.   —Maude Adams

Children see things very well sometimes—and idealists even better.
—Lorraine Hansbury

Freedom is always and exclusively freedom for the one who thinks differently.   —Rosa Luxemburg

The person who can combine frames of reference and draw connections between ostensibly unrelated points of view is likely to be the one who makes the creative breakthrough.
—Denise Shekerjian

Art is the signature of civilizations.
—Beverly Sills

Every single one of us can do things that no one else can do—can love things that no one else can love. We are like violins. We can be used for doorstops, or we can make music.
—Barbara Sher

We Are Who We Are

If God had wanted me otherwise, He would have created me otherwise.
—Johann von Goethe

Love your self's self where it lives.
—Anne Sexton

I am what I am, so take me as I am!
—Johann von Goethe

Be content with what you are, and wish not change; nor dread your last day, nor long for it.   —Martial

It is the chiefest point of happiness that a man is willing to be what he is.
    —Erasmus

Who I am is the best I can be.
    —Leontyne Price

Oh, I'm so inadequate. And I love myself!   —Meg Ryan

Learn what you are and be such.
    —Pindar

What thou art, that thou art.
    —Thomas à Kempis

I is who I is.   —Tom Peterson

People remain what they are, even when their faces fall to pieces.
    —Bertolt Brecht

You have to deal with the fact that your life is your life.   —Alex Hailey

The search for a new personality is futile; what is fruitful is the interest the old personality can take in new activities.   —Cesare Pavese

IT'S OK TO BE
WHOMEVER WE ARE

I seldom think about my limitations, and they never make me sad. Perhaps there is just a touch of yearning at times; but it is vague, like a breeze among flowers.   —Helen Keller

In order to be irreplaceable one must always be different.   —Coco Chanel

The courage to be is the courage to accept oneself, in spite of being unacceptable.   —Paul Tillich

Contentment, and indeed usefulness, comes as the infallible result of great acceptances, great humilities—of not trying to conform to some dramatized version of ourselves.
    —David Grayson

A man should not strive to eliminate his complexes but to get into accord with them, for they are legitimately what directs his conduct in the world.   —Sigmund Freud

Resolve to be thyself ... he who finds himself loses his misery!
    —Matthew Arnold

There's a period of life when we swallow a knowledge of ourselves and it becomes either good or sour inside.   —Pearl Bailey

There is always a certain peace in being what one is, in being that completely.   —Ugo Betti

I'm not OK, you're not OK—and that's OK.   —William Sloane Coffin

We will discover
the nature of our particular genius when we stop trying to conform to our own or to other people's models, learn to be ourselves, and allow our natural channel to open.
    —Shakti Gawain

All the discontented people I know are trying to be something they are not, to do something they cannot do.
    —David Grayson

Be yourself. The world worships the original.   —Ingrid Bergman

Best be yourself, imperial, plain, and true!   —Elizabeth Barrett Browning

She soothed and solaced and celebrated, destroying her gift by maiming it to suit her hearers.
          —Martha Bacon

It is better to be hated for what you are than loved for what you are not.
          —André Gide

Borrowed thoughts, like borrowed money, only show the poverty of the borrower.
          —Lady Marguerite Blessington

Do not wish to be anything but what you are.   —Saint Francis de Sales

Every man must at last accept himself for his portion, and learn to do his work with the tools and talents with which he has been endowed.
          —Charles A. Hawley

No person has the right to rain on your dreams.
          —Marian Wright Edelman

Of all our infirmities, the most savage is to despise our being.
          —Michel de Montaigne

Our entire life . . . consists ultimately in accepting ourselves as we are.
          —Jean Anouilh

The secret of my success is that at an early age I discovered I was not God.
          —Oliver Wendell Holmes, Jr.

To find the good life you must become yourself.   —Dr. Bill Jackson

Man has to live with the body and soul which have fallen to him by chance.   —José Ortega y Gasset

Be content with what you are, and wish not change; nor dread your last day, nor long for it.   —Martial

Change occurs when one becomes what she is, not when she tries to become what she is not.
          —Ruth P. Freedman

A man can stand a lot as long as he can stand himself.   —Axel Munthe

I've finally stopped running away from myself. Who else is there better to be?   —Goldie Hawn

HAVING REALISTIC EXPECTATIONS OF OURSELVES

Human beings aren't orchids; we must draw something from the soil we grow in. —Sara Jeannette Duncan

We expect more of ourselves than we have any right to.
          —Oliver Wendell Holmes, Jr.

I think knowing what you cannot do is more important than knowing what you can.   —Lucille Ball

Try as hard as we may for perfection, the net result of our labors is an amazing variety of imperfectness. We are surprised at our own versatility in being able to fail in so many different ways.   —Samuel McChord Crothers

Most of us have trouble juggling. The woman who says she doesn't is someone whom I admire but have never met. —Barbara Walters

A sobering thought: what if, right at this very moment, I am living up to my full potential? —Jane Wagner

Do not lose courage in considering your own imperfections. —Saint Francis de Sales

We set up harsh and unkind rules against ourselves. No one is born without faults. That man is best who has fewest. —Horace

One must not hope to be more than one can be. —Nicolas de Chamfort

I long to see everything, to know everything, to learn everything! —Marie Bashkirtseff

I can't write a book commensurate with Shakespeare, but I can write a book by me. —Sir Walter Raleigh

I have done what I could do in life, and if I could not do better, I did not deserve it. In vain I have tried to step beyond what bound me. —Maurice Maeterlinck

Don't try to teach a whole course in one lesson. —Kathryn Murray

The man with insight enough to admit his limitations comes nearest to perfection. —Johann von Goethe

Growth begins when we start to accept our own weakness. —Jean Vanier

To dream of the person you would like to be is to waste the person you are. —Anon.

Shall a man go and hang himself because he belongs to the race of pygmies, and not be the biggest pygmy that he can? —Henry David Thoreau

Of all the young men in America only a few hundred can get into major league baseball, and of these only a handful in a decade can get into the Hall of Fame. So it goes in all human activity. . . . Some become multimillionaires and chairmen of the board, and some of us must be content to play baseball at company picnics or manage a credit union without pay. —William Feather

At thirty a man should know himself like the palm of his hand, know the exact number of his defects and qualities. . . . And above all, accept these things. —Albert Camus

You can't make the Duchess of Windsor into Rebecca of Sunnybrook Farm. The facts of life are very stubborn things. —Cleveland Amory

Learn to . . . be what you are, and learn to resign with a good grace all that you are not. —Henri Frederic Amiel

We cannot all be masters. —William Shakespeare

No man can climb out beyond the limitations of his own character. —John Morley

Sometimes it is more important to discover what one cannot do, than what one can do.   —Lin Yutang

To do all that one is able to do is to be a man; to do all that one would like to do is to be a god.
                —Napoleon Bonaparte

No one is expected to achieve the impossible.   —French proverb

A hero is a man who does what he can.   —Romain Rolland

It is only fools who keep straining at high C all their lives.
                —Charles Dudley Warner

May God . . . let me strive for attainable things.   —Pindar

Despair is the price one pays for setting himself an impossible aim.
                —Graham Greene

We would have to settle for the elegant goal of becoming ourselves.
                —William Styron

A great obstacle to happiness is to expect too much happiness.
                —Bernard de Fontenelle

I cannot do everything, but still I can do something; and because I cannot do everything, I will not refuse to do something I can do.
                —Edward Everett Hale

I hope to work, support my children and die quietly without pain.
                —Sean Connery

As we advance in life, we learn the limits of our abilities.   —J.A. Froud

Striving for excellence motivates you; striving for perfection is demoralizing.
                —Dr. Harriet Braiker

There is a proper balance between not asking enough of oneself and asking or expecting too much.
                —May Sarton

It is enough that I am of value to somebody today.   —Hugh Prather

A tomb now suffices him for whom the whole world was not sufficient.
                —Epitaph of Alexander the Great

To wish to act like angels while we are still in this world is nothing but folly.   —Teresa of Avila

It isn't important to come out on top, what matters is to be the one who comes out alive.   —Bertolt Brecht

I long to accomplish a great and noble task, but it my chief duty to accomplish small tasks as if they were great and noble.   —Helen Keller

The one important thing I have learned over the years is the difference between taking one's work seriously and taking one's self seriously. The first is imperative and the second is disastrous.   —Margaret Fontey

SELF-ACCEPTANCE IS CRITICAL TO OUR RELATIONS WITH OTHER PEOPLE

Friendship with oneself is all-important, because without it one cannot be friends with anyone else.
                —Eleanor Roosevelt

How I relate to my inner self influences my relationships with all others. My satisfaction with myself and my satisfaction with other people are directly proportional.
—Sue Atchley Ebaugh

I was always looking outside myself for strength and confidence, but it comes from within. It is there all the time. —Anna Freud

If you want to be respected by others, the great thing is to respect yourself.
—Fyodor Dostoyevsky

If one is cruel to himself, how can we expect him to be compassionate with others? —Hasdai Ibn Shaprut

Let a man's talents or virtues be what they may, he will only feel satisfaction in his society as he is satisfied in himself. —William Hazlitt

To succeed is nothing—it's an accident. But to feel no doubts about oneself is something very different: it is character. —Marie Lenéru

No matter what age you are, or what your circumstances might be, you are special, and you still have something unique to offer. Your life, because of who you are, has meaning.
—Barbara De Angelis

The worst walls are never the ones you find in your way. The worst walls are the ones you put there— you build yourself. Those are the high ones, the thick ones, the ones with no doors in.
—Ursula K. LeGuin

Interest in the lives of others, the high evaluation of these lives, what are they but the overflow of the interest a man finds in himself, the value he attributes to his own being?
—Sherwood Anderson

I want to be remembered as the person who helped us restore faith in ourselves. —Wilma Pearl Mankiller

Those people who are uncomfortable in themselves are disagreeable to others.
—William Hazlitt

Self-love is not opposed to the love of other people. You cannot really love yourself and do yourself a favor without doing other people a favor, and vice versa. —Dr. Karl Menninger

Healthy personalities accept themselves not in any self-idolizing way, but in the sense that they see themselves as persons who are worth giving to another and worthy to receive from another. —William Klassen

We should try to bring to any power what we have as women. We will destroy it all if we try to imitate that absolutely unfeeling, driving ambition that we have seen coming at us across the desk. —Colleen Dewhurst

A man needs self-acceptance or he can't live with himself; he needs self-criticism or others can't live with him. —James A. Pike

Nobody holds a good opinion of a man who has a low opinion of himself. —Anthony Trollope

To love others, we must first learn to love ourselves. —Anon.

There is overwhelming evidence that the higher the level of self-esteem, the more likely one will treat others with respect, kindness, and generosity. People who do not experience self-love have little or no capacity to love others. —Nathaniel Branden

SELF-ACCEPTANCE AND HUMOR

You grow up the day you have your first real laugh at yourself.
—Ethel Barrymore

Imagination was given to us to compensate for what we are not; a sense of humor was provided to console us for what we are.
—Mack McGinnis

GENERAL QUOTATIONS ABOUT SELF-ACCEPTANCE

It is the duty of youth to bring its fresh powers to bear on social progress. Each generation of young people should be to the world like a vast reserve force to a tired army. They should lift the world forward. That is what they are for.
—Charlotte P. Gilman

I looked always outside of myself to see what I could make the world give me instead of looking within myself to see what was there.
—Belle Livingstone

A true man never frets about his place in the world, but just slides into it by the gravitation of his nature, and swings there as easily as a star.
—Edwin H. Chapin

My recipe for life is not being afraid of myself, afraid of what I think or of my opinions. —Eartha Kitt

Accept the place the divine providence has found for you.
—Ralph Waldo Emerson

I needed to find my way to write. I need about six hours of uninterrupted time in order to produce about two hours of writing, and when I accepted that and found the way to do it, then I was able to write.
—Robert B. Parker

When one is pretending the entire body revolts. —Anaïs Nin

When you affirm your own rightness in the universe, then you co-operate with others easily and automatically as part of your own nature. You, being yourself, help others be themselves. —Jane Roberts

So prodigal was I of youth,
Forgetting I was young;
I worshipped dead men for their
    strength,
Forgetting I was strong.
—Vita Sackville-West

Life is a very sad piece of buffoonery, because we have . . . the need to fool ourselves continuously by the spontaneous creation of a reality . . . which, from time to time, reveals itself to be vain and illusory. —Luigi Pirandello

The deepest principle in human nature is the craving to be appreciated.
—William James

It's OK if you mess up. You should give yourself a break. —Billy Joel

Who we are never changes. Who we think we are does.
—Mary S. Almanac

It is not easy to be sure that being yourself is worth the trouble, but [we do know] it is our sacred duty.
—Florida Scott-Maxwell

Each of us has a day . . . when he has to accept, finally, the fact that he is a man.
—Jean Anouilh

Nature never repeats herself, and the possibilities of one human soul will never be found in another.
—Elizabeth Cady Stanton

Style is something peculiar to one person; it expresses one personality and one only; it cannot be shared.
—Freya Stark

If you put a woman in a man's position, she will be more efficient, but no more kind.
—Fay Weldon

Accept your humanness as well as your divinity, totally and without reserve.
—Emmanuel

The things we hate about ourselves aren't more real than things we like about ourselves.
—Ellen Goodman

Why can a man not act himself, be himself, and think for himself? It seems to me that naturalness alone is power; that a borrowed word is weaker than our own weakness, however small we may be.
—Maria Mitchell

Until you make peace with who you are, you'll never be content with what you have.
—Doris Mortman

If you make friends with yourself you will never be alone.
—Maxwell Maltz

It is a sign of strength, not of weakness, to admit that you don't know all the answers. —John P. Loughrane

The fundamental problem most patients have is an inability to love themselves, having been unloved by others during some crucial part of their lives. —Bernie S. Siegel, M.D.

Who you are is a necessary step to being who you will be. —Emmanuel

Ultimately, love is self approval.
—Sondra Ray

Unless I accept my faults, I will most certainly doubt my virtues.
—Hugh Prather

Too many people overvalue what they are not and undervalue what they are. —Malcolm Forbes

If I am not for myself, who is for me? And if I am only for myself, what am I? And if not now, when? —Hillel

Accept your defeats
With your head up and your eyes open
With the grace of woman, not the grief of a child . . .
—Kara DiGiovanna

He who despises himself esteems himself as a self-despiser.
—Susan Sontag

Your problem is you're . . . too busy holding onto your unworthiness.
—Ram Dass

Self-Control

DEVELOPING SELF-CONTROL

You must learn to be still in the midst
of activity, and to be vibrantly alive
in repose. —Indira Gandhi

When the fight begins within himself,
a man's worth something.
—Robert Browning

To put a tempting face aside when
duty demands every faculty is a lesson which takes most men longest
to learn. —Gertrude Atherton

Lack of discipline leads to frustration
and self-loathing. —Marie Chapian

You must have discipline to have fun.
—Julia Child

Self-command is the main elegance.
—Ralph Waldo Emerson

A little kingdom I possess,
Where thoughts and feelings dwell;
And very hard the task I find
Of governing it well.
—Louisa May Alcott

Everybody's business is nobody's
business, and nobody's business is my
business. —Clara Barton

I listen and give input only if somebody asks. —Barbara Bush

The man who masters his own soul
will forever be called conqueror of
conquerors. —Plautus

Temptations come, as a general rule,
when they are sought.
—Margaret Oliphant

A mind which really lays hold of a
subject is not easily detached from it.
—Ida Tarbell

There is little that can withstand a
man who can conquer himself.
—Louis XIV

Too often in ironing out trouble
someone gets scorched.
—Marcelene Cox

When you borrow trouble you give
your peace of mind as security.
—Myrtle Reed

Don't be curious of matters that
don't concern you; never speak of
them, and don't ask about them.
—Teresa of Avila

I will write of him who fights and
vanquishes his sins, who struggles on
through weary years against himself
...and wins.
—Caroline Begelow LeRow

What we do upon some great occasion will probably depend on what
we already are; and what we are will
be the result of previous years of self-
discipline.   —H.P. Liddon

Man who man would be, must rule
the empire of himself.
—Percy Bysshe Shelley

He that hath no rule over his own
spirit is like a city that is broken
down, and without walls.
—Proverbs 25:28

Most powerful is he who has himself
in his own power.
—Marcus Annaeus Seneca

It goes without saying that you
should never have more children than
you have car windows.
—Erma Bombeck

If you can't write your message in a
sentence, you can't say it in an hour.
—Dianna Booher

Sweet words are like honey, a little
may refresh, but too much gluts the
stomach.   —Anne Bradstreet

I am, indeed, a king, because I know
how to rule myself.   —Pietro Aretino

He who conquers others is strong; he
who conquers himself is mighty.
—Lao-tzu

A woman that's too soft and sweet is
like tapioca pudding—fine for them
as likes it.   —Osa Johnson

A little of what you fancy does you
good.   —Marie Lloyd

Gammy used to say, "Too much
scrubbing takes the life right out of
things."   —Betty MacDonald

Who is apt, on occasion, to assign a
multitude of reasons when one will
do? This is a sure sign of weakness in
argument.   —Harriet Martineau

The point of good writing is knowing
when to stop.
—L.M. Montgomery

Superior people never make long visits.
—Marianne Moore

The longest absence is less perilous to
love than the terrible trials of incessant proximity.   —Ouida

Never eat more than you can lift.
—Miss Piggy

What lies in our power to do, it lies
in our power not to do.   —Aristotle

It isn't until you come to a spiritual
understanding of who you are—not
necessarily a religious feeling, but
deep down, the spirit within—that
you can begin to take control.
—Oprah Winfrey

Anger is only one letter short of
danger.   —Anon.

Without discipline, there's no life at all.　　—Katharine Hepburn

Self-control is the quality that distinguishes the fittest to survive.
　　—George Bernard Shaw

Many people have the ambition to succeed; they may even have a special aptitude for their job. And yet they do not move ahead. Why? Perhaps they think that since they can master the job, there is no need to master themselves.　　—John Stevenson

Waiting is one of the great arts.
　　—Margery Allingham

Never fail to know that if you are doing all the talking, you are boring somebody.　　—Helen Gurley Brown

I know too well the poison and the
　　sting
Of things too sweet.
　　—Adelaide Proctor

Would that there were an award for people who come to understand the concept of enough. Good enough. Successful enough. Thin enough. Rich enough. Socially responsible enough. When you have self-respect you have enough.　　—Gail Sheehy

Transformation also means looking for ways to stop pushing yourself so hard professionally or inviting so much stress.　　—Gail Sheehy

To wear your heart on your sleeve isn't a very good plan; you should wear it inside, where it functions best.
　　—Margaret Thatcher

For fast-acting relief try slowing down.　　—Lily Tomlin

This is the gist of what I know:
Give advice and buy a foe.
　　—Phyllis McGinley

Don't give advice unless you're asked.
　　—Amy Alcott

The Only Thing We Can Control Is Ourselves

We don't want to push our ideas on to customers, we simply want to make what they want.
　　—Laura Ashley

The passion for setting people right is in itself an afflictive disease.
　　—Marianne Moore

There is only one corner of the universe you can be certain of improving, and that's your own self.
　　—Aldous Huxley

He that hath no rule over his own spirit is like a city that is broken down and without walls.
　　—Taylor Caldwell

Not being able to govern events, I govern myself.
　　—Michel de Montaigne

As far as your self-control goes, as far goes your freedom.
　　—Marie von Ebner-Eschenbach

That is always our problem, not how to get control of people, but how all together we can get control of a situation.　　—Mary Parker Follett

There is no hierarchy of values by which one culture has the right to insist on all its own values and deny those of another.   —Margaret Mead

He that would govern others should first be the master of himself.
                —Philip Massinger

You've got to ensure that the holders of an opinion, however unpopular, are allowed to put across their points of view.   —Betty Boothroyd

There is space within sisterhood for likeness and difference, for the subtle differences that challenge and delight; there is space for disappointment— and surprise.   —Christine Downing

It takes a disciplined person to listen to convictions which are different from their own.
                —Dorothy Fuldheim

The highest result of education is tolerance.   —Helen Keller

In a society where the rights and potential of women are constrained, no man can be truly free. He may have power, but he will not have freedom.   —Mary F. Robinson

Ambition, old as mankind, the immemorial weakness of the strong.
                —Vita Sackville-West

When one clings to the myth of superiority, one must constantly overlook the virtues and abilities of others.
                —Anne Wilson Schaef

The desire to conquer is itself a sort of subjection.   —George Eliot

The only people who would be in government are those who care more about people than they do about power.   —Millicent Fenwick

Leaders can be moral—and they should be moral—without imposing their morality on others.
                —Geraldine Ferraro

SILENCE IS GOLDEN

The fool shouts loudly, thinking to impress the world.
                —Marie de France

Blessed is the man who, having nothing to say, abstains from giving wordy evidence of the fact.
                —George Eliot

It was enough just to sit there without words.   —Louise Erdrich

Talking too much, too soon, and with too much self-satisfaction has always seemed to me a sure way to court disaster.   —Meg Greenfield

A story is told as much by silence as by speech.   —Susan Griffin

Talk uses up ideas. . . . Once I have spoken them aloud, they are lost to me, dissipated into the noisy air like smoke. Only if I bury them, like bulbs, in the rich soil of silence do they grow.   —Doris Grumbach

Next to entertaining or impressive talk, a thoroughgoing silence manages to intrigue most people.
                —Florence Hurst Harriman

Love understands love; it needs no talk.   —Frances Ridley Havergal

I like people who refuse to speak until they are ready to speak.
                    —Lillian Hellman

The strokes of the pen need deliberation as much as the sword needs swiftness.   —Julia Ward Howe

Handle them carefully, for words have more power than atom bombs.
                    —Pearl Strachan Hurd

One sees intelligence far more than one hears it. People do not always say transcendental things, but if they are capable of saying them, it is always visible.   —Marie Lenéru

The silence of a man who loves to praise is a censure sufficiently severe.
                    —Charlotte Lennox

Silence is one of the great arts of conversation.   —Hannah Moore

Silence and reserve will give anyone a reputation for wisdom.
                    —Myrtle Reed

It is impossible to persuade a man who does not disagree, but smiles.
                    —Muriel Spark

All the feeling which my father could not put into words was in his hand—any dog, child, or horse would recognize the kindness of it.
                    —Freya Stark

Nothing could bother me more than the way a thing goes dead once it has been said.   —Gertrude Stein

Minimum information given with maximum politeness.
                    —Jacqueline Kennedy Onassis

A gossip is one who talks to you about others; a bore is one who talks to you about himself; and a brilliant conversationalist is one who talks to you about yourself.   —Lisa Kirk

Beware of allowing a tactless word, rebuttal, a rejection to obliterate the whole sky.   —Anaïs Nin

Violence of the tongue is very real—sharper than any knife.
                    —Mother Teresa

Don't confuse being stimulating with being blunt.   —Barbara Walters

The less said the better.
                    —Jane Austen

Self-Control and Freedom

No man is free who is not master of himself.   —Epictetus

You were once wild here. Don't let them tame you!   —Isadora Duncan

Freedom is not procured by a full enjoyment of what is desired, but by controlling that desire.   —Epictetus

Self-Control and Passion

The happiness of a man in this life does not consist in the absence, but in the mastery, of his passions.
                    —Alfred, Lord Tennyson

When we start deceiving ourselves
into thinking not that we want something or need something, not that it is
a pragmatic necessity for us to have
it, but that it is a moral imperative
that we have it. Then is when we join
the fashionable madmen, and then
is when the thin whine of hysteria is
heard in the land, and then is when
we are in bad trouble.

—Joan Didion

I count him braver who overcomes
his desires than him who conquers
his enemies; the hardest victory is the
victory over self.   —Aristotle

The basic difference between being
assertive and being aggressive is how
our words and behavior affect the
rights and well-being of others.

—Sharon Anthony Bower

The strong man is the one who is
able to intercept at will the communication between the senses and the
mind.   —Napoleon Bonaparte

He that would be superior to external
influences must first become superior
to his own passions.

—Samuel Johnson

He who reigns within himself and
rules his passions, desires, and fears is
more than a king.   —John Milton

Self-Confidence

SELF-CONFIDENCE ISN'T CONCEIT OR EGOMANIA

Conceit spoils the finest genius. There is not much danger that real talent or goodness will be overlooked long; even if it is, the consciousness of possessing and using it well should satisfy one. —Louisa May Alcott

People in big empty places are likely to behave very much as the gods did on Olympus. —Edna Ferber

What makes humility so desirable is the marvelous thing it does to us; it creates in us a capacity for the closest possible intimacy with God. —Monica Baldwin

Calm self-confidence is as far from conceit as the desire to earn a decent living is remote from greed. —Channing Pollock

Big egos are big shields for lots of empty space. —Diana Black

Self-love, my liege, is not so vile a sin as self-neglecting. —William Shakespeare

The nice thing about egotists is that they don't talk about other people. —Lucille S. Harper

There is nothing so skillful in its own defense as imperious pride. —Helen Hunt Jackson

Wounded vanity knows when it is mortally hurt; and limps off the field, piteous, all disguises thrown away. But pride carries its banner to the last; and fast as it is driven from one field unfurls it in another. —Helen Hunt Jackson

In our society those who are in reality superior in intelligence can be accepted by their fellows only if they pretend they are not. —Marya Mannes

It is as proper to have pride in oneself as it is ridiculous to show it to others. —Francois de La Rochefoucauld

If a man doesn't delight in himself and the force in him and feel that he and it are wonders, how is all life to become important to him? —Sherwood Anderson

Your father used to say, "Never give away your work. People don't value what they don't have to pay for."
　　　　　　　　　　—Nancy Hale

Pride . . . is the direct appreciation of oneself.　　　　—Arthur Schopenhauer

Proud people breed sad sorrows for themselves.　　　　—Emily Brontë

Beware of over-great pleasure in being popular or even beloved.
　　　　　　　　　—Margaret Fuller

Soften my hard self-opinionatedness, which time has hardened so exceedingly!　　　　—Gertrude the Great

WITHOUT SELF-CONFIDENCE, WE'RE DONE FOR

Self-esteem isn't everything; it's just that there's nothing without it.
　　　　　　　　　—Gloria Steinem

As soon as you trust yourself, you will know how to live.
　　　　　　　—Johann von Goethe

It is far more impressive when others discover your good qualities without your help.
　　　　—Judith Martin (Miss Manners)

Humility is like underwear, essential but indecent if it shows.
　　　　　　　　　—Helen Nielsen

The more important the title, the more self-important the person, the greater the amount of time spent on the Eastern shuttle, the more suspicious the man and the less vitality in the organization.　　　—Jane O'Reilly

I'm glad I never feel important, it does complicate life.
　　　　　　　—Eleanor Roosevelt

More people are ruined by victory, I imagine, than by defeat.
　　　　　　　—Eleanor Roosevelt

Vanity is the quicksand of reason.
　　　　　　　　　—George Sand

I was somewhat drunk with what I had done. And I am always one to prefer being sober.　—Gertrude Stein

Our vanity is the constant enemy of our dignity.
　　　　　—Anne-Sophie Swetchine

He who has lost confidence can lose nothing more.　　　　—Boiste

To have that sense of one's intrinsic worth which constitutes self-respect is potentially to have everything.
　　　　　　　　　—Joan Didion

It is best to act with confidence, no matter how little right you have to it.
　　　　　　　　—Lillian Hellman

I've always seen myself as a winner, even as a kid. If I hadn't, I just might have gone down the drain a couple of times. I've got something inside of me, peasantlike and stubborn, and I'm in it 'til the end of the race.
　　　　　　　—Truman Capote

Success doesn't necessarily make you a happy person . . . but without the confidence and security that comes from being totally happy, I believe you cannot achieve your true potential and ultimate success.
　　　　　　　　　—Jinger Heath

Self-respect will keep a man from being abject when he is in the power of enemies, and will enable him to feel that he may be in the right when the world is against him.
—Bertrand Russell

'Tis the ignorant who boast.
—Carmen Sylva

Being powerful is like being a lady. If you have to tell people you are, you aren't.   —Margaret Thatcher

There's one blessing only, the source and cornerstone of beatitude: confidence in self.
—Marcus Annaeus Seneca

If arrogance is the heady wine of youth, then humility must be its eternal hangover.   —Helen Van Slyke

Conquer but never triumph.
—Marie von Ebner-Eschenbach

Only so far as a man believes strongly, mightily, can he act cheerfully, or do anything worth doing.
—Frederick W. Robertson

Experience tells you what to do; confidence allows you to do it.
—Stan Smith

Your success depends mainly upon what you think of yourself and whether you believe in yourself.
—William J.H. Boetcker

Success can make you go one of two ways. It can make you a prima donna, or it can smooth the edges, take away the insecurities, let the nice things come out.   —Barbara Walters

Humility is attentive patience.
—Simone Weil

The man who cannot believe in himself cannot believe in anything else.
—Roy L. Smith

A man cannot be comfortable without his own approval. —Mark Twain

Believe that you can whip the enemy, and you have won half the battle.
—General J.E.B. Stuart

As is our confidence, so is our capacity.
—William Hazlitt

AGE AND EXPERIENCE
BRING CONFIDENCE

Such to me is the new image of aging; growth in self, and service for all mankind.   —Ethel Percy Andrus

The older I get, the greater power I seem to have to help the world; I am like a snowball—the further I am rolled, the more I gain.
—Susan B. Anthony

The real evidence of growing older is that things level off in importance.
—Gladys Taber

It is sad to grow old but nice to ripen.
—Brigitte Bardot

Oh, yes. I'd do it all again; the spirit is willing yet; I feel the same desire to do the work but the flesh is weak. It's too bad that our bodies wear out while our interests are just as strong as ever.   —Susan B. Anthony

I'm not interested in age. People who tell me their age are silly. You're as old as you feel.   —Elizabeth Arden

It is sad to grow old, but nice to ripen.
                    —Brigitte Bardot

Maturity is coming to terms with that other part of yourself.
        —Dr. Ruth Tiffany Barnhouse

I believe the true function of age is memory. I'm recording as fast as I can.
                    —Rita Mae Brown

A woman's always younger than a man of equal years.
        —Elizabeth Barrett Browning

It is often the case with finer natures, that when the fire of the spirit dies out with increasing age, the power of the intellect is unaltered or increased.
                    —Margaret Gatty

I'm like old wine. They don't bring me out very often, but I'm well preserved.   —Rose Fitzgerald Kennedy

The great thing about getting older is that you don't lose all the other ages you've been.   —Madeleine L'Engle

Perhaps middle age is, or should be, a period of shedding shells; the shell of ambition, the shell of material accumulations and possessions, the shell of the ego.
                —Anne Morrow Lindbergh

Age is totally unimportant. The years are really irrelevant. It's how you cope with them.   —Shirley Lord

We are always the same age inside.
                    —Gertrude Stein

There is a fountain of youth: it is your mind, your talents, the creativity you bring to your life and the lives of the people you love. When you learn to tap this source, you will truly have defeated age.   —Sophia Loren

I am much younger now than I was at twelve or anyway, less burdened.
                —Flannery O'Connor

There are no old people nowadays; they are either "wonderful for their age" or dead.
            —Mary Pettibone Poole

For inside all the weakness of old age, the spirit, God knows, is as mercurial as it ever was.   —May Sarton

Age puzzles me. I thought it was a quiet time. My seventies were interesting and fairly serene, but my eighties are passionate. I grow more intense as I age.
            —Florida Scott-Maxwell

We who are old know that age is more than a disability. It is an intense and varied experience, almost beyond our capacity at times, but something to be carried high.
            —Florida Scott-Maxwell

Character contributes to beauty. It fortifies a woman as her youth fades. A mode of conduct, a standard of courage, discipline, fortitude and integrity can do a great deal to make a woman beautiful.
                —Jacqueline Bisset

Be on the alert to recognize your prime at whatever time of your life it may occur.   —Muriel Spark

Women may be the one group that grows more radical with age.
—Gloria Steinem

So much has been said and sung of beautiful young girls, why doesn't somebody wake up to the beauty of old women? —Harriet Beecher Stowe

Old age is that night of life, as night is the old age of day. Still night is full of magnificence and, for many, it is more brilliant than the day.
—Anne-Sophie Swetchine

In youth we learn; in age we understand.—Marie von Ebner-Eschenbach

Change excites me. I am fifty years old. It's when the mind catches up with the body.   —Raquel Welch

Don't buy the garbage that you're over the hill at fifty. This country makes such a big thing about age, particularly if you're a woman. What I think is relevant is your experience, what you have to offer. I hope people will recognize that and keep going.
—Molly Yard

I refuse to admit that I am more than fifty-two, even if that does make my sons illegitimate.   —Nancy Astor

I used to dread getting older because I thought I would not be able to do all the things I wanted to do, but now that I am older I find that I don't want to do them.
—Nancy Astor

I am immortal! I know it! I feel it!
—Margaret Witter Fuller

Another belief of mine: that everyone else my age is an adult, whereas I am merely in disguise.
—Margaret Atwood

I think your whole life shows in your face and you should be proud of that.
—Lauren Bacall

Youth is not a time of life, it is a state of mind. You are as old as your doubt, your fear, your despair. The way to keep young is to keep your faith young. Keep your self-confidence young. Keep your hope young.
—Luella F. Phean

WE CAN'T AFFORD TO DOUBT OURSELVES

I have become my own version of an optimist. If I can't make it through one door, I'll go through another door—or I'll make a door. Something terrific will come no matter how dark the present.   —Joan Rivers

Our doubts are traitors, and make us lose the good we oft might win, by fearing to attempt.
—William Shakespeare

Doubt indulged soon becomes doubt realized.   —Frances Ridley Havergal

Kill the snake of doubt in your soul, crush the worms of fear in your heart, and mountains will move out of your way.   —Kate Seredy

A man's doubts and fears are his worst enemies.
—William Wrigley, Jr.

Doubt whom you will, but never yourself. —Christian Bovee

I have never been nervous in all my life and I have no patience with people who are. If you know what you are going to do, you have no reason to be nervous. And I knew what I was going to do. —Mary Garden

Our self-conceit sustains, and always must sustain us. —Samuel Butler

Self-distrust is the cause of most of our failures . . . they are the weakest, however strong, who have no faith in themselves or their own powers. —Christian Bovee

Faith in oneself . . . is the best and safest course. —Michelangelo

Self-Confidence Is Essential to Success

Strong people don't need strong leaders. —Ella Baker

Might, could, would—they are contemptible auxiliaries. —George Eliot

You've got to take the initiative and play your game . . . confidence makes the difference. —Chris Evert

Shyness is just egotism out of its depth. —Penelope Keith

Self-trust is the first secret of success. —Ralph Waldo Emerson

Self-confidence is the first requisite to great undertakings. —Samuel Johnson

I felt a comedy ego beginning to grow, which gave me the courage to begin tentatively looking into myself for material. —Joan Rivers

My mother taught me very early to believe I could achieve any accomplishment I wanted to. The first was to walk without braces. —Wilma Rudolph

If there be a faith that can move mountains, it is faith in one's own power. —Marie von Ebner-Eschenbach

They are able because they think they are able. —Virgil

Nothing splendid has ever been achieved except by those who dared believe that something inside them was superior to circumstances. —Bruce Barton

Confidence is that feeling by which the mind embarks on great and honorable courses with a sure hope and trust in itself. —Cicero

One's self-image is very important because if that's in good shape, then you can do anything, or practically anything. —Sir John Gielgud

I've never had a humble opinion in my life. If you're going to have one, why bother to be humble about it? —Joan Baez

They conquer who believe they can. —John Dryden

The big gap between the ability of actors is confidence. —Kathleen Turner

Women who are confident of their abilities are more likely to succeed than those who lack confidence, even though the latter may be much more competent and talented and industrious.   —Dr. Joyce Brothers

It's so important to believe in yourself. Believe that you can do it, under any circumstances. Because if you believe you can, then you really will. That belief just keeps you searching for the answers, and then pretty soon you get it.   —Wally "Famous" Amos

Search and you will find that at the base and birth of every great business organization was an enthusiast, a man consumed with earnestness of purpose, with confidence in his powers, with faith in the worthwhileness of his endeavors.   —B.C. Forbes

Self-reverence, self-knowledge, self-control. These three alone lead to sovereign power.
     —Alfred, Lord Tennyson

Optimism is the faith that leads to achievement. Nothing can be done without hope and confidence.
     —Helen Keller

Confidence imparts a wonderful inspiration to its possessor.
     —John Milton

Great poetry is always written by somebody straining to go beyond what he can do.   —Stephen Spender

Immense power is acquired by assuring yourself in your secret reveries that you were born to control affairs.
     —Andrew Carnegie

If one advances confidently in the direction of his dreams, and endeavors to live the life which he has imagined, he will meet with a success unexpected in common hours.
     —Henry David Thoreau

SELF-CONFIDENCE IS CRITICAL TO OUR RELATIONS WITH OTHER PEOPLE

The confidence which we have in ourselves gives birth to much of that which we have in others.
     —Francois de La Rochefoucauld

The way in which we think of ourselves has everything to do with how our world sees us.   —Arlene Raven

Once you get rid of the idea that you must please other people before you please yourself, and you begin to follow your own instincts—only then can you be successful. You become more satisfied, and when you are other people tend to be satisfied by what you do.   —Raquel Welch

Ideal conversation must be an exchange of thought, and not, as many of those who worry about their shortcomings believe, an eloquent exhibition of wit or oratory.
     —Emily Post

There is overwhelming evidence that the higher the level of self-esteem, the more likely one will treat others with respect, kindness, and generosity. People who do not experience self-love have little or no capacity to love others.   —Nathaniel Branden

Nobody holds a good opinion of a man who has a low opinion of himself. —Anthony Trollope

Only the person who has faith in himself is able to be faithful to others. —Erich Fromm

He can inspire a group only if he himself is filled with confidence and hope of success. —Floyd V. Filson

A good sweat, with the blood pounding through my body, makes me feel alive, revitalized. I gain a sense of mastery and assurance. I feel good about myself. Then I can feel good about others. —Arthur Dobrin

Nothing is a greater impediment to being on good terms with others than being ill at ease with yourself. —Honore de Balzac

SOME SOURCES OF SELF-CONFIDENCE

Measure yourself by your best moments, not by your worst. We are too prone to judge ourselves by our moments of despondency and depression. —Robert Johnson

Oftentimes nothing profits more than self-esteem, grounded on what is just and right and well-managed. —John Milton

Confidence . . . is directness and courage in meeting the facts of life. —John Dewey

The gain in self-confidence of having accomplished a tiresome labour is immense. —Arnold Bennett

The way to develop self-confidence is to do the thing you fear and get a record of successful experiences behind you. —William Jennings Bryan

Believe that with your feelings and your work you are taking part in the greatest; the more strongly you cultivate this belief, the more will reality and the world go forth from it. —Rainer Maria Rilke

Class is an aura of confidence that is being sure without being cocky. Class has nothing to do with money. Class never runs scared. It is self-discipline and self-knowledge. It's the sure-footedness that comes with having proved you can meet life. —Ann Landers

In forty hours I shall be in battle, with little information, and on the spur of the moment will have to make the most momentous decisions, but I believe that one's spirit enlarges with responsibility and that, with God's help, I shall make them and make them right. —General George S. Patton

Be always sure you're right, then go ahead. —Davy Crockett

GENERAL QUOTATIONS ABOUT SELF-CONFIDENCE

I always thought I should be treated like a star. —Madonna

Perhaps I am stronger than I think. —Thomas Merton

The ability to take pride in your own
work is one of the hallmarks of sanity.
                    —Nikki Giovanni

Confidence is contagious. So is lack
of confidence.   —Vince Lombardi

"Glamour" is assurance. It is a kind
of knowing that you are all right in
every way, mentally and physically
and in appearance, and that, whatever the occasion or the situation, you
are equal to it.   —Marlene Dietrich

Never bend your head. Hold it high.
Look the world straight in the eye.
                    —Helen Keller

To be confident is to act in faith.
                    —Bernard Bynion

Skill and confidence are an uncon-
quered army.   —George Herbert

Self-Reliance

The Importance of Self-Reliance

It is better to be tied to any thorny bush than to be with a cross man.
—Augusta Gregory

I don't follow precedent, I establish it.
—Fanny Ellen Holtzman

Your future depends on many things, but mostly on you.   —Frank Tyger

The woman who can create her own job is the one who will win fame and fortune.   —Amelia Earhart

Don't ask of your friends what you yourself can do.   —Quintus Ennius

The thing women have got to learn is that nobody gives you power. You just take it.   —Roseanne

Who ever walked behind anyone to freedom?   —Hazel Scott

A man who finds no satisfaction in himself, seeks for it in vain elsewhere.
—Francois de La Rochefoucauld

The wise don't expect to find life worth living; they make it that way.
—Anon.

I do not wish women to have power over men; but over themselves.
—Mary Wollstonecraft Shelley

I am learning that if I just go on accepting the framework for life that others have given me, if I fail to make my own choices, the reason for my life will be missing. I will be unable to recognize that which I have the power to change.   —Liv Ullmann

To be a man is, precisely, to be responsible.
—Antoine de Saint-Exupery

Real adulthood is the result of two qualities: self-discipline and self-reliance. The process of developing them together in balance is called maturing.   —J.W. Jepson

He who would be well taken care of must take care of himself.
—William Graham Sumner

What we say and what we do ultimately comes back to us so let us
own our responsibility, place it in our
hands, and carry it with dignity and
strength.
        —Gloria Evangelina Anzaldua

We are free up to the point of choice,
then the choice controls the chooser.
        —Mary Crowley

To be born free is an accident; to live
free a responsibility; to die free is an
obligation.   —Mrs. Hubbard Davis

The best bet is to bet on yourself.
        —Arnold Glasow

It is not fair to ask of others what
you are not willing to do yourself.
        —Eleanor Roosevelt

Do for yourself or do without.
        —Gaylord Perry

Intimate relationships cannot substitute for a life plan. but to have any
meaning or viability at all, a life plan
must include intimate relationships.
        —Harriet Lerner

The great law of denial belongs to
the powerful forces of life, whether
the case be one of coolish baked
beans, or an unrequited affection.
        —Elizabeth Stuart Phelps

For the great benefits of our being—
our life, health, and reason—we look
upon ourselves.
        —Marcus Annaeus Seneca

I have always regarded myself as the
pillar of my life.   —Meryl Streep

A secure individual . . . knows that the
responsibility for anything concerning
his life remains with himself—and he
accepts that responsibility.
        —Harry Browne

An axe at home saves hiring a carpenter.   —J.C.F. von Schiller

We're all in this together . . . alone.
        —Lily Tomlin

No one can really pull you up very
high—you lose your grip on the rope.
But on your own two feet you can
climb mountains.   —Louis Brandeis

We need to find the courage to say
no to the things and people that are
not serving us if we want to rediscov-
er ourselves and live our lives with
authenticity.   —Barbara De Angelis

No one is in control of your happiness but you; therefore, you have
the power to change anything about
yourself or your life that you want to
change.   —Barbara De Angelis

Women share with men the need for
personal success, even the taste for
power, and no longer are we willing
to satisfy those needs through the
achievements of surrogates, whether
husbands, children, or merely role
models.   —Elizabeth Dole

There is no dependence that can be
sure but a dependence upon one's self.
        —John Gay

Getting fit is a political act—you are
taking charge of your life.
        —Jane Fonda

It is easier to live life through someone else than to become complete yourself. —Betty Friedan

Being black does not stop you. You can sit out in the world and say, "Well, white people kept me back, and I can't do this." Not so. You can have anything you want if you make up your mind and you want it. —Clara McBride Hale

The future is not in the hands of fate, but in ours. —Jules Jusserano

Men are made stronger on realization that the helping hand they need is at the end of their own arm. —Sidney J. Phil

I never really address myself to any image anybody has of me. That's like fighting with ghosts. —Sally Field

There is no such thing as vicarious experience. —Mary Parker Follett

I love being single. It's almost like being rich. —Sue Grafton

The best place to find a helping hand is at the end of your own arm. —Swedish proverb

Every tub must stand on its own bottom. —Thomas Fuller

You've got to do your own growing, no matter how tall your grandfather was. —Irish proverb

Do not rely completely on any other human being, however dear. We meet all of life's greatest tests alone. —Agnes MacPhail

Only those means of security are good, are certain, are lasting, that depend on yourself and your own vigor. —Niccolo Machiavelli

I don't want to be a passenger in my own life. —Diane Ackerman

Independence is happiness. —Susan B. Anthony

Woman must not depend upon the protection of man, but must be taught to protect herself. —Susan B. Anthony

Every man paddles his own canoe. —Frederick Marryat

If you would have a faithful servant, and one that you like, serve yourself. —Benjamin Franklin

If you want a thing done, go; if not, send. —Benjamin Franklin

I am not afraid of storms, for I am learning how to sail my ship. —Louisa May Alcott

Our remedies oft in ourselves do lie. —William Shakespeare

If it is to be, it is up to me. —Anon.

There are three types of baseball players—those who make it happen, those who watch it happen, and those who wonder what happened. —Tommy Lasorda

Rogers sees daylight. Campbell makes daylight. —Bum Phillips

I leave before being left. I decide. —Brigitte Bardot

No man may make another free.
—Zora Neale Hurston

Living by proxy is always a precarious expedient.
—Simone de Beauvoir

When I saw something that needed doing, I did it.   —Nellie Cashman

The only discipline that lasts is self-discipline.   —Bum Phillips

The destiny of man is in his own soul.
—Herodotus

My future is one I must make myself.
—Louis L'Amour

Faced with crisis, the man of character falls back on himself.
—Charles de Gaulle

If there is no wind, row.
—Latin proverb

No bird soars too high if he soars on his own wings.   —William Blake

WE MUST RELY ON WHAT'S INSIDE US

Seek not good from without: seek it within yourselves, or you will never find it.   —Bertha von Suttner

We carry with us the wonders we seek without us.
—Sir Thomas Browne

As far as beauty is concerned, in order to be confident we must accept that the way we look and feel is our own responsibility.   —Sophia Loren

The best things in life must come by effort from within, not by gifts from the outside.   —Fred Corson

Ruin and recovery are both from within.   —Epictetus

Learn to get in touch with silence within yourself and know that everything in life has a purpose.
—Elisabeth Kubler-Ross

People are like stained-glass windows. They sparkle and shine when the sun is out, but when the darkness sets in, their true beauty is revealed only if there is a light from within.
—Elisabeth Kubler-Ross

If you can't change your fate, change your attitude.   —Amy Tan

He who is plenteously provided for from within needs but little from without.   —Johann von Goethe

What pulls the strings is the force hidden within; there lies ... the real man.   —Marcus Aurelius

The foundations which we would dig about and find are within us, like the Kingdom of Heaven, rather than without.   —Samuel Butler

No external advantages can supply self-reliance. The force of one's being ... must come from within.
—R.W. Clark

Every time I start a picture ... I feel the same fear, the same self-doubts ... and I have only one source on which I can draw, because it comes from within me.   —Federico Fellini

There is no man so low down that the cure for his condition does not lie strictly within himself.
—Thomas L. Masson

It is what you are inside that matters. You, yourself, are your only real capital.
—Vladimir Zworykin

Look well into thyself; there is a source which will always spring up if thou wilt always search there.
—Marcus Aurelius

I've never met a person, I don't care what his condition, in whom I could not see possibilities. I don't care how much a man may consider himself a failure, I believe in him, for he can change the thing that is wrong in his life anytime he is prepared and ready to do it. Whenever he develops the desire, he can take away from his life the thing that is defeating it. The capacity for reformation and change lies within.
—Preston Bradley

You will not find poetry anywhere unless you bring some of it with you.
—Joseph Joubert

God, why do I storm heaven for answers that are already in my heart? Every grace I need has already been given me. Oh, lead me to the Beyond within.
—Macrina Wiederkehr

The only Zen you find on the tops of mountains is the Zen you bring up there.
—Robert M. Pirsig

There ain't nothing from the outside can lick any of us.
—Margaret Mitchell

Man must be arched and buttressed from within, else the temple wavers to dust.
—Marcus Aurelius

There is no reality except the one contained within us.
—Herman Hesse

Religious faith, indeed, relates to that which is above us, but it must arise from that which is within us.
—Josiah Royce

CREATING OURSELVES

God creates the animals, man creates himself.
—Georg Christoph Lichtenberg

Let women be provided with living strength of their own.
—Simone de Beauvoir

Man cannot remake himself without suffering, for he is both the marble and the sculptor.
—Dr. Alexis Carrel

Every man is his own ancestor, and every man his own heir. He devises his own future, and he inherits his own past.
—H.F. Hedge

In the long run we shape our lives and we shape ourselves. The process never ends until we die. And the choices we make are ultimately our own responsibility.
—Eleanor Roosevelt

Our awesome responsibility to ourselves, to our children, and to the future is to create ourselves in the image of goodness, because the future depends on the nobility of our imaginings.
—Barbara Grizzuti Harrison

Up to a point a man's life is shaped by environment, heredity, and movements and changes in the world about him; then there comes a time when it lies within his grasp to shape the clay of his life into the sort of thing he wishes to be. . . . Everyone has it within his power to say, this I am today, that I shall be tomorrow.
—Louis L'Amour

We either make ourselves miserable, or we make ourselves strong. The amount of work is the same.
—Carlos Castaneda

I, woman, give birth: and this time to myself.   —Alma Villanueva

Exude happiness and you will feel it back a thousand times.
—Joan Lunden

What you have become is the price you paid to get what you used to want.   —Mignon McLaughlin

You are the product of your own brainstorm.
—Rosemary Konner Steinbaum

I long to put the experience of fifty years at once into your young lives, to give you at once the key to that treasure chamber every gem of which has cost me tears and struggles and prayers, but you must work for these inward treasures yourselves.
—Harriet Beecher Stowe

There's only one corner of the universe you can be certain of improving, and that's your own self.
—Aldous Huxley

Parents can only give good advice or put them on the right paths, but the final forming of a person's character lies in their own hands.
—Anne Frank

CREATING AND USING OUR CIRCUMSTANCES

You need to claim the events in your life to make yourself yours. When you truly possess all you have been and done, which may take some time, you are fierce with reality.
—Florida Scott-Maxwell

I would not sit waiting for some value tomorrow, nor for something to happen. One could wait a lifetime. . . . I would make something happen.
—Louis L'Amour

I truly believe that women of my generation can bring a new cleansing element to American public life.
—Georgie Anne Geyer

Circumstances are the rulers of the weak; they are but the instruments of the wise.   —Samuel Lover

Sometimes you gotta create what you want to be a part of.
—Geri Weitzman

Circumstances—what are circumstances? I make circumstances.
—Napoleon Bonaparte

Man is not the creature of circumstances, circumstances are the creature of man. We are free agents, and man is more powerful than matter.
—Benjamin Disraeli

It is our relation to circumstances that determines their influence over us. The same wind that carries one vessel into port may blow another off shore. —Christian Bovee

We will either find a way, or make one. —Hannibal

People are always blaming their circumstances for what they are. The people who get on in this world are they who get up and look for the circumstances they want, and, if they can't find them, make them. —George Bernard Shaw

Choice of attention—to pay attention to this and ignore that—is to the inner life what choice of action is to the outer. In both cases, a man is responsible for his choice and must accept the consequences. —W.H. Auden

Heaven and hell is right now. . . . You make it heaven or you make it hell by your actions. —George Harrison

Freedom means choosing your burden. —Hephzibah Menuhin

We create our fate every day . . . most of the ills we suffer from are directly traceable to our own behavior. —Henry Miller

You have to take it as it happens, but you should try to make it happen the way you want to take it. —Old German proverb

The winds and waves are always on the side of the ablest navigators. —Edward Gibbon

A life of reaction is a life of slavery, intellectually and spiritually. One must fight for a life of action, not reaction. —Rita Mae Brown

Life is raw material. We are artisans. We can sculpt our existence into something beautiful, or debase it into ugliness. It's in our hands. —Cathy Better

The proverb warns that "You should not bite that hand that feeds you." But maybe you should, if it prevents you from feeding yourself. —Thomas Szasz

If we live good lives, the times are also good. As we are, such are the times. —Saint Augustine

Change and growth take place when a person has risked himself and dares to become involved with experimenting with his own life. —Herbert Otto

They have rights who dare defend them. —Roger Baldwin

Make good use of bad rubbish. —Elizabeth Beresford

Things alter for the worse spontaneously, if they be not altered for the better designedly. —Francis Bacon

Things don't turn up in this world until somebody turns them up. —James A. Garfield

Is life so wretched? Isn't it rather your hands which are too small, your vision which is muddied? You are the one who must grow up. —Dag Hammarskjold

Some leaders are born women.
—Geraldine Ferraro

Be thine own palace, or the world's
thy jail.   —John Donne

A filly who wants to run will always
find a rider.   —Jacques Audiberti

Each of us makes his own weather,
determines the color of the skies in
the emotional universe which he
inhabits.   —Fulton J. Sheen

RELYING ON OUR OWN THINKING

Thinking is like loving and dying.
Each of us must do it for himself.
—Josiah Royce

Be yourself and think for yourself;
and while your conclusions may not
be infallible, they will be nearer right
than the conclusions forced upon
you.   —Elbert Hubbard

Though reading and conversation
may furnish us with many ideas of
men and things, our own meditation
must form our judgement.
—Isaac Watts

He who has no opinion of his own,
but depends upon the opinion and
taste of others, is a slave.
—Friedrich Klopstock

How much time he gains who does
not look to see what his neighbor
says or does or thinks, but only at
what he does himself, to make it just
and holy.   —Marcus Aurelius

Let me listen to me and not to them.
—Gertrude Stein

The efficient man is the man who
thinks for himself.
—Charles W. Eliot

Learn to depend upon yourself by
doing things in accordance with your
own way of thinking.
—Grenville Kleiser

If we are not responsible for the
thoughts that pass our doors, we
are at least responsible for those we
admit and entertain.
—Charles B. Newcomb

Think wrongly, if you please, but in
all cases think for yourself.
—Doris Lessing

Each man must for himself alone
decide what is right and what is
wrong, which course is patriotic and
which isn't. You cannot shirk this
and be a man. To decide against your
conviction is to be an unqualified and
excusable traitor, both to yourself
and to your country, let men label
you as they may.   —Mark Twain

WE'RE RESPONSIBLE FOR OUR
OWN HAPPINESS

The man who makes everything that
leads to happiness depend upon himself, and not upon other men, has
adopted the very best plan for living
happily.   —Plato

Happiness must be cultivated. It is
like character. It is not a thing to be
safely let alone for a moment, or it
will run to weeds.
—Elizabeth Stuart Phelps

256

We are taught you must blame your father, your sisters, your brothers, the school, the teachers—you can blame anyone, but never blame yourself. It's never your fault. But it's always your fault, because if you want to change, you're the one who has got to change. It's as simple as that, isn't it?
—Katharine Hepburn

Discontent is want of self-discipline; it is infirmity of will.
—Ralph Waldo Emerson

Happiness is a conscious choice, not an automatic response.
—Mildred Barthel

The essence of philosophy is that a man should so live that his happiness shall depend as little as possible on external things. —Epictetus

Most folks are about as happy as they make up their minds to be.
—Abraham Lincoln

Happiness is not in our circumstances, but in ourselves. It is not something we see, like a rainbow, or feel, like the heat of a fire. Happiness is something we are.
—John B. Sheerin

When I have been unhappy, I have heard an opera . . . and it seemed the shrieking of winds; when I am happy, a sparrow's chirp is delicious to me. But it is not the chirp that makes me happy, but I that make it sweet.
—John Ruskin

The U.S. Constitution doesn't guarantee happiness, only the pursuit of it. You have to catch up with it yourself.
—Benjamin Franklin

To believe that if only we had this or that we would be happy, or to pursue any excessive desire, diverts us from seeing that happiness depends on an adequate self. —Eric Hoffer

Nothing can bring you peace but yourself. —Ralph Waldo Emerson

Happiness belongs to those who are sufficient unto themselves. For all external sources of happiness and pleasure are, by their very nature, highly uncertain, precarious, ephemeral, and subject to chance.
—Arthur Schopenhauer

All times are beautiful for those who maintain joy within them; but there is no happy or favorable time for those with disconsolate or orphaned souls.
—Rosalia Castro

Felicity, felicity . . . is quaffed out of a golden cup . . . the flavour is with you alone, and you can make it as intoxicating as you please.
—Joseph Conrad

Some pursue happiness— others create it. —Anon.

To be obliged to beg our daily happiness from others bespeaks a more lamentable poverty than that of him who begs his daily bread.
—Charles Caleb Colton

Man is the artificer of his own happiness. —Henry David Thoreau

To wait for someone else, or to expect someone else to make my life richer, or fuller, or more satisfying, puts me in a constant state of suspension.
—Kathleen Tierney Andrus

I am my own heaven and hell!
　　　　　—J.C.F. von Schiller

I am responsible for my own well-being, my own happiness. The choices and decisions I make regarding my life directly influence the quality of my days. —Kathleen Tierney Andrus

If you do not find peace in yourself you will never find it anywhere else.
　　　　　—Paula A. Bendry

To know what you prefer, instead of humbly saying Amen to what the world tells you that you ought to prefer, is to have kept your soul alive.
　　　　　—Robert Louis Stevenson

If people are suffering, then they must look within themselves. . . . Happiness is not something ready-made [Buddha] can give you. It comes from your own actions.
　　　　　—The Dalai Lama

Blame yourself if you have no branches or leaves; don't accuse the sun of partiality. —Chinese proverb

The opportunities for enjoyment in your life are limitless. If you feel you are not experiencing enough joy, you have only yourself to blame.
　　　　　—David E. Bresler

Happiness is like time and space—we make and measure it ourselves; it is as fancy, as big, as little, as you please, just a thing of contrasts and comparisons. —George du Marier

It is not easy to find happiness in ourselves, and it is not possible to find it elsewhere. —Agnes Repplier

The greatest griefs are those we cause ourselves. —Sophocles

No human being can really understand another, and no one can arrange another's happiness.
　　　　　—Graham Greene

No-one gives joy or sorrow. . . . We gather the consequences of our own deeds. —Garuda Purana

Happiness depends upon ourselves.
　　　　　—Aristotle

IT'S UP TO US
TO DEFEAT BOREDOM

The amount of satisfaction you get from life depends largely on your own ingenuity, self-sufficiency, and resourcefulness. People who wait around for life to supply their satisfaction usually find boredom instead.
　　　　　—Dr. William Menninger

Somebody's boring me; I think it's me.
　　　　　—Dylan Thomas

Being bored is an insult to oneself.
　　　　　—Jules Renard

When people are bored, it is primarily with their own selves that they are bored. —Jules Renard

If your daily life seems poor, do not blame it; blame yourself, tell yourself that you are not poet enough to call forth its riches.
　　　　　—Rainer Maria Rilke

Life's under no obligation to give us what we expect.
　　　　　—Margaret Mitchell

258

One has to handle these negative experiences alone. You can't get help from your friends or family. You're finally alone with it, and you have to come to grips with misfortune and go on.   —Shirley Temple Black

Expect nothing. Live frugally on surprise.   —Alice Walker

SELF-RELIANCE AND SUCCESS

If you want to succeed, you must make your own opportunities as you go.   —John B. Gough

It is sometimes the man who opens the door who is the last to enter the room.   —Elizabeth Asquith Bibesco

If, after all, men cannot always make history have a meaning, they can always act so that their own lives have one.   —Albert Camus

Every man is the architect of his own fortune.   —Sallust

A wise man will make more opportunities than he finds.   —Francis Bacon

Man is still responsible. . . . His success lies not with the stars, but with himself. He must carry on the fight of self-correction and discipline.   —Frank Curtis Williams

No one can help you in holding a good job except Old Man You.   —Edgar Watson Howe

No man will succeed unless he is ready to face and overcome difficulties and prepared to assume responsibilities.   —William J.H. Boetcker

The brave man carves out his fortune, and every man is the sum of his own works.   —Miguel de Cervantes

Under normal periods, any man's success hinges about 5 percent on what others do for him and 95 percent on what he does.   —James A. Worsham

If a man wants his dreams to come true, he must wake up.   —Anon.

Pa, he always said a man had to look spry for himself, because nobody would do it for him; your opportunities didn't come knocking around, you had to hunt them down and hogtie them.   —Louis L'Amour

Destiny is not a matter of chance, it is a matter of choice; it is not a thing to be waited for, it is a thing to be achieved.   —William Jennings Bryan

Men at some time are masters of their fates.   —William Shakespeare

The people who get on in this world are the people who get up and look for the circumstances they want, and, if they can't find them, make them.   —George Bernard Shaw

ACCEPTING RESPONSIBILITY FOR OUR ERRORS AND MISTAKES

Mistakes fail in their mission of helping the person who blames them on the other fellow.   —Henry S. Haskins

We have not passed that subtle line between childhood and adulthood until . . . we have stopped saying "It got lost," and say "I lost it."   —Sydney J. Harris

Do not blame anybody for your mistakes and failures.
—Bernard M. Baruch

The day you take complete responsibility for yourself, the day you stop making excuses, that's the day you start your move to the top.
—O.J. Simpson

It is a painful thing to look at your own trouble and know that you yourself, and no one else, has made it.
—Sophocles

When you blame others, you give up your power to change. —Anon.

Take your life in your own hands, and what happens? A terrible thing: no one to blame. —Erica Jong

What fate can be worse than to know we have no one but ourselves to blame for our misfortunes!
—Sophocles

Fair play with others is primarily not blaming them for anything that is wrong with us. —Eric Hoffer

How we love to blame others for our misfortunes! Almost every individual who has lost money in stock speculation has on the tip of his tongue an explanation which he trots out to show that it wasn't his own fault at all. ... Hardly one loser has the manliness to say frankly, "I was wrong."
—B.C. Forbes

Man must cease attributing his problems to his environment and learn again to exercise ... his personal responsibility in the realm of faith and morals. —Albert Schweitzer

The greatest griefs are those we cause ourselves. —Sophocles

The fault, dear Brutus, is not in our stars, but in ourselves.
—William Shakespeare

A chief is a man who assumes responsibility. He does not say, "My men were beaten," he says, "I was beaten." —Antoine de Saint-Exupery

Debt is a trap which man sets and baits himself, and then deliberately gets into. —Josh Billings

WE SHOULD RELY ON GOD ... UP TO A POINT

God helps those who help themselves. —German proverb

I feel no need for any other faith than my faith in human beings.
—Pearl S. Buck

It is vain to ask of the gods what man is capable of supplying for himself.
—Epicurus

The gods help those who help themselves. —Marcus Terentius Varro

Ask God's blessing on your work, but don't ask him to do it for you.
—Dame Flora Robson

He who prays and labours lifts his heart to God with his hands.
—Saint Bernard

God gives every bird its food, but he does not throw it into the nest.
—Josiah G. Holland

God gives the nuts, but he does not crack them.   —German proverb

Trust in Allah, but tie your camel first.   —Arab proverb

Put your trust in God, my boys, and keep your powder dry!
          —Valentine Blacker

God loves to help him who strives to help himself.   —Aeschylus

Religious faith, indeed, relates to that which is above us, but it must arise from that which is within us.
          —Josiah Royce

Even God lends a hand to honest boldness.   —Menander

Help yourself and heaven will help you.   —Jean de La Fontaine

God has entrusted me with myself.
          —Epictetus

The Ancient Mariner said to Neptune during a great storm, "O God, you will save me if you wish, but I am going to go on holding my tiller straight."   —Michel de Montaigne

If your ship doesn't come in, swim out to it.   —Jonathan Winters

To character and success, two things, contradictory as they may seem, must go together—humble dependence and manly independence; humble dependence on God and manly reliance on self.
          —William Wordsworth

I am a moonbeam, free to go whenever I choose.   —Marina Tsvetaeva

GENERAL QUOTATIONS ABOUT SELF-RELIANCE

My will shall shape my future. Whether I fail or succeed shall be no man's doing but my own. I am the force; I can clear any obstacle before me or I can be lost in the maze. My choice, my responsibility; win or lose, only I hold the key to my destiny.
          —Elaine Maxwell

I had never been as resigned to ready-made ideas as I was to ready-made clothes, perhaps because although I couldn't sew, I could think.
          —Jane Rule

Self-reliance is the only road to true freedom, and being one's own person is its ultimate reward.
          —Patricia Sampson

The basic freedom of the world is woman's freedom. —Margaret Sanger

Never grow a wishbone, daughter, where your backbone ought to be.
          —Clementine Paddleford

You are the handicap you must face. You are the one who must choose your place.   —James Lane Allen

The best and most efficient pharmacy is within your own system.
          —Robert C. Peale, M.D.

I am the master of my fate; I am the captain of my soul.
          —William E. Henley

Champions take responsibility. When the ball is coming over the net, you can be sure I want the ball.
          —Billie Jean King

Simplicity

The Importance of Keeping Things Simple

A speech does not need to be eternal to be immortal. —Muriel Humphrey

Simplicity is the ultimate sophistication.   —Leonardo da Vinci

To be simple is to be great.
          —Ralph Waldo Emerson

It helped me in the air to keep my small mind contained in earthly human limits, not lost in vertiginous space and elements unknown.
          —Diana Cooper

A man must be able to cut a knot, for everything cannot be untied; he must know how to disengage what is essential from the detail in which it is enwrapped, for everything cannot be equally considered; in a word, he must be able to simplify his duties, his business and his life.
          —Henri Frederic Amiel

Simplicity is an exact medium between too little and too much.
          —Sir Joshua Reynolds

Simplicity and naturalness are the truest marks of distinction.
          —W. Somerset Maugham

The trouble about man is twofold. He cannot learn truths which are too complicated; he forgets truths which are too simple.
          —Dame Rebecca West

Everything should be made as simple as possible . . . but not simpler.
          —Albert Einstein

To be simple is the best thing in the world.   —G.K. Chesterton

Simplicity and Living

If we live, we live; if we die, we die; if we suffer, we suffer; if we are terrified, we are terrified. There is no problem about it.   —Alan Watts

I have a simple philosophy. Fill what's empty. Empty what's full. And scratch where it itches.
          —Alice Roosevelt Longworth

Keep breathing.   —Sophie Tucker

I go about looking at horses and cattle. They eat grass, make love, work
when they have to, bear their young.
I am sick with envy of them.
—Sherwood Anderson

What you do not want done to yourself, do not do to others. —Confucius

I know only that what is moral is
what you feel good after and what is
immoral is what you feel bad after.
—Ernest Hemingway

My formula for living is quite simple.
I get up in the morning and I go to
bed at night. In between I occupy
myself as best I can.   —Cary Grant

Keep doing what you're doing and
you'll keep getting what you're getting.
—Anon.

Life is one long struggle to disinter
oneself, to keep one's head above the
accumulations, the ever deepening
layers of objects . . . which attempt to
cover one over, steadily, almost irresistibly, like falling snow.
—Rose Macaulay

Is nothing in life ever straight and
clear, the way children see it?
—Rosie Thomas

There is no cure for birth or death
save to enjoy the interval.
—George Santayana

We cannot solve life's problems
except by solving them.
—M. Scott Peck

Eat when you're hungry. Drink when
you're thirsty. Sleep when you're tired.
—Buddhist proverb

I believe that a simple and unassum-
ing manner of life is best for everyone, best both for the body and the
mind.   —Albert Einstein

If it's working, keep doing it.
If it's not working, stop doing it.
If you don't know what to do, don't
do anything.
—Dr. Melvin Konner

If you don't like something about
yourself, change it. If you can't
change it, accept it.
—Ted Shackelford

The great business of life is to be, to
do, to do without, and to depart.
—John, Viscount Morley
of Blackburn

There is only one meaning of life, the
act of living itself.   —Erich Fromm

I have a simple philosophy. Fill
what's empty. Empty what's full.
Scratch where it itches.
—Alice Roosevelt Longworth

Simplicity is making the journey of
this life with just baggage enough.
—Anon.

The boy and girl going hand in hand
through a meadow; the mother washing her baby; the sweet simple things
in life. We have almost lost track of
them. On the one side, we overintel-
lectualize everything; on the other
hand, we are over-mechanized. We
can understand the danger of the
atomic bomb, but the danger of our
misunderstanding the meaning of life
is much more serious.
—Edward Steichen

Fear less, hope more; eat less, chew
more; whine less, breathe more; talk
less, say more; love more, and all
good things will be yours.
                    —Swedish proverb

I take a simple view of living.
It is, keep your eyes open and
get on with it.   —Sir Laurence Olivier

Love, and do what you like.
                    —Saint Augustine

Reduce the complexity of life by
eliminating the needless wants of life,
and the labors of life reduce themselves.   —Edwin Way Teale

Manifest plainness, Embrace
simplicity, Reduce selfishness,
Have few desires.   —Lao-tzu

Simplicity, clarity, singleness: these
are the attributes that give our lives
power and vividness and joy.
                    —Richard Halloway

I searched through rebellion, drugs,
diet, mysticism, religion, intellectualism and much more, only to find that
truth is basically simple and feels
good, clear and right. —Chick Corea

If you walk, just walk. If you sit,
just sit. But whatever you do, don't
wobble.   —Anon.

To keep a lamp burning, we have to
keep putting oil in it.
                    —Mother Teresa

If a Plant's Roots Are Too Tight,
Repot.   —Gardening headline,
              The New York Times

WE COMPLICATE LIFE

Fame is a pearl many dive for and
only a few bring up. Even when they
do, it is not perfect, and they sigh for
more, and lose better things in struggling for them.   —Louisa May Alcott

Life is not complex. We are complex.
Life is simple, and the simple thing is
the right thing.   —Oscar Wilde

God made man simple, but how he
changed and got complicated is hard
to say.   —Johann von Goethe

Making the simple complicated is
commonplace; making the complicated simple, awesomely simple, that's
creativity.   —Charles Mingus

The man of fixed ingrained principles who has mapped out a straight
course, and has the courage and self-
control to adhere to it, does not find
life complex. Complexities are all of
our own making.   —B.C. Forbes

The whole is simpler than the sum of
its parts.   —Willard Gibbs

The course of every intellectual, if
he pursues his journey long and unflinchingly enough, ends in the obvious, from which the non-intellectuals
have never stirred.   —Aldous Huxley

Any intelligent fool can make things
bigger, more complex, and more violent. It takes a touch of genius—and
a lot of courage—to move in the
opposite direction.
                    —E.F. Schumacher

At times almost all of us envy the animals. They suffer and die, but do not seem to make a "problem" of it.
—Alan Watts

First Things First

First say to yourself what you would be, and then do what you have to do.
—Epictetus

Do what you can, with what you have, where you are.
—Theodore Roosevelt

Do the duty which lies nearest thee. . . . Thy second duty will already have become clearer.
—Thomas Carlyle

Start by doing what's necessary, then what's possible and suddenly you are doing the impossible.
—Saint Francis of Assisi

When you see a rattlesnake poised to strike, you do not wait until he has struck before you crush him.
—Franklin Delano Roosevelt

If a madman were to come into this room with a stick in his hand, no doubt we should pity the state of his mind; but our primary consideration would be to take care of ourselves. We should knock him down first, and pity him afterwards.
—Samuel Johnson

You decide what it is you want to accomplish and then you lay out your plans to get there, and then you just do it. It's pretty straightforward.
—Nancy Ditz

There is a point at which everything becomes simple and there is no longer any question of choice, because all you have staked will be lost if you look back. Life's point of no return.
—Dag Hammarskjold

Eliminating Non-Essentials

The ability to simplify means to eliminate the unnecessary so that the necessary may speak.
—Hans Hofmann

The sculptor produces the beautiful statue by chipping away such parts of the marble block as are not needed— it is a process of elimination.
—Elbert Hubbard

A great man is one who seizes the vital issue in a complex question, what we might call the jugular vein of the whole organism, and spends his energies upon that.
—Joseph Rickaby

The more we reduce the size of our world, the more we shall be its master.
—Jacinto Benavente

Simplicity, simplicity, simplicity! I say, let your affairs be as two or three, and not a hundred or a thousand. . . . Simplify, simplify.
—Henry David Thoreau

There is no greatness where there is not simplicity.   —Leo Tolstoy

The wisdom of life consists in the elimination of nonessentials.
—Lin Yutang

SIMPLICITY AND HAPPINESS

All animals except man know that
the ultimate of life is to enjoy it.
—Samuel Butler

I finally figured out the only reason
to be alive is to enjoy it.
—Rita Mae Brown

Happiness comes of the capacity to
feel deeply, to enjoy simply, to think
freely, to risk life, to be needed.
—Storm Jameson

The main obligation is to amuse
yourself.   —S.J. Perelman

There is no cure for birth or death
save to enjoy the interval.
—George Santayana

SIMPLICITY AND SUCCESS

Success is simple. Do what's right, the
right way, at the right time.
—Arnold Glasow

There is a master key to success with
which no man can fail. Its name is
simplicity . . . reducing to the simplest
possible terms every problem.
—Henri Deterding

If you want to be found, stand where
the seeker seeks.   —Sidney Lanier

Many things are lost for want of
asking.   —English proverb

Economy, prudence, and a simple life
are the sure masters of need, and will
often accomplish that which their
opposites, with a fortune at hand,
will fail to do.   —Clara Barton

Wealth consists not in having great
possessions but in having few wants.
—Esther de Waal

If you aren't going all the way, why
go at all?   —Joe Namath

What I do, I do very well, and what I
don't do well, I don't do at all.
—Anon.

SIMPLICITY IN SPORTS

Players have two things to do: Play
and keep their mouths shut.
—Sparky Anderson

Hitting is timing. Pitching is upsetting
timing.   —Warren Spahn

All I had to do was keep turning left.
—George Robson,
after winning the Indianapolis 500

The rules of soccer are very simple.
Basically it's this: If it moves, kick it; if
it doesn't move, kick it until it does.
—Phil Woosnam

You've got a lot of cute stuff. But son,
there's only one thing we're looking
for, and that's a pitcher who can tear
the catcher's head off with a fastball.
You get one of those, come on back.
—Baseball scout,
quoted by Tom Wolfe

If you don't throw it, they can't hit it.
—Lefty Gomez

Football is blocking and tackling.
Everything else is mythology.
—Vince Lombardi

It's a round ball and a round bat, and you got to hit it square.   —Pete Rose

There are only five things you can do in baseball: run, throw, catch, hit, and hit with power.   —Leo Durocher

Losers have tons of variety. Champions take pride in just learning to hit the same old boring winners.
—Vic Braden

The way you get better at playing football is to play football.
—Gene Brodie

I just take my three swings and go sit on the bench. I don't ever want to mess up my swing.   —Dick Allen

SIMPLICITY IN ACTING

Just learn your lines and don't bump into the furniture.   —Spencer Tracy

My advice about acting? Speak clearly, don't bump into people, and if you must have motivation, think of your pay packet on Friday.
—Noel Coward

Just sit out there and have them go through the moves. When you see something you don't like, change it.
—Joshua Logan's
advice to directors

Don't let go of the vine.
—John Weissmuller,
who played Tarzan,
giving advice to acting students

Stay out of jail. —Alfred Hitchcock's
advice to directors

SIMPLICITY AND WARFARE

Putting aside all the fancy words and academic doubletalk, the basic reason for having a military is to do two jobs—to kill people and to destroy the works of man.
—Thomas S. Power

The first law of war is to preserve ourselves and destroy the enemy.
—Mao Tse-Tung

In combat, life is short, nasty and brutish. The issues of national policy which brought him into war are irrelevant to the combat soldier; he is concerned with his literal life chances.
—Charles E. Moskos, Jr.

You don't hurt 'em if you don't hit 'em.
—General Lewis "Chesty" Puller

There is nothing certain about war except that one side won't win.
—Sir Ian Hamilton

I can always make it a rule to get there first with the most men.
—Nathan Bedford Forrest

The object of war is not to die for your country, but to make the other bastard die for his.
—General George S. Patton

The object of war is to survive it.
—John Irving

SIMPLICITY AND WRITING

When ideas come, I write them; when they don't come, I don't.
—William Faulkner

267

The idea is to get the pencil moving quickly. —Bernard Malamud

I never thought of myself as a writer, but the simplest thing seemed to be to put a piece of paper in the roller and start typing. —Cynthia Friedman

The niftiest turn of phrase, the most elegant flight of rhetorical fancy, isn't worth beans next to a clear thought clearly expressed. —Jeff Greenfield

Get black on white.
    —Guy de Maupassant

Art, it seems to me, should simplify.
    —Willa Cather

It's a simple formula; do your best and somebody might like it.
    —Dorothy Baker

Simplicity, carried to an extreme, becomes elegance. —Jon Franklin

THE SIMPLEST IDEAS AND SAYINGS ARE OFTEN THE BEST AND MOST PROFOUND

All the great things are simple, and many can be expressed in a single word: freedom; justice; honor; duty; mercy; hope. —Sir Winston Churchill

It is the essence of genius to make use of the simplest ideas.
    —Charles Peguy

Genius is the ability to reduce the complicated to the simple.
    —C.W. Ceram

The simplest things give me ideas.
    —Joan Miro

If you can't write your idea on the back of my calling card, you don't have a clear idea. —David Belasco

It is proof of high culture to say the greatest matters in the simplest way.
    —Ralph Waldo Emerson

The art of art, the glory of expression and the sunshine of the light of letters is simplicity: nothing is better than simplicity. —Walt Whitman

True eloquence consists of saying all that should be said, and that only.
    —Francois de La Rochefoucauld

Simplicity of character is no hindrance to subtlety of intellect.
    —John Morley

Simplicity of character is the natural result of profound thought.
    —William Hazlitt

The obvious is that which is never seen until someone expresses it simply. —Kahlil Gibran

Simple style is like white light. It is complex, but its complexity is not obvious. —Anatole France

When an idea is too weak to support a simple statement, it is a sign that it should be rejected. —Vauvenargues

When thought is too weak to be simply expressed, it's clear proof that it should be rejected. —Luc de Claplers

The great artist and thinker are the simplifiers. —Henri Frederic Amiel

Simple truths are a relief from grand speculations. —Vauvenargues

PART 2

Living One Day at a Time

One Day

It's Impossible to Overstate the Value of One Day

No one can confidently say that he will still be living tomorrow.
—Euripides

Youth troubles over eternity, age grasps at a day and is satisfied to have even the day.
—Dame Mary Gilmore

Nothing is worth more than this day.
—Johann von Goethe

I have come to understand that every day is something to cherish.
—Kerri Strug

What a folly to dread the thought of throwing away life at once, and yet have no regard to throwing it away by parcels and piecemeal.
—John Howe

Not a day passes over this earth but men and women of note do great deeds, speak great words and suffer noble sorrows.
—Charles Reed

We create our fate every day we live.
—Henry Miller

Who loses a day loses life.
—Ralph Waldo Emerson

May you live all the days of your life.
—Jonathan Swift

If we only knew the real value of a day.
—Joseph Farrell

We are involved in a life that passes understanding: our highest business is our daily life.
—John Cage

We die daily. Happy those who daily come to life as well.
—George MacDonald

He who has lived a day has lived an age.
—Jean de La Bruyère

Life, we learn too late, is in the living, in the tissue of every day and hour.
—Stephen Leacock

To sensible men, every day is a day of reckoning.
—John W. Gardner

270

A day's impact is better than a month of dead pull.

—Oliver Wendell Holmes

They deem me mad because I will not sell my days for gold; and I deem them mad because they think my days have a price.　—Kahlil Gibran

The proper function of man is to live, not to exist. I shall not waste my days in trying to prolong them.

—Jack London

A day, an hour, of virtuous liberty is worth a whole eternity in bondage.

—Joseph Addison

Live mindful of how brief your life is.

—Horace

Gladly accept the gifts of the present hour.　　　　　　　　—Horace

There is but a step between me and death.　　　　　　—1 Samuel 20:3

Everyone once, once only. Just once and no more. And we also once. Never again.　—Rainer Maria Rilke

Most of us spend our lives as if we had another one in the bank.

—Ben Irwin

It's better to be a lion for a day than a sheep all your life.

—Sister Elizabeth Kenny

While we live, let us live.

—D.H. Lawrence

No objects of value . . . are worth risking the priceless experience of waking up one more day.

—Jack Smith

Every possession and every happiness is but lent by chance for an uncertain time, and may therefore be demanded back the next hour.

—Arthur Schopenhauer

Some days you tame the tiger. And some days the tiger has you for lunch.　　　　　—Tug McGraw

So teach us to number our days, that we may apply our hearts unto wisdom.　　　　—Psalms 90:12

You have got to own your days and live them, each one of them, every one of them, or else the years go right by and none of them belong to you.

—Herb Gardner

The ideal never comes. Today is ideal for him who makes it so.

—Horatio W. Dresser

True wisdom lies in gathering the precious things out of each day as it goes by.　　　　—E.S. Bouton

The most important thing in our lives is what we are doing now.　—Anon.

Write it on your heart that every day is the best day in the year.

—Ralph Waldo Emerson

He possesses dominion over himself, and is happy, who can every day say, "I have lived." Tomorrow the heavenly Father may either involve the world in dark clouds, or cheer it with clear sunshine; he will not, however, render ineffectual the things which have already taken place.　—Horace

Each day, each hour, an entire life.

—Juan Ramon Jimenel

The days come and go like muffled and veiled figures sent from a distant friendly party, but they say nothing, and if we do not use the gifts they bring, they carry them as silently away.　　　—Ralph Waldo Emerson

Your daily life is your temple and your religion.　　　—Kahlil Gibran

He is only rich who owns the day. There is no king, rich man, fairy, or demon who possesses such power as that.　　　—Ralph Waldo Emerson

Life is now . . . this day, this hour . . . and is probably the only experience of the kind one is to have.
　　　—Charles Macomb Flandrau

Gather ye rose-buds while ye may,
Old time is still a-flying.
And this same flower that smiles today,
Tomorrow will be dying.
　　　—Robert Herrick

Seize the hour.　　　—Sophocles

The Value of Time

Time, like money, is measured by our needs.　　　—George Eliot

Nothing is ours except time.
　　　—Marcus Annaeus Seneca

Nothing in business is so valuable as time.　　　—John H. Patterson

Many people take no care of their money till they come nearly to the end of it, and others do just the same with their time.
　　　—Johann von Goethe

Possessions dwindle: I mourn their loss. But I mourn the loss of time much more, for anyone can save his purse, but none can win back lost time.　　　—Latin proverb

Riches are chiefly good because they give us time.　　　—Charles Lamb

One realizes the full importance of time only when there is little of it left. Every man's greatest capital asset is his unexpired years of productive life.
　　　—Paul W. Litchfield

Know the true value of time; snatch, seize, and enjoy every moment of it. No idleness, no laziness, no procrastination: never put off till tomorrow what you can do today.
　　　—Lord Chesterfield

A sense of the value of time . . . is an essential preliminary to efficient work; it is the only method of avoiding hurry.　　　—Arnold Bennett

All my possessions for a moment of time.　　　—Queen Elizabeth I

Let me tell thee, time is a very precious gift of God; so precious that it's only given to us moment by moment.
　　　—Amelia Barr

Pick my left pocket of its silver dime, but spare the right—it holds my golden time!
　　　—Oliver Wendell Holmes

We work not only to produce, but to give value to time.
　　　—Eugene Delacroix

Dollars cannot buy yesterday.
　　　—Admiral Harold R. Stark

As every thread of gold is valuable,
so is every moment of time.
—John Mason

Minutes are worth more than money.
Spend them wisely.
—Thomas P. Murphy

Time is the coin of your life. It is the
only coin you have, and only you can
determine how it will be spent. Be
careful lest you let other people spend
it for you.   —Carl Sandburg

Every minute of life carries with it its
miraculous value, and its face of eternal youth.   —Albert Camus

Lost time is never found again.
—Benjamin Franklin

If a person gives you his time, he can
give you no more precious gift.
—Frank Tyger

You may ask me for anything you
like except time.
—Napoleon Bonaparte

The laboring man and the artificer
knows what every hour of his time is
worth, and parts not with it but for
the full value.   —Lord Clarendon

Time isn't a commodity, something
you pass around like cake. Time is
the substance of life. When anyone
asks you to give your time, they're
really asking for a chunk of your life.
—Antoinette Bosco

Love and time—those are the only
two things in all the world and all of
life that cannot be bought, but only
spent.   —Gary Jennings

There is nothing good in this world
which time does not improve.
—Alexander Smith

Time is the most valuable thing a
man can spend.   —Laertius Diogenes

The great rule of moral conduct is,
next to God, to respect Time.
—Johann Kaspar Lavater

It is the time you have wasted for
your rose that makes your rose so
important.
—Antoine de Saint-Exupery

One hour of life, crowded to the full
with glorious action and filled with
noble risks, is worth whole years of
those mean observances of paltry
decorum.   —Sir Walter Scott

Don't be fooled by the calendar.
There are only as many days in the
year as you make use of. One man
gets only a week's value out of a year
while another man gets a full year's
value out of a week.
—Charles Richards

Our costliest expenditure is time.
—Theophrastus

THE IMPORTANCE OF
USING TIME WELL

How pleasant it is, at the end of the
      day,
No follies to have to repent;
But reflect on the past, and be able
      to say,
That my time has been properly
      spent.   —Ann Taylor

273

I must govern the clock, not be governed by it. —Golda Meir

You are no more exempt from time's inexorable passing than Macbeth. Whether time is your friend or foe depends on how you use it —Patricia Fripp

Millions long for immortality who do not know what to do with themselves on a rainy Sunday afternoon. —Susan Ertz

The organized person . . . makes the most of his time and goes to his bed for the night perfectly relaxed for rest and renewal. —George Matthew Adams

Have regular hours for work and play; make each day both useful and pleasant, and prove that you understand the worth of time by employing it well. Then youth will be delightful, old age will bring few regrets, and life will become a beautiful success. —Louisa May Alcott

He who every morning plans the transactions of the day and follows out that plan carries a thread that will guide him through the labyrinth of the most busy life. . . . If the disposal of time is surrendered merely to the chance of incident, chaos will soon reign. —Victor Hugo

Have a time and place for everything, and do everything in its time and place, and you will not only accomplish more, but have far more leisure than those who are always hurrying. —Tyron Edwards

It is not how many years we live, but rather what we do with them. —Evangeline Cory Booth

During a very busy life I have often been asked, "How did you manage to it all?" The answer is very simple: it is because I did everything promptly. —Sir Richard Tangye

Time cannot be expanded, accumulated, mortgaged, hastened, or retarded. —Anon.

Seize time by the forelock. —Pittacus

Time is a tyranny to be abolished. —Eugene Jolus

The time which we have at our disposal every day is elastic; the passions that we feel expand it, those that we inspire contract it; and habit fills up the rest. —Marcel Proust

The ability to concentrate and to use time well is everything. —Lee Iacocca

Time is an equal opportunity employer. Each human being has exactly the same number of hours and minutes every day. Rich people can't buy more hours. Scientists can't invent new minutes. And you can't save time to spend it on another day. Even so, time is amazingly fair and forgiving. No matter how much time you've wasted in the past, you still have an entire tomorrow. Success depends upon using it wisely—by planning and setting priorities. —Denis Waitely

An Italian philosopher said that "time was his estate"; an estate indeed which will produce nothing without cultivation, but will always abundantly repay the labors of industry, and generally satisfy the most extensive desires, if no part of it be suffered to lie in waste by negligence, to be overrun with noxious plants, or laid out for show rather than for use.
—Samuel Johnson

Timely service, like timely gifts, is doubled in value.
—George MacDonald

Time is the one thing that can never be retrieved.   —C.R. Lawton

We must use time as a tool, not as a crutch.   —John F. Kennedy

Make use of time, let not advantage slip.   —William Shakespeare

O, for an engine to keep back all clocks!   —Ben Johnson

You may delay, but time will not.
—Benjamin Franklin

He who would make serious use of his life must always act as though he had a long time to live and schedule his time as though he were about to die.   —Emile Littre

The highest value in life is found in the stewardship of time.
—Robert M. Fine

WASTING TIME

A stale mind is the devil's breadbox.
—Mary Bly

I wish I could stand on a busy corner, hat in hand, and beg people to throw me all their wasted hours.
—Bernard Berenson

Every day I live I am more convinced that the waste of life lies in the love we have not given, the powers we have not used, the selfish prudence that will risk nothing and which, shirking pain, misses happiness as well.   —Mary Cholmondeley

Wasted time means wasted lives.
—R. Shannon

Regret for time wasted can become a power for good in the time that remains, if we will only stop the waste and the idle, useless regretting.
—Arthur Brisbane

Economy is the thief of time.
—Ethel Watts Mumford

I wasted time, and now doth time waste me.   —William Shakespeare

All that time is lost which might be better employed.
—Jean-Jacques Rousseau

Lost, yesterday, somewhere between sunrise and sunset, two golden hours, each set with sixty diamond minutes. No reward is offered, for they are gone forever.   —Horace Mann

Thrift of time will repay you in afterlife, with a usury of profit beyond your most sanguine dreams; waste of it will make you dwindle, alike in intellectual and moral stature, beyond your darkest reckoning.
—William Gladstone

The clock upbraids me with the
waste of time.
                —William Shakespeare

Time is lost when we have not lived
a full human life, time unenriched by
experience, creative endeavor, enjoyment, and suffering.
                —Dietrich Bonhoeffer

Still on it creeps,
Each little moment at another's heels,
Till hours, days, years, and ages are
    made up
Of such small parts as these, and men
    look back
Worn and bewilder'd, wondering
    how it is.
                —Joanna Baillie

Does't thou love life? Then do not
squander time, for that is the stuff
life is made of.   —Benjamin Franklin

Time wasted is a theft from God.
                —Henri Frederic Amiel

Lost time is like a run in a stocking.
It always gets worse.
                —Anne Morrow Lindbergh

As if you could kill time without
injuring eternity.
                —Henry David Thoreau

Killing time is the chief end of our
society.   —Ugo Betti

You can kill time or kill yourself, it
comes to the same thing in the end.
                —Elsa Triolet

No person will have occasion to complain of the want of time who never
loses any.   —Thomas Jefferson

Time is that which man is always trying to kill, but which ends in killing
him.   —Herbert Spencer

Do not wait for leaders; do it alone,
person to person.   —Mother Teresa

Men talk of killing time, while time
quietly kills them.
                —Dion Boucicault

Modern man thinks he loses something—time—when he does not do
things quickly. Yet he does not know
what to do with the time he gains—
except kill it.   —Erich Fromm

If you want to kill time, try working
it to death.   —Sam Levenson

A man who dares to waste one hour
of life has not discovered the value of
life.   —Charles Darwin

If time be of all things most precious,
wasting time must be the greatest
prodigality, since lost time is never
found again.   —Benjamin Franklin

Don't agonize. Organize.
                —Florynce Kennedy

THERE'S NEVER ENOUGH TIME

Curse ruthless time! Curse our mortality. How cruelly short is the allotted span for all we must cram into it!
                —Sir Winston Churchill

Death and taxes and childbirth!
There's never any convenient time for
any of them!   —Margaret Mitchell

There is a time for work. And a time for love. That leaves no other time.
—Coco Chanel

You will never "find" time for anything. If you want time you must make it.
—Charles Buxton

We have as much time as we need.
—Melody Beattie

Ah! the clock is always slow; it is later than you think.
—Robert W. Service

The forty-four-hour week has no charm for me. I'm looking for a forty-hour day.
—Nicholas Murray Butler

Those who make the worst use of their time most complain of its brevity.
—Jean de La Bruyère

I still find each day too short for all the thoughts I want to think, all the walks I want to take, all the books I want to read, and all the friends I want to see.
—John Burroughs

HAVING ENOUGH TIME

What we love to do we find time to do.
—John Lancaster Spalding

Time stays long enough for anyone who will use it.
—Anon.

There is time for everything.
—Thomas A. Edison

It is nonsense to say there is not enough time to be fully informed. . . . Time given to thought is the greatest timesaver of all.
—Norman Cousins

We all find time to do what we really want to do.
—William Feather

Time is a fixed income and, as with any income, the real problem facing most of us is how to live successfully within our daily allotment.
—Margaret B. Johnstone

We shall never have more time. We have, and have always had, all the time there is. No object is served in waiting until next week or even until to-morrow. Keep going. . . . Concentrate on something useful.
—Arnold Bennett

There is time enough for everything in the course of the day if you do but one thing at once; but there is not time enough in the year if you will do two things at a time.
—Lord Chesterfield

USING SMALL PIECES OF TIME

Much may be done in those little shreds and patches of time which every day produces, and which most men throw away.
—Charles Caleb Colton

Learn to use ten minutes intelligently. It will pay you huge dividends.
—William A. Irwin

It is better to do the most trifling thing in the world than to regard half an hour as trifle.
—Johann von Goethe

I recommend you to take care of the minutes, for the hours will take care of themselves.
—Lord Chesterfield

The real secret of how to use time is to pack it as you would a portmanteau, filling up the small spaces with small things.   —Sir Henry Haddow

One must learn a different . . . sense of time, one that depends more on small amounts than big ones.
—Sister Mary Paul

An earnest purpose finds time, or makes it. It seizes on spare moments, and turns fragments to golden account.   —William Ellery Channing

Guard well your spare moments. They are like uncut diamonds. Discard them and their value will never be known. Improve them and they will become the brightest gems in a useful life.
—Ralph Waldo Emerson

The butterfly counts not months but moments, and has time enough.
—Rabindranath Tagore

LIVING ONE DAY AT A TIME IS A KEY TO HAPPINESS

That man is happiest who lives from day to day and asks no more, garnering the simple goodness of life.
—Euripides

It is only possible to live happily-ever-after on a day-to-day basis.
—Margaret Bonnano

Happiness is produced not so much by great pieces of good fortune that seldom happen, as by little advantages that occur every day.
—Benjamin Franklin

All the great blessings of my life are present in my thoughts today.
—Phoebe Cary

The best way to secure future happiness is to be as happy as is rightfully possible today.   —Charles W. Eliot

A fool bolts pleasure, then complains of indigestion.   —Minna Antrim

Happiness is to be found along the way, not at the end of the road, for then the journey is over and it is too late. Today, this hour, this minute is the day, the hour, the minute for each of us to sense the fact that life is good, with all of its trials and troubles, and perhaps more interesting because of them.
—Robert R. Updegraff

Each day provides its own gifts.
—Martial

Let us savour the swift delights of the most beautiful of our days!
—Alphonse de Lamartine

Death accompanies us at every step and enables us to use those moments when life smiles at us to feel more deeply the sweetness of life. The more certain the end, the more tempting the minute.   —Theodore Fontane

Happiness is not a state to arrive at, but a manner of traveling.
—Margaret Lee Runbeck

My advice to you is not to inquire why or whither, but just to enjoy your ice cream while it's on your plate.
—Thornton Wilder

Those who face that which is actually before them, unburdened by the past, undistracted by the future, these are they who live, who make the best use of their lives; these are those who have found the secret of contentment.
—Alban Goodier

And that was victory. The freedom to sprawl loosely upon a city street, heat his coffee and eat a can of beans . . . with no enemy bullets forcing him to toss the can aside while diving behind another wall for momentary survival.
—David Douglas Duncan

Taking time to live is taking time to appreciate simple silence as better than any kind of talk, or watching a flower, or watching a guy wash the windows on a skyscraper and wondering what he is thinking.
—Gersi Douchan

If you observe a really happy man, you will find . . . that he is happy in the course of living life twenty-four crowded hours each day.
—W. Beran Wolfe

To fill the hour, that is happiness; to fill the hour, and leave no crevice for a repentance or an approval.
—Ralph Waldo Emerson

Live your life each day as you would climb a mountain. An occasional glance toward the summit keeps the goal in mind, but many beautiful scenes are to be observed from each new vantage point. Climb slowly, steadily, enjoying each passing moment; and the view from the summit will serve as a fitting climax for the journey.   —Harold B. Melchart

One day of pleasure is worth two of sorrow.   —Anon.

Present joys are more to flesh and blood
Than the dull prospect of a distant good.   —John Dryden

In order to be utterly happy the only thing necessary is to refrain from comparing this moment with other moments in the past, which I often did not fully enjoy because I was comparing them with other moments of the future.   —André Gide

Live in day-tight compartments.
—Dale Carnegie

If you are not happy here and now, you never will be.
—Taisen Deshimaru

People who postpone happiness are like children who try chasing rainbows in an effort to find the pot of gold at the rainbow's end. . . . Your life will never be fulfilled until you are happy here and now.
—Ken Keyes, Jr.

He's one of those Christmas Eve guys. There are people like that . . . every day in their lives is Christmas Eve.
—Joe Garagiola,
talking about Yogi Berri

Learn to drink the cup of life as it comes.   —Agnes Turnbull

SOME BASIC THINGS
TO DO EACH DAY

Every day give yourself a good mental shampoo.   —Sara Jordan, M.D.

There is no other solution to man's progress but the day's honest work, the day's honest decisions, the day's generous utterances and the day's good deed.   —Clare Boothe Luce

Leisure for reverie, gay or somber, does much to enrich life.
    —Miriam Beard

A man should hear a little music, read a little poetry, and see a fine picture every day of his life, in order that worldly cares may not obliterate the sense of the beautiful which God has implanted in the human soul.
    —Johann von Goethe

You have to set new goals every day.
    —Julie Krone

I have resolved that from this day on, I will do all the business I can honestly, have all the fun I can reasonably, do all the good I can willingly, and save my digestion by thinking pleasantly.   —Robert Louis Stevenson

Make the most of today. Translate your good intentions into actual deeds.   —Grenville Kleiser

Today is the day in which to express your noblest qualities of mind and heart, to do at least one worthy thing which you have long postponed.
    —Grenville Kleiser

Do what you can, with what you have, where you are.
    —Theodore Roosevelt

Our grand business undoubtedly is not to see what lies dimly at a distance but to do what lies clearly at hand.   —Thomas Carlyle

My formula for living is quite simple. I get up in the morning and I go to bed at night. In between I occupy myself as best I can.   —Cary Grant

What you are afraid to do is a clear indicator of the next thing you need to do.   —Anon.

If we cannot meet our everyday surroundings with equanimity and pleasure and grow each day in some useful direction, then . . . life is on the road toward misfortune, misery and destruction.   —Luther Burbank

A day's work is a day's work, neither more nor less, and the man who does it needs a day's sustenance, a night's repose and due leisure, whether he be painter or ploughman.
    —George Bernard Shaw

Add each day something to fortify you against poverty and death.
    —Marcus Annaeus Seneca

It isn't hard to be good from time to time in sports. What's tough is being good every day.   —Willie Mays

Make it a point to do something every day that you don't want to do. This is the golden rule for acquiring the habit of doing your duty without pain.   —Mark Twain

Realize life as an end in itself. Functioning is all there is.
    —Oliver Wendell Holmes, Jr.

He has not learned the first lesson of life who does not every day surmount a fear.   —Ralph Waldo Emerson

A homer a day will boost my pay.
—Josh Gibson

Act well at the moment, and you have performed a good action to all eternity.   —Johann Kaspar Lavater

If I had my life to live over, I would start barefoot earlier in the spring and stay that way later in the fall. I would go to more dances. I would ride more merry-go-rounds. I would pick more daisies.   —Nadine Stair

Nothing determines who we will become so much as those things we choose to ignore.   —Sandor Minab

Love, and do what you like.
—Saint Augustine

Take the time to come home to your-self everyday.   —Robin Casarjean

The power of a man's virtue should not be measured by his special efforts, but by his ordinary doing.
—Blaise Pascal

The great business of life is to be, to do, to do without, and to depart.
—John, Viscount Morley
of Blackburn

Know what you want to do, hold the thought firmly, and do every day what should be done, and every sun-set will see you that much nearer the goal.   —Elbert Hubbard

It is no easy thing for a principle to become a man's own unless each day he maintains it and works it out in his life.   —Epictetus

Follow your bliss. —Joseph Campbell
Resolve to perform what you ought. Perform without fail what you resolve.   —Benjamin Franklin

Resolve to edge in a little reading every day, if it is but a single sen-tence. If you gain fifteen minutes a day, it will make itself felt at the end of the year.   —Horace Mann

I work every day—or at least I force myself into my office or room. I may get nothing done, but you don't earn bonuses without putting in time. Nothing may come for three months, but you don't get the fourth without it.
—Mordecai Richler

Take short views, hope for the best, and trust in God.   —Sydney Smith

Each day can be one of triumph if you keep up your interests.
—George Matthew Adams

If you always do what interests you, at least one person is pleased.
—Katharine Hepburn's mother

When action grows unprofitable, gather information; when informa-tion grows unprofitable, sleep.
—Ursula K. LeGuin

I long to accomplish a great and noble task, but it is my chief duty to accomplish small tasks as if they were great and noble.   —Helen Keller

To do the useful thing, to say the courageous thing, to contemplate the beautiful thing: that is enough for one man's life.   —T.S. Eliot

Showing up is 80 percent of life.
                           —Woody Allen

Do you know that disease and death
must needs overtake us, no matter
what we are doing? ... What do you
wish to be doing when it overtakes
you? If you have anything better to
be doing when you are so overtaken,
get to work on that.   —Epictetus

Have patience with all things, but
chiefly have patience with yourself.
Do not lose courage in considering
your own imperfections, but instantly
set about remedying them—every day
begin the task anew.
             —Saint Francis de Sales

Without duty, life is soft and boneless.   —Joseph Joubert

A man may fulfill the object of his
existence by asking a question he
cannot answer, and attempting a task
he cannot achieve.
             —Oliver Wendell Holmes

And each man stands with his face
in the light of his own drawn sword.
Ready to do what a hero can.
             —Elizabeth Barrett Browning

Be strong!
We are not here to play, to dream, to
    drift;
We have hard work to do and loads
    to lift;
Shun not the struggle—face it; 'tis
    God's gift.
             —Maltbie D. Babcock

Man goeth forth unto his work and
to his labor until the evening.
             —Psalms 104:23

Every day give yourself a good mental shampoo.   —Sara Jordan, M.D.

To look up and not down,
To look forward and not back,
To look out and not in, and
To lend a hand.
             —Edward Everett Hale

Do all the good you can,
By all the means you can,
In all the ways you can,
In all the places you can,
At all the times you can.

                           —Anon.

I like the man who faces what he
    must,
With steps triumphant and a heart of
    cheer;
Who fights the daily battle without
    fear.
             —Sarah Knowles Bolton

To accomplish our destiny ... [w]e
must cover before nightfall the distance assigned to each of us.
             —Dr. Alexis Carrel

Fulfill your works, your daily tasks.
             —Exodus 5:13

Man goeth forth unto his work and
to his labor until the evening.
             —Psalms 104:23

LIVING EACH DAY AS THOUGH IT WERE OUR LAST

Each day should be passed as though
it were our last.   —Publilius Syrus

Learn as if you were going to live forever. Live as if you were going to die
tomorrow.   —Anon.

One should count each day a separate life. —Marcus Annaeus Seneca

If, every day, I dare to remember that I am here on loan, that this house, this hillside, these minutes are all leased to me, not given, I will never despair. —Erica Jong

To live each day as though one's last, never flustered, never apathetic, never attitudinizing—here is perfection of character. —Marcus Aurelius

Look at everything as though you were seeing it for the first time or the last time. Then your time on earth will be filled with glory.
—Betty Smith

The years seem to rush by now, and I think of death as a fast approaching end of a journey—double and treble reason for loving as well as working while it is day. —George Eliot

Study as if you were going to live forever; live as if you were going to die tomorrow. —Maria Mitchell

Every day is a little life . . . live every day as if it would be the last. Those that dare lose a day are dangerously prodigal; those that dare misspend it are desperate. —Joseph Hall

You have to count on living every single day in a way you believe will make you feel good about your life— so that if it were over tomorrow, you'd be content with yourself.
—Jane Seymour

No one can confidently say that he will still be living tomorrow.
—Euripides

Happy the man, and happy he alone
He who can call today his own
He who, secure within, can say
"Tomorrow, do thy worst
For I have lived today."
—Henry Fielding

DOING OUR BEST EVERY DAY

Do your best every day and your life will gradually expand into satisfying fullness. —Horatio W. Dresser

There are only three colors, ten digits, and seven notes; it's what we do with them that's important.
—Ruth Ross

Any man's life will be filled with constant and unexpected encouragement if he makes up his mind to do his level best each day.
—Booker T. Washington

Do each daily task the best we can; act as though the eye of opportunity were always upon us.
—William Feather

What a man accomplishes in a day depends upon the way in which he approaches his tasks. When we accept tough jobs as a challenge to our ability and wade into them with joy and enthusiasm, miracles can happen. —Arland Gilbert

Look at a day when you are supremely satisfied at the end. It's not a day when you lounge around doing nothing; it's when you've had everything to do, and you've done it.
—Margaret Thatcher

So get a few laughs and do the best you can. —Will Rogers

I come to the office each morning and stay for long hours doing what has to be done to the best of my ability. And when you've done the best you can, you can't do any better. So when I go to sleep I turn everything over to the Lord and forget it.
—Harry S. Truman

That man is blest who does his best and leaves the rest. —Charles F. Deems

Do Something for Someone Else, Every Day

When you rise in the morning, form a resolution to make the day a happy one for a fellow creature.
—Sydney Smith

He who allows his day to pass by without practicing generosity and enjoying life's pleasures is like a blacksmith's bellows; he breathes, but does not live. —Sanskrit proverb

You have not lived a perfect day, even though you have earned your money, unless you have done something for someone who will never be able to repay you. —Ruth Smeltzer

Think that day lost whose descending sun, views from thy hand no noble action done. —Joseph Joubert

I expect to pass through life but once. If, therefore, there can be any kindness I can show, or any good thing I can do to any fellow human being, let me do it now. —William Penn

Be ashamed to die until you have won some victory for humanity.
—Horace Mann

Have Some Fun, Some Relaxation, Each Day

The most thoroughly wasted of all days is that on which one has not laughed. —Nicolas de Chamfort

Each day, and the living of it, has to be a conscious creation in which discipline and order are relieved with some play and pure foolishness.
—May Sarton

Sweets are good for the nerves.
—Margarete Bieber

Fat gives things flavor. —Julia Child

Friends, I beg you do not shirk your daily task of indolence.
—Don Marquis

If someone said, "Write a sentence about your life," I'd write, "I want to go outside and play." —Jenna Elfman

We should consider every day lost on which we have not danced at least once. —Friedrich Nietzsche

Life is about enjoying yourself and having a good time. —Cher

Put a little fun into your life. Try dancing. —Kathryn Murray

He who does not get fun and enjoyment out of every day . . . needs to reorganize his life.
—George Matthew Adams

Unless each day can be looked back upon by an individual as one in which he has had some fun, some joy, some real satisfaction, that day is a loss.
—Anon.

Take time every day to do something silly.　　　　　—Philipa Walker

It's fun to get together and have something good to eat at least once a day. That's what human life is all about—enjoying things.
—Julia Child

Come, let us give a little time to folly ...and even in a melancholy day let us find time for an hour of pleasure.
—Saint Bonaventura

No matter what looms ahead, if you can eat today, enjoy the sunlight today, mix good cheer with friends today, enjoy it and bless God for it.
—Henry Ward Beecher

Be Satisfied with a Good Day's Work
There are hundreds of tasks we feel we must accomplish in the day, but if we do not take them one at a time ...we are bound to break our own physical or mental structure.
—Ted Bengermino

A man can do only what he can do. But if he does that each day he can sleep at night and do it again the next day.　　　　—Albert Schweitzer

If I had my life to live over, I would start barefoot earlier in the spring and stay that way later in the fall. I would go to more dances. I would ride more merry-go-rounds. I would pick more daisies.　　—Nadine Stair

I finally figured out the only reason to be alive is to enjoy it.
—Rita Mae Brown

We cannot do everything at once, but we can do something at once.
—Calvin Coolidge

Always do one thing less than you think you can do. —Bernard M. Baruch

I come to the office each morning and stay for long hours doing what has to be done to the best of my ability. And when you've done the best you can, you can't do any better. So when I go to sleep I turn everything over to the Lord and forget it.
—Harry S. Truman

A day's work is a day's work, neither more nor less, and the man who does it needs a day's sustenance, a night's repose and due leisure, whether he be painter or ploughman.
—George Bernard Shaw

Sufficient to each day are the duties to be done and the trials to be endured.　　　　　—T.L. Gayler

I have fought a good fight, I have finished my course, I have kept the faith.
—2 Timothy 4:7

I look back on my life like a good day's work; it is done, and I am satisfied with it.　　—Grandma Moses

GOOD HABITS MAKE OUR
DAILY LIVES EASIER

The moment we pass out of our habits we lose all sense of permanency and routine.　　—George Moore

Manners are a sensitive awareness of the feelings of others. If you have that awareness, you have good manners, no matter what fork you use.
—Emily Post

And hearts have been broken from harsh words spoken
That sorrow can ne'er set right.
—Margaret Elizabeth Sangster

That which is horrifying to you don't do to anybody else.
—Dr. Laura Schlessinger

It is too bad if you have to do everything upon reflection and can't do anything from early habit.
—Georg Christoph Lichtenberg

Most of life is routine—dull and grubby, but routine is the mountain that keeps a man going. If you wait for inspiration you'll be standing on the corner after the parade is a mile down the street.   —Ben Nicholas

Good habits, which bring our lower passions and appetites under automatic control, leave our natures free to explore the larger experiences of life.   —Ralph W. Sockman, D.D.

Without the aid of prejudice and custom, I should not be able to find my way across the room.
—William Hazlitt

Motivation is what gets you started. Habit is what keeps you going.
—Jim Ryuh

Habits are safer than rules; you don't have to watch them. And you don't have to keep them, either; they keep you.   —Dr. Frank Crane

Habit is not mere subjugation, it is a tender tie; when one remembers habit it seems to have been happiness.
—Elizabeth Bowen

To learn new habits is everything, for it is to reach the substance of life. Life is but a tissue of habits.
—Henri Frederic Amiel

Choose always the way that seems the best, however rough it may be; custom will soon render it easy and agreeable.   —Pythagoras

Quality is not an act. It is a habit.
—Aristotle

It is not in novelty but in habit that we find the greatest pleasure.
—Raymond Radiguet

Habit is stronger than reason.
—George Santayana

Character is simply habit long enough continued.   —Plutarch

Nothing is more powerful than habit.
—Ovid

If you do the same thing every day at the same time for the same length of time, you'll save yourself from many a sink. Routine is a condition of survival.   —Flannery O'Connor

Have a time and place for everything, and do everything in its time and place, and you will not only accomplish more, but have far more leisure than those who are always hurrying.
—Tyron Edwards

SOMETIMES, THE BEST WE CAN DO IS JUST MAKE IT THROUGH THE DAY

Anyone can carry his burden, however hard, until nightfall. Anyone can do his work, however hard, for one day. Anyone can live sweetly, patiently, lovingly, purely, till the sun goes down. And this is all life really means.   —Robert Louis Stevenson

Come what may, time and the hour runs through the roughest day.
        —William Shakespeare

At any rate, you can bear it for a quarter of an hour!
            —Theodore Haecker

The longest day is soon ended.
            —Pliny, the Younger

The secret of my success is that I always managed to live to fly another day.   —Chuck Yeager

HOW LONG IS A DAY?

The time which we have at our disposal every day is elastic; the passions that we feel expand it, those that we inspire contract it; and habit fills up what remains.   —Marcel Proust

A day is a miniature eternity.
            —Ralph Waldo Emerson

One day, with life and heart, is more than time enough to find a world.
            —James Russell Lowell

A day is a span of time no one is wealthy enough to waste.   —Anon.

TIME IS RELATIVE

When a man sits with a pretty girl for an hour, it seems like a minute. But let him sit on a hot stove for a minute, and it's longer than any hour. That's relativity.   —Albert Einstein

Time is
Too slow for those who wait,
Too swift for those who fear,
Too long for those who grieve,
Too short for those who rejoice.
But for those who love, time is not.
            —Henry Van Dyke

The less one has to do, the less time one finds to do it in. One yawns, one procrastinates, one can do it when one will, and, therefore, one seldom does it at all; whereas those who have a great deal of business must buckle to it; and then they always find time enough to do it.   —Lord Chesterfield

Time is nothing absolute; its duration depends on the rate of thought and feeling.   —John Draper

Time is a fluid condition which has no existence except in the momentary avatars of individual people.
            —William Faulkner

What then is time? If no one asks me, I know what it is. If I wish to explain it to him who asks, I do not know.
            —Saint Augustine

Time is the product of changing realities, beings, existences.
            —Nicholas Berdyaev

Time is the relationship between events.   —Yakima Indian Nation

Time is the arbitrary division of eternity.   —Anon.

Time is a part of eternity, and of the same piece with it.
—Moses Mendelssohn

Time is eternity begun.
—James Montgomery

Time is not a line, but a series of now-points.   —Taisen Deshimaru

You can't measure time in days the way you can money in dollars, because each day is different.
—Phillip Hewett

An hour of pain is as long as a day of pleasure.   —Anon.

The value of life lies not in the length of days, but in the use we make of them; a man may live long yet live very little.   —Michel de Montaigne

Reality is a staircase going neither up nor down, we don't move; today is today, always is today. —Octavio Paz

OTHER DEFINITIONS OF ONE DAY

What runs through a person like water through a sieve.
—Samuel Butler

Scrolls: write on them what you want to be remembered for.
—Joseph Ibn Pakuda

Every day is a messenger of God.
—Russian proverb

A little space of time before time expires; a little way of breath.
—Algernon Swinburne

Each day is a little life; every waking and rising a little birth; every fresh morning a little youth; every going to rest and sleep a little death.
—Arthur Schopenhauer

OTHER DEFINITIONS OF TIME

Time is an avid gambler who has no need to cheat to win every time.
—Charles Baudelaire

Time is the only critic without ambition.   —John Steinbeck

Time is the most valuable thing a man can spend.   —Theophrastus

Time is a storm in which we are all lost.   —William Carlos Williams

Time is the wisest counsellor of all.
—Pericles

Time is the moving image of eternity.
—Plato

Time is the soul of this world.
—Plutarch

Time is a sandpile we run our fingers in.   —Carl Sandburg

Time is one kind of robber whom the law does not strike at, and who steals what is most precious to men.
—Napoleon Bonaparte

Time is the tyrant of the body.
—Anon.

Time is that in which all things pass away.   —Arthur Schopenhauer

Time is a file that wears and makes
no noise.   —English proverb

Time is what we want most, but . . .
what we use worst.   —William Penn

Time is the king of men.
                —William Shakespeare

Time . . . is the life of the soul.
        —Henry Wadsworth Longfellow

Time is the dressing room for eternity.
                            —Anon.

Time is an available instrument for
reaching the eternal.
                    —John W. Lynch

Time itself is an element.
                —Johann von Goethe

Time is the devourer of all things.
                            —Ovid

Time is the subtle thief of youth.
                    —John Milton

Time is the rider that breaks youth.
                    —George Herbert

Time is an eternal guest that banquets
on our ideals and bodies.
                    —Elbert Hubbard

Time is an illusion—to orators.
                    —Elbert Hubbard

The surest poison is time.
                —Ralph Waldo Emerson

Time is a great manager: it arranges
things well.   —Pierre Corneille

Time is a river without banks.
                    —Marc Chagall

Time is the greatest and longest-
established spinner of all. . . . His fac-
tory is a secret place, his work noise-
less, and his hands are mutes.
                    —Charles Dickens

Time is the stuff life's made of.
                    —David Belasco

Time is my estate: to Time I'm heir.
                —Johann von Goethe

Time is change, transformation, evo-
lution.   —Isaac L. Peretz

Time is a circus always packing up
and moving away.   —Ben Hecht

Time is a dressmaker specializing in
alterations.   —Faith Baldwin

Time is the greatest innovator.
                    —Francis Bacon

Time is a wealth of change, but the
clock in its parody makes it mere
change and no wealth.
                —Rabindranath Tagore

Time is but the stream I go a-fishing
in.   —Henry David Thoreau

Time is the silent, never-resting thing
. . . rolling, rushing on, swift, silent,
like an all-embracing oceantide, on
which we and all the universe swim.
                    —Thomas Carlyle

Time is a flowing river. Happy those
who allow themselves to be carried,
unresisting, with the current. They
float through easy days. They live,
unquestioning, in the moment.
                —Christopher Morley

Time is a very shadow that passeth
away.   —Apocrypha

Time is the author of authors.
                    —Francis Bacon

Time is a stream which glides smoothly on and is past before we know.
                    —Ovid

Time is a sort of river of passing
events, and strong is its current; no
sooner is a thing brought to sight
than it is swept by and another takes
its place, and this too will be swept
away.   —Marcus Aurelius

Time is the sea in which men grow,
are born, or die.   —Freya Stark

Time is the longest distance between
two places.   —Tennessee Williams

Yesterday: The Past

WE SHOULD REMEMBER MORE OF THE GOOD THAN OF THE BAD OR THE DIFFICULT

Vanity plays lurid tricks with our memory. —Joseph Conrad

Nostalgia is a seductive liar.
—George W. Ball

Was it always my nature to take a bad time and block out the good times, until any success became an accident and failure seemed the only truth?
—Lillian Hellman

Nostalgia: A device that removes the ruts and potholes from memory lane.
—Doug Larson

What was hard to bear is sweet to remember.   —Portuguese proverb

The heart's memory eliminates the bad and magnifies the good; and thanks to this artifice we manage to endure the burdens of the past.
—Gabriel Garcia Marquez

Some folks never exaggerate—they just remember big.   —Audrey Snead

A man's memory may almost become the art of continually varying and misrepresenting his past, according to his interest in the present.
—George Santayana

Praising what is lost makes the remembrance dear.
—William Shakespeare

God gave us memory that we might have roses in December.
—Sir James M. Barrie

PEOPLE HAVE ALWAYS TTHOUGHT "THE GOOD OLD DAYS" WERE BETTER

There has never been an age that did not applaud the past and lament the present.   —Lillian Eichler Watson

Only sick music makes money today.
—Friedrich Nietzsche (in 1888)

Let others praise ancient times; I am glad I was born in these.
—Ovid (81 B.C.)

291

Children today are tyrants. They contradict their parents, gobble their food, and tyrannize their teachers.
　　　　　—Socrates (470–399 B.C.)

Posterity will say as usual: "In the past things were better, the present is worse than the past."
　　　　　—Anton Chekhov (1860–1904)

Our ignorance of history makes us libel to our own times. People have always been like this.
　　　　　—Gustave Flaubert (1821–1880)

Oh, this age! How tasteless and ill-bred it is!　　—Catullus (87–54 B.C.)

This strange disease of modern life, with its sick hurry, its divided aims.
　　　　　—Matthew Arnold (1822–1888)

The illusion that times that were are better than those that are has probably pervaded all ages.
　　　　　—Horace Greeley (1811–1872)

Oh, what times! Oh, what standards!
　　　　　—Cicero (106–43 B.C.)

Probably no one alive hasn't at one time or another brooded over the possibility of going back to an earlier, ideal age in his existence and living a different kind of life.　　—Hal Boyle

The Golden Age was never the present Age.
　　　　　—Thomas Fuller (1608–1661)

The worst time is always the present.
　—Jean de La Fontaine (1621–1695)

The "good old times"—all times, when old, are good.
　　　　　—Lord Byron (1788–1824)

"The good old days." The only good days are ahead.　　—Alice Childress

REGRETS

Very frequently, feminine activity also expresses itself in what is largely a retrospectively oriented pondering over what we ought to have done differently in life, and how we ought to have done it; or, as if under compulsion, we make up strings of causal connections. We like to call this thinking; though, on the contrary, it is a form of mental activity that is strangely pointless and unproductive, a form that really leads only to self-torture.　　—Emma Jung

The only causes of regret are laziness, outbursts of temper, hurting others, prejudice, jealousy, and envy.
　　　　　—Germaine Greer

If you have behaved badly, repent, make what amends you can and address yourself to the task of behaving better next time. On no account brood over your wrongdoing. Rolling in the muck is not the best way of getting clean.　　—Aldous Huxley

You always feel when you look it straight in the eye that you could have put more into it, could have let yourself go and dug harder.
　　　　　—Emily Carr

When one door closes another opens. But we often look so long and so regretfully upon the closed door that we fail to see the one that has opened for us.　　—Alexander Graham Bell

No doing without some ruing.
—Sigrid Undset

Nobody gets to live life backward.
Look ahead, that is where your
future lies.   —Ann Landers

Were it not better to forget
Than to remember and regret?
—L.E. Landon

Regret for the things we did can be
tempered by time; it is regret for the
things we did not do that is inconsol-
able.   —Sydney J. Harris

Always repenting of wrongs done
will never bring my heart to rest.
—Ji Kang

Should-haves solve nothing. It's the
next thing to happen that needs
thinking about.   —Alexandra Ripley

The error of the past is the success of
the future. A mistake is evidence that
someone tried to do something.
—Anon.

Regret is an appalling waste of energy; you can't build on it; it is good
only for wallowing.
—Katherine Mansfield

I have always found that each step
we take in life is to be regretted—if
we once begin to wonder how many
other steps might have been possible.
—John Oliver Hobbes

If you cannot get rid of the family
skeleton, you may as well make it
dance.   —George Bernard Shaw

Let the dead Past bury its dead!
—Henry Wadsworth Longfellow

"The horror of that moment," the
King went on, "I shall never forget."
"You will, though," the Queen said,
"if you don't make a memorandum
of it."   —Lewis Carroll

Reflect upon your present blessings,
of which every man has many—not
on your past misfortunes, of which
all men have some.
—Charles Dickens

They say you should not suffer
through the past. You should be able
to wear it like a loose garment, take
it off and let it drop.   —Eva Jessye

Your past is always going to be the
way it was. Stop trying to change it.
—Anon.

The only thing I regret about my past
is the length of it. If I had to live my
life again, I'd make the same mistakes, only sooner.
—Tallulah Bankhead

There is no greater sorrow than to
recall a happy time in the midst of
wretchedness.   —Dante Alighieri

We should have no regrets. . . . The
past is finished. There is nothing to
be gained by going over it. Whatever
it gave us in the experiences it
brought us was something we had to
know.   —Rebecca Beard

One must never lose time in vainly
regretting the past or in complaining
against the changes which cause us
discomfort, for change is the essence
of life.   —Anatole France

Yesterday's errors let yesterday cover.
—Susan Coolidge

This is another day! Are its eyes blurred with maudlin grief for any wasted past? A thousand thousand failures shall not daunt! Let dust clasp dust, death, death; I am alive!
—Don Marquis

Whatever with the past has gone, the best is always yet to come.
—Lucy Larcom

Hindsight is always 20/20.
—Billy Wilder

LEARNING FROM THE PAST

There are two kinds of stones, as everyone knows, one which rolls.
—Amelia Earhart

Recognizing what we have done in the past is a recognition of ourselves. By conducting a dialogue with our past, we are searching how to go forward.
—Kiyoko Takeda

I know of no way of judging the future but by the past.
—Patrick Henry

Those who cannot remember the past are condemned to repeat it.
—George Santayana

To look backward for a while is to refresh the eye, to restore it, and to render it more fit for its prime function of looking forward.
—Margaret Fairless Barber

The past is never dead—it is not even past.
—William Faulkner

The past is the best way to suppose what may come.
—Lord Halifax

We can never go back again, that much is certain. The past is still too close to us. The things we have tried to forget and put behind us would stir again, and that sense of fear, of furtive unrest . . . might in some manner unforeseen become a living companion, as it had before.
—Daphne du Maurier

Past: Our cradle, not our prison, and there is danger as well as appeal in its glamour. The past is for inspiration, not imitation; for continuation, not repetition.
—Israel Zangwill

Life can only be understood backwards, but it must be lived forward.
—Søren Kierkegaard

When I want to understand what is happening today or try to decide what will happen tomorrow, I look back.
—Oliver Wendell Holmes

We live in the present, we dream of the future, but we learn eternal truths from the past.
—Madame Chiang Kai-Shek

The past is the best prophet of the future.
—Lord Byron

Truth, however bitter, can be accepted, and woven into a design for living.
—Agatha Christie

The past will not tell us what we ought to do, but . . . what we ought to avoid.
—José Ortega y Gasset

Tomorrow hopes we have learned something from yesterday.
—John Wayne

Judgement comes from experience, and great judgement comes from bad experience.   —Robert Packwood

The only use of a knowledge of the past is to equip us for the present.
    —Alfred North Whitehead

When the past has taught us that we have more within us than we have ever used, our prayer is a cry to the divine to come to us and fill us with its power.   —Rudolph Steiner

IT'S IMPORTANT TO BURY THE PAST, TO LET IT GO— TO MOVE ON

Don't ruin the present with the ruined past.   —Ellen Gilchrist

Ah tell me not that memory
Sheds gladness o'er the past;
What is recalled by faded flowers
Save that they did not last?
    —Letitia Landon

Here lies my past,
Goodbye I have kissed it;
Thank you kids,
I wouldn't have missed it.
    —Ogden Nash

Forget the past and live the present hour.   —Sarah Knowles Bolton

Living in the past is a dull and lonely business; looking back strains the neck muscles, causes you to bump into people not going your way.
    —Edna Ferber

I demolish my bridges behind me . . . then there is no choice but forward.
    —Firdtjof Nansen

Looking repeatedly into the past, you do not necessarily become fascinated with your own life, but rather with the phenomenon of memory.
    —Patricia Hampl

Let the past drift away with the water.   —Japanese saying

The past cannot be changed. The future is yet in your power.
    —Mary Pickford

I have very strong feelings about how you lead your life. You always look ahead, you never look back.
    —Ann Richards

Not the power to remember, but its very opposite, the power to forget, is a necessary condition for our existence.   —Sholem Asch

You cannot step twice into the same river, for other waters are continually flowing on.   —Heraclitus

Better by far you should forget and smile, than that you should remember and be sad.   —Christina Rosetti

The past should be culled like a box of fresh strawberries, rinsed of debris, sweetened judiciously and served in small portions, not very often.
    —Laura Palmer

May I forget what ought to be forgotten; and recall, unfailing, all that ought to be recalled, each kindly thing, forgetting what might sting.
    —Maty Caroline Davies

Here's to the past. Thank God it's past!   —Anon.

One must be thrust out of a finished cycle in life, and that leap is the most difficult to make—to part with one's faith, one's love, when one would prefer to renew the faith and recreate the passion.   —Anaïs Nin

The biggest thing in today's sorrow is the memory of yesterday's joy.
                    —Kahlil Gibran

It's but little good you'll go a-watering the last year's crop.
                    —George Eliot

The worst thing you can do is to try to cling to something that's gone, or to recreate it. —Johnette Napolitano

Ne'er look for the birds of this year in the nests of the last.
                    —Miguel de Cervantes

Don't look back. Something may be gaining on you.   —Satchel Paige

Anyone who limits her vision to memories of yesterday is already dead.   —Lillie Langtry

I like the dreams for the future better than the history of the past.
                    —Thomas Jefferson

The first recipe for happiness is: Avoid too lengthy meditations on the past.
                    —André Maurois

The past is a funeral gone by.
                    —Edmund Gosse

Never let yesterday use up today.
                    —Richard H. Nelson

How the past perishes is how the future becomes.
                    —Alfred North Whitehead

The dogmas of the quiet past are inadequate to the stormy present.
                    —Abraham Lincoln

The Past as Prologue—
As Beginning

In the life of the spirit there is no ending that is not a beginning.
                    —Henrietta Zolde

The past is but the beginning of a beginning, and all that is and has been is but the twilight of the dawn.
                    —H. G. Wells

Anyone who limits her vision to memories of yesterday is already dead.
                    —Lillie Langtry

Nor deem the irrevocable Past
As wholly wasted, wholly vain,
If, rising on its wrecks, at last
To something nobler we attain.
                    —Henry Wadsworth Longfellow

Youth is, after all, just a moment, but it is the moment, the spark that you always carry in your heart.
                    —Raisa M. Gorbachev

Nothing is predestined: The obstacles of your past can become the gateways that lead to new beginnings.
                    —Ralph Blum

No star is ever lost we once have
    seen,
We always may be what we might
    have been.
                    —Adelaide Proctor

What's past is prologue.
—William Shakespeare

In my end is my beginning.
—Mary Stuart

Visualize yourself standing before a gateway on a hilltop. Your entire life lies out before you and below. Before you step through, pause and review the past; the learning and the joys, the victories and the sorrows—everything it took to bring you here.
—*The Book of Runes*

The good old days were never that good, believe me. The good new days are today, and better days are coming tomorrow. Our greatest songs are still unsung.   —Hubert H. Humphrey

The past is never completely lost, however extensive the devastation. Your sorrows are the bricks and mortar of a magnificent temple. What you are today and what you will be tomorrow are because of what you have been.   —Gordon Wright

YESTERDAY AND TOMORROW

Fear not for the future, weep not for the past.   —Percy Bysshe Shelley

There are two days about which nobody should ever worry, and these are yesterday and tomorrow.
—Robert Jones Burdette

We crucify ourselves between two thieves: regret for yesterday and fear of tomorrow.   —Fulton Oursler

Every saint has a past, and every sinner has a future.   —Oscar Wilde

When I am anxious it is because I am living in the future. When I am depressed it is because I am living in the past.   —Anon.

MANY THINGS REMAIN THE SAME

I'm not convinced that the world is in any worse shape than it ever was. It's just that in this age of almost instantaneous communication, we bear the weight of problems our forefathers only read about after they were solved.   —Burton Hillis

Truth has no beginning.
—Mary Baker Eddy

The world's history is constant, like the laws of nature, and simple, like the souls of men.
—J.C.F. von Schiller

These are the stories that never, never die, that are carried like seed into a new country, are told to you and me and make in us new and lasting strengths.   —Meridel Le Sueur

What one loves in childhood stays in the heart forever.   —Mary Jo Putney

This time, like all times, is a very good one if we but know what to do with it.   —Ralph Waldo Emerson

In times like these, it helps to recall that there have always been times like these.   —Paul Harvey

Our ignorance of history makes us libel our own times. People have always been like this.
—Gustave Flaubert

The good old days are neither better nor worse than the ones we're living through right now.   —Artie Shaw

GENERAL QUOTATIONS ABOUT THE PAST

Where I was born and where and how I have lived is unimportant. It is what I have done with where I have been that should be of interest.
    —Georgia O'Keefe

Respect the past in the full measure of its deserts, but do not make the mistake of confusing it with the present, nor seek in it the ideals of the future.   —José Ingenieros

It's a pleasure to share one's memories. Everything remembered is dear, endearing, touching, precious. At least the past is safe—though we didn't know it at the time. We know it now. Because it's in the past; because we have survived.
    —Susan Sontag

The events in our lives happen in a sequence in time, but in their significance to ourselves, they find their own order . . . the continuous thread of revelation.   —Eudora Welty

The best compliment we can pay our past is to prophetically and bravely face today and tomorrow.
    —Bernie Wiebe

Some memories are realities, and are better than anything that can ever happen to one again.
    —Willa Cather

Fortunate are the people whose roots are deep.   —Agnes Meyer

As the dew to the blossom, the bud to the bee,
As the scent to the rose, are those memories to me.
    —Amelia C. Welby

Heirlooms we don't have in our family. But stories we've got.
    —Rose Chernin

We have to do with the past only as we can make it useful to the present and the future.
    —Frederick Douglass

The past is a guidepost, not a hitching post.   —L. Thomas Holdcroft

The past in retrospect holds manifold disenchantments, failures and even tragedies; and yet the worse may be forgotten and the best held fast.
    —W. Robertson Neicoll

The road was new to me, as roads always are, going back.
    —Sarah Orne Jewett

No yesterdays are ever wasted for those who give themselves to today.
    —Brendan Francis

Yesterday I lived, today I suffer, tomorrow I die; but I still think fondly, today and tomorrow, of yesterday.
    —Gotthold Ephraim Lessing

Each has his past shut in him like the leaves of a book shown to him by heart, and his friends can only read the title.   —Virginia Woolf

We are well advised to keep on nodding terms with the people we used to be, whether we find them attractive company or not. . . . We forget all too soon the things we thought we could never forget. —Joan Didion

The past is a work of art, free of irrelevancies and loose ends.
—Max Beerbohm

The past is a foreign country; they do things differently there.
—Leslie Poles Hartley

The past with its pleasures, its rewards, its foolishness, its punishments, is there for each of us forever, and it should be. —Lillian Hellman

The past is that which we possess fully and in whole. —Isidor Eliashev

Our deeds still travel with us from afar, and what we have been makes us what we are. —George Eliot

The past is the tomorrow that got away. —Leonard L. Levinson

Our life is like some vast lake that is slowly filling with the stream of our years. As the waters creep surely upward the landmarks of the past are one by one submerged. But there shall always be memory to lift its head above the tide until the lake is overflowing.
—Alexandre Charles Auguste Bisson

Why should we grope among the dry bones of the past, or put the living generation into masquerade out of its faded wardrobe?
—Ralph Waldo Emerson

No past is dead for us, but only sleeping, love.
—Helen Hunt Jackson

I look back on my life like a good day's work; it is done and I am satisfied with it. —Grandma Moses

Of all sad words of tongue or pen, the saddest are these: It might have been. —John Greenleaf Whittier

That sign of old age, extolling the past at the expense of the present.
—Sydney Smith

The past is one evil less and one memory more. —Elbert Hubbard

Then is then. Now is now. We must grow to learn the difference. —Anon.

Say not thou, what is the cause that the former days were better than these, for thou dost not inquire wisely concerning this. —Ecclesiastes 7:10

The past not merely is not fugitive, it remains present. —Marcel Proust

The past which is so presumptuously brought forward as a precedent for the present was itself founded on some past that went before it.
—Madame de Staël

"Old times" never come back and I suppose it's just as well. What comes back is a new morning every day in the year, and that's better.
—George E. Woodberry

We have inherited new difficulties because we have inherited more privileges. —Dr. Abram Sacher

People are always asking about the
good old days. I say, why don't you
say the good "now" days? Isn't
"now" the only time you're living?
　　　　　　　—Robert M. Young

Life in the twentieth century undeni-
ably has . . . such richness, joy and
adventure as were unknown to our
ancestors except in their dreams.
　　　　　　　—Arthur H. Campton

Enjoy yourself. These are the "good
old days" you're going to miss in the
years ahead.　　　　　　　—Anon.

The past is our very being.
　　　　　　　—David Ben-Gurion

To disdain today is to prove that yesterday has been misunderstood.
　　　　　　　—Maurice Maeterlinck

The universe is made of stories, not
of atoms.　　　　　—Muriel Rukeyser

Today: The Present

The Importance of Today

This is not a dress rehearsal. This is It.
—Tom Cunningham

Only when your consciousness is totally focused on the moment you are in can you receive whatever gift, lesson, or delight that moment has to offer. —Barbara De Angelis

Seize the day, and put the least possible trust in tomorrow. —Horace

Tomorrow's life is too late. Live today.
—Martial

One today is worth two tomorrows.
—Benjamin Franklin

Half of today is better than all of tomorrow. —Jean de La Fontaine

Never put off until tomorrow what you can do today, because if you enjoy it today, you can do it again, tomorrow. —Anon.

Today is the first day of the rest of your life. —Abbie Hoffman

The present moment is significant, not as the bridge between past and future, but by reason of its contents, which can fill our emptiness and become ours, if we are capable of receiving them
—Dag Hammarskjold

All of us tend to put off living. We are all dreaming of some magical rose garden over the horizon instead of enjoying the roses that are blooming outside our windows today.
—Dale Carnegie

It's not that "today is the first day of the rest of my life," but that now is all there is of my life.
—Hugh Prather

We want to live in the present, and the only history that is worth a tinker's damn is the history we make today. —Henry Ford

Now is the only time we own; give, love, toil with a will.
And place no faith in tomorrow, for the clock may then be still.
—Anon.

Enjoy yourself, drink, call the life you live today your own—but only that; the rest belongs to chance.
—Euripides

You are younger today than you ever will be again. Make use of it for the sake of tomorrow.   —Anon.

If we are ever to enjoy life, now is the time, not tomorrow or next year. . . . Today should always be our most wonderful day.   —Thomas Dreier

Live now, believe me, wait not till tomorrow, gather the roses of life today.   —Pierre de Ronsard

So often we rob tomorrow's memories by today's economies.
—John Mason Brown

You had better live your best and act your best and think your best today; for today is the sure preparation for tomorrow and all the other tomorrows that follow.
—Harriet Martineau

Happy the man, and happy he alone
He can call today his own.
He who, secure within can say,
"Tomorrow, do thy worst, for I have
    lived today."   —Henry Fielding

Forget mistakes. Forget failures. Forget everything except what you're going to do now and do it. Today is your lucky day.   —Will Durant

Yesterday is ashes; tomorrow wood. Only today does the fire burn brightly.
—Old Eskimo proverb

One of these days is none of these days.   —H.G. Bohn

Look lovingly upon the present, for it holds the only things that are forever true.   —*A Course in Miracles*

This is the day which the Lord has made. Let us rejoice and be glad in it.
—Psalms 118:24

He growled at morning, noon, and
    night,
And trouble sought to borrow;
Although today the sky was bright,
He knew t'would storm tomorrow;
A thought of joy he could not stand,
And struggled to resist it;
Though sunshine dappled all the land
This sorry pessimist it.
—Nixon Waterman

To those leaning on the sustaining infinite, to-day is big with blessings.
—Mary Baker Eddy

The here-and-now is no mere filling of time, but a filling of time with God.   —John Foster

In the present, every day is a miracle.
—James Gould Cozzens

Life is only this place, this time, and these people right here and now.
—Vincent Collins

I believe that only one person in a thousand knows the trick of really living in the present.
—Storm Jameson

There is one thing we can do, and the happiest people are those who do it to the limit of their ability. We can be completely present. We can be all here. We can . . . give all our attention to the opportunity before us.
—Mark Van Doren

The more I give myself permission to live in the moment and enjoy it without feeling guilty or judgmental about any other time, the better I feel about the quality of my work.
—Wayne Dyer

Act—act in the living Present!
—Henry Wadsworth Longfellow

Are not my days few? Cease then, and let me alone, that I may take comfort a little, Before I go to the place from which I shall not return.
—Job 10:21–22

Now or never was the time.
—Laurence Sterne

And now, Lord, what wait I for?
—Psalms 39:7

The future belongs to those who live intensely in the present. —Anon.

The present is elastic to embrace infinity. —Louis Anspacher

The present is the living sum-total of the whole past. —Thomas Carlyle

The present is an eternal now.
—Abraham Cowley

The present is all the ready money Fate can give. —Abraham Cowley

The present is an edifice which God cannot rebuild.
—Ralph Waldo Emerson

The present is the blocks with which we build. —Henry W. Longfellow

The present is the symbol and vehicle of the future. —Joseph McSorely

The present is all you have for your certain possession. —Anon.

We are here and it is now. Further than that, all knowledge is moonshine.
—H.L. Mencken

Having spent the better part of my life trying either to relive the past or experience the future before it arrives, I have come to believe that in between these two extremes is peace.
—Anon.

This time, like all times, is a very good one if we but know what to do with it. —Ralph Waldo Emerson

The time is always right to do what is right. —Martin Luther King, Jr.

One realm we have never conquered: the pure present. —D.H. Lawrence

He who lives in the present lives in eternity. —Ludwig Wittgenstein

I am in the present. I cannot know what tomorrow will bring forth. I can know only what the truth is for me today. That is what I am called upon to serve. —Igor Stravinsky

The present offers itself to our touch for only an instant of time and then eludes the senses. —Plutarch

A life uncommanded now is uncommanded; a life unenjoyed now is unenjoyed; a life not lived wisely now is not lived wisely. —David Grayson

The word "now" is like a bomb thrown through the window, and it ticks. —Arthur Miller

Whether it's the best of times or the worst of times, it's the only time we've got. —Art Buchwald

It is now, and in this world, that we must live. —André Gide

Who cares about great marks left behind? We have one life. . . . Just one. Our life. We have nothing else. —Ugo Betti

This—the immediate, everyday, and present experience—is IT, the entire and ultimate point for the existence of a universe. —Alan Watts

Let us live today. —J.C.F. von Schiller

Work accomplished means little. It is in the past. What we all want is the glorious and living present. —Sherwood Anderson

Yesterday is a cancelled check. Tomorrow is a promissory note. Today is cash in hand. Spend It! —John W. Newbern

Today Relative to Yesterday or Tomorrow

The future is made of the same stuff as the present. —Simone Weil

Yesterday is but a dream, tomorrow is only a vision. But today, well lived, makes every yesterday a dream of happiness, and every tomorrow a vision of hope. Look well, therefore, to this day, for it is life, the very life of life. —The Sanskrit

Be glad today. Tomorrow may bring tears.
Be brave today. The darkest night will pass.
And golden rays will usher in the dawn. —Sarah Knowles Bolton

Do not look back on happiness, or dream of it in the future. You are only sure of today; do not let yourself be cheated out of it. —Henry Ward Beecher

Existence is no more than the precarious attainment of relevance in an intensely mobile flux of past, present, and future. —Susan Sontag

I am not afraid of tomorrow, for I have seen yesterday and I love today. —William Allen White

The past, the present and the future are really one: they are today. —Harriet Beecher Stowe

The present contains all that there is. It is holy ground; for it is the past, and it is the future. —Alfred North Whitehead

There is no justification for present existence other than its expansion into an indefinitely open future. —Simone de Beauvoir

With the past, I have nothing to do; nor with the future. I live now. —Ralph Waldo Emerson

Children have neither a past nor a future. Thus they enjoy the present, which seldom happens to us. —Jean de La Bruyère

The past is a bucket of ashes, so live not in your yesterdays, nor just for tomorrow, but in the here and now.
—Carl Sandburg

Youth is the time of getting, middle age of improving, and old age of spending.   —Anne Bradstreet

It is not the weight of the future or the past that is pressing upon you, but ever that of the present alone. Even this burden, too, can be lessened if you confine it strictly to its own limits.   —Marcus Aurelius

Reappraise the past, reevaluate where we've been, clarify where we are, and predict or anticipate where we are headed.   —Toni Cade Bambara

We can easily manage if we will only take, each day, the burden appointed to it. But the load will be too heavy for us if we carry yesterday's burden over again today, and then add the burden of the morrow before we are required to bear it.   —John Newton

Take in the ideas of the day, drain off those of yesterday. As to the morrow, time enough to consider it when it becomes today.
—Edward Bulwer-Lytton

Tomorrow I will live, the fool does say; today itself's too late, the wise lived yesterday.   —Martial

The cares of today are seldom those of tomorrow.   —William Cowper

Yesterday is a cancelled check; tomorrow is a promissory note; today is the only cash you have—so spend it wisely.   —Kay Lyons

Everyman's life lies within the present, for the past is spent and done with, and the future is uncertain.
—Marcus Aurelius

The flesh endures the storms of the present alone, the mind those of the past and future as well.   —Epicurus

I try to learn from the past, but I plan for the future by focusing exclusively on the present. That's where the fun is.
—Donald Trump

No mind is much employed upon the present; recollection and anticipation fill up almost all our moments.
—Samuel Johnson

The only living life is in the past and future—the present is an interlude—strange interlude in which we call on past and future to bear witness that we are living.   —Eugene O'Neill

Past, and to come, seems best; things present, worst.
—William Shakespeare

The past cannot be regained, although we can learn from it; the future is not yet ours even though we must plan for it. . . . Time is now. We have only today.   —Charles Hummell

Look not mournfully into the past, it comes not back again. Wisely improve the present, it is thine. Go forth to meet the shadowy future without fear and with a manly heart.
—Henry Wadsworth Longfellow

No longer forward nor behind I look in hope or fear; but grateful, take the good I find, the best of now and here.   —John Greenleaf Whittier

The present, like a note in music, is
nothing but as it appertains to what
is past and what is to come.
—Walter Savage Landor

We can see well into the past; we can
guess shrewdly in to the future; but
that which is rolled up and muffled
in impenetrable folds is today.
—Ralph Waldo Emerson

The present time is seldom able to fill
desire or imagination with immediate
enjoyment, and we are forced to supply its deficiencies by recollection or
anticipation.   —Samuel Johnson

Be satisfied, and pleased with what
        thou art,
Act cheerfully and well thy allotted
        part;
Enjoy the present hour, be thankful
        for the past,
And neither fear, nor wish, the
        approaches of the last.   —Martial

It is difficult to live in the present,
ridiculous to live in the future and
impossible to live in the past.
—Jim Bishop

If you have one eye on yesterday, and
one eye on tomorrow, you're going to
be cockeyed today.   —Anon.

Yesterday has gone. Tomorrow may
never come. There is only the miracle
of this moment. Savor it. It is a gift.
—Anon.

Don't waste today regretting yesterday instead of making a memory for
tomorrow.   —Laura Palmer

Light tomorrow with today.
—Elizabeth Barrett Browning

I just take one day. Yesterday is gone.
Tomorrow has not come. We have
only today to love Jesus.
—Mother Teresa

Patterns of the past echo in the present and resound through the future.
—Dhyani Ywahoo

Who controls the past controls the
future; who controls the present controls the past.   —George Orwell

If we spend our time with regrets
over yesterday, and worries over
what might happen tomorrow, we
have no today in which to live.
—Anon.

Now is all we have. Everything that
has ever happened to you, and anything that is ever going to happen to
you, is just a thought.   —Wayne Dyer

The present is the necessary product
of all the past, the necessary cause of
all the future.   —Robert G. Ingersoll

If we open a quarrel between the past
and the present, we shall find we
have lost the future.
—Sir Winston Churchill

Few of us ever live in the present, we
are forever anticipating what is to
come or remembering what has gone.
—Louis L'Amour

The secret of health for both mind
and body is not to mourn for the
past, not to worry about the future,
nor to anticipate troubles, but to live
the present moment wisely and
earnestly.   —Buddha

When we have a world of only now, with no shadows of yesterdays or clouds of tomorrow, then saying what we can do will work.
—Goldie Ivener

I can feel guilty about the past, apprehensive about the future, but only in the present can I act. The ability to be in the present moment is a major component of mental wellness.
—Abraham Maslow

The idea of "twenty-four-hour living" applies primarily to the emotional life of the individual. Emotionally speaking, we must not live in yesterday, nor in tomorrow.   —As Bill Sees It

I have realized that the past and the future are real illusions, that they exist only in the present, which is what there is and all that there is.
—Alan Watts

There is no present or future, only the past, happening over and over again, now.   —Eugene O'Neill

Today was once the future from which you expected so much in the past.   —Anon.

Today is yesterday's pupil.
—Benjamin Franklin

Today is yesterday's effect and tomorrow's cause.   —Phillip Gribble

Through loyalty to the past, our mind refuses to realize that tomorrow's joy is possible only if today's makes way for it; that each wave owes the beauty of its line only to the withdrawal of the preceding one.
—André Gide

The present is the now, the here, through which all future plunges to the past.   —James Joyce

I have everything I need to enjoy my here and now—unless I am letting my consciousness be dominated by demands and expectations based on the dead past or the imagined future.
—Ken Keyes, Jr.

Today is the blocks with which we build.
—Henry Wadsworth Longfellow

In order to be utterly happy, the only thing necessary is to refrain from comparing this moment with other moments in the past, which I often did not fully enjoy because I was comparing them with other moments of the future.   —André Gide

DON'T WASTE TODAY
PREPARING FOR TOMORROW

Seize from every moment its unique novelty, and do not prepare your joys.   —André Gide

You don't need endless time and perfect conditions. Do it now. Do it today. Do it for twenty minutes and watch your heart start beating.
—Barbara Sher

Do not manage as if you had ten thousand years before you. Look you, death stands at your elbow; make the most of your minute, and be good for something while it is in your power.
—Charles Palmer

And if not now, when?   —Talmud

As we are always preparing to be happy, it is inevitable that we should never be so. —Blaise Pascal

Why not seize the pleasure at once? How often is happiness destroyed by preparation, foolish preparation! —Jane Austen

When shall we live if not now? —M.F.K. Fisher

We cannot put off living until we are ready. The most salient characteristic of life is its coerciveness: it is always urgent, "here and now," without any possible postponement. Life is fired at us point-blank. —José Ortega y Gasset

Very few men, properly speaking, live at present, but are providing to live another time. —Jonathan Swift

Real generosity toward the future lies in giving all to the present. —Albert Camus

Freedom from worries and surcease from strain are illusions that always inhabit the distance. —Edwin Way Teale

Study as if you were to live forever. Live as if you were to die tomorrow. —Saint Isidore of Seville

The best preparation for a better life next year is a full, complete, harmonious, joyous life this year. —Thomas Dreier

If you spend your whole life waiting for the storm, you'll never enjoy the sunshine. —Morris West

Some people are making such thorough preparation for rainy days that they aren't enjoying today's sunshine. —William Feather

The greater part of our lives is spent in dreaming over the morrow, and when it comes, it, too, is consumed in the anticipation of a brighter morrow, and so the cheat is prolonged, even to the grave. —Mark Rutherford

It is cheap generosity which promises the future in compensation for the present. —J.A. Spender

Who knows if the gods above will add tomorrow's span to this day's sum? —Horace

Defer not till tomorrow to be wise, tomorrow's sun to thee may never rise. —William Congreve

My head is buried in the sands of tomorrow, while my tail feathers are singed by the hot sun of today. —John Barrymore

Today, well lived, will prepare me for both the pleasure and the pain of tomorrow. —Anon.

The future belongs to those who live intensely in the present. —Anon.

Every moment that I am centered in the future, I suffer a temporary loss of this life. —Hugh Prather

We know nothing of tomorrow; our business is to be good and happy today. —Sydney Smith

We are always beginning to live, but are never living. —Manilius

Live wastes itself while we are preparing to live.
—Ralph Waldo Emerson

I have always been waiting for something better—sometimes to see the best I had snatched from me.
—Dorothy Reed Mendenhall

Men spend their lives in anticipation, in determining to be vastly happy at some period when they have time. But the present time has one advantage over every other—it is our own. . . . We may lay in a stock of pleasures, as we would lay in a stock of wine; but if we defer the tasting of them too long, we shall find that both are soured by age.
—Charles Caleb Colton

You do well to have visions of a better life than of every day, but it is the life of every day from which the elements of a better life must come.
—Maurice Maeterlinck

The most effective way to ensure the value of the future is to confront the present courageously and constructively. —Rollo May

The habit of looking into the future and thinking that the whole meaning of the present lies in what it will bring forth is a pernicious one. There can be no value in the whole unless there is value in the parts.
—Bertrand Russell

You don't save a pitcher for tomorrow. Tomorrow it may rain.
—Leo Durocher

Very strange is this quality of our human nature which decrees that unless we feel a future before us we do not live completely in the present.
—Phillips Brooks

Just do your best today and tomorrow will come . . . tomorrow's going to be a busy day, a happy day.
—Helen Boehm

Do today's duty, fight today's temptation; do not weaken and distract yourself by looking forward to things you cannot see, and could not understand if you saw them.
—Charles Kingsley

The best preparation for good work tomorrow is to do good work today.
—Elbert Hubbard

Live for today. Multitudes of people have failed to live for today. . . . What they have had within their grasp today they have missed entirely, because only the future has intrigued them. —William Allen White

Present opportunities are neglected, and attainable good is slighted, by minds busied in extensive ranges and intent upon future advantages.
—Samuel Johnson

Light tomorrow with today.
—Elizabeth Barrett Browning

A preoccupation with the future not only prevents us from seeing the present as it is, but often prompts us to rearrange the past. —Eric Hoffer

The man least dependent upon the morrow goes to meet the morrow most cheerfully. —Epicurus

Today's egg is better than tomorrow's
hen.   —Turkish proverb

T'were too absurd to slight for the
hereafter, the day's delight!
                    —Robert Browning

The best part of our lives we pass in
counting on what is to come.
                    —William Hazlitt

It seems to be the fate of man to seek
all his consolations in futurity.
                    —Samuel Johnson

The prospect of being pleased tomorrow will never console me for the
boredom of today.
                    —Francois de La Rochefoucauld

To live only for some future goal is
shallow. It's the sides of the mountain
that sustain life, not the top.
                    —Robert M. Pirsig

We steal if we touch tomorrow. It is
God's.   —Henry Ward Beecher

The past and present are only our
means; the future is always our end.
Thus we never really live, but only
hope to live.   —Blaise Pascal

This Moment

THE PRECIOUSNESS OF EACH MOMENT

The bliss e'en of a moment still is bliss.
—Joanna Baillie

Every second is of infinite value.
—Johann von Goethe

The bliss e'en of a moment still is bliss.
—Joanna Baillie

Let me tell thee, time is a very precious gift of God; so precious that it's only given to us moment by moment.
—Amelia Barr

There are half hours that dilate to the importance of centuries.
—Mary Catherwood

This—this was what made life: a moment of quiet, the water falling in the fountain, the girl's voice . . . a moment of captured beauty. He who is truly wise will never permit such moments to escape.
—Louis L'Amour

We do not remember days, we remember moments. —Cesare Pavese

Life is a succession of moments. To live each one is to succeed.
—Corita Kent

The span of life is waning fast;
Beware, unthinking youth, beware!
Thy soul's eternity depends
Upon the record moments bear!
—Eliza Cook

Florence Farr once said to me, "If we could say to ourselves, with sincerity, 'this passing moment is as good as any I shall ever know,' we could die upon the instant and be united with God." —William Butler Yeats

Sometimes I would almost rather have people take away years of my life than take away a moment.
—Pearl Bailey

Life is not lost by dying; life is lost minute by minute, day by day, in all the thousand small, uncaring ways.
—Stephen Vincent Benet

I have the happiness of the passing moment, and what more can mortal ask? —George R. Gissing

The sole life which a man can lose is that which he is living at the moment.
—Marcus Aurelius

I always say to myself, what is the most important thing we can think about at this extraordinary moment.
—Francois de La Rochefoucauld

Fill the unforgiving minute with sixty seconds worth of distance run.
—Rudyard Kipling

The present moment is creative, creating with an unheard-of intensity.
—Le Corbusier

The only way to live is to accept each minute as an unrepeatable miracle, which is exactly what it is: a miracle and unrepeatable. —Storm Jameson

Who makes quick use of the moment is a genius of prudence.
—Johann Kaspar Lavater

I live now and only now, and I will do what I want to do this moment and not what I decided was best for me yesterday. —Hugh Prather

But what minutes! Count them by sensation, and not by calendars, and each moment is a day.
—Benjamin Disraeli

It may be life is only worthwhile at moments. Perhaps that is all we ought to expect.
—Sherwood Anderson

To finish the moment, to find the journey's end in every step of the road, to live the greatest number of good hours, is wisdom.
—Ralph Waldo Emerson

Our latest moment is always our supreme moment. Five minutes delay in dinner now is more important than a great sorrow ten years gone.
—Samuel Butler

God speaks to all individuals through what happens to them moment by moment. —J.P. DeCaussade

Be always resolute with the present hour. Every moment is of infinite value. —Johann von Goethe

A player's effectiveness is directly related to his ability to be right there, doing that thing, in the moment. . . . He can't be worrying about the past or the future or the crowd or some other extraneous event. He must be able to respond in the here and now.
—John Brodie

OUR MOMENTS PASS TOO QUICKLY

We inhabit ourselves without valuing ourselves, unable to see that here, now, this very moment is sacred; but once it's gone—its value is incontestable. —Joyce Carol Oates

Life is all memory except for the one present moment that goes by so quick you can hardly catch it going.
—Tennessee Williams

The trouble is not that we are never happy—it is that happiness is so episodical. —Ruth Benedict

Non-cooks think it's silly to invest two hours' work in two minutes' enjoyment; but if cooking is evanescent, so is the ballet. —Julia Child

We have only this moment, sparkling like a star in our hand . . . and melting like a snowflake. Let us use it before it is too late.
—Marie Beynon Ray

It is privilege of living to be . . . acutely, agonizingly conscious of the moment that is always present and always passing.　—Marya Mannes

The passing moment is all we can be sure of; it is only common sense to extract its utmost value from it.
—W. Somerset Maugham

He is blessed over all mortals who loses no moment of the passing life.
—Henry David Thoreau

GENERAL QUOTATIONS ABOUT MOMENTS

We must not wish anything other than what happens from moment to moment, all the while, however, exercising ourselves in goodness.
—Saint Catherine of Genoa

The only courage that matters is the kind that gets you from one moment to the next.　—Mignon McLaughlin

The moment of change is the only poem.　　　—Adrienne Rich

If it weren't for the last minute, nothing would get done.　　　—Anon.

Once to every man and nation comes
　　the moment to decide. . . .
And the choice goes by forever t'wixt
　　that darkness and that light.
—James Russell Lowell

I have always felt that the moment when first you wake up in the morning is the most wonderful of the twenty-four hours. No matter how weary or dreary you may feel, you possess the certainty that . . . absolutely anything may happen. And the fact that it practically always doesn't, matters not one jot. The possibility is always there.　　—Monica Baldwin

Every age can be enchanting, provided you live within it.　—Brigitte Bardot

To live exhilaratingly in and for the moment is deadly serious work, fun of the most exhausting sort.
—Barbara Grizzuti Harrison

Love the moment and the energy of the moment will spread beyond all boundaries.　　　—Corita Kent

Life isn't a matter of milestones, but of moments.
—Rose Fitzgerald Kennedy

Mornings

No Matter How Bad Things Look at Night, They Usually Look Better in the Morning

There never was night that had no morn. —Dinah Maria Mulock Craik

Weeping may endure for a night, but joy cometh in the morning.
— Psalms 30:5

Sadness flies on the wings of the morning, and out of the heart of darkness comes the light.
—Jean Giraudoux

Out of the scabbard of the night,
By God's hand drawn,
Flashes his shining sword of light,
And lo, the dawn!
—Frank Dempster Sherman

For what human ill does not dawn seem to be an alleviation?
—Thornton Wilder

The weariest night, the longest day, sooner or later must perforce come to an end.   —Baroness Orczy

Beware of desp'rate steps; the darkest day lived till tomorrow will have pass'd away.   —William Cowper

Have hope. Though clouds environs now,
And gladness hides her face in scorn,
Put thou the shadow from thy brow—
No night but hath its morn.
—J.C.F. von Schiller

Snow endures but for a season, and joy comes with the morning.
—Marcus Aurelius

The morning is wiser than the evening.
—Russian proverb

For the mind disturbed, the still beauty of dawn is nature's finest balm.
—Edwin Way Teale

Hold your head high, stick your chest out. You can make it. It gets dark sometimes, but morning comes. . . . Keep hope alive.   —Jesse Jackson

Each day the world is born anew for him who takes it rightly.
—James Russell Lowell

It is a common experience that a problem difficult at night is resolved in the morning after the committee of sleep has worked on it.

—John Steinbeck

WE'RE REBORN EACH MORNING

Each day is a new life. Seize it. Live it.

—David Guy Powers

We sail, at sunrise, daily, "outward bound."   —Helen Hunt Jackson

Always begin anew with the day, just as nature does. It is one of the sensible things that nature does.

—George E. Woodberry

With each sunrise, we start anew.

—Anon.

I have always been delighted at the prospect of a new day, a fresh try, one more start, with perhaps a bit of magic waiting somewhere behind the morning.   —J.B. Priestly

Relying on God has to begin all over again every day as if nothing had yet been done.   —C.S. Lewis

Have patience with all things, but chiefly have patience with yourself. Do not lose courage in considering your own imperfections, but instantly set about remedying them—every day begin the task anew.

—Saint Francis de Sales

Each day is a little life; every waking and rising a little birth; every fresh morning a little youth; every going to rest and sleep a little death.

—Arthur Schopenhauer

I love the challenge of starting at zero every day and seeing how much I can accomplish.   —Martha Stewart

Whether one is twenty, forty, or sixty; whether one has succeeded, failed or just muddled along; whether yesterday was full of sun or storm, or one of those dull days with no weather at all, life begins each morning! . . . Each morning is the open door to a new world—new vistas, new aims, new tryings.   —Leigh Mitchell Hodges

To be seeing the world made new every morning, as if it were the morning of the first day, and then to make the most of it for the individual soul as if each were the last day, is the daily curriculum of the mind's desire.

—John H. Finley

Do not say, "It is morning," and dismiss it with a name of yesterday. See it for the first time as a newborn child that has no name.

—Rabindranath Tagore

God had infinite time to give us. . . . He cut it up into a near succession of new mornings, and, with each, therefore, a new idea, new inventions, and new applications.

—Ralph Waldo Emerson

We are new every day.

—Irene Claremont de Castillego

GET UP QUICKLY

No matter how big or soft or warm your bed is, you still have to get out of it.   —Grace Slick

Spill not the morning (the quintessence of the day!) in recreations, for sleep is a recreation. Add not, therefore, sauce to sauce. . . . Pastime, like wine, is poison in the morning. It is then good husbandry to sow the head, which hath lain fallow all night, with some serious work.
—Thomas Fuller

Do not shorten the morning by getting up late; look upon it as the quintessence of life, and to a certain extent sacred.
—Arthur Schopenhauer

Let us then be up and doing, with a heart for any fate.
—Henry Wadsworth Longfellow

He'd jolt up in bed every morning, sit quietly for a moment, and you could feel those wheels spinning in his mind as he planned his day. Then he'd hit the floor almost on the run.
—Sasha Stallone,
describing Sylvester's
early Hollywood days

Clay lies still, but blood's a rover
Breath's a ware that will not keep.
Up lad: when the journey's over
There'll be time enough to sleep.
—A.E. Housman

Even if a farmer intends to loaf, he gets up in time to get an early start.
—Edgar Watson Howe

GIVE THANKS

Wake at dawn with a winged heart and give thanks for another day of loving.   —Kahlil Gibran

I thank You God for this most amazing day; for the leaping greenly spirits of trees and a blue true dream of sky; and for everything which is natural which is infinite which is yes.
—e.e. cummings

I get up and I bless the light thin clouds and the first twittering of birds, and the breathing air and smiling face of the hills.
—Giacomo Leopardi

I'm a most lucky and thankful woman. Lucky and thankful for each morning I wake up. For three wonderful daughters and one son. For an understanding and very loving husband with whom I've shared fifty-two blessed years, all in good health.
—Thelma Elliott

If God adds another day to our life, let us receive it gladly.
—Marcus Annaeus Seneca

CHOOSING HOW
OUR DAY WILL BE

Here we stand between two eternities of darkness. What are we to do with this glory while it is still ours?
—Gilbert Murray

Your morning thoughts may determine your conduct for the day. Optimistic thoughts will make your day bright and productive, while pessimistic thinking will make it dull and wasteful. Face each day cheerfully, smilingly and courageously, and it will naturally follow that your work will be a real pleasure and progress will be a delightful accomplishment.
—William M. Peck

You should always know when you're shifting gears in life. You should leave your era; it should never leave you.   —Leontyne Price

The first thing each morning, and the last thing each night, suggest to yourself specific ideas that you wish to embody in your character and personality. Address such suggestions to yourself, silently or aloud, until they are deeply impressed upon your mind.   —Grenville Kleiser

Everyday ask yourself the question, "Do I want to experience Peace of Mind or do I want to experience Conflict?"   —Gerald Jampolsky

It was only a sunny smile,
And little it cost in the giving.
But like morning light, it scattered
    the night,
And made the day worth living.
                              —Anon.

To get up each morning with the resolve to be happy . . . is to set our own conditions to the events of each day. To do this is to condition circumstances instead of being conditioned by them.
                    —Ralph Waldo Trine

Today is a new day. You will get out of it just what you put into it. . . . If you have made mistakes, even serious mistakes, there is always another chance for you. And supposing you have tried and failed again and again, you may have a fresh start any moment you choose, for this thing that we call "failure" is not the falling down, but the staying down.
                    —Mary Pickford

When you rise in the morning, form a resolution to make the day a happy one for a fellow creature.
                    —Sydney Smith

As soon as you open your eyes in the morning, you can square away for a happy and successful day. It's the mood and the purpose at the inception of each day that are the important facts in charting your course for the day. We can always square away for a fresh start, no matter what the past has been.
              —George Matthew Adams

This is the beginning of a new day. God has given me this day to use as I will. I can waste it or use it for good, but what I do today is important, because I am exchanging a day of my life for it! When tomorrow comes, this day will be gone forever, leaving in its place something that I have traded for it. I want it to be gain, and not loss; good, and not evil; success, and not failure; in order that I shall not regret the price I have paid for it.
                              —Anon.

I think in terms of the day's resolutions, not the year's.   —Henry Moore

Every new day begins with possibilities. It's up to us to fill it with the things that move us toward progress and peace.   —Ronald Reagan

Here hath been dawning another blue day: think, wilt thou let it slip useless away?   —Thomas Carlyle

Be pleasant until ten o'clock in the morning and the rest of the day will take care of itself. —Elbert Hubbard

Today a thousand doors of enterprise are open to you, inviting you to useful work. To live at this time is an inestimable privilege, and a sacred obligation devolves upon you to make right use of your opportunities. Today is the day in which to attempt and achieve something worthwhile.

—Grenville Kleiser

Get out of bed forcing a smile. You may not smile because you are cheerful; but if you will force yourself to smile you'll . . . be cheerful because you smile. Repeated experiments prove that when man assumes the facial expression of a given mental mood, any given mood, then that mental mood itself will follow.

—Kenneth Goode

He who every morning plans the transactions of the day and follows that plan carries thread that will guide him through the labyrinth of the most busy life. —Victor Hugo

A man without a plan for the day is lost before he starts.

—Lewis K. Bendele

Never be afraid to sit awhile and think. —Lorraine Hansbury

Only the thinking man lives his life, the thoughtless man's life passes him by. —Marie von Ebner-Eschenbach

My credo is etched on my mirror in my bathroom and I see it when I brush my teeth in the morning. It says, "Don't worry, Be Happy, Feel Good." When you see that first thing, and you reflect on it, the rest of the day seems to glide by pretty well.

—Larry Hagman

Only that day dawns to which we are awake. —Henry David Thoreau

The day returns and brings us the petty round of irritating concerns and duties. Help us to play the man, help us to perform them with laughter and kind faces; let cheerfulness abound with industry. Give us to go blithely on our business all this day, bring us to our resting beds weary and content and undishonored, and grant us in the end the gift of sleep.

—Robert Louis Stevenson

REMAINING OPEN TO UNFORESEEN OPPORTUNITIES AND GIFTS

A day dawns, quite like other days; in it, a single hour comes, quite like other hours; but in that day and in that hour the chance of a lifetime faces us. —Maltbie D. Babcock

One never knows what each day is going to bring. The important thing is to be open and ready for it.

—Henry Moore

Great opportunities come to all, but many do not know they have met them. The only preparation to take advantage of them is . . . to watch what each day brings.

—Albert E. Dunning

There will be something, anguish or elation, that is peculiar to this day alone. I rise from sleep and say: Hail to the morning! Come down to me, my beautiful unknown.

—Jessica Powers

The Morning Sun

The sun is new each day.
>—Heraclitus

Someday the sun is going to shine
down on me in some faraway place.
>—Mahalia Jackson

With every rising of the sun, think of
your life as just begun.   —Anon.

I feel very happy to see the sun come
up every day. I feel happy to be
around. . . . I like to take this day—
any day—and go to town with it.
>—James Dickey

Look to the East, where up the lucid
   sky
The morning climbs! The day shall
   yet be fair.
>—Celia Thaxter

Each golden sunrise ushers in new
opportunities for those who retain
faith in themselves, and keep their
chins up. . . . Meet the sunrise with
confidence. Fill every golden minute
with right thinking and worthwhile
endeavor. Do this and there will be
joy for you in each golden sunset.
>—Alonzo Newton Benn

Today a new sun rises for me; everything lives, everything is animated,
everything seems to speak to me of
my passion, everything invites me to
cherish it.   —Anne De Lenclos

What humbugs we are, who pretend
to live for Beauty, and never see the
Dawn!   —Logan Pearsall Smith

Sunrise: day's great progenitor.
>—Emily Dickinson

General Quotations about Mornings

Put yourself in competition with
yourself each day. Each morning look
back upon your work of yesterday
and then try to beat it.
>—Charles M. Sheldon

The morning has gold in its mouth.
>—German proverb

Do you know what the greatest test
is? Do you still get excited about
what you do when you get up in the
morning?   —David Halberstam

Oft when the white, still dawn lifted
the skies and pushed the hills apart, I
have felt it like a glory in my heart.
>—Edwin Markham

Sometimes I have believed as many
as six impossible things before breakfast.   —Lewis Carroll

The mind is found most acute
and most uneasy in the morning.
Uneasiness is, indeed, a species of
sagacity—a passive sagacity. Fools
are never uneasy.
>—Johann von Goethe

Day's sweetest moments are at dawn.
>—Ella Wheeler Wilcox

Evenings

NIGHTLY ASSESSMENTS

We should every night call ourselves
to an account: What infirmity have
I mastered today? What passions
opposed! What temptation resisted?
What virtue acquired?
　　　　—Marcus Annaeus Seneca

Each morning puts man on trial and
each evening passes judgement.
　　　　—Roy L. Smith

I think, what has this day brought
me, and what have I given it?
　　　　—Henry Moore

Every night before I turn out the
lights to sleep, I ask myself this question: Have I done everything that I
can. . . . Have I done enough?
　　　　—Lyndon B. Johnson

Each morning sees some task begin,
each evening sees it close;
Something attempted, something
done, has earned a night's repose.
　　　　—Henry Wadsworth Longfellow

Judge each day not by it's harvest,
but by the seeds you plant.　—Anon.

Sum up at night what thou has done
by day.　　　　—Edward Herbert

TAKING OFF OUR CARES AND NEGATIVE EMOTIONS WITH OUR CLOTHING

Put off thy cares with thy clothes; so
shall thy rest strengthen thy labor,
and so thy labor sweeten thy rest.
　　　　—Francis Quarles

One of the secrets of a long and fruitful life is to forgive everybody everything every night before you go to
bed.　　　　—Anon.

The camel, at the close of day,
Kneels down upon the sandy plain
To have his burden lifted off
And rest again.
My soul, thou too should to thy
　knees
When daylight draweth to a close,
And let thy Master lift the load
And grant repose.　　　　—Anon.

To carry care to bed is to sleep with a
pack on your back.
　　　　—Thomas C. Haliburton

Let not the sun go down upon your wrath.   —Ephesians 14:26

Don't fight with the pillow, but lay
    down your head
And kick every worriment out of the
    bed.   —Edmund Vance Cooke

Shed, as you do your garments, your daily sins, whether of omission or commission, and you will wake a free man, with a new life.
    —Sir William Osler

Sleep

Thou driftest gently down the tides of sleep.
    —Henry Wadsworth Longfellow

Go to bed early, get up early—this is wise.   —Mark Twain

Come Sleep! Oh Sleep, the certain
    knot of peace,
The baiting-place of wit, the balm of
    woe,
The poor man's wealth, the prisoner's
    release,
The indifferent judge between the
    high and low.   —Sir Philip Sidney

Blessings on him that invented sleep! It covers a man, thoughts and all, like a cloak; it is meat for the hungry, drink for the thirsty, heat for the cold, and cold for the hot. It is the currency with which everything may be purchased, and the balance that sets even king and shepherd, simpleton and sage.   —Miguel de Cervantes

Health is the first muse, and sleep is the condition to produce it.
    —Ralph Waldo Emerson

O bed! O bed! Delicious bed! That heaven on earth to the weary head!
    —Thomas Hood

Fatigue is the best pillow.
    —Benjamin Franklin

A well-spent day brings happy sleep.
    —Leonardo da Vinci

It is a delicious moment, certainly, that of being well-nestled in bed and feeling that you shall drop gently to sleep. The good is to come, not past; the limbs are tired enough to render the remaining in one posture delightful; the labor of the day is gone.
    —Leigh Hunt

Sleep, Silence's child, sweet father of
    soft rest,
Prince whose approach peace to all
    mortals brings,
Indifferent host to shepherds and
    kings,
Sole comforter to minds with grief
    oppressed.
    —William Drummond

Sleep, that knits up the ravell'd slave
    of care,
The death of each day's life, sore
    labour's bath,
Balm of hurt minds, great nature's
    second course,
Chief nourisher in life's feast.
    —William Shakespeare

There is only one thing people like that is good for them; a good night's sleep.   —Edgar Watson Howe

Sleep is the most blessed and blessing of all natural graces.
    —Aldous Huxley

It is a common experience that a problem difficult at night is resolved in the morning after the committee of sleep has worked on it.
—John Steinbeck

Sleep: The golden chain that ties health and our bodies together.
—Thomas Dekker

Thank God for sleep! And when you cannot sleep, still thank Him that you live to lie awake.   —John Oxenham

Sleep . . . peace of the soul, who puttest care to flight.   —Ovid

Now I lay me down to sleep, I pray the Lord my soul to keep.   —Anon.

There may be those on earth who dress better or eat better, but those who enjoy the peace of God sleep better.   —L. Thomas Holdcroft

General Quotations about Evenings
Let us add this one more night to our lives.   —Suetonius

Fools look to tomorrow; wise men use tonight.   —Scottish proverb

Tomorrow: The Future

We're Not Supposed to See Too Far Ahead

It is a mistake to look too far ahead. Only one link in the chain of destiny can be handled at a time.
—Sir Winston Churchill

It is seldom in life that one knows that a coming event is to be of crucial importance. —Anya Seton

Neither in the life of the individual nor in that of mankind is it desirable to know the future.
—Jakob Burckhardt

There is only one large circle that we march in, around and around, each of us with our own little picture—in front of us—our own little mirage that we think is the future.
—Lorraine Hansbury

God made the world round so we would never be able to see too far down the road. —Isak Dinesen

The future comes one day at a time.
—Dean Acheson

There is a case, and a strong case, for that particular form of indolence that allows us to move through life knowing only what immediately concerns us. —Alec Waugh

Cease to inquire what the future has in store, and take as a gift whatever the day brings forth. —Horace

There is no data on the future.
—Laurel Cutler

The best thing about the future is that it comes only one day at a time.
—Abraham Lincoln

Hardly anyone knows how much is gained by ignoring the future.
—Bernard de Fontenelle

The future is hidden even from those who make it. —Anatole France

Tomorrow's Always Another Day

They who lose today may win tomorrow. —Miguel de Cervantes

Be of good cheer. Do not think of today's failures, but of the success that may come tomorrow. You have set yourselves a difficult task, but you will succeed if you persevere; and you will find a joy in overcoming obstacles. Remember, no effort that we make to attain something beautiful is ever lost. —Helen Keller

When all else is lost, the future still remains. —Christian Bovee

There is hope for all of us. Well, anyway, if you don't die you live through it, day in, day out. —Mary Beckett

Our faith in the present dies out long before our faith in the future. —Ruth Benedict

I have been nothing . . . but there is tomorrow. —Louis L'Amour

After all, tomorrow is another day. —Scarlett O'Hara, *Gone wWith the Wind*

Everyone has it within his power to say, this I am today, that I shall be tomorrow. —Louis L'Amour

WE CAN'T BE AFRAID OF THE FUTURE

He who foresees calamities suffers them twice over. —Beilby Porteous

Only man clogs his happiness with care, destroying what is with thoughts of what may be. —John Dryden

It is never safe to look into the future with eyes of fear. —E.H. Harriman

If you are afraid for your future, you don't have a present. —James Petersen

He that fears not the future may enjoy the present. —Thomas Fuller

Cowards die many times before their deaths; the valiant never taste of death but once. —William Shakespeare

The future is called "perhaps," which is the only possible thing to call the future. And the important thing is not to allow that to scare you. —Tennessee Williams

To relinquish a present good through apprehension of a future evil is in most instances unwise . . . from a fear which may afterwards turn out groundless, you lost the good that lay within your grasp. —Francesco Guicciardini

Nothing in life is more remarkable than the unnecessary anxiety which we endure, and generally create ourselves. —Benjamin Disraeli

Every man, through fear, mugs his aspirations a dozen times a day. —Brendan Francis

The mere apprehension of a coming evil has put many into a situation of the utmost danger. —Lucan

We need not be afraid of the future, for the future will be in our own hands. —Thomas E. Dewey

I am not afraid of tomorrow, for I have seen yesterday and I love today. —William Allen White

Go forth to meet the shadowy Future
without fear and with a manly heart.
　　　—Henry Wadsworth Longfellow

WE MUST LEARN TO
TRUST THE FUTURE

We grow in time to trust the future
for our answers.　　　—Ruth Benedict

Every tomorrow has two handles. We
can take hold of it with the handle of
anxiety or the handle of faith.
　　　　　—Henry Ward Beecher

Put aside the need to know some
future design and simply leave your
life open to what is needed of it by
the Divine forces.　　　—Emmanuel

See how time makes all grief decay.
　　　　　—Adelaide Proctor

The only limit to our realization
of tomorrow will be our doubts of
today. Let us move forward with
strong and active faith.
　　　—Franklin Delano Roosevelt

It is not the cares of today, but the
cares of tomorrow, that weigh a man
down. For the needs of today we
have corresponding strength given.
For the morrow we are told to trust.
It is not ours yet.
　　　　　—George MacDonald

Take therefore no thought of the
morrow; for the morrow shall take
thought for the things of itself.
　　　　　—Matthew 6:34

OTHER DEFINITIONS OF
TOMORROW AND THE FUTURE

Tomorrow is the day when idlers
work, and fools reform, and mortal
men lay hold on heaven.
　　　　　—Edward Young

Tomorrow is the mysterious,
unknown guest.
　　　—Henry Wadsworth Longfellow

Tomorrow is the only day in the year
that appeals to a lazy man.
　　　　　—Jimmy Lyons

The future is something which
everyone reaches at the rate of sixty
minutes an hour, whatever he does,
whoever he is.　　　—C.S. Lewis

The future is a world limited by ourselves—in it we discover only what
concerns us.　—Maurice Maeterlinck

The future is only the past again,
entered through another gate.
　　　　　—Arthur Wing Pinero

The future is the most expensive
luxury in the world.
　　　　　—Thornton Wilder

The future is the shape of things to
come.　　　　　—H. G. Wells

The future is the past in preparation.
　　　　　—Pierre Dac

To the being of fully alive, the future
is not ominous but a promise; it surrounds the present like a halo.
　　　　　—John Dewey

The future is hope!　　　—John Fiske

The future is a great land. —Anon.

The future is wider than vision, and has no end. —Donald G. Mitchell

General Quotations about Tomorrow and the Future

Losing the future is the best thing that ever happened to me.
—Marilyn French

Grow old along with me! The best is yet to be. —Robert Browning

I have always been driven by some distant music—a battle hymn no doubt—for I have been at war from the beginning. I've never looked back before. I've never had the time and it has always seemed so dangerous.
—Bette Davis

He who lives in the future lives in a featureless blank; he lives in impersonality; he lives in Nirvana. The past is democratic, because it is a people. The future is despotic, because it is a caprice. Every man is alone in his prediction, just as each man is alone in a dream. —G.K. Chesterton

The future belongs to those who believe in the beauty of their dreams.
—Eleanor Roosevelt

When I look to the future, it's so bright, it burns my eyes.
—Oprah Winfrey

I like the dreams of the future better than the history of the past.
—Thomas Jefferson

I never think of the future. It comes soon enough. —Albert Einstein

You cannot plan the future by the past. —Edmund Burke

It is when tomorrow's burden is added to the burden of today that the weight is more than a man can bear.
—George MacDonald

My interest is in the future because I am going to spend the rest of my life there. —Charles F. Kettering

Yesterday is not ours to recover, but tomorrow is ours to win or lose.
—Lyndon B. Johnson

The possibilities for tomorrow are usually beyond our expectations.
—Anon.

Where will I be five years from now? I delight in not knowing. That's one of the greatest things about life—its wonderful surprises.
—Marlo Thomas

When I look at the future, it's so bright, it burns my eyes.
—Oprah Winfrey

Everyone's future is, in reality, uncertain and full of unknown treasures from which all may draw unguessed prizes. —Lord Dunsany

The future is made of the same stuff as the present. —Simone Weil

The future is much like the present, only longer. —Dan Quisenberry

By-and-by never comes.
—Saint Augustine

The bridges you cross before you
come to them are over rivers that
aren't there.   —Gene Brown

Strike when thou wilt, the hour of
rest, but let my last days be my best.
                    —Robert Browning

For you and me, today is all we have;
tomorrow is a mirage that may never
become reality.   —Louis L'Amour

I fear there will be no future for those
who do not change.
                    —Louis L'Amour

If a man carefully examines his
thoughts he will be surprised to find
how much he lives in the future. His
well-being is always ahead.
          —Ralph Waldo Emerson

I got the blues thinking of the future,
so I left off and made some marmalade. It's amazing how it cheers one
up to shred oranges and scrub the
floor.   —D.H. Lawrence

You learn to build your roads on
today, because tomorrow's ground is
too uncertain for plans, and futures
have a way of falling down in mid-
flight.   —Veronica Shoffstal

Fortunately for children, the uncertainties of the present always give
way to the enchanted possibilities of
the future.   —Gelsey Kirkland

Average, "Boring" Days

AVERAGE DAYS

Normal day, let me be aware of the
treasure you are. Let me learn from
you, love you, bless you before you
depart. Let me not pass you by in
quest of some rare and perfect tomorrow. Let me hold you while I may,
for it may not always be so. One day
I shall dig my nails into the earth, or
bury my face in the pillow, or stretch
myself taut, or raise my hands to
the sky and want, more than all the
world, your return.
                    —Mary Jean Iron

Either you reach a higher point today,
or you exercise your strength in order
to be able to climb higher tomorrow.
                    —Friedrich Nietzsche

One appreciates that daily life is
really good when one wakes from a
horrible dream, or when one takes
the first outing after a sickness. Why
not realize it now?
                    —William Lyon Phelps

This is the day which the Lord hath
made; we will rejoice and be glad.
                    —Psalms 118:24

That man is happiest who lives from
day to day and asks no more, garnering the simple goodness of a life.
                    —Euripides

Write it on your heart that every day
is the best day in the year.
                    —Ralph Waldo Emerson

Sunshine is delicious, rain is refreshing, wind braces us, snow is exhilarating; there is no such thing as bad
weather, only different kinds of good
weather.   —John Ruskin

DAY-TO-DAY LIVING IS HARDER THAN AN EMERGENCY

A man can stand almost anything
except a succession of ordinary days.
                    —Johann von Goethe

We look wishfully to emergencies,
to eventful, revolutionary times ...
and think how easy to have taken
our part when the drum was rolling
and the house was burning over our
heads.   —Ralph Waldo Emerson

Poets are like baseball pitchers. Both have their moments. The intervals are the tough things. —Robert Frost

Any idiot can face a crisis—it's day to day living that wears you out.
—Anton Chekhov

They sicken of the calm that know the storm. —Ralph Waldo Emerson

Peace is not only better than war, but infinitely more arduous.
—George Bernard Shaw

Peace hath higher tests of manhood
Than battle ever knew.
—John Greenleaf Whittier

Man lives by habits indeed, but what he lives for is thrill and excitements. ... From time immemorial war has been ... the supremely thrilling excitement. —William James

It is not merely cruelty that leads men to love war, it is excitement.
—Henry Ward Beecher

The statistics of suicide show that, for non-combatants at least, life is more interesting in war than in peace.
—William Ralph Inge

The Problems and Dangers of Boredom

Boredom is rage spread thin.
—Paul Tillich

Ennui has made more gamblers than avarice, more drunkards than thirst, and perhaps as many suicides as despair. —Charles Caleb Colton

Boredom ... causes us to neglect more duties than does interest.
—Francois de La Rochefoucauld

Boredom is a vital problem for the moralist, since at least half of the sins of mankind are caused by the fear of it. —Bertrand Russell

Boredom slays more of existence than war. —Norman Mailer

One of the worst forms of mental suffering is boredom, not knowing what to do with oneself and one's life. Even if man had no monetary, or any other reward, he would be eager to spend his energy in some meaningful way because he could not stand the boredom which inactivity produces.
—Erich Fromm

Monotony is the awful reward of the careful. —A.G. Buckham

Boredom is the most horrible of wolves. —Jean Giono

We Bore Ourselves, and It's Up to Us to Overcome Boredom

If your daily life seems poor, do not blame it; blame yourself, tell yourself that you are not poet enough to call forth its riches.
—Rainer Maria Rilke

Banality is a terribly likely consequence of the underuse of a good mind.
—Cynthia Propper Seton

Somebody's boring me; I think it's me.
—Dylan Thomas

329

The cure for boredom is curiosity.
There is no cure for curiosity.
—Ellen Parr

Being bored is an insult to oneself.
—Jules Renard

The amount of satisfaction you get
from life depends largely on your
own ingenuity, self-sufficiency, and
resourcefulness. People who wait
around for life to supply their satisfaction usually find boredom instead.
—Dr. William Menninger

When you stop learning, stop listening, stop looking and asking questions, always new questions, then it is
time to die.   —Lillian Smith

When people are bored, it is primarily with their own selves that they are
bored.   —Eric Hoffer

Is not life a hundred times too short
for us to bore ourselves?
—Friedrich Nietzsche

Nothing is interesting if you're not
interested.   —Helen MacInness

Boredom is a sickness of the soul.
—Anon.

Boredom is simply the lack of imagination.   —Julie O. Smith

Perhaps the world's second worst
crime is boredom. The first is being a
bore.   —Cecil Beaton

SOME REMEDIES FOR BOREDOM

In the ancient recipe, the three anti-
dotes for dullness or boredom are
sleep, drink, and travel. It is rather
feeble. From sleep you wake up, from
drink you become sober, and from
travel you come home again. And
then where are you? No, the two sovereign remedies for dullness are love
or a crusade.   —D.H. Lawrence

You can learn new things at any time
in your life if you're willing to be a
beginner. If you actually learn to like
being a beginner, the whole world
opens up to you.   —Barbara Sher

As for boredom . . . I notice that it
leaves me as soon as I am doing
something that has got to be done.
—John Jay Chapman

Uncertainty and mystery are energies of life. Don't let them scare you
unduly, for they keep boredom at bay
and spark creativity.
—R.I. Fitzhenry

If something is boring after two minutes, try it for four. If still boring, try
it for eight, sixteen, thirty-two, and
so on. Eventually, one discovers that
it is not boring, but very interesting.
—Zen saying

Nobody is bored when he is trying to
make something that is beautiful, or
to discover something that is true.
—William Ralph Inge

The one sure means of dealing with
boredom is to care for someone else,
to do something kind and good.
—Theodore Haecker

Everything considered, work is less boring than amusing oneself.
—Charles Baudelaire

General Quotations about Boredom

Man is the only animal that can be bored.
—Erich Fromm

The only unhappiness is a life of boredom.
—Stendhal

Getting bored is not allowed.
—Kay Thompson

One can be bored until boredom becomes a mystical experience.
—Logan Pearsall Smith

One must choose in life between boredom and suffering.
—Madame de Staël

We often forgive those who bore us, but can't forgive those whom we bore.
—Francois de La Rochefoucauld

Dullness is a misdemeanor.
—Ethel Wilson

Over-excitement and boredom are states of mind which I equally shun.
—E.V. Knox

Passions are less mischievous than boredom, for passions tend to diminish and boredom increase.
—Jules Barbey d'Aurevilly

It is better to be happy for the moment and be burned up with beauty than to live a long time and be bored all the while.
—Don Marquis

Boredom: the desire for desires.
—Leo Tolstoy

The only menace is inertia.
—Saint John Perse

Boredom is useful to me when I notice it and think: Oh I'm bored; there must be something else I want to be doing . . . boredom acts as an initiator of originality by pushing me into new activities or new thoughts.
—Hugh Prather

Boredom, like necessity, is very often the mother of invention.
—Anon.

One of man's finest qualities is described by the simple word "guts"—the ability to take it. If you have the discipline to stand fast when your body wants to run, if you can control your temper and remain cheerful in the face of monotony or disappointments, you have "guts" in the soldiering sense.
—Colonel John S. Roosman

Life is as tedious as a twice-told tale, vexing the dull ear of a drowsy man.
—William Shakespeare

An enthusiast may bore others, but he has never a dull moment himself.
—John Kieran

Three-quarters of a soldier's life is spent in aimlessly waiting about.
—Eugene Rosenstock-Huessy

Difficult Days

DIFFICULT DAYS

Everyone gets their rough day. No
one gets a free ride. Today so far, I
had a good day. I got a dial tone.
— Rodney Dangerfield

Thy fate is the common fate of all,
Into each life some rain must fall,
Some days must be dark and dreary.
— Henry Wadsworth Longfellow

Some days you tame the tiger. And
some days the tiger has you for lunch.
— Tug McGraw

Some days the dragon wins. — Anon.

EVERYTHING CHANGES

The one law that does not change
is that everything changes, and the
hardship I was bearing today was
only a breath away from the pleasures I would have tomorrow, and
those pleasures would be all the
richer because of the memories of this
I was enduring.   — Louis L'Amour

Experience cold or heat, pleasure
or pain. These experiences are fleeting; they come and go. Bear them
patiently.
— Sri Krishna, (Bhagavad Gita)

To everything there is a season,
A time for every purpose under
heaven. . . .
A time to weep, and a time to laugh,
A time to mourn, and a time to
dance.   — Ecclesiastes 3:1, 4

Let nothing disturb thee,
Let nothing affright thee,
All things are passing,
God changeth never.
— Teresa of Avila

This, too, shall pass.
— William Shakespeare

The present will not long endure.
— Pindar

We do not live an equal life, but one
of contrasts and patchwork; now a
little joy, then a sorrow, now a sin,
then a generous or brave action.
— Ralph Waldo Emerson

I feel successful when the writing goes well. This lasts five minutes. Once, when I was number one on the bestseller list, I also felt successful. That lasted three minutes.
—Jacqueline Briskin

To those who shall sit here rejoicing, and to those who shall sit here lamenting, greetings and sympathy. So have we done in our time.
—Bench inscription, Cornell University

Sadness and gladness succeed each other.
—Anon.

Sadness flies away on the wings of time.
—Jean de La Fontaine

I don't think that ... one gets a flash of happiness once, and never again; it is there within you, and it will come as certainly as death. . . .
—Isak Dinesen

Life comes in clusters, clusters of solitude, then clusters when there is hardly time to breathe.
—May Sarton

THE CONDITIONS OF OUR LIVES CHANGE LIKE NATURE'S SEASONS

If winter comes, can spring be far behind?
—Percy Bysshe Shelley

Human misery must somewhere have a stop; there is no wind that always blows a storm.
—Euripides

No winter lasts forever; no spring skips its turn.
—Hal Borland

There are trees that seem to die at the end of autumn. There are also the evergreens.
—Gilbert Maxwell

Our Lord has written the promise of resurrection, not in books alone, but in every leaf in springtime.
—Martin Luther

For, lo, the winter is past, the rain is over and gone; the flowers appear on the earth.
—Song of Solomon 2:11–12

Sitting quietly, doing nothing, Spring comes, and the grass grows by itself.
—*The Gospel According to Zen*

There ain't no cloud so thick that the sun ain't shinin' on t'other side.
—Rattlesnake, an 1870s mountain man

If matters go badly now, they will not always be so.
—Horace

PAIN AND SUFFERING

Pain is never permanent.
—Teresa of Avila

You will suffer and you will hurt. You will have joy and you will have peace.
—Alison Cheek

Pain is part of being alive, and we need to learn that. Pain does not last forever, nor is it necessarily unbearable, and we need to be taught that.
—Rabbi Harold Kushner

Pain is hard to bear. . . .
But with patience, day by day,
Even this shall pass away.
—Theodore Tilton

Everything in life that we really accept undergoes a change. So suffering must become love. That is the mystery.   —Katherine Mansfield

FAILURE AND FINANCIAL PROBLEMS

I've been failing for, like, ten or eleven years. When it turns, it'll turn. Right now I'm just tryin' to squeeze through a very tight financial period, get the movie out, and put my things in order.   —Francis Ford Coppola

I've never been poor, only broke. Being poor is a frame of mind. Being broke is a temporary situation.
    —Mike Todd

GOOD THINGS OFTEN RESULT FROM DIFFICULT THINGS

In the darkest hour the soul is replenished and given strength to continue and endure.   —Heart Warrior Chosa

He that can't endure the bad will not live to see the good.
    —Yiddish proverb

Our toil is sweet with thankfulness,
Our burden is our boon;
The curse of earth's gray morning is
The blessing of its noon.
    —John Greenleaf Whittier

Were it possible for us to see further than our knowledge reaches, perhaps we would endure our sadnesses with greater confidence than our joys. For they are moments when something new has entered into us, something unknown.   —Rainer Maria Rilke

We may draw good outof evil; we must not do evil, that good may come.
    —Maria Weston Chapman

You will find a joy in overcoming obstacles.   —Helen Keller

ENDINGS ARE ALSO BEGINNINGS

What we call the beginning is often an end. And to make an end is to make a beginning. The end is where we start from.   —T.S. Eliot

When one door of happiness closes, another opens; but often we look so long at the closed door that we do not see the one which has been opened for us.   —Helen Keller

Death is a door life opens.
    —Adela Rogers St. Johns

The world is round, and the place which may seem like the end may also be only the beginning.
    —Ivy Baker Priest

SOMEDAY, WE'LL LOOK BACK AND THINGS WON'T SEEM AS DIFFICULT AS THEY DO NOW

Perhaps someday it will be pleasant to remember even this.   —Virgil

One day in retrospect the years of struggle will strike you as the most beautiful.   —Sigmund Freud

The crisis of today is the joke of tomorrow.   —H.G. Wells

Sadness flies away on the wings of time.   —Jean de La Fontaine

Sometimes I found that in my happy moments I could not believe that I had ever been miserable.

—Joanna Field

It Just Takes Time

If our education had included training to bear unpleasantness and to let the first shock pass until we could think more calmly, many an unbearable situation would become manageable, and many a nervous illness avoided. There is a proverb expressing this. It says, trouble is a tunnel through which we pass and not a brick wall against which we must break our head. —Claire Weeks

Time, in the turning-over of days, works change, for better or worse.

—Pindar

Experience is what really happens to you in the long run; the truth that finally overtakes you.

—Katherine Anne Porter

Time is like a river of fleeting events, and its current is strong; as soon as something comes into sight, it is swept past us, and something else takes its place, and that too will be swept away. —Marcus Aurelius

Time cools, time clarifies; no mood can be maintained quite unaltered through the course of hours.

—Thomas Mann

Time bears away all things. —Virgil

Come what come may, time and the hour runs through the roughest day.

—William Shakespeare

Time brings all things to pass.

—Aeschylus

We undo ourselves by impatience. Misfortunes have their life and their limits, their sickness and their health.

—Michel de Montaigne

The future is something which everyone reaches at the rate of sixty minutes an hour, whatever he does, whoever he is. —C.S. Lewis

That's the advantage of having lived sixty-five years. You don't feel the need to be impatient any longer.

—Thornton Wilder

Your three best doctors are faith, time, and patience.

—From a fortune cookie

Patience Is a Key to Success, to Victory

Who longest waits most surely wins.

—Helen Hunt Jackson

Patience is a bitter plant, but it has sweet fruit. —German proverb

No emergency excuses you from exercising tolerance.

—Phyllis Bottome

I believe the sign of maturity is accepting deferred gratification.

—Peggy Cahn

He that can have patience can have what he will. —Benjamin Franklin

Being human, we should bear all we can. —Norma Meacock

Adopt the pace of nature, her secret is patience.   —Ralph Waldo Emerson

You can't have genius without patience.   —Margaret Deland

The most potent and sacred command which can be laid upon any artist is the command: wait.
                —Iris Murdoch

How poor are they that have not patience? What wound did ever heal but by degrees?
                —William Shakespeare

All things come round to him who will but wait.
        —Henry Wadsworth Longfellow

Panic is not an effective long-term organizing strategy.   —Starhawk

Self-denial is painful for a moment, but very agreeable in the end.
                —Jane Taylor

And he shall reign a goodly king
And sway his hand o'er every clime
With peace writ on his signet ring,
Who bides his time.
                —James Whitcomb Riley

It takes time to succeed because success is merely the natural reward of taking time to do anything well.
                —Joseph Ross

Patience and fortitude conquer all things.   —Ralph Waldo Emerson

Be not afraid of growing slowly, be afraid only of standing still.
                —Chinese proverb

Wisely and slow. They stumble that run fast.   —William Shakespeare

No great thing is created suddenly, any more than a bunch of grapes or a fig. If you tell me that you desire a fig, I answer you that there must be time. Let it first blossom, then bear fruit, then ripen.   —Epictetus

Time deals gently only with those who take it gently.   —Anatole France

Hold on; hold fast; hold out. Patience is genius.   —Georges de Buffon

Genius is nothing but a greater aptitude for patience.
                —Benjamin Franklin

All human wisdom is summed up in two words: wait and hope.
                —Alexandre Dumas

Genius is eternal patience.
                —Michelangelo

Serene I fold my hands and wait.
                —John Burroughs

The race is not to the swift, nor the battle to the strong. —Ecclesiastes 9:11

Everything comes if a man will only wait.   —Benjamin Disraeli

BEING PRODUCTIVE
WHILE WE'RE BEING PATIENT

Everything comes to him who hustles while he waits.   —Thomas A. Edison

The secret of patience . . . to do something else in the meantime.   —Anon.

Have patience with all things, but chiefly have patience with yourself. Do not lose courage in considering your own imperfections, but instantly set about remedying them—every day begin the task anew.
—Saint Francis de Sales

Let us then be up and doing,
With a heart for any fate,
Still achieving, still pursuing,
Learn to labor and to wait.
—Henry Wadsworth Longfellow

General Quotations about Difficult Days

God will wait as long as it takes for us.
—Reverend R. Walters

Waiting is not mere empty hoping. It has the inner certainty of reaching the goal.
—I Ching

All things come to him who waits—provided he knows what he is waiting for.
—Woodrow Wilson

Hope and patience are two sovereign remedies for all, the surest reposals, the softest cushions to lean on in adversity.
—Robert Burton

The strongest of all warriors are these two—Time and Patience.
—Leo Tolstoy

Who bides his time tastes the sweet
Of honey in the saltiest tear;
And though he fares with slowest feet
Joy runs to meet him drawing near.
—James Whitcomb Riley

God grant us patience!
—William Shakespeare

Better is the end of a thing than the beginning thereof: and the patient in spirit is better than the proud in spirit.
—Ecclesiastes 7:8

There is nothing so bitter that a patient mind cannot find some solace for it.
—Marcus Annaeus Seneca

Patience is the best remedy for every trouble.
—Plautus

For ye have need of patience. . . .
—Hebrews 10:36

They are ill discoverers that think there is no land, when they see nothing but sea.
—Francis Bacon

PART 3

Preparing for Success

Positive Thinking
and Self-Fulfilling
Prophecies and Actions

OUR FAITH AND BELIEF
CREATE OUR REALITY

Beauty to me is being comfortable in your own skin.   —Gwyneth Paltrow

Man is what he believes.
—Anton Chekhov

Believe that life is worth living, and your belief will help create that fact.
—William James

Dream lofty dreams, and as you dream, so shall you become. Your vision is the promise of what you shall at last unveil.   —John Ruskin

Our belief at the beginning of a doubtful undertaking is the one thing that ensures the successful outcome of our venture.   —William James

We are what we believe we are.
—Benjamin N. Cardozo

If you constantly think of illness, you eventually become ill; if you believe yourself to be beautiful, you become so.   —Shakti Gawain

You have to believe in happiness, or happiness never comes.
—Douglas Malloch

If you keep on saying things are going to be bad, you have a good chance of being a prophet.
—Isaac Bashevis Singer

What one believes to be true either is true or becomes true within limits to be found experientially and experimentally. These limits are beliefs to be transcended.   —John Lilly

The thing always happens that you really believe in; and the belief in a thing makes it happen.
—Frank Lloyd Wright

OUR ATTITUDES
CREATE OUR LIVES

The name we give to something
shapes our attitude toward it.
                    —Katherine Paterson

This I know. This I believe with
all my heart. If we want a free and
peaceful world, if we want to make
the deserts bloom and man grow to
greater dignity as a human being—
we can do it!   —Eleanor Roosevelt

The name we give to something
shapes our attitude toward it.
                    —Katherine Paterson

This I know. This I believe with
all my heart. If we want a free and
peaceful world, if we want to make
the deserts bloom and man grow to
greater dignity as a human being—we
can do it!   —Eleanor Roosevelt

Failure is impossible.
                    —Susan B. Anthony

If you think you can, you can. And if
you think you can't, you're right.
                    —Mary Kay Ash

When you look at the world in a
narrow way, how narrow it seems!
When you look at it in a mean way,
how mean it is! When you look at it
selfishly, how selfish it is! But when
you look at it in a broad, generous,
friendly spirit, what wonderful people
you find in it.   —Horace Rutledge

Always keep that happy attitude.
Pretend that you are holding a beautiful fragrant bouquet.
                    —Candice M. Pope

She was one of those happily created
beings who please without effort,
make friends everywhere, and take
life so gracefully and easily that less
fortunate souls are tempted to believe
that such are born under a lucky star.
                    —Louisa May Alcott

It was completely fruitless to quarrel
with the world, whereas the quarrel
with oneself was occasionally fruitful
and always, she had to admit, interesting.   —May Sarton

Each of us makes his own weather,
determines the color of the skies in
the emotional universe which he
inhabits.   —Fulton J. Sheen

One of the things I learned the hard
way was that it doesn't pay to get
discouraged. Keeping busy and making optimism a way of life can restore
your faith in yourself.   —Lucille Ball

Life is raw material. We are artisans.
We can sculpt our existence into
something beautiful, or debase it into
ugliness. It's in our hands.
                    —Cathy Better

I invented my life by taking for
granted that everything I did not like
would have an opposite, which I
would like.   —Coco Chanel

If you look at life one way, there is
always cause for alarm.
                    —Elizabeth Bowen

Being tall is an advantage, especially in business. People will always
remember you. And if you're in a
crowd, you'll always have some clean
air to breathe.   —Julia Child

It is only in sorrow bad weather masters us; in joy we face the storm and defy it.　　　　—Amelia Barr

The pure, the beautiful, the bright,
That stirred our hearts in youth,
The impulse to a wordless prayer,
The dreams of love and truth,
The longings after something lost,
The spirit's yearning cry,
The strivings after better hopes,
These things can never die.
　　　　　　　—Sarah Doudney

I actually remember feeling delight, at two o'clock in the morning, when the baby woke for his feed, because I so longed to have another look at him.
　　　　　　—Margaret Drabble

Teenagers travel in droves, packs, swarms. . . . To the librarian, they're a gaggle of geese. To the cook, they're a scourge of locusts. To department stores, they're a big beautiful exaltation of larks . . . all lovely and loose and jingly.　　—Bernice Fitz-Gibbon

Both abundance and lack exist simultaneously in our lives, as parallel realities. It is always our conscious choice which secret garden we will tend . . . when we choose not to focus on what is missing from our lives but are grateful for the abundance that's present—love, health, family, friends, work, the joys of nature, and personal pursuits that bring us pleasure—the wasteland of illusion falls away and we experience heaven on earth.　　—Sarah Ban Breathnach

Exude happiness and you will feel it back a thousand times.
　　　　　　　—Joan Lunden

I keep my ideals, because in spite of everything I still believe that people are really good at heart.
　　　　　　　—Anne Frank

Man's rise or fall, success or failure, happiness or unhappiness depends on his attitude . . . a man's attitude will create the situation he imagines.
　　　　　　—James Lane Allen

A good heart will help you to a bonny face, my lad . . . and a bad one will turn the bonniest into something worse than ugly.　　—Emily Brontë

The greatest discovery of my generation is that man can alter his life simply by altering his attitude of mind.
　　　　　　—William James

I think there is a choice possible to us at any moment, as long as we live. But there is no sacrifice. There is a choice, and the rest falls away. Second choice does not exist. Beware of those who talk about sacrifice.
　　　　　　—Muriel Rukeyser

Life has, indeed, many ills, but the mind that views every object in its most cheering aspect, and every doubtful dispensation as replete with latent good, bears within itself a powerful and perpetual antidote.
　　　　　—Lydia H. Sigourney

Immense power is acquired by assuring yourself in your secret reveries that you were born to control affairs.
　　　　　　—Andrew Carnegie

A woman's hopes are woven of sunbeams; a shadow annihilates them.
　　　　　　　—George Eliot

Keep your face to the sunshine and you cannot see the shadow.
—Helen Keller

Man's real life is happy, chiefly because he is ever expecting that it soon will be so.   —Edgar Allan Poe

Some folks never exaggerate—they just remember big.   —Audrey Snead

I expect some new phases of life this summer, and shall try to get the honey from each moment.
—Lucy Stone

Love is much nicer to be in than an automobile accident, a tight girdle, a higher tax bracket, or a holding pattern over Philadelphia.
—Judith Viorst

I am optimistic and confident in all that I do. I affirm only the best for myself and others. I am the creator of my life and my world. I meet daily challenges gracefully and with complete confidence. I fill my mind with positive, nurturing, and healing thoughts.   —Alice Potter

'Tis very certain the desire of life prolongs it.   —Lord Byron

Happiness is the ability to recognize it.
—Carolyn Wells

The saddest day hath gleams of light,
The darkest wave hath bright foam
    beneath it,
The twinkles o'er the cloudiest night,
Some solitary star to cheer it.
—Sarah Winnemucca

Every thought we think is creating our future.   —Louise L. Hay

Could we change our attitude, we should not only see life differently, but life itself would come to be different. Life would undergo a change of appearance because we ourselves had undergone a change in attitude.
—Katherine Mansfield

The words "I am . . . " are potent words; be careful what you hitch them to. The thing you're claiming has a way of reaching back and claiming you.   —A.L. Kitselman

Self-image sets the boundaries of individual accomplishment.
—Maxwell Maltz

We are not interested in the possibilities of defeat.
—Victoria, Queen of England

To think of losing is to lose already.
—Sylvia Townsend Warner

Nothing can stop the man with the right mental attitude from achieving his goal; nothing on earth can help the man with the wrong mental attitude.   —W.W. Ziege

If you expect nothing, you're apt to be surprised. You'll get it.
—Malcolm Forbes

Life is like a mirror. Smile at it and it smiles back at you.   —Peace Pilgrim

Since the human body tends to move in the direction of its expectations—plus or minus—it is important to know that attitudes of confidence and determination are no less a part of the treatment program than medical science and technology.
—Norman Cousins

They can because they think they can.
—Virgil

I do think that being the second [female Supreme Court Justice] is wonderful, because it is a sign that being a woman in a place of importance is no longer extraordinary.
—Ruth Bader Ginsberg

Women forget all the things they don't want to remember, and remember everything they don't want to forget.   —Zora Neale Hurston

When you're in love, you put up with things that, when you're out of love you cite.
—Judith Martin (Miss Manners)

To the timid and hesitating everything is impossible because it seems so.
—Sir Walter Scott

Work is either fun or drudgery. It depends on your attitude. I like fun.
—Colleen C. Barrett

We Find What We Look For

What we see depends mainly on what we look for.   —John Lubbock

People only see what they are prepared to see.
—Ralph Waldo Emerson

For years I wanted to be older, and now I am.   —Margaret Atwood

Look for the ridiculous in everything and you find it.   —Jules Renard

He that seeks trouble always finds it.
—English proverb

The more wary you are of danger, the more likely you are to meet it.
—Jean de La Fontaine

Lifting as they climb, onward and upward they go, struggling and striving and hoping that the buds and blossoms of their desires may burst into glorious fruition ere long.
—Mary Church Terrell

We are always paid for our suspicion by finding what we suspect.
—Henry David Thoreau

The unthankful heart . . . discovers no mercies; but the thankful heart . . . will find, in every hour, some heavenly blessings.
—Henry Ward Beecher

If you are possessed by an idea, you find it expressed everywhere, you even smell it.   —Thomas Mann

All seems infected that the infected spy, as all looks yellow to the jaundiced eye.   —Alexander Pope

The faultfinder will find faults even in paradise. —Henry David Thoreau

Those see nothing but faults that seek for nothing else.   —Thomas Fuller

Life Is Like a Mirror

The world is a looking glass and gives back to every man the reflection of his own face. Frown at it and it will in turn look sourly upon you; laugh at it and with it, and it is a jolly, kind companion.
—William Makepeace Thackeray

Life is a mirror and will reflect back to the thinker what he thinks into it.
—Ernest Holmes

The world is a great mirror. It reflects back to you what you are. If you are loving, if you are friendly, if you are helpful, the world will prove loving and friendly and helpful to you. The world is what you are.
—Thomas Dreier

The world is like a mirror; frown at it, and it frowns at you. Smile and it smiles, too.   —Herbert Samuels

OUR THOUGHTS
DETERMINE OUR LIVES

If enough people think of a thing and work hard enough at it, I guess it's pretty nearly bound to happen, wind and weather permitting.
—Laura Ingalls Wilder

If you are going to think black, think positive about it. Don't think down on it, or think it is something in your way. And this way, when you really do want to stretch out and express how beautiful black is, everybody will hear you.   —Leontyne Price

Our minds can shape the way a thing will be because we act according to our expectations.   —Federico Fellini

I like living. I have sometimes been wildly, despairingly, acutely miserable, racked with sorrow, but through it all I still know quite certainly that just to be alive is a grand thing.
—Agatha Christie

A man is literally what he thinks.
—James Lane Allen

Although none of the rules for becoming alive is valid, it is healthy to keep on formulating them.
—Susan Sontag

The happiness of your life depends upon the quality of your thoughts ...take care that you entertain no notions unsuitable to virtue and reasonable nature.   —Marcus Aurelius

All that a man does outwardly is but the expression and completion of his inward thought. To work effectively, he must think clearly; to act nobly, he must think nobly.
—William Ellery Channing

You cannot escape the results of your thoughts. . . . Whatever your present environment may be, you will fall, remain or rise with your thoughts, your vision, your ideal. You will become as small as your controlling desire, as great as your dominant aspiration.   —James Lane Allen

The life each of us lives is the life within the limits of our own thinking. To have life more abundant, we must think in limitless terms of abundance.
—Thomas Dreier

A man's life is what his thoughts make it.   —Marcus Aurelius
Before a painter puts a brush to his canvas he sees his picture mentally.... If you think of yourself in terms of a painting, what do you see? . . . Is the picture one you think worth painting? . . . You create yourself in the image you hold in your mind.
—Thomas Dreier

A man is what he thinks about all day long.   —Ralph Waldo Emerson

All that we are is the result of what we have thought. The mind is everything. What we think, we become.
—Buddha

I believe that if you think about disaster, you will get it. Brood about death and you hasten your demise. Think positively and masterfully with confidence and faith, and life becomes more secure, more fraught with action, richer in achievement and experience.
—Eddie Rickenbacker

Think you can, think you can't; either way, you'll be right. —Henry Ford

Our destiny changes with our thoughts; we shall become what we wish to become, do what we wish to do, when our habitual thoughts correspond with our desires.
—Orison Swett Marden

Our best friends and our worst enemies are our thoughts. A thought can do us more good than a doctor or a banker or a faithful friend. It can also do us more harm than a brick.
—Dr. Frank Crane

The way a man's mind runs is the way he is sure to go.
—Henry B. Wilson

Nothing befalls us that is not of the nature of ourselves. There comes no adventure but wears to our soul the shape of our everyday thoughts.
—Maurice Maeterlinck

The mere apprehension of a coming evil has put many into a situation of the utmost danger. —Lucan

The soul contains the event that shall befall it, for the event is only the actualization of its thoughts, and what we pray to ourselves for is always granted.
—Ralph Waldo Emerson

If you think it's going to rain, it will.
—Clint Eastwood

As you think, you travel, and as you love, you attract. You are today where your thoughts have brought you; you will be tomorrow where your thoughts take you.
—James Lane Allen

God will help you if you try, and you can if you think you can.
—Anna Delaney Peale

To expect defeat is nine-tenths of defeat itself.
—Francis Marion Crawford

The quality of our expectations determines the quality of our action.
—André Godin

What a man thinks of himself, that is what determines, or rather indicates, his fate. —Henry David Thoreau

Man, being made reasonable, and so a thinking creature, there is nothing more worthy of his being than the right direction and employment of his thoughts; since upon this depends both his usefulness to the public, and his own present and future benefit in all respects. —William Penn

Great men are they who see that the spiritual is stronger than any material force, that thoughts rule the world.
—Ralph Waldo Emerson

Never think any oldish thoughts. It's oldish thoughts that make a person old.   —James A. Farley

They can because they think they can.   —Virgil

As a man thinketh, so is he, and as a man chooseth, so is he.
                —Ralph Waldo Emerson

Thoughts lead on to purposes; purposes go forth in action; actions form habits; habits decide character; and character fixes our destiny.
                —Tyron Edwards

Keep your thoughts right, for as you think, so are you. Therefore, think only those things that will make the world better, and you unashamed.
                —Henry H. Buckley

Every man is free to rise as far as he's able or willing, but the degree to which he thinks determines the degree to which he'll rise.   —Ayn Rand

What you think means more than anything else in your life.
                —George Matthew Adams

Change your thoughts and you change your world.
                —Norman Vincent Peale

Baseball is 90 percent mental. The other half is physical.   —Yogi Berra

The way in which we think of ourselves has everything to do with how our world sees us.   —Arlene Raven

Be careful of your thoughts; they may become words at any moment.
                —Ira Gassen

The wisdom of all ages and cultures emphasizes the tremendous power our thoughts have over our character and circumstances.   —Liane Cordes

There comes no adventure but wears to our soul the shape of our everyday thoughts.   —Maurice Maeterlinck

OUR THOUGHTS DETERMINE OUR HAPPINESS

We exaggerate misfortune and happiness alike. We are never either so wretched or so happy as we say we are.   —Honore de Balzac

Think of all the beauty that's still left in and around you and be happy!
                —Anne Frank

We are never so happy or so unhappy as we think.
                —Francois de La Rochefoucauld

Man is only miserable so far as he thinks himself so.
                —Jacopo Sannazaro

A man's as miserable as he thinks he is.
                —Marcus Annaeus Seneca

The most unhappy of all men is he who believes himself to be so.
                —David Hume

The mind is its own place, and in itself can make a heaven of hell, a hell of heaven.   —John Milton

All happiness is in the mind. —Anon.

Happiness is not a matter of events, it depends upon the tides of the mind.
                —Alice Meynell

The greater part of our happiness or misery depends on our dispositions, and not our circumstances.
—Martha Washington

I am happy and content because I think I am. —Alain-Rene Lesage

A happy life consists in tranquility of mind. —Cicero

The happiest person is the person who thinks the most interesting thoughts. —William Lyon Phelps

Unhappiness indicates wrong thinking, just as ill health indicates a bad regimen. —Paul Bourge

Happiness does not depend on outward things, but on the way we see them. —Leo Tolstoy

Happiness will never be any greater than the idea we have of it.
—Maurice Maeterlinck
He is happy that knoweth not himself to be otherwise. —Thomas Fuller

Misery is almost always the result of thinking. —Joseph Joubert

A great obstacle to happiness is to expect too much happiness.
—Bernard de Fontenelle

It isn't our position, but our disposition, that makes us happy. —Anon.

OUR THOUGHTS, OUR BODIES, AND OUR HEALTH

God prefers your health, and your obedience, to your penance.
—Teresa of Avila

After you're older, two things are possibly more important than any others: health and money.
—Helen Gurley Brown

The best course was to buy a house across a road from a cemetery and look at it every morning. Reminding yourself where it all ended anyway, you'd never get upset about anything again. —Mildred Davis

Some patients I see are actually draining into their bodies the diseased thoughts of their minds.
—Zachary T. Bercovitz, M.D.

A sneer is like a flame; it may occasionally be curative because it cauterizes, but it leaves a bitter scar.
—Margaret Deland

Hate is like acid. It can damage the vessel in which it is stored as well as destroy the object on which it is poured. —Ann Landers

The body manifests what the mind harbors. —Jerry Augustine

Since the human body tends to move in the direction of its expectations—plus or minus—it is important to know that attitudes of confidence and determination are no less a part of the treatment program than medical science and technology.
—Norman Cousins

Tragedy had its compensations. Once the worst misfortune occurred, one never worried about the minor ones.
—Mildred Davis

Give me good health and I'll take care of the rest. —Marilyn Horne

When people asked, I used to tell them how sick I was. The more I talked about being sick, the worse I got. Finally, I started saying, "I'm getting better." It took a while, but then I started to feel better, too.
  —Michael Hirsch, person with AIDS

You can promote your healing by your thinking.   —James E. Sweeney

Most of the time we think we're sick it's all in the mind.   —Thomas Wolfe

My gift is that I'm not beautiful. My career was never about looks. It's about health and being in good shape.   —Shirley MacLaine

NEGATIVE, CYNICAL, PESSIMISTIC THINKING IS DANGEROUS

The pessimist is half-licked before he starts.   —Thomas A. Buckner

In rejecting secrecy I had also rejected the road to cynicism.
  —Catharine Marshall

An ass may bray a good while before he shakes the stars down.
  —George Eliot

It is healthier to see the good points of others than to analyze our own bad ones.   —Françoise Sagan

Pessimism is a luxury that a Jew can never afford himself.   —Golda Meir

Never say anything on the phone that you wouldn't want your mother to hear at your trial.
  —Sydney Biddle Barrows

You can either give in to negative feelings or fight them, and I'm of the belief that you should fight them.
  —Dr. Ruth Westheimer

A critic is someone who never actually goes to the battle, yet who afterwards comes out shooting the wounded.   —Tyne Daly

They never raised a statue to a critic.
  —Martha Graham

The weak are the most treacherous of us all. They come to the strong and drain them. They are bottomless. They are insatiable. They are always parched and always bitter. They are everyone's concern and like vampires they suck our life's blood.
  —Bette Davis

No one can defeat us unless we first defeat ourselves.
  —Dwight D. Eisenhower

Play not with paradoxes. That caustic which you handle in order to scorch others may happen to sear your own fingers and make them dead to the quality of things.   —George Eliot

Discussing how old you are is the temple of boredom.   —Ruth Gordon

You can't be pessimistic, because there are so many things that go wrong every day that if you were to be negative or pessimistic, you'd go out of business.   —John DePasquale

We criticize and separate ourselves from the process. We've got to jump right in there with both feet.
  —Dolores Huerta

Wit is the salt of conversation, not the food, and few things in the world are more wearying than a sarcastic attitude towards life.
—Agnes Repplier

You can't pay attention to your mistakes. I made a mistake today, I made a mistake yesterday. I think it's . . . very important to ignore the negative.
—Jerry Rubin

You just can't complain about being alive. It's self-indulgent to be unhappy.
—Gena Rowland

We can destroy ourselves by cynicism and disillusion, just as affectively as by bombs.
—Kenneth Clark

One of the most devastating experiences in human life is disillusionment.
—Art Sisson

The pessimist sees the difficulty in every opportunity; the optimist sees the opportunity in every difficulty.
—L.P. Jacks

No pessimist ever discovered the secrets of the stars, or sailed to an uncharted land, or opened a new heaven to the human spirit.
—Helen Keller

There are people who have an appetite for grief; pleasure is not strong enough and they crave pain. They have mithridatic stomachs which must be fed on poisoned bread, natures so doomed that no prosperity can sooth their ragged and dishevelled desolation.
—Ralph Waldo Emerson

I don't believe in pessimism.
—Clint Eastwood

If any has a stone to throw
It is not I, ever or now.
—Elinor Wylie

Cynicism is intellectual dandyism.
—George Meredith

When one door of happiness closes, another opens; but often we look so long at the closed door that we do not see the one which has been opened for us.
—Helen Keller

Do not sit long with a sad friend. When you go to a garden do you look at the weeds? Spend more time with the roses and jasmines.
—Jelaluddin Rumi

WE ARE RESPONSIBLE FOR OUR THOUGHTS

If we are not responsible for the thoughts that pass our doors, we are at least responsible for those we admit and entertain.
—Charles B. Newcomb

Optimism is an intellectual choice.
—Diana Schneider

Think of only three things: your God, your family and the Green Bay Packers—in that order.
—Vince Lombardi, to his team

You live with your thoughts—so be careful what they are.
—Eva Arrington

We must dare to think unthinkable thoughts.
—James W. Fulbright

Politeness is the art of choosing among one's real thoughts.
—Abel Stevens

Thoughts have power; thoughts are energy. And you can make your world or break it by your own thinking.
—Susan Taylor

Your imagination has much to do with your life. . . . It is for you to decide how you want your imagination to serve you.   —Philip Conley

A vacant mind invites dangerous inmates, as a deserted mansion tempts wandering outcasts to enter and take up their abode in its desolate apartments.   —Nicholas Hilliard

Great things are not something accidental, but must certainly be willed.
—Vincent van Gogh

If We're Not Part of the Solution, We're Part of the Problem

It takes two flints to make a fire.
—Louisa May Alcott

Cease to be a drudge, seek to be an artist.   —Mary McLeod Bethune

True revolutions . . . restore more than they destroy.   —Louise Bogan

There are seeds of self-destruction in all of us that will bear only unhappiness if allowed to grow.
—Dorothea Brande

We have seen too much defeatism, too much pessimism, too much of a negative approach.   —Margo Jones

This is the way of peace—overcome evil with good, and falsehood with truth, and hatred with love.
—Peace Pilgrim

The evil of the world is made possible by nothing but the sanction you give it.   —Ayn Rand

If you make fun of bad persons you make yourself beneath them. . . . Be kind to bad and good, for you don't know your own heart.
—Sarah Winnemucca

The Importance and Value of Positive Thinking

We have learned that power is a positive force if it is used for positive purposes.   —Elizabeth Dole

The optimism of a healthy mind is indefatigable.   —Margery Allingham

If I were to wish for anything, I should not wish for wealth and power, but for the passionate sense of the potential, for the eye which, ever young and ardent, sees the possible . . . what wine is so sparkling, so fragrant, so intoxicating, as possibility!
—Søren Kierkegaard

What after all has maintained the human race on this old globe, despite all the calamities of nature and all the tragic failings of mankind, if not the faith in new possibilities and the courage to advocate them?
—Jane Adams

The basic success orientation is having an optimistic attitude.
—John DePasquale

Think positively and masterfully, with confidence and faith, and life becomes more secure, more fraught with action, richer in achievement and experience.
—Eddie Rickenbacker

Am I like the optimist who, while falling ten stories from a building, says at each story, "I'm all right so far"?
—Gretel Ehrlich

It doesn't hurt to be optimistic. You can always cry later.
—Lucimar Santos de Lima

The biggest quality in successful people, I think, is an impatience with negative thinking . . . my feeling was, even if it's as bad as I think it is, we'll make it work.   —Edward McCabe

Optimism and humor are the grease and glue of life. Without both of them we would never have survived our captivity.
—Philip Butler, Vietnam powPOW

Optimism is the faith that leads to achievement. Nothing can be done without hope and confidence.
—Helen Keller

Positive thinking is the key to success in business, education, pro football, anything that you can mention. I go out there thinking that I am going to complete every pass. —Ron Jaworski

Positive Thinking Is Practical
There is in the worst of fortune the best of chances for a happy change.
—Euripides

Every noble work is at first impossible.   —Thomas Carlyle

Optimism is essential to achievement and is also the foundation of courage and of true progress.
—Nicholas Murray Butler

I cannot discover that anyone knows enough to say definitely what is and what is not possible.   —Henry Ford

I have learned to use the word impossible with the greatest caution.
—Wernher von Braun

The Wright brothers flew right through the smoke screen of impossibility. —Charles Franklin Kettering

On the human chessboard, all moves are possible.   —Miriam Schiff

In the long run, the pessimist may be proved to be right, but the optimist has a better time on the trip.
—Daniel L. Reardon

All things are possible until they are proved impossible—and even the impossible may only be so as of now.
—Pearl S. Buck

But Positive Thinking Alone Isn't Enough

Optimism, unaccompanied by personal effort, is merely a state of mind and not fruitful. —Edward L. Curtis

I believe that . . . all that can be, will be, if man helps.   —André Gide

We Create Our Own Situations and Circumstances

One is not born a genius, one becomes a genius.   —Simone de Beauvoir

Like begets like; honesty begets honesty; trust, trust; and so on.
                    —James F. Bell

Honor begets honor; trust begets trust; faith begets faith; and hope is the mainspring of life.
                    —Henry L. Stimson

Mankind's greatest gift . . . is that we have free choice.
                    —Elisabeth Kubler-Ross

If you haven't been happy very young, you can still be happy later on, but it's much harder. You need more luck.   —Simone de Beauvoir

Events, circumstances, etc., have their origin in ourselves. They spring from seeds which we have sown.
                    —Henry David Thoreau

Hope is like a road in the country; there was never a road, but when many people walk on it, the road comes into existence.   —Lin Yutang

If fear is cultivated it will become stronger, if faith is cultivated it will achieve mastery.   —John Paul Jones

The process of maturing is an art to be learned, an effort to be sustained. By the age of fifty, you have made yourself what you are, and if it is good, it is better than your youth.
                    —Marya Mannes

A human being fashions his consequences as surely as he fashions his goods or his dwelling. Nothing that he says, thinks or does is without consequences.   —Norman Cousins

We create our fate every day . . . most of the ills we suffer from are directly traceable to our own behavior.
                    —Henry Miller

It seems to me probably that any one who has a series of intolerable positions to put up with must have been responsible for them to some extent . . . they have contributed to it by impatience or intolerance, or brusqueness—or some provocation.
                    —Robert Hugh Benson

If we live good lives, the times are also good. As we are, such are the times.
                    —Saint Augustine

Opportunities multiply as they are seized; they die when neglected. Life is a long line of opportunities.
                    —John Wicker

I have found that if you love life, life will love you back.
                    —Arthur Rubinstein

A man is a method, a progressive arrangement; a selecting principle, gathering his like unto him wherever he goes. What you are comes to you.
                    —Ralph Waldo Emerson

Thousands upon thousands are yearly brought into a state of real poverty by their great anxiety not to be thought poor.   —William Cobbett

We are made kind by being kind.
                    —Eric Hoffer

The world has a way of giving what is demanded of it. If you are frightened and look for failure and poverty, you will get them, no matter how hard you may try to succeed. Lack of faith in yourself, in what life will do for you, cuts you off from the good things of the world. Expect victory and you make victory. Nowhere is this truer than in business that is, where bravery and faith bring both material and spiritual rewards.
—Preston Bradley

Choice is the essence of what I believe it is to be human.
—Liv Ullmann

Kindness gives birth to kindness.
—Sophocles

IN MANY CASES, WE DETERMINE WHAT WILL HAPPEN TO US

We choose our joys and sorrows long before we experience them.
—Kahlil Gibran

Once a human being has arrived on this earth, communication is the largest single factor determining what kinds of relationships he makes with others and what happens to him in the world about him. —Virginia Satir

Man does not simply exist, but always decides what his existence will be, what he will become in the next moment. —Viktor Frankl

You end up as you deserve. In old age you must put up with the face, the friends, the health, and the children you have earned. —Fay Weldon

Liberty cannot be caged into a charter and handed on ready-made to the next generation. Each generation must recreate liberty for its own times. Whether or not we establish freedom rests with ourselves.
—Florence Ellinwood Allen

I am one of those people who are blessed . . . with a nature which has to interfere. If I see a thing that needs doing I do it. —Margery Allingham

The principle of life is that life responds by corresponding; your life becomes the thing you have decided it shall be.
—Raymond Charles Barker

If we choose to be no more than clods of clay, then we shall be used as clods of clay for braver feet to tread on.
—Marie Corelli

WHAT WE PREPARE FOR OFTEN HAPPENS

Preparing for the worst is an activity I have taken up since I turned thirty-five, and the worst actually began to happen. —Delia Ephron

If you prepare for old age, old age comes sooner. —Anon.

It is no use blaming the men—we made them what they are—and now it is up to us to try and make ourselves—the makers of men—a little more responsible. —Nancy Astor

Lead me not into temptation; I can find the way myself.
—Rita Mae Brown

Believe there is a great power silently working all things for good, behave yourself and never mind the rest.
—Beatrix Potter

I made the decision. I'm accountable.
—Janet Reno

What we prepare for is what we shall get.   —William Graham Sumner

We make our own criminals, and their crimes are congruent with the national culture we all share. It has been said that a people get the kind of political leadership they deserve. I think they also get the kinds of crime and criminals they themselves bring into being.   —Margaret Mead

If one asks for success and prepares for failure, he will get the situation he has prepared for.
—Florence Scovel Shinn

We are accountable only to ourselves for what happens to us in our lives.
—Mildred Newman

I attribute my success to this: I never gave or took an excuse.
—Florence Nightingale

The world has a way of giving what is demanded of it. If you are frightened and look for failure and poverty, you will get them, no matter how hard you may try to succeed. Lack of faith in yourself, in what life will do for you, cuts you off from the good things of the world. Expect victory and you make victory. Nowhere is this truer than in business life, where bravery and faith bring both material and spiritual rewards.
—Preston Bradley

Carry on, carry on, for the men and boys are gone,
But the furrow shan't lie fallow while the women carry on.
—Janet Begbie

The willingness to accept responsibility for one's own life is the source from which self-respect springs.
—Joan Didion

If you don't like the way the world is, you change it. You have an obligation to change it. You just do it one step at a time.
—Marian Wright Edelman

Whoso diggeth a pit shall fall therein.
—Proverbs 26:27

Debt is a trap which man sets and baits himself, and then deliberately gets into.   —Josh Billings

It is not our circumstances that c reate our discontent or contentment. It is us.   —Vivian Greene

Fortunately the family is a human institution: humans made it and humans can change it.   —Shere Hite

Any committee is only as good as the most knowledgeable, determined, and vigorous person on it. There must be somebody who provides the flame.
—Lady Bird Johnson

Self-image sets the boundaries of individual accomplishment.
—Maxwell Maltz

If you expect nothing, you're apt to be surprised. You'll get it.
—Malcolm Forbes

My father instilled in me that if you don't see things happening the way you want them to, you get out there and make them happen.

—Susan Powter

To heal ourselves we also have to heal society. —Riane Eisler

Here is where some entrepreneurs fail. They are filled with creative juices and total commitment to their business, but too often they don't understand that they must also be managers, administrators, even gofers—at least for a while.

—Lillian Vernon

WHAT WE TALK ABOUT OFTEN OCCURS

A voice is a human gift; it should be cherished and used, to utter as fully human speech as possible. Powerlessness and silence go together.

—Margaret Atwood

Persistent prophecy is a familiar way of assuring the event.

—George R. Gissing

The words "I am . . . " are potent words; be careful what you hitch them to. The thing you're claiming has a way of reaching back and claiming you. —A.L. Kitselman

A word after a word after a word is power. —Margaret Atwood

A person who can write a long letter with ease, cannot write ill.

—Jane Austen

If you keep saying things are going to be bad, you have a good chance of being a prophet.

—Isaac Bashevis Singer

Our lives preserved. How it was; and how it will be. Passing it along in the relay. That is what I work to do: to produce stories that save our lives.

—Toni Cade Bambara

When people asked, I used to tell them how sick I was. The more I talked about being sick, the worse I got. Finally, I started saying, "I'm getting better." It took a while, but then I started to feel better, too.

—Michael Hirsch, person with AIDS

Journal writing is a voyage to the interior. —Christina Baldwin

To know how to say what others only know how to think is what makes men poets or sages; and to dare to say what others only dare to think makes men martyrs or reformers—or both. —Elizabeth Charles

My voice is still the same, and this makes me beside myself with Joy! Oh, mon Dieu, when I think what I might be able to do with it!

—Jenny Lind

WE GET OUT OF LIFE WHAT WE PUT INTO IT

Men will get no more out of life than they put into it.

—William J.H. Boetcker

He who sows courtesy reaps friendship, and he who plants kindness gathers love. —Saint Basil

Who soweth good seed shall surely reap; The year grows rich as it groweth old, And life's latest sands are its sands of gold!   —Julia Dorr

Whatsoever a man soweth, that shall he also reap.   —Galatians 6:7

There is a very real relationship, both quantitatively and qualitatively, between what you contribute and what you get out of this world.
      —Oscar Hammerstein II

If a man plants melons he will reap melons; if he sows beans, he will reap beans.   —Chinese proverb

Give to the world the best you have and the best will come back to you.
      —Madeline Bridges

WE DETERMINE HOW OTHER PEOPLE RELATE TO US

Trust men and they will be true to you; treat them greatly and they will show themselves great.
      —Ralph Waldo Emerson

While you don't need a formal written contract before you get married, I think it's important for both partners to spell out what they expect from each other. . . . There are always plenty of surprises—and lots of give and take—once you're married.
      —Muriel Fox

We awaken in others the same attitude of mind we hold toward them.
      —Elbert Hubbard

He who has not faith in others shall find no faith in them.   —Lao-tzu

Any man will usually get from other men just what he is expecting of them. If he is looking for friendship he will likely receive it. If his attitude is that of indifference, it will beget indifference. And if a man is looking for a fight, he will in all likelihood be accommodated in that.
      —John Richelsen

A man would prefer to come home to an unmade bed and a happy woman than to a neatly made bed and an angry woman.   —Marlene Dietrich

They say, "You can't give a smile away; it always comes back." The same is true of a kind word or a conversation starter. What goes around, comes around.   —Susan RoAne

Revolve your world around the customer and more customers will revolve around you.
      —Heather Williams

Charm is the ability to make someone else think that both of you are pretty wonderful. —Kathleen Winsor

Power without [the people's] confidence is nothing.
      —Catherine the Great

To make the world a friendly place, one must show it a friendly face.
      —James Whitcomb Riley

People are not going to love you unless you love them.   —Pat Carroll

Getting people to like you is merely the other side of liking them.
      —Norman Vincent Peale

If you would be loved, love and be lovable.   —Benjamin Franklin

People, by and large, will relate to the image you project.   —Anon.

The confidence which we have in ourselves gives birth to much of that which we have in others.
          —Francois de La Rochefoucauld

Self-Doubt Will Create the Very Failure We Fear

He who fears he shall suffer, already suffers what he fears.
          —Michel de Montaigne

Fear to let fall a drop and you spill a lot.   —Malay proverb

A person who doubts himself is like a man who would enlist in the ranks of his enemies and bear arms against himself. He makes his failure certain by himself being the first person to be convinced of it.   —Alexandre Dumas

To be ambitious for wealth, and yet always expecting to be poor; to be always doubting your ability to get what you long for, is like trying to reach east by travelling west. There is no philosophy which will help a man to succeed when he is always doubting his ability to do so, and thus attracting failure. No matter how hard you work for success, if your thought is saturated with the fear of failure, it will kill your efforts, neutralize your endeavors and make success impossible.
          —Charles Baudouin

He who fears being conquered is sure of defeat.   —Napoleon Bonaparte

Dangers by being despised grow great.   —Edmund Burke

If one asks for success and prepares for failure, he will get the situation he has prepared for.
          —Florence Scovel Shinn

Doubt breeds doubt.
          —Franz Grillparzer

Doubt indulged soon becomes doubt realized.   —Frances Ridley Havergal

Proust has pointed out that the predisposition to love creates its own objects; is this not also true of fear?
          —Elizabeth Bowen

Fear breeds fear.   —Byron Janis

The thing we fear we bring to pass.
          —Elbert Hubbard

Those who foresee the future and recognize it as tragic are often seized by a madness which forces them to commit the very acts which makes it certain that what they dread shall happen.   —Dame Rebecca West

There are certain people who so ardently and passionately desire a thing, that from dread of losing it they leave nothing undone to make them lose it.   —Jean de La Bruyère

People Often Become What Is Expected of Them

A great manager has a knack for making ballplayers think they are better than they think they are. He forces you to have a good opinion of yourself. He lets you know he believes in you. He makes you get more out of yourself. And once you learn how good you really are, you never settle for playing anything less than your very best.
—Reggie Jackson

The only way to make a man trustworthy is to trust him.
—Henry L. Stimson

Children are likely to live up to what you believe of them.
—Lady Bird Johnson

However much we guard against it, we tend to shape ourselves in the image others have of us.
—Eric Hoffer

If you want your children to improve, let them overhear the nice things you say about them to others.
—Haim Ginott

It is the nature of man to rise to greatness if greatness is expected of him.
—John Steinbeck

I dare you to be the strongest boy in this class.
—William H. Danforth's teacher

Men have a trick of coming up to what is expected of them, good or bad.
—Jacob A. Riis

Treat people as if they were what they should be, and you help them become what they are capable of becoming.
—Johann von Goethe

Where much is expected from an individual, he may rise to the level of events and make the dream come true.
—Elbert Hubbard

People have a way of becoming what you encourage them to be—not what you nag them to be.
—S.N. Parker

Our self-image, strongly held, essentially determines what we become.
—Maxwell Maltz

Act so as to elicit the best in others and thereby in thyself.
—Felix Adler

Act "As If"

To keep our faces toward change, and behave like free spirits in the presence of fate, is strength undefeatable.
—Helen Keller

We planted flowers last year, and I didn't know if I'd be alive to see them come up.
—Neal McHugh,
person with AIDS

Act as if it were impossible to fail.
—Dorothea Brande

If you want a quality, act as if you already had it.
—William James

If you would be powerful, pretend to be powerful.
—Horne Tooke

Assume a virtue, if you have it not.
—William Shakespeare

We must laugh before we are happy, for fear of dying without having laughed at all.   —Jean de La Bruyère

If you want to be a big company tomorrow, you have to start acting like one today.   —Thomas Watson

If one advances confidently in the direction of his dreams, and endeavors to live the life which he has imagined, he will meet with a success unexpected in common hours.
—Henry David Thoreau

We are what we pretend to be, so we must be careful about what we pretend to be.   —Kurt Vonnegut

Act as if you were already happy, and that will tend to make you happy.
—Dale Carnegie

Always imitate the behavior of the winner when you lose.   —Anon.

I couldn't hit a wall with a sixgun, but I can twirl one. It looks good.
—John Wayne

It is good to act as if. It is even better to grow to the point where it is no longer an act.
—Charles Caleb Colton

It is easy enough to be pleasant, when life flows by like a song. But the man worthwhile is one who will smile, when everything goes dead wrong.
—Ella Wheeler Wilcox

To find oneself jilted is a blow to one's pride. One must do one's best to forget it and if one doesn't succeed, at least one must pretend to.
—Moliere

Attempt easy tasks as if they were difficult, and difficult as if they were easy; in the one case that confidence may not fall asleep, in the other that it may not be dismayed.
—Baltasar Gracian

It is best to act with confidence, no matter how little right you have to it.
—Lillian Hellman

If you've got it, flaunt it. If you do not, pretend.   —Wally Phillips

If you wish to live a life free from sorrow, think of what is going to happen as if it had already happened.
—Epictetus

To establish oneself in the world, one has to do all one can to appear established.
—Francois de La Rochefoucauld

To believe in God is to yearn for His existence, and furthermore, it is to act as if He did exist.
—Miguel de Unamuno

Our deeds determine us, as much as we determine our deeds.
—George Eliot

Illusory joy is often worth more than genuine sorrow.   —Rene Descartes

Live as if you like yourself, and it may happen.   —Marge Piercy

If I had a party to attend and didn't want to be there, I would play the part of someone who was having a lovely time.   —Shirley MacLaine

Make your judgement trustworthy by trusting it.   —Grenville Kleiser

Fake feeling good. . . . You're going to have to learn to fake cheerfulness. Believe it or not, eventually that effort will pay off: you'll actually start feeling happier. —Jean Bach

I long to accomplish a great and noble task, but it is my chief duty to accomplish small tasks as if they were great and noble. —Helen Keller

We become just by performing just actions, temperate by performing temperate actions, brave by performing brave actions. —Aristotle

SOME INCREDIBLY POSITIVE APPROACHES

They've got us surrounded again, the poor bastards.
—General Creighton W. Abrams

My center is giving way, my right is in retreat: situation excellent. I am attacking. —Marshal Ferdinand Foch

If you act like you're rich, you'll get rich. —Adnan Koashoggi

I'll just hit the dry side of the ball.
—Stan Musial,
on how to handle a spitball

My disease is one of the best things that has happened to me; it has pulled me out of a quietly desperate life toward one full of love and hope.
—Tom O'Connor,
person with ARC

I've never been poor, only broke. Being poor is a frame of mind. Being broke is a temporary situation.
—Mike Todd

Retreat? We're coming out of here as a Marine division. We're bring . . . our dead. Retreat, hell! We're just advancing in another direction.
—General Oliver Prince Smith

I'm in a wonderful position: I'm unknown, I'm underrated, and there's nowhere to go but up.
—Pierre S. DuPont IV

I am dying, but otherwise I am quite well. —Edith Sitwell,
when asked how she felt

I can't say I was ever lost, but I was bewildered once for three days.
—Daniel Boone

Sunshine is delicious, rain is refreshing, wind braces us up, snow is exhilarating; there is really no such thing as bad weather, only different kinds of good weather. —John Ruskin

If they do kill me, I shall never die another death. —Abraham Lincoln

We are so outnumbered there's only one thing to do. We must attack.
—Sir Andrew Cunningham

Circumstances—what are circumstances? I make circumstances.
—Napoleon Bonaparte

Focus is important. Focus on those parts of yourself that are working. Look at yourself as someone whose body is in the process of healing. Concentrate on the positive parts.
—Will Garcia,
person with AIDS

I never lost a game. I just ran out of time. —Bobby Layne

Disease can be seen as a call for personal transformation through metamorphosis. It is a transition from the death of your old self into the birth of your new.   —Tom O'Connor, person with ARC

I'm not overweight, I'm just nine inches too short.   —Shelley Winters

Anyone can have an off decade.
      —Larry Cole

Practice being excited.   —Bill Foster

GENERAL QUOTATIONS
ABOUT POSITIVE THINKING,
AND SELF-FULFILLING PROPHESIES
AND ACTIONS

The person who says it cannot be done should not interrupt the person doing it.   —Chinese proverb

Knock the "t" off the "can't."
      —George Reeves

Being an optimist after you've got everything you want doesn't count.
      —Kin Hubbard

There are more defects in temperament than in the mind.
      —Francois de La Rochefoucauld

I make the most of all that comes and the least of all that goes.
      —Sara Teasdale

Clear your mind of "can't."
      —Samuel Johnson

Rosiness is not a worse windowpane than gloomy gray when viewing the world.   —Grace Paley

It is never too late to be what you might have been.   —George Eliot

I will say this about being an optimist: even when things don't turn out well, you are certain they will get better.
      —Frank Hughes

We have a problem. "Congratulations." But it's a tough problem. "Then double congratulations."
      —W. Clement Stone

One should . . . be able to see things as hopeless and yet be determined to make them otherwise.
      —F. Scott Fitzgerald

Isn't it splendid to think of all the things there are to find out about? It just makes me feel glad to be alive— it's such an interesting world.
      —L.M. Montgomery

To every disadvantage there is a corresponding advantage.
      —W. Clement Stone

I learned really to practice mustard seed faith, and positive thinking, and remarkable things happened.
      —Sir John Walton

Failure is impossible.
      —Susan B. Anthony

The only prison we need to escape from is the prison of our own minds.
      —Anon.

Whatever the ups and downs of detail within our limited experience, the larger whole is primarily beautiful.
      —Gregory Bateson

He was a "how" thinker, not an "if" thinker. —Anon.

No man can think clearly when his fists are clenched.
—George Jean Nathan

We think in generalities, but we live in detail. —Alfred North Whitehead

Some folks think they are thinking when they are only rearranging their prejudices. —Anon.

How things look on the outside of us depends on how things are on the inside of us. —Park Cousins

This I conceive to be the chemical function of humor: to change the character of our thought.
—Lin Yutang

Think like a man of action, act like a man of thought. —Henri Bergson

As is our confidence, so is our capacity.
—William Hazlitt

The more we do, the more we can do; the more busy we are, the more leisure we have. —William Hazlitt

The young do not know enough to be prudent, and therefore they attempt the impossible—and achieve it, generation after generation.
—Pearl S. Buck

What we love, we shall grow to resemble. —Bernard of Clairvaux

How much shall I be changed, before I am changed! —John Donnell

It is by sitting down to write every morning that he becomes a writer. Those who do not do this remain amateurs. —Gerald Brenan

There is no miraculous change that takes place in a boy that makes him a man. He becomes a man by being a man. —Louis L'Amour

Skill to do comes of doing.
—Ralph Waldo Emerson

In the end, the love you take is equal to the love you make.
—Song lyric, "Abbey Road,"
Paul McCartney

The quality of our expectations determines the quality of our actions.
—André Godin

Success produces success, just as money produces money.
—Nicolas de Chamfort

Once you begin to believe there is help "out there," you will know it to be true. —Saint Bartholomew

Enthusiasm

ENTHUSIASM IS ONE OF THE
MOST IMPORTANT THINGS IN LIFE

With renunciation life begins.
—Amelia Barr

As I grow older, part of my emotional survival plan must be to actively seek inspiration instead of passively waiting for it to find me.
—Bebe Moore Campbell

Enthusiasm signifies God in us.
—Madame de Staël

Enthusiasm is life.   —Paul Scofield

To sing is to love and affirm, to fly and soar, to coast into the hearts of the people who listen, to tell them that life is to live, that love is there, that nothing is a promise, but that beauty exists, and must be hunted for and found.   —Joan Baez

O lovely Sisters! is it true
That they are all inspired by you,
And write by inward magic charm'd,
And high enthusiasm warm'd?
—Joanna Baillie

Enthusiasm is the most important thing in life.   —Tennessee Williams

Enthusiasm signifies God in us.
—Madame de Staël

Life is enthusiasm, zest.
—Sir Laurence Olivier

There is only one big thing—desire. And before it, when it is big, all is little.   —Willa Cather

There is nothing greater than enthusiasm.   —Henry Moore

Enthusiasm is the most beautiful word on earth.
—Christian Morgenstern

Boredom is the fear of self.
—Comtesse Diane

It is not opposition but indifference which separates men.
—Mary Parker Follett

Exuberance is beauty.
—William Blake

Enthusiasm moves the world.
—J. Balfour

A man can be short and dumpy and getting bald but if he has fire, women will like him.   —Mae West

What a man knows only through feeling can be explained only through enthusiasm.   —Joseph Joubert

My enthusiasms . . . constitute my reserves, my unexploited resources, perhaps my future.   —E.M. Cioran

I have always had a dread of becoming a passenger in life.
—Margareth II, Queen of Denmark

A continued atmosphere of hectic passion is very trying if you haven't got any of your own.
—Dorothy L. Sayers

Nothing is so contagious as enthusiasm; it moves stones, it charms brutes. Enthusiasm is the genius of sincerity, and truth accomplishes no victories without it.
—Edward Bulwer-Lytton

The clue is not to ask in a miserly way—the key is to ask in a grand manner.   —Ann Wigmore

Energy is equal to desire and purpose.
—Sheryl Adams

What counts is not necessarily the size of the dog in the fight, but the size of the fight in the dog.
—Dwight D. Eisenhower

All we need to make us really happy is something to be enthusiastic about.
—Charles Kingsley

Most great men and women are not perfectly rounded in their personalties, but are instead people whose one driving enthusiasm is so great it makes their faults seem insignificant.
—Charles A. Cerami

Winning isn't everything. Wanting to win is.   —Catfish Hunter

Vitality! That's the pursuit of life, isn't it?   —Katharine Hepburn

In things pertaining to enthusiasm, no man is sane who does not know how to be insane on proper occasions.   —Henry Ward Beecher

Enthusiasm is the divine particle in our composition: with it we are great, generous, and true; without it, we are little, false, and mean.
—L.E. Landon

The great man is he who does not lose his childlike heart.   —Mencius

Zest is the secret of all beauty. There is no beauty that is attractive without zest.   —Christian Dior

What hunger is in relation to food, zest is in relation to life.
—Bertrand Russell

Wake up with a smile and go after life. . . . Live it, enjoy it, taste it, smell it, feel it.   —Joe Knapp

What one has, one ought to use; and whatever he does, he should do with all his might.   —Cicero

Let us go singing as far as we go; the road will be less tedious.   —Virgil

And whatsoever ye do, do it heartily.
—Colossians 3:23

You will do foolish things, but do
them with enthusiasm.   —Colette

Whatever you attempt, go at it with
spirit. Put some in!
—David Starr Jordan

Passion Is a Vital Force

Every man without passions has
within him no principle of action, nor
motive to act.   —Claude Helvetius

What is man but his passion?
—Robert Penn Warren

We always attract into our lives
whatever we think about most,
believe in most strongly, expect on
the deepest level, and imagine most
vividly.   —Shakti Gawain

You can have anything you want if
you want it desperately enough. You
must want it with an inner exuberance that erupts through the skin
and joins the energy that created the
world.   —Sheila Graham

Only passions, great passions, can
elevate the soul to great things.
—Denis Diderot

No one has it who isn't capable of
genuinely liking others, at least at the
actual moment of meeting and speaking. Charm is always genuine; it may
be superficial but it isn't fake.
—P.D. James

A willing heart adds feather to the
heel.   —Joanna Baillie

I really do believe I can accomplish
a great deal with a big grin. I know
some people find that disconcerting,
but that doesn't matter.
—Beverly Sills

Charm is a cunning self-forgetfulness.
—Christina Stead

Charm is the measure of attraction's
    power
To chain the fleeting fancy of the
    hour.   —Louisa Thomas

I'm convinced that it's energy and
humor. The two of them combined
equal charm.   —Judith Krantz

Nothing great in the world has been
accomplished without passion.
—George Hegel

If you're a champion, you have to
have it in your heart.   —Chris Evert

Human nature, if it healthy, demands
excitement; and if it does not obtain
its thrilling excitement in the right
way, it will seek it in the wrong. God
never makes bloodless stoics; He
makes no passionless saints.
—Oswald Chambers

All passions exaggerate; it is because
they do that they are passions.
—Nicolas de Chamfort

If we resist our passions, it is more
from their weakness than from our
strength.
—Francois de La Rochefoucauld

Be still when you have nothing to
say; when genuine passion moves
you, say what you've got to say, and
say it hot.   —D.H. Lawrence

The passions are the only orators
which always persuade.
—Francois de La Rochefoucauld

Passion, though a bad regulator, is a
powerful spring.
—Ralph Waldo Emerson

Our passions are ourselves.
—Anatole France

People who never get carried away
should be.   —Malcolm Forbes

But Enthusiasm Must
Be Channeled

This, indeed, is one of the eternal
paradoxes of both life and literature—that without passion little
gets done; yet, without control of
that passion, its effects are largely ill
or null.   —F.L. Lucas

When the habitually even-tempered
suddenly fly into a passion, that
explosion is apt to be more impressive than the outburst of the most
violent amongst us.
—Margery Allingham

Optimism, unaccompanied by personal effort, is merely a state of mind
and not fruitful.   —Edward L. Curtis

When enthusiasm is inspired by reason; controlled by caution; sound
in theory; practical in application;
reflects confidence; spreads good
cheer; raises morale; inspires associates; arouses loyalty; and laughs at
adversity, it is beyond price.
—Coleman Cox

The world belongs to the enthusiast
who keeps cool.   —William McFee

Without passion man is a mere latent
force and possibility, like the flint
which awaits the shock of the iron
before it can give forth its spark.
—Henri Frederic Amiel

Enthusiasm and Work

If you aren't fired with enthusiasm,
you will be fired with enthusiasm.
—Vince Lombardi

You've got to sing like you don't need
the money. You've got to love like
you'll never get hurt. You've got to
dance like there's nobody watching.
You've got to come from the heart, if
you want it to work.
—Susanna Clark

When his enthusiasm goes, he's
through as a player.   —Pete Rose

Every production of genius must be
the production of enthusiasm.
—Benjamin Disraeli

Give me a man who sings at his work.
—Thomas Carlyle

Enthusiasm and Success

A man can succeed at almost anything for which he has unlimited
enthusiasm.   —Charles M. Schwab

Drama is very important in life: You
have to come on with a bang. You
never want to go out with a whimper.
—Julia Child

The world belongs to the energetic.
—Ralph Waldo Emerson

The real difference between men is energy. —Thomas Fuller

A faint endeavor ends in a sure defeat.
—Hannah Moore

Flaming enthusiasm, backed up by horse sense and persistence, is the quality that most frequently makes for success. —Dale Carnegie

Success is going from failure to failure without loss of enthusiasm.
—Sir Winston Churchill

There is a passion for perfection which you rarely see fully developed, but . . . in successful lives it is never wholly lacking. —Bliss Carman

Many of the most successful men I have known have never grown up. They have retained bubbling-over boyishness. They have relished wit, they have indulged in humor. They have not allowed "dignity" to depress them into moroseness. Youthfulness of spirit is the twin brother of optimism, and optimism is the stuff of which American business success is fashioned. Resist growing up!
—B.C. Forbes

If you have the will to win, you have achieved half your success; if you don't, you have achieved half your failure. —David V.A. Ambrose

Someone's always saying, "It's not whether you win or lose," but if you feel that way, you're as good as dead.
—James Caan

To bring one's self to a frame of mind and to the proper energy to accomplish things that require plain hard work continuously is the one big battle that everyone has. When this battle is won for all time, then everything is easy. —Thomas A. Buckner

We would accomplish many more things if we did not think of them as impossible. —C. Malesherbez

Faith that the thing can be done is essential to any great achievement.
—Thomas N. Carruther

We can accomplish almost anything within our ability if we but think that we can! —George Matthew Adams

Optimism is essential to achievement and it is also the foundation of courage and of true progress.
—Nicholas Murray Butler

Morale is the greatest single factor in successful wars.
—Dwight D. Eisenhower

The will to conquer is the first condition of victory.
—Marshal Ferdinand Foch

The real secret of success is enthusiasm. Yes, more than enthusiasm, I would say excitement. I like to see men get excited. When they get excited they make a success of their lives.
—Walter Chrysler

Always bear in mind that your own resolution to success is more important than any other one thing.
—Abraham Lincoln

It is fatal to enter any war without
the will to win it.
　　　—General Douglas MacArthur

The measure of an enthusiasm must
be taken between interesting events.
It is between bites that the lukewarm
angler loses heart.
　　　—Edwin Way Teale

Enthusiasm for one's goal to lessens the disagreeableness of working
toward it. 　　　—Thomas Eakins

To burn always with this hard gem-
like flame. To maintain this ecstasy, is
success in life. 　　　—Walter Pater

Every man is enthusiastic at times.
One man has enthusiasm for thirty
minutes, another man has it for thirty
days. But it is the man who has it for
thirty years who makes a success in
life. 　　　—Edward B. Butler

Man never rises to great truths without enthusiasm. 　　　—Vauvenargues

Success is due less to ability than to
zeal. 　　　—Charles Buxton

I rate enthusiasm even above professional skill. 　　—Sir Edward Appleton

He did it with all his heart, and prospered. 　　　—2 Chronicles 31:21

A strong passion for any object will
ensure success, for the desire of the
end will point out the means.
　　　—William Hazlitt

Nothing great was ever achieved
without enthusiasm.
　　　—Ralph Waldo Emerson

What a man accomplishes in a day
depends upon the way in which
he approaches his tasks. When we
accept tough jobs as a challenge to
our ability and wade into them with
joy and enthusiasm, miracles can
happen. When we do our work with
a dynamic, conquering spirit, we get
things done. 　　　—Arland Gilbert

If you're not happy every morning
when you get up, leave for work, or
start to work at home—if you're not
enthusiastic about doing that, you're
not going to be successful.
　　　—Donald M. Kendall

The method of the enterprising is to
plan with audacity and execute with
vigor. 　　　—Christian Bovee

Do it big or stay in bed.
　　　—Larry Kelly

Sometimes success is due less to ability than to zeal. 　　—Charles Buxton

ENTHUSIASM AND KNOWLEDGE

Zeal will do more than knowledge.
　　　—William Hazlitt

Let a man in a garret burn with
enough intensity, and he will set fire
to the world.
　　　—Antoine de Saint-Exupery

Knowledge is power, but enthusiasm
pulls the switch. 　　　—Ivern Ball

Through zeal, knowledge is gotten;
through lack of zeal, knowledge is
lost. 　　　—Buddha

I prefer the errors of enthusiasm to the indifference of wisdom.
—Anatole France

ENTHUSIASM AND ENERGY

It is energy, the central element of which is will, that produces the miracles of enthusiasm in all ages. It is the mainspring of what is called force of character and the sustaining power of all great action.   —Samuel Smiles

The difference between one man and another is not mere ability . . . it is energy.   —Thomas Arnold

You see me in my most virile moment when you see me doing what I do. When I am directing, a special energy comes upon me. . . . It is only when I am doing my work that I feel truly alive. It is like having sex.
—Federico Fellini

Energy, even like the Biblical grain of mustard-seed, will move mountains.
—Hosea Ballou

Energy and persistence conquer all things.   —Benjamin Franklin

Energy will do anything that can be done in this world.
—Johann von Goethe

The only thing that keeps a man going is energy. And what is energy but liking life?   —Louis Auchincloss

ENTHUSIASM AND AGE

No one grows old by living, only by losing interest in living.
—Marie Beynon Ray

None are so old as those who have outlived enthusiasm.
—Henry David Thoreau

Years wrinkle the face, but to give up enthusiasm wrinkles the soul.
—Watterson Lowe

ENTHUSIASM AND WARFARE

He fights with spirit as well as with the sword.   —Latin proverb

It is fatal to enter any war without the will to win it.
—General Douglas MacArthur

Morale is the greatest single factor in successful wars.
—Dwight D. Eisenhower

The will to conquer is the first condition of victory.
—Marshal Ferdinand Foch

The aim of military training is not just to prepare men for battle, but to make them long for it.
—Louis Simpson

Wars may be fought with weapons, but they are won by men. It is the spirit of men who follow and of the man who leads that gains the victory.
—General George S. Patton

Primary Sources of Enthusiasm

Enthusiasm can only be aroused by two things: first, an ideal which takes the imagination by storm, and second, a definite, intelligible plan for carrying that ideal into practice.
—Arnold J. Toynbee

Earnestness and sincereness are synonymous.
—Corita Kent

Opposition inflames the enthusiast, never converts him.
—J.C.F. von Schiller

No one keeps up his enthusiasm automatically. Enthusiasm must be nourished with new actions, new aspirations, new efforts, new vision. Compete with yourself; set your teeth and dive into the job of breaking your own record. It is one's own fault if his enthusiasm is gone; he has failed to feed it.
—Anon.

The same reason makes a man a religious enthusiast that makes a man an enthusiast in any other way . . . an uncomfortable mind in an uncomfortable body.
—William Hazlitt

The great composer does not set to work because he is inspired, but becomes inspired because he is working. Beethoven, Wagner, Bach and Mozart settled down day after day to the job in hand with as much regularity as an accountant settles down each day to his figures. They didn't waste time waiting for inspiration.
—Ernest Newman

Enthusiasm is nothing more or less than faith in action.
—Henry Chester

Whatever course you have chosen for yourself, it will not be a chore but an adventure if you bring to it a sense of the glory of striving, if your sights are set far above the merely secure and mediocre.
—David Sarnoff

Vigor is contagious, and whatever makes us either think or feel strongly adds to our power and enlarges our field of action.
—Ralph Waldo Emerson

Practice being excited.
—Bill Foster

It is the greatest shot of adrenaline to be doing what you've wanted to do so badly. You almost feel like you could fly without the plane.
—Charles Lindbergh

Reason alone is insufficient to make us enthusiastic in any matter.
—Francois de La Rochefoucauld

Hope

The Importance and Value of Hope

It is characteristic of genius to be hopeful and aspiring.
—Harriet Martineau

If it were not for hopes, the heart would break.   —Thomas Fuller

None are completely wretched but those who are without hope, and few are reduced so low as that.
—William Hazlitt

Wonder . . . music heard in the heart, is voiceless.   —Rosemary Dobson

To all the living there is hope, for a living dog is better than a dead lion.
—Ecclesiastes 9:4

Everybody lives for something better to come.   —Anon.

Hope is itself a species of happiness, and, perhaps, the chief happiness which this world affords.
—Samuel Johnson

At first we hope too much; later on, not enough.   —Joseph Roux

Lord save us all from . . . a hope tree that has lost the faculty of putting out blossoms.   —Mark Twain

He who does not hope to win has already lost.
—José Joaquin Olmedo

We should not let our fears hold us back from pursuing our hopes.
—John F. Kennedy

Man needs, for his happiness, not only the enjoyment of this or that, but hope and enterprise and change.
—Bertrand Russell

Without hope men are only half alive. With hope they dream and think and work.   —Charles Sawyer

They say a person needs just three things to be truly happy in this world. Someone to love, something to do, and something to hope for.
—Tom Bodett

In all pleasure hope is a considerable part. —Samuel Johnson

Great hopes make great men. —Thomas Fuller

Hope is one of those things in life you cannot do without. —LeRoy Douglas

A leader is a dealer in hope. —Napoleon Bonaparte

The important thing is not that we can live on hope alone, but that life is not worth living without it. —Harvey Milk

Hope and patience are two sovereign remedies for all, the surest reposals, the softest cushions to lean on in adversity. —Robert Burton

It has never been, and never will be, easy work! But the road that is built in hope is more pleasant to the traveler than the road built in despair, even though they both lead to the same destination. —Marion Zimmer Bradley

Optimism is the faith that leads to achievement. Nothing can be done without hope or confidence. —Helen Keller

We want to create hope for the person . . . we must give hope, always hope. —Mother Teresa, on AIDS

Take hope from the heart of man and you make him a beast of prey. —Ouida

And thou shalt be secure because there is hope. —Job 11:18

Hope! Of all the ills that men endure, the only cheap and universal cure. —Abraham Cowley

Our greatest good, and what we least can spare, is hope. —John Armstrong

WITHOUT HOPE WE DIE

Hope is the last thing that dies in man. —Francois de La Rochefoucauld

Hope is the major weapon against the suicide impulse. —Dr. Karl Menninger

Refusal to hope is nothing more than a decision to die. —Bernie S. Siegel, M.D.

We must have hope or starve to death. —Pearl S. Buck

When hope is taken away from the people, moral degeneration follows swiftly after. —Pearl S. Buck

Man can live about forty days without food, about three days without water, about eight minutes without air . . . but only for one second without hope. —Hal Lindsey

To eat bread without hope is still slowly to starve to death. —Pearl S. Buck

Strong hope is a much greater stimulant of life than any single realized joy could be. —Friedrich Nietzsche

Hope is the last thing ever lost. —Italian proverb

Hope, Faith, and Belief

Faith walks simply, childlike, between the darkness of human life and the hope of what is to come.
—Catherine de Hueck Doherty

Now the God of hope fills you with all joy and peace in believing, that ye may abound in hope.
—Romans 15:13

Hope is putting faith to work when doubting would be easier.   —Anon.

My faith is important. I have nothing without it.   —Kathy Ireland

Hope is the belief, more or less strong, that joy will come; desire is the wish it may come.
—Sydney Smith

There is nothing that fear or hope does not make men believe.
—Vauvenargues

Hope is the parent of faith.
—C.A. Bartol

Hope is faith holding out its hand in the dark.   —George Iles

Hope Is a Great Motivator

No hope, no action.   —Peter Levi

Hope is one of the principal springs that keep mankind in motion.
—Thomas Fuller

Hope arouses, as nothing else can arouse, a passion for the possible.
—William Sloane Coffin, Jr.

Hope is the first thing to take some sort of action.   —John Armstrong

Hope is the anchor of the soul, the stimulus to action, and the incentive to achievement.   —Anon.

Hope is a vigorous principle . . . it sets the head and heart to work, and animates a man to do his utmost.
—Jeremy Collier

It is the around-the-corner brand of hope that prompts people to action, while the distant hope acts as an opiate.   —Eric Hoffer

Hope As a Dream

Hope is the pillar that holds up the world. Hope is the dream of a waking man.   —Pliny, the Elder

Hope is a waking dream.   —Aristotle

Hope is but the dream of those that wake.   —Matthew Prior

Hope is not a dream, but a way of making dreams become reality.
—L.J. Cardinal Suenens

Hope and Happiness

Hope is grief's best music.   —Anon.

Hope is the last thing to abandon the unhappy.   —Anon.

The miserable have no medicine but hope.   —William Shakespeare

Hope is the second soul of the unhappy.   —Johann von Goethe

Hope and the Future

Hope is the positive mode of awaiting the future.   —Emil Brunner

All shall be well, and all shall be well,
and all manner of things shall be
well.   —Julian of Norwich

If we were logical, the future would
be bleak indeed. But we are more
than logical. We are human beings,
and we have faith, and we have hope,
and we can work.

          —Jacques Cousteau

Clouds and darkness surround us, yet
heaven is just, and the day of triumph
will surely come, when justice and
truth will be vindicated. Our wrongs
will be made right, and we will once
more taste the blessings of freedom.
          —Mary Todd Lincoln

If winter comes, can spring be far
behind?   —Percy Bysshe Shelley

There is no medicine like hope, no
incentive so great, and no tonic so
powerful as expectation of something
tomorrow.   —Orison Swett Marden

"Wait'll next year!" is the favorite
cry of baseball fans, football fans,
hockey fans, and gardeners.
          —Robert Orben

Hope and Patience

Hope and patience are two sovereign
remedies for all, the surest reposals,
the softest cushions to lean on in
adversity.   —Robert Burton

Stars will blossom in the darkness,
Violets bloom beneath the snow.
          —Julia Dorr

Patience is the art of hoping.
          —Vauvenargues

Hope is patience with the lamp lit.
          —Tertullian

All human wisdom is summed up in
two words—wait and hope.
          —Alexandre Dumas

Hope and Fear

Hope is some extraordinary spiritual
grace that God gives us to control
our fears, not to oust them.
          —Vincent NcNabb

Where no hope is left, is left no fear.
          —John Milton

There is no hope unmingled with fear,
and no fear unmingled with hope.
          —Baruch Spinoza

I steer my bark with hope in my
heart, leaving fear astern.
          —Thomas Jefferson

Hopelessness

When you say a situation or a person
is hopeless, you are slamming the
door in the face of God.
          —Charles L. Allen

There are no hopeless situations;
there are only men who have grown
hopeless about them.
          —Clare Boothe Luce

Hope never abandons you, you abandon it. —George Weinberg

Other men see only a hopeless end, but the Christian rejoices in an endless hope. —Gilbert M. Beeken

Never despair. —Horace

One should . . . be able to see things as hopeless and yet be determined to make them otherwise.
—F. Scott Fitzgerald

Hell is the place where one has ceased to hope. —A.J. Cronin

Primary Sources of Hope

Extreme hopes are born of extreme misery. —Bertrand Russell

Hope is brightest when it dawns from fears. —Sir Walter Scott

Hope is like a road in the country; there was never a road, but when many people walk on it, the road comes into existence. —Lin Yutang

Hope works in these ways: it looks for the good in people instead of harping on the worst; it discovers what can be done instead of grumbling about what cannot; it regards problems, large or small, as opportunities; it pushes ahead when it would be easy to quit; it "lights the candle" instead of "cursing the darkness."
—Anon.

While there's life, there's hope.
—Terence

When you're depressed, the whole body is depressed, and it translates to the cellular level. The first objective is to get your energy up, and you can do it through play. It's one of the most powerful ways of breaking up hopelessness and bringing energy into the situation. —O. Carl Simonton

Every area of trouble gives out a ray of hope, and the one unchangeable certainty is that nothing is certain or unchangeable. —John F. Kennedy

Other Definitions of Hope

Hope is the poor man's bread.
—Gary Herbert

Oh, what a valiant faculty is hope.
—Michel de Montaigne

Hope is necessary in every condition. The miseries of poverty, sickness and captivity would, without this comfort, be insupportable.
—Samuel Johnson

Hope is a risk that must be run.
—Georges Bernanos

Hope is an adventure, a going forward, a confident search for a rewarding life. —Dr. Karl Menninger

Appetite, with an opinion of attaining, is called hope; the same, without such opinion, despair.
—Thomas Hobbes

Hope is a satisfaction unto itself, and need not be fulfilled to be appreciated.
—Dr. Fred O. Henker

Hope is desire and expectation rolled into one. —Ambrose Bierce

To hope is to enjoy.
　　　　　　　—Jacques Delille

Hope, that star of life's tremulous ocean. —Paul Moon James

Hope is the word which God has written on the brow of every man.
　　　　　　　—Victor Hugo

Hope is the thing with feathers that perches in the soul and sings the tune without words and never stops at all.
　　　　　　　—Emily Dickinson

Hope is not the conviction that something will turn out well but the certainty that something makes sense, regardless of how it turns out.
　　　　　　　—Vaclav Havel

Hope is a light diet, but very stimulating. —Honore de Balzac

Hope is the power of being cheerful in circumstances which we know to be desperate. —G.K. Chesterton

Honor begets honor, trust begets trust, faith begets faith, and hope is the mainspring of life.
　　　　　　　—Henry L. Stimson

GENERAL QUOTATIONS ABOUT HOPE

Hope is a song in a weary throat.
　　　　　　　—Pauli Murray

Hope . . . is not a feeling; it is something you do. —Katherine Paterson

Hope is the thing with feathers
That perches in the soul,
And sings the tune without the
　　words,
And never stops at all.
　　　　　　　—Emily Dickinson

Hope, like the gleaming taper's light, adorns and cheers our way;
And still, as darker grows the night, emits a lighter ray.
　　　　　　　—Oliver Goldsmith

Grass grows at last above all graves.
　　　　　　　—Julia Dorr

The happy ending is our national belief. —Mary McCarthy

Nobody really cares if you're miserable, so you might as well be happy.
　　　　　　　—Cynthia Nelms

Hope springs eternal in the human breast. —Alexander Pope

Just as dumb creatures are snared by food, human beings would not be caught unless they had a nibble of hope. —Petronius

True hope is swift and flies with
　　swallow's wings;
Kings it makes Gods, and meaner
　　creatures kings.
　　　　　　　—William Shakespeare

Ten thousand men possess ten thousand hopes. —Euripides

Hope has as many lives as a cat or a king.
　　　　　　　—Henry Wadsworth Longfellow

Have hope. Though clouds environs
now,
And gladness hides her face in scorn,
Put thou the shadow from thy
brow—
No night but hath its morn.
—J.C.F. von Schiller

In time of trouble avert not thy face
from hope, for the soft marrow abi-
deth in the hard bone. —Hafez

Faith, hope, and charity—if we had
more of the first two, we'd need less
of the last. —Anon.

In the face of uncertainty, there is
nothing wrong with hope.
—O. Carl Simonton

Hope is the only bee that makes
honey without flowers.
—Robert G. Ingersoll

They sailed. They sailed. Then spoke
the mate:
"This mad sea shows its teeth to-
night
He curls his lip, he lies in wait,
With lifted teeth, as if to bite!
Brave admiral, say but one good
word:
What shall we do when hope is
gone?"
The words leapt like a leaping sword:
"Sail on! sail on! and on!"
—Joaquin Miller

Hope is a very unruly emotion.
—Gloria Steinem

The hopeful man sees success where
others see failure, sunshine where
others see shadows and storm.
—Orison Swett Marden

The wind was cold off the mountains
and I was a naked man with enemies
behind me, and nothing before me
but hope. —Louis L'Amour

Hope sees the invisible, feels the intan-
gible and achieves the impossible.
—Anon.

I always entertain great hopes.
—Robert Frost

To hope is not to demand. —Anon.

Hold your head high, stick your chest
out. You can make it. It gets dark
sometimes but morning comes. . . .
Keep hope alive. —Jesse Jackson

Forgiving means to pardon the
unpardonable,
Faith means believing the unbelievable,
And hoping means to hope when
things are hopeless.
—G.K. Chesterton

The gift we can offer others is so
simple a thing as hope.
—Daniel Berrigan

Even the cry from the depths is an
affirmation: why cry if there is no
hint of hope of hearing?
—Martin Marty

It's never too late—in fiction or in
life—to revise. —Nancy Thayer

In the night of death, hope sees a star,
and listening love can hear the rustle
of a wing. —Robert G. Ingersoll

Vision Doesn't Depend on Our Eyes

Vision is the art of seeing things invisible. —Jonathan Swift

Man's mind is not a container to be filled but rather a fire to be kindled. —Dorothea Brande

You can't depend on your eyes when your imagination is out of focus. —Mark Twain

We live on the leash of our senses. —Diane Ackerman

Just because a man lacks the use of his eyes doesn't mean he lacks vision. —Stevie Wonder

True vision is always twofold. It involves emotional comprehensions as well as physical perception. —Ross Parmenter

We Don't All Visualize the Same Things

We all live under the same sky, but we don't all have the same horizon. —Konrad Adenauer

A genius is one who shoots at something no one else can see—and hits it. —Anon.

My imagination makes me human and makes me a fool; it gives me all the world and exiles me from it. —Ursula K. LeGuin

A fool sees not the same tree that a wise man sees. —William Blake

Little girls are cute and small only to adults. To one another they are not cute. They are life-sized. —Margaret Atwood

You can always trust information given you by people who are crazy; they have an access to truth not available through regular channels. —Sheila Ballantyne

Who is the wise man? He who sees what's going to be born. —Solomon

A feeble man can see the farms that are fenced and tilled, the houses that are built. The strong man sees the possible houses and farms. His eye makes estates as fast as the sun breeds clouds. —Ralph Waldo Emerson

Guido the plumber and Michelangelo obtained their marble from the same quarry, but what each saw in the marble made the difference between a nobleman's sink and a brilliant sculpture. —Bob Kall

We Must Visualize Before We Act or Create

A rock pile ceases to be a rock pile the moment a single man contemplates it, bearing within him the image of a cathedral. —Antoine de Saint-Exupery

By going over your day in imagination before you begin it, you can begin acting successfully at any moment. —Dorothea Brande

A daydreamer is prepared for most things. —Joyce Carol Oates

All acts performed in the world begin
in the imagination.
                —Barbara Grizzuti Harrison

The engineering is secondary to the
vision.   —Cynthia Ozick

Dreams grow holy put in action; work
grows fair through starry dreaming.
But where each flows on unmingling,
both are fruitless and in vain.
                —Adelaide Proctor

Man can only become what he is able
to consciously imagine, or to "image
forth."   —Dane Rudhyar

I believe that you cannot go any further than you can think. I certainly
believe if you don't desire a thing,
you will never get it.
                —Charleszetta Waddles

Visualization

VISUALIZING GOALS

Before you begin a thing remind yourself that difficulties and delays quite impossible to foresee are ahead. . . . You can only see one thing clearly, and that is your goal. Form a mental vision of that and cling to it through thick and thin.   —Kathleen Norris

Man can only receive what he sees himself receiving.
                —Florence Scovel Shinn

A person can grow only as much as his horizon allows.   —John Powell

All prosperity begins in the mind and is dependent only upon the full use of our creative imagination.
                            —Ruth Ross

If we have not achieved our early dreams, we must either find new ones or see what we can salvage from the old. If we have accomplished what we set out to do in our youth, we need not weep like Alexander the Great that we have no more worlds to conquer.   —Rosalynn Carter

What man can imagine he may one day achieve.   —Nancy Hale

Envisioning the end is enough to put the means in motion.
                —Dorothea Brande

VISUALIZATION AND DREAMS

Our visions begin with our desires.
                —Audre Lorde

It is in our idleness, in our dreams, that the submerged truth sometimes comes to the top.   —Virginia Woolf

One must desire something to be alive: perhaps absolute satisfaction is only another name for Death.
                —Margaret Deland

The truth isn't always beauty, but the hunger for it is.   —Nadine Gordimer

When your dreams tire, they go underground and out of kindness that's where they stay.
                —Libby Houston

Nothing happens unless first a dream.
—Carl Sandburg

The very least you can do in your life is to figure out what you hope for. And the most you can do is live inside that hope. Not admire it from a distance but live right in it, under its roof. —Barbara Kingsolver

The history of all times, and of today especially, teaches that . . . women will be forgotten if they forget to think about themselves.
—Louise Otto

Instead of thinking about where you are, think about where you want to be. It takes twenty years of hard work to become an overnight success.
—Diana Rankin

To the lack of incentive to effort, which is the awful shadow under which we live, may be traced the wreck and ruin of scores of colored youth. —Mary Church Terrell

The moment of enlightenment is when a person's dreams of possibilities become images of probabilities.
—Vic Braden

Reach high, for stars lie hidden in your soul. Dream deep, for every dream precedes the goal.
—Pamela Vaull Starr

When we can't dream any longer, we die. —Emma Goldman

Hold fast to dreams, for if dreams die, life is a broken-winged bird that cannot fly. —Langston Hughes

I think, at a child's birth, if a mother could ask a fairy godmother to endow it with the most useful gift, that gift should be curiosity.
—Eleanor Roosevelt

You know, my children, that humanity advances only by forming itself an ideal and endeavoring to realize it. Every passion has its ideal, which is modified by that of the whole.
—Jenny P. d'Hericourt

It seems to me we can never give up longing and wishing while we are alive. There are certain things we feel to be beautiful and good, and we must hunger for them.
—George Eliot

The best antidote I have found is to yearn for something. As long as you yearn, you can't congeal: there is a forward motion to yearning.
—Gail Godwin

Every woman dreams of her own political career and her own place in life. —Raisa M. Gorbachev

Dream lofty dreams, and as you dream, so shall you become. Your vision is the promise of what you shall at last unveil. —John Ruskin

Imagination is the highest kite that can fly. —Lauren Bacall

Who would ever give up the reality of dreams for relative knowledge?
—Alice James

Dreams are the sources of action, the meeting and the end, a resting place among the flight of things.
—Muriel Rukeyser

Within your heart, keep one still, secret spot where dreams may go.
—Louise Driscoll

I've dreamt in my life dreams that have stayed with me ever after, and changed my ideas: they've gone through and through me, like wine through water, and altered the color of my mind.
—Emily Brontë

It may be that those who do most, dream most.
—Stephen Leacock

I've dreamt in my life dreams that have stayed with me ever after, and changed my ideas: they've gone through and through me, like wine through water, and altered the color of my mind.
—Emily Brontë

It's our dreams that keep us going, that separate us from the beasts. I wouldn't even want to live if I thought it was all just eating and sleeping and taking off my clothes.
—Mary Chase

GENERAL QUOTATIONS ABOUT VISION

A couple of times a day I sit quietly and visualize my body fighting the AIDS virus. It's the same as me sitting and seeing myself hit the perfect serve. I did that often when I was an athlete.
—Arthur Ashe

Is life so wretched? Isn't it rather your hands which are too small, your vision which is muddled? You are the one who must grow up.
—Dag Hammarskjold

Imagination has always had powers of resurrection that no science can match.
—Ingrid Bengis

The artist doesn't see things as they are, but as he is.
—Anon.

Make-believe colors the past with innocent distortion, and it swirls ahead of us in a thousand ways—in science, in politics, in every bold intention. It is part of our collective lives, entwining our past and our future . . . a particularly rewarding aspect of life itself.
—Shirley Temple Black

We are governed not by armies, but by ideas.
—Mona Caird

One of your most powerful inner resources is your own creativity. Be willing to try on something new and play the game full-out.
—Marcia Wieder

No vision and you perish;
No ideal, and you're lost;
Your heart must ever cherish
Some faith at any cost.
Some hope, some dream to cling to,
Some rainbow in the sky,
Some melody to sing to,
Some service that is high.
—Harriet Du Autermont

Five minutes, just before going to sleep, given to a bit of directed imagination regarding achievement possibilities of the morrow, will steadily and increasingly bear fruit, particularly if all ideas of difficulty, worry or fear are resolutely ruled out and replaced by those of accomplishment and smiling courage.
—Frederick Pierce

With our progress we have destroyed
our only weapon against tedium: that
rare weakness we call imagination.
                    —Oriana Fallaci

You can vitally influence your life
from within by auto-suggestion. The
first thing each morning, and the last
thing each night, suggest to yourself
specific ideas that you wish to embody
in your character and personality.
Address such suggestions to yourself,
silently or aloud, until they are deeply
impressed upon your mind.
                    —Grenville Kleiser

Leaders are visionaries with a poorly
developed sense of fear and no concept of the odds against them. They
make the impossible happen.
                    —Dr. Robert Jarvik

Where there is no vision, the people
perish.   —Proverbs 29:18

Role Models

THE RIGHT ROLE MODEL CAN BE VERY INSPIRATIONAL

My playground was the theatre. I'd sit and watch my mother pretend for a living. As a young girl, that's pretty seductive.　　—Gwyneth Paltrow

What you teach your own children is what you really believe in.
　　　　—Cathy Warner Weatherford

Nothing arouses ambition so much as the trumpet clang of another's fame.
　　　　—Baltasar Gracian

I studied the lives of great men and famous women, and I found that the men and women who got to the top were those who did the jobs they had in hand, with everything they had of energy and enthusiasm and hard work.
　　　　—Harry S. Truman

It's true that heroes are inspiring, but mustn't they also do some rescuing if they are to be worthy of their name? Would Wonder Woman matter if she only sent commiserating telegrams to the distressed?　—Jeanette Winterson

I believe in recovery, and I believe that as a role model I have the responsibility to let young people know that you can make a mistake and come back from it.
　　　　—Ann Richards

People never improve unless they look to some standard or example higher and better than themselves.
　　　　—Tyron Edwards

My heart is happy, my mind is free. I had a father who talked with me.
　　　　—Hilde Bigelow

If a child is too keep alive his inborn sense of wonder . . . he needs the companionship of at least one adult who can share it, rediscovering with him the joy, excitement, and mystery of the world we live in.
　　　　—Rachel Carson

Examine the personality of the mother, who is the medium through which the primitive infant transforms herself into a socialized human being.
　　　　—Beata Rank

385

That some should be rich shows that others may become rich, and hence is just encouragement to industry and enterprise.   —Abraham Lincoln

The best teachers of humanity are the lives of great men.
                    —Charles H. Fowler

As it is our nature to be more moved by hope than fear, the example of one we see abundantly rewarded cheers and encourages us far more than the sight of many who have not been well treated disquiets us.
                    —Francesco Guicciardini

Keep away from people who try to belittle your ambitions. Small people always do that, but the really great make you feel that you, too, can become great.   —Mark Twain

To be ignorant of the lives of the most celebrated men of antiquity is to continue in a state of childhood.
                    —Plutarch

People seldom improve when they have no other model but themselves to copy.   —Oliver Goldsmith

As you get older it is harder to have heroes, but it is sort of necessary.
                    —Ernest Hemingway

The most important single influence in the life of a person is another person . . . who is worthy of emulation.
                    —Paul D. Shafer

Lives of great men all remind us we can make our lives sublime; and, departing, leave behind us, footprints on the sands of time.
                    —Henry Wadsworth Longfellow

Very few men are wise by their own counsel, or learned by their own teaching. For he that was only taught by himself had a fool for his master.
                    —Ben Johnson

Call the roll in your memory of conspicuously successful business giants and . . . you will be struck by the fact that almost every one of them encountered inordinate difficulties sufficient to crush all but the gamest of spirits. Edison went hungry many times before he became famous.
                    —B.C. Forbes

Without heroes, we are all plain people, and don't know how far we can go.   —Bernard Malamud

We All Need Good Examples

If you can't be a good example, then you'll just have to be a horrible warning.   —Catherine Aird

A good example is the best sermon.
                    —Anon.

Children have more need of models than of critics.   —Carolyn Coats

Kill reverence and you've killed the hero in man.   —Ayn Rand

We deceive ourselves when we fancy that only weakness needs support. Strength needs it far more.
                    —Anne-Sophie Swetchine

Example has more followers than reason.   —Christian Bovee

Example moves the world more than doctrine.   —Henry Miller

Example is the school of mankind,
and they will learn at no other.
—Burke

Example is not the main thing in
influencing others. It is the only thing.
—Albert Schweitzer

We travel to learn; and I have never
been in any country where they did
not do something better than we do
it, think some thoughts better than
we think, catch some inspiration
from heights above our own.
—Maria Mitchell

Judgment can be acquired only by
acute observation, by actual experience in the school of life, by ceaseless
alertness to learn from others, by
study of the activities of men who
have made notable marks, by striving to analyze the everyday play of
causes and effects, by constant study
of human nature.   —B.C. Forbes

We need to teach the next generation
of children from day one that they
are responsible for their lives.
—Elisabeth Kubler-Ross

When you are a mother, you are
never really alone in your thoughts
. . . A mother has to think twice, once
for herself and once for her child.
—Sophia Loren

Our mothers and our grandmothers,
some of them: moving to music not
yet written.   —Alice Walker

Nothing is so infectious as example.
—Francois de La Rochefoucauld

There is a need for heroism in
American life today.   —Agnes Meyer

One filled with joy preaches without
preaching.   —Mother Teresa

IMITATION

There is a difference between imitating a good man and counterfeiting
him.   —Benjamin Franklin

Imitation is for shirkers, like-minded-
ness for the comfort lovers, unifying
for the creators.
—Mary Parker Follett

Each of us is in fact what he is almost
exclusively by virtue of his imitative-
ness.   —William James

Go to the ant, thou sluggard, learn
to live, and by her busy ways, reform
thy own.   —Elizabeth Smart

Imitation is a necessity of human
nature. —Oliver Wendell Holmes, Jr.

When people are free to do as they
please, they usually imitate each other.
—Eric Hoffer

Whatever good I have accomplished
as an actress I believe came in direct
proportion to my efforts to portray
black women who have made positive contributions to my heritage.
—Cicely Tyson

Emulation is a noble and just passion, full of appreciation.
—J.C.F. von Schiller

Emulation admires and strives to imitate great actions; envy is only moved
to malice.   —Honore de Balzac

'Tis no shame to follow the better precedent. —Ben Johnson

Imitation can acquire pretty much everything but the power which created the thing imitated.
—Henry S. Haskins

Almost all absurdity of conduct arises from the imitation of those whom we cannot resemble. —Samuel Johnson

To do exactly as your neighbors do is the only sensible rule. —Emily Post

Is there anyone so wise as to learn by the experience of others? —Voltaire

If . . . you can't be a good example, then you'll just have to be a horrible warning. —Catherine Aird

LEARNING FROM OTHERS' MISTAKES

From the errors of others, a wise man corrects his own. —Publilius Syrus

Learn from the mistakes of others— you can't live long enough to make them all yourself. —Martin Vanbee

Wise men learn by other men's mistakes, fools by their own.
—H.G. Bohn

A man is fortunate if he encounters living examples of vice, as well as of virtue, to inspire him.
—Brendan Francis

Learn to see in another's calamity the ills which you should avoid.
—Publilius Syrus

Don't use the conduct of a fool as a precedent. —Talmud

A prudent person profits from personal experience, a wise one from the experience of others.
—Dr. Joseph Collins

PART 4

Knowing What to Do

Change

CHANGE IS INEVITABLE

Everything passes; everything wears out; everything breaks.
　　　　　　—French proverb

I've learned only that you never say never.
　　—Marina von Neumann Whitman

Always! That is the dreadful word . . . it is a meaningless word, too.
　　　　　　—Oscar Wilde

The most ominous of fallacies: the belief that things can be kept static by inaction. 　　—Freya Stark

What is actual is actual only for one time, and only for one place.
　　　　　　—T.S. Eliot

Our days are a kaleidoscope. Every instant a change takes place. . . . New harmonies, new contrasts, new combinations of every sort. . . . The most familiar people stand each moment in some new relation to each other, to their work, to surrounding objects.
　　　　—Henry Ward Beecher

Just when I think I have learned the way to live, life changes.
　　　　　　—Hugh Prather

We change, whether we like it or not.
　　　　—Ralph Waldo Emerson

The one unchangeable certainty is that nothing is certain or unchangeable.
　　　　　—John F. Kennedy

All things must change to something new, to something strange.
　　—Henry Wadsworth Longfellow

Because things are the way they are, things will not stay the way they are.
　　　　　—Bertolt Brecht

The moral world is as little exempt as the physical world from the law of ceaseless change, of perpetual flux.
　　　　　—Sir James Frazer

Wherever we are, it is but a stage on the way to somewhere else, and whatever we do, however well we do it, it is only a preparation to do something else that shall be different.
　　　—Robert Louis Stevenson

All is change; all yields its place
and goes.   —Euripides

O visionary world, condition strange,
Where naught abiding is but only
change.   —James Russell Lowell

Things alter for the worse spontaneously, if they be not altered for the
better designedly.   —Francis Bacon

For good and evil, man is a free creative spirit. This produces the very
queer world we live in, a world in
continuous creation and therefore
continuous change and insecurity.
          —Joyce Cary

All things change, nothing is extinguished.   —Ovid

Life is always at some turning point.
          —Irwin Edman

Everything flows, nothing stays still.
          —Heraclitus

Nothing in this world is permanent.
          —German proverb

There are no permanent changes
because change itself is permanent.
          —Ralph L. Woods

Nothing is permanent but change.
          —Heraclitus

Time, in the turning-over of days,
works change for better or worse.
          —Pindar

Impermanence is the law of the
universe.   —Carlene Hatcher Polite

Everything changes but change itself.
          —John F. Kennedy

CHANGE IS LIFE ITSELF

Would that life were like the shadow
cast by a wall or a tree, but it is like
the shadow of a bird in flight.
          —Talmud

Some people are still unaware that
reality contains unparalleled beauties.
The fantastic and unexpected, the ever-
changing and renewing is nowhere so
exemplified as in real life itself.
          —Berenice Abbott

Life is change. Growth is optional.
Choose wisely.   —Karen Kaiser Clark

Change is the law of life.
          —John F. Kennedy

Life is measured by the rapidity of
change, the succession of influences
that modify the being. —George Eliot

To live is to change, and to be perfect
is to change often.
          —John Henry Cardinal Newman

One must never lose time in vainly
regretting the past or in complaining
against the changes which cause us
discomfort, for change is the essence
of life.   —Anatole France

A living thing is distinguished from a
dead thing by the multiplicity of the
changes at any moment taking place
in it.   —Herbert Spencer

When you're through changing,
you're through.   —Bruce Barton

Change is the only evidence of life.
          —Evelyn Waugh

To exist is to change, to change is to mature, to mature is to go on creating oneself endlessly.
—Henri Bergson

Life belongs to the living, and he who lives must be prepared for changes.
—Johann von Goethe

Someday change will be accepted as life itself.   —Shirley MacLaine

What is more enthralling to the human mind than this splendid, boundless, colored mutability!—Life in the making?   —David Grayson

You must change in order to survive.
—Pearl Bailey

The basic fact of today is the tremendous.   —Jawaharlal Nehru

Each new season grows from the leftovers from the past. That is the essence of change, and change is the basic law.   —Hal Borland

Arriving at one goal is the starting point to another.   —John Dewey

All that is not eternal is eternally out of date.   —C.S. Lewis

WHY WE SHOULD
WELCOME CHANGE

When people shake their heads because we are living in a restless age, ask them how they would like to life in a stationary one, and do without change. —George Bernard Shaw

Variety is the soul of pleasure.
—Aphra Behn

If one sticks too rigidly to one's principles, one would hardly see anybody.
—Agatha Christie

I'm tired of playing worn-out depressing ladies in frayed bathrobes. I'm going to get a new hairdo and look terrific and go back to school and even if nobody notices, I'm going to be the most self-fulfilled lady on the block.   —Joanne Woodward

The healthy being craves an occasional wildness, a jolt from normality, a sharpening of the edge of appetite, his own little festival of the Saturnalia, a brief excursion from his way of life.   —Robert MacIver

Impermanence is the very essence of joy—the drop of bitterness that enables one to perceive the sweet.
—Myrtle Reed

There is a certain relief in change, even though it be from bad to worse; as I have found in traveling in a stagecoach, it is often a comfort to shift one's position and be bruised in a new place.   —Washington Irving

None of us knows what the next change is going to be, what unexpected opportunity is just around the corner, waiting to change all the tenor of our lives.   —Kathleen Norris

The art of living does not consist in preserving and clinging to a particular mood of happiness, but in allowing happiness to change its form … happiness, like a child, must be allowed to grow up.
—Charles L. Morgan

In embracing change, entrepreneurs ensure social and economic stability.
—George Gilder

Fluidity and discontinuity are central to the reality in which we live.
—Mary Bateson

Change does not change tradition. It strengthens it. Change is a challenge and an opportunity, not a threat.
—Prince Phillip of England

Changes are not only possible and predictable, but to deny them is to be an accomplice to one's own unnecessary vegetation.
—Gail Sheehy

I have found that sitting in a place where you have never sat before can be inspiring.
—Dodie Smith

Continuity gives us roots; change gives us branches, letting us stretch and grow and reach new heights.
—Pauline R. Kezer

I've learned that you'll never be disappointed if you always keep an eye on uncharted territory, where you'll be challenged and growing and having fun.
—Kirstie Alley

The things we fear most in organizations—fluctuations, disturbances, imbalances—are the primary sources of creativity.
—Margaret J. Wheatley

It is in changing that things find purpose.
—Heraclitus

Turbulence is a life force. It is opportunity. Let's love turbulence and use it for change.
—Ramsay Clark

In all change, well looked into, the germinal good out-vails the apparent ill.
—Francis Thompson

The time is ripe, and rotten-ripe, for change; then let it come.
—James Russell Lowell

Society can only pursue its normal course by means of a certain progression of changes.
—John, Viscount Morley of Blackburn

Continuity in everything is unpleasant.
—Blaise Pascal

We emphasize that we believe in change because we were born of it, we have lived by it, we prospered and grew great by it. So the status quo has never been our god, and we ask no one else to bow down before it.
—Carl T. Rowan

If you do what you've always done, you'll get what you've always gotten.
—Anon.

Man needs, for his happiness, not only the enjoyment of this or that, but hope and enterprise and change.
—Bertrand Russell

To remain young one must change.
—Alexander Chase

Where the old tracks are lost, new country is revealed with its wonders.
—Rabindranath Tagore

Weep not that the world changes—did it keep a stable, changeless state, it were a cause indeed to weep.
—William Cullen Bryant

Only in growth, reform, and change, paradoxically enough, is true security to be found.
—Anne Morrow Lindbergh

CHANGE AND PROGRESS

If folks can learn to be racist, then they can learn to be antiracist. If being sexist ain't genetic, then, dad gum, people can learn about gender equality.   —Johnnetta Betsch Cole

Change is inevitable in a progressive society. Change is constant.
—Benjamin Disraeli

All bonafide revolutions are of necessity revolutions of the spirit.
—Sonia Johnson

We can say "Peace on Earth." We can sing about it, preach about it or pray about it, but if we have not internalized the mythology to make it happen inside us, then it will not be.
—Betty Shabazz

We're just getting started. We're just beginning to meet what will be the future—we've got the Model T.
—Grace Murray Hopper

Why do we shrink from change? What can come into being save by change?   —Marcus Aurelius

The challenges of change are always hard. It is important that we begin to unpack those challenges that confront this nation and realize that we each have a role that requires us to change and become more responsible for shaping our own future.
—Hillary Rodham Clinton

Progress is impossible without change, and those who cannot change their minds cannot change anything.
—George Bernard Shaw

The mind of the most logical thinker goes so easily from one point to another that it is not hard to mistake motion for progress.
—Margaret Collier Graham

The world hates change, yet it is the only thing that has brought progress.
—Charles F. Kettering

The art of progress is to preserve order amid change, and to preserve change amid order.
—Alfred North Whitehead

Change is the watchword of progression. When we tire of well-worn ways, we seek for new. This restless craving in the souls of men spurs them to climb, and to seek the mountain view.   —Ella Wheeler Wilcox

He that will not apply new remedies must expect new evils.
—Francis Bacon

In a moving world readaptation is the price of longevity.
—George Santayana

PEOPLE CHANGE

A person needs at intervals to separate himself from family and companions and go to new places. He must go without his familiars in order to be open to influences, to change.
—Katherine Butler Hathaway

Every saint has a past, and every sinner has a future.   —Oscar Wilde

It's quite possible to leave your home for a walk in the early morning air and return a different person—beguiled, enchanted.   —Mary Chase

We must always change, renew, rejuvenate ourselves; otherwise we harden.   —Johann von Goethe

On the human chessboard, all moves are possible.   —Miriam Schiff

There is nobody who totally lacks the courage to change.   —Rollo May

I've never met a person, I don't care what his condition, in whom I could not see possibilities. I don't care how much a man may consider himself a failure, I believe in him, for he can change the thing that is wrong in his life anytime he is prepared and ready to do it. Whenever he develops the desire, he can take away from his life the thing that is defeating it. The capacity for reformation and change lies within.   —Preston Bradley

The most amazing thing about little children . . . was their fantastic adaptability.   —Kristin Hunter

Let a man turn to his own childhood—no further—if he will renew his sense of remoteness, and of the mystery of change.   —Alice Meynell

All love shifts and changes. I don't know if you can be wholeheartedly in love all the time.   —Julie Andrews

People change and forget to tell each other.   —Lillian Hellman

When you have a baby, you set off an explosion in your marriage, and when the dust settles, your marriage is different from what it was. Not better, necessarily; not worse, necessarily; but different.   —Nora Ephron

There is change in all things. You yourself are subject to continual change and some decay, and this is common to the entire universe.
      —Marcus Aurelius

No one can persuade another to change. Each of us guards a gate of change that can only be opened from the inside. We cannot open the gate of another, either by argument or emotional appeal.
      —Marilyn Ferguson

We measure success and depth by length and time, but it is possible to have a deep relationship that doesn't always stay the same.
      —Barbara Hershey

One of the dreariest spots on life's road is the point of conviction that nothing will ever again happen to you.
      —Faith Baldwin

I realized that if what we call human nature can be changed, then absolutely anything is possible. And from that moment, my life changed.
      —Shirley MacLaine

A woman's life can really be a succession of lives, each revolving around some emotionally compelling situation or challenge, and each marked off by some intense experience.
      —Wallis Simpson,
      Duchess of Windsor

Readjusting is a painful process, but most of us need it at one time or another.
—Arthur Christopher Benson

For many men, the acquisition of wealth does not end their troubles, it only changes them.
—Marcus Annaeus Seneca

Our being is continually undergoing and entering upon changes. . . . We must, strictly speaking, at every moment give each other up and let each other go and not hold each other back. —Rainer Maria Rilke

Change the fabric of your own soul and your own visions, and you change all. —Vachel Lindsay

A person needs at intervals to separate himself from family and companions and go to new places. He must go without his familiars in order to be open to influence, to change.
—Katharine Butler Hathaway

There are people who not only strive to remain static themselves, but strive to keep everything else so . . . their position is almost laughably hopeless.
—Odell Shepard

The curious paradox is that when I accept myself just as I am, then I can change. —Carl Rogers

Very often a change of self is needed more than a change of scene.
—Arthur Christopher Benson

There is not a single ill-doer who could not be turned to some good.
—Jean-Jacques Rousseau

Things do not change; we change.
—Henry David Thoreau

We do not succeed in changing things according to our desire, but gradually our desire changes. —Marcel Proust

The old woman I shall become will be quite different from the woman I am now. Another I is beginning.
—George Sand

The absurd man is he who never changes. —Auguste Barthelemy

Man would be "otherwise." That's the essence of the specifically human.
—Antonio Machado

CREATING POSITIVE CHANGE

The reality is that changes are coming. . . . They must come. You must share in bringing them.
—John Hersey

After you've done a thing the same way for two years, look it over carefully. After five years, look at it with suspicion. And after ten years, throw it away and start all over.
—Alfred Edward Perlman

All that philosophers have done is interpret the world in different ways. It is our job to change it.
—Karl Marx

Christians are supposed not merely to endure change, nor even to profit by it, but to cause it.
—Harry Emerson Fosdick

If you have no will to change it, you have no right to criticize it. —Anon.

Changes are not predictable; but to deny them is to be an accomplice to one's own unnecessary vegetation.
—Gail Sheehy

We must learn to view change as a natural phenomenon—to anticipate it and to plan for it. The future is ours to channel in the direction we want to go . . . we must continually ask ourselves, "What will happen if . . . ?" or better still, "How can we make it happen?" —Lisa Taylor

One must change one's tactics every ten years if one wishes to maintain one's superiority.
—Napoleon Bonaparte

WE MUST OFTEN GIVE UP SOMETHING TO GET SOMETHING BETTER

New things cannot come where there is no room. —Marlo Morgan

The important thing is this: to be able at any moment to sacrifice what we are for what we could become.
—Charles Du Bos

When patterns are broken, new worlds emerge. —Tuli Kupferberg

One must lose one's life in order to find it. —Anne Morrow Lindbergh

This Mouse must give up one of his Mouse ways of seeing things in order that he may grow.
—Hyemeyohsts Storm

Compromise, if not the spice of life, is its solidity. —Phyllis McGinley

The only alternative to war is peace and the only road to peace is negotiations. —Golda Meir

Every one should keep a mental wastepaper basket and the older he grows the more things he will consign to it—torn up to irrecoverable tatters.
—Samuel Butler

Unless one says goodbye to what one loves, and unless one travels to completely new territories, one can expect merely a long wearing away of oneself and an eventual extinction.
—Jean Dubuffet

"How does one become a butterfly?" she asked pensively. "You must want to fly so much that you are willing to give up being a caterpillar."
—Trina Paulus

WE SHOULD CHANGE COURSE AS SOON AS WE REALIZE IT'S WRONG FOR US

No matter how far you have gone on a wrong road, turn back.
—Turkish proverb

Duration is not a test of true or false.
—Anne Morrow Lindbergh

It is only an error in judgement to make a mistake, but it shows infirmity of character to adhere to it when discovered. —Christian Bovee

If you board the wrong train, it is no use running along the corridor in the other direction.
—Dietrich Bonhoeffer

It's never too late—in fiction or in life—to revise.   —Nancy Thayer

Any path is only a path, and there is no affront, to oneself or to others, in dropping it if that is what your heart tells you.   —Carlos Castaneda

Sometimes We Must Make Changes Before We Know What to Do Next

There is a time for departure even when there's no certain place to go.
        —Tennessee Williams

Being stuck is a position few of us like. We want something new but cannot let go of the old—old ideas, beliefs, habits, even thoughts. We are out of contact with our own genius. Sometimes we know we are stuck; sometimes we don't. In both cases we have to do something.
        —Inga Teekens

My success was not based so much on any great intelligence but on great common sense.
        —Helen Gurley Brown

Lose yourself wholly; and the more you lose, the more you will find.
        —Saint Catherine of Siena

Heroes take journeys, confront dragons, and discover the treasure of their true selves.   —Carol Pearson

Life's challenges are not supposed to paralyze you, they're supposed to help you discover who you are.
        —Bernice Johnson Reagon

Just as we outgrow a pair of trousers, we outgrow acquaintances, libraries, principles, etc., at times before they're worn out and times—and this is the worst of all—before we have new ones.
        —Georg Christoph Lichtenberg

It is best to learn as we go, not go as we have learned.
        —Leslie Jeanne Sahler

Those interested in perpetuating present conditions are always in tears about the marvelous past that is about to disappear, without having so much as a smile for the young future.
        —Simone de Beauvoir

But Don't Make Changes Just for the Sake of Making Changes

I will not change just to court popularity.   —Margaret Thatcher

Innovation! One cannot be forever innovating. I want to create classics.
        —Coco Chanel

Have no fear of change as such and, on the other hand, no liking for it merely for its own sake.
        —Robert Moses

If you want to stand out, don't be different, be outstanding.
        —Meredith West

The main dangers in this life are the people who want to change everything . . . or nothing.   —Lady Astor

To change and to improve are two different things.   —German proverb

Our fathers valued change for the sake of its results; we value it in the act.
—Alice Meynell

We must beware of needless innovations, especially when guided by logic.   —Sir Winston Churchill

All change is not growth, as all movement is not forward.
—Ellen Glasgow

Just because everything is different doesn't mean anything has changed.
—Irene Peter

None are happy but by the anticipation of change. The change itself is nothing; when we have made it, the next wish is to change again.
—Samuel Johnson

We accept the verdict of the past until the need for change cries out loudly enough to force upon us a choice between the comforts of further inertia and the irksomeness of action.
—Learned Hand

To some will come a time when change itself is beauty, if not heaven.
—Edwin Arlington Robinson

IT'S OFTEN MORE IMPORTANT TO CHANGE OUR MINDS AND OPINIONS THAN TO STICK WITH THEM

Today is not yesterday; how can our works and thoughts, if they are always to be the fittest, continue always the same? Change, indeed, is painful, yet ever needful.
—Thomas Carlyle

Security can only be achieved through constant change, through discarding old ideas that have outlived their usefulness and adapting others to current facts.
—William O. Douglas

Loyalty to petrified opinion never yet broke a chain or freed a human soul.
—Mark Twain

They were so strong in their beliefs that there came a time when it hardly mattered what exactly those beliefs were; they all fused into a single stubbornness.
—Louise Erdrich

We are chameleons, and our partialities and prejudices change place with an easy and blessed facility.
—Mark Twain

Our firmest convictions are apt to be the most suspect; they mark our limitations and our bounds. Life is a petty thing unless it is moved by the indomitable urge to extend its boundaries.
—José Ortega y Gasset

It often takes more courage to change one's opinion than to stick to it.
—Georg Christoph Lichtenberg

All our final resolutions are made in a state of mind which is not going to last.   —Marcel Proust

It's an ill plan that cannot be changed.
—Latin proverb

The death of dogma is the birth of reality.   —Immanuel Kant

If anyone accuses me of contradict-
ing myself, I reply: Because I have
been wrong once, or oftener, I do not
aspire to be always wrong.
—Vauvenargues

He who cannot change the very fabric of his thought will never be able
to change reality.   —Anwar Sadat

It is in the uncompromisingness with
which dogma is held, and not in the
dogma or want of dogma, that the
danger lies.   —Samuel Butler

I wish to say what I think and feel
today, with the proviso that tomorrow perhaps I shall contradict it all.
—Ralph Waldo Emerson

Progress is impossible without
change, and those who cannot change
their minds cannot change anything.
—George Bernard Shaw

The most significant change in a
person's life is a change of attitude.
Right attitudes produce right actions.
—William J. Johnston

You had better be ready to change
your mind when needed, or your
mind will change you.
—Henry B. Wilson

The most fatal illusion is the settled
point of view. Since life is growth and
motion, a fixed point of view kills
anybody who has one.
—Brooks Atkinson

The world does not have to change....
The only thing that has to change is
our attitude.   —Gerald Jampolsky

Oh, would that my mind could let
fall its dead ideas, as the tree does its
withered leaves!   —André Gide

Convictions are more dangerous
enemies of truth than lies.
—Friedrich Nietzsche

A foolish consistency is the hobgoblin
of little minds, adored by little states-
men and philosophers and divines.
—Ralph Waldo Emerson

A man should never be ashamed to
own that he has been in the wrong,
which is but saying . . . that he is
wiser today than yesterday.
—Jonathan Swift

We have to live today by what truth
we can get today and be ready
tomorrow to call it falsehood.
—William James

It is well for people who think to
change their minds occasionally in
order to keep them clean. For those
who do not think, it is best at least to
rearrange their prejudices once in a
while.   —Luther Burbank

New opinions are always suspected,
and usually opposed, without any
other reason but because they are not
already common.   —John Locke

Do I contradict myself? Very well
then, I contradict myself (I am large,
I contain multitudes).
—Walt Whitman

I shall try to correct errors when
shown to be errors, and I shall adopt
new views so fast as they shall appear
to be new views.
—Abraham Lincoln

Contradiction is not a sign of falsity, nor the lack of contradiction a sign of truth. —Blaise Pascal

My opinion is a view I hold until . . . well, until I find something that changes it. —Luigi Pirandello

He that never changes his opinions, and never corrects his mistakes, will never be wiser on the morrow than he is today. —Tyron Edwards

CONSISTENCY

Inconsistency is the only thing in which men are consistent.
—Horatio Smith

There is nothing in this world constant but inconstancy.
—Jonathan Swift

Consistency is only suitable for ridicule. —Moliere

The world is quite right. It does not have to be consistent.
—Charlotte P. Gilman

The world's a scene of changes, and to be constant, in nature, is inconstancy. —Abraham Cowley

We cannot remain consistent with the world save by growing inconsistent with our past selves.
—Havelock Ellis

Consistency is the last refuge of the unimaginative. —Oscar Wilde

The world is quite right. It does not have to be consistent.
—Charlotte P. Gilman

True consistency, that of the prudent and the wise, is to act in conformity with circumstances, and not to act always the same way under a change of circumstances.
—John C. Calhoun

Consistency is a paste jewel that only cheap men cherish.
—William Allen White

Consistency requires you to be as ignorant today as you were a year ago.
—Bernard Berenson

Consistency is contrary to nature, contrary to life. The only completely consistent people are the dead.
—Aldous Huxley

There are those who would misteach us that to stick in a rut is consistency, and a virtue, and that to climb out of the rut is inconsistency, and a vice.
—Mark Twain

Too much consistency is as bad for the mind as for the body.
—Aldous Huxley

With consistency a great soul has simply nothing to do. . . . Speak what you think today in words as hard as cannon balls, and tomorrow speak what tomorrow thinks in hard words again, though it contradicts everything you said today.
—Ralph Waldo Emerson

People who honestly mean to be true really contradict themselves much more rarely than those who try to be "consistent."
—Oliver Wendell Holmes

To be honest, one must be inconsistent.   —H.G. Wells

What Not Changing Our Opinions May Indicate

The only man who can't change his mind is a man who hasn't got one.
—Edward Noyes Westcott

Like all weak men, he laid an exaggerated stress on not changing one's mind.   —W. Somerset Maugham

Nothing should be permanent except struggle with the dark side within ourselves.   —Shirley MacLaine

The foolish and the dead alone never change their opinion.
—James Russell Lowell

A fanatic is one who can't change his mind and won't change the subject.
—Sir Winston Churchill

The circumstances of the world are so variable that an irrevocable purpose or opinion is almost synonymous with a foolish one.
—William H. Seward

If in the last few years you haven't discarded a major opinion or acquired a new one, check your pulse. You may be dead.
—Gelett Burgess

A stiff attitude is one of the phenomena of rigor mortis.
—Henry S. Haskins

Those who never retract their opinions love themselves more than they love truth.   —Joseph Joubert

It's the most unhappy people who most fear change.
—Mignon McLaughlin

Obstinacy and heat in sticking to one's opinions is the surest proof of stupidity. Is there anything so cocksure, so immovable, so disdainful, so contemplative, so solemn and serious as an ass?   —Michel de Montaigne

The man who never alters his opinion is like standing water, and breeds reptiles of the mind.   —William Blake

When people are least sure, they are often most dogmatic.
—John Kenneth Galbraith

A conclusion is a place where you got tired of thinking.   —Fischer's Law

Only fools and dead men don't change their minds. Fools won't. Dead men can't. —John H. Patterson

The consistent thinker ... is either a walking mummy or else, if he has not succeeded in stifling all his vitality, a fanatical monomaniac.
—Aldous Huxley

Life is not a static thing. The only people who do not change their minds are incompetents in asylums, and those in cemeteries.
—Everett M. Dirksen

To hold the same views at forty as we held at twenty is to have been stupefied for a score of years and to take rank, not as a prophet, but as an unteachable brat, well birched and none the wiser.
—Robert Louis Stevenson

Why Change Is Hard

To do things today exactly the way you did them yesterday saves thinking.
—Woodrow Wilson

Any change, even a change for the better, is always accompanied by drawbacks and discomforts.
—Arnold Bennett

Old habits are strong and jealous.
—Dorothea Brande

Every new adjustment is a crisis in self-esteem.   —Eric Hoffer

Every new truth begins in a shocking heresy.   —Margaret Deland

Birth is violent, whether it be the birth of a child or the birth of an idea.
—Marianne Williamson

Any truth creates a scandal.
—Marguerite Yourcenar

Even in slight things the experience of the new is rarely without some stirring of foreboding.   —Eric Hoffer

Change is not made without inconvenience, even from worse to better.
—Richard Hooker

All changes, even the most longed for, have their melancholy, for what we leave behind us is a part of ourselves; we must die to one life before we can enter into another.   —Anatole France

How to Make Change Easier

The key to change . . . is to let go of fear.   —Rosanne Cash

Tears are sometimes an inappropriate response to death. When a life has been lived completely honestly, completely successfully, or just completely, the correct response to death's perfect punctuation mark is a smile.
—Julie Burchill

Since changes are going on anyway, the great thing is to learn enough about them so that we will be able to lay hold of them and turn them in the direction of our desires. Condi-tions and events are neither to be fled from nor passively acquiesced in; they are to be utilized and directed.
—John Dewey

He that has energy enough to root out a vice should go further, and try to plant a virtue in its place.
—Charles Caleb Colton

To change skins, evolve into new cycles, I feel one has to learn to discard. If one changes internally, one should not continue to live with the same objects. They reflect one's mind and psyche of yesterday. I throw away what has no dynamic, living use.
—Anaïs Nin

Today changes must come fast; and we must adjust our mental habits, so that we can accept comfortably the idea of stopping one thing and beginning another overnight. . . . We must assume that there is probably a better way to do almost everything. We must stop assuming that a thing which has never been done before probably cannot be done at all.
—Donald M. Nelson

We must therefore take account of this changeable nature of things and of human institutions, and prepare for them with enlightened foresight.
—Pope Pius XI

You don't have to be afraid of change. You don't have to worry about what's being taken away. Just look to see what's been added.
—Jackie Greer

When you're stuck in a spiral, to change all aspects of the spin you need only to change one thing.
—Christina Baldwin

The first step toward change is acceptance. Once you accept yourself, you open the door to change. That's all you have to do. Change is not something you do, it's something you allow.
—Will Garcia, person with AIDS

STILL, SOME THINGS DON'T CHANGE

The more things change, the more they remain the same.
—Alphonse Karr

Things good in themselves . . . perfectly valid in the integrity of their origins, become fetters if they cannot alter.
—Freya Stark

Change lays her hand not upon the truth.
—Algernon Swinburne

The spectacle has changed, but our eyes remain the same.
—Joseph Joubert

OTHER DEFINITIONS OF CHANGE

Change is the constant, the signal for rebirth, the egg of the phoenix.
—Christina Baldwin

Change is what people fear most.
—Fyodor Dostoyevsky

Change means the unknown.
—Eleanor Roosevelt

Nature's mighty law is change.
—Robert Burns

GENERAL QUOTATIONS ABOUT CHANGE

A human being does not cease to exist at death. It is change, not destruction, which takes place.
—Florence Nightingale

The old order changeth yielding place to new, and God fulfills himself in many ways.
—Alfred, Lord Tennyson

The only people in the world who can change things are those who can sell ideas.
—Lois Wyse

Everybody thinks of changing humanity and nobody thinks of changing himself.
—Leo Tolstoy

One person's constant is another person's variable.
—Susan Gerhart

The mill wheel turns, it turns forever, though what is uppermost remains not so.
—Bertolt Brecht

It's a bad plan that can't be changed.
—Publilius Syrus

In a way, winter is the real spring, the
time when the inner things happen,
the resurge of nature. —Edna O'Brien

Mourning is not forgetting. . . . It is
an undoing. Every minute tie has to
be untied and something permanent
and valuable recovered and assimi-
lated from the dust.
                    —Margery Allingham

It is never any good dwelling on
goodbyes. It is not the being together
that it prolongs, it is the parting.
            —Elizabeth Asquith Bibesco

Such is the state of life that none
are happy but by the anticipation of
change. The change itself is nothing.
When we have made it, the next wish
is to change again. —Samuel Johnson

New links must be forged as old ones
rust.   —Jane Howard

The hearts of great men can be
changed.   —Homer

You cannot step twice into the same
river, for other waters are continually
flowing on.   —Heraclitus

A man's fortune must first be
changed from within.
                    —Chinese proverb

One change always leaves the way
open for the establishment of others.
                —Niccolo Machiavelli

There is danger in reckless change; but
greater danger in blind conservatism.
                    —Henry George

Without imagination, nothing is dangerous.   —Georgette Leblanc

Everything in life that we really
accept undergoes a change.
                —Katherine Mansfield

The moment of change is the only
poem.   —Adrienne Rich

I have accepted fear as a part of
life—specifically the fear of change.
. . . I have gone ahead despite the
pounding in the heart that says: turn
back. . . .   —Erica Jong

As we learn we always change, and
so our perception. This changed perception then becomes a new Teacher
inside each of us.
                —Hyemeyohsts Storm

We are restless because of incessant
change, but we would be frightened if
change were stopped.
                —Lyman Lloyd Bryson

One must be thrust out of a finished
cycle in life, and that leap is the most
difficult to make—to part with one's
faith, one's love, when one would
prefer to renew the faith and recreate
the passion.   —Anaïs Nin

When one door of happiness closes,
another opens; but often we look
so long at the closed door that we
do not see the one which has been
opened for us.   —Helen Keller

If you want to make enemies, try to
change something.
                —Woodrow Wilson

God, grant me the serenity to accept
the things I cannot change, the courage to change the things I can, and
the wisdom to know the difference.
                —Reinhold Niebuhr

Decisions

WE MUST ALL MAKE DECISIONS

Men and women everywhere must exercise deliberate selection to live wisely. —Robert Grant

Decision and determination are the engineer and fireman of our train to opportunity and success.
—Burt Lawlor

AIDS presents me with a choice: the choice either to be a hopeless victim and die of AIDS, or to make my life right now what it always ought to have been.
—Graham, person with AIDS

The last of the human freedoms: to choose one's attitude in any given set of circumstances, to choose one's own way. —Viktor Frankl

Choice of attention . . . is to the inner life what choice of action is to the outer. In both cases, a man is responsible for his choice and must accept the consequences, whatever they may be.
—W.H. Auden

You are the one who must choose your place. —James Lane Allen

Man does not simply exist, but always decides what his existence will be, what he will become in the next moment. —Viktor Frankl

Full maturity . . . is achieved by realizing that you have choices to make.
—Angela Barron McBride

Wherever you see a successful business, someone once made a courageous decision. —Peter Drucker

DECISIONS ARE LIFE ITSELF

Life is just a series of trying to make up your mind. —Timothy Fuller

Life is just an endless chain of judgements. . . . The more imperfect our judgement, the less perfect our success.
—B.C. Forbes

To know just what has do be done, then to do it, comprises the whole philosophy of practical life.
—Sir William Osler

Life is like a game of cards. The hand that is dealt you represents determinism; the way you play it is free will.
—Jawaharlal Nehru

Somehow we learn who we really are and then live with that decision.
—Eleanor Roosevelt

Living is a constant process of deciding what we are going to do.
—José Ortega y Gasset

Life is the sum of all your choices.
—Albert Camus

Life is the art of drawing sufficient conclusions from insufficient premises.
—Samuel Butler

The difficulty of life is in the choice.
—George Moore

The strongest principle of growth lies in human choice.　　—George Eliot

As a man thinketh, so is he, and as a man chooseth, so is he.
—Ralph Waldo Emerson

Decisions determine destiny.
—Frederick Speakman

Choices are the hinges of destiny.
—Edwin Markham

Many of life's circumstances are created by three basic choices: the disciplines you choose to keep, the people you chose to be with, and the laws you choose to obey.　　—Charles Millhuff

You don't get to choose how you're going to die. Or when. You can only decide how you're going to live. Now.
—Joan Baez

SOME GOOD WAYS TO MAKE DECISIONS

Look for your choices, pick the best one, then go with it.　　—Pat Riley

Rules of society are nothing; one's conscience is the umpire.
—Madame Dudevant

No matter how lovesick a woman is, she shouldn't take the first pill that comes along.　　—Dr. Joyce Brothers

Form the habit of making decisions when your spirit is fresh . . . to let dark moods lead is like choosing cowards to command armies.
—Charles Horton Cooley

One must either accept some theory or else believe one's own instinct or follow the world's opinion.
—Gertrude Stein

Decide which is the line of conduct that presents the fewest drawbacks and then follow it out as being the best one, because one never finds anything perfectly pure and unmixed, or exempt from danger.
—Niccolo Machiavelli

A problem clearly stated is a problem half solved.　　—Dorothea Brande

We must make the choices that enable us to fulfill the deepest capacities of our real selves.
—Thomas Merton

Choose always the way that seems the best, however rough it may be; custom will soon render it easy and agreeable.　　—Pythagoras

Where an opinion is general, it is usually correct.　　—Jane Austen

In forty hours I shall be in battle, with little information, and on the spur of the moment will have to make the most momentous decisions. But I believe that one's spirit enlarges with responsibility and that, with God's help, I shall make them, and make them right.
　　—General George S. Patton

Once the "what" is decided, the "how" always follows. We must not make the "how" an excuse for not facing and accepting the "what."
　　—Pearl S. Buck

In each action we must look beyond the action at our past, present and future state, and at others whom it affects, and see the relation of all those things. And then we shall be very cautious.　　—Blaise Pascal

One's mind has a way of making itself up in the background, and it suddenly becomes clear what one means to do.
　　—Arthur Christopher Benson

Not all of your decisions will be correct. None of us is perfect. But if you get into the habit of making decisions, experience will develop your judgment to a point where more and more of your decisions will be right. After all, it is better to be right 51 percent of the time and get something done, than it is to get nothing done because you fear to reach a decision.
　　—H.W. Andrews

Decide on what you think is right, and stick to it.　　—George Eliot

Continually one faces the horrible matter of making decisions. The solution . . . is, as far as possible, to avoid conscious rational decisions and choices; simply to do what you find yourself doing; to float in the great current of life with as little friction as possible; to allow things to settle themselves, as indeed they do with the most infallible certainty.
　　—Christopher Morley

When making a decision of minor importance, I have always found it advantageous to consider all the pros and cons. In vital matters, however, such as the choice of a mate or a profession, the decision should come from the unconscious, from somewhere within ourselves. In the important decisions of personal life, we should be governed, I think, by the deep inner needs of our nature.
　　—Sigmund Freud

Pick battles big enough to matter, small enough to win.
　　—Jonathan Kozel

Wisdom consists in being able to distinguish among dangers and make a choice of the least harmful.
　　—Niccolo Machiavelli

I think we should follow a simple rule: if we can take the worst, take the risk.　　—Dr. Joyce Brothers

Human foresight often leaves its proudest possessor only a choice of evils.　　—Charles Caleb Colton

When one bases his life on principle, 99 percent of his decisions are already made.　　—Anon.

The best we can do is size up the chances, calculate the risks involved, estimate our ability to deal with them, and then make our plans with confidence.   —Henry Ford

In case of doubt, decide in favor of what is correct.   —Karl Kraus

Each man must for himself alone decide what is right and what is wrong, which course is patriotic and which isn't. You cannot shirk this and be a man. To decide against your conviction is to be an unqualified and inexcusable traitor, both to yourself and to your country, let men label you as they may.   —Mark Twain

People "died" all the time. . . . Parts of them died when they made the wrong kinds of decisions—decisions against life. Sometimes they died bit by bit until finally they were just living corpses walking around. If you were perceptive you could see it in their eyes; the fire had gone out ... you always knew when you made a decision against life. . . . The door clicked and you were safe inside— safe and dead.
          —Anne Morrow Lindbergh

What I emphasize is for people to make choices based not on fear, but on what really gives them a sense of fulfillment.   —Pauline Rose Chance

We lose the fear of making decisions, great and small, as we realize that should our choice prove wrong we can, if we will, learn from the experience.   —Bill W.

Our Decisions Have Consequences

History is a stern judge.
          —Svetlana Alliluyeva

I get a little angry about this high-handed scrapping of the look of things. What else have we to go by? How else can the average person form an opinion of a girl's sense of values or even of her chastity except by the looks of her conduct?
          —Margaret Culkin Banning

You wouldn't want to be caught wearing cheap perfume, would you? Then why do you want to wear cheap perfume on your conduct?
          —Margaret Culkin Banning

The difference between weakness and wickedness is much less than people suppose; and the consequences are nearly always the same.
          —Lady Marguerite Blessington

Authority without wisdom is like a heavy axe without an edge, fitter to bruise than to polish.
          —Anne Bradstreet

One faces the future with one's past.
          —Pearl S. Buck

Our deeds still travel with us from afar, and what we have been makes us what we are.   —George Eliot

You must not change one thing, one pebble, one grain of sand, until you know what good and evil will follow on that act.   —Ursula K. LeGuin

The beginning of compunction is the beginning of a new life.—George Eliot

We Must Often Decide and Do Important Things with Very Little Knowledge or Experience

The Pilgrims didn't have any experience when they landed here. Hell, if experience was that important, we'd never have anybody walking on the moon. —Doug Rader

Each person has a literature inside them. But when people lose language, when they have to experiment with putting their thoughts together on the spot——that's what I love most. That's where character lives.
—Anna Deavere Smith

There is no data on the future.
—Laurel Cutler

The most important fact about Spaceship Earth: an instruction book didn't come with it.
—R. Buckminster Fuller

Life is the only art that we are required to practice without preparation, and without being allowed the preliminary trials, the failures and botches, that are essential for the training of a mere beginner.
—Lewis Mumford

Time has told me less than I need to know. —Gwen Harwood

I learn by going where I have to go.
—Theodore Roethke

Life is like playing a violin in public and learning the instrument as one goes on. —Samuel Butler

We don't have enough time to premeditate all our actions.
—Vauvenargues

Every year, if not every day, we have to wager our salvation upon some prophecy based upon imperfect knowledge.
—Oliver Wendell Holmes, Jr.

Faith . . . acts promptly and boldly on the occasion, on slender evidence.
—John Henry Cardinal Newman

A decision is an action you must take when you have information so incomplete that the answer does not suggest itself. —Arthur Radford

We Can't Rely on Just Logic and Reason and Statistics

She knew in her heart that to be without optimism, that core of reasonless hope in the spirit, rather than the brain, was a fatal flaw, the seed of death. —Anne Perry

When faith is supported by facts or by logic it ceases to be faith.
—Edith Hamilton

How far would Moses have gone if he had taken a poll in Egypt?
—Harry S. Truman

Better to be without logic than without feeling. —Charlotte Brontë

The will to be totally rational is the will to be made out of glass and steel: and to use others as if they were glass and steel. —Marge Piercy

In the three years I played ball, we won six, lost seventeen and tied two. Some statistician . . . calculated that we won 75 percent of the games we didn't lose.   —Roger M. Blough

Imagination took the reins, and Reason, slow-paced, though sure-footed, was unequal to a race with so eccentric and flighty a companion.
        —Fanny Burney

Many persons of high intelligence have notoriously poor judgement.
        —Sydney J. Harris

How dangerous can false reasoning prove!   —Sophocles

The tendency of modern science is to reduce proof to absurdity by continually reducing absurdity to proof.
        —Samuel Butler

Say you were standing with one foot in the oven and one foot in an ice bucket. According to the percentage people, you would be perfectly comfortable.   —Bobby Bragan

Logic is the art of going wrong with confidence.   —Joseph Wood Krutch

Reason, with most people, means their own opinions.
        —William Hazlitt

Logic pervades the world; the limits of the world are also the limits of logic.   —Ludwig Wittgenstein

Man is a reasoning, rather than a reasonable, animal.
        —Alexander Hamilton

False conclusions which have been reasoned out are infinitely worse than blind impulse.   —Horace Mann

If you do everything you should do, and do not do anything you should not do, you will, according to the best available statistics, live exactly eighteen hours longer than you would otherwise.
        —Dr. Logain Clendening,
                in 1944

Decisions, particularly important ones, have always made me sleepy, perhaps because I know that I will have to make them by instinct, and thinking things out is only what other people tell me I should do.
        —Lillian Hellman

Statistics are no substitute for judgement.   —Henry Clay

It is the heart always that sees before the head can see.   —Thomas Carlyle

Facts are stubborn things, but statistics are more pliable.
        —Laurence J. Peter

A true history of human events would show that a far larger proportion of our acts are the result of sudden impulse and accident than of that reason of which we so much boast.
        —Peter Cooper

It is always thus, impaled by a state of mind which is destined not to last, that we make our irrevocable decisions.   —Marcel Proust

A power greater than any human being helped make this decision.
        —Herbert J. Steifel

Don't Deliberate Too Long

He who reflects too much will achieve little.   —J.C.F. von Schiller

The opportunity is often lost by deliberating.   —Publilius Syrus

The percentage of mistakes in quick decisions is no greater than in long-drawn-out vacillations, and the effect of decisiveness itself "makes things go" and creates confidence.
     —Anne O'Hare McCormick

Deliberation often loses a good chance.   —Latin proverb

The mania of thinking renders one unfit for every activity.
     —Anatole France

When possible make the decisions now, even if action is in the future. A revised decision usually is better than one reached at the last moment.
     —William B. Given, Jr.

We spend our days in deliberating, and we end them without coming to any resolve.   —L'Estrange

If you think too long, you think wrong.   —Jim Kaat

You decide you'll wait for your pitch. Then as the ball starts toward the plate, you think about your stance. And then you think about your swing. And then you realize that the ball that went past you for a strike was your pitch.   —Bobby Mercer

The soul of dispatch is decision.
     —William Hazlitt

The moment a question comes to your mind, see yourself mentally taking hold of it and disposing of it. In that moment . . . you learn to become the decider and not the vacillator. Thus you build character.
     —H. Van Anderson

So what do we do? Anything. Something. So long as we just don't sit there. If we screw it up, start over. Try something else. If we wait until we've satisfied all the uncertainties, it may be too late.   —Lee Iacocca

Often greater risk is involved in postponement than in making a wrong decision.   —Harry A. Hopf

Some persons are very decisive when it comes to avoiding decisions.
     —Brendan Francis

Do not wait for ideal circumstances, nor the best opportunities; they will never come.   —Janet Erskine Stuart

There comes a time when you've got to say, "Let's get off our asses and go . . . " I have always found that if I move with 75 percent or more of the facts I usually never regret it. It's the guys who wait to have everything perfect that drive you crazy.
     —Lee Iacocca

Conditions are never just right. People who delay action until all factors are favorable do nothing.
     —William Feather

Common sense does not ask an impossible chessboard, but takes the one before it and plays the game.
     —Wendell Phillips

He who postpones the hour of living
is like the rustic who waits for the
river to run out before he crosses.
—Horace

If you wait for inspiration you'll
be standing on the corner after the
parade is a mile down the street.
—Ben Nicholas

Nothing at all will be attempted if all
possible objections must first be overcome.   —Samuel Johnson

ALTERNATIVES

It is the characteristic excellence of
the strong man that he can bring
momentous issues to the fore and
make a decision about them. The
weak are always forced to decide
between alternatives they have not
chosen themselves.
—Dietrich Bonhoeffer

Alternatives, and particularly desirable alternatives, grow only on imaginary trees.   —Saul Bellow

The more one does and sees and
feels, the more one is able to do, and
the more genuine may be one's own
appreciation of fundamental things
like home, and love, and understanding companionship.
—Amelia Earhart

Our danger is not too few, but too
many options . . . to be puzzled by
innumerable alternatives.
—Sir Richard Livingstone

The absence of alternatives clears the
mind marvelously. —Henry Kissinger

I couldn't claim that I have never felt
the urge to explore evil, but when
you descend into hell you have to be
very careful.   —Kathleen Raine

If decisions were a choice between
alternatives, decisions would come
easy. Decision is the selection and
formulation of alternatives.
—Kenneth Burke

WHEN WE'RE DOWN TO
TWO CHOICES

You cannot have your cake and eat it.
—Anon.

It is better to arm and strengthen
your hero, than to disarm and enfee-
ble your foe.   —Anne Brontë

You cannot sell the cow and sup
the milk.   —Anon.

There is only one answer to destruc-
tiveness and that is creativity.
—Sylvia Ashton-Warner

A door must either be shut or open.
—Anon.

Here's a rule I recommend. Never
practice two vices at once.
—Tallulah Bankhead

You cannot serve God and Mammon.
—Matthew 6:24

Between two stools one sits on the
ground.   —French proverb

When you cannot make up your
mind between two evenly balanced
courses of action, choose the bolder.
—W.J. Slim

When confronted with two courses of action I jot down on a piece of paper all the arguments in favor of each one, then on the opposite side I write the arguments against each one. Then by weighing the arguments pro and con and cancelling them out, one against the other, I take the course indicated by what remains.
—Benjamin Franklin

There are two ways of spreading light: to be the candle or the mirror that reflects it.　　—Edith Wharton

You cannot have it both ways.
—Anon.

I would sort out all the arguments and see which belonged to fear and which to creativeness. Other things being equal, I would make the decision which had the larger number of creative reasons on its side.
—Katharine Butler Hathaway

Of two evils, choose the less.—Anon.

Of two evils, choose the prettier.
—Carolyn Wells

Where bad's the best, bad must be the choice.　　　　—Anon.

Both choices are painful, but only one is therapeutic.
—Albert M. Wells, Jr.

God offers to every mind its choice between truth and repose. Take which you please—you can never have both.
—Ralph Waldo Emerson

Necessity relieves us from the embarrassment of choice.　—Vauvenargues

WHAT NOT DECIDING MAY MEAN

When you have to make a choice and don't make it, that is in itself a choice.
—William James

A man without decision can never be said to belong to himself; he is as a wave of the sea, or a feather in the air which every breeze blows about.
—John Foster

Nothing is so exhausting as indecision, and nothing is so futile.
—Bertrand Russell

Not to decide is to decide.
—Harvey Cox

Decision is a sharp knife that cuts clean and straight; indecision, a dull one that hacks and tears and leaves ragged edges behind it.
—Gordon Graham

There is no more miserable human being than one in whom nothing is habitual but indecision.
—William James

In not making the decision, you've made one. Not doing something is the same as doing it.　—Ivan Bloch

There is a time when we must firmly choose the course we will follow, or the relentless drift of events will make the decision for us.
—Herbert B. Prochnow

DECISIONS CAN'T BE EVALUATED UNTIL THEY ARE IMPLEMENTED

You can only predict things after they've happened.　—Eugene Ionesco

It is the mark of a good action that it appears inevitable, in retrospect.
—Robert Louis Stevenson

No one knows what he can to do until he tries.   —Publilius Syrus

GENERAL QUOTATIONS ABOUT DECISIONS

Of all paths a man could strike into, there is, at any given moment, a best path which, here and now, it were of all things wisest for him to do. To find this path, and walk in it, is the one thing needful for him.
—Thomas Carlyle

Decisions, particularly important ones, have always made me sleepy, perhaps because I know that I will have to make them by instinct, and thinking things out is only what other people tell me I should do.
—Lillian Hellman

After a battle is over people talk a lot about how decisions were methodically reached, but actually there's always a hell of a lot of groping around.
—Admiral Frank Jack Fletcher

No question is ever settled until it is settled right.   —Ella Wheeler Wilcox

No man who has not sat in the assemblies of men can know the light, odd and uncertain ways in which decisions are often arrived at.
—Sir Arthur Helps

No trumpets sound when the important decisions of our life are made. Destiny is made known silently.
—Agnes de Mille

A man must be able to cut a knot, for everything cannot be untied.
—Henri Frederic Amiel

Once to every man and nation comes the moment to decide . . .
And the choice goes by forever t'wixt that darkness and that light.
—James Russell Lowell

Necessity is not an established fact, but an interpretation.
—Friedrich Nietzsche

We are not permitted to choose the frame of our destiny. But what we put into it is ours.
—Dag Hammarskjold

There is a point at which everything becomes simple and there is no longer any question of choice, because all you have staked will be lost if you look back. Life's point of no return.
—Dag Hammarskjold

Optimism is an intellectual choice.
—Diana Schneider

The lame man who keeps the right road outstrips the runner who takes a wrong one . . . the more active and swift the latter is, the further he will go astray.   —Francis Bacon

Nothing is more difficult, and therefore more precious, than to be able to decide.   —Napoleon Bonaparte

There is one quality more important than know-how. . . . This is know-how by which we determine not only how to accomplish our purposes, but what our purposes are to be.
—Norbert Weiner

Destiny is not a matter of chance, it
is a matter of choice; it is not a thing
to be waited for, it is a thing to be
achieved.   —William Jennings Bryan

What must be, shall be; and that
which is a necessity to him that struggles is little more than choice to him
that is willing.
          —Marcus Annaeus Seneca

A wiser rule would be to make up
your mind soberly what you want,
peace or war, and then to get ready
for what you want; for what we prepare for is what we shall get.
          —William Graham Sumner

We have resolved to endure the unendurable and suffer what is insuffer-
able.   —Emperor Hirohito,
          after the Hiroshima bombing

Choose your rut carefully; you'll be
in it for the next ten miles.
          —Road sign in upstate New York

Once a decision was made, I did not
worry about it afterward.
          —Harry S. Truman

No country can act wisely simultaneously in every part of the globe at
every moment of time.
          —Henry Kissinger

The last, if not the greatest, of the
human freedoms: to choose their own
attitude in any given circumstance.
          —Bruno Bettelheim

He who has a choice has trouble.
          —Dutch proverb

Instincts

WE MUST TRUST OUR INSTINCTS

Trust your own instinct. Your mistakes might as well be your own, instead of someone else's.
—Billy Wilder

I feel there are two people inside of me—me and my intuition. If I go against her, she'll screw me every time, and if I follow her, we get along quite nicely. —Kim Basinger

I give myself, sometimes, admirable advice, but I am incapable of taking it.
—Lady Mary Wortley Montagu

Some of the finest moral intuitions come to quite humble people. The visiting of lofty ideas doesn't depend on formal schooling. Think of those Galilean peasants.
—Alfred North Whitehead

I'm the foe of moderation, the champion of excess. If I may lift a line from a die-hard whose identity is lost in the shuffle, "I'd rather be strongly wrong than weakly right."
—Tallulah Bankhead

Conviction without experiences makes for harshness.
—Flannery O'Connor

Without fanaticism we cannot accomplish anything. —Eva Perón

To have character is to be big enough to take life on.
—Mary Caroline Richards

The trouble is that not enough people have come together with the firm determination to live the things which they say they believe.
—Eleanor Roosevelt

All I can do is act according to my deepest instinct, and be whatever I must be—crazy or ribald or sad or compassionate or loving or indifferent. That is all anybody can do.
—Katharine Butler Hathaway

Instinct is untaught ability.
—Alexander Bain

Trusting our intuition often saves us from disaster. —Anne Wilson Schaef

Trust your gut. —Barbara Walters

It is our business to go as we are impelled.   —D.H. Lawrence

Intuition . . . appears to be the extra-sensory perception of reality.
                    —Dr. Alexis Carrel

Common sense is instinct. Enough of it is genius.   —George Bernard Shaw

A goose flies by a chart which the Royal Geographical Society could not improve.   —Holmes

I go by instinct. . . . I don't worry about experience.   —Barbra Streisand

Unconsciousness, spontaneity, instinct . . . hold us to the earth and dictate the relatively good and useful.
                    —Henri Frederic Amiel

Every time you don't follow your inner guidance, you feel a loss of energy, loss of power, a sense of spiritual deadness.   —Shakti Gawain

Every time a resolve or fine glow of feeling evaporates without bearing fruit, it is worse than a chance lost; it works to hinder future emotions from taking the normal path of discharge.   —William James

It is only by following your deepest instinct that you can lead a rich life.
                    —Katharine Butler Hathaway

Instinct is the nose of the mind.
                    —Madame de Girardin

One of the reasons why so few of us ever act, instead of react, is because we are continually stifling our deepest impulses.   —Henry Miller

A man should not strive to eliminate his complexes but to get into accord with them, for they are legitimately what directs his conduct in the world.
                    —Sigmund Freud

If you let your fear of consequence prevent you from following your deepest instinct, your life will be safe, expedient and thin.
                    —Katharine Butler Hathaway

Everyone was searching for a formula for survival . . . and the only formula that worked was no formula. Instinct . . . that's all you had to go on.
                    —Carolyn Kenmore

I feel there are two people inside me—me and my intuition. If I go against her, she'll screw me every time, and if I follow her, we get along quite nicely.   —Kim Basinger

To be faithful to your instincts and the impulses that carry you in the direction of the excellence you most desire and value . . . surely that is to lead the noble life.
                    —George E. Woodberry

We each need to let our intuition guide us, and then be willing to follow that guidance directly and fearlessly.   —Shakti Gawain

By learning to contact, listen to, and act on our intuition, we can directly connect to the higher power of the universe and allow it to become our guiding force.   —Shakti Gawain

The struggle to learn to listen to and respect our own intuitive, inner promptings is the greatest challenge of all.   —Herb Goldberg

Once you get rid of the idea that you must please other people before you please yourself, and you begin to follow your own instincts—only then can you be successful. You become more satisfied, and when you are, other people tend to be satisfied by what you do.   —Raquel Welch

If you do not express your own original ideas, if you do not listen to your own being, you will have betrayed yourself.   —Rollo May

Every human being has, like Socrates, an attendant spirit; and wise are they who obey its signals. If it does not always tell us what to do, it always cautions us what not to do.
          —Lydia M. Child

Trust the instinct to the end, though you can render no reason.
          —Ralph Waldo Emerson

The truth of a thing is the feel of it, not the think of it.
          —Stanley Kubrick

Spend time every day listening to what your muse is trying to tell you.
          —Saint Bartholomew

Spontaneity

When I do things without any explanation, but just with spontaneity . . . I can be sure that I am right.
          —Federico Fellini

Analysis kills spontaneity. The grain once ground into flour germinates no more.   —Henri Frederic Amiel

Spontaneity is the quality of being able to do something just because you feel like it at the moment, of trusting your instincts, of taking yourself by surprise and snatching from the clutches of your well-organized routine a bit of unscheduled pleasure.   —Richard Iannelli

Instincts, Facts, and Statistics

I never believe facts; Canning said nothing was so fallacious as facts, except figures.   —Sydney Smith

Trust your hunches. . . . Hunches are usually based on facts filed away just below the conscious level. Warning! Do not confuse your hunches with wishful thinking. This is the road to disaster.   —Dr. Joyce Brothers

Facts are not truths; they are not conclusions; they are not even premisses, but in the nature and parts of premisses.
          —Samuel Taylor Coleridge

Statistics are no substitute for judgement.   —Henry Clay

The Relationship between Instinct and Reason

You cannot know what you cannot feel.   —Marya Mannes

We should chiefly depend not upon that department of the soul which is most superficial and fallible (our reason), but upon that department that is deep and sure, which is instinct.
          —Charles Sanders Peirce

I make all my decisions on intuition. I throw a spear into the darkness. That is intuition. Then I must send an army into the darkness to find the spear. That is intellect.

—Ingmar Bergman

Instinct is intelligence incapable of self-consciousness.   —John Sterling

Every advance in social progress removes us more and more from the guidance of instinct, obliging us to depend upon reason for the assurance that our habits are really agreeable to the laws of health.

—Emily Blackwell

Follow your instincts. That's where true wisdom manifests itself.

—Oprah Winfrey

Impulse without reason is not enough, and reason without impulse is a poor makeshift.

—William James

The shrewd guess, the fertile hypothesis, the courageous leap to a tentative conclusion—these are the most valuable coin of the thinker at work.

—Jerome S. Bruner

A trembling in the bones may carry a more convincing testimony than the dry, documented deductions of the brain.   —Llewelyn Powers

Calculation never made a hero.

—John Henry Cardinal Newman

We are so clothed in rationalization and dissemblance that we can recognize but dimly the deep primal impulses that motivate us.

—James Ramsey Ullman

All our reasoning ends in surrender to feeling.   —Blaise Pascal

Reason, ruling alone, is a force confining; and passion, unattended, is a flame that burns to its own destruction.   —Kahlil Gibran

Modern man's besetting temptation is to sacrifice his direct perceptions and spontaneous feelings to his reasoned reflections; to prefer in all circumstances the verdict of his intellect to that of his immediate intuitions.

—Aldous Huxley

Decisions, particularly important ones, have always made me sleepy, perhaps because I know that I will have to make them by instinct, and thinking things out is only what other people tell me I should do.

—Lillian Hellman

Systems die; instincts remain.

—Oliver Wendell Holmes, Jr.

I do not believe that the deeper problems of living can ever be answered by the process of thought. I believe that life itself teaches us either patience with regard to them, or reveals to us possible solutions when our hearts are pressed close against duties and sorrows and experiences of all kinds.

—Hamilton Wright Mabie

Life is one long struggle between conclusions based on abstract ways of conceiving cases, and opposite conclusions prompted by our instinctive perception of them.

—William James

Nothing reaches the intellect before making its appearance in the senses.
—Latin proverb

Instinct guides the animal better than the man. In the animal it is pure, in man it is led astray by his reason and intelligence. —Denis Diderot

Ideas pull the trigger, but instinct loads the gun. —Don Marquis

Well-bred instinct meets reason halfway. —George Santayana

Good instincts usually tell you what to do long before your head has figured it out. —Michael Burke

Pure logic is the ruin of the spirit.
—Antoine de Saint-Exupery

When a man begins to reason, he ceases to feel. —French proverb

A mind all logic is like a knife all blade. It makes the hand bleed that uses it. —Rabindranath Tagore

The mind can assert anything, and pretend it has proved it. My beliefs I test on my body, on my intuitional consciousness, and when I get a response there, then I accept.
—D.H. Lawrence

People who lean on logic and philosophy and rational exposition end by starving the best part of the mind.
—William Butler Yeats

The brain is not, and cannot be, the sole or complete organ of thought and feeling.
—Antoinette Brown Blackwell

Imagination is more important than knowledge. —Albert Einstein

Some other faculty than the intellect is necessary for the apprehension of reality. —Henri Bergson

Command by instinct is swifter, subtler, deeper, more accurate, more in touch with reality than command by conscious mind. The discovery takes one's breath away.
—Michael Novak

No one is more liable to make mistakes than the man who acts only on reflection. —Vauvenargues

Nothing is impossible when we follow our inner guidance, even when its direction may threaten us by reversing our usual logic.
—Gerald Jampolsky

A true history of human events would show that a far larger proportion of our acts are the results of sudden impulses and accident than of that reason of which we so much boast.
—Peter Cooper

Instincts and the Heart

It is wisdom to believe the heart.
—George Santayana

I follow my heart, for I can trust it.
—J.C.F. von Schiller

The intellect is always fooled by the heart.
—Francois de La Rochefoucauld

There are no rules. Just follow your heart. —Robin Williams

Man becomes man only by his intelligence, but he is man only by his heart.   —Henri Frederic Amiel

It is the heart always that sees, before the head can see.   —Thomas Carlyle

It is only with the heart that one can see rightly; what is essential is invisible to the eye.
      —Antoine de Saint-Exupery

Great thoughts always come from the heart.   —Vauvenargues

It is the heart which experiences God, not the reason.   —Blaise Pascal

The heart has reasons which reason cannot understand.   —Blaise Pascal

In making our decisions, we must use the brains that God has given us. But we must also use our hearts, which He also gave us.   —Fulton Oursler

Just be what you are and speak from your guts and heart—it's all a man has.   —Hubert H. Humphrey

INSTINCTS AND LOVE

When love is not madness, it is not love.   —Pedro Calderón de la Barca

To live is like to love: all reason is against it, and all healthy instinct is for it.   —Samuel Butler

The thinker philosophizes as the lover loves. Even were the consequences not only useless but harmful, he must obey his impulse.   —William James

What you intuitively desire, that is possible to you.   —D.H. Lawrence

Falling in love is one of the activities forbidden that tiresome person, the consistently reasonable man.
      —Sir Arthur Eddington

INSTINCTS, DESIRES, AND PASSIONS

If you really want something you can figure out how to make it happen.
      —Cher

Our real duty is always found running in the direction of our worthiest desires.   —Randolph Bourne

The essential conditions of everything you do must be choice, love, passion.
      —Nadia Boulanger

Passion and prejudice govern the world, only under the name of reason.
      —John Wesley

The conclusions of passion are the only reliable ones.
      —Søren Kierkegaard

Man is a passion which brings a will into play, which works an intelligence.
      —Henri Frederic Amiel

Life is not governed by will or intention. Life is a question of nerves, and fibers, and slowly built-up cells in which thought hides itself, and passion has its dreams.   —Oscar Wilde

We do not wish ardently for what we desire only through reason.
      —Francois de La Rochefoucauld

INSTINCTS DON'T JUST OCCUR— THEY RESULT FROM OTHER INFLUENCES

Trust your hunches. They're usually based on facts filed away just below the conscious level.
—Dr. Joyce Brothers

Inspiration does not come like a bolt, nor is it kinetic energy striving, but it comes to us slowly and quietly and all the time. —Brenda Ueland

Intuition is given only to him who has undergone long preparation to receive it. —Louis Pasteur

You must train your intuition—you must trust the small voice inside you which tells you exactly what to say, what to decide. —Ingrid Bergman

You have first an instinct, then an opinion, then a knowledge, as the plant has root, bud and fruit. Trust the instinct to the end, though you can render no reason.
—Ralph Waldo Emerson

GENERAL QUOTATIONS ABOUT INSTINCTS

A hunch is creativity trying to tell you something. —Anon.

I move on feeling and have learned to distrust those who don't.
—Nikki Giovanni

Advice is what we ask for when we already know the answer but wish we didn't. —Erica Jong

Instinct is a powerful form of natural energy, perhaps comparable in humans to electricity or even atomic energy in the mechanical world.
—Margaret A. Ribble

Cherish your emotions and never undervalue them. —Robert Henri

But are not this struggle and even the mistakes one may make better, and do they not develop us more, than if we kept systematically away from emotions? —Vincent van Gogh

Many a man gets weary of clamping down on his rough impulses, which if given occasional release would encourage the living of life with salt in it, in place of dust.
—Henry S. Haskins

We shall keep our horizon perfectly, absolutely, crystallinely open, ready every day for the scouring gales of impulse. —John Mistletoe

Intuition is a spiritual faculty and does not explain, but simply points the way. —Florence Scovel Shinn

Every time I've done something that doesn't feel right, it's ended up not being right. —Mario Cuomo

None of us can estimate what we do when we do it from instinct.
—Luigi Pirandello

I write out of instinct.
—Jerome Weidman

Doing What's Right for Us

WE MUST DO WHAT'S RIGHT FOR US

The great thing to learn about life is, first, not to do what you don't want to do, and, second, to do what you do want to do.
—Margaret Anderson

Men can starve from a lack of self-realization as much as they can from a lack of bread.   —Richard Wright

[There] is a need to find and sing our own song, to stretch our limbs and shake them in a dance so wild that nothing can roost there, that stirs the yearning for solitary voyage.
—Barbara Lazear Ascher

Every man has his own destiny; the only imperative is to follow it, to accept it, no matter where it leads him.   —Henry Miller

You don't get to choose how you're going to die. Or when. You can only decide how you're going to live.
—Joan Baez

Ya gotta do what ya gotta do.
—Sylvester Stallone

I want to do it because I want to do it.
—Amelia Earhart

Personality, too, is destiny.
—Erik H. Erikson

The door that nobody else will go in at, seems always to swing open widely for me.   —Clara Barton

I don't go by the rule book—I lead from the heart, not the head.
—Diana, Princess of Wales

A man should not strive to eliminate his complexes but to get into accord with them, for they are legitimately what directs his conduct in the world.   —Sigmund Freud

When she stopped conforming to the conventional picture of femininity she finally began to enjoy being a woman.   —Betty Friedan

Live as you will wish to have lived when you are dying.
—Christian Furchtegott Gellert

The history of human growth is at the same time the history of every new idea heralding the approach of a brighter dawn, and the brighter dawn has always been considered illegal, outside of the law.

—Emma Goldman

The first thing is to love your sport. Never do it to please someone else. It has to be yours. —Peggy Fleming

There is just one life for each of us: our own. —Euripides

People are ridiculous only when they try or seem to be that which they are not. —Giacomo Leopardi

Men are created different; they lose their social freedom and their individual autonomy in seeking to become like each other. —David Riesman

The pain of leaving those you grow to love is only the prelude to understanding yourself and others.

—Shirley MacLaine

Of all the paths a man could strike into, there is, at any given moment, a best path . . . a thing which, here and now, it were of all things wisest for him to do . . . to find this path, and walk in it, is the one thing needful for him. —Thomas Carlyle

I don't tell the truth any more to those who can't make use of it. I tell it mostly to myself, because it always changes me. —Anaïs Nin

To feel that one has a place in life solves half the problem of contentment. —George E. Woodberry

In my clinical experience, the greatest block to a person's development is his having to take on a way of life which is not rooted in his own powers.

—Rollo May

This is the chief thing: be not perturbed, for all things are according to the nature of the universal.

—Marcus Aurelius

Dedication to one's work in the world is the only possible sanctification. Religion in all its forms is dedication to Someone Else's work, not yours. —Cynthia Ozick

What's a joy to the one is a nightmare to the other. —Bertolt Brecht

Nothing is good for everyone, but only relatively to some people.

—André Gide

What's important is finding out what works for you. —Henry Moore

Everyone has a right to his own course of action. —Moliere

Freedom and constraint are two aspects of the same necessity, the necessity of being the man you are, and not another. You are free to be that man, but not free to be another.

—Antoine de Saint-Exupery

What one man does, another fails to do; what's fit for me may not be fit for you. —Anon.

Let them know a real man, who lives as he was meant to live.

—Marcus Aurelius

The one thing that doesn't abide by majority rule is a person's conscience.
—Harper Lee

There's no right way of writing. There's only your way.
—Milton Lomask

Every man must get to heaven his own way.
—Frederick the Great

There are as many ways to live and grow as there are people. Our own ways are the only ways that should matter to us.
—Evelyn Mandel

Only he who keeps his eye fixed on the far horizon will find his right road.
—Dag Hammarskjold

Those who love a cause are those who love the life which has to be led in order to serve it.
—Simone Weil

If you always do what interests you, at least one person is pleased.
—Katharine Hepburn's mother

Why not be oneself? That is the whole secret of a successful appearance. If one is a greyhound, why try to look like a Pekingese?
—Edith Sitwell

Do you know that disease and death must needs overtake us, no matter what we are doing? . . . What do you wish to be doing when it overtakes you? . . . If you have anything better to be doing when you are so overtaken, get to work on that.
—Epictetus

I'll walk where my own nature would be leading; it vexes me to choose another guide.
—Emily Brontë

If you go to heaven without being naturally qualified for it, you will not enjoy it there.
—George Bernard Shaw

He who walks in another's tracks leaves no footprints.
—Joan L. Brannon

To be what we are, and to become what we are capable of becoming, is the only end of life.
—Robert Louis Stevenson

Follow your bliss. Find where it is and don't be afraid to follow it.
—Joseph Campbell

To have no set purpose in one's life is harlotry of the will.
—Stephen McKenna

[A] rose is a rose is a rose.
—Gertrude Stein

BEING TRUE TO OURSELVES

Somehow we learn who we really are and then live with that decision.
—Eleanor Roosevelt

True inward quietness . . . is not vacancy, but stability—the steadfastness of a single purpose.
—Caroline Stephen

Seek out that particular mental attitude which makes you feel most deeply and vitally alive, along with which comes the inner voice which says, "This is the real me," and when you have found that attitude, follow it.
—William James

Most of our platitudes notwithstanding, self-deception remains the most difficult deception. The tricks that worked on others count for nothing in that very well-lit back alley where one keeps assignations with oneself: no winning smiles will do here, no prettily drawn list of good intentions.
—Joan Didion

No matter where I run, I meet myself there.　　　—Dorothy Fields

A woman who is willing to be herself and pursue her own potential runs not so much the risk of loneliness as the challenge of exposure to more interesting men—and people in general.
—Lorraine Hansbury

There is always a certain peace in being what one is, in being that completely. The condemned man has that joy.　　　—Ugo Betti

Be what you are. This is the first step toward becoming better than you are.
—Julius Charles Hare

As you go along your road in life, you will, if you aim high enough, also meet resistance . . . but no matter how tough the opposition may seem, have courage still—and persevere.
—Madeleine Albright

When a just cause reaches its flood-tide, as ours has done . . . , whatever stands in the way must fall before its overwhelming power.
—Carrie Chapman Catt

The first and worst of all frauds is to cheat one's self. All sin is easy after that.　　　—Pearl Bailey

To keep your character intact you cannot stoop to filthy acts. It makes it easier to stoop the next time.
—Katharine Hepburn

Keep integrity and your work ethics intact. So what if that means working a little harder; an honorable character is your best calling card, and that's something anyone can have!
—Kathy Ireland

The world may take your reputation from you, but it cannot take your character.　　—Emma Dunham Kelley

We must remember that one determined person can make a significant difference, and that a small group of determined people can change the course of history.　　—Sonia Johnson

I am only one, but still I am one. I cannot do everything, but still I can do something. And because I cannot do everything I will not refuse to do the something that I can do.
—Helen Keller

Keep your promises to yourself.
—David Harold Fink

The possibilities are unlimited as long as you are true to your life's purpose.
—Marcia Wieder

Put your ear down close to your soul and listen hard.　　—Anne Sexton

Like the winds of the sea are the
　　ways of fate;
As the voyage along thru life;
'Tis the will of the soul
That decides its goal,
And not the calm or the strife.
—Ella Wheeler Wilcox

I believe there's an inner power that makes winners or losers. And the winners are the ones who really listen to the truth of their hearts.
—Sylvester Stallone

I was and I always shall be hampered by what I think other people will say.
—Violette Leduc

No matter how ill we may be, nor how low we may have fallen, we should not change identity with any other person.   —Samuel Butler

Here I stand. I can do no other. God help me. Amen.   —Martin Luther

Whatever you want in life, other people are going to want it too. Believe in yourself enough to accept the idea that you have an equal right to it.
—Diane Sawyer

I argue that we deserve the choice to do whatever we want with our faces and bodies without being punished by an ideology that is using attitudes, economic pressure, and even legal judgments regarding women's appearance to undermine us psychologically and politically.   —Naomi Wolf

Nobody is so miserable as he who longs to be somebody other than the person he is.   —Angelo Patri

To be nobody-but-yourself—in a world which is doing its best, night and day, to make you everybody else—means to fight the hardest battle which any human being can fight; and never stop fighting.
—e.e. cummings

To aim at the best and to remain essentially ourselves is one and the same thing.   —Janet Erskine Stuart

We had as lief not be, as not be ourselves.   —William Hazlitt

No man can produce great things who is not thoroughly sincere in dealing with himself.
—James Russell Lowell

The most exhausting thing in life is being insincere.
—Anne Morrow Lindbergh

Misfortunes occur only when a man is false. . . . Events, circumstances, etc., have their origin in ourselves. They spring from seeds which we have sown.   —Henry David Thoreau

Man has no nobler function than to defend the truth.   —Mahalia Jackson

Every human being is intended to have a character of his own; to be what no others are, and to do what no other can do.
—William Ellery Channing

Do not wish to be anything but what you are.   —Saint Francis de Sales

I think God rarely gives to one man, or one set of men, more than one great moral victory to win.
—Lucy Stone

Truth has beauty, power, and necessity.
—Sylvia Townsend Warner

It is necessary to the happiness of man that he be mentally faithful to himself.   —Thomas Paine

Integrity simply means a willingness
not to violate one's identity.
—Erich Fromm

Don't compromise yourself. You are
all you've got.   —Janis Joplin

The greatest thing in the world is to
know how to be one's own self
—Michel de Montaigne

Theories are like scaffolding: they are
not the house, but you cannot build
the house without them.
—Constance Fenimore Woolson

To know what you prefer, instead of
humbly saying "Amen" to what the
world tells you you ought to prefer, is
to keep your soul alive.
—Robert Louis Stevenson

Do what thy manhood bids thee do.
—Sir Richard Burton

We live counterfeit lives in order to
resemble the idea we first had of ourselves.   —André Gide

The moment that any life, however
good, stifles you, you may be sure it
isn't your real life.
—Arthur Christopher Benson

All is disgust when one leaves his
own nature and does things that mis-
fit it.   —Sophocles

What does reason demand of a man?
A very easy thing—to live in accord
with his own nature.
—Marcus Annaeus Seneca

We are sure to be losers when we
quarrel with ourselves; it is civil war.
—Charles Caleb Colton

With begging and scrambling we find
very little, but with being true to ourselves we find a great deal more.
—Rabindranath Tagore

While you cannot resolve what you
are, at last you will be nothing.
—Martial

The highest courage is to dare to
appear to be what one is.
—John Lancaster Spalding

Choose always the way that seems
the best, however rough it may be;
custom will soon render it easy and
agreeable.   —Pythagoras

Our whole life is an attempt to discover when our spontaneity is whim-
sical, sentimental irresponsibility and
when it is a valid expression of our
deepest desires and values.
—Helen Merrell Lynd

Until you know that life is interesting, and find it so, you haven't found
your soul.   —Geoffrey Fisher

It is better to be hated for what you
are than loved for what you are not.
—André Gide

Learn what you are, and be such.
—Pindar

We are betrayed by what is false
within.   —George Meredith

If I trim myself to suit others I will
soon whittle myself away.   —Anon.

This above all: to thine own self be
true.   —William Shakespeare

In the world to come they will not ask me, "Why were you not Moses?" They will ask me, "Why were you not Zusya?"   —Zusya of Hanipoli

A man must be obedient to the promptings of his innermost heart.
    —Robertson Davies

All life is the struggle, the effort to be itself.   —José Ortega y Gasset

What's a man's first duty? The answer is brief: To be himself.
    —Henrik Ibsen

Any path is only a path, and there is no affront, to oneself or to others, in dropping it if that is what your heart tells you.   —Carlos Castaneda

It is possible to be different and still be all right.   —Anne Wilson Schaef

Let me listen to me and not to them.
    —Gertrude Stein

She lacks confidence, she craves admiration insatiably. She lives on the reflections of herself in the eyes of others. She does not dare to be herself.   —Anaïs Nin

I will not cut my conscience to fit this year's fashions.   —Lillian Hellman

The crow that mimics a cormorant gets drowned.   —Japanese proverb

Let the world know you as you are, not as you think you should be, because sooner or later, if you are posing, you will forget the pose, and then where are you?   —Fanny Brice

I was raised to sense what someone wanted me to be and be that kind of person. It took me a long time not to judge myself through someone else's eyes.   —Sally Field

Education should be the process of helping everyone to discover his uniqueness.   —Leo Buscaglia

Philosophy is a purely personal matter. A genuine philosopher's credo is the outcome of a single complex personality; it cannot be transferred. No two persons, if sincere, can have the same philosophy.   —Havelock Ellis

Remember always that you have not only the right to be an individual, you have an obligation to be one.
    —Eleanor Roosevelt

WE CAN'T BE HAPPY IF WE'RE NOT BEING OURSELVES

It is the chiefest point of happiness that a man is willing to be what he is.
    —Erasmus

Follow what you love! Don't deign to ask what "they" are looking for out there. Ask what you have inside. Follow not your interests, which change, but what you are and what you love, which will and should not change.   —Georgie Anne Geyer

All the discontented people I know are trying to be something they are not, to do something they cannot do.
    —David Graydon

Dress to please yourself. . . . Forget you are what you wear. . . . Wear what you are.   —Elizabeth Hawkes

Resolve to be thyself . . . he who finds himself loses his misery!
—Matthew Arnold

If we do not rise to the challenge of our unique capacity to shape our lives, to seek the kinds of growth that we find individually fulfilling, then we can have no security: we will live in a world of sham, in which our selves are determined by the will of others, in which we will be constantly buffeted and increasingly isolated by the changes round us.
—Nena O'Neil

Happiness, that grand mistress of the ceremonies in the dance of life, impels us through all its mazes and meanderings, but leads none of us by the same route.
—Charles Caleb Colton

A happy life is one which is in accordance with its own nature.
—Marcus Annaeus Seneca

Different men seek after happiness in different ways and by different means, and so make for themselves different modes of life.   —Aristotle

All men have happiness as their object: there is no exception. However different the means they employ, they aim at the same end.
—Blaise Pascal

Be not imitator; freshly act thy part;
Through this world be thou an independent ranger;
Better is the faith that springeth from thy heart
Than a better faith belonging to a stranger.
—Persian proverb

There is always a certain peace in being what one is, in being that completely.   —Ugo Betti

Posterity weaves no garlands for imitators.   —J.C.F. von Schiller

Why feignest thou thyself to be another?   —1 Kings 14:6

'Tis a gift to be simple, 'tis a gift to be free.
'Tis a gift to come round to where we ought to be.
And when we find a place that feels just right,
We will be in the valley of love and delight.
—Appalachian folk song

You have to deal with the fact that your life is your life.   —Alex Hailey

I is who I is.   —Tom Peterson

There are as many ways to live and grow as there are people. Our own ways are the only ways that should matter to us.   —Evelyn Mandel

The white light streams down to be broken up by those human prisms into all the colors of the rainbow. Take your own color in the pattern and be just that.
—Charles R. Brown

The search for a new personality is futile; what is fruitful is the human interest the old personality can take in new activities.   —Cesare Pavese

We would have to settle for the elegant goal of becoming ourselves.
—William Stryon

Our concern must be to live while we're alive . . . to release our inner selves from the spiritual death that comes with living behind a facade designed to conform to external definitions of who and what we are.
—Elisabeth Kubler-Ross

I searched through rebellion, drugs, diets, mysticism, religions, intellectualism and much more, only to begin to find . . . that truth is basically simple—and feels good, clean and right.
—Chick Corea

If you're gonna be a failure, at least be one at something you enjoy.
—Sylvester Stallone

That suit is best that best suits me.
—John Clark

The self is not something that one finds. It is something one creates.
—Thomas Szasz

Your readiest desire is your path to joy . . . even if it destroys you.
—Holbrook Jackson

WE CAN'T LET OTHERS TELL US WHAT'S RIGHT FOR US

Individuals learn faster than institutions and it is always the dinosaur's brain that is the last to get the new messages.   —Hazel Henderson

Go ahead and do it. It's much easier to apologize after something's been done than to get permission ahead of time.   —Grace Murray Hopper

Innovators are inevitably controversial.
—Eva Le Gallienne

I'm not going to limit myself just because some people won't accept the fact that I can do something else.
—Dolly Parton

Criticism . . . makes very little dent upon me, unless I think there is some real justification and something should be done.
—Eleanor Roosevelt

It is healthier, in any case, to write for the adults one's children will become than for the children one's "mature" critics often are.
—Alice Walker

I was the kind nobody thought could make it. I had a funny Boston accent. I couldn't pronounce my R's. I wasn't a beauty.   —Barbara Walters

Power is strength and the ability to see yourself through your own eyes and not through the eyes of another.
—Agnes Whistling Elk

WE FEEL GOOD WHEN WE DO WHAT'S RIGHT FOR US

Getting fit is a political act—you are taking charge of your life.
—Jane Fonda

I'm uncomfortable when I'm comfortable . . . I can't help it, it's my personality.   —Jay Chiat

For a long time the only time I felt beautiful—in the sense of being complete as a woman, as a human being, and even female—was when I was singing.   —Leontyne Price

The source of continuing aliveness was to find your passion and pursue it, with whole heart and single mind.
—Gail Sheehy

I look at ordinary people in their suits, them with no scars, and I'm different. I don't fit with them. I'm where everybody's got scar tissue on their eyes and got noses like saddles. I go to conventions of old fighters like me and I see the scar tissue and all them flat noses and it's beautiful. . . . They talk like me, like they got rocks in their throats. Beautiful!
—Willie Pastrano

I have the feeling when I write poetry that I'm doing what I'm supposed to do. You don't think about whether you're going to get money or fame, you just do it.   —Doris Lund

A door that seems to stand open must be of a man's size, or it is not the door that providence means for him.
—Henry Ward Beecher

I have the true feeling of myself only when I am unbearably unhappy.
—Franz Kafka

Mountains should be climbed with as little effort as possible and without desire. The reality of your own nature should determine the speed. If you become restless, speed up. If you become winded, slow down. You climb the mountain in an equilibrium between restlessness and exhaustion. Then, when you're no longer thinking ahead, each footstep isn't just a means to an end, but a unique event in itself.   —Robert M. Pirsig

It is the soul's duty to be loyal to its own desires.   —Rebecca West

Finding Work That Will Use Our Abilities and Talents

In the first grade, I already knew the pattern of my life. I didn't know the living of it, but I knew the line. . . . From the first day in school until the day I graduated, everyone gave me one hundred plus in art. Well, where do you go in life? You go to the place where you got one hundred plus.
—Louise Nevelson

I am a writer because writing is the thing I do best.
—Flannery O'Connor

Each of us has some unique capability waiting for realization. Every person is valuable in his own existence, for himself alone . . . each of us can bring to fruition these innate, God-given abilities.   —George H. Bender

All of us attain the greatest success and happiness possible in this life whenever we use our native capacities to their fullest extent. . . . And every life must be chalked up at least a partial failure when it does not succeed in reaching its inherent destiny.
—Smiley Blanton

The same man cannot be skilled in everything; each has his special excellence.   —Euripides

Any talent that we are born with eventually surfaces as a need.
—Marsha Sinetar

The best career advice given to the young . . . is "Find out what you like doing best and get someone to pay you for doing it."
—Katharine Whitehorn

Skills vary with the man. We must . . . strive by that which is born in us.
—Pindar

People are always neglecting something they can do in trying to do something they can't do.
—Edgar Watson Howe

A man like Verdi must write like Verdi.
—Verdi

I write lustily and humorously. It isn't calculated; it's the way I think. I've invented a writing style that expresses who I am.
—Erica Jong

Each citizen should play his part in the community according to his individual gifts.
—Plato

Genius does what it must, talent does what it can. —Edward Bulwer-Lytton

Everything keeps its best nature only by being put to its best use.
—Phillips Brooks

We don't see many fat men walking on stilts.
—Bud Miller

I was playing it like Willie Wilson, but I forgot that I'm in Clint Hurdle's body.
—Clint Hurdle

We succeed in enterprises which demand the positive qualities we possess, but we excel in those which can also make use of our defects.
—Alexis de Tocqueville

I wrote because I had to. I couldn't stop. There wasn't anything else I could do. If no one ever bought anything, anything I ever did, I'd still be writing. It's beyond a compulsion.
—Tennessee Williams

To every man according to his ability.
—Matthew 25:4

If a man is called to be a streetsweeper, he should sweep streets even as Michelangelo painted, or Beethoven composed music, or Shakespeare wrote poetry. He should sweep streets so well that all the hosts of heaven and earth will pause to say, here lived a great streetsweeper who did his job well. —Martin Luther King, Jr.

Men whose trade is rat-catching, love to catch rats; the bug destroyer seizes on his bug with delight; and the suppressor is gratified by finding his vice.
—Sydney Smith

Brutes find out where their talents lie; a bear will not attempt to fly.
—Jonathan Swift

We may fail of our happiness, strive we ever so bravely; but we are less likely to fail if we measure with judgment our chances and our capabilities.
—Agnes Repplier

The greatest achievement of the human spirit is to live up to one's opportunities and make the most of one's resources.
—Vauvenargues

The test of a vocation is the love of the drudgery it involves.
—Logan Pearsall Smith

Are you doing the kind of work you were built for, so that you can expect to be able to do very large amounts of that kind and thrive under it? Or are you doing a kind of which you can do comparatively little?
—B.C. Forbes

Starting out to make money is the greatest mistake in life. Do what you feel you have a flair for doing, and if you are good enough at it, the money will come. —Greer Garson

Whenever it is possible, a boy should choose some occupation which he should do even if he did not need the money. —William Lyon Phelps

The fun of being alive is realizing you have a talent and you can use it every day so it grows stronger. . . . And if you're in an atmosphere where this talent is appreciated instead of just tolerated, why, it's just as good as sex.
—Lou Centlivre

It is only when I am doing my work that I feel truly alive. It is like having sex. —Federico Fellini

If a man has a talent and cannot use it, he has failed. If he has a talent and uses only half of it, he has partly failed. If he has a talent and learns somehow to use the whole of it, he has gloriously succeeded, and won a satisfaction and a triumph few men ever know. —Thomas Wolfe

The high prize of life, the crowning fortune of a man, is to be born with a bias to some pursuit which finds him in employment and happiness.
—Ralph Waldo Emerson

Everybody undertakes what he sees another successful in, whether he has the aptitude for it or not.
—Johann von Goethe

To find out what one is fitted to do, and to secure an opportunity to do it, is the key to happiness.
—John Dewey

The road to happiness lies in two simple principles: find what interests you and that you can do well, and put your whole soul into it—every bit of energy and ambition and natural ability you have.
—John D. Rockefeller III

One should stick to the sort of thing for which one was made; I tried to be an herbalist, whereas I should keep to the butcher's trade.
—Jean de La Fontaine

If you have to support yourself, you had bloody well better find some way that is going to be interesting.
—Katharine Hepburn

When men are rightfully occupied, then their amusement grows out of their work as the color petals out of a fruitful garden. —John Ruskin

A musician must make music, an artist must paint, a poet must write, if he to be at peace with himself. What a man can be, he must be.
—Abraham Maslow

We do not write as we want but as we can. —W. Somerset Maugham

Never desert your own line of talent. Be what nature intended you for, and you will succeed. —Sydney Smith

Nature arms each man with some faculty which enables him to do easily some feat impossible to any other.
—Ralph Waldo Emerson

It is not a dreamlike state, but the somehow insulated state, that a great musician achieves in a great performance. He's aware of where he is and what he's doing, but his mind is on the playing of his instrument with an internal sense of rightness—it is not merely mechanical, it is not only spiritual; it is something of both, on a different plane and a more remote one.
—Arnold Palmer

We will discover the nature of our particular genius when we stop trying to conform to our own or to other people's models, learn to be ourselves, and allow our natural channel to open.
—Shakti Gawain

It requires a certain kind of mind to see beauty in a hamburger bun. Yet, is it any more unusual to find grace in the texture and softly curved silhouette of a bun than to reflect lovingly on ... the arrangement of textures and colors in a butterfly's wing?
—Ray Kroc

The question "Who ought to be boss" is like asking "Who ought to be tenor in the quartet?" Obviously, the man who can sing tenor.
—Henry Ford

I'm a salami writer. I try to write good salami, but salami is salami.
—Stephen King

I'd rather be a failure at something I enjoy than a success at something I hate.
—George Burns

WE CAN ONLY DO WHAT WE'RE CAPABLE OF DOING

I cannot do everything, but still I can do something; and because I cannot do everything, I will not refuse to do the something that I can do.
—Edward Everett Hale

What really matters is what you do with what you have.   —Shirley Lord

I know that I haven't powers enough to divide myself into one who earns and one who creates.   —Tillie Olsen

Man is not born to solve the problems of the universe, but to find out what he has to do ... within the limits of his comprehension.
—Johann von Goethe

The weakest among us has a gift, however seemingly trivial, which is peculiar to him and which worthily used will be a gift also to his race.
—John Ruskin

Every person is responsible for all the good within the scope of his abilities, and for no more.   —Gail Hamilton

Me, I'm just a hack. I'm just a schlepper. I just do what I can do.
—Bette Midler

The great law of culture: Let each become all that he was created capable of being.   —Thomas Carlyle

Don't bother just to be better than your contemporaries or predecessors. Try to be better than yourself.
—William Faulkner

God requires a faithful fulfillment of
the merest trifle given us to do, rather
than the most ardent aspiration to
things to which we are not called.
　　　　—Saint Francis de Sales

When I was young, I said to God,
"God, tell me the mystery of the
universe." But God answered, "That
knowledge is reserved for me alone."
So I said, "God, tell me the mystery
of the peanut." Then God said, "Well
George, that's more nearly your size."
And he told me.
　　　　—George Washington Carver

I long to accomplish a great and
noble task, but it is my chief duty to
accomplish small tasks as if they were
great and noble.　　　　—Helen Keller

We may fail of our happiness, strive
we ever so bravely; but we are less
likely to fail if we measure with judgment our chances and our capabilities.
　　　　—Agnes Repplier

No amount of study or learning will
make a man a leader unless he has
the natural qualities of one.
　　　　—Sir Archibald Wavell

Choose a subject equal to your abilities; think carefully what your shoulders may refuse, and what they are
capable of bearing.　　　　—Horace

In efforts to soar above our nature,
we invariably fall below it.
　　　　—Edgar Allan Poe

The driver knows how much the ox
can carry, and keeps the ox from
being overloaded. You know your
way and your state of mind. Do not
carry too much.　　　　—Zen saying

If you could once make up your mind
never to undertake more work . . .
than you can carry on calmly, quietly,
without hurry or flurry . . . and if
the instant you feel yourself growing nervous and . . . out of breath,
you would stop and take breath, you
would find this simple common-sense
rule doing for you what no prayers
or tears could ever accomplish.
　　　　—Elizabeth Prentiss

The deepest personal defeat suffered
by human beings is constituted by
the difference between what one was
capable of becoming, and what one
has in fact become.
　　　　—Ashley Montagu

SUCCESS IS DOING
WHAT'S RIGHT FOR US

What I wanted was to be allowed
to do the thing in the world that I
did best—which I believed then and
believe now is the greatest privilege
there is. When I did that, success
found me.　　　　—Debbi Fields

I had already learned from more than
a decade of political life that I was
going to be criticized no matter what
I did, so I might as well be criticized
for something I wanted to do.
　　　　—Rosalynn Carter

There is only one success—to be able
to spend your life in your own way.
　　　　—Christopher Morley

The only success worth one's powder
was success in the line of one's idiosyncrasy . . . what was talent but the
art of being completely whatever one
happened to be?　　　　—Henry James

We are traditionally rather proud of ourselves for having slipped creative work in there between the domestic chores and obligations. I'm not sure we deserve such big A-pluses for all that. —Toni Morrison

Success based on anything but internal fulfillment is bound to be empty.
—Dr. Martha Friedman

We succeed in enterprises which demand the positive qualities we possess, but we excel in those which can also make use of our defects.
—Alexis de Tocqueville

All I would tell people is to hold on to what was individual about themselves, not to allow their ambition for success to cause them to try to imitate the success of others. You've got to find in on your own terms.
—Harrison Ford

For me, writing is the only thing that passes the three tests of metier: (1) when I'm doing it, I don't feel that I should be doing something else instead; (2) it produces a sense of accomplishment and, once in a while, pride; and (3) it's frightening.
—Gloria Steinem

One can never consent to creep when one feels an impulse to soar.
—Helen Keller

My mother said to me, "If you become a soldier, you'll be a general, if you become a monk you'll end up as the pope." Instead, I became a painter and wound up as Picasso.
—Pablo Picasso

We only do well the things we like doing. —Colette

Abasement, degradation is simply the manner of life of the man who has refused to be what it is his duty to be.
—José Ortega y Gasset

Different people have different duties assigned to them by Nature; Nature has given one the power or the desire to do this, the other that. Each bird must sing with his own throat.
—Anon.

A first rate soup is better than a second rate painting.
—Abraham Maslow

We can't all be heroes, because someone has to sit on the curb and clap as they go by. —Will Rogers

Nature magically suits a man to his fortunes, by making them the fruit of his character.
—Ralph Waldo Emerson

I'd rather be a lamppost in Chicago than a millionaire in any other city.
—William A. Hulbert

Whatever you are by nature, keep to it; never desert your own line of talent. Be what nature intended you for, and you will succeed; be anything else and you will be ten thousand times worse than nothing.
—Sydney Smith

Ask yourself the secret of your success. Listen to your answer, and practice it. —Richard Bach

Do what you love, the money will follow. —Marsha Sinetar

I am only one, but still I am one. I cannot do everything, but still I can do something; and because I cannot do everything, I will not refuse to do something I can do.

—Edward Everett Hale

Starting out to make money is the greatest mistake in life. Do what you feel you have a flair for doing, and if you are good enough at it, the money will come.   —Greer Garson

If a man has a talent and cannot use it, he has failed. If he has a talent and uses only half of it, he has partly failed. If he has a talent and learns somehow to use the whole of it, he has gloriously succeeded, and won a satisfaction and a triumph few men ever know.   —Thomas Wolfe

A man can do only what he can do. But if he does that each day he can sleep at night and do it again the next day.   —Albert Schweitzer

Don't take anyone else's definition of success as your own. (This is easier said than done.) —Jacqueline Briskin

GENERAL QUOTATIONS ABOUT DOING WHAT'S RIGHT FOR US

You must be holy in the way God asks you to be holy. God does not ask you to be a Trappist monk or a hermit. He wills that you sanctify your everyday life.

—Saint Vincent Pallotti

Bloom where you are planted.

—Anon.

The first duty of a human being is to assume the right relationship to society—more briefly, to find your real job, and do it. —Charlotte P. Gilman

The great enemy of clear language is insincerity. When there is a gap between one's real and one's declared aims, one turns, as it were, instinctively to long words and exhausted idioms, like a cuttlefish squirting out ink.

—George Orwell

We don't know who we are until we see what we can do.

—Martha Grimes

If Heaven made him, earth can find some use for him.

—Chinese proverb

Don't do anything that someone else can do for you because there are only so many things that only you can do.

—Jinger Heath

The hole and the patch should be commensurate.   —Thomas Jefferson

The things that one most wants to do are the things that are probably most worth doing.   —Winifred Holtby

If all misfortunes were laid in one common heap whence everyone must take an equal portion, most people would be contented to take their own and depart.   —Socrates

Every true man, sir, who is a little above the level of the beasts and plants, lives so as to give a meaning and a value to his own life.

—Luigi Pirandello

Motivation

The Importance and Value of Motivation

What makes life dreary is want of motive. —George Eliot

They never die, who have the future in them. —Meridel Le Sueur

As long as I have a want, I have a reason for living. Satisfaction is death. —George Bernard Shaw

One must not lose desires. They are mighty stimulants to creativeness, to love and to long life. —Alexander A. Bogomoletz

Take away the cause, and the effect ceases. —Miguel de Cervantes

Every true man, sir, who is a little above the level of the beasts and plants, lives so as to give a meaning and a value to his own life. —Luigi Pirandello

The secret of discipline is motivation. When a man is sufficiently motivated, discipline will take care of itself. —Sir Alexander Paterson

Where the willingness is great, the difficulties cannot be great. —Niccolo Machiavelli

Talent isn't enough. You need motivation—and persistence, too: what Steinbeck called a blend of faith and arrogance. When you're young, plain old poverty can be enough, along with an insatiable hunger for recognition. You have to have that feeling of "I'll show them." If you don't have it, don't become a writer. —Leon Uris

Never let go of that fiery sadness called desire. —Patti Smith

It seems to me we can never give up longing and wishing while we are alive. There are certain things we feel to be beautiful and good, and we must hunger for them. —George Eliot

One man with a dream, at pleasure, Shall go forth and conquer a crown, And three with a new song's measure, Can trample an empire down. —Arthur O'Shaughnessy

We can do whatever we wish to do provided our wish is strong enough. . . . What do you want most to do? That's what I have to keep asking myself, in the face of difficulties.
—Katherine Mansfield

Winning isn't everything. Wanting to win is. —Catfish Hunter

Different People Are Motivated by Different Things

If you can learn from hard knocks, you can also learn from soft touches.
—Carolyn Kenmore

For every man there exists a bait which he cannot resist swallowing.
—Friedrich Nietzsche

Accurate information is a key part of motivation. —Mary Ann Allison

Football linemen are motivated by a more complicated, self-determining series of factors than the simple fear of humiliation in the public gaze, which is the emotion that galvanizes the backs and receivers.
—Merlin Olsen

Love makes the wildest spirit tame, and the tamest spirit wild.
—Alexis Delp

I tried to treat them like me, and some of them weren't.
—Bill Russell,
on why he had difficulty
coaching some of his players

Your wits make others witty.
—Catherine the Great

To be what we are, and to become what we are capable of becoming, is the only end of life.
—Baruch Spinoza

I believe in using words, not fists.
—Susan Sarandon

Every man is said to have his peculiar ambition. —Abraham Lincoln

The moment somebody says to me, "This is very risky," is the moment it becomes attractive to me.
—Kate Capshaw

Some people are molded by their admirations, others by their hostilities.
—Elizabeth Bowen

A man will fight harder for his interests than for his rights.
—Napoleon Bonaparte

Good humor, like the jaundice, makes every one of its own complexion.
—Elizabeth Inchbald

All I want out of life is that when I walk down the street, folks will say, "There goes the greatest hitter who ever lived." —Ted Williams

Your distress about life might mean you have been living for the wrong reason, not that you have no reason for living. —Tom O'Connor,
person with ARC

Great men undertake great things because they are great; fools, because they think them easy.
—Vauvenargues

Love teaches even asses to dance.
—French proverb

There are only two stimulants to one's best efforts: the fear of punishment, and the hope of reward.
—John M. Wilson

When you get hungry enough, you find yourself speaking Spanish pretty well.
—Josh Gibson, on playing baseball in Cuba

Discontent is the first step in progress. No one knows what is in him till he tries, and many would never try if they were not forced to.
—Basil W. Maturin

I never work better than when I am inspired by anger; when I am angry, I can write, pray, and preach well, for then my whole temperament is quickened, my understanding sharpened, and all mundane vexations and temptations depart.
—Martin Luther

It is for the superfluous things of life that men sweat.
—Marcus Annaeus Seneca

Happiness is in the taste, and not in the things themselves; we are happy from possessing what we like, not from possessing what others like.
—Francois de La Rochefoucauld

We must each find our separate meaning in the persuasion of our days until we meet in the meaning of the world.
—Christopher Fry

Don't let other people tell you what you want.
—Pat Riley

COMMON MOTIVATORS

Men are more often bribed by their loyalties and ambitions than by money.
—Robert H. Jackson

In my experience, there is only one motivation, and that is desire. No reasons or principle contain it or stand against it.
—Jane Smiley

All progress is based upon a universal, innate desire on the part of every living organism to live beyond its income.
—Samuel Butler

Those who are lifting the world upward and onward are those who encourage more than criticize.
—Elizabeth Harrison

Everyone expects to go further than his father went; everyone expects to be better than he was born and every generation has one big impulse in its heart—to exceed all the other generations of the past in all the things that make life worth living.
—William Allen White

To feel valued, to know, even if only once in a while, that you can do a job well is an absolutely marvelous feeling.
—Barbara Walters

The speed of the leader is the speed of the gang.
—Mary Kay Ash

To sink a six-foot putt with thirty million people looking over your shoulder, convince yourself that, if you miss it, you will be embarrassed and poor.
—Jack Nicklaus

I want to do it because I want to do it.
—Amelia Earhart

Fear, desire, hope still push us on toward the future.
—Michel de Montaigne

Money never remains just coins and pieces of paper. Money can be translated into the beauty of living, a support in misfortune, an education, or future security. —Sylvia Porter

Human behavior flows from three main sources: desire, emotion, and knowledge. —Plato

Lust and force are the source of all our actions; lust causes voluntary actions, force involuntary ones.
—Blaise Pascal

I don't make deals for the money. I've got enough, much more than I'll never need. I do it to do it. Other people paint beautifully on canvas or write wonderful poetry. I like making deals, preferably big deals. That's how I get my kicks. —Donald Trump

Wealth . . . and poverty: the one is the parent of luxury and indolence, and the other of meanness and viciousness, and both of discontent. —Plato

Anxiety and conscience are a powerful pair of dynamos. Between them, they have ensured that I shall work hard, but they cannot ensure that one shall work at anything worthwhile.
—Arnold J. Toynbee

It is the spur of ignorance, the consciousness of not understanding, and the curiosity about that which lies beyond that are essential to our progress. —John Pierce

We all live with the objective of being happy; our lives are all different, and yet the same. —Anne Frank

Love teaches even asses to dance.
—French proverb

Money and women. They're the two strongest things in the world. There are things you do for a woman you wouldn't do for anything else. Same with money. —Satchel Paige

It is for the superfluous things of life that men sweat.
—Marcus Annaeus Seneca

It is not merely cruelty that leads men to love war, it is excitement.
—Henry Ward Beecher

I am not sending messages with my feet. All I ever wanted was not to come up empty. I did it for the dough, and the old applause.
—Fred Astaire

My advice about acting? Speak clearly, don't bump into people, and if you must have motivation, think of your pay packet on Friday.
—Noel Coward

I take it that what all men are really after is some form of, perhaps only some formula of, peace.
—Joseph Conrad

It is the north wind that lashes men into Vikings; it is the soft, luscious south wind which lulls them to lotus dreams. —Ouida

One starts an action simply because one must do something. —T.S. Eliot

Action springs not from thought, but from a readiness for responsibility.
—Dietrich Bonhoeffer

The breakfast of champions is not cereal, it's the opposition.
—Nick Seitz

There's only one good reason to be a writer—we can't help it! We'd all like to be successful, rich and famous, but if those are our goals, we're off on the wrong foot. . . . I just wanted to earn enough money so I could work at home on my writing.
—Phyllis Whitney

I wish it, I command it. Let my will take the place of a reason.   —Juvenal

NECESSITY AND DISCONTENT ARE BASIC MOTIVATORS

Necessity, who is the mother of our invention.   —Plato

Urgent necessity prompts many to do things.   —Miguel de Cervantes

I always felt that I hadn't achieved what I wanted to achieve. I always felt I could get better. That's the whole incentive.   —Virginia Wade

Discontent is the first step in the progress of a man or a nation.
—Oscar Wilde

To have a grievance is to have a purpose in life.   —Eric Hoffer

What you are must always displease you, if you would attain to that which you are not. —Saint Augustine

We accept the verdict of the past until the need for change cries out loudly enough to force upon us a choice between the comforts of further inertia and the irksomeness of action.
—Louis L'Amour

I can't concentrate on golf or bowling. Those bowling pins aren't going to hurt me. I can concentrate in the ring because someone is trying to kill me.
—Carmen Basilio

I happened on the idea of fitting an engine to a bicycle simply because I did not want to ride crowded trains and buses.   —Soichire Honda

Always in a moment of extreme danger things can be done which had previously been thought impossible.
—Field Marshal Erwin Rommel

Acting was a way out at first. A way out of not knowing what to do, a way of focusing ambitions. And the ambition wasn't for fame. The ambition was to do an interesting job.
—Harrison Ford

A loafer never works except when there is a fire; then he will carry out more furniture than anybody.
—Edgar Watson Howe

Hardships, poverty and want are the best incentives, and the best foundation, for the success of man.
—Bradford Merrill

Poverty, Frost, Famine, Rain, Disease, are the beadles and guardsmen that hold us to Common Sense.
—Ralph Waldo Emerson

Necessity is the mother of taking chances. —Mark Twain

PRAISE AND RECOGNITION ARE COMMON MOTIVATORS

If you're good to your staff when things are going well, they'll rally when times go bad. —Mary Kay Ash

Praise is the only gift for which people are really grateful.
—Lady Marguerite Blessington

I praise loudly; I blame softly.
—Catherine II

There are two things that people want more than sex and money—recognition and praise.
—Mary Kay Ash

To hear how special and wonderful we are is endlessly enthralling.
—Gail Sheehy

Words are less needful to sorrow than to joy. —Helen Hunt Jackson

Sandwich every bit of criticism between two heavy layers of praise.
—Mary Kay Ash

There isn't much that tastes better than praise from those who are wise and capable. —Selma Lagerlöf

We treat our people like royalty. If you honor and serve the people who work for you, they will honor and serve you. —Mary Kay Ash

What you praise you increase.
—Catherine Ponder

What men and women need is encouragement. . . . Instead of always harping on a man's faults, tell him of his virtues. Try to pull him out of his rut of bad habits.
—Eleanor H. Porter

Everyone has an invisible sign hanging from their neck saying, "Make me feel important." Never forget this message when working with people.
—Mary Kay Ash

We are all motivated by a keen desire for praise, and the better a man is, the more he is inspired by glory.
—Cicero

Applause is the spur of noble minds, the end and aim of weak ones.
—Charles Caleb Colton

Most people would rather be seen through than not seen at all.
—Ada Leverson

When we are listened to, it creates us, makes us unfold and expand. Ideas actually begin to grow within us and come to life. —Brenda Ueland

Praise out of season, or tactlessly bestowed, can freeze the heart as much as blame. —Pearl S. Buck

We do not content ourselves with the life we have in ourselves; we desire to live an imaginary life in the minds of others, and for this purpose we endeavor to shine. —Blaise Pascal

The greatest efforts of the race have always been traceable to the love of praise, as the greatest catastrophes to the love of pleasure. —John Ruskin

If each of us were to confess his most secret desire, the one that inspires all his plans, all his actions, he would say: "I want to be praised."
—E.M. Cioran

OUR INTERESTS ARE POWERFUL MOTIVATORS

We talk on principle, but we act on interest.   —Walter Savage Landor

What allows us, as human beings, to psychologically survive life on earth, with all of its pain, drama, and challenges, is a sense of purpose and meaning.   —Barbara De Angelis

A man will fight harder for his interests than for his rights.
—Napoleon Bonaparte

The pitcher cries for water to carry and a person for work that is real.
—Marge Piercy

The virtues and the vices are all put in motion by interest.
—Francois de La Rochefoucauld

It's so hard when I have to, and so easy when I want to.
—Sondra Anice Barnes

Just don't give up trying to do what you really want to do. Where there is love and inspiration, I don't think you can go wrong.   —Ella Fitzgerald

You have to know exactly what you want out of your career. If you want to be a star, you don't bother with other things.   —Marilyn Horne

Interest speaks all sorts of tongues, and plays all sorts of parts, even that of disinterestedness.
—Francois de La Rochefoucauld

FEAR IS A FUNDAMENTAL MOTIVATOR

Men's actions depend to a great extent upon fear. We do things either because we enjoy doing them or because we are afraid not to do them.
—John F. Milburn

Some people change their ways when they see the light, others when they feel the heat.   —Caroline Schoeder

There are only two forces that unite men—fear and interest.
—Napoleon Bonaparte

The passion to get ahead is sometimes born of the fear lest we be left behind.   —Eric Hoffer

You can't underestimate the power of fear.   —Patricia Nixon

There are only two stimulants to one's best efforts: the fear of punishment, and the hope of reward.
—John M. Wilson

A man who is afraid will do anything.   —Jawaharlal Nehru

Fear of losing is what makes competitors so great. Show me a gracious loser and I'll show you a permanent loser.   —O.J. Simpson

General Quotations about Motivation

A team that has character doesn't need stimulation.   —Tom Landry

Beware of trying to accomplish anything by force.   —Angela Merici

People who fight fire with fire usually end up with ashes.
                    —Abigail Van Buren

Because it's there.   —G.H.L. Mallory, on why he wanted to climb Matthew Everest

Diplomacy is the art of letting someone have your way.   —Daniele Vare

It is easier to influence strong than weak characters in life.
                    —Margot Asquith

Men are not against you; they are merely for themselves.
                    —Gene Fowler

No punishment has ever possessed enough power of deterrence to prevent the commission of crimes. On the contrary, whatever the punishment, once a specific crime has appeared for the first time, its reappearance is more likely than its initial emergence could ever have been.
                    —Hannah Arendt

When the flag is unfurled, all reason is in the trumpet.
                    —Ukrainian proverb

No leader can be too far ahead of his followers.   —Eleanor Roosevelt

You will accomplish more by kind words and a courteous manner than by anger or sharp rebuke, which should never be used except in necessity.   —Angela Merici

Realistic Expectations

WE NEED TO HAVE REALISTIC EXPECTATIONS ABOUT OTHER PEOPLE AND LIFE

Expect nothing and life will be velvet.
—Lisa Gardiner

What is destructive is impatience, haste, expecting too much too fast.
—May Sarton

No one has ever loved anyone the way everyone wants to be loved.
—Mignon McLaughlin

If you expect perfection from other people, your whole life is a series of disappointments, grumbling and complaints. If, on the contrary, you pitch your expectations low, taking folks as the inefficient creatures which they are, you are frequently surprised by having them perform better than you had hoped.   —Bruce Barton

A pint can't hold a quart—if it holds a pint it is doing all that can be expected of it.   —Margaret Deland

Truth has rough flavors if we bite it through.   —George Eliot

What had seemed easy in imagination was rather hard in reality.
—L.M. Montgomery

You can't move so fast that you try to change [a situation] faster than people can accept it. That doesn't mean you do nothing, but it means that you do the things that need to be done according to priority.
—Eleanor Roosevelt

He that will have a perfect brother must resign himself to remaining brotherless.   —Italian proverb

Who ever is adequate? We all create situations which others can't live up to, then break our hearts at them because they don't.
—Elizabeth Bowen

It is a rough road that leads to the heights of greatness.
—Lucius Annaeus Seneca

Friendships aren't perfect, and yet they are very precious. For me, not expecting perfection all in one place was a great release.
—Letty Cottin Pogrebin

The way to achieve happiness is to have a high standard for yourself and a medium one for everyone else.
—Marcelene Cox

Life is not a spectacle or a feast; it is a predicament.   —George Santayana

To expect too much is to have a sentimental view of life, and this is a softness that ends in bitterness.
—Flannery O'Connor

Because you're not what I would have you be, I blind myself to who, in truth, you are.
—Madeleine L'Engle

No one from the beginning of time has had security. —Eleanor Roosevelt

No one is happy all his life long.
—Euripides

Vex not thy spirit at the course of things; they heed not thy vexation. How ludicrous and outlandish is astonishment at anything that may happen in life.   —Marcus Aurelius

There are philosophies which are unendurable not because men are cowards, but because they are men.
—Ludwig Lewisohn

When I decided to go into politics I weighed the cost: I would get criticism. But I went ahead. So when the virulent criticism came I wasn't surprised. I was better able to handle it.
—Herbert Hoover

If you want a place in the sun, you've got to put up with a few blisters.
—Abigail Van Buren

Never let life's hardships disturb you . . . no one can avoid problems, not even saints or sages.
—Nichiren Daishonen

Life is made up of sobs, sniffles, and smiles, with sniffles predominating.
—O. Henry

The scornful nostril and the high head gather not the odors that lie on the track of truth.   —George Eliot

Expecting the world to treat you fairly because you are a good person is a little like expecting the bull not to attack you because you're a vegetarian.   —Dennis Wholey

When nobody around you seems to measure up, it's time to check your yardstick.   —Bill Lemley

Life to the great majority is only a constant struggle for mere existence, with the certainty of losing it at last.
—Arthur Schopenhauer

Marriage is not just spiritual communion and passionate embraces; marriage is also three meals a day, sharing the workload and remembering to carry out the trash.
—Dr. Joyce Brothers

We [Americans] cheerfully assume that in some mystic way love conquers all, that good outweighs evil in the just balances of the universe and that at the eleventh hour something gloriously triumphant will prevent the worst before it happens.
—Brooks Atkinson

There is no such thing as something for nothing.   —Napoleon Hill

The mass of men lead lives of quiet desperation. —Henry David Thoreau

Free man is by necessity insecure; thinking man is by necessity uncertain. —Erich Fromm

It is arrogance to expect that life will always be music. . . . Harmony, like a following breeze at sea, is the exception. In a world where most things wind up broken or lost, our lot is to tack and tune. —Harvey Oxenhorn

Being unready and ill-equipped is what you have to expect in life. It is the universal predicament. It is your lot as a human being to lack what it takes. Circumstances are seldom right. You never have the capacities, the strength, the wisdom, the virtue you ought to have. You must always do with less than you need in a situation vastly different from what you would have chosen as appropriate for your special endowments. —Charlton Ogburn, Jr.

In nature there are neither rewards or punishments—there are consequences. —Robert G. Ingersoll

Hope for a miracle. But don't depend on one. —Talmud

Life guarantees a chance—not a fair shake. —Anon.

Life is a perilous voyage. —Palladas

HAVING REALISTIC EXPECTATIONS OF OURSELVES

One must not hope to be more than one can be. —Nicolas de Chamfort

The whole point of getting things done is knowing what to leave undone. —Lady Stella Reading

We expect more of ourselves than we have any right to. —Oliver Wendell Holmes, Jr.

Don't fool yourself that you are going to have it all. You are not. Psychologically, having it all is not even a valid concept. The marvelous thing about human beings is that we are perpetually reaching for the stars. The more we have, the more we want. And for this reason, we never have it all. —Dr. Joyce Brothers

Try as hard as we may for perfection, the net result of our labors is an amazing variety of imperfectness. We are surprised at our own versatility in being able to fail in so many different ways. —Samuel McChord Crothers

We set up harsh and unkind rules against ourselves. No one is born without faults. That man is best who has fewest. —Horace

I can't write a book commensurate with Shakespeare, but I can write a book by me. —Sir Walter Raleigh

I have done what I could do in life, and if I could not do better, I did not deserve it. In vain I have tried to step beyond what bound me. —Maurice Maeterlinck

Shall a man go and hang himself because he belongs to the race of pygmies, and not be the biggest pygmy that he can?
—Henry David Thoreau

The man with insight enough to admit his limitations comes nearest to perfection.   —Johann von Goethe

The one important thing I have learned over the years is the difference between taking one's work seriously and taking one's self seriously. The first is imperative, and the second is disastrous. —Margaret Fontey

Growth begins when we start to accept our own weakness.
—Jean Vanier

To dream of the person you would like to be is to waste the person you are.   —Anon.

Of all the young men in America, only a few hundred can get into major league baseball, and of these only a handful in a decade can get into the Hall of Fame. So it goes in all human activity. . . . Some become multimillionaires and chairmen of the board, and some of us must be content to play baseball at company picnics or manage a credit union without pay.   —William Feather

At thirty a man should know himself like the palm of his hand, know the exact number of his defects and qualities. . . . And, above all, accept these things.   —Albert Camus

No man can climb out beyond the limitations of his own character.
—John Morley

You can't make the Duchess of Windsor into Rebecca of Sunnybrook Farm. The facts of life are very stubborn things.   —Cleveland Amory

Sometimes it is more important to discover what one cannot do, than what one can do.   —Lin Yutang

Learn to . . . be what you are, and learn to resign with a good grace all that you are not.
—Henri Frederic Amiel

We cannot all be masters.
—William Shakespeare

To do all that one is able to do is to be a man; to do all that one would like to do is to be a god.
—Napoleon Bonaparte

No one is expected to achieve the impossible.   —French proverb

A hero is a man who does what he can.   —Romain Rolland

It is only fools who keep straining at high C all their lives.
—Charles Dudley Warner

May God . . . let me strive for attainable things.   —Pindar

Despair is the price one pays for setting himself an impossible aim.
—Graham Greene

We would have to settle for the elegant goal of becoming ourselves.
—William Styron

A great obstacle to happiness is to expect too much happiness.
—Bernard de Fontenelle

There is a proper balance between not asking enough of oneself and asking or expecting too much.
—May Sarton

I hope to work, support my children and die quietly without pain.
—Sean Connery

As we advance in life, we learn the limits of our abilities. —J.A. Froud

Striving for excellence motivates you; striving for perfection is demoralizing. —Dr. Harriet Braiker

It is enough that I am of value to somebody today. —Hugh Prather

A tomb now suffices him for whom the whole world was not sufficient.
—Epitaph of Alexander the Great

To wish to act like angels while we are still in this world is nothing but folly. —Teresa of Avila

It isn't important to come out on top; what matters is to be the one who comes out alive. —Bertolt Brecht

I long to accomplish a great and noble task, but it is my chief duty to accomplish small tasks as if they were great and noble. —Helen Keller

I cannot do everything, but still I can do something; and because I cannot do everything, I will not refuse to do something I can do.
—Edward Everett Hale

Do not lose courage in considering your own imperfections.
—Saint Francis de Sales

WE MUST ACCEPT THE SPREAD BETWEEN OUR WISHES AND LIFE'S REALITIES

Happy the man who early learns the wide chasm that lies between his wishes and his powers.
—Johann von Goethe

[Being a parent] is tough. If you just want a wonderful little creature to love, you can get a puppy.
—Barbara Walters

You never conquer a mountain. You stand on the summit a few moments; then the wind blows your footprints away. —Arlene Blum

If we are to survive on this planet, there must be compromises.
—Storm Jameson

Real life is, to most men . . . a perpetual compromise between the ideal and the possible. —Bertrand Russell

He who cannot do what he wants must make do with what he can.
—Terence

What has always made a hell on earth has been that man has tried to make it his heaven.
—Friedrich Holderlin

Good is not good, where better is expected. —Thomas Fuller

Nobody has things just as he would like them. The thing to do is to make a success with what material I have. It is a sheer waste of time and soul-power to imagine what I would do if things were different. They are not different. —Dr. Frank Crane

452

People are lucky and unlucky . . . according to the ratio between what they get and what they have been led to expect. —Samuel Butler

We must like what we have when we don't have what we like.
—Bussy-Rabutin

Better is the enemy of the good.
—Voltaire

If you aspire to the highest place, it is no disgrace to stop at the second, or even the third, place. —Cicero

Genius does what it must, talent does what it can. —Edward Bulwer-Lytton

A hero is a man who does what he can. —Romain Rolland

Nature is what you may do. There is much you may not do.
—Ralph Waldo Emerson

Results are what you expect; consequences are what you get. —Anon.

The resistance to the unpleasant situation is the root of suffering.
—Ram Dass and Paul Gorman

To expect life to be tailored to our specifications is to invite frustration.
—Anon.

Each of us does, in effect, strike a series of "deals," or compromises, between the wants and longings of the inner self, and an outer environment that offers certain possibilities and sets certain limitations.
—Maggie Scarf

Man is the only animal that laughs and weeps, for he is the only animal that is struck with the difference between what things are, and what they might have been.
—William Hazlitt

We do not write as we want, but as we can. —W. Somerset Maugham

Every creator painfully experiences the chasm between his inner vision and its ultimate expression. The chasm is never completely bridged. We all have the conviction, perhaps illusory, that we have much more to say than appears on the paper.
—Isaac Bashevis Singer

A body shouldn't heed what might be. He's got to do with what is.
—Louis L'Amour

The chief pang of most trials is not so much the actual suffering itself as our own spirit of resistance to it.
—Jean Nicholas Grou

The greatest and most important problems in life are all in a certain sense insoluble. They can never be solved, but only outgrown.
—Carl Jung

The art of living lies less in eliminating our troubles than in growing with them. —Bernard M. Baruch

DOING WHAT'S RIGHT WON'T GUARANTEE HAPPINESS OR SUCCESS

Doing what's right is no guarantee against misfortune. —William McFee

Life has not taught me to expect nothing, but she has taught me not to expect success to be the inevitable result of my endeavors. —Alan Paton

WE HAVE TO DEAL WITH WHAT'S POSSIBLE

Knowledge of what is possible is the beginning of happiness.
—George Santayana

Don't spend time beating on a wall, hoping to transform it into a door.
—Dr. Laura Schlessinger

If I were to wish for anything, I should not wish for wealth and power, but for the passionate sense of the potential, for the eye which, ever young and ardent, sees the possible . . . what wine is so sparkling, so fragrant, so intoxicating, as possibility!
—Søren Kierkegaard

Wisdom never kicks at the iron walls it can't bring down.
—Olive Schreiner

It is impossible to control creation.
—Evelyn Scott

To seek fulfillment is to invite frustration. —Jiddu Krishnamurti

Half the unhappiness in the world is due to the failure of plans which were never reasonable, and often impossible. —Edgar Watson Howe

There is an illusion that has much to do with . . . most of our unhappiness. . . . We expect too much.
—Joseph Farrell

A fool or idiot is one who expects things to happen that never can happen. —George Eliot

Shall a man go and hang himself because he belongs to the race of pygmies, and not be the biggest pygmy that he can?
—Henry David Thoreau

Life is a compromise of what your ego wants to do, what experience tells you to do, and what your nerves let you do. —Bruce Crampton

We almost made it, but we wanted it all. —From the song "We Wanted It All,"Burt Bachrach and Carole Bayer Sager

No, Doctor, I don't want to grow young again. I just want to keep on growing old.
—Madame de Rothschild

What we call reality is an agreement that people have arrived at to make life more livable. —Louise Nevelson

There is no such thing as pure pleasure; some anxiety always goes with it.
—Ovid

When somebody tells you nothing is impossible, ask him to dribble a football. —Anon.

No country can act wisely simultaneously in every part of the globe at every moment of time.
—Henry Kissinger

The most important thing in marriage is not happiness, but stability.
—Gabriel Garcia Marquez

So often we search out the impossible, and then throw ourselves into trying to do it. —Anon.

ANTICIPATION IS OFTEN MORE ENJOYABLE THAN REALIZATION

Nothing is so good as it seems beforehand. —George Eliot

Prospect is often better than possession. —Thomas Fuller

The hours we pass with happy prospects in view are more pleasing than those crowned with fruition. —Oliver Goldsmith

'Tis expectation makes a blessing dear; heaven were not heaven if we knew what it were. —Sir John Sucking

Life is so constructed that the event does not, cannot, will not, match the expectation. —Charlotte Brontë

There is no greater enemy to those who would please than expectation. —Michel de Montaigne

To dream too much of the person you would like to be is to waste the person you are. —Anon.

Too many people miss the silver lining because they're expecting gold. —Maurice Setter

For people who live on expectations, to face up to their realization is something of an ordeal. —Elizabeth Bowen

My expectations—which I extended whenever I came close to accomplishing my goals—made it impossible ever to feel satisfied with my success. —Ellen Sue Stern

REALITY AND WARFARE

Every attempt to make war easy and safe will result in humiliation and disaster. —General William Sherman

I sincerely wish war was a pleasanter and easier business than it is, but it does not admit of holidays. —Abraham Lincoln

There is many a boy here today who looks on war as all glory, but boys, it is all hell. —General William T. Sherman

War is not an adventure. It is a disease. It is like typhus. —Antoine de Saint-Exupery

In combat, life is short, nasty and brutish. The issues of national policy which brought him into war are irrelevant to the combat soldier; he is concerned with his literal life chances. —Charles E. Moskos, Jr.

In war, more than anywhere else in the world, things happen differently from what we had expected, and look differently when near from what they did at a distance. —Karl Von Clausewitz

In spite of all of the training you get and the precautions you take to keep yourself alive, it's largely a matter of luck that decides whether or not you get killed. —James Jones

Moderation in war is imbecility.
—Admiral John Fisher

GENERAL QUOTATIONS ABOUT
REALISTIC EXPECTATIONS

When one's expectations are reduced
to zero, one really appreciates everything one does have.
—Stephen Hawking

I like trees because they seem more
resigned to the way they have to live
than other things do. —Willa Cather

Life didn't promise to be wonderful.
—Teddy Pendergrass

We never enjoy perfect happiness; our
most fortunate successes are mingled
with sadness; some anxieties always
perplex the reality of our satisfaction.
—Pierre Corneille

Do not commit the error, common
among the young, of assuming that
if you cannot save the whole of mankind you have failed.
—Jan de Hartog

The art of living lies less in eliminating our troubles than in growing with
them.   —Bernard M. Baruch

If one considered life as a simple loan,
one would perhaps be less exacting.
—Eugene Delacroix

Why are we surprised when fig trees
bear figs?   —Margaret Titzel

Those who aim at great deeds must
also suffer greatly.   —Plutarch

I have nothing to offer but blood,
toil, tears, and sweat.
—Sir Winston Churchill

There's no map, there's no master
plan, there's just people.   —Stingray

Every writer I know has trouble
writing.   —Joseph Heller

Men expect too much, do too little.
—Allen Tate

Goals

It's Tremendously Important to Have Good Goals

An aim in life is the only fortune worth finding.
—Jacqueline Kennedy Onassis

You have to have a dream so you can get up in the morning. —Billy Wilder

What an immense power over the life is the power of possessing distinct aims. The voice, the dress, the look, the very motions of a person, define and alter when he or she begins to live for a reason.
—Elizabeth Stuart Phelps

If I had one wish for my children, it would be that each of them would reach for goals that have meaning for them as individuals. —Lillian Carter

The tragedy of life doesn't lie in not reaching your goal. The tragedy lies in having no goal to reach.
—Benjamin Mays

Purpose is what gives life a meaning.
—C.H. Parkhurst

Nothing contributes so much to tranquilize the mind as a steady purpose—a point on which the soul may fix its intellectual eye.
—Mary Wollstonecraft Shelley

The poor man is not he who is without a cent, but he who is without a dream. —Harry Kemp

He is conscious of touching the highest pinnacle of fulfillment . . . when he is consumed in the service of an idea, in the conquest of the goal pursued.
—R. Briffault

He who has a why to live for can bear almost any how.
—Friedrich Nietzsche

The great and glorious masterpiece of man is to know how to live to purpose. —Michel de Montaigne

Great minds have purposes, others have wishes. —Washington Irving

Unless you give yourself to some great cause, you haven't even begun to live. —William P. Merrill

If we could only give, just once, the same amount of reflection to what we want to get out of life that we give to the question of what to do with a two weeks' vacation, we would be startled at our false standards and the aimless procession of our busy days.
—Dorothy Canfield Fisher

Be a life long or short, its completeness depends on what it was lived for.
—David Starr Jordan

To live means to have . . . a mission to fulfill—and in the measure in which we avoid setting our life to something, we make it empty.
—José Ortega y Gasset

To seek one's goals and to drive toward it, steeling one's heart, is most uplifting!   —Henrik Ibsen

The true worth of a man is to be measured by the objects he pursues.
—Marcus Aurelius

A useless life is an early death.
—Johann von Goethe

My father used to play with my brother and me in the yard. Mother would come out and say, "You're tearing up the grass." "We're not raising grass," Dad would reply. "We're raising boys."
—Harmon Killebrew

Without a purpose, nothing should be done.   —Marcus Aurelius

To grow and know what one is growing towards—that is the source of all strength and confidence in life.
—James Baillie

Our plans miscarry because they have no aim. When a man does not know what harbor he is making for, no wind is the right wind.
—Marcus Annaeus Seneca

Every true man, sir, who is a little above the level of the beasts and plants, lives so as to give a meaning and a value to his own life.
—Luigi Pirandello

Men cannot for long live hopefully unless they are embarked upon some great unifying enterprise, one for which they may pledge their lives, their fortunes and their honor.
—C.A. Dykstra

No pleasure philosophy, no sensuality, no place nor power, no material success can for a moment give such inner satisfaction as the sense of living for good purpose.
—Minot Simons

Many are stubborn in pursuit of the path they have chosen, few in pursuit of the goal.   —Friedrich Nietzsche

There is one thing which gives radiance to everything. It is the idea of something around the corner.
—G.K. Chesterton

Lack of something to feel important about is almost the greatest tragedy a man may have.   —Charles C. Noble

There are three ingredients in the good life: learning, earning and yearning.   —Christopher Morely

If you cry "Forward," you must make plain in what direction to go.
—Anton Chekhov

Men, like nails, lose their usefulness when they lose direction and begin to bend. —Walter Savage Landor

A novelist must know what his last chapter is going to say and one way or another work toward that last chapter. . . . To me it is utterly basic, yet it seems like it's a great secret. —Leon Uris

Obstacles are those frightful things you see when you take your eyes off the goal. —Hannah More

You must have long-range goals to keep you from being frustrated by short-range failures. —Charles C. Noble

The world stands aside to let anyone pass who knows where he is going. —David Starr Jordan

This is true joy of life—the being used for a purpose that is recognized by yourself as a right one, instead of being a feverish, selfish little clod of ailments and grievances, complaining that the world will not devote itself to making you happy. —George Bernard Shaw

Not only must we be good, but we must also be good for something. —Henry David Thoreau

It is when things go hardest, when life becomes most trying, that there is greatest need for having a fixed goal. When few comforts come from without, it is all the more necessary to have a fount to draw on from within. —B.C. Forbes

In everything one must consider the end. —Jean de La Fontaine

A straight path never leads anywhere except to the objective. —André Gide

There's some end at last for the man who follows a path; mere rambling is interminable. —Marcus Annaeus Seneca

Having a goal is a state of happiness. —E.J. Bartek

The American people can have anything they want; the trouble is, they don't know what they want. —Eugene V. Debs

Life has a meaning only if one barters it day by day for something other than itself. —Antoine de Saint-Exupery

To have a reason to get up in the morning, it is necessary to possess a guiding principle. A belief of some kind. A bumper sticker, if you will. —Judith Guest

An aspiration is a joy forever, a possession as solid as a landed estate, a fortune which we can never exhaust and which gives us year by year a revenue of pleasurable activity. —Robert Louis Stevenson

The soul that has no established aim loses itself. —Michel de Montaigne

Life has a value only when it has something valuable as its object. —George Hegel

He turns not back who is bound to a star. —Leonardo da Vinci

He might never really do what he said, but at least he had it in mind. He had somewhere to go.
—Louis L'Amour

The great and glorious masterpiece of man is how to live with a purpose.
—Michel de Montaigne

What most counts is not to live, but to live aright.
—Socrates

Choosing a goal and sticking to it changes everything.
—Scott Reed

No wind serves him who addresses his voyage to no certain port.
—Michel de Montaigne

Laboring toward distant aims sets the mind in a higher key, and puts us at our best.
—C.H. Parkhurst

Everything's in the mind. That's where it all starts. Knowing what you want is the first step toward getting it.
—Mae West

Set short term goals and you'll win games. Set long term goals and you'll win championships!
—Anon.

We act as though comfort and luxury were the chief requirements of life, when all that we need to make us really happy is something to be enthusiastic about.
—Charles Kingsley

Unhappiness is in not knowing what we want and killing ourselves to get it.
—Don Herold

Having a dream isn't stupid. . . . It's not having a dream that's stupid.
—Anon.

Happiness is the overcoming of not unknown obstacles toward a known goal.
—L. Ron Hubbard

To have no set purpose in one's life is the harlotry of the will.
—Stephen McKenna

There is no happiness except in the realization that we have accomplished something.
—Henry Ford

Strong lives are motivated by dynamic purposes.
—Kenneth Hildebrand

One of the sources of pride in being a human being is the ability to bear present frustrations in the interests of longer purposes.
—Helen Merrell Lynd

Only he who can see the invisible can do the impossible.
—Frank Gaines

If you don't know where you are going, how can you expect to get there?
—Basil S. Walsh

The only people who attain power are those who crave for it.
—Erich Kastner

Destiny is not a matter of chance, it is a matter of choice; it is not a thing to be waited for, it is a thing to be achieved.
—William Jennings Bryan

In this life we get only those things for which we hunt, for which we strive, and for which we are willing to sacrifice.
—George Matthew Adams

You seldom get what you go after unless you know in advance what you want.
—Maurice Switzer

Where no plan is laid, where the disposal of time is surrendered merely to the chance of incident, chaos will soon reign. —Victor Hugo

A life that hasn't a definite plan is likely to become driftwood.
—David Sarnoff

Only he who keeps his eye fixed on the far horizon will find his right road.
—Dag Hammarskjold

Fortunate is the person who has developed the self-control to steer a straight course toward his objective in life, without being swayed from his purpose by either commendation or condemnation. —Napoleon Hill

Nothing is more terrible than activity without insight. —Thomas Carlyle

If we would only give, just once, the same amount of reflection to what we want to get out of life that we give to the question of what to do with a two weeks' vacation, we would be startled at our false standards and the aimless procession of our busy days.
—Dorothy Canfield Fisher

The purpose of life is a life of purpose. —Robert Byrne

Aim at nothing and you'll succeed.
—Anon.

The purpose of life is life.
—Karl Lagerfeld

GOALS REQUIRE A PLAN

Goals are dreams with deadlines.
—Diana Scharf Hunt

So long as I believe I have to do certain things, I will just go right ahead. That's how I run my life.
—Corazan Aquino

A schedule defends from chaos and whim. It is a net for catching days. It is a scaffolding on which a worker can stand and labor with both hands at sections of time. —Annie Dillard

You decide what it is you want to accomplish and then you lay out your plans to get there, and then you just do it. It's pretty straightforward.
—Nancy Ditz

What does so-called success or failure matter if only you have succeeded in doing the thing you set out to do. The doing is all that really counts.
—Eva Le Gallienne

Get out of the blocks, run your race, stay relaxed. If you run your race, you'll win. Channel your energy. Focus. —Carol Lewis

Know what you want to do—then do it. Make straight for your goal and go undefeated in spirit to the end.
—Ernestine Schumann-Heink

WE EACH HAVE OUR OWN GOALS

There is a place in God's sun for the youth "farthest down" who has the vision, the determination, and the courage to reach it.
—Mary McLeod Bethune

Every man is said to have his peculiar ambition. —Abraham Lincoln

We all live with the objective of being happy; our lives are all different, and yet the same.   —Anne Frank

Follow your bliss. Find where it is and don't be afraid to follow it.
          —Joseph Campbell

You can't assume the responsibility for everything you do—or don't do.
          —Simone de Beauvoir

There were angry men confronting me and I caught the flashing of defiant eyes, but above me and within me, there was a spirit stronger than them all.
          —Antoinette Brown Blackwell

A woman finds the natural lay of the land almost unconsciously; and not feeling it incumbent on her to be guide and philosopher to any successor, she takes little pains to mark the route by which she is making her ascent.
          —Antoinette Brown Blackwell

No matter what the competition is, I try to find a goal that day and better that goal.   —Bonnie Blair

It doesn't matter what anybody thinks of what I do. The clock doesn't lie.
          —Bonnie Blair

You can have your titular recognition. I'll take money and power.
          —Helen Gurley Brown

Normal is not something to aspire to, it's something to get away from.
          —Jodie Foster

I'm always making a comeback but nobody ever tells me where I've been.
          —Billie Holiday

My passions were all gathered together like fingers that made a fist. Drive is considered aggression today; I knew it then as purpose.
          —Bette Davis

In the multitude of middle-aged men who go about their vocations in a daily course determined for them much in the same way as they tie their cravats, there is always a good number who once meant to shape their own deeds and alter the world a little.   —George Eliot

Remember if people talk behind your back, it only means you're two steps ahead!   —Fannie Flagg

It's a sign of your own worth sometimes if you are hated by the right people.   —Miles Franklin

For me it's the challenge—the challenge to try to beat myself or do better than I did in the past. I try to keep in mind not what I have accomplished but what I have to try to accomplish in the future.
          —Jackie Joyner-Kersee

There's a very fine line between a groove and a rut; a fine line between eccentrics and people who are just plain nuts.   —Christine Lavin

Promises that you make to yourself are often like the Japanese plum tree—they bear no fruit.
          —Frances Marion

I am not sending messages with my feet. All I ever wanted was not to come up empty. I did it for the dough, and the old applause.
          —Fred Astaire

First say to yourself what you would be, and then do what you have to do.
—Epictetus

I can honestly say that I was never affected by the question of the success of an undertaking. If I felt it was the right thing to do, I was for it regardless of the possible outcome.
—Golda Meir

What exactly is success? For me it is to be found not in applause, but in the satisfaction of feeling that one is realizing one's ideal. —Anna Pavlova

We can do whatever we wish to do provided our wish is strong enough. . . . What do you want most to do? That's what I have to keep asking myself, in the face of difficulties.
—Katherine Mansfield

To be what we are, and to become what we are capable of becoming, is the only end of life.
—Baruch Spinoza

You have to define success in your own way. What maintains your dignity and integrity and what is your life's plan, where do you want to put your efforts. I could be richer and more famous, but I would have to give up things that are of infinitely more value. —Dr. Laura Schlessinger

You cannot do good work if you take your mind off the work to see how the community is taking it.
—Dorothy L. Sayers

When the shriveled skin of the ordinary is stuffed out with meaning, it satisfies the senses amazingly.
—Virginia Woolf

Ambition means longing and striving to attain some purpose. Therefore, there are as many brands of ambition as there are human aspirations.
—B.C. Forbes

The aim of life is self-development, to realize one's nature perfectly.
—Oscar Wilde

Our victory is sure to come, and I can endure anything but recreancy to principle. —Lucy Stone

If you just set out to be liked, you would be prepared to compromise on anything at any time, and you would achieve nothing.
—Margaret Thatcher

Concentrate on finding your goal, then concentrate on reaching it.
—Colonel Michael Friedman

Enthusiasm for one's goal lessens the disagreeableness of working toward it.
—Thomas Eakins

I'm not going to let my life revolve around losing weight. I have other things to do. —Rosie O'Donnell

WE CAN HAVE TOO MANY GOALS

The streams which would otherwise diverge to fertilize a thousand meadows, must be directed into one deep narrow channel before they can turn a mill. —Anna Jameson

He who wants to do everything will never do anything. —André Maurois

As you emphasize your life, you must localize and define it . . . you cannot do everything. —Phillips Brooks

There are people who want to be everywhere at once, and they get nowhere. —Carl Sandburg

Leader and followers are both following the invisible leader—the common purpose. —Mary Parker Follett

A windmill is eternally at work to accomplish one end, although it shifts with every variation of the weathercock, and assumes ten different positions in a day.
—Charles Caleb Colton

People can have many different kinds of pleasure. The real one is that for which they will forsake the others.
—Marcel Proust

Nations, like individuals, have to limit their objectives or take the consequences. —James Reston

One of the most important factors, not only in military matters but in life as a whole, is . . . the ability to direct one's whole energies towards the fulfillment of a particular task.
—Field Marshal Erwin Rommel

It is in self-limitation that a master first shows himself.
—Johann von Goethe

One cannot manage too many affairs: like pumpkins in the water, one pops up while you try to hold down the other. —Chinese proverb

One principle reason why men are so often useless is that they . . . divide and shift their attention among a multitude of objects and pursuits.
—Nathaniel Emmons

I can tell you how to get what you want: You've just got to keep a thing in view and go for it and never let your eyes wander to right or left or up or down. And looking back is fatal.
—William J. Lock

He who begins many things finishes but few. —Italian proverb

Who begins too much accomplishes little. —German proverb

Never try to catch two frogs with one hand. —Chinese proverb

If you run after two hares, you will catch neither. —Thomas Fuller

The greyhound that starts many hares kills none. —Spanish proverb

A bull does not enjoy fame in two herds. —Rhodesian proverb

The man who seeks one thing in life, and but one
May hope to achieve it before life be done.
But he who seeks all things wherever he goes
Only reaps from the hopes which around him he sows
A harvest of barren regrets.
—Owen Meredith

Those who attain any excellence commonly spend life in one pursuit; for excellence is not often granted upon easier terms. —Samuel Johnson
No man can serve two masters: for either he will hate the one, and love the other; or else he will hold to the one, and despise the other.
—Matthew 6:24

He who wishes to fulfill his mission in the world must be a man of one idea, one great overmastering purpose, overshadowing all his aims, and guiding and controlling his entire life.
—Julius Bate

Firmness of purpose is one of the most necessary sinews of character and one of the best instruments of success. Without it, genius wastes its efforts in a maze of inconsistencies.
—Lord Chesterfield

A double-minded man is unstable in all his ways. . . . A determinate purpose in life, and a steady adhesion to it through all disadvantages, are indispensable conditions of success.
—William M. Punshion

If you would be Pope, you must think of nothing else.
—Spanish proverb

One should want only one thing and want it constantly. Then one is sure of getting it. But I desire everything, and consequently get nothing.
—André Gide

I care not what your education is, elaborate or nothing, what your mental calibre is, great or small, that man who concentrates all his energies of body, mind and soul in one direction is a tremendous man.
—T. DeWitt Talmage

He who hunts two hares leaves one and loses the other.
—Japanese proverb

He who serves two masters has to lie to one.   —Portuguese proverb

MAKE THE ENJOYMENT OF LIFE A PRIMARY GOAL

All animals except man know that the ultimate of life is to enjoy it.
—Samuel Butler

What does so-called success or failure matter if only you have succeeded in doing the thing you set out to do. The doing is all that really counts.
—Eva Le Gallienne

Catching something is purely a by-product of our fishing. It is the act of fishing that wipes away all grief, lightens all worry, dissolves all fear and anxiety.   —Gladys Taber

Let us live, while we are alive!
—Johann von Goethe

Since we must all die sooner or later, let us enjoy life while we can!
—Otoma no Tabito

Life is an end in itself, and the only question as to whether it is worth living is whether you have had enough of it.   —Oliver Wendell Holmes, Jr.

I take it as a prime cause of the present confusion of society that it is too sickly and too doubtful to use pleasure as a test of value.
—Rebecca West

There is no cure for birth and death save to enjoy the interval.
—George Santayana

Life is about enjoying yourself and having a good time.   —Cher

All men seek one goal: success or happiness.   —Aristotle

What I'm out for is a good time. All the rest is propaganda.

—*Saturday Night and Sunday Morning*

The goal of all civilization, all religious thought, and all that sort of thing is simply to have a good time. But man gets so solemn over the process that he forgets the end.

—Don Marquis

The business of life is to enjoy oneself; everything else is a mockery.

—Norman Douglas

The true object of human life is play.

—G.K. Chesterton

Use your health, even to the point of wearing it out. That is what it is for. Spend all you have before you die; do not outlive yourself.

—George Bernard Shaw

Pleasure is the object, duty and the goal of all rational creatures.

—Voltaire

Pleasure is the only thing to live for. Nothing ages like happiness.

—Oscar Wilde

I finally figured out the only reason to be alive is to enjoy it.

—Rita Mae Brown

Life exists for the love of music or beautiful things. —G.K. Chesterton

There is only one meaning of life: the act of living itself. —Erich Fromm

The main obligation is to amuse yourself. —S.J. Perelman

GOALS AND PEACE OF MIND

From his cradle to the grave, a man never does a single thing which has any first and foremost object save one—to secure peace of mind, spiritual comfort, for himself.

—Mark Twain

I take it that what all men are really after is some form of, perhaps only some formula of, peace.

—James Conrad

ALWAYS AIM HIGH

There is no such thing as expecting too much. —Susan Cheever

Your goal should be out of reach but not out of sight. —Anita DeFrantz

Why should I deem myself to be a chisel, when I could be the artist?

—J.C.F. von Schiller

I've always had such high expectations for myself. I'm aware of them, but I can't relax them.

—Mary Decker Slaney

I want to be great, or nothing. I won't be a commonplace dauber, so I don't intend to try any more.

—Louisa May Alcott

We're half the people, we should be half the Congress.

—Jeannette Rankin

I think the key is for women not to set any limits. —Martina Navratilova

It's expectation that differentiates you from the dead. —Sheila Ballantyne

The state of the world today demands that women become less modest and dream/plan/act/risk on a larger scale.   —Charlotte Bunch

Aim at the sun, and you may not reach it; but your arrow will fly far higher than if aimed at an object on a level with yourself.   —J. Hawes

When one paints an ideal, one does not need to limit one's imagination.
          —Ellen Key

If you would hit the mark, you must aim a little above it; every arrow that flies feels the attraction of earth.
          —Henry Wadsworth Longfellow

People don't pay much attention to you when you are second best. I wanted to see what it felt like to be number one.
          —Florence Griffith Joyner

Nearly every glamorous, wealthy, successful career woman you might envy now started out as some kind of schlepp.   —Helen Gurley Brown

The fact that I was a girl never damaged my ambitions to be a pope or an emperor.   —Willa Cather

In the long run men hit only what they aim at. Therefore, though they should fall immediately, they had better aim at something high.
          —Henry David Thoreau

Each time I leaped I seemed to touch the sky and when I regained earth it seemed to be mine alone.
          —Josephine Baker

The tragedy of life doesn't lie in not reaching your goal. The tragedy lies in having no goal to reach. It isn't a calamity to die with dreams unfulfilled, but it is a calamity not to dream. It is not disgrace to reach the stars, but it is a disgrace to have no stars to reach for. Not failure, but low aim, is a sin.   —Benjamin Mays

I have an almost complete disregard of precedent and a faith in the possibility of something better. It irritates me to be told how things always have been done. . . . I defy the tyranny of precedent. I cannot afford the luxury of a closed mind. I go for anything new that might improve the past.
          —Clara Barton

It's not enough to just swing at the ball. You've got to loosen your girdle and really let it fly.
          —Babe Didrikson Zaharias

I am comforted by life's stability, by earth's unchangeableness. What has seemed new and frightening assumes its place in the unfolding of knowledge.   —Pearl S. Buck

Someday, someone will follow in my footsteps and preside over the White House as the President's spouse. And I wish him well.   —Barbara Bush

The most absurd and reckless aspirations have sometimes led to extraordinary success.   —Vauvenargues

When you reach for the stars, you may not quite get one, but you won't come up with a handful of mud, either.   —Leo Burnett

I might have been born in a hovel but I am determined to travel with the wind and the stars.
—Jacqueline Cochran

The brain is wider than the sky.
—Emily Dickinson

My motto: sans limites.
—Isadora Duncan

A lot of young girls have looked to their career paths and have said they'd like to be chief. There's been a change in the limits people see.
—Wilma Pearl Mankiller

[My father] said, Don't grow up to be a woman, and what he meant by that was, a housewife . . . without any interests.   —Maria Goeppert Mayer

Our being is subject to all the chances of life. There are so many things we are capable of, that we could be or do. The potentialities are so great that we never, any of us, are more than one-fourth fulfilled.
—Katherine Anne Porter

What else are we gonna live by if not dreams? We need to believe in something. What would really drive us crazy is to believe this reality we run into every day is all there is. If I don't believe that there's a happy ending out there—that will-you-marry-me in the sky—I can't keep working today.
—Jill Robinson

People think that at the top there isn't much room. They tend to think of it as an Everest. My message is that there is tons of room at the top.
—Margaret Thatcher

I am always more interested in what I am about to do than in what I have already done.   —Rachel Carson

We have believed—and we do believe now—that freedom is indivisible, that peace is indivisible, that economic prosperity is indivisible.
—Indira Gandhi

I always ask the question, "Is this what I want in my life?"
—Kathy Ireland

Tell them that as soon as I can walk I'm going to fly!   —Bessie Coleman

He who demands little gets it.
—Ellen Glasgow

Unless in one thing or another we are straining toward perfection, we have forfeited our manhood.
—Stephen McKenna

It is necessary to try to surpass one's self always; this occupation ought to last as long as life.
—Christina Augusta,
Queen of Sweden

I was born to be a remarkable woman; it matters little in what way or how. . . . I shall be famous or I will die.   —Marie Bashkirtseff

I never intended to become a run-of-the-mill person.   —Barbara Jordaon

There is only one real sin and that is to persuade oneself that the second best is anything but second best.
—Doris Lessing

Too low they build, who build beneath the stars.   —Edward Young

468

I have the same goal I've had ever since I was a little girl. I want to rule the world. —Madonna

Your world is as big as you make it. —Georgia Douglas Johnson

Whatever course you have chosen for yourself, it will not be a chore but an adventure if you bring to it a sense of the glory of striving, if your sights are set far above the merely secure and mediocre. —David Sarnoff

Once you say you're going to settle for second, that's what happens to you. —John F. Kennedy

Aim at heaven and you get earth thrown in; aim at earth and you get neither. —C.S. Lewis

I truly believe that before I retire from public office, I'll be voting for a woman for president. —Barbara Mikulski

We are all in the gutter, but some of us are looking at the stars. —Oscar Wilde

If I smashed the traditions it was because I knew no traditions. —Maude Adams

Aim at perfection in everything, though in most things it is unattainable. However they who aim at it, and persevere, will come much nearer to it than those whose laziness and despondency make them give it up as unattainable. —Lord Chesterfield

One may miss the mark by aiming too high, as too low. —Thomas Fuller

Shoot for the moon. Even if you miss it, you will land among the stars. —Les Brown

We aim above the mark to hit the mark. Every act hath some falsehood or exaggeration in it. —Ralph Waldo Emerson

Life is a petty thing unless it is moved by the indomitable urge to extend its boundaries. —José Ortega y Gasset

Far away in the sunshine are my highest inspirations. I many not reach them, but I can look up and see the beauty, believe in them and try to follow where they lead. —Louisa May Alcott

A man's worth is no greater than the worth of his ambitions. —Marcus Aurelius

Not failure, but low aim, is crime. —James Russell Lowell

On the human chessboard, all moves are possible. —Miriam Schiff

Great is the road I climb, but . . . the garland offered by an easier effort is not worth the gathering. —Propertius

I never took a position we were going to be a good ball club. I took the position we were going to be a winning ball club. —Red Auerbach

Man's reach should exceed his grasp, or what's a heaven for? —Robert Browning

We Must Visualize Our Goals

Before you begin a thing, remind yourself that difficulties and delays quite impossible to foresee are ahead. . . . You can only see one thing clearly and that is your goal. Form a mental vision of that and cling to it through thick and thin.   —Kathleen Norris

You have to erect a fence and say, "Okay, scale this." —Linda Ronstadt

You can change your beliefs so they empower your dreams and desires. Create a strong belief in yourself and what you want.   —Marcia Wieder

Man can only receive what he sees himself receiving.
                    —Florence Scovel Shinn

A person can grow only as much as his horizon allows.   —John Powell

You must learn day by day, year by year, to broaden your horizon. The more things you love, the more you are interested in, the more you enjoy, the more you are indignant about, the more you have left when anything happens.   —Ethel Barrymore

Goals and Happiness

Enjoyment is not a goal, it is a feeling that accompanies important ongoing activity.   —Paul Goodman

What our deepest self craves is not mere enjoyment, but some supreme purpose that will enlist all our powers and give unity and direction to our life.   —Henry J. Golding

The very first condition of lasting happiness is that a life should be full of purpose, aiming at something outside self.   —Hugh Black

The only true happiness comes from squandering ourselves for a purpose.
                    —John Mason Brown

There is more to life than just existing and having a pleasant time.
                    —J.C.F. von Schiller

Happiness is not the end of life; character is.   —Henry Ward Beecher

Many persons have a wrong idea of what constitutes true happiness. It is not attained through self-gratification, but through fidelity to a worthy purpose.   —Helen Keller

Enjoying the Effort it Takes to Achieve Our Goals

A good goal is like a strenuous exercise—it makes you stretch.
                    —Mary Kay Ash

It's weak and despicable to go on wanting things and not trying to get them.   —Joanna Field

Growth is not concerned with itself.
                    —Meridel Le Sueur

The self-confidence one builds from achieving difficult things and accomplishing goals is the most beautiful thing of all.   —Madonna

If ambition doesn't hurt you, you haven't got it.   —Kathleen Norris

Doing Our Duty and Pursuing Goals Leads to Happiness

We need to restore the full meaning of that old word, duty. It is the other side of rights. —Pearl S. Buck

This is true joy of life—being used for a purpose that is recognized by yourself as a mighty one . . . instead of being a feverish, selfish little clod of ailments and grievances, complaining that the world will not devote itself to making you happy.
—George Bernard Shaw

That is happiness: to be dissolved into something completely great.
—Willa Cather

I looked on child rearing not only as a work of love and duty but as a profession that was fully as interesting and challenging as any honorable profession in the world and one that demanded the best I could bring to it.
—Rose Fitzgerald Kennedy

Human happiness and moral duty are inseparably connected.
—George Washington

The measure of a life, after all, is not its duration, but its donation.
—Corrie ten Boom

When we . . . devote ourselves to the strict and unsparing performance of duty, then happiness comes of itself.
—Wilhelm von Humboldt

Duties are what make life most worth living. Lacking them, you are not necessary to anyone.
—Marlene Dietrich

Seek happiness for its own sake, and you will not find it; seek for duty, and happiness will follow, as the shadow comes with the sunshine.
—Tyron Edwards

True happiness . . . is not attained through self-gratification, but through fidelity to a worthy purpose.
—Helen Keller

The only true happiness comes from squandering ourselves for a purpose.
—William Cowper

True happiness, we are told, consists in getting out of one's self, but the point is not only to get out; you must stay out, and to stay out, you must have some absorbing errand.
—Henry James

Happiness is the natural flower of duty. —Phillips Brooks

The happiest excitement in life is to be convinced that one is fighting for all one is worth on behalf of some clearly seen and deeply felt good.
—Ruth Benedict

The secret of living is to find . . . the pivot of a concept on which you can make your stand. —Luigi Pirandello

The only ones among you who will be really happy are those who will have sought and found how to serve.
—Albert Schweitzer

He who never sacrificed a present to a future good, or a personal to a general one, can speak of happiness only as the blind speak of color.
—Horace Mann

There is no happiness except in the realization that we have accomplished something.   —Henry Ford

The full-grown modern human being . . . is conscious of touching the highest pinnacle of fulfillment . . . when he is consumed in the service of an idea, in the conquest of the goal pursued.
     —R. Briffault

Happiness is essentially a state of going somewhere, wholeheartedly, one-directionally, without regret or reservation.   —William H. Sheldon

A man's happiness: to do the things proper to man.   —Marcus Aurelius

Happy the man who knows his duties!
     —Christian Furchtegott Gellert

I believe half the unhappiness in life comes from people being afraid to go straight at things.   —William J. Locke

Happiness is the overcoming of not unknown obstacles toward a known goal.   —L. Ron Hubbard

Give a man health and a course to steer, and he'll never stop to trouble about whether he's happy or not.
     —George Bernard Shaw

Having a goal is a state of happiness.
     —E.J. Bartek

Happiness lies in the joy of achievement and the thrill of creative effort.
     —Franklin Delano Roosevelt

Without duty, life is soft and boneless.
     —Joseph Joubert

Never mind your happiness; do your duty.   —Will Durant

SUCCESS

I probably hold the distinction of being one movie star who, by all laws of logic, should never have made it. At each stage of my career, I lacked the experience.   —Audrey Hepburn

The man who succeeds above his fellows is the one who early in life discerns his object and toward that object habitually directs his powers. Even genius itself is but fine observation strengthened by fixity of purpose.
     —Edward Bulwer-Lytton

If one advances confidently in the direction of his dreams, and endeavors to live the life which he has imagined, he will meet with a success unexpected in common hours.
     —Henry David Thoreau

A determinate purpose of life, and steady adhesion to it through all disadvantages, are indispensable conditions of success.
     —William M. Punshion

The secret of success is constancy to purpose.   —Benjamin Franklin

The man who fails because he aims astray, or because he does not aim at all, is to be found everywhere.
     —Frank Swinnerton

Life has . . . taught me not to expect success to be the inevitable result of my endeavors. She taught me to seek sustenance from the endeavor itself, but to leave the result to God.
     —Alan Paton

GOALS AND WARFARE

The object of war is not to die for your country, but to make the other bastard die for his.
—General George S. Patton

The object of war is to survive it.
—John Irving

ULTIMATE GOALS

If we want a free and peaceful world, if we want to make the deserts bloom and man grow to greater dignity as a human being—we can do it.
—Eleanor Roosevelt

The most comprehensive formulation of therapeutic goals is the striving for wholeheartedness: to be without pretense, to be emotionally sincere, to be able to put the whole of oneself into one's feelings, one's work, one's beliefs.
—Karen Horney

I think the purpose of life is to be useful, to be responsible, to be honorable, to be compassionate. It is, after all, to matter: to count, to stand for something, to have made some difference that you lived at all.
—Leo C. Rosten

Only when men are connected to large, universal goals are they really happy—and one result of their happiness is a rush of creative activity.
—Joyce Carol Oates

The great business of life is to be, to do, to do without, and to depart.
—John Morley

Much pleasure and little grief is every man's desire.
—Spanish proverb

The proper function of man is to live—not to exist.
—Jack London

Life's objective is life itself.
—Johann von Goethe

I seek the utmost pleasure and the least pain.
—Plautus

There are two things to aim at in life: first, to get what you want, and after that to enjoy it. Only the wisest of mankind achieve the second.
—Logan Pearsall Smith

I am searching for that which every man seeks—peace and rest.
—Dante Alighieri

Reach high, for stars lie hidden in your soul. Dream deep, for every dream precedes the goal.
—Pamela Vaull Starr

Never undertake anything for which you wouldn't have the courage to ask the blessings of heaven.
—Georg Christoph Lichtenberg

The one thing worth living for is to keep one's soul pure.
—Marcus Aurelius

The greatest use of life is to spend it for something that will outlast it.
—William James

PART 5

Overcoming Negatives and Uncertainties

Fear

All Living Creatures Fear Something

The horse does abominate the camel; the mighty elephant is afraid of a mouse; and they say that the lion, which scorneth to turn his back upon the stoutest animal, will tremble at the crowing of a cock.

—Increase Mather

The flocks fear the wolf, the crops the storm, and the trees the wind.

—Virgil

We all choke, and the man who says he doesn't choke is lying like hell.

—Lee Trevino

A man who says he has never been scared is either lying or else he's never been any place or done anything.

—Louis L'Amour

All men are afraid in battle. The coward is the one who lets his fear overcome his sense of duty. Duty is the essence of manhood.

—General George S. Patton

Only the self-deceived will claim perfect freedom from fear.   —Bill W.

Every day I wake up a little afraid. Only a fool is never afraid.

—Ron Meyer

This is the century of fear.

—Albert Camus

Fear Is One of the Most Terrible Things in Life

There is perhaps nothing so bad and so dangerous in life as fear.

—Jawaharlal Nehru

The trouble with most people is that they think with their hopes or fears or wishes rather than with their minds.   —Nancy Astor

Fear, true fear, is a savage frenzy. Of all the insanities of which we are capable, it is surely the most cruel.

—Georges Bernanos

Fear is the fire that melts Icarian wings.   —Florence Earle Coates

476

There seemed to be endless obstacles—it seemed that the root cause of them all was fear.   —Joanna Field

How very little can be done under the spirit of fear.
                    —Florence Nightingale

The most destructive element in the human mind is fear. Fear creates aggressiveness; aggressiveness engenders hostility; hostility engenders fear—a disastrous circle.
                    —Dorothy Thompson

A man's doubts and fears are his worst enemies. —William Wrigley, Jr.

Great self-destruction follows upon unfounded fear. —Ursula K. LeGuin

Fear is the most devastating of all human emotions. Man has no trouble like the paralyzing effects of fear.
                    —Paul Parker

Only when we are no longer afraid do we begin to live.
                    —Dorothy Thompson

Neither a man nor a crowd nor a nation can be trusted to act humanely or to think sanely under the influence of a great fear.   —Bertrand Russell

The worst sorrows in life are not in its losses and misfortunes, but its fears. —Arthur Christopher Benson

No passion so effectually robs the mind of all its powers of acting and reasoning as fear. —Edmund Burke

The thing I fear most is fear.
                    —Michel de Montaigne

Nothing is so much to be feared as fear.   —Henry David Thoreau

Nothing is terrible except fear itself.
                    —Francis Bacon

The only thing we have to fear is fear itself—nameless, unreasoning, unjustified terror which paralyzes needed efforts to convert retreat into advance.
                    —Franklin Delano Roosevelt

It is better by noble boldness to run the risk of being subject to half the evils we anticipate than to remain in cowardly listlessness for fear of what might happen.   —Herodotus

There is no devil but fear.
                    —Elbert Hubbard

Men who look young, act young, and everlastingly harp on the fact that they are young—but who nevertheless think and act with a degree of caution what would be excessive in their grandfathers—are the curses of the world.   —Robertson Davies

There's nothing I'm afraid of like scared people.   —Robert Frost

God! Is there anything uglier than a frightened man!   —Jean Anouilh

The only thing I am afraid of is fear.
                    —Arthur Wellesley,
                    Duke of Wellington

THE HORRIBLE EFFECTS OF FEAR

Of all the passions, fear weakens judgment most.   —Cardinal de Retz

All forms of fear produce fatigue.
—Bertrand Russell

The more I traveled the more I realized that fear makes strangers of people who should be friends.
—Shirley MacLaine

Power does not corrupt. Fear corrupts, perhaps the fear of a loss of power.
—John Steinbeck

When men are ruled by fear, they strive to prevent the very changes that will abate it.
—Alan Paton

Fear, if allowed free rein, would reduce all of us to trembling shadows of men, for whom only death could bring release.
—John M. Wilson

If we let things terrify us, life will not be worth living.
—Marcus Annaeus Seneca

When fear is excessive it can make many a man despair.
—Saint Thomas Aquinas

Fear makes the wolf bigger than he is.
—German proverb

One of the effects of fear is to disturb the senses and cause things to appear other than what they are.
—Miguel de Cervantes

What begins in fear usually ends in folly.
—Samuel Taylor Coleridge

In doubt, fear is the worst of prophets.
—Statius

Fear is the most damnable, damaging thing to human personality in the whole world.
—William Faulkner

Fear is the main source of superstition, and one of the main sources of cruelty.
—Bertrand Russell

Fear is like fire. If controlled it will help you; if uncontrolled, it will rise up and destroy you. Men's actions depend to a great extent upon fear. We do things either because we enjoy doing them or because we are afraid not to do them.
—John F. Milburn

To hate and to fear is to be psychologically ill . . . it is, in fact, the consuming illness of our time.
—Harry A. Overstreet

Fear is an acid which is pumped into one's atmosphere. It causes mental, moral and spiritual asphyxiation, and sometimes death; death to energy and all growth.
—Horace Fletcher

Fear is the proof of a degenerate mind.
—Virgil

Fear is an insidious virus. Given a breeding place in our minds . . . it will eat away our spirit and block the forward path of our endeavors.
—James F. Bell

A man who is afraid will do anything.
—Jawaharlal Nehru

Excessive fear is always powerless.
—Aeschylus

Fear makes strangers of people who should be friends.
—Shirley MacLaine

O, how vain and vile a passion is this fear! What base, uncomely things it makes men do.
—Samuel Johnson

The unknown is what it is. And to be frightened of it is what sends everybody scurrying around chasing dreams, illusions, wars, peace, love, hate, all that. Unknown is what it is. Accept that it's unknown, and it's plain sailing.   —John Lennon

No passion so effectively robs the mind of its powers of acting and reasoning as fear.   —Edmund Burke

As many people die from an excess of timidity as from bravery.
          —Norman Mailer

If a man harbors any sort of fear, it percolates through all his thinking, damages his personality, makes him landlord to a ghost.
          —Lloyd C. Douglas

If you let fear of consequence prevent you from following your deepest instinct, then your life will be safe, expedient and thin.
          —Katharine Butler Hathaway

There is nothing that fear or hope does not make men believe.
          —Vauvenargues

Fear is the prison of the heart.
          —Anon.

I have come to realize that all my trouble with living has come from fear and smallness within me.
          —Angela L. Wozniak

He who fears something gives it power over him.   —Moorish proverb

How very little can be done under the spirit of fear.
          —Florence Nightingale

All fear is bondage.   —Anon.

We promise according to our hopes, and perform according to our fears.
          —Francois de La Rochefoucauld

There seemed to be endless obstacles . . . it seemed that the root cause of them all was fear.   —Joanna Field

No power is strong enough to be lasting if it labors under the weight of fear.   —Cicero

Where fear is, happiness is not.
          —Marcus Annaeus Seneca

Primary Sources of Fear

Many fears are born of fatigue and loneliness.   —Max Ehrmann

We're frightened of what makes us different.   —Anne Rice

Fear always springs from ignorance.
          —Ralph Waldo Emerson

We are always afraid to start something that we want to make very good, true, and serious.
          —Brenda Ueland

The craven's fear is but selfishness, like his merriment.
          —John Greenleaf Whittier

When did reason ever direct our desires or our fears?   —Juvenal

Fear is created not by the world around us, but in the mind, by what we think is going to happen.
          —Elizabeth Gawain

Fear is secured by a dread of punishment. —Niccolo Machiavelli

We are largely the playthings of our fears. To one, fear of the dark; to another, of physical pain; to a third, of public ridicule; to a fourth, of poverty; to a fifth, of loneliness . . . for all of us, our particular creature waits in ambush. —Horace Walpole

If your desires be endless, your cares and fears will be so, too.
—Thomas Fuller

We fear the thing we want the most.
—Dr. Robert Anthony

We are more often frightened than hurt; and we suffer more from imagination than from reality.
—Marcus Annaeus Seneca

Fear, born of that stern matron, Responsibility. —William McFee

Only your mind can produce fear.
—*A Course in Miracles*

Fear follows crime, and is its punishment. —Voltaire

All infractions of love and equity in our social relations are . . . punished by fear. —Ralph Waldo Emerson

The only thing we have to fear on this planet is man. —Carl Jung

There is nothing in the universe that I fear, but that I shall not know all my duty or fail to do it. —Mary Lyon

UNCERTAINTY CAN FILL PEOPLE WITH FEAR

I can stand what I know. It's what I don't know that frightens me.
—Frances Newton

I am never afraid of what I know.
—Anna Sewell

Fear comes from uncertainty. When we are absolutely certain, whether of our worth or worthlessness, we are almost impervious to fear.
—William Congreve

Let us not fear the hidden. Or each other. —Muriel Rukeyser

We all fear what we don't know—it's natural. —Leo Buscaglia

ANXIETY ABOUT THE FUTURE

He that fears not the future may enjoy the present. —Thomas Fuller

Grief and constant anxiety kill nearly as many women as men die on the battlefield. —Mary Bokin Chesnut

To tremble before anticipated evils is to bemoan what thou hast never lost.
—Johann von Goethe

He who foresees calamities suffers them twice over. —Beilby Porteous

He who fears he shall suffer already suffers what he fears.
—Michel de Montaigne

If you are afraid for your future, you don't have a present.
—James Petersen

Nothing in life is more remarkable than the unnecessary anxiety which we endure, and generally create ourselves. —Benjamin Disraeli

Do not think of all your anxieties, you will only make yourself ill.
—*The Shih King*

Only man clogs his happiness with care, destroying what is with thoughts of what may be.
—John Dryden

I care. I care a lot. I think of "Cosmopolitan" all day, and I run scared. So it's a combination of fright, caring, and anxiety.
—Helen Gurley Brown

Cowards die many times before their deaths; the valiant never taste of death but once.
—William Shakespeare

Every man, through fear, mugs his aspirations a dozen times a day.
—Brendan Francis

The mind that is anxious about the future is miserable.
—Marcus Annaeus Seneca

I am not afraid of tomorrow, for I have seen yesterday and I love today.
—William Allen White

We are more disturbed by a calamity which threatens us than by one which has befallen us.
—John Lancaster Spalding

We need not be afraid of the future, for the future will be in our own hands. —Thomas E. Dewey

It is never safe to look into the future with eyes of fear. —E.H. Harriman

The future is called "perhaps," which is the only possible thing to call the future. And the important thing is not to allow that to scare you.
—Tennessee Williams

Grief has limits, whereas apprehension has none. For we grieve only for what we know has happened, but we fear all that possibly may happen.
—Pliny, the Younger

Cowardice . . . is almost always simply a lack of ability to suspend the functioning of the imagination.
—Ernest Hemingway

Anxiety is a thin stream of fear trickling through the mind. If encouraged, it cuts a channel into which all other thoughts are drained.
—Arthur Somers Roche

Most of the fear that spoils our life comes from attacking difficulties before we get to them.
—Dr. Frank Crane

Fear is created not by the world around us, but in the mind, by what we think is going to happen.
—Elizabeth Gawain

FEAR CAN BE A
SELF-FULFILLING PROPHECY

Proust has pointed out that the predisposition to love creates it's own objects: is this not also true of fear?
—Elizabeth Bowen

Fear breeds fear. —Byron Janis

Fear to let fall a drop and you spill a lot. —Malay proverb

The truly fearless think of themselves as normal. —Margaret Atwood

Be not afraid of life. Believe that life is worth living, and your belief will help create the fact. —William James

We are terrified by the idea of being terrified. —Friedrich Nietzsche

That fear of missing out on things makes you miss out on everything. —Etty Hillesum

He who fears being conquered is sure of defeat. —Napoleon Bonaparte

What we fear comes to pass more speedily than what we hope. —Publilius Syrus

The greatest mistake you can make is to be continually fearing you will make one. —Elbert Hubbard

The mere apprehension of a coming evil has put many into a situation of the utmost danger. —Lucan

The thing we fear we bring to pass. —Elbert Hubbard

How often the fear of one evil leads into a worse. —Nicolas Bouleau-Despreaux

FEARS CAN BE UNLEARNED

Fears are educated into us, and can, if we wish, be educated out. —Dr. Karl Menninger

Love is what we are born with. Fear is what we learn. —Marianne Williamson

Human beings are born with just two basic fears. One is the fear of loud noises. The other is the fear of falling. All other fears must be learned. —Ronald Rood

Needless fear and panic over disease or misfortune that seldom materialize are simply bad habits. By proper ventilation and illumination of the mind it is possible to cultivate tolerance, poise and real courage. —Elie Metchnikoff

Nothing in life is to be feared. It is only to be understood. —Marie Curie

We have to start teaching ourselves not to be afraid. —William Faulkner

Victory over fear is the first spiritual duty of man. —Nicholas Berdyaev

I am not afraid of storms, for I am learning how to sail my ship. —Louisa May Alcott

WE CAN'T FEAR EITHER FAILURE OR SUCCESS

One of the marks of a gift is to have the courage of it. —Katherine Anne Porter

Part of being a champ is acting like a champ. You have to learn how to win and not run away when you lose. Everyone has bad stretches and real successes. —Nancy Kerrigan

Fear of success can also be tied into the idea that success means someone else's loss. Some people are unconsciously guilty because they believe their victories are coming at the expense of another.
—Joan C. Harvey

Most people are afraid of failing. I think there's nothing wrong in failing.
—Mark N. Cohen

True success is overcoming the fear of being unsuccessful.   —Paul Sweeney

I'm afraid of being lazy and complacent. I'm afraid of taking myself too seriously.   —Barbara Hershey

The sheer rebelliousness in giving ourselves permission to fail frees a childlike awareness and clarity. . . . When we give ourselves permission to fail, we at the same time give ourselves permission to excel.
—Eloise Ristad

He is much to be dreaded who stands in dread of poverty.   —Publilius Syrus

I was nervous and confident at the same time, nervous about going out there in front of all of those people, with so much at stake, and confident that I was going to go out there and win.   —Althea Gibson

There are those who are so scrupulously afraid of doing wrong that they seldom venture to do anything.
—Vauvenargues

Real courage is when you know you're licked before you begin, but you begin anyway and see it through no matter what.   —Harper Lee

To be ambitious for wealth, and yet always expecting to be poor, to be always doubting your ability to get what you long for, is like trying to reach east by traveling west. . . . No matter how hard you work for success, if your thought is saturated with the fear of failure, it will kill your efforts, neutralize your endeavors and make success impossible.
—Charles Baudouin

Studies by Medical Corps psychiatrists of combat fatigue cases . . . found that fear of killing, rather than fear of being killed, was the most common cause of battle failure, and that fear of failure ran a strong second.
—S.L.A. Marshall

Think like a queen. A queen is not afraid to fail. Failure is another steppingstone to greatness.
—Oprah Winfrey

Half the things that people do not succeed in are through fear of making the attempt.   —James Northcote

A champion is afraid of losing. Everyone else is afraid of winning.
—Billie Jean King

We fear our highest possibility (as well as our lowest one). We are generally afraid to become that which we can glimpse in our most perfect moments.   —Abraham Maslow

We fear the thing we want the most.
—Dr. Robert Anthony

We should not let our fears hold us back from pursuing our hopes.
—John F. Kennedy

The ambitious climb high and perilous stairs, and never care how to come down; the desire of rising hath swallowed up their fear of a fall.
—Thomas Adams

WE CAN'T FEAR EITHER DYING OR LIVING

It is not death that a man should fear, he should fear never beginning to live.
—Marcus Aurelius

Don't be afraid your life will end; be afraid it will never begin.
—Grace Hansen

Some people are so afraid to die that they never begin to live.
—Henry Van Dyke

Death is the last enemy: once we've got past that I think everything will be all right.   —Alice Thomas Ellis

The worst of all fears is the fear of living.   —Theodore Roosevelt

Life is to life in such a way that we are not afraid to die.
—Teresa of Avila

Those who fear life are already three parts dead.   —Bertrand Russell

Fear not that thy life shall come to an end, but rather that it shall never have a beginning.
—John Henry Cardinal Newman

People living deeply have no fear of death.   —Anaïs Nin

Fear of death is worse than dying.
—J.C.F. von Schiller

The fear of life is the favorite disease of the twentieth century.
—William Lyon Phelps

Too many people are thinking of security instead of opportunity. They are more afraid of life than death.
—James F. Byrnes

Death does not frighten me, but dying obscurely and above all uselessly does.   —Isabelle Eberhardt

Fear of life in one form or another is the great thing to exorcise.
—William James

If we let things terrify us, life will not be worth living.
—Marcus Annaeus Seneca

A good life fears not life, nor death.
—Thomas Fuller

He who fears death cannot enjoy life.
—Spanish proverb

Healthy children will not fear life if their elders have integrity enough not to fear death.   —Erik H. Erikson

To live your life in the fear of losing it is to lose the point of life.
—Malcolm Forbes

It is not death we fear, but the thought of it.
—Marcus Annaeus Seneca

It is not death or pain that is to be dreaded, but the fear of pain or death.   —Epictetus

Death is not the enemy, living in constant fear of it is.   —Norman Cousins

We Must Go on Despite Our Fear

We must act in spite of fear . . . not because of it. —Anon.

I have accepted fear as a part of life—specifically the fear of change. . . . I have gone ahead despite the pounding in the heart that says: turn back. . . . —Erica Jong

Go forth to meet the shadowy Future without fear and with a manly heart. —Henry Wadsworth Longfellow

I may be compelled to face danger, but never fear it, and while our soldiers can stand and fight, I can stand and feed and nurse them. —Clara Barton

The fishermen know that the sea is dangerous and the storm terrible, but they have never found these dangers sufficient reason for remaining ashore. —Vincent van Gogh

Fear is one thing. To let fear grab you and swing you around by the tail is another. —Katherine Paterson

I have not ceased being fearful, but I have ceased to let fear control me. —Erica Jong

Success and Happiness Depend on Facing Our Fears Directly

You gain strength, courage and confidence by every experience in which you really stop to look fear in the face. . . . You must do the thing you think you cannot do. —Eleanor Roosevelt

If you banish fear, nothing terribly bad can happen to you. —Margaret Bourke-White

I believe that anyone can conquer fear by doing the things he fears to do, provided he keeps doing them until he gets a record of successful experiences behind him. —Eleanor Roosevelt

When in fear, it is safest to force the attack. —Marcus Annaeus Seneca

The way to develop self-confidence is to do the thing you fear, and get a record of successful experiences behind you. —William Jennings Bryan

He that fleeth from the fear shall fall into the pit. —Jeremiah 48:44

To live with fear and not be afraid is the final test of maturity. —Edward Weeks

Constant exposure to dangers will breed contempt for them. —Marcus Annaeus Seneca

To do anything in this world worth doing, we must not stand back shivering and thinking of the cold and danger, but jump in and scramble through as well as we can. —Sydney Smith

Do the thing you fear, and the death of fear is certain. —Ralph Waldo Emerson

I wanted to be scared again . . . I wanted to feel unsure again. That's the only way I learn, the only way I feel challenged. —Connie Chung

You cannot run away from a weakness. You must sometimes fight it out or perish; and if that be so, why not now, and where you stand?
—Robert Louis Stevenson

Often I have found that the one thing that can save is the thing which appears most to threaten . . . one has to go down into what one most fears and in that process . . . comes a saving flicker of light and energy that, even if it does not produce the courage of a hero, at any rate enables a trembling mortal to take one step further.
—Laurens Van Der Post

I was afraid to write Fear of Flying; ergo, I had to write it. I have lived my life according to this principle: If I'm afraid of it, then I must do it.
—Erica Jong

One ought never to turn one's back on a threatened danger and try to run away from it. If you do that, you will double the danger. But if you meet it promptly and without flinching, you will reduce the danger by half. Never run away from anything. Never!
—Sir Winston Churchill

Being "brave" means doing or facing something frightening. . . . Being "fearless" means being without fear.
—Penelope Leach

From a distance it is something, and nearby it is nothing.
—Jean de La Fontaine

What you are afraid to do is a clear indicator of the next thing you need to do.
—Anon.

He that is afraid to shake the dice will never throw a six.
—Chinese proverb

ACTION IS A GREAT ANTIDOTE TO FEAR

The most drastic, and usually the most effective, remedy for fear is direct action.
—William Burnham

To be busy with material affairs is the best preservative against reflection, fears, doubts. . . . I suppose a fellow proposing to cut his throat would experience a sort of relief while occupied in stropping his razor carefully.
—Joseph Conrad

I think we should follow a simple rule: if we can take the worst, take the risk.
—Dr. Joyce Brothers

Happiness is to take up the struggle in the midst of the raging storm, not to pluck the lute in the moonlight or recite poetry among the blossoms.
—Ding Ling

Winners take chances. Like everyone else, they fear failing, but they refuse to let fear control them.
—Nancy Simms

Many of our fears are tissuepaper-thin, and a single courageous step would carry us clear through them.
—Brendan Francis

The habit of doing one's duty drives away fear.
—Charles Baudelaire

Become so wrapped up in something that you forget to be afraid.
—Lady Bird Johnson

Things done well and with care
exempt themselves from fear.
                —William Shakespeare

Ultimately we know deeply that the
other side of every fear is freedom.
                —Marilyn Ferguson

One had to take some action against
fear when once it laid hold of one.
                —Rainer Maria Rilke

Too busy with the crowded hour to
fear to live or die.
                —Ralph Waldo Emerson

A life of action and danger moderates
the dread of death. It not only gives
us fortitude to bear pain, but teaches
us at every step the precarious tenure
on which we hold our present being.
                —William Hazlitt

If you want to conquer fear, don't sit
at home and think about it. Go out
and get busy.   —Dale Carnegie

Most Fears Are Useless

Half our fears are baseless, the other
half discreditable. —Christian Bovee

We poison our lives with fear of
burglary and shipwreck and . . . the
house is never burgled, and the ship
never goes down.   —Jean Anouilh

To relinquish a present good through
apprehension of a future evil is in
most instances unwise . . . from a
fear which may afterwards turn out
groundless, you lost the good that lay
within your grasp.
                —Francesco Guicciardini

Envy and fear are the only passions
to which no pleasure is attached.
                —John Churton Collins

There is often less danger in the things
we fear than in the things we desire.
                —John Churton Collins

Needless fear and panic over disease
or misfortune that seldom materialize
are simply bad habits. By proper ventilation and illumination of the mind
it is possible to cultivate tolerance,
poise and real courage.
                —Elie Metchnikoff

There are very few monsters who
warrant the fear we have of them.
                —André Gide

When thinking won't cure fear, action
will.   —W. Clement Stone

The Competition
Is Afraid, Too

Above all things, never be afraid.
The enemy who forces you to retreat
is himself afraid of you at that very
moment.   —André Maurois

Every great batter works on the theory that the pitcher is more afraid of
him than he is of the pitcher.
                —Ty Cobb

The superpowers often behave like
two heavily armed blind men feeling their way around a room, each
believing himself in mortal peril from
the other, whom he assumes to have
perfect vision.   —Henry Kissinger

General Grant had a simple, child-like recipe for meeting life . . . "I am terribly afraid, but the other fellow is afraid, too."   —Sherwood Anderson

If you knew how cowardly your enemy is, you would slap him. Bravery is knowledge of the coward-ice in the enemy.
—Edgar Watson Howe

Mountains appear more lofty the nearer they are approached, but great men resemble them not in this par-ticular.
—Lady Marguerite Blessington

FAITH IS ESSENTIAL TO OVERCOMING FEAR

I have found adventure in flying, in world travel, in business, and even close at hand. . . . Adventure is a state of mind—and spirit. It comes with faith, for with complete faith there is no fear of what faces you in life or death.   —Jacqueline Cochran

There is much in the world to make us afraid. There is much more in our faith to make us unafraid.
—Frederick W. Cropp

Deep faith eliminates fear.
—Lech Walesa

Fear knocked at the door. Faith answered. And lo, no one was there.
—Anon.

A perfect faith would lift us abso-lutely above fear.
—George MacDonald

If fear is cultivated it will become stronger. If faith is cultivated it will achieve the mastery . . . faith is the stronger emotion because it is posi-tive, whereas fear is negative.
—John Paul Jones

Fear imprisons, faith liberates; fear paralyzes, faith empowers; fear dis-heartens, faith encourages; fear sick-ens, faith heals; fear makes useless, faith makes serviceable.
—Harry Emerson Fosdick

Fear is faith that it won't work out.
—Sister Mary Tricky

Fear is the absence of faith.
—Paul Tillich

Faith in yourself and faith in God are the key to mastery of fear.
—Harold Sherman

God is our refuge and strength, a very present help in trouble. Therefore we will not fear.
—Psalms 36:1–2

I will not fear, for you are ever with me, and you will never leave me to face my perils alone.
—Thomas Merton

Fear is faithlessness.
—George MacDonald

OTHER WAYS TO OVERCOME FEAR

If you wish to fear nothing, consider that everything is to be feared.
—Marcus Annaeus Seneca

I am deliberate and afraid of nothing.
—Audre Lorde

I survived my childhood by birth-
ing many separate identities to stand
in for one another in times of great
stress and fear.   —Roseanne

How does one kill fear? . . . How
do you shoot a specter through the
heart, slash off its spectral head, take
it by its spectral throat?
                          —Joseph Conrad

The brave man is not he who feels no
    fear,
For that were stupid and irrational;
But he, whose noble soul its fear sub-
    dues,
And barely dares the danger nature
    shrinks from.
                          —Joanna Baillie

Perhaps the most important thing we
can undertake toward the reduction
of fear is to make it easier for people
to accept themselves; to like themselves.   —Bonaro Overstreet

When fear seizes, change what you
are doing. You are doing something
wrong.   —Jean Craighead George

Grab the broom of anger and drive
off the beast of fear.
                          —Zora Neale Hurston

We will not be driven by fear . . . if we
remember that we are not descended
from fearful men.
                          —Edward R. Murrow

When we are afraid we ought not to
occupy ourselves with endeavoring to
prove that there is no danger, but in
strengthening ourselves to go on in
spite of the danger.
                          —Mark Rutherford

Every time I start a picture . . . I feel
the same fear, the same self-doubts . . .
and I have only one source on which
I can draw, because it comes from
within me.   —Federico Fellini

Fear is met and destroyed with
courage.   —James F. Bell

A cheerful frame of mind, reinforced
by relaxation, which in itself banishes
fatigue, is the medicine that puts all
ghosts of fear on the run.
                          —George Matthew Adams

To hell with pleasure that's haunted
by fear!   —Jean de La Fontaine

What I emphasize is for people to
make choices based not on fear, but
on what really gives them a sense of
fulfillment.   —Pauline Rose Chance

I steer my bark with hope in my
heart, leaving fear astern.
                          —Thomas Jefferson

Why should a man fear, since chance
is all in all for him, and he can clearly fore-know nothing? Best to live
lightly as one can, unthinking.
                          —Sophocles

I sought the Lord, and He heard me,
and delivered me from all my fears.
                          —Psalms 34:4

Any device whatever by which one
frees himself from fear is a natural
good.   —Epicurus

Joking about death—or anything
else that oppresses us—makes it less
frightening.   —Allen Klein

Humor acts to relieve fear.
—Dr. William F. Fry, Jr.

Good Things to Be Gained from Fear

If you can keep your head when all about are losing theirs, it's just possible you haven't grasped the situation.
—Jean Kerr

Fear is a kind of bell, or gong, which rings the mind into quick life and avoidance upon the approach of danger. It is the soul's signal for rallying.
—Henry Ward Beecher

If you can keep your head when all about are losing theirs, it's just possible you haven't grasped the situation.
—Jean Kerr

Fear is an emotion indispensable for survival.　—Hannah Arendt

Fear is the single strongest motivating force in our lives. . . . The more frightened you become, the better your chances of achieving success.
—Lois Korey

We only really face up to ourselves when we are afraid.
—Thomas Bernhard

If you're never scared or embarrassed or hurt, it means you never take any chances.　—Julia Sorel

Fear makes us feel our humanity.
—Benjamin Disraeli

A coward's fear can make a coward valiant.　—Thomas Fuller

Fear drives you and makes you better.
—Donna E. Shalala

Fear is an instructor of great sagacity, and the herald of all revolutions.
—Ralph Waldo Emerson

Just as courage imperils life, fear protects it.　—Leonardo da Vinci

In order to feel anything, you need strength.　—Anna Maria Ortese

There are times when fear is good. It must keep its watchful place at the heart's controls.　—Aeschylus

A danger foreseen is half avoided.
—Thomas Fuller

A good scare is worth more to a man than good advice.
—Edgar Watson Howe

Fear is a fine spur.　—Irish proverb

Fear is a question: What are you afraid of, and why? Just as the seed of health is an illness, because illness contains information, our fears are a treasure house of self-knowledge if we explore them.
—Marilyn Ferguson

Men who fear God face life fearlessly. Men who do not fear God end up fearing everything.
—Richard Halverson

It is only the fear of God that can deliver us from the fear of men.
—John Witherspoon

Being scared can keep a man from getting killed, and often makes a better fighter of him.　—Louis L'Amour

Nerves provide me with energy. . . .
It's when I don't have them, when I
feel at ease, that I get worried.
—Mike Nichols

Fear is an emotion indispensable for
survival. —Hannah Arendt

Fear gives sudden instincts of skill.
—Samuel Taylor Coleridge

I quit being afraid when my first
venture failed and the sky didn't fall
down. —Allen H. Neuharth

Fear of losing is what makes competitors so great. Show me a gracious
loser and I'll show you a permanent
loser. —O.J. Simpson

Fear is the father of courage and the
mother of safety.
—Henry H. Tweedy

Other Definitions of Fear

Fear is the needle that pierces us, that
it may carry a thread to bind us to
heaven. —James Hastings

Fear is the thought of admitted inferiority. —Elbert Hubbard

Fear is nature's warning signal to get
busy. —Henry Link

Fear is an uneasiness of the mind,
upon the thought of a future evil
likely to befall us. —John Locke

Fear is a cloak which old men huddle
about their love, as if to keep it
warm. —William Wordsworth

Fear is the tax that conscience pays
to guilt. —Anon.

Fear is pain arising from the anticipation of evil. —Aristotle

Fear is the soul's signal for rallying.
—Henry Ward Beecher

Fear is an instructor of great sagacity,
and the herald of all revolutions.
—Ralph Waldo Emerson

Fear is static that prevents me from
hearing myself. —Samuel Butler

FEAR: False Evidence Appearing Real.
—Anon.

Fear is the main source of superstition, and one of the main sources of
cruelty. —Bertrand A. Russell

Fear is a slinking cat I find beneath
the lilacs of my mind.
—Sophie Tunnell

Fear is the start of wisdom.
—Miguel de Unamuno

Fear is the lengthened shadow of
ignorance. —Arnold Glasow

Fear is the highest fence.
—Dudley Nichols

Fear is uncertainty. —Eric Hoffer

Fear is sand in the machinery of life.
—E. Stanley Jones

Fear is the dark room in which negatives are developed. —Anon.

General Quotations about Fear

Nothing is more despicable than respect based on fear.
—Albert Camus

I am not afraid. . . . I was born to do this.
—Joan of Arc

I have a lot of things to prove to myself. One is that I can live my life fearlessly.
—Oprah Winfrey

Fear betrays unworthy souls. —Virgil

Fear is not a good teacher. The lessons of fear are quickly forgotten.
—Mary Bateson

Fear could never make a virtue.
—Voltaire

Considering how dangerous everything is, nothing is really very frightening.
—Gertrude Stein

Were the diver to think on the jaws of the shark, he would never lay hands on the precious pearl. —Sa'di

Every problem in your life goes away in front of a bull because this problem, the bull, is bigger than all other problems. Of course, I have fear, but it is fear that I will fail the responsibility I have taken on in front of all those people—not fear of the bull.
—Cristina Sanchez

Fear is stronger than arms.
—Aeschylus

Fear is sharp-sighted, and can see things under ground, and much more in the skies. —Miguel de Cervantes

It is better to have a right destroyed than to abandon it because of fear.
—Phillip Mann

Better a fearful end than fear without end. —Anon.

A great philosophy is not a philosophy without reproach; it is philosophy without fear. —Charles Peguy

There is a time to take counsel of your fears, and there is a time to never listen to any fear.
—General George S. Patton

I, a stranger and afraid, in a world I never made. —A.E. Housman

While we wait in silence for that final luxury of fearlessness, the weight of that silence will choke us.
—Audre Lorde

All we are asked to bear we can bear. That is a law of the spiritual life. The only hindrance to the working of this law, as of all benign laws, is fear.
—Elizabeth Goudge

"But" is a fence over which few leap.
—German proverb

There are always two voices sounding in our ears—the voice of fear and the voice of confidence. One is the clamor of the senses, the other is the whispering of the higher self.
—Charles B. Newcomb

Fear nothing, for every renewed effort raises all former failures into lessons, all sins into experience.
—Katherine Tingley

Better hazard once than always be in fear. —Thomas Fuller

Pitching is the art of instilling fear by making a man flinch.
—Sandy Koufax

Fear has a large shadow, but he himself is small. —J. Ruth Gendler

Stripped of all their masquerades, the fears of men are quite identical: the fear of loneliness, rejection, inferiority, unmanageable anger, illness and death. —Joshua L. Liebman

What is there to be afraid of? The worst thing that can happen is you fail. So what? I failed at a lot of things. My first record was horrible.
—John Mellencamp

There is no hope unmingled with fear, and no fear unmingled with hope. —Baruch Spinoza

Leaders are visionaries with a poorly developed sense of fear and no concept of the odds against them. They make the impossible happen.
—Dr. Robert Jarvik

Those who love to be feared, fear to be loved. Some fear them, but they fear everyone. —Jean Pierre Camus

Keep your fears to yourself, but share your courage with others.
—Robert Louis Stevenson

There is a courageous wisdom; there is also a false reptile prudence, the result, not of caution, but of fear.
—Edmund Burke

The man who fears nothing is as powerful as he who is feared by everybody. —J.C.F. von Schiller

To conquer fear is the beginning of wisdom. —Bertrand Russell

Who is more foolish, the child afraid of the dark, or the man afraid of the light? —Maurice Freehill

The one permanent emotion of the inferior man is fear—fear of the unknown, the complex, the inexplicable. What he wants beyond everything else is safety. —H.L. Mencken

Fear is only an illusion. It is the illusion that creates the feeling of separateness—the false sense of isolation that exists only in your imagination.
—Jeraldine Saunders

A fool without fear is sometimes wiser than an angel with fear.
—Nancy Astor

Fear can be headier than whiskey, once man has acquired a taste for it.
—Donald Dowes

The first and great commandment is, don't let them scare you.
—Elmer Davis

Worry

Some Negative, Harmful Effects of Worry

Worry affects the circulation, the heart, the glands, the whole nervous system, and profoundly affects the health. You have never known a man who died from overwork, but many who died from doubt.
—Charles W. Mayo, M.D.

Everybody knows if you are too careful you are so occupied in being careful that you are sure to stumble over something.   —Gertrude Stein

Worry is a god, invisible but omnipotent. It steals the bloom from the cheek and lightness from the pulse; it takes away the appetite, and turns the hair gray.   —Benjamin Disraeli

A worried man could borrow a lot of trouble with practically no collateral.
—Helen Nielsen

If your eyes are blinded with your worries, you cannot see the beauty of the sunset.   —Jiddu Krishnamurti

Worry often gives a small thing a big shadow.   —Swedish proverb

If you worry about what might be, and wonder what might have been, you will ignore what is.   —Anon.

Bacteria and other microorganisms find it easier to infect people who worry and fret.   —Leo Rangell

Worry Is Useless and Wasteful

Worry is a funky luxury when a lot has to be done.   —Melvin Peebles

Worries are the most stubborn habits in the world. Even after a poor man has won a huge lottery prize, he will still for months wake up in the night with a start, worrying about food and rent.   —Vicki Baum

There is nothing so wretched or foolish as to anticipate misfortunes. What madness is it in expecting evil before it arrives? —Marcus Annaeus Seneca

Worry is like racing the engine of an automobile without letting in the clutch. —Corrie ten Boom

Worry is evidence of an ill-controlled brain; it is merely a stupid waste of time in unpleasantness.
—Arnold Bennett

It ain't no use putting up your umbrella till it rains!
—Alice Caldwell Rice

When speculation has done its worst, two and two still make four.
—Samuel Johnson

Worry a little bit every day and in a lifetime you will lose a couple of years. If something is wrong, fix it if you can. But train yourself not to worry. Worry never fixes anything.
—Mary Hemingway

Worry is like a rocking chair—it keeps you moving but doesn't get you anywhere. —Anon.

Anxiety is the poison of human life, the parent of many sins and of more miseries.... Can it alter the cause, or unravel the mystery of human events?
—Paxton Blair

It only seems as if you are doing something when you're worrying.
—L.M. Montgomery

A hundredload of worry will not pay an ounce of debt. —George Herbert

Worry is a futile thing, it's somewhat
like a rocking chair,
Although it keeps you occupied, it
doesn't get you anywhere.
—Anon.

Worry never climbed a hill, worry
never paid a bill,
Worry never dried a tear, worry never
calmed a fear,
Worry never darned a heel, worry
never cooked a meal,
It never led a horse to water, nor ever
did a thing it "oughter."
—Anon.

I am reminded of the advice of my neighbor. "Never worry about your heart 'til it stops beating."
—E.B. White

Worry is as useless as a handle on a snowball. —Mitzi Chandler

When you worry, you go over the same ground endlessly and come out the same place you started. Thinking, on the other hand, makes progress from one place to another.... The problem of life is to change worry into thinking, and anxiety into creative action. —Harold B. Walker

Which of you by being anxious can add one cubit unto his stature?
—Matthew 6:27

I think these difficult times have helped me to understand better than before how infinitely rich and beautiful life is in every way, and that so many things that one goes around worrying about are of no importance whatsoever. —Isak Dinesen

You always get negative reactions. If you worry about that, you would never do anything.
—Tom Monaghan

Anxiety never yet successfully bridged any chasm. —Giovanni Ruffini

WORRY AND TOMORROW

Cast away care; he that loves sorrow lengthens not a day, nor can he buy tomorrow. —Thomas Dekker

Worry doesn't help tomorrow's troubles, but it does ruin today's happiness. —Anon.

You can't start worrying about what's going to happen. You get spastic enough worrying about what's happening now. —Lauren Bacall

There are two days in the week about which and upon which I never worry. ... One of these days is Yesterday ... And the other day I do not worry about is Tomorrow.
—Robert Jones Burdette

We have to fight them daily, like fleas, those many small worries about the morrow, for they sap our energies. —Etty Hillesum

T'ain't worthwhile to wear a day all out before it comes.
—Sarah Orne Jewett

Worry never robs tomorrow of its sorrow, but only saps today of its strength. —A.J. Cronin

The really frightening thing about middle age is that you know you'll grow out of it! —Doris Day

Be, therefore, not anxious about tomorrow; for tomorrow will be anxious for the things of itself.
—Matthew 6:34

WORRY AND WORK

Never despair, but if you do, work on in despair. —Edmund Burke

If you are doing your best, you will not have time to worry about failure.
—Robert Hillyer

It is not work that kills men, it is worry. Work is healthy; you can hardly put more upon a man that he can bear. Worry is rust upon the blade. —Henry Ward Hughes

No good work is ever done while the heart is hot and anxious and fretted.
—Olive Schreiner

A day of worry is more exhausting than a day of work. —John Lubbock

The reason why worry kills more people than work is that more people worry than work. —Robert Frost

WORRY AND FEAR

Worry is a form of fear.
—Bertrand A. Russell

Worry is a complete cycle of inefficient thought revolving about a pivotal fear.
—Anon.

Worry is a state of mind based on fear. —Napoleon Hill

Worry is a thin stream of fear trickling through the mind. If encouraged, it cuts a channel into which all other thoughts are drained.
—Arthur Somers Roche

BASIC WAYS TO EASE YOUR WORRIES

If we would keep filling our minds with the picture of happy things ahead, many worries and anxieties, and perhaps ill health, would naturally melt away. . . . Always expect the best. Then if you have to hurdle a few tough problems, you will have generated the strength and courage to do so.　　—George Matthew Adams

Turn resolutely to work, to recreation, or in any case to physical exercise till you are so tired you can't help going to sleep, and when you wake up you won't want to worry.
—B.C. Forbes

A great many worries can be diminished by realizing the unimportance of the matter which is causing anxiety.
—Bertrand Russell

A problem not worth praying about is not worth worrying about.
—Anon.

We can always get along better by reason and love of truth than by worry of conscience and remorse. Harmful are these, and evil.
—Baruch Spinoza

As a cure for worrying, work is better than whiskey.
—Thomas A. Edison

Every morning I spend fifteen minutes filling my mind full of God, and so there's no room left for worry thoughts.
—Howard Chandler Christy

Worry compounds the futility of being trapped on a dead-end street. Thinking opens new avenues.
—Cullen Hightower

Rule No. 1 is, don't sweat the small stuff. Rule No. 2 is, it's all small stuff.
—Robert Eliot

If only the people who worry about their liabilities would think about the riches they do possess, they would stop worrying. Would you sell both your eyes for a million dollars . . . or your two legs . . . or your hands . . . or your hearing? Add up what you do have, and you'll find that you won't sell them for all the gold in the world. The best things in life are yours, if you can appreciate yourself.
—Dale Carnegie

ACCEPT THE WORST THAT CAN HAPPEN

You'll break the worry habit the day you decide you can meet and master the worse that can happen to you.
—Arnold Glasow

Peace of mind is that mental condition in which you have accepted the worst.　　—Lin Yutang

Of course I realized there was a measure of danger. Obviously I faced the possibility of not returning when I first considered going. Once faced and settled there really wasn't any good reason to refer to it again.
—Amelia Earhart

The worst is not so long as we can say, "This is the worst."
—William Shakespeare

What is there to be afraid of? The worst thing that can happen is you fail. So what? I failed at a lot of things. My first record was horrible.
—John Mellencamp

When you first learn to love hell, you will be in heaven. —Thaddeus Golas

Accept that all of us can be hurt, that all of us can—and surely will at times—fail. Other vulnerabilities, like being embarrassed or risking love, can be terrifying, too. I think we should follow a simple rule: if we can take the worst, take the risk.
—Dr. Joyce Brothers

A wise man fights to win, but he is twice a fool who has no plan for possible defeat. —Louis L'Amour

MOST THINGS WE WORRY ABOUT NEVER HAPPEN

There are people who are always anticipating trouble, and in this way they manage to enjoy many sorrows that never really happen.
—Josh Billings

The expectation of an unpleasantness is more terrible than the thing itself.
—Marie Bashkirtseff

Our worst misfortunes never happen, and most miseries lie in anticipation.
—Honore de Balzac

Some men storm imaginary Alps all their lives, and die in the foothills cursing difficulties which do not exist. —Edgar Watson Howe

Most people go through life dreading they'll have a traumatic experience.
—Diane Arbus

How much pain they have cost us, the evils which have never happened.
—Thomas Jefferson

The misfortunes hardest to bear are those which never happen.
—James Russell Lowell

What torments of grief you endured, from evils that never arrived.
—Ralph Waldo Emerson

We poison our lives with fear of burglary and shipwreck, and the house is never burgled, and the ship never goes down. —Jean Anouilh

Do we not all spend the greater part of our lives under the shadow of an event that has not yet come to pass?
—Maurice Maeterlinck

This was a great year for preventive worrying. Seldom in recent history have so many people worried about so many things that didn't happen in the end. —James Reston

I remember the story of the old man who said on his deathbed that he had had a lot of trouble in his life, most of which never happened.
—Sir Winston Churchill

Needless fear and panic over disease or misfortune that seldom materialize are simply bad habits. By proper ventilation and illumination of the mind it is possible to cultivate tolerance, poise and real courage.
—Elie Metchnikoff

Some of your hurts you have cured,
And the sharpest you still have
   survived,
But what torments of grief you
   endured
From the evil which never arrived.
                    —Ralph Waldo Emerson

I am an old man and have known
a great many troubles, but most of
them never happened. —Mark Twain

My life has been full of terrible misfortunes, most of which never happened.   —Michel de Montaigne

Though life is made up of mere
   bubbles
'Tis better than many have,
For while we've a whole lot of
   troubles
The most of them never occur.
                    —Nixon Waterman

If you see ten troubles coming down
the road, you can be sure that nine
will run into the ditch before they
reach you.   —Calvin Coolidge

The crisis you have to worry about
most is the one you don't see coming.
                    —Mike Mansfield

Other Definitions of Worry
Anxiety is the great modern plague.
But faith can cure it.
                    —Smiley Blanton, M.D.

Worry is the only insupportable misfortune of life.   —Henry Saint John

Worry is the cross which we make for
ourselves by overanxiety.
                    —Francois de Fenelon

Worry is interest paid on trouble
before it comes due.
                    —William Ralph Inge

Worry is a morbid anticipation of
events which never happen.
                    —Russell Green

Worry is the sin we're not afraid to
commit.   —Anon.

GENERAL QUOTATIONS ABOUT WORRY

That man is blest
Who does his best
And leaves the rest,
Then—do not worry.
                    —Charles F. Deems

Happy the man who has broken the
chains which hurt the mind, and has
given up worrying, once and for all.
                    —Ovid

If things happen all the time you are
never nervous. It is when they are not
happening that you are nervous.
                    —Gertrude Stein

Stop worrying about the potholes in
the road and celebrate the journey!
                    —Barbara Hoffman

A request not to worry . . . is perhaps
the least soothing message capable of
human utterance.
                    —Mignon G. Eberhart

It is the little things that fret and
worry us; you can dodge an elephant,
but not a fly.   —Josh Billings

To be rich is not the end, but only a
change, of worries.   —Epicurus

A man ninety years old was asked
to what he attributed his longevity.
"I reckon," he said, with a twinkle
in his eye, "it's because most nights I
went to bed and slept when I should
have sat up and worried."
—Dorothea Kent

Worry less about what other people
think about you, and more about
what you think about them.
—Fay Weldon

Don't hurry, don't worry. You're only
here for a short visit. So be sure to
stop and smell the flowers.
—Walter Hagen

Every faculty and virtue I possess can
be used as an instrument with which
to worry myself. —Mark Rutherford

What worries you, masters you.
—Haddon W. Robinson

Worry is most apt to ride you ragged
not when you are in action, but when
the day's work is done. Your imagination can run riot then . . . your
mind is like a motor operating without its load.   —James L. Muresell

"Worry" is a word that I don't allow
myself to use.
—Dwight D. Eisenhower

Real difficulties can be overcome, it
is only the imaginary ones that are
unconquerable. —Theodore N. Vail

Doubts and Uncertainties

UNCERTAINTY IS PART OF LIFE

Unrest and uncertainty are our lot.
—Johann von Goethe

Life is uncertain. Eat dessert first.
—Ernestine Ulmer

If we insist on being as sure as is conceivable . . . we must be content to creep along the ground, and can never soar.
—John Henry Cardinal Newman

Nothing, perhaps, is strange, once you have accepted life itself, the great strange business which includes all lesser strangeness.   —Rose Macaulay

The shortest period of time lies between the minute you put some money away for a rainy day and the unexpected arrival of rain.
—Jane Bryant Quinn

Our lives are never certain, even for an hour.   —Ferrant Sanchez Calavera

Throughout this life, you can never be certain of living long enough to take another breath.   —Huang Po

I wanted a perfect ending. Now I've learned, the hard way, that some poems don't rhyme, and some stories don't have a clear beginning, middle, and end. Life is about not knowing, having to change, taking the moment and making the best of it without knowing what's going to happen next.   —Gilda Radner

Where will I be five years from now? I delight in not knowing.
—Marlo Thomas

The longing for certainty . . . is in every human mind. But certainty is generally illusion.
—Oliver Wendell Holmes

No great deed is done by falterers who ask for certainty.
—George Eliot

Every year, if not every day, we have to wager our salvation upon some prophecy based upon imperfect knowledge.
—Oliver Wendell Holmes, Jr.

We are not certain, we are never certain.   —Albert Camus

We live in an epoch in which the solid ground of our preconceived ideas shakes daily under our certain feet.
—Barbara Ward

All business proceeds on beliefs, or judgment of probabilities, and not on certainties.　　—Charles W. Eliot

The man who insists upon seeing with perfect clearness before he decides, never decides.
—Henri Frederic Amiel

There is nothing certain in a man's life but that he must lose it.
—Owen Meredith

Ah, what a dusty answer gets the soul when hot for certainties in this, our life!　　—George Meredith

When I was young I was sure of everything; in a few years, having been mistaken a thousand times, I was not half so sure of most things as I was before; at present, I am hardly sure of anything but what God has revealed.　　—John Wesley

We can be absolutely certain only about things we do not understand.
—Eric Hoffer

You are all you will ever have for certain.　　—June Havoc

Certitude is not the test of certainty. We have been cock-sure of many things that were not so.
—Oliver Wendell Holmes, Jr.

A reasonable probability is the only certainty.　　—Edgar Watson Howe

Doubt is not a pleasant state, but certainty is a ridiculous one.
—Voltaire

Being unready and ill-equipped is what you have to expect in life. It is the universal predicament. It is your lot as a human being to lack what it takes. Circumstances are seldom right. You never have the capacities, the strength, the wisdom, the virtue you ought to have. You must always do with less than you need in a situation vastly different from what you would have chosen.
—Charlton Ogburn, Jr.

To be absolutely certain about something, one must know everything, or nothing, about it.　　—Olin Miller

Free man is by necessity insecure, thinking man by necessity uncertain.
—Erich Fromm

We sail within a vast sphere, ever drifting in uncertainty, driven from end to end.　　—Blaise Pascal

Something must be left to chance; nothing is sure in a sea fight.
—Horatio Nelson

There is nothing certain about war except that one side won't win.
—Sir Ian Hamilton

UNCERTAINTY IS THE
ONLY CERTAINTY

There is only one thing about which I am certain, and this is that there is very little about which one can be certain.　　—W. Somerset Maugham

The only certainty is that nothing is certain. —Pliny, the Elder

I'm often wrong, but never in doubt. —Ivy Baker Priest

There is one thing certain, namely, that we can have nothing certain; therefore it is not certain that we can have nothing certain. —Samuel Butler

Every area of trouble gives out a ray of hope, and the one unchangeable certainty is that nothing is certain or unchangeable. —John F. Kennedy

NEEDING CERTAINTY CAN BE COWARDICE

Any coward can fight a battle when he's sure of winning. —George Eliot

The demand is for certainty is a sign of weakness. —Mark Rutherford

The unknown is what it is. And to be frightened of it is what sends everybody scurrying around chasing dreams, illusions, wars, peace, love, hate, all that. . . . Accept that it's unknown, and it's plain sailing. —John Lennon

Only a weak mind seeks ultimate answers. —Agnes Thornton

When nothing is sure, everything is possible. —Margaret Drabble

DEMANDING CERTAINTY CAN BE PARALYZING

He who forecasts all perils will never sail the sea. —Anon.

There is a time for departure, even when there's no certain place to go. —Tennessee Williams

One doesn't discover new lands without consenting to lose sight of shore for a very long time. —André Gide

To teach how to live with uncertainty, yet without being paralyzed by hesitation, is perhaps the chief thing that philosophy can do. —Bertrand Russell

Faith . . . acts promptly and boldly on the occasion, on slender evidence. —John Henry Cardinal Newman

If we wait until we've satisfied all the uncertainties, it may be too late. —Lee Iacocca

The successful man is he who, when he sees that no further certainty is attainable, promptly decides on the most probable side, as if he were completely sure it was right. —Mark Rutherford

WE SHOULDN'T WORRY IF WE CAN'T SEE THE FINAL RESULT

Not seeing is half-believing. —Vita Sackville-West

The best and most beautiful things in the world cannot be seen or even touched—they must be felt with the heart. —Helen Keller

There is no advancement to him who stands trembling because he cannot see the end from the beginning.
—E.J. Klemme

I am a woman who understands the necessity of an impulse whose goal or origin still lie beyond me.
—Olga Broumas

To end with certainty, we must begin with doubting.
—Stanislaus

Gardening is an exercise in optimism.
—Maria Schinz

In the face of uncertainty, there is nothing wrong with hope.
—Bernie S. Siegel, M.D.

No object is mysterious. The mystery is your eye.
—Elizabeth Bowen

Faith hasn't got no eyes, but she's long-legged.
—Zora Neale Hurston

Maturity of mind is the capacity to endure uncertainty.
—John H. Finley

Don't be afraid of the space between your dreams and reality. If you can dream it, you can make it so.
—Belva Davis

If a man will begin with certainties, he shall end in doubts, but if he will content to begin with doubts, he shall end in certainties.
—Francis Bacon

I said here's the river I want to flow on, here's the direction I want to go, and put my boat in. I was ready for the river to take unexpected turns and present obstacles.
—Nancy Woodhull

UNCERTAINTY AND THE FUTURE

The future is no more uncertain than the present.
—Walt Whitman

Nobody can really guarantee the future. The best we can do is size up the chances, calculate the risks involved, estimate our ability to deal with them and make our plans with confidence.
—Henry Ford II

Every time I think that I'm getting old, and gradually going to the grave, something else happens.
—Lillian Carter

Many live in dread of what is coming. Why should we? The unknown puts adventure into life. . . . The unexpected around the corner gives a sense of anticipation and surprise. Thank God for the unknown future.
—E. Stanley Jones

WE CAN'T BE INTIMIDATED BY DOUBTS

I think I look good out there. I'm strong, powerful, and artistic. But I have my doubts as much as anyone.
—Jill Trenary

If I ever felt inclined to be timid as I was going into a room full of people, I would say to myself, "You're the cleverest member of one of the cleverest families in the cleverest class of the cleverest nation. . . . Why should you be frightened?"
—Beatrice Potter Webb

Action will remove the doubts that theory cannot solve.
—Tehyi Hsieh

To Death I yield, but not to Doubt,
who slays before!
— Edith M. Thomas

Soon after a heart-wrung decision,
something inevitably occurs to cast
doubt on your choice. Holding steady
against that doubt usually proves
your decision.   — R.I. Fitzhenry

Doubt breeds doubt.
— Franz Grillparzer

It's the moment you think you can't
that you realize you can.
— Celine Dion

From a shy, timid girl I had become
a woman of resolute character, who
could no longer be frightened by the
struggle with troubles.
— Anna Dostoevsky

Doubt is a pain too lonely to know
that faith is his twin brother.
— Kahlil Gibran

Doubts and mistrust are the mere
panic of timid imagination, which the
steadfast heart will conquer, and the
large mind transcend.   — Helen Keller

Doubt indulged soon becomes doubt
realized.   — Frances Ridley Havergal

When one devotes oneself to meditation, mental burdens, unnecessary
worries, and wandering thoughts
drop off one by one; life seems to run
smoothly and pleasantly. A student
may now depend on intuition to
make decisions. As one acts on intuition, second thought, with its dual-
ism, doubt and hesitation, does not
arise.   — Nyogen Senzaki

In doubt, fear is the worst of prophets.
— Statius

The only limit to our realization
of tomorrow will be our doubts of
today. Let us move forward with
strong and active faith.
— Franklin Delano Roosevelt

In case of doubt, decide in favor of
what is correct.   — Karl Kraus

Faith and doubt both are needed, not
as antagonists, but working side by
side to take us around the unknown
curve.   — Lillian Smith

Our doubts are traitors, and make us
lose the good we often might win, by
fearing to attempt.
— William Shakespeare

A man's doubts and fears are his
worst enemies.
— William Wrigley, Jr.

When in doubt, do it.
— Oliver Wendell Holmes, Jr.

WE MUSTN'T DOUBT OURSELVES

Yes, I have doubted. I have wandered
off the path, but I always return. It is
intuitive, an intrinsic, built-in sense
of direction. I seem always to find my
way home.   — Helen Hayes

A person who doubts himself is like
a man who would enlist in the ranks
of his enemies and bear arms against
himself.   — Alexandre Dumas

Doubt whom you will, but never
yourself.   — Christian Bovee

Self distrust is the cause of most of our failures. In the assurance of strength, there is strength, and they are the weakest, however strong, who have no faith in themselves or their own powers.   —Christian Bovee

Doubt yourself and you doubt everything you see. Judge yourself and you see judges everywhere. But if you listen to the sound of your own voice, you can rise above doubt and judgment. And you can see forever.
                —Nancy Kerrigan

To be ambitious for wealth, and yet always expecting to be poor; to be always doubting your ability to get what you long for, is like trying to reach east by traveling west. There is no philosophy which will help a man to succeed when he is always doubting his ability to do so, and thus attracting failure. No matter how hard you work for success, if your thought is saturated with the fear of failure, it will kill your efforts, neutralize your endeavors and make success impossible.
                —Charles Baudouin

FOCUS ON THE POSITIVE ASPECTS OF UNCERTAINTY

Uncertainty and expectation are the joys of life. Security is an insipid thing.   —William Congreve

I used to tremble from nerves so badly that the only way I could hold my head steady was to lower my chin practically to my chest and look up at Bogie. That was the beginning of "The Look."   —Lauren Bacall

When nothing is sure, everything is possible.   —Margaret Drabble

Uncertainty and mystery are energies of life. Don't let them scare you unduly, for they keep boredom at bay and spark creativity. —R.I. Fitzhenry

The quest for certainty blocks the search for meaning. Uncertainty is the very condition to impel man to unfold his powers.   —Erich Fromm

All uncertainly is fruitful . . . so long as it is accompanied by the wish to understand.   —Antonio Machado

I'm delighted that the future is unsure. That's the way it should be.
                —William Sloane Coffin

When we are not sure, we are alive.
                —Graham Greene

Freedom is nothing else but a chance to be better, whereas enslavement is a certainty of the worst.
                —Albert Camus

The only thing that makes life possible is permanent, intolerable uncertainty, not knowing what comes next.
                —Ursula K. LeGuin

In the face of uncertainty, there is nothing wrong with hope.
                —Bernie S. Siegel, M.D.

Security

SECURITY DOESN'T EXIST

Security is mostly superstition. It does not exist in nature. . . . Avoiding danger is no safer in the long run than outright exposure. The fearful are caught as often as the bold.
——Helen Keller

Security is a false god; begin making sacrifices to it and you are lost.
——Paul Bowles

God Himself is not secure, having given man dominion over His works.
——Helen Keller

The man who looks for security, even in the mind, is like a man who would chop off his limbs in order to have artificial ones which will give him no pain or trouble.   ——Henry Miller

Never think you've seen the last of anything.   ——Eudora Welty

If you want total security, go to prison. There you're fed, clothed, given medical care and so on. The only thing lacking . . . is freedom.
——Dwight D. Eisenhower

Life is not orderly. No matter how we try to make life so, right in the middle of it we die, lose a leg, fall in love, drop a jar of applesauce.
——Natalie Goldberg

Truly nothing is to be expected but the unexpected.   ——Alice James

Happiness, greatness, pride—nothing is secure, nothing keeps.   ——Euripides

There is no security, no assurance that because we wrote something good two months ago, we will do it again. Actually, every time we begin, we wonder how we ever did it before.
——Natalie Goldberg

There is no security on this earth. Only opportunity.
——General Douglas MacArthur

There is no way to take the danger out of human relationships.
——Barbara Grizzuti Harrison

Safety Isn't Security

It is the risk element which ensures security. Risk brings out the ingenuity and resourcefulness which insure success. —Robert Rawls

The way to be safe is never to be secure. —Benjamin Franklin

We are never more in danger than when we think ourselves most secure, nor in reality more secure than when we seem to be most in danger. —William Cowper

It is when we all play safe that we create a world of utmost insecurity. —Dag Hammarskjold

To keep oneself safe does not mean to bury oneself. —Marcus Annaeus Seneca

"Safety first" has been the motto of the human race for half a million years; but it has never been the motto of leaders. —Anon.

Security and Money

If money is your hope for independence you will never have it. The only real security that a man can have in this world is a reserve of knowledge, experience and ability. —Henry Ford

Our greatest illusion is reliance upon the security and permanence of material possessions. We must search for some other coin. —John Cudahy

The only peace, the only security, is in fulfillment. —Henry Miller

Solvency is entirely a matter of temperament, not of income. —Logan Pearsall Smith

Security depends not so much upon how much you have, as upon how much you can do without. —Joseph Wood Krutch

Other Sources of Security

Security can only be achieved through constant change, through discarding old ideas that have outlived their usefulness and adapting others to current facts. —William O. Douglas

Truth is the only safe ground to stand upon. —Elizabeth Cady Stanton

Only in growth, reform, and change, paradoxically enough, is true security to be found. —Anne Morrow Lindbergh

Security is not the absence of danger, but the presence of God, no matter what the danger. —Anon.

I'm in love with the potential of miracles. For me, the safest place is out on a limb. —Shirley MacLaine

We Are Our Own Security

Man's security comes from within himself. —Manly Hall

You are all you will ever have for certain. —June Havoc

No one can build her security upon the nobleness of another person. —Willa Cather

Your real security is yourself. You know you can do it, and they can't ever take that away from you.
—Mae West

Only those means of security are good, are certain, are lasting, that depend on yourself and your own vigor. —Niccolo Machiavelli

LACK OF SECURITY CAN BE A POSITIVE FORCE

Uncertainty and expectation are the joys of life. Security is an insipid thing.
—William Congreve

Freedom works. —Jeane Kirkpatrick

To be on the alert is to live; to be lulled into security is to die.
—Oscar Wilde

Prudence keeps life safe, but does not often make it happy.
—Samuel Johnson

Whatever course you have chosen for yourself, it will not be a chore but an adventure if you bring to it a sense of the glory of striving . . . if your sights are set far above the merely secure and mediocre. —David Sarnoff

Security is a kind of death.
—Tennessee Williams

Without danger we cannot get beyond danger. . . . Each one of us requires the spur of insecurity to force us to do our best.
—Dr. Harold W. Dodds

Nerves provide me with energy. . . . It's when I don't have them, when I feel at ease, that I get worried.
—Mike Nichols

Protection and security are only valuable if they do not cramp life excessively. —Carl Jung

GENERAL QUOTATIONS ABOUT SECURITY

Too many people are thinking of security instead of opportunity; they seem more afraid of life than of death.
—James F. Byrnes

The one permanent emotion of the inferior man is fear—fear of the unknown, the complex, the inexplicable. What he wants beyond everything else is safety. —H.L. Mencken

We spend our time searching for security and hate it when we get it.
—John Steinbeck

Be like the bird that, passing on her flight awhile on boughs too slight, feels them give way beneath her, and yet sings, knowing that she hath wings. —Victor Hugo

We hear of a silent generation, more concerned with security than integrity, with conforming than performing, with imitating than creating.
—Thomas J. Watson

Risks

RISKS ARE PART OF LIFE

You risk just as much in being credulous as in being suspicious.
—Denis Diderot

Our whole way of life today is dedicated to the removal of risk. Cradle to grave we are supported, insulated, and isolated from the risks of life—and if we fall, our government stands ready with Band-Aids of every size.
—Shirley Temple Black

Any life truly lived is a risky business, and if one puts up too many fences against the risks one ends by shutting out life itself. —Kenneth S. Davis

However well organized the foundations of life may be, life must always be full of risks. —Havelock Ellis

Dancing on the edge is the only place to be. —Trisha Brown

It is so tempting to try the most difficult thing possible.
—Jennie Jerome Churchill

Do not be too timid and squeamish. . . . All life is an experiment. The more experiments you make, the better.
—Ralph Waldo Emerson

To laugh is to risk appearing the fool.
To weep is to risk appearing sentimental.
To reach for another is to risk involvement.
To expose your ideas, your dreams, before a crowd, is to risk their loss.
To love is to risk not being loved in return.
To live is to risk dying.
To believe is to risk failure.
But risks must be taken, because the greatest hazard in life is to risk nothing.
The people who risk nothing do nothing, have nothing, are nothing.
They may avoid suffering and sorrow, but they cannot learn, feel, change, grow, love, live.
Chained by their attitudes, they are slaves; they have forfeited their freedom.
Only a person who risks is free.
—Poem quoted in "Dear Abby"

510

All life is a chance. So take it! The person who goes furthest is the one who is willing to do and dare.
—Dale Carnegie

I postpone death by living, by suffering, by error, by risking, by giving, by losing.   —Anaïs Nin

If you don't take chances, you can't do anything in life. —Michael Spinks

Only those who dare, truly live.
—Ruth P. Freedman

Life has no romance without risk.
—Sarah Doherty

We love because it is the only true adventure.   —Nikki Giovanni

If your life is ever going to get better, you'll have to take risks. There is simply no way you can grow without taking chances.   —David Viscot

You've got to keep fighting—you've got to risk your life every six months to stay alive.   —Elia Kazan

It takes courage to lead a life. Any life.
—Erica Jong

There's no such thing as a sure thing. That's why they call it gambling.
—Neil Simon

It is only by risking . . . that we live at all.   —William James

Life is a risk.
—Diane von Furstenberg

To be alive at all involves some risk.
—Harold MacMillan

This nation was built by men who took risks—pioneers who were not afraid of the wilderness, business men who were not afraid of failure, scientists who were not afraid of the truth, thinkers who were not afraid of progress, dreamers who were not afraid of action.   —Brooks Atkinson

To live without risk for me would be tantamount to death.
—Jacqueline Cochran

DANGER IS PART OF LIFE

It is the business of the future to be dangerous.
—Alfred North Whitehead

To achieve anything, you must be prepared to dabble on the boundary of disaster.   —Stirling Moss

He that will not sail till all dangers are over must never put to sea.
—Thomas Fuller

The fishermen know that the sea is dangerous and the storm terrible, but they have never found these dangers sufficient reason for remaining ashore.   —Vincent van Gogh

If we are intended for great ends, we are called to great hazards.
—John Henry Cardinal Newman

Liberty is always dangerous, but it is the safest thing we have.
—Harry Emerson Fosdick

As soon as there is life, there is danger.
—Ralph Waldo Emerson

One never finds anything perfectly pure and ... exempt from danger.
—Niccolo Machiavelli

He that is not in the war is not out of danger. —Anon.

WE MUST FACE RISKS AND DANGERS DIRECTLY

Danger itself is the best remedy for danger. —Anon.

A sharp knife cuts the quickest and hurts the least.
—Katharine Hepburn

It's only when we have nothing else to hold onto that we're willing to try something very audacious and scary.
—Sonia Johnson

Without danger we cannot get beyond danger. —Anon.

Constant exposure to dangers will breed contempt for them.
—Marcus Annaeus Seneca

Avoiding danger is no safer in the long run than outright exposure. The fearful are caught as often as the bold. —Helen Keller

All reformations seem formidable before they are attempted.
—Hannah Moore

What one has not experienced, one will never understand in print.
—Isadora Duncan

Doing is a quantum leap from imagining. —Barbara Sher

It is not manly to turn one's back on fortune. —Marcus Annaeus Seneca

Be bold, and mighty forces will come to your aid. —Basil King

A leader must face danger. He must take the risk and the blame, and the brunt of the storm.
—Herbert N. Casson

Fortune and love befriend the bold.
—Ovid

Our safety is not in blindness, but in facing our danger.
—J.C.F. von Schiller

Of course people are afraid. But honestly facing that fear, seeing it for what it is, is the only way of putting it to rest. —Harvey Fierstein

Unless you enter the tiger's den, you cannot take the cubs.
—Japanese proverb

All work of man is as the swimmer's: a vast ocean threatens to devour him; if he front it not bravely, it will keep its word. —Thomas Carlyle

They are surely to be esteemed the bravest spirits who, having the clearest sense of both the pains and pleasures of life, do not on that account shrink from danger. —Thucydides

PUTTING RISKS INTO PERSPECTIVE

If one is forever cautious, can one remain a human being?
—Aleksandr Solzhenitsyn

An individual dies . . . when, instead of taking risks and hurling himself toward being, he cowers within, and takes refuge there.   —E.M. Cioran

Few are they who have never had a chance to achieve happiness—and fewer those who have taken that chance.   —André Maurois

You have all eternity to be cautious in when you're dead. —Lois Platford

Without risk, faith is an impossibility.
—Søren Kierkegaard

Who dares nothing, need hope for nothing.   —J.C.F. von Schiller

If you're never scared or embarrassed or hurt, it means you never take any chances.   —Julia Sorel

It is not because things are difficult that we do not dare, it is because we do not dare that they are difficult.
—Marcus Annaeus Seneca

Only those who will risk going too far can possibly find out how far one can go.   —T.S. Eliot

In order to find the edge, you must risk going over the edge.
—Dennis Dugan

Make voyages. Attempt them. There's nothing else. —Tennessee Williams

The faster you go, the more chance there is of stubbing your toe, but the more chance you have of getting somewhere.   —Charles F. Kettering

Taking risks gives me energy.
—Jay Chiat

The torment of precautions often exceeds the dangers to be avoided. It is sometimes better to abandon one's self to destiny.
—Napoleon Bonaparte

What is necessary is never a risk.
—Cardinal de Retz

To render ourselves insensible to pain we must forfeit also the possibilities of happiness.   —John Lubbock

Take risks: if you win, you will be happy; if you lose, you will be wise.
—Anon.

WE CAN'T SUCCEED WITHOUT TAKING RISKS

Women must think strategically about creating ongoing pressure for change.   —Mary Baker Eddy

Anything I've ever done that ultimately was worthwhile . . . initially scared me to death.   —Betty Bender

Attempt the impossible in order to improve your work.   —Bette Davis

When you make a commitment to a relationship, you invest your attention and energy in it more profoundly because you now experience ownership of that relationship.
—Barbara De Angelis

The men who have done big things are those who were not afraid to attempt big things, who were not afraid to risk failure in order to gain success.   —B.C. Forbes

Security is not the meaning of my life. Great opportunities are worth the risks. —Shirley Hufstedler

I'll always push the envelope. To me, the ultimate sin in life is to be boring. I don't play it safe. —Cybil Shepherd

If the risk-reward ratio is right, you can make big money buying trouble. —Anon.

What isn't tried won't work. —Claude McDonald

It is better to die on your feet than to live on your knees! —Delores Ibarruri

Security is mostly superstition. It does not exist in nature. —Helen Keller

All great reforms require one to dare a lot to win a little. —William L. O'Neill

Competition can damage self-esteem, create anxiety, and lead to cheating and hurt feelings. But so can romantic love. —Mariah Burton Nelson

I am willing to put myself through anything; temporary pain or discomfort means nothing to me as long as I can see that the experience will take me to a new level. I am interested in the unknown, and the only path to the unknown is through breaking barriers, an often painful process. —Diana Nyad

If you limit your actions in life to things that nobody can possibly find fault with, you will not do much. —Charles Lutwidge Dodgson

Those lose least who have least to lose. —Rose O'Neil

The ambitious climb high and perilous stairs, and never care how to come down; the desire of rising hath swallowed up their fear of a fall. —Thomas Adams

He that would have fruit must climb the tree. —Thomas Fuller

Love, like a chicken salad or restaurant hash, must be taken with blind faith or it loses its flavor. —Helen Rowland

Every noble acquisition is attended with its risks; he who fears to encounter the one must not expect to obtain the other —Pietro Metastasio

Providence has hidden a charm in difficult undertakings, which is appreciated only by those who dare to grapple with them. —Anne-Sophie Swetchine

To get profit without risk, experience without danger and reward without work is as impossible as it is to live without being born. —A.P. Gouthey

The method of the enterprising is to plan with audacity and execute with vigor. —Christian Bovee

Great deeds are usually wrought at great risks. —Herodotus

Life is a risk. —Diane von Furstenberg

Only those who dare to fail greatly can ever achieve greatly. —Robert F. Kennedy

He that is overcautious will accomplish little.   —J.C.F. von Schiller

No one reaches a high position without daring.   —Publilius Syrus

Cadillacs are down at the end of the bat.   —Ralph Kiner,
when asked why he
didn't choke up
and hit "for average"

It is impossible to win the great prizes of life without running risks.
        —Theodore Roosevelt

You can't expect to hit the jackpot if you don't put a few nickels in the machine.   —Flip Wilson

Who dares nothing, need hope for nothing.   —J.C.F. von Schiller

Progress always involves risks. You can't steal second base and keep your foot on first.   —Frederick B. Wilcox

You can't catch trout with dry breeches.   —Spanish proverb

I don't think about risks much. I just do what I want to do. If you gotta go, you gotta go.   —Lillian Carter

Behold the turtle. He makes progress only when he sticks his neck out.
        —James Bryant Conant

Nothing ventured, nothing gained.
        —Anon.

Don't be afraid to take a big step if one is indicated. You can't cross a chasm in two small steps.
        —David Lloyd George

TAKE SMART—NOT CRAZY—RISKS

There is little place in the political scheme of things for an independent, creative personality, for a fighter. Anyone who takes that role must pay a price.   —Shirley Chisholm

Take calculated risks. That is quite different from being rash.
        —General George S. Patton

Valour lies just halfway between rashness and cowardice.
        —Miguel de Cervantes

I compensate for big risks by always doing my homework and being well-prepared. I can take on larger risks by reducing the overall risk.
        —Donna E. Shalala

Accept that all of us can be hurt, that all of us can—and surely will at times—fail. Other vulnerabilities, like being embarrassed or risking love, can be terrifying, too. I think we should follow a simple rule: if we can take the worst, take the risk.
        —Dr. Joyce Brothers

Every man has the right to risk his own life in order to preserve it. Has it ever been said that a man who throws himself out the window to escape a fire is guilty of suicide?
        —Jean-Jacques Rousseau

Courage is rarely reckless or foolish ... courage usually involves a highly realistic estimate of the odds that must be faced.   —Margaret Truman

You can no more win a war than you can win an earthquake.
—Jeannette Rankin

PARADOX: RISKS CAN PROVIDE SAFETY

It is the risk element which ensures security. Risk brings out the ingenuity and resourcefulness which ensure success.
—Robert Rawls

Entrepreneurs, in accepting risk, achieve security for all. In embracing change, they ensure social and economic stability.
—George Gilder

Those who cling to life die, and those who defy death live.
—Uyesugi Kenshin

And the trouble is, if you don't risk anything, you risk even more.
—Erica Jong

Danger can never by overcome without taking risks.
—Latin proverb

TAKING RISKS CAN BE INVIGORATING

The rewards go to the risk-takers, those who are willing to put their egos on the line and reach out to other people and to a richer, fuller life for themselves.
—Susan RoAne

Every minute of life I take a risk; it's part of the enjoyment.
—Otto Preminger

Everything is sweetened by risk.
—Alexander Smith

My favorite thing is to go where I have never gone.
—Diane Arbus

The power of habit and the charm of novelty are the two adverse forces which explain the follies of mankind.
—Maria De Beausacq

The soul should always stand ajar, ready to welcome the ecstatic experience.
—Emily Dickinson

Adventure is worthwhile in itself.
—Amelia Earhart

We may by our excessive prudence squeeze out of the life we are guarding so anxiously all the adventurous quality that makes it worth living.
—Randolph Bourne

A dreamer—you know—it's a mind that looks over the edges of things.
—Mary O'Hara

I feel very adventurous. There are so many doors to be opened, and I'm not afraid to look behind them.
—Elizabeth Taylor

Danger and delight grow on one stalk.
—English proverb

Life has no romance without risk.
—Sarah Doherty,
the first one-legged
person to scale Matthew McKinley

The moment somebody says "this is very risky" is the moment it becomes attractive to me.
—Kate Capshaw

One can never consent to creep when one feels an impulse to soar.
—Helen Keller

Prudence keeps life safe, but does not often make it happy.
—Samuel Johnson

Between two evils, I always picked the one I never tried before.
—Mae West

Life is either always a tightrope or a feather bed. Give me the tightrope.
—Edith Wharton

WORTHY VICTORIES

The greater the difficulty, the more glory in surmounting it.   —Epicurus

Victories that are cheap are cheap. Those only are worth having which come as the result of hard fighting.
—Henry Ward Beecher

The greater the obstacle, the more glory in overcoming it.   —Moliere

People who are born even-tempered, placid and untroubled—secure from violent passions or temptations to evil—those who have never needed to struggle all night with the angel to emerge lame but victorious at dawn, never become great saints.
—Eva Le Gallienne

The harder the conflict, the more glorious the triumph. What we obtain too cheaply, we esteem too lightly; 'tis dearness only that gives everything its value.   —Thomas Paine

The fiery trials through which we pass will light us down in honor or dishonor to the last generation.
—Abraham Lincoln

To conquer without risk is to triumph without glory.   —Pierre Corneille

There could be no honor in a sure success, but much might be wrested from a sure defeat.
—T.E. Lawrence
(Lawrence of Arabia)

ABOUT THE RISKS WE DON'T TAKE . . .

The follies which a man regrets most in his life are those which he didn't commit when he had the opportunity.
—Helen Rowland

There is no memory with less satisfaction than the memory of some temptation we resisted.
—James Branch Cabell

The only things one never regrets are one's mistakes.   —Oscar Wilde

The only things you regret are the things you don't do.
—Michael Curtiz

The defense force inside of us wants us to be cautious, to stay away from anything as intense as a new kind of action. Its job is to protect us, and it categorically avoids anything resembling danger. But it's often wrong.
—Barbara Sher

For of all sad words of tongues or pen the saddest are these: It might have been.
—John Greenleaf Whittier

Calculation never made a hero.
—John Henry Cardinal Newman

To play it safe is not to play.
　　　　　　　　—Robert Altman

Better hazard once than always be in
fear.　　　　　　　—Thomas Fuller

Sometimes We Must
Risk Everything

No one would have crossed the ocean
if he could have gotten off the ship in
the storm.　　　—Charles F. Kettering

Nine times out of ten the best thing
that can happen to a young man is to
be tossed overboard and compelled
to sink or swim.
　　　　　　　—James A. Garfield

Life is either a daring adventure or
nothing.　　　　　　—Helen Keller

When something does not insist
on being noticed, when we aren't
grabbed by the collar or struck on
the skull by a presence or an event,
we take for granted the very things
that most deserve our gratitude.
　　　　　　　　—Cynthia Ozick

There are those who have discovered
that fear is death in life, and have
willingly risked physical death and
loss of all that is considered valuable
in order to live in freedom.
　　　　　　—Virginia Burden Tower

I tore myself away from the safe comfort of certainties through my love
for truth; and truth rewarded me.
　　　　　　—Sylvia Ashton-Warner

In danger there is great power.
　　　　　　—Agnes Whistling Elk

Why not go out on a limb? Isn't that
where the fruit is?　　—Frank Scully

You might as well fall flat on your
face as lean over too far backward.
　　　　　　　　—James Thurber

Defensive strategy never has produced ultimate victory.
　　　—General Douglas MacArthur

We stand now where two roads
diverge. But unlike the roads in
Robert Frost's familiar poem, they
are not equally fair. The road we
have long been traveling is decep-
tively easy, a smooth superhighway
on which we progress with great
speed, but at its end lies disaster. The
other fork of the road—the one less
traveled by—offers our last, our only
chance to reach a destination that
assures the preservation of the earth.
　　　　　　　　—Rachel Carson

To gain that which is worth having,
it may be necessary to lose everything
else.　　　　　—Bernadette Devlin

We fail far more often by timidity
than by over-daring.
　　　　　　　—David Grayson

Nothing can resist a will which will
stake even existence upon its fulfillment.　　　　　—Benjamin Disraeli

Risk always brings its own rewards:
the exhilaration of breaking through,
of getting to the other side; the relief
of a conflict healed; the clarity when
a paradox dissolves.
　　　　　　　—Marilyn Ferguson

No guts, no glory.　　　　—Anon.

Sometimes I think we can tell how important it is to risk by how dangerous it is to do so.   —Sonia Johnson

He gets a good hold on the paintbrush, then confidently has the ladder removed.   —Roger Vaughan, speaking of Ted Turner

The important thing is this: to be able at any moment to sacrifice what we are for what we could become.   —Charles Du Bos

Better that we should die fighting than be outraged and dishonored. Better to die than to live in slavery.   —Emmeline Pankhurst

The fixed determination to have acquired the warrior soul, to either conquer or perish with honor, is the secret of victory.   —General George S. Patton

If man is not ready to risk his life, where is his dignity?   —André Malraux

GENERAL QUOTATIONS ABOUT RISKS

All serious daring starts from within.   —Eudora Welty

To avoid an occasion for our virtues is a worse degree of failure than to push forward pluckily and make a fall.   —Robert Louis Stevenson

Risk! Risk anything! . . . Do the hardest thing on earth for you. Act for yourself. Face the truth.   —Katherine Mansfield

Living at risk is jumping off the cliff and building your wings on the way down.   —Ray Bradbury

We owe something to extravagance, for thrift and adventure seldom go hand in hand.   —Jennie Jerome Churchill

There was never a place for her in the ranks of the terrible, slow army of the cautious. She ran ahead, where there were no paths.   —Dorothy Parker

I prefer liberty with danger to peace with slavery.   —The Palatine of Posnan

Do not follow where the path may lead. Go instead where there is no path and leave a trail.   —Muriel Strode

Be wary of the man who urges an action in which he himself incurs no risk.   —Joaquin Setanti

Creativity is inventing, experimenting, growing, taking risks, breaking rules, making mistakes, and having fun.   —Mary Lou Cook

Necessity is the mother of taking chances.   —Mark Twain

I am one of those people who can't help getting a kick out of life—even when it's a kick in the teeth.   —Polly Adler

Something must be left to chance; nothing is sure in a sea fight beyond all others.   —Horatio Nelson

You do not have to be superhuman
to do what you believe in.

> —Debbi Fields

We can only do what is possible for
us to do. But still it is good to know
what the impossible is.

> —Maria Irene Fornés

I love the challenge.   —Nancy Lopez

We must dare, and dare again, and
go on daring.

> —Georges Jacques Danton

Into the darkness they go, the wise
and the lovely.

> —Edna Saint Vincent Millay

Dare to be naive.

> —R. Buckminster Fuller

Courage

COURAGE IS THE FOUNDATION OF ALL OUR VIRTUES

I'm not funny. What I am is brave.
—Lucille Ball

Courage is the first of the human qualities because it is the quality which guarantees all the others.
—Sir Winston Churchill

Courage to be is the key to revelatory power of the feminist revolution.
—Mary Daly

Without courage, all other virtues lose their meaning.
—Sir Winston Churchill

A brave man is seldom unkind.
—Pretty-Shield,
Crow medicine woman

Success is never found. Failure is never fatal. Courage is the only thing.
—Sir Winston Churchill

Courage is the most important of all virtues, because without it we can't practice any other virtue with consistency.
—Maya Angelou

Courage is not simply one of the virtues, but the form of every virtue at the testing point.
—C.S. Lewis

Courage is the ladder on which all other virtues mount.
—Clare Boothe Luce

Courage is the basic virtue for everyone so long as he continues to grow, to move ahead.
—Rollo May

Courage is the greatest of all the virtues. Because if you haven't courage, you may not have an opportunity to use any of the others.
—Samuel Johnson

The courage of life is often a less dramatic spectacle than the courage of a final moment, but it is no less a magnificent mixture of triumph and tragedy. A man does what he must—in spite of personal consequences, in spite of obstacles and dangers and pressures—and that is the basis of all morality.
—John F. Kennedy

Nothing but courage can guide life.
—Vauvenargues

Wealth lost—something lost; Honor lost—much lost; Courage lost—all lost. —Old German proverb

BOLDNESS AND BRAVERY ARE VITAL QUALITIES

Why not go out on a limb? Isn't that where the fruit is? —Frank Scully

In politics, guts is all.
—Barbara Castle

In difficult situations, when hope seems feeble, the boldest plans are safest. —Livy

Courage is the best slayer—courage which attacketh, for in every attack there is the sound of triumph.
—Friedrich Nietzsche

He who finds Fortune on his side should go briskly ahead, for she is wont to favor the bold.
—Baltasar Gracian

That's what being young is all about. You have the courage and the daring to think that you can make a difference. —Ruby Dee

It is better by noble boldness to run the risk of being subject to half of the evils we anticipate than to remain in cowardly listlessness for fear of what might happen. —Herodotus

A decent boldness ever meets with friends. —Homer

In times of stress, be bold and valiant.
—Horace

The brave venture anything. —Anon.

It is the bold man who every time does best, at home or abroad.
—Homer

Attacking is the only secret. Dare and the world always yields; or if it beats you sometimes, dare it again, and it will succumb.
—William Makepeace Thackeray

You don't learn to hold your own in the world by standing on guard, but by attacking, and getting well-hammered yourself.
—George Bernard Shaw

Fortune helps the brave. —Virgil

Audacity augments courage; hesitation, fear. —Publilius Syrus

Fortune reveres the brave, and overwhelms the cowardly.
—Marcus Annaeus Seneca

God helps the brave.
—J.C.F. von Schiller

Fortune befriends the bold.
—John Dryden

Fortune and love favor the brave.
—Ovid

Fortune favors the audacious.
—Erasmus

Audacity has made kings.
—Prosper Jolyot de Crebillion

Audacity, more audacity, always audacity.
—Georges Jacques Danton

With audacity one can undertake anything. —Napoleon Bonaparte

Bravery and faith bring both material and spiritual rewards.
—Preston Bradley

He who loses wealth loses much; he who loses a friend loses more; but he who loses his courage loses all.
—Miguel de Cervantes

True miracles are created by men when they use the courage and intelligence that God gave them.
—Jean Anouilh

THE COURAGE TO FACE LIFE DIRECTLY

Tender-handed stroke a nettle, and it stings you for your pains;
Grasp it like a man of mettle, and it soft as silk remains.
—Thomas Fuller

Be content to stand in the light, and let the shadow fall where it will.
—Mary W. Stewart

Never forget that life can only be nobly inspired and rightly lived if you take it bravely and gallantly, as a splendid adventure in which you are setting out into an unknown country, to meet many a joy, to find many a comrade, to win and lose many a battle.
—Annie Besant

Life is the acceptance of responsibilities, or their evasion; it is a business of meeting obligations, or avoiding them.
—Ben Ames Williams

The superior man makes the difficulty to be overcome his first interest; success comes only later.
—Confucius

There were always in me, two women at least, one woman desperate and bewildered, who felt she was drowning and another who would leap into a scene, as upon a stage, conceal her true emotions because they were weaknesses, helplessness, despair, and present to the world only a smile, an eagerness, curiosity, enthusiasm, interest.
—Anaïs Nin

Facing it—always facing it—that's the way to get through. Face it!
—Joseph Conrad

If one is willing to do a thing he is afraid to do, he does not have to . . . face a situation fearlessly, and [if] there is no situation to face; it falls away of its own weight.
—Florence Scovel Shinn

He shall fare well who confronts circumstances aright.
—Plutarch

He that handles a nettle tenderly is soonest stung.
—Thomas Fuller

He who is afraid of every nettle should not piss in the grass.
—Thomas Fuller

Let us be brave in the face of adversity.
—Marcus Annaeus Seneca

Only one feat is possible: not to have run away.
—Dag Hammarskjold

There is something healthy and invigorating about direct action.
—Henry Miller

Confidence . . . is directness and courage in meeting the facts of life.
—John Dewey

The man who most vividly realizes
a difficulty is the man most likely to
overcome it.   —Joseph Farrell

I believe half the unhappiness in life
comes from people being afraid to go
straight at things.   —William J. Lock

No man will succeed unless he is
ready to face and overcome difficulties, and is prepared to assume
responsibilities.
          —William J.H. Boetcker

The fly that doesn't want to be swat-
ted is most secure when it lights on
the fly-swatter.
          —Georg Christoph Lichtenberg

The fly ought to be used as the symbol of impertinence and audacity, for
whilst all other animals shun man
more than anything else, and run
away even before he comes near them,
the fly lights upon his very nose.
          —Arthur Schopenhauer

All problems become smaller if you
don't dodge them, but confront them.
          —William F. Halsey

The best way out of a problem is
through it.   —Anon.

We cannot solve life's problems
except by solving them.
          —M. Scott Peck

The truth will set you free, but first it
will make you miserable.
          —James A. Garfield

Have the courage to face a difficulty
lest it kick you harder than you bargain for.   —Stanislaus

A great man is one who seizes the
vital issue in a complex question,
what we might call the jugular vein
of the whole organism, and spends
his energies upon that.
          —Joseph Rickaby

It is often wonderful how putting
down on paper a clear statement of a
case helps one to see, not perhaps the
way out, but the way in.
          —Arthur Christopher Benson

As a rule, what is out of sight disturbs men's minds more seriously
than what they see.   —Julius Caesar

Every difficulty slurred over will be a
ghost to disturb your repose later on.
          —Frédéric Chopin

Life is a battle in which we fall from
wounds we receive in running away.
          —William L. Sullivan

Fools, through false shame, conceal
their open wounds.   —Horace

Let us not look back in anger, nor
forward in fear, but around us in
awareness.   —James Thurber

It takes courage to know when you
ought to be afraid.
          —James A. Michener

However mean your life is, meet it and
live it; do not shun it and call it hard
names. It is not so bad as you are.
          —Henry David Thoreau

Genius is an infinite capacity for taking life by the scruff of the neck.
          —Katharine Hepburn

If you suppress grief too much, it can well redouble. —Moliere

Bad weather always looks worse through a window. —Anon.

The frontiers are not east or west, north or south, but wherever a man fronts a fact.
—Henry David Thoreau

Should I, after tea and cakes and ices, have the strength to force the moment to its crisis? —T.S. Eliot

Whatever you are trying to avoid won't go away until you confront it.
—Anon.

None are so blind as those who will not see. —Anon.

You don't change the course of history by turning the faces of portraits to the wall. —Jawaharlal Nehru

Soldiers, strike the foe in the face!
—Florus

Get in front of the ball, you won't get hurt. That's what you've got a chest for, young man. —John McGraw

Knowledge of sin is the beginning of salvation. —Marcus Annaeus Seneca

Courage is a quietness, not martial
    music made
Born of facing up to life, even when
    afraid.
—Emily Sargent Councilman

The great virtue in life is real courage that knows how to face facts and live beyond them. —D.H. Lawrence

Risk! Risk anything! . . . Do the hardest thing on earth for you. Act for yourself. Face the truth.
—Katherine Mansfield

The first rule is to keep an untroubled spirit. The second is to look things in the face and know them for what they are. —Marcus Aurelius

It is courage, courage, courage, that raises the blood of life to crimson splendor. Live bravely and present a brave front to adversity! —Horace

It is easy to be brave from a safe distance. —Aesop

THE COURAGE TO BE TRUTHFUL, AND TO FACE THE TRUTH

Defending the truth is not something one does out of a sense of duty or to allay guilt complexes, but is a reward in itself. —Simone de Beauvoir

No blame should attach to telling the truth. —Anita Brookner

The elegance of honesty needs no adornment. —Merry Browne

Truth is always exciting. Speak it, then; life is dull without it.
—Pearl S. Buck

You cannot weave truth on a loom of lies. —Suzette Haden Elgin

You're only as sick as your secrets.
—Anon.

You can't expect to win unless you know why you lose.
—Benjamin Lipson

525

It takes great courage to break with one's past history and stand alone.
—Marion Woodman

We run away all the time to avoid coming face to face with ourselves.
—Anon.

Awakening begins when a man realizes that he is going nowhere, and does not know where to go.
—Georges Gurdjieff

The naked truth is always better than the best-dressed lie.   —Ann Landers

If the word frankly or sincerely is not uttered in the first ten minutes—or let us speak openly—then you are not in the presence of a genuine businessman, and he will certainly go bankrupt.
—Françoise Mallet-Joris

The man with insight enough to admit his limitations comes nearest to perfection.   —Johann von Goethe

If I ever said in grief or pride,
I tired of honest things, I lied.
—Edna Saint Vincent Millay

Truth, that fair goddess who comes always with healing in her wings.
—Anne Shannon Monroe

The confession of evil works is the first beginning of good works.
—Saint Augustine

Admitting errors clears the score and proves you wiser than before.
—Arthur Guiterman

There is in the end no remedy but truth. It is the one course that cannot be evil.   —Ellis Peters

There is no power on earth more formidable than the truth.
—Margaret Lee Runbeck

If one cannot invent a really convincing lie, it is often better to stick to the truth.   —Angela Thirkell

An excuse is a lie guarded.
—Jonathan Swift

Honesty is the first chapter of the book of wisdom.
—Thomas Jefferson

Truth is the vital breath of Beauty;
Beauty the outward form of Truth.
—Grace Aguilar

The trouble with lying and deceiving is that their efficiency depends entirely upon a clear notion of the truth that the liar and deceiver wishes to hide.
—Hannah Arendt

There is at least one thing more brutal than the truth, and that is the consequence of saying less than the truth.
—Ti-Grace Atkinson

The real gift of love is self disclosure.
—John Powell

We only really face up to ourselves when we are afraid.
—Thomas Bernhard

EMOTIONAL, SPIRITUAL, AND MENTAL COURAGE

It takes a lot of courage to show your dreams to someone else.
—Erma Bombeck

It takes more courage to reveal insecurities than to hide them, more
strength to relate to people than to
dominate them, more "manhood"
to abide by thought-out principles
rather than blind reflex. Toughness is
in the soul and spirit, not in muscles
and an immature mind.
—Alex Karras

I have often though morality may
perhaps consist solely in the courage
of making a choice.   —Leon Blum

Introversion, at least if extreme,
is a sign of mental and spiritual
immaturity.   —Pearl S. Buck

The highest courage is to dare to
appear to be what one is.
—John Lancaster Spalding

It isn't for the moment you are stuck
that you need courage, but for the
long uphill climb back to sanity and
faith and security.
—Anne Morrow Lindbergh

True courage is not the brutal force
of vulgar heroes, but the firm resolve
of virtue and reason.
—Alfred North Whitehead

Greatness, in the last analysis, is
largely bravery—courage in escaping
from old ideas and old standards.
—James Harvey Robinson

The highest courage is not to be
found in the instinctive acts of men
who risk their lives to save a friend
or slay a foe; the physical fearlessness of a moment or an hour is not
to be compared with immolation of
months or years for the sake of wisdom or art.   —Joseph H. Odell

I have met brave women who are
exploring the outer edge of human
possibility, with no history to guide
them, and with a courage to make
themselves vulnerable that I find
moving beyond words.
—Gloria Steinem

Valour is nobleness of the mind.
—Anon.

Courage . . . is nothing less than the
power to overcome danger, misfortune, fear, injustice, while continuing
to affirm inwardly that life, with all
its sorrows, is good; that everything
is meaningful, even if in a sense
beyond our understanding; and that
there is always tomorrow.
—Dorothy Thompson

This is the art of courage: to see
things as they are and still believe
that the victory lies not with those
who avoid the bad, but those who
taste, in living awareness, every drop
of the good.   —Victoria Lincoln

God grant me the courage not to give
up what I think is right, even though
I think it is hopeless.
—Admiral Chester W. Nimitz

The great virtue in life is real courage
that knows how to face facts and live
beyond them.   —D.H. Lawrence

Physical courage, which despises all
danger, will make a man brave in
one way; and moral courage, which
despises all opinion, will make a man
brave in another. The former would
seem most necessary for the camp; the
latter for the council; but to constitute
a great man, both are necessary.
—Charles Caleb Colton

Courage is the power to let go of the familiar. —Raymond Lindquist

Valor is stability, not of legs and arms, but of courage and the soul.
—Michel de Montaigne

One of man's finest qualities is described by the simple word "guts"—the ability to take it. If you have the discipline to stand fast when your body wants to run, if you can control your temper and remain cheerful in the face of monotony or disappointment, you have "guts" in the soldiering sense.
—Colonel John S. Roosman

Whatever course you decide upon, there is always someone to tell you that you are wrong. There are always difficulties arising which tempt you to believe that your critics are right. To map out a course of action and follow it to an end requires . . . courage. —Ralph Waldo Emerson

COURAGE AND CONVICTION

Courage is more than standing for a firm conviction. It includes the risk of questioning that conviction.
—Julian Weber Gordon

The hallmark of courage in our age of conformity is the capacity to stand on one's convictions—not obstinately or defiantly (these are gestures of defensiveness, not courage) nor as a gesture of retaliation, but simply because these are what one believes.
—Rollo May

Courage is what it takes to stand up and speak; courage is also what it takes to sit down and listen. —Anon.

COURAGE IN REACTING TO DIFFICULT SITUATIONS

The greatest test of courage on earth is to bear defeat without losing heart.
—Robert G. Ingersoll

Courage is to take hard knocks like a man when occasion calls. —Plautus

You don't develop courage by being happy in your relationships everyday. You develop it by surviving difficult times and challenging adversity.
—Barbara De Angelis

This is courage . . . to bear unflinchingly what heaven sends.
—Euripides

Courage, in the final analysis, is nothing but an affirmative answer to the shocks of existence.
—Dr. Kurt Goldstein

Courage is a perfect sensibility of the measure of danger, and a mental willingness to endure it.
—General William T. Sherman

To have courage for whatever comes in life—everything lies in that.
—Teresa of Avila

To accept whatever comes, regardless of the consequences, is to be unafraid.
—John Cage

The Courage of the Minority

The test of courage comes when we are in the minority.
—Ralph W. Sockman

One man with courage makes a majority.   —Andrew Jackson

Courage and Happiness

Many women miss their greatest chance of happiness through a want of courage in a decisive moment.
—Winifred Gordon

We must have the courage to be happy.   —Henri Frederic Amiel

There is a courage of happiness as well as a courage of sorrow.
—Maurice Maeterlinck

Happy the man who ventures boldly to defend what he holds dear.
—Ovid

All happiness depends on courage and work.   —Honore de Balzac

There is nothing in the world so much admired as a man who knows how to bear unhappiness with courage.
—Marcus Annaeus Seneca

We must have courage to bet on our ideas, on the calculated risk, and to act. Everyday living requires courage if life is to be effective and bring happiness.   —Maxwell Maltz

Courage and Love

Faint heart never won fair lady.
—Miguel de Cervantes

The last thing a woman will consent to discover in a man whom she loves, or on whom she simply depends, is want of courage.   —Joseph Conrad

None but the brave deserve the fair.
—John Dryden

Fortune and love favor the brave.
—Ovid

The bravest are the tenderest.
The loving are the daring.
—Henry Wadsworth Longfellow

Courage and Warfare

The weapon of the brave is in his heart.   —Anon.

The guts carry the feet, not the feet the guts.   —Miguel de Cervantes

I am not afraid of a fight; I have to do my duty, come what may.
—Thérèse of Lisieux

War is fear cloaked in courage.
—General William Westmoreland

A bold heart is half the battle.
—Anon.

Courage in danger is half the battle.
—Plautus

A man of courage never wants weapons.   —Anon.

A brave arm makes a short sword long. —Anon.

Courage which goes against military expediency is stupidity, or, if it is insisted upon by a commander, irresponsibility.
—Field Marshal Erwin Rommel

LIVING CAN TAKE MORE COURAGE THAN DYING

There is, in addition to a courage with which men die, a courage by which men must live.
—John F. Kennedy

Where life is more terrible than death, it is the truest valor to dare to live.
—Sir Thomas Browne

The courage we desire and prize is not the courage to die decently, but to live manfully. —Thomas Carlyle

Often the test of courage is not to die, but to live.
—Conte Vittorio Alfieri

He who has the courage to laugh is almost as much the master of the world as he who is ready to die.
—Giacomo Leopardi

Life shrinks or expands in proportion to one's courage. —Anaïs Nin

Only those are fit to live who are not afraid to die.
—General Douglas MacArthur

Sometimes even to live is an act of courage. —Marcus Annaeus Seneca

To say yes, you have to sweat and roll up your sleeves and plunge both hands into life up to the elbows. It is easy to say no, even if saying no means death. —Jean Anouilh

Have the courage to live. Anyone can die. —Robert Cody

WE CAN'T SUCCEED WITHOUT COURAGE

Because a fellow has failed once or twice or a dozen times, you don't want to set him down as a failure till he's dead or loses his courage—and that's the same thing.
—George Horace Lorimer

What is more mortifying than to feel that you have missed the plum for want of courage to shake the tree?
—Logan Pearsall Smith

Yesterday I dared to struggle. Today I dare to win. —Bernadette Devlin

To persevere, trusting in what hopes he has, is courage. The coward despairs.
—Euripides

It takes vision and courage to create— it takes faith and courage to prove.
—Owen D. Young

Whatever you do, you need courage. . . . To map out a course of action and follow it to an end requires some of the same courage which a soldier needs. —Ralph Waldo Emerson

Who dares nothing, need hope for nothing. —J.C.F. von Schiller

Have the courage of your desire.
—George R. Gissing

To see what is right, and not do it, is want of courage. —Confucius

No great thing comes to any man unless he has courage.
—Cardinal James Gibbons

Great things are done more through courage than through wisdom.
—German proverb

Courage permits the caliber of performance to continue at its peak, until the finish line is crossed.
—Stuart Walker

Failure is only postponed success as long as courage "coaches" ambition. The habit of persistence is the habit of victory. —Herbert Kaufman

Courage and perseverance have a magical talisman, before which difficulties disappear, and obstacles vanish into air. —John Quincy Adams

There are a lot of fellas with all the ability it takes to play in the major leagues, but . . . they always get stuck in the minor leagues because they haven't got the guts to make the climb.
—Cookie Lavagetto

Where there is a brave man, in the thickest of the fight, there is the post of honor. —Henry David Thoreau

It takes as much courage to have tried and failed as it does to have tried and succeeded.
—Anne Morrow Lindbergh

You will never do anything in this world without courage.
—James Lane Allen

Whenever you see a successful business, someone once made a courageous decision. —Peter Drucker

Courage to start and willingness to keep everlasting at it are the requisites for success.
—Alonzo Newton Benn

One of the biggest factors in success is the courage to undertake something.
—James A. Worsham

WITHOUT COURAGE, ABILITY AND TALENT WON'T BE ENOUGH

Everyone has a talent. What is rare is the courage to follow that talent to the dark place where it leads.
—Erica Jong

The world is not perishing for the want of clever or talented or well-meaning men. It is perishing for the want of men of courage and resolution. —Robert J. McCracken

Talent is helpful in writing, but guts are absolutely necessary.
—Jessamyn West

Knowledge without courage is sterile.
—Baltasar Gracian

To create one's own world in any of the arts takes courage.
—Georgia O'Keefe

Courage is the thing. All goes if courage goes. —Sir James M. Barrie

We Must Have the Courage to Begin

It's weak and despicable to go on wanting things and not trying to get them. —Joanna Field

How many feasible projects have miscarried through despondency, and been strangled in their birth by a cowardly imagination? —Jeremy Collier

It is brave to be involved. —Gwendolyn Brooks

One of the biggest factors in success is the courage to undertake something. —James A. Worsham

When it comes to betting on yourself ... you're a chicken-livered coward if you hesitate. —B.C. Forbes

What would life be if we had no courage to attempt anything? —Vincent van Gogh

Be courageous! ... I have seen many depressions in business. Always America has come out stronger and more prosperous. Be as brave as your fathers before you. Have faith! Go forward. —Thomas A. Edison

Dare to begin! He who postpones living rightly is like the rustic who waits for the river to run out before he crosses. —Horace

Nothing ventured, nothing gained. —Anon.

The brave venture anything. —Anon.

The difference between getting somewhere and nowhere is the courage to make an early start. —Charles M. Schwab

Life is to be entered upon with courage. —Alexis de Tocqueville

We ought to face our destiny with courage. —Friedrich Nietzsche

You can surmount the obstacles in your path if you are determined, courageous and hardworking. . . . Do not fear to pioneer, to venture down new paths of endeavor. —Ralph J. Bunche

The great man is the man who does a thing for the first time. —Alexander Smith

Imposing limitations on yourself is cowardly because it protects you from having to try, and perhaps failing. —Vladimir Zworykin

What you can do, or dream you can do, begin it; boldness has genius, power and magic in it. —Johann von Goethe

We need the courage to start and continue what we should do, and courage to stop what we shouldn't do. —Richard L. Evans

Caution, Prudence, Safety

Prudence which degenerates into timidity is very seldom the path to safety. —Viscount Cecil

He that is overcautious will accomplish little. —J.C.F. von Schiller

532

We can easily become as much slaves to precaution as we can to fear.
—Randolph Bourne

To the timid and hesitating everything is impossible because it seems so.
—Sir Walter Scott

Do not be too timid and squeamish. . . . All life is an experiment. The more experiments you make, the better.
—Ralph Waldo Emerson

Courage is rarely reckless or foolish . . . courage usually involves a highly realistic estimate of the odds that must be faced.   —Margaret Truman

Valour lies just halfway between rashness and cowardice.
—Miguel de Cervantes

COURAGE AND FEAR

When you're my size in the pros, fear is a sign that you're not stupid.
—Jerry Levias

Keep your fears to yourself, but share your courage with others.
—Robert Louis Stevenson

Courage leads starward, fear toward death.   —Marcus Annaeus Seneca

Go forth to meet the shadowy Future without fear and with a manly heart.
—Henry Wadsworth Longfellow

Fate loves the fearless.
—James Russell Lowell

There is no such thing as bravery, only degrees of fear.
—John Wainwright

Courage is a peculiar kind of fear.
—Charles Kennedy

Courage is fear that has said its prayers.   —Dorothy Bernard

Courage is fear holding on a minute longer.   —General George S. Patton

Courage is the ability to solve problems realistically in the presence of fear.   —Stuart Walker

Courage is resistance to fear, mastery of fear—not absence of fear.
—Mark Twain

Courage is . . . the knowledge of how to fear what ought to be feared and how not to fear what ought not to be feared.   —David Ben-Gurion

Courage is knowing what not to fear.
—Plato

Courage is the right disposition toward fear.   —Anon.

Courage is a scorner of things which inspire fear.
—Marcus Annaeus Seneca

We must constantly build dykes of courage to hold back the flood of fear.
—Martin Luther King, Jr.

Courage is never letting your actions be influenced by your fears.
—Arthur Koestler

COWARDICE

Cowards cannot see that their greatest safety lies in dauntless courage.
—Johann Kaspar Lavater

A coward turns away, but a brave man's choice is danger. —Euripides

Cowardice is the mother of cruelty. —Michel de Montaigne

Optimism and self-pity are the positive and negative poles of modern cowardice. —Cyril Connolly

Cowards die many times before their deaths; the valiant never taste of death but once. —William Shakespeare

To say a person is a coward has no more meaning than to say he is lazy: It simply tells us that some vital potentiality is unrealized or blocked. —Rollo May

There are at least two kinds of cowards. One kind always lives with himself, afraid to face the world. The other kind lives with the world, afraid to face himself. —Roscoe Snowden

There is a time when to avoid trouble is to store up trouble, and when to seek for a lazy and a cowardly peace is to court a still greater danger. —William Barclay

To know what is right and not do it is the worst cowardice. —Confucius

Spiritual cowardice is not only weakness but wickedness. —J.B. Gambrell

The most mortifying infirmity in human nature . . . is, perhaps, cowardice. —Charles Lamb

Men perish by the sword, cowards by disease. —Phillippus

Between cowardice and despair, valour is gendered. —John Donne

If you knew how cowardly your enemy is, you would slap him. —Edgar Watson Howe

Bravery is the knowledge of the cowardice in the enemy. —Edgar Watson Howe

Any coward can fight a battle when he's sure of winning. —George Eliot

The coward despairs. —Euripides

Cowardice, as distinguished from panic, is almost always simply a lack of ability to suspend the functioning of the imagination. —Ernest Hemingway

The only cowards are sinners; fighting the fight is all. —John G. Neihardt

All men would be cowards if they durst. —John Wilmot, Earl of Rochester

That cowardice is incorrigible which the love of power cannot overcome. —Charles Caleb Colton

WE CAN'T BE BRAVE IF WE'RE NOT AFRAID

Courage is doing what you're afraid to do. There can be no courage unless you're scared. —Eddie Rickenbacker

Courage is being scared to death . . . and saddling up anyway. —John Wayne

You look at a guy who's being brave. He's afraid, or he wouldn't be brave. If he isn't afraid, he's stupid.
—Joe Torre

To fight a bull when you are not scared is nothing. And to not fight a bull when you are scared is nothing. But to fight a bull when you are scared is something. —Anon.

Being "brave" means doing or facing something frightening. . . . Being "fearless" means being without fear.
—Penelope Leach

It takes courage to know when you ought to be afraid.
—James A. Michener

Everyone thought I was bold and fearless and even arrogant, but inside I was always quaking.
—Katharine Hepburn

Perfect courage means doing unwitnessed what we would be capable of with the world looking on.
—Francois de La Rochefoucauld

Fear is the single strongest motivating force in our lives. . . . The more frightened you become, the better your chances of achieving success.
—Lois Korey

Bravery is the capacity to perform properly even when scared half to death. —General Omar N. Bradley
This morning I threw up at a board meeting. I was sure the cat was out of the bag, but no one seemed to think anything about it; apparently it's quite common for people to throw up at board meetings. —Jane Wagner

I'm a real pussycat—with an iron tail.
—Rona Barrett

Bravery is being the only one who knows you're afraid.
—Franklin P. Jones

COURAGE CAN COME FROM NECESSITY

Necessity makes even the timid brave.
—Sallust

Necessity does the work of courage.
—Nicholas Murray Butler

I became more courageous by doing the very things I needed to be courageous for—first, a little, and badly. Then, bit by bit, more and better. Being avidly—sometimes annoyingly—curious and persistent about discovering how others were doing what I wanted to do. —Audre Lorde

When it comes to the pinch, human beings are heroic. —George Orwell

Many become brave when brought to bag. —Norwegian proverb

Courage mounteth with occasion.
—William Shakespeare

When you have no choice, mobilize the spirit of courage.
—Jewish proverb

DREAMS FUEL COURAGE

Courage is sustained by calling up anew the vision of the goal.
—A.G. Sertillanges

Women have to summon up courage
to fulfill dormant dreams.
—Alice Walker

Courage is like love, it must have
hope for nourishment.
—Napoleon Bonaparte

Optimism is the foundation of courage.
—Nicholas Murray Butler

COWARDICE CAN CREATE COURAGE

I would often be a coward, but for
the shame of it.   —Ralph Connor

At the bottom of a good deal of
bravery . . . lurks a miserable cowardice. Men will face powder and steel
because they cannot face public opinion.   —Edwin H. Chapin

We would be cowards, if we had
courage enough.   —Thomas Fuller

A coward's fear can make a coward
valiant.   —Thomas Fuller

OTHER SOURCES OF COURAGE

Courage is as often the outcome of
despair as of hope; in the one case
we have nothing to lose, in the other
everything to gain.
—Diane De Pottiers

Despair gives courage to a coward.
—Anon.

No one has yet computed how many
imaginary triumphs are silently celebrated by people each year to keep
up their courage. —Henry S. Haskins

I'm not afraid of too many things,
and I got that invincible kind of attitude from my father. —Queen Latifah

If we survive danger, it steels our
courage more than anything else.
—Reinhold Niebuhr
Courage is the fear of being thought
a coward.   —Horace Smith

How, then, find the courage for
action? By slipping a little into unconsciousness, spontaneity, instinct which
holds one to the earth and dictates
the relatively good and useful. . . . By
accepting the human condition more
simply, and candidly, by dreading
troubles less, calculating less, hoping
more.   —Henri Frederic Amiel

It takes courage to live—courage and
strength and hope and humor. And
courage and strength and hope and
humor have to be bought and paid
for with pain and work and prayers
and tears.   —Jerome P. Fleishman

Courage that grows from constitution often forsakes a man . . . courage
which arises from a sense of duty acts
in a uniform manner.
—Joseph Addison

He who knows how to suffer everything can dare everything.
—Vauvenargues

Courage does not always march
to airs blown by a bugle, it is not
always wrought out of the fabric
ostentation wears.
—Frances Rodman

We learn courageous action by going
forward whenever fear urges us back.
—David Seabury

The paradox of courage is that a man must be a little careless of his life in order to keep it. —G.K. Chesterton

All men are afraid in battle. The coward is the one who lets his fear overcome his sense of duty. Duty is the essence of manhood.
—General George S. Patton

OTHER DEFINITIONS OF COURAGE

Courage isrequired not only in a person's occasional crucial decision for his own freedom, but in the little hour-to-hour decisions which place the bricks in the structure of his building of himself into a person who acts with freedom and responsibility.
—Rollo May

Courage does not consist in calculation, but in fighting against chances.
—John Henry Cardinal Newman

Courage is its own reward. —Plautus

Courage is the price that life exacts for granting peace. —Amelia Earhart

Courage is a kind of salvation.
—Plato

Courage is grace under pressure.
—Ernest Hemingway

Courage is the lovely virtue—the rib of Himself that God sent down to His children. —Sir James M. Barrie

Courage is the integrating strength that causes one to overcome tragedy.
—Eugene E. Brussell

Courage is almost a contradiction in terms. It means a strong desire to live taking the form of readiness to die.
—G.K. Chesterton

Courage is the virtue which champions the cause of right. —Cicero

Courage is generosity of the highest order, for the brave are prodigal of the most precious things.
—Charles Caleb Colton

Courage is clearly a readiness to risk self-humiliation. —Nigel Dennis

Courage is fire, and bullying is smoke.
—Benjamin Disraeli

Courage consists of the power of self-recovery. —Ralph Waldo Emerson

Courage is a virtue only so far as it is directed by prudence.
—Francois de Fenelon

Courage is a quality so necessary for maintaining virtue that it is always respected even when it is associated with vice. —Samuel Johnson

Courage is the footstool of the Virtues, upon which they stand.
—Robert Louis Stevenson

Courage is to feel the daily daggers of relentless steel and keep on living.
—Douglas Malloch

Courage is what preserves our liberty, safety, life, and our homes and parents, our country and children. Courage comprises all things.
—Plautus

Courage is a peculiar kind of fear.
—Charles Kennedy

GENERAL QUOTATIONS
ABOUT COURAGE

There is plenty of courage among us for the abstract, but not for the concrete. —Helen Keller

Every man has his own courage, and is betrayed because he seeks in himself the courage of other persons.
—Ralph Waldo Emerson

If we have the courage and tenacity of our forebears, who stood firmly like a rock against the lash of slavery, we shall find a way to do for our day what they did for theirs.
—Mary McLeod Bethune

If you are brave too often, people will come to expect it of you.
—Mignon McLaughlin

The best protection any woman can have . . . is courage.
—Elizabeth Cady Stanton

Valor is a gift. Those having it never know for sure if they have it till the test comes. And those having it in one test never know for sure if they will have it when the next test comes.
—Carl Sandburg

Until the day of his death, no man can be sure of his courage.
—Jean Anouilh

Among wellborn spirits courage does not depend on age.
—Pierre Corneille

Courage can't see around corners, but goes around them anyway.
—Mignon McLaughlin

Freedom is not for the timid.
—Vijaya Lakshmi Pandit

Courage easily finds its own eloquence.
—Plautus

In true courage there is always an element of choice, of an ethical choice, and of anguish, and also of action and deed. There is always a flame of spirit in it, a vision of some necessity higher than oneself. —Brenda Ueland

But screw your courage to the sticking place and we'll not fail.
—William Shakespeare

Courage is always the surest wisdom.
—Wilfred Grenfell

Courage is very important. Like a muscle, it is strengthened by use.
—Ruth Gordon

There are some women who seem to be born without fear, just as there are people who are born without the ability to feel pain. . . . Providence appears to protect such women, maybe out of astonishment.
—Margaret Atwood

On many of the great issues of our time, men have lacked wisdom because they have lacked courage.
—William Benton

Catch courage. —Carolyn Heilbrun

If you are scared to go to the brink, you are lost. —John Foster Dulles

538

It takes courage to lead a life. Any life.
—Erica Jong

Nothing is as valuable to a man as
courage.   —Terence

I'd rather give my life than be afraid
to give it.   —Lyndon B. Johnson

The only courage that matters is the
kind that gets you from one moment
to the next.   —Mignon McLaughlin

Courage ought to have eyes as well
as arms.   —H.G. Bohn

GOD MATCHES OUR PROBLEMS
TO OUR CAPABILITIES

Sorrow is a fruit. God does not allow
it to grow on a branch that is too
weak to bear it.   —Victor Hugo

The will of God will not take you
where the grace of God cannot keep
you.   —Anon.

Act, and God will act. —Joan of Arc

So when the crisis is upon you,
remember that God, like a trainer of
wrestlers, has matched you with a
tough and stalwart antagonist . . . that
you may prove a victor at the Great
Games.   —Epictetus

Act boldly and unseen forces will
come to your aid.
—Dorothea Brande

What God expects us to attempt, He
also enables us to achieve.
—Stephen Olford

God gave burdens, also shoulders.
—Yiddish proverb

With them I gladly shared my all and
learned the great truth that where
God guides, He provides.
—Frank N.D. Buchman

The Bible tells us that a sparrow does
not fall without God's notice. I know
he will help us meet our responsibilities through his guidance.
—Michael Cardone, Sr.

Leap, and the net will appear.
—Julie Cameron

Cowards falter, but danger is often
overcome by those who nobly dare.
—Queen Elizabeth I

God gives us always strength enough,
and sense enough, for everything He
wants us to do.   —John Ruskin

OUR ABILITIES WILL ALWAYS BE
EQUAL TO OUR CHALLENGES

Fatalism is a lazy man's way of
accepting the inevitable.
—Natalie Clifford Barney

In this unbelievable universe in which
we live, there are no absolutes. Even
parallel lines, reaching into infinity,
meet somewhere yonder.
—Pearl S. Buck

Instead of looking at life as a narrow-
ing funnel, we can see it ever widening to choose the things we want to
do, to take the wisdom we've learned
and create something.

—Liz Carpenter

Nothing befalls a man except what is in his nature to endure.
—Marcus Aurelius

Life only demands from you the strength you possess.
—Dag Hammarskjold

Everyone will be taxed according to his means. —J.C.F. von Schiller

I discovered I always have choices and sometimes it's only a choice of attitude. —Judith M. Knowlton

The burden is equal to the horse's strength. —Talmud

Experience shows that exceptions are as true as rules.
—Edith Ronald Mirrielees

What we call reality is an agreement that people have arrived at to make their lives more livable.
—Louise Nevelson

All we are asked to bear we can bear. That is a law of the spiritual life. The only hindrance to the working of this law, as of all benign laws, is fear.
—Elizabeth Goudge

When it comes to the pinch, human beings are heroic. —George Orwell

The incurable ills are the imaginary ills —Marie von Ebner-Eschenbach

However confused the scene of our life appears, however torn we may be who now do face that scene, it can be faced, and we can go on to be whole.
—Muriel Rukeyser

A change of heart is the essence of all other change, and it has brought about me a reeducation of the mind.
—Emmeline Pethick-Lawrence

We Can Do Whatever We Have to Do

The human spirit is stronger than anything that can happen to it.
—George. C. Scott

What one has to do usually can be done. —Eleanor Roosevelt

Man performs and engenders so much more than he can or should have to bear. That's how he finds that he can bear anything.
—William Faulkner

If you have enough fantasies, you're ready, in the event that something happens. —Sheila Ballantyne

The peril of the hour moved the British to tremendous exertions, just as always in a moment of extreme danger things can be done which had previously been thought impossible. Mortal danger is an effective antidote for fixed ideas.
—Field Marshal Erwin Rommel

What We Need Is Already within Us

We all carry it within us: supreme strength, the fullness of wisdom, unquenchable joy. It is never thwarted, and cannot be destroyed.
—Huston Smith

Within us all there are wells of thought and dynamos of energy which are not suspected until emergencies arise. Then oftentimes we find that it is comparatively simple to double or triple our former capacities and to amaze ourselves by the results achieved.　　—Thomas J. Watson

The spirit of man is an inward flame; a lamp the world blows upon but never puts out.　　—Margot Asquith

We have what we seek. It is there all the time, and if we give it time, it will make itself known to us.
　　　　　　—Thomas Merton

Truth is not introduced into the individual from without, but was within him all the time.
　　　　　　—Søren Kierkegaard

Nature arms each man with some faculty which enables him to do easily some feat impossible to any other.
　　　　　　—Ralph Waldo Emerson

Our Problems Themselves Contain the Resources to Overcome Them

When we know what we want to prove, we go out and find our facts. They are always there.
　　　　　　—Pearl S. Buck

Nature reacts not only to physical disease, but also to moral weakness; when the danger increases, she gives us greater courage.
　　　　　　—Johann von Goethe

rouble creates a capacity to handle it.
　　　—Oliver Wendell Holmes, Jr.

Trouble, like the hill ahead, straightens out when you advance upon it.
　　　　　　—Marcelene Cox

In the darkest hour the soul is replenished and given strength to continue and endure.　　—Heart Warrior Chosa

Our energy is in proportion to the resistance it meets. We attempt nothing great but from a sense of the difficulties we have to encounter; we persevere in nothing great but from a pride in overcoming them.
　　　　　　—William Hazlitt

We shall draw from the heart of suffering itself the means of inspiration and survival.
　　　　　　—Sir Winston Churchill

Exigencies create the necessary ability to meet and conquer them.
　　　　　　—Wendell Philips

The moment one definitely commits oneself, then Providence moves too. All sorts of things occur to help that would never otherwise have occurred. A stream of events issues from the decision, raising unforeseen incidents and meetings and material assistance, which no man could have dreamt would have come his way.
　　　　　　—W.H. Murray

In forty hours I shall be in battle, with little information, and on the spur of the moment will have to make the most momentous decisions. But I believe that one's spirit enlarges with responsibility and that, with God's help, I shall make them, and make them right.
　　　　　　—General George S. Patton

Ignorance

We Musn't Feign Ignorance

Truth can be outraged by silence quite as cruelly as by speech.
—Amelia Barr

You can do one of two things; just shut up, which is something I don't find easy, or learn an awful lot very fast, which is what I tried to do.
—Jane Fonda

Ignorance is no excuse—it's the real thing.
—Irene Peter

My doctrine is this, that if we see cruelty or wrong that we have the power to stop, and do nothing, we make ourselves sharers in the guilt.
—Anna Sewell

Whenever two good people argue over principles, they are both right.
—Marie von Ebner-Eschenbach

Not Knowing That Something Is "Impossible" Can Be a Blessing

Progress results only from the fact that there are some men and women who refuse to believe that what they know to be right cannot be done.
—Russell W. Davenport

The Wright brothers flew through the smoke screen of impossibility.
—Dorothea Brande

Most of the basic truths of life sound absurd at first hearing.
—Elizabeth Goudge

The good thing about being young is that you are not experienced enough to know you cannot possibly do the things you are doing. —Gene Brown

The young do not know enough to be prudent, and therefore they attempt the impossible—and achieve it, generation after generation.
—Pearl S. Buck

Sometimes it proves the highest understanding not to understand.
—Baltasar Gracian

Aerodynamically, the bumblebee shouldn't be able to fly, but the bumble bee doesn't know it so it goes on flying anyway. —Mary Kay Ash

Lack of understanding is a great power. Sometimes it enables men to conquer the world. —Anatole France

An impossibility does not disturb us until its accomplishment shows what fools we were. —Henry S. Haskins

Once you start asking questions, innocence is gone. —Mary Astor

God may have been waiting for centuries for somebody ignorant enough of the impossible to do that thing.
—Dr. J.A. Holmes

To some people, the impossible is impossible.
—Elizabeth Asquith Bibesco

Some of my best friends are illusions. Been sustaining me for years.
—Sheila Ballantyne

Great things are accomplished by those who do not feel the impotence of man. This . . . is a precious gift.
—Valery

At first people refuse to believe that a strange new thing can be done, then they begin to hope it can be done, then they see it can be done—then it is done and all the world wonders why it was not done centuries ago.
—Frances Hodgson Burnett

Ordinary people believe only in the possible. Extraordinary people visualize not what is possible or probable, but rather what is impossible. And by visualizing the impossible, they begin to see it as possible.
—Cherie Carter-Scott

Success is often achieved by those who don't know that failure is inevitable. —Coco Chanel

It is our duty as men and women to proceed as though limits to our abilities do not exist.
—Pierre Teilhard de Chardin

So long as we think dugout canoes are the only possibility—all that is real or can be real—we will never see the ship, we will never feel the free wind blow. —Sonia Johnson

Men are always averse to enterprises in which they foresee difficulties.
—Niccolo Machiavelli

The greatest wisdom often consists in ignorance. —Baltasar Gracian

Not Knowing How to Do Something Can Be a Gift

Painting is easy when you don't know how, but very difficult when you do.
—Edgar Degas

To measure up to all that is demanded of him, a man must overestimate his capacities. —Johann von Goethe

Every true genius is bound to be naive.
—J.C.F. von Schiller

To write a good love letter you ought to begin without knowing what you mean to say, and to finish without knowing what you have written.
—Jean-Jacques Rousseau

Today, if you are not confused, you are not thinking clearly. —Irene Peter

When we are not sure, we are alive.
—Graham Greene

FAMOUS PEOPLE WHO ADMITTED THEY SOMETIMES DIDN'T KNOW WHAT THEY WERE DOING

Basic research is what I'm doing when I don't know what I'm doing.
—Wernher von Braun

I have always wanted to be somebody, but I see now I should have been more specific.   —Lily Tomlin

I don't know what I'm doing. I don't know what actors do.
—Geraldine Page

In baseball, you don't know nothing.
—Yogi Berra

I know it was wonderful, but I don't know how I did it.
—Sir Laurence Olivier,
after a brilliant performance

What makes a good pinch hitter? I wish the hell I knew.
—Bobby Mercer

We couldn't possibly know where it would lead, but we knew it had to be done.   —Betty Friedan,
on the Women's Movement

People think the Beatles know what's going on. We don't. We're just doing it.   —John Lennon

I don't know what humor is.
—Will Rogers

Unprovided with original learning, unformed in the habits of thinking, unskilled in the arts of composition, I resolved to write a book.
—Edward Gibbon

When Columbus started out he didn't know where he was going, when he got there he didn't know where he was, and when he got back he didn't know where he had been.   —Anon.

All I know about humor is that I don't know anything about it.
—Fred Allen

It is a sign of strength, not of weakness, to admit that you don't know all the answers. —John P. Loughrane

WE LEARN AS WE GO ALONG

I learn by going where I have to go.
—Theodore Roethke

Whatever people in general do not understand, they are always prepared to dislike; the incomprehensible is always the obnoxious.
—L.E. Landon

One learns by doing the thing; for though you think you know it, you have no certainty until you try.
—Sophocles

No one knows what he can do until he tries.   —Publilius Syrus

I don't know much about being a
millionaire, but I'll bet I'd be darling
at it.   —Dorothy Parker

All decisions are made on insufficient
evidence.   —Rita Mae Brown

Education is learning what you didn't
even know you didn't know.
                    —Daniel Boorstin

Intelligence is really a kind of taste:
taste in ideas.   —Susan Sontag

Curiosity is the one thing invincible
in Nature.   —Freya Stark

The true test of character is . . . how
we behave when we don't know what
to do.   —John Holt

Nothing in this world can one imagine beforehand, not the least thing.
Everything is made up of so many
unique particulars that cannot be
foreseen.   —Rainer Maria Rilke

The work will teach you how to do it.
                    —Estonian proverb

Life is my college. May I graduate
well, and earn some honors!
                 —Louisa May Alcott

Living is a form of not being sure,
not knowing what next or how. The
moment you know how, you begin to
die a little. The artist never entirely
knows. We guess. We may be wrong,
but we take leap after leap in the
dark.   —Agnes de Mille

Where there is an unknowable, there
is a promise.   —Thornton Wilder

Dare to be naive.
            —R. Buckminster Fuller

545

Getting Going

WE MUSTN'T HESITATE

Act decidedly and take the consequences. No good is ever done by hesitation.
—Thomas Henry Huxley

How lovely to think that no one need wait a moment, we can start now, start slowly changing the world!
—Anne Frank

To know what has to be done, then do it, comprises the whole philosophy of practical life.
—Sir William Osler

If you want to do something, do it!
—Plautus

Something must happen!
—Heinrich Böll

Putting off an easy thing makes it hard. Putting off a hard thing makes it impossible.
—George Claude Lorimer

Delay always breeds danger, and to protract a great design is often to ruin it.
—Miguel de Cervantes

The wise man does at once what the fool does finally.
—Baltasar Gracian

In putting off what one has to do, one runs the risk of never being able to do it.
—Charles Baudelaire

Getting an idea should be like sitting down on a pin; it should make you jump up and do something.
—E.L. Simpson

Procrastination is opportunity's assassin.
—Victor Kiam

To do anything in this world worth doing, we must not stand back shivering and thinking of the cold and danger, but jump in and scramble through as well as we can.
—Sydney Smith

The man who will not execute his resolutions when they are fresh upon him can have no hope from them afterwards; they will be dissipated, lost and perish in the hurry and scurry of the world, or sunk in the slough of indolence.
—Maria Edgeworth

Why always, "not yet"? Do flowers in spring say, "not yet"?
—Norman Douglas

We are very near to greatness: one step and we are safe; can we not take the leap?   —Ralph Waldo Emerson

The keen spirit seizes the prompt occasion.   —Hannah Moore

The hour is ripe, and yonder lies the way.   —Virgil

Delay not to seize the hour!
—Aeschylus

I was seldom able to see an opportunity until it had ceased to be one.
—Mark Twain

This one makes a net, this one stands and wishes.
Would you like to make a bet which one gets the fishes?
—Chinese rhyme

Inspirations never go in for long engagements; they demand immediate marriage to action.
—Brendan Francis

If we really want to live, we'd better start at once to try.   —W.H. Auden

The rewards in business go to the man who does something with an idea.   —William Benton

The important thing is somehow to begin.   —Henry Moore

Eighty percent of success is showing up.   —Woody Allen

As long as you can start, you are all right. The juice will come.
—Ernest Hemingway

The way to get ahead is to start now.
—William Feather

Begin doing what you want to do now.
—Marie Beynon Ray

It is no good hearing an inner voice or getting an inner prompting if you do not immediately act on that inner prompting.   —David Spangler

Even if you're on the right track, you'll get run over if you just sit there.
—Will Rogers

THE FIRST STEP

The first step is the hardest.
—Anon.

The art of writing is the art of applying the seat of the pants to the seat of the chair.   —Mary Heaton Vorse

Every beginning is hard.   —Anon.

A journey of a thousand miles must begin with a single step.
—Chinese proverb

Whenever you take a step forward, you are bound to disturb something.
—Indira Gandhi

If you miss the first buttonhole, you will not succeed in buttoning up your coat.   —Johann von Goethe

If you don't place your foot on the rope, you'll never cross the chasm.
—Anon.

He who is outside the door has already a good part of his journey behind him.   —Dutch proverb

The beginning is half of every action.
                    —Greek proverb

The man who removes a mountain begins by carrying away small stones.
                    —Chinese proverb

WE MUST BEGIN WHEREVER WE ARE

Everyone who got where he is had to begin where he was.
                    —Robert Louis Stevenson

Change your life today. Don't gamble on the future, act now, without delay.
                    —Simone de Beauvoir

The most important thing about getting somewhere is starting right where we are.   —Bruce Barton

Sometimes we look so intently toward the pinnacle that we stumble over the steps leading to it. Development begins just where you are.
                    —Mrs. Herman Stanley

WE MUST BEGIN, EVEN IF WE'RE NOT EXACTLY SURE WHERE WE'RE GOING

Few begin with anything like a clear view of what they want to do, and the fortune they seek may come in a very different form from that which they have kept in view.
                    —*The Independent*

The most effective way to do it, is to do it.   —Toni Cade Bambara

Beginnings are apt to be shadowy.
                    —Rachel Carson

We will not know unless we begin.
                    —Howard Zinn

Let us watch well our beginnings, and results will manage themselves.
                    —Alexander Clark

TO GET WHAT WE WANT, WE MUST TAKE ACTION

"Mean to" don't pick no cotton.
                    —Anon.

You cannot contribute anything to the ideal condition of mind and heart known as Brotherhood, however much you preach, posture, or agree, unless you live it.   —Faith Baldwin

The secret of getting ahead is getting started.   —Sally Berger

To always be intending to live a new life, but never to find time to set about it; this is as if a man should put off eating and drinking and sleeping from one day and night to another, till he is starved and destroyed.
                    —Tillotson

To choose is also to begin.
                    —Starhawk

Knowing is not enough, we must apply. Willing is not enough, we must do.   —Johann von Goethe

Wisdom is harder to do than it is to know.   —Yula Moses

Justice is a concept. Muscle is the reality. —Linda Blandford

No one has a right to sit down and feel hopeless. There's too much work to do. —Dorothy Day

Do noble things, do not dream them all day long. —Charles Kingsley

That is the principal thing: not to remain with the dream, with the intention, with the being in the mood, but always forcibly to convert it into all things.
—Rainer Maria Rilke

Don't wait for your "ship to come in," and feel angry and cheated when it doesn't. Get going with something small. —Irene Kassorla

Don't sit down and wait for the opportunities to come; you have to get up and make them.
—Madame C.J. Walker

The individual activity of one man with backbone will do more than a thousand men with a mere wishbone.
—William J.H. Boetcker

With mere good intentions hell is proverbially paved. —William James

All the beautiful sentiments in the world weigh less than a single lovely action. —James Russell Lowell

It is vain to say human beings ought to be satisfied with tranquility: they must have action; and they will have it if they cannot find it.
—George Eliot

Now, go take on the day!
—Dr. Laura Schlessinger

You can't steal second base and keep one foot on first.
—Frederick B. Wilson

You cannot dream yourself into a character; you must hammer and forge one for yourself.
—James A. Froude

What the Puritans gave the world was not thought, but action.
—Wendell Phillips

Stagnation is something worse than death. It is corruption, also.
—William Gilmore Simms

I myself must mix with action, lest I wither by despair.
—Alfred, Lord Tennyson

Psychology is action, not thinking about oneself. —Albert Camus

The great end of life is not knowledge, but action.
—Thomas Henry Huxley

The biggest sin is sitting on your ass.
—Florynce Kennedy

This is a world of action, and not for moping and droning in.
—Charles Dickens

Honors and rewards fall to those who show their good qualities in action. —Aristotle

Share the passion and action of your time, at peril of being judged not to have lived.
—Oliver Wendell Holmes Jr.

Action is eloquence.
—William Shakespeare

The end of man is action.
—Thomas Carlyle

Optimism, unaccompanied by personal effort, is merely a state of mind, and not fruitful.   —Edward L. Curtis

To attain happiness in another world we need only to believe something, while to secure it in this world, we must do something.
—Charlotte P. Gilman

The only menace is inertia.
—Saint John Perse

One of the reasons why so few of us ever act, instead of react, is because we are continually stifling our deepest impulses.   —Henry Miller

If a man wants his dreams to come true, he must wake them up. —Anon.

Men expect too much, do too little.
—Allen Tate

Action may not always bring happiness, but there is no happiness without action.   —William James

Things don't turn up in this world until somebody turns them up.
—James A. Garfield

Act—act in the living present!
—Henry Wadsworth Longfellow

Life is essentially a series of events to be lived through rather than intellectual riddles to be played with and solved.   —George A. Buttrick

The shortest answer is doing.
—English proverb

THE RISKS OF TAKING ACTION
CAN BE LESS THAN THE
RISKS OF INACTION

There are risks and costs to a program of action. But they are far less than the long-range risks and costs of comfortable inaction.
—John F. Kennedy

What you don't do can be a destructive force.   —Eleanor Roosevelt

He that is overcautious will accomplish little.   —J.C.F. von Schiller

Untilled ground, however rich, will bring forth thistles and thorns; so also the mind of man.
—Thérèse of Lisieux

Often greater risk is involved in postponement than in making a wrong decision.   —Harry A. Hopf

The bitterest tears shed over graves are for words left unsaid and deeds left undone. —Harriet Beecher Stowe

And all that you are sorry for is what you haven't done.
—Margaret Widdemer

Can anything be sadder than work unfinished? Yes; work never begun.
—Christina Rossetti

The only things you regret are the things you didn't do.
—Michael Curtiz

Above all, try something.
—Franklin Delano Roosevelt

To avoid an occasion for our virtues is a worse degree of failure than to push forward pluckily and make a fall.
—Robert Louis Stevenson

Indifference and inaction must always pay a penalty. —William Feather

Shun idleness. It is a rust that attaches itself to the most brilliant metals.
—Voltaire

I do not believe in a fate that falls on men however they act, but I do believe in a fate that falls on men unless they act. —G.K. Chesterton

We Can't Let Talking Get in the Way of Action

Deeds, not words.
—Motto of the McRarie family

The real nature of an ethic is that it does not become an ethic unless and until it goes into action.
—Margaret Halsey

For it isn't enough to talk about peace. One must believe in it. And it isn't enough to believe in it. One must work at it. —Eleanor Roosevelt

Words are mere bubbles of water, but deeds are drops of gold.
—Chinese proverb

Ef women want any rights more'n dey got, why don't dey jes' take 'em and not be talkin' about it.
—Sojourner Truth

All talk of women's rights is moonshine. Women have every right. They have only to exercise them.
—Victoria Claffin Woodhull

A man of words and not of deeds is like a garden full of weeds. —Anon.

Life is worth being lived, but not worth being discussed all the time.
—Isabelle Adfani

Action, not words, are the true criterion of the attachment of friends.
—George Washington

Words without actions are the assassins of idealism. —Herbert Hoover

If you have something to do that is worthwhile doing, don't talk about it ...do it. —George W. Biount

If deeds are wanting, all words appear mere vanity and emptiness.
—Greek proverb

Talking is easy, action difficult.
—Spanish proverb

One's feelings waste themselves in words; they ought all to be distilled into action ... which bring results.
—Florence Nightingale

Boast not of what thou would'st have done, but do. —John Milton

I like to deliver more than I promise instead of the other way around.
—Dorothy Uhnak

When I talked, no one listened to me. But as soon as I acted I became persuasive, and I no longer find anyone incredulous. —Giosue Borsi

551

If you can talk brilliantly about a problem, it can create the consoling illusion that it has been mastered.
—Stanley Kubrick

Words gain credibility by deed.
—Terence

Men are alike in their promises. It is only in their deeds that they differ.
—Moliere

An acre of performance is worth a whole world of promise.
—W.D. Howells

Well done is better than well said.
—Benjamin Franklin

Our chief defect is that we are more given to talking about things than to doing them. —Jawaharlal Nehru

We have too many sounding words and too few actions that correspond with them. —Abigail Adams

WE CAN'T LET PLANNING GET IN THE WAY OF ACTION

Activity in back of a very small idea will produce more than inactivity and the planning of a genius.
—James A. Worsham

When it comes to getting things done, we need fewer architects and more bricklayers. —Colleen C. Barrett

Get good counsel before you begin; and when you have decided, act promptly. —Sallust

Ideas are one thing, and what happens is another. —John Cage

Thinking about swimming isn't much like actually getting in the water. Actually getting in the water can take your breath away. —Barbara Sher

All worthwhile men have good thoughts, good ideas and good intentions, but precious few of them ever translate those into action.
—John Hancock Field

A thought which does not result in an action is nothing much, and an action which does not proceed from a thought is nothing at all.
—Georges Bernanos

To think is easy. To act is difficult. To act as one thinks is the most difficult of all. —Johann von Goethe

Unless a capacity for thinking be accompanied by a capacity for action, a superior mind exists in torture.
—Benedetto Croce

Contemplation often makes life miserable. We should act more, think less, and stop watching ourselves live.
—Nicolas de Chamfort

What you theoretically know, vividly realize. —Francis Thompson

We must not waste life in devising means. It is better to plan less and do more. —William Ellery Channing

The best way to prepare for life is to begin to live. —Elbert Hubbard

We are always getting ready to live, but never living.
—Ralph Waldo Emerson

Action will remove the doubt that theory cannot solve.   —Tehyi Hsieh

It is a common observation that those who dwell continually upon their expectations are apt to become oblivious to the requirements of their actual situation.
                —Charles Sanders Peirce

He who deliberates fully before taking a step will spend his entire life on one leg.   —Chinese proverb

We don't have enough time to premeditate all our actions.
                        —Vauvenargues

The opportunity is often lost by deliberating.   —Publilius Syrus

To think too long about doing a thing often becomes its undoing.
                            —Eva Young

We Can't Wait Too Long for "The Right Circumstances," or for Inspiration

Do not wait for ideal circumstances, nor the best opportunities; they will never come.   —Janet Erskine Stuart

Do what you can, with what you have, where you are.
                    —Theodore Roosevelt

Anything worth doing is worth doing too soon.   —Barbara Sher

"Now" is the operative word. Everything you put in your way is just a method of putting off the hour when you could actually be doing your dream.   —Barbara Sher

Common sense does not ask an impossible chessboard, but takes the one before it and plays the game.
                        —Wendell Phillips

I don't wait for moods. You accomplish nothing if you do that. Your mind must know it has got to get down to earth.   —Pearl S. Buck

My evil genius Procrastination has whispered me to tarry 'til a more convenient season.
                    —Mary Todd Lincoln

I realize that if I wait until I am no longer afraid to act, write, speak, be, I'll be sending messages on a ouija board, cryptic complaints from the other side.   —Audre Lorde

He who postpones the hour of living is like the rustic who waits for the river to run out before he crosses.
                            —Horace

Being unready and ill-equipped is what you have to expect in life. It is the universal predicament. It is your lot as a human being to lack what it takes. Circumstances are seldom right. You never have the capacities, the strength, the wisdom, the virtue you ought to have. You must always do with less than you need in a situation vastly different from what you would have chosen.
                    —Charlton Ogburn, Jr.

He who hesitates is last.   —Mae West

Conditions are never just right. People who delay action until all factors are favorable do nothing.
                        —William Feather

You decide you'll wait for your pitch. Then as the ball starts toward the plate, you think about your stance. And then you think about your swing. And then you realize that the ball that went past you for a strike was your pitch.   —Bobby Murcer

So what do we do? Anything. Something. So long as we just don't sit there. If we screw it up, start over. Try something else. If we wait until we've satisfied all the uncertainties, it may be too late.   —Lee Iacocca

Nothing at all will be attempted if all possible objections must first be overcome.   —Samuel Johnson

No age or time of life, no position or circumstance, has a monopoly on success. Any age is the right age to start doing!   —Anon.

Everyone must row with the oars he has.   —English proverb

The question for each man is not what he would do if he had the means, time, influence and educational advantages, but what he will do with the things he has.
        —Frank Hamilton

How many opportunities come along? If you wait for the right one, that's wrong, because it may never be right, and what have you got to lose? Even if it's a disaster, you've tried, you've learned something, you've had an adventure. And that doesn't mean you can't do it again.
        —Edward McCabe

And now, Lord, what wait I for?
        —Psalms 39:7

We should be taught not to wait for inspiration to start a thing. Action always generates inspiration. Inspiration seldom generates action.
        —Frank Tibolt

If you wait for inspiration you'll be standing on the corner after the parade is a mile down the street.
        —Ben Nicholas

The best place to succeed is where you are with what you have.
        —Charles M. Schwab

One of these days is none of these days.   —H.G. Bohn

Who waits until the wind shall silent keep
Will never find the ready hour to sow.
        —Helen Hunt Jackson

Begin somewhere; you cannot build a reputation on what you intend to do.
        —Liz Smith

If you wait for the perfect moment when all is safe and assured, it may never arrive. Mountains will not be climbed, races won, or lasting happiness achieved.   —Maurice Chevalier

There is nothing to be gained by waiting for a better situation. You see where you are and you do what you can with that.   —Jacob K. Javits

WE ARE OUR ACTIONS

It is in your act that you exist, not in your body. Your act is yourself, and there is no other you.
        —Antoine de Saint-Exupery

554

The things people discard tell more about them than the things they keep.
—Hilda Lawrence

The test of any man lies in action.
—Pindar

Every action we take, everything we do, is either a victory or defeat in the struggle to become what we want to be.   —Anne Byrhhe

It's where we go, and what we do when we get there, that tells us who we are.   —Joyce Carol Oates

By his deeds we know a man.
—African proverb

A human being has no discernible character until he acts.
—Constantine Nash and Virginia Oakley

What we make is more important than what we are, particularly if making is our profession.
—Dorothy L. Sayers

To do is to be.   —Socrates

You can't build a reputation on what you intend to do.   —Liz Smith

To be is to do.   —Plato

The way to do is to be.   —Lao-tzu

The ordinary man is involved in action, the hero acts. An immense difference.   —Henry Miller

We judge ourselves by what we feel capable of doing, while others judge us by what we have already done.
—Henry Wadsworth Longfellow

Our deeds determine us, as much as we determine our deeds.
—George Eliot

We Feel Better When We Take Action

The emotions are not always subject to reason . . . but they are always subject to action. When thoughts do not neutralize an undesirable emotion, action will.   —William James

Silences have a climax, when you have got to speak.
—Elizabeth Bowen

He who desires but acts not breeds pestilence.   —William Blake

When I am idle and shiftless, my affairs become confused; when I work, I get results . . . not great results, but enough to encourage me.
—Edgar Watson Howe

To be busy with material affairs is the best preservative against reflection, fears, doubts . . . all these things which stand in the way of achievement. I suppose a fellow proposing to cut his throat would experience a sort of relief while occupied in stropping his razor carefully.   —Joseph Conrad

Acting can work a peculiar magic on the actor . . . it can cure you (at least for the length of a performance) of a whole variety of ailments. Migraine headaches, miserable colds or toothaches will suddenly disappear as you're up there going through your paces.   —Barbara Harris

It is only when I dally with what I am about, look back and aside instead of keeping my eyes straight forward, that I feel these cold sinkings of the heart. But the first broadside puts all to rights. —Sir Walter Scott

Action is the antidote to despair.
—Joan Baez

Action is the only reality; not only reality, but morality as well.
—Abbie Hoffman

Performance releases pressure.
—Anon.

ACTION AND WEALTH

Wishing does not make a poor man rich. —Arab proverb

You can't get rich sitting on the bench.
—Phil Linz

Action makes more fortunes than caution. —Vauvenargues

HOW TO GET GOING

For purposes of action, nothing is more useful than narrowness of thought combined with energy of will.
—Henri Frederic Amiel

How, then, find the courage for action?... By accepting the human condition more simply and candidly, by dreading troubles less, calculating less, hoping more.
—Henri Frederic Amiel

Necessity of action takes away the fear of the act. —Francis Quarles

Commitment leads to action. Action brings your dream closer.
—Marcia Wieder

One starts an action simply because one must do something. —T.S. Eliot

We couldn't possibly know where it would lead, but we knew it had to be done. —Betty Friedan,
speaking of the Women's Movement

Action springs not from thought, but from a readiness for responsibility.
—Dietrich Bonhoeffer

COURAGE IS ESSENTIAL
TO BEGINNING

What you can do, or dream you can do, begin it; boldness has genius, power and magic in it.
—Johann von Goethe

There are people who put their dreams in a little box and say, "Yes, I've got dreams, of course, I've got dreams." Then they put the box away and bring it out once in a while to look in it, and yep, they're still there. These are great dreams, but they never even get out of the box. It takes an uncommon amount of guts to put your dreams on the line, to hold them up and say, "How good or how bad am I?" That's where courage comes in. —Erma Bombeck

The difference between getting somewhere and nowhere is the courage to make an early start.
—Charles M. Schwab

All glory comes from daring to begin.
—Anon.

How many feasible projects have miscarried through despondency, and been strangled in their birth by a cowardly imagination?
—Jeremy Collier

More powerful than the will to win is the courage to begin. —Anon.

Courage to start and willingness to keep everlasting at it are the requisites for success.
—Alonzo Newton Benn

There is no such thing as a long piece of work, except one that you dare not start. —Charles Baudelaire

To the timid and hesitating everything is impossible because it seems so.
—Sir Walter Scott

He who begun has half done. Dare to be wise; begin. —Horace

It's weak and despicable to go on wanting things and not trying to get them. —Joanna Field

When it comes to betting on yourself . . . you're a chicken-livered coward if you hesitate. —B.C. Forbes

Imposing limitations on yourself is cowardly because it protects you from having to try, and perhaps failing.
—Vladimir Zworykin

All know the way, few actually walk it.
—Bodhidharma

The distance doesn't matter, only the first step is difficult.
—Madame Marquise du Deffand

GENERAL QUOTATIONS ABOUT GETTING GOING

Seize opportunity by the beard, for it is bald behind. —Bulgarian proverb

Procrastination usually results in sorrowful regret. Today's duties put off until tomorrow give us a double burden to bear; the best way is to do them in their proper time.
—Ida Scott Taylor

If you dam a river it stagnates. Running water is beautiful water.
—English proverb

Never mistake motion for action.
—Ernest Hemingway

A person who has not done one half his day's work by ten o' clock, runs a chance of leaving the other half undone. —Emily Brontë

There is clearly much left to be done, and whatever else we are going to do, we had better get on with it.
—Rosalynn Carter

Procrastination is the thief of time.
—Edward Young

Slaying the dragon of delay is no sport for the short-winded.
—Sandra Day O'Connor

If a man would move the world, he must first move himself. —Socrates

Who hesitate and falter life away, and lose tomorrow the ground won today. —Matthew Arnold

Now or never was the time.
—Laurence Sterne

Can anything be sadder than work
unfinished? Yes; work never begun.
                    —Christina Rossetti

Fear not that thy life shall come to
an end, but rather that it shall never
have a beginning.
        —John Henry Cardinal Newman

Go ahead with your life, your
plans.... Don't waste time by stopping
before the interruptions have started.
                    —Richard L. Evans

A hard beginning makes a good
ending.   —John Heywood

We may our ends by our beginnings
know.   —Sir John Denham

The only joy in the world is to begin.
                    —Cesare Pavese

Every artist was first an amateur.
                    —Ralph Waldo Emerson

The best way to prepare for life is to
begin to live.   —Elbert Hubbard

PART 6

Making Dreams Come True

Success

Basic Success Techniques

Find a need and fill it.
—Ruth Stafford Peale

The successful person is the individual who forms the habit of doing what the failing person doesn't like to do.
—Donald Riggs

The victory of success is half done when one gains the habit of work.
—Sarah Knowles Bolton

The secret of every man who has ever been successful lies in the fact that he formed the bait of doing those things that failures don't like to do.
—A. Jackson King

Nature gave men two ends—one to sit on, and one to think with. Ever since then man's success or failure has been dependent on the one he used most.   —George R. Kirkpatrick

Make yourself indispensable and you'll be moved up. Act as if you're indispensable and you'll be moved out.
—Anon.

What is the recipe for successful achievement? To my mind there are just four essential ingredients: Choose a career you love. . . . Give it the best there is in you. . . . Seize your opportunities. . . . And be a member of the team.   —Benjamin F. Fairless

Vacillating people seldom succeed. They seldom win the solid respect of their fellows. Successful men and women are very careful in reaching decisions, and very persistent and determined in action thereafter.
—L.G. Elliott

Many people have the ambition to succeed; they may even have a special aptitude for their job. And yet they do not move ahead. Why? Perhaps they think that since they can master the job, there is no need to master themselves.   —John Stevenson

I've been polite and I've always shown up. Somebody asked me if I had any advice for young people entering the business. I said: "Yeah, show up."   —Tom T. Hall

560

The wise man puts all his eggs in one basket and watches the basket.
—Andrew Carnegie

I know the price of success: dedication, hard work and an unremitting devotion to the things you want to see happen.   —Frank Lloyd Wright

Success is that old ABC—Ability, Breaks and Courage.
—Charles Luckman

The secret of success in life is for a man to be ready for his opportunity when it comes.   —Benjamin Disraeli

If one advances confidently in the direction of his dreams, and endeavors to live the life which he has imaged, he will meet with success unexpected in common hours.
—Henry David Thoreau

Before everything else, getting ready is the secret of success. —Henry Ford

To be ambitious for wealth, and yet always expecting to be poor; to be always doubting your ability to get what you long for, is like trying to reach east by traveling west. There is no philosophy which will help man to succeed when he is always doubting his ability to do so, and thus attracting failure. No matter how hard you work for success, if your thought is saturated with the fear of failure, it will kill your efforts, neutralize your endeavors and make success impossible.   —Charles Baudouin

I cannot give you the formula for success, but I can give you the formula for failure, which is—try to please everybody.   —Herbert Bayard Swope

We may fail of our happiness, strive we ever so bravely, but we are less likely to fail if we measure with judgement our chances and our capabilities.
—Agnes Repplier

A double-minded man is unstable in all his ways. . . . A determinate purpose in life and a steady adhesion to it through all disadvantages are indispensable conditions of success.
—William M. Punshion

The conditions of conquest are always easy. We have but to toil awhile, endure awhile, believe always, and never turn back.
—Marcus Annaeus Seneca

The very first step towards success in any occupation is to become interested in it.   —Sir William Osler

I studied the lives of great men and famous women; and I found that the men and women who got to the top were those who did the jobs they had in hand, with everything they had of energy and enthusiasm and hard work.   —Harry S. Truman

Without ambition one starts nothing. Without work one finishes nothing. The prize will not be sent to you. As to methods there may be a million and then some, but the principles are few. The man who grasps principles can successfully select his own methods. The man who tries methods, ignoring principles, is sure to have trouble.   —Ralph Waldo Emerson

There are no secrets to success. It is the result of preparation, hard work, learning from failure.
—General Colin L. Powell

Success is blocked by concentrating on it and planning for it. . . . Success is shy—it won't come out while you're watching.

—Tennessee Williams

Three outstanding qualities make for success: judgement, industry, health. And the greatest of these is judgement.

—William Maxwell Aitken,
Lord Beaverbrook

Thirteen virtues necessary for true success: temperance, silence, order, resolution, frugality, industry, sincerity, justice, moderation, cleanliness, tranquility, chastity, and humility.

—Benjamin Franklin

Find a need and fill it.

—Ruth Stafford Peale

Put your heart, mind, intellect and soul even to your smallest acts. This is the secret of success.

—Swami Sivananda

Four steps to achievement: plan purposefully, prepare prayerfully, proceed positively, pursue persistently.

—William A. Ward

Success follows doing what you want to do. There is no other way to be successful.   —Malcolm Forbes

Always aim for achievement, and forget about success.   —Helen Hayes

Success, which is something so simple in the end, is made up of thousands of things, we never fully know what.

—Rainer Maria Rilke

Self-trust is the first secret of success.

—Ralph Waldo Emerson

The man who will use his skill and constructive imagination to see how much he can give for a dollar, instead of how little he can give for a dollar, is bound to succeed.   —Henry Ford

The Importance of Interpersonal Relations

So once I shut down my privilege of disliking anyone I choose and holding myself aloof if I could manage it, greater understanding, growing compassion came to me.

—Catharine Marshall

The most important single ingredient in the formula of success is knowing how to get along with people.

—Theodore Roosevelt

Remember, the bread you meet each day is still rising. Don't scare the dough.   —Macrina Wiederkehr

The art of dealing with people is the foremost secret of successful men. A man's success in handling people is the very yardstick by which the outcome of his whole life's work is measured.

—Paul C. Packe

The ability to form friendships, to make people believe in you and trust you is one of the few absolutely fundamental qualities of success. Selling, buying, negotiating are so much smoother and easier when the parties enjoy each other's confidence. The young man who can make friends quickly will find that he will glide, instead of stumble, through life.

—John J. McGuirk

Networking is an enrichment program, not an entitlement program.
—Susan RoAne

Respect for people is the cornerstone of communication and networking.
—Susan RoAne

No matter how much a man can do, no matter how engaging his personality may be, he will not advance far in business if he cannot work through others.
—John Craig

The way to rise is to obey and please.
—Ben Johnson

Skill is fine, and genius is splendid, but the right contacts are more valuable than either.
—Sir Archibald McIndoe

Whatever your grade or position, if you know how and when to speak, and when to remain silent, your chances of real success are proportionately increased.
—Ralph C. Smedley

The Importance of Desire, Enthusiasm, Zeal, Optimism, and Energy

That they can strengthen through the empowerment of others is essential wisdom often gathered by women.
—Mary Field Belenky

A man can succeed at almost anything for which he has unlimited enthusiasm.
—Charles M. Schwab

You have to block everything out and be extremely focused and be relaxed and mellow too.
—Jennifer Capriati

I've never sought success in order to get fame and money; it's the talent and the passion that count in success.
—Ingrid Bergman

Flaming enthusiasm, backed up by horse sense and persistence, is the quality that most frequently makes for success.
—Dale Carnegie

Anyone who has gumption knows what it is, and anyone who hasn't can never know what it is.
—L.M. Montgomery

The world belongs to the energetic.
—Ralph Waldo Emerson

I feel that one must deliberate then act, must scan every life choice with rational thinking but then base the decision on whether one's heart will be in it.
—Jean Shinoda Bolen

Since everything is in our heads, we better not lose them.
—Coco Chanel

There is a passion for perfection which you rarely see fully developed; but you may note this fact, that in successful lives it is never wholly lacking.
—Bliss Carman

Many of the most successful men I have known have never grown up. They have retained bubbling-over boyishness. They have relished wit, they have indulged in humor. They have not allowed "dignity" to depress them into moroseness. Youthfulness of spirit is the twin brother of optimism, and optimism is the stuff of which American business success is fashioned. Resist growing up!
—B.C. Forbes

People are subject to moods, to temptations and fears, lethargy and aberration and ignorance, and the staunchest qualities shift under the stresses and strains of daily life.
—Ilka Chase

Whoever said, "It's not whether you win or lose that counts," probably lost. —Martina Navratilova

If you have the will to win, you have achieved half your success; if you don't, you have achieved half your failure. —David V.A. Ambrose

Someone's always saying, "It's not whether you win or lose," but if you feel that way, you're as good as dead.
—James Caan

The real difference between men is energy. —Thomas Fuller

Success is going from failure to failure without loss of enthusiasm.
—Sir Winston Churchill

To bring one's self to a frame of mind and to the proper energy to accomplish things that require plain hard work continuously is the one big battle that everyone has. When this battle is won for all time, then everything is easy. —Thomas A. Buckner

We would accomplish many more things if we did not think of them as impossible. —C. Malesherbez

Faith that the thing can be done is essential to any great achievement.
—Thomas N. Carruther

Sometimes success is due less to ability than to zeal. —Charles Buxton

We can accomplish almost anything within our ability if we but think that we can! —George Matthew Adams

Optimism is essential to achievement and it is also the foundation of courage and of true progress.
—Nicholas Murray Butler

Morale is the greatest single factor in successful wars.
—Dwight D. Eisenhower

The will to conquer is the first condition of victory.
—Marshal Ferdinand Foch

Always bear in mind that your own resolution to success is more important than any other one thing.
—Abraham Lincoln

The real secret of success is enthusiasm. Yes, more than enthusiasm, I would say excitement. I like to see men get excited. When they get excited, they make a success of their lives.
—Walter Chrysler

It is fatal to enter any war without the will to win it.
—General Douglas MacArthur

The measure of an enthusiasm must be taken between interesting events. It is between bites that the lukewarm angler loses heart.
—Edwin Way Teale

Enthusiasm for one's goal lessens the disagreeableness of working toward it.
—Thomas Eakins

To burn always with this hard gem-like flame, to maintain this ecstasy, is success in life. —Walter Pater

Every man is enthusiastic at times. One man has enthusiasm for thirty minutes, another man has it for thirty days. But it is the man who has it for thirty years who makes a success in life. —Edward B. Butler

Man never rises to great truths without enthusiasm. —Vauvenargues

Success is due less to ability than to zeal. —Charles Buxton

I rate enthusiasm even above professional skill. —Sir Edward Appleton

He did it with all his heart, and prospered. —2 Chronicles 31:21

Do it big or stay in bed. —Larry Kelly

Nothing great was ever achieved without enthusiasm. —Ralph Waldo Emerson

What a man accomplishes in a day depends upon the way in which he approaches his tasks. When we accept tough jobs as a challenge to our ability and wade into them with joy and enthusiasm, miracles can happen. When we do our work with a dynamic conquering spirit, we get things done. —Arland Gilbert

If you're not happy every morning when you get up, leave for work, or start to work at home, if you're not enthusiastic about doing that, you're not going to be successful. —Donald M. Kendall

The method of the enterprising is to plan with audacity and execute with vigor. —Christian Bovee

A strong passion for any object will ensure success, for the desire of the end will point out the means. —William Hazlitt

SELF-RELIANCE AND SUCCESS

If you want to succeed, you must make your own opportunities as you go. —John B. Gough

A wise man will make more opportunities than he finds. —Francis Bacon

No man will succeed unless he is ready to face and overcome difficulties and prepared to assume responsibilities. —William J.H. Boetcker

Man is still responsible. . . . His success lies not with the stars, but with himself. He must carry on the fight of self-correction and discipline. —Frank Curtis Williams

No one can help you in holding a good job except Old Man You. —Edgar Watson Howe

Under normal periods, any man's success hinges about five percent on what others do for him and 95 percent on what he does. —James A. Worsham

If, after all, men cannot always make history have a meaning, they can always act so that their own lives have one. —Albert Camus

The brave man carves out his fortune, and every man is the sum of his own works. —Miguel de Cervantes

If a man wants his dreams to come true, he must wake up. —Anon.

Pa, he always said a man had to look spry for himself, because nobody would do it for him; your opportunities didn't come knocking around, you had to hunt them down and hog-tie them. —Louis L'Amour

Men at some time are masters of their fates. —William Shakespeare

Destiny is not a matter of chance, it is a matter of choice; it is not a thing to be waited for, it is a thing to be achieved. —William Jennings Bryan

The people who get on in this world are the people who get up and look for the circumstances they want, and, if they can't find them, make them. —George Bernard Shaw

Every man is the architect of his own fortune. —Sallust

We Must Take Risks to Succeed

The men who have done big things are those who were not afraid to attempt big things, who were not afraid to risk failure in order to gain success. —B.C. Forbes

If the risk-reward ratio is right, you can make big money buying trouble. —Anon.

What isn't tried won't work. —Claude McDonald

He that is overcautious will accomplish little. —J.C.F. von Schiller

All great reforms require one to dare a lot to win a little. —William L. O'Neill

If you limit your actions in life to things that nobody can possibly find fault with, you will not do much. —Charles Lutwidge Dodgson

The ambitious climbs high and perilous stairs and never cares how to come down; the desire of rising hath swallowed up his fear of a fall. —Thomas Adams

He that would have fruit must climb the tree. —Thomas Fuller

To get profit without risk, experience without danger and reward without work is as impossible as it is to live without being born. —A.P. Gouthey

Every noble acquisition is attended with its risks; he who fears to encounter the one must not expect to obtain the other. —Pietro Metastasio

The method of the enterprising is to plan with audacity and execute with vigor. —Christian Bovee

Great deeds are usually wrought at great risks. —Herodotus

Only those who dare to fail greatly can ever achieve greatly. —Robert F. Kennedy

No one reaches a high position without daring. —Publilius Syrus

Cadillacs are down at the end of the bat. —Ralph Kiner, when asked why he didn't choke up and hit for average

It is impossible to win the great prizes of life without running risks.
—Theodore Roosevelt

You can't expect to hit the jackpot if you don't put a few nickels in the machine. —Flip Wilson

Who dares nothing, need hope for nothing. —J.C.F. von Schiller

Progress always involves risks. You can't steal second base and keep your foot on first. —Frederick B. Wilcox

I don't think about risks much. I just do what I want to do. If you gotta go, you gotta go. —Lillian Carter

Behold the turtle. He makes progress only when he sticks his neck out.
—James Bryant Conant

Nothing ventured, nothing gained.
—Anon.

You can't catch trout with dry breeches. —Spanish proverb

Don't be afraid to take a big step if one is indicated. You can't cross a chasm in two small jumps.
—David Lloyd George

We Can't Succeed without Courage

Because a fellow has failed once or twice or a dozen times, you don't want to set him down as a failure till he's dead or loses his courage—and that's the same thing.
—George Horace Lorimer

What is more mortifying than to feel that you have missed the plum for want of courage to shake the tree?
—Logan Pearsall Smith

To persevere, trusting in what hopes he has, is courage. The coward despairs. —Euripides

Whatever you do, you need courage. . . . To map out a course of action and follow it to an end requires some of the same courage which a soldier needs. —Ralph Waldo Emerson

Who dares nothing, need hope for nothing. —J.C.F. von Schiller

Have the courage of your desire.
—George R. Gissing

To see what is right, and not do it, is want of courage. —Confucius

It takes vision and courage to create—it takes faith and courage to prove.
—Owen D. Young

No great thing comes to any man unless he has courage.
—Cardinal James Gibbons

Great things are done more through courage than through wisdom.
—German proverb

Courage permits the caliber of performance to continue at its peak, until the finish line is crossed.
—Stuart Walker

Failure is only postponed success as long as courage "coaches" ambition. The habit of persistence is the habit of victory. —Herbert Kaufman

Courage and perseverance have a magical talisman, before which difficulties disappear, and obstacles vanish into air.   —John Quincy Adams

You will never do anything in this world without courage.
                —James Lane Allen

It takes as much courage to have tried and failed as it does to have tried and succeeded.
        —Anne Morrow Lindbergh

Where there is a brave man, in the thickest of the fight, there is the post of honor.   —Henry David Thoreau

Whenever you see a successful business, someone once made a courageous decision.   —Peter Drucker

There are a lot of fellas with all the ability it takes to play in the major leagues, but they never make it, they always get stuck in the minor leagues because they haven't got the guts to make the climb.   —Cookie Lavagetto

Courage to start and willingness to keep everlasting at it are the requisites for success.
            —Alonzo Newton Benn

One of the biggest factors in success is the courage to undertake something.
                —James A. Worsham

It is weak and despicable to go on wanting things and not trying to get them.   —Joanna Field

Work and Success

The measure of achievement is not winning awards. It's doing something that you appreciate, something you believe is worthwhile. I think of my strawberry soufflé. I did that at least twenty-eight times before I finally conquered it.   —Julia Child

Nothing worthwhile comes easily. Half effort does not produce half results. It produces no results. Work, continuous work and hard work, is the only way to accomplish results that last.   —Hamilton Holt

If a man wakes up famous he hasn't been sleeping.   —Wes Izzard

What it comes down to is that anybody can win with the best horse. What makes you good is if you can take the second or third best horse and win.   —Vicky Aragon

Success is dependent on effort.
                —Sophocles

Success comes before work only in the dictionary.   —Anon.

Success is having a flair for the thing that you are doing, knowing that is not enough, that you have got to have hard work and a sense of purpose.
            —Margaret Thatcher

Striving for success without hard work is like trying to harvest where you haven't planted.   —David Bly

Sweat plus sacrifice equals success.
            —Charles O. Finley

Success usually comes to those who are too busy to be looking for it.
—Henry David Thoreau

Excellence in any pursuit is the late, ripe fruit of toil. —W.M.L. Jay

It's in the preparation—in those dreary pedestrian virtues they taught you in seventh grade and you didn't believe. It's making the extra call and caring a lot. —Diane Sawyer

In all human affairs there are efforts, and there are results, and the strength of the effort is the measure of the result. —James Lane Allen

WE MUST WORK ON THE RIGHT THINGS

It is no use saying "we are doing our best." You have got to succeed in doing what is necessary.
—Sir Winston Churchill

Social advance depends as much upon the process through which it is secured as upon the result itself.
—Jane Addams

Children use the fist
Until they are of the age to use the brain. —Elizabeth Barrett Browning

Crime seems to change character when it crosses a bridge or a tunnel. In the city, crime is taken as emblematic of class and race. In the suburbs, though, it's intimate and psychological—resistant to generalization, a mystery of the individual soul.
—Barbara Ehrenreich

Since when do grown men and women, who presume to hold high government office and exercise what they think of as "moral leadership," require ethics officers to tell them whether it is or isn't permissible to grab the secretary's behind or redirect public funds to their own personal advantage? —Meg Greenfield

Vice
Is nice
But a little virtue
Won't hurt you. —Felicia Lamport

The lesser evil is also evil.
—Naomi Mitchison

The great majority of successful business men and women have been and are possessors of strong personalities of the right sort, and by analyzing their climb to success it is amazing to discover how large a part good manners, good breeding, and correct behavior have had in helping them to win the goal. —Ida White Parker

I don't eat junk food and I don't think junk thoughts. —Peace Pilgrim

The Department of Justice is committed to asking one central question of everything we do: What is the right thing to do? Now that can produce debate, and I want it to be spirited debate. I want the lawyers of America to be able to call me and tell me: Janet, have you lost your mind?
—Janet Reno

The voice of conscience is so delicate that it is easy to stifle it; but it is also so clear that it is impossible to mistake it. —Madame de Staël

Many people who wonder why they don't amount to more than they do have good stuff in them, and are energetic, persevering, and have ample opportunities. It is all a case of trimming the useless branches and throwing the whole force of power into the development of something that counts.   —Walter J. Johnston

Noble deeds and hot baths are the best cures for depression.
                    —Dodie Smith

Will you be satisfied with the fruit of your life's work? Will the efforts you are making now bring you satisfaction when the things of time are receding, and eternity looms ahead?
                    —Raymond L. Cox

The act of acting morally is behaving as if everything we do matters.
                    —Gloria Steinem

I place a high moral value on the way people behave. I find it repellent to have a lot, and to behave with anything other than courtesy in the old sense of the word—politeness of the heart, a gentleness of the spirit.
                    —Emma Thompson

SUCCESS AND CHARACTER

Success . . . depends on your ability to make and keep friends.
                    —Sophie Tucker

Some men succeed by what they know; some by what they do; and a few by what they are.
                    —Elbert Hubbard

Try not to become a man of success, but rather a man of value.
                    —Albert Einstein

It is abundantly clear that success tends to negate humility.
                    —Landrum P. Leavell

Success seems to be that which forms the distinction between confidence and conceit.   —Charles Caleb Colton

The common idea that success spoils people by making them vain, egotistic, and self-complacent is erroneous; on the contrary, it makes them, for the most part, humble, tolerant, and kind. Failure makes people cruel and bitter.   —W. Somerset Maugham

Character cannot be developed in ease and quiet. Only through experience of trial and suffering can the soul be strengthened, vision cleared, ambition inspired, and success achieved.   —Helen Keller

If a man be self-controlled, truthful, wise, and resolute, is there aught that can stay out of reach of such a man?
                    —The Panchatantra

Character is the real foundation of all worthwhile success.
                    —John Hays Hammond

TO SUCCEED, WE MUST LEARN TO ADMIT AND ACCEPT FAILURE

One of the first businesses of a sensible man is to know when he is beaten, and to leave off fighting at once.
                    —Samuel Butler

If you can't accept losing, you can't win. —Vince Lombardi

You can't have any successes unless you can accept failure.
—George Cukor

We have fought this fight as long, and as well, as we know how. We have been defeated . . . there is now but one course to pursue. We must accept the situation. —Robert E. Lee

The most considerable difference I note among men is not in their readiness to fall into error, but in their readiness to acknowledge these inevitable lapses.
—Thomas Henry Huxley

An error gracefully acknowledged is a victory won.
—Caroline L. Gascoigne

The man who can own up to his error is greater than he who merely knows how to avoid making it.
—Cardinal de Retz

I have made mistakes, but I have never made the mistake of claiming that I never made one.
—James Gordon Bennett

WE MUST PERSEVERE TO BE SUCCESSFUL

I am not the smartest or most talented person in the world, but I succeeded because I keep going, and going, and going.
—Sylvester Stallone

Victory belongs to the most persevering. —Napoleon Bonaparte

You can imprison a man, but not an idea. You can exile a man, but not an idea. You can kill a man, but not an idea. —Benazir Bhutto

It never pays to deal with the flyweights of the world. They take far too much pleasure in thwarting you at every turn. —Sue Grafton

I know the price of success: dedication, hard work and an unremitting devotion to the things you want to see happen. —Frank Lloyd Wright

There is no point at which you can say, "Well, I'm successful now. I might as well take a nap."
—Carrie Fisher

I wrote for twelve years and collected 250 rejection slips before getting any fiction published, so I guess outside reinforcement isn't all that important to me. —Lisa Alther

I used to want the words "She tried" on my tombstone. Now I want "She did it." —Katherine Dunham

Success generally depends upon knowing how long it takes to succeed.
—Charles de Montesquieu

I am not afraid of the pen, or the scaffold, or the sword. I will tell the truth whenever I please.
—Mother Jones

Once I decide to do something, I can't have people telling me I can't. If there's a roadblock, you jump over it, walk around it, crawl under it.
—Kitty Kelley

Success seems to be largely a matter of hanging on after others have let go.
—William Feather

Call the roll in your memory of conspicuously successful business giants and . . . you will be struck by the fact that almost every one of them encountered inordinate difficulties sufficient to crush all but the gamest of spirits. Edison went hungry many times before he became famous.
—B.C. Forbes

Problems arise in that one has to find a balance between what people need from you and what you need for yourself.
—Jessye Norman

If your efforts are sometimes greeted with indifference, don't lose heart. The sun puts on a wonderful show at daybreak, yet most of the people in the audience go on sleeping.
—Ada Teixeira

If you wish success in life, make perseverance your bosom friend.
—Joseph Addison

Perseverance is failing nineteen times and succeeding the twentieth.
—Julie Andrews

The only thing that happens overnight is recognition. Not talent.
—Carol Haney

If you rest, you rust.   —Helen Hayes

If you don't quit, and don't cheat, and don't run home when trouble arrives, you can only win.
—Shelley Long

They who are the most persistent, and work in the true spirit, will invariably be the most successful.
—Samuel Smiles

If at first you don't succeed, try, try, try again.   —W.E. Hickson

If at first you don't succeed, you're running about average.
—M.H. Alderson

The only way to the top is by persistent, intelligent, hard work.
—A.T. Mercier

The heights by great men reached
    and kept
Were not attained by sudden flight,
But they, while their companions
    slept
Were toiling upward in the night.
—Henry Wadsworth Longfellow

I realized early on that success was tied to not giving up. Most people in this business gave up and went on to other things. If you simply didn't give up, you would outlast the people who came in on the bus with you.
—Harrison Ford

Perseverance is a great element of success. If you only knock long enough and loud enough at the gate, you are sure to wake up somebody.
—Henry Wadsworth Longfellow

Four steps to achievement: plan purposefully, prepare prayerfully, proceed positively, pursue persistently.
—William A. Ward

The secret of success is constancy of purpose.   —Benjamin Disraeli

I'm hardnosed about luck. I think it sucks. Yeah, if you spend seven years looking for a job as a copywriter, and then one day somebody gives you a job, you can say, "Gee, I was lucky I happened to go up there today." But dammit, I was going to go up there sooner or later in the next seventy years. . . . If you're persistent in trying and doing and working, you almost make your own fortune.
—Jerry Della Femina

Flaming enthusiasm, backed up by horse sense and persistence, is the quality that most frequently makes for success.   —Dale Carnegie

It's the plugging away that will win
    you the day
So don't be a piker, old pard!
Just draw on your grit, it's so easy to
    quit—
It's the keeping your chin up that's
    hard.
                —Robert W. Service

No one succeeds without effort. . . . Those who succeed owe their success to their perseverance.
                —Ramana Maharshi

Big shots are only little shots who keep shooting. —Christopher Morley

Entrepreneurs average 3.8 failures before final success. What sets the successful ones apart is their amazing persistence. There are a lot of people out there with good and marketable ideas, but pure entrepreneurial types almost never accept defeat.
                —Lisa M. Amos

There are no shortcuts to any place worth going.   —Beverly Sills

Be of good cheer. Do not think of today's failures, but of the success that may come tomorrow. You have set yourselves a difficult task, but you will succeed if you persevere; and you will find a joy in overcoming obstacles. Remember, no effort that we make to attain something beautiful is ever lost.   —Helen Keller

The way to succeed is never quit. That's it. But really be humble about it. . . . You start out lowly and humble and you carefully try to learn an accretion of little things that help you get there.   —Alex Hailey

Continuous effort—not strength or intelligence—is the key to unlocking our potential.
                —Sir Winston Churchill

Plodding wins the race.   —Aesop

The difficulties and struggles of today are but the price we must pay for the accomplishments and victories of tomorrow.   —William J.H. Boetcker

Let me tell you the secret that has led me to my goal. My strength lies solely in my tenacity. —Louis Pasteur

A winner never quits, and a quitter never wins.   —Anon.

It isn't hard to be good from time to time in sports. What's tough is being good every day.   —Willie Mays

If you start to take Vienna, take Vienna.   —Napoleon Bonaparte

There's such a thin line between winning and losing.   —John R. Tunis

Men who have attained things worth having in this world have worked while others idled, have persevered when others gave up in despair, have practiced early in life the valuable habits of self-denial, industry, and singleness of purpose. As a result, they enjoy in later life the success so often erroneously attributed to good luck.
—Grenvill Kleiser

In the realm of ideas, everything depends on enthusiasm; in the real world, all rests on perseverance.
—Johann von Goethe

SUCCESS TAKES TIME

It takes time to be a success. —Anon.

Actually, I'm an overnight success. But it took twenty years.
—Monty Hall

It takes time to succeed because success is merely the natural reward for taking time to do anything well.
—Joseph Ross

Success generally depends upon knowing how long it takes to succeed.   —Charles de Montesquieu

It takes twenty years to make an overnight success.   —Eddie Cantor

SUCCESS IS RELATIVE

Success is to be measured not so much by the position that one has reached in life as by the obstacles which he has overcome.
—Booker T. Washington

Our business in life is not to get ahead of others but to get ahead of ourselves—to break our own records, to outstrip our yesterdays by our today, to do our work with more force than ever before.
—Steward B. Johnson

Success has always been easy to measure. It is the distance between one's origins and one's final achievement.
—Michael Korda

How can they say my life is not a success? Have I not for more than sixty years got enough to eat and escaped being eaten?
—Logan Pearsall Smith

Survival is triumph enough.
—Harry Crews

Success is peace of mind, which is a direct result of knowing you did your best to become the best that you are capable of becoming.
—John Wooden

Success is relative: It is what we can make of the mess we have made of things.   —T.S. Eliot

The conventional army loses if it does not win. The guerrilla wins if he does not lose.   —Henry Kissinger

The man who has done his level best, and who is conscious that he has done his best, is a success, even though the world may write him down a failure.   —B.C. Forbes

My success is measured by my willingness to keep trying.   —Anon.

If you've had a good time playing the game, you're a winner even if you lose.
—Malcolm Forbes

Success is living up to your potential. That's all. Wake up with a smile and go after life. . . . Live it, enjoy it, taste it, smell it, feel it.
—Joe Kapp

I have fought a good fight, I have finished my course, I have kept the faith.
—2 Timothy 4:7

On earth we have nothing to do with success or results, but only with being true to God, and for God. Defeat in doing right is nevertheless victory.
—Frederick W. Robertson

The reward of a thing well done is to have done it.
—Ralph Waldo Emerson

I'd rather be a lamppost in Chicago than a millionaire in any other city.
—William A. Hulbert

A successful man is he who receives a great deal from his fellow men, usually incomparably more than corresponds to his service to them. The value of a man, however, should be seen in what he gives, and not in what he is able to receive.
—Albert Einstein

SUCCESS IS DOING WHAT'S RIGHT FOR US

There is only one success—to be able to spend your life in your own way.
—Christopher Morley

We only do well the things we like doing.
—Colette

The only success worth one's powder was success in the line of one's idiosyncrasy . . . what was talent but the art of being completely whatever one happened to be?
—Henry James

Success based on anything but internal fulfillment is bound to be empty.
—Dr. Martha Friedman

All I would tell people is to hold on to what was individual about themselves, not to allow their ambition for success to cause them to try to imitate the success of others. You've got to find it on your own terms.
—Harrison Ford

For me, writing is the only thing that passes the three tests of metier: (1) when I'm doing it, I don't feel that I should be doing something else instead; (2) it produces a sense of accomplishment and, once in a while, pride; and (3) it's frightening.
—Gloria Steinem

My mother said to me, "If you become a soldier, you'll be a general, if you become a monk you'll end up as the pope." Instead, I became a painter and wound up as Picasso.
—Pablo Picasso

Abasement, degradation is simply the manner of life of the man who has refused to be what it is his duty to be.
—José Ortega y Gasset

Different people have different duties assigned to them by Nature; Nature has given one the power or the desire to do this, the other that. Each bird must sing with his own throat.
—Henrik Ibsen

A first rate soup is better than a second rate painting.
—Abraham Maslow

We can't all be heroes because someone has to sit on the curb and clap as they go by. —Will Rogers

Nature magically suits a man to his fortunes, by making them the fruit of his character.
—Ralph Waldo Emerson

I'd rather be a lamppost in Chicago than a millionaire in any other city.
—William A. Hulbert

We succeed in enterprises which demand the positive qualities we possess, but we excel in those which can also make use of our defects.
—Alexis de Tocqueville

A man can do only what he can do. But if he does that each day he can sleep at night and do it again the next day. —Albert Schweitzer

Don't take anyone else's definition of success as your own. (This is easier said than done.) —Jacqueline Briskin

Whatever you are by nature, keep to it; never desert your own line of talent. Be what nature intended you for, and you will succeed; be anything else and you will be ten thousand times worse than nothing.
—Sydney Smith

Ask yourself the secret of your success. Listen to your answer, and practice it. —Richard Bach

I cannot do everything, but still I can do something; and because I cannot do everything I will not refuse to do something that I can do.
—Edward Everett Hale

Starting out to make money is the greatest mistake in life. Do what you feel you have a flair for doing, and if you are good enough at it, the money will come. —Greer Garson

If a man has a talent and cannot use it, he has failed. If he has a talent and uses only half of it, he has partly failed. If he has a talent and learns somehow to use the whole of it, he has gloriously succeeded, and won a satisfaction and a triumph few men ever know. —Thomas Wolfe

One can never consent to creep when one feels an impulse to soar.
—Helen Keller

BEFORE WE CAN SUCCEED, WE HAVE TO NOT FAIL

Oh! Much may be done by defying
The ghosts of Despair and Dismay
And much may be gained by relying
On "Where there's a Will There's a Way." —Eliza Cook

We can never give up the belief that good guys always win. And that we are the good guys. —Faith Popcorn

I know there will be spring, as surely as the birds know it when they see above the snow two tiny, quivering green leaves. Spring cannot fail us.
—Olive Schreiner

Most ball games are lost, not won.
—Casey Stengel

Never face facts; if you do you'll
never get up in the morning.
—Marlo Thomas

Before you can win a game, you have
to not lose it.   —Chuck Noll

Football games aren't won, they're
lost.   —Fielding Yost

THE JOURNEY IS MORE IMPORTANT THAN ARRIVING

Success is a journey, not a destination.
—Ben Sweetland

The journey is my home.
—Muriel Rukeyser

To travel hopefully is a better thing
than to arrive, and the true success is
to labor.   —Robert Louis Stevenson

The man who goes fishing gets something more than the fish he catches.
—Mary Astor

Despite the success cult, men are
most deeply moved not by the reaching of the goal, but by the grandness
of effort involved in getting there—or
failing to get there.   —Max Lerner

To live only for some future goal is
shallow. It's the sides of the mountain
that sustain life, not the top.
—Robert M. Pirsig

The reward of the general is not a
bigger tent, but command.
—Oliver Wendell Holmes, Jr.

It is good to have an end to journey
toward; but it is the journey that
matters, in the end.
—Ursula K. LeGuin

We're still not where we're going, but
we're not where we were.
—Natash Jasefowitz

'Tis the motive exalts the action,
'Tis the doing, and not the deed.
—Margaret Junkin Preston

Arriving at one goal is the starting
point to another.   —John Dewey

I think that wherever your journey
takes you, there are new gods waiting there, with divine patience—and
laughter.   —Susan M. Watkins

It has never been, and never will be,
easy work! But the road that is built
in hope is more pleasant to the traveler than the road built in despair,
even though they both lead to the
same destination.
—Marion Zimmer Bradley

In the long run, the pessimist may be
proved to be right, but the optimist
has a better time on the trip.
—Daniel L. Reardon

The excursion is the same when you
go looking for your sorrow as when
you go looking for your joy.
—Eudora Welty

The reward of a thing well done is to
have done it.
—Ralph Waldo Emerson

The struggle alone pleases us, not the
victory.   —Blaise Pascal

The problem is not that you cannot have what you think you want. The problem is that when you get what you think you want, it won't satisfy.
—Anon.

We should scarcely desire things ardently if we were perfectly acquainted with what we desire.
—Francois de La Rochefoucauld

With the catching ends the pleasures of the chase.　　—Abraham Lincoln

To have realized your dream makes you feel lost.　　—Oriana Fallaci

Need and struggle are what excite and inspire us; our hour of triumph is what brings the void.
—William James

We spend our time searching for security, and hate it when we get it.
—John Steinbeck

Happiness is not a station to arrive at, but a manner of traveling.
—Margaret Lee Runbeck

Happiness is to be found along the way, not at the end of the road, for then the journey is over and it is too late.　　—Robert R. Updegraff

The really happy man is one who can enjoy the scenery on a detour.
—Anon.

You wear yourself out in the pursuit of wealth or love or freedom, you do everything to gain some right, and once it's gained you take no pleasure in it.　　—Oriana Fallaci

SUCCESS ISN'T THE TOTAL ANSWER

Success is counted sweetest by those who ne'er succeed.
—Emily Dickinson

Granting our wish is one of Fate's saddest jokes. —James Russell Lowell

Now that I'm here, where am I?
—Janis Joplin

Success is not greedy, as people think, but insignificant. That's why it satisfies nobody.
—Marcus Annaeus Seneca

Is there anything in life so disenchanting as attainment?
—Robert Louis Stevenson

Nothing fails like success; nothing is so defeated as yesterday's triumphant cause.　　—Phyllis McGinley

There are two tragedies in life. One is to lose your heart's desire. The other is to gain it. —George Bernard Shaw

Success has ruined many a man.
—Benjamin Franklin

Fame always brings loneliness. Success is as ice cold and lonely as the North Pole.　　—Vicki Baum

Success has killed more men than bullets.　　—Texas Guinan

Achievement: The death of an endeavor, and the birth of disgust.
—Ambrose Bierce

Success and failure are equally disastrous.　　—Tennessee Williams

The problems of victory are more agreeable than those of defeat, but they are no less difficult.
—Sir Winston Churchill

We are never further from our wishes than when we imagine that we possess what we have desired.
—Johann von Goethe

Some aspects of success seem rather silly as death approaches.
—Donald A. Miller

Unless a man has been taught what to do with success after getting it, the achievement of it must inevitably leave him a prey to boredom.
—Bertrand Russell

If I had known what it would be like to have it all, I might have been willing to settle for less.   —Lily Tomlin

Success and failure are both difficult to endure. Along with success come drugs, divorce, fornication, bullying, travel, meditation, medication, depression, neurosis and suicide. With failure comes failure.
—Joseph Heller

The two hardest things to handle in life are failure and success.   —Anon.

The best thing that can come with success is the knowledge that it is nothing to long for.   —Liv Ullmann

The closer one gets to the top, the more one finds there is no "top."
—Nancy Barcus

Oh, how quickly the world's glory passes away.   —Thomas à Kempis

The minute you think you've got it made, disaster is just around the corner.   —Joe Paterno

Creating success is tough. But keeping it is tougher. You have to keep producing, you can't ever stop.
—Pete Rose

Out of every fruition of success, no matter what, comes forth something to make a new effort necessary.
—Walt Whitman

The toughest thing about success is that you've got to keep on being a success. Talent is only a starting point in business. You've got to keep working that talent.   —Irving Berlin

We would often be sorry if our wishes were gratified.   —Aesop

Nothing except a battle lost can be half so melancholy as a battle won.
—Arthur Wellesley,
Duke of Wellington

Being frustrated is disagreeable, but the real disasters of life begin when you get what you want.
—Irving Kristol

We grow weary of those things (and perhaps soonest) which we most desire.   —Samuel Butler

Our desires always increase with our possessions. The knowledge that something remains yet unenjoyed impairs our enjoyment of the good before us.   —Samuel Johnson

Oddly enough, success over a period of time is more expensive than failure.
—Grant Tinker

There must be more to life than having everything! —Maurice Sendak

It's not that I'm not grateful for all this attention. It's just that fame and fortune ought to add up to more than fame and fortune. —Robert Fulghum

If you live long enough, you'll see that every victory turns into a defeat.
—Simone de Beauvoir

One more such victory and we are undone. —Pyrrhus

Pray that success will not come any faster than you are able to endure it.
—Elbert Hubbard

The prospect of success in achieving our most cherished dream is not without its terrors. Who is more deprived and alone than the man who has achieved his dream?
—Brendan Francis

Success can also cause misery. The trick is not to be surprised when you discover it doesn't bring you all the happiness and answers you thought it would. —Prince

Adversity is sometimes hard upon a man, but for one man who can stand prosperity, there are a hundred that will stand adversity.
—Thomas Carlyle

OTHER DEFINITIONS OF SUCCESS

To me success means effectiveness in the world, that I am able to carry my ideas and values into the world—that I am able to change it in positive ways. —Maxine Hong Kingston

If you have a good name, if you are right more often than you are wrong, if your children respect you, if your grandchildren are glad to see you, if your friends can count on you and you can count on them in time of trouble, if you can face your God and say "I have done my best," then you are a success. —Ann Landers

Success is getting what you want; happiness is wanting what you get.
—Anon.

Life is a succession of moments. To live each one is to succeed.
—Corita Kent

To laugh often and much;
To win the respect of intelligent
    people, and the affection of
    children;
To earn the appreciation of honest
    critics, and endure the betrayal of
    false friends;
To appreciate beauty;
To find the best in others;
To leave the world a bit better,
    whether by a healthy child, a
    garden patch, or a redeemed
    social condition;
To know that even one life has
    breathed easier because you lived.
This is to have succeeded.
—Ralph Waldo Emerson

I personally measure success in terms of the contributions an individual makes to his or her fellow human beings. —Margaret Mead

He has achieved success, who has lived well, laughed often, and loved much; who has gained the respect of intelligent men and the love of little children. —Bessie A. Stanley

Success has nothing to do with what you gain in life or accomplish for yourself. It's what you do for others.
—Danny Thomas

If you have a good name, if you are right more often than you are wrong, if your children respect you, if your grandchildren are glad to see you, if your friends can count on you and you can count on them in time of trouble, if you can face your God and say, "I have done my best," then you are a success.   —Ann Landers

Success is the sweetest revenge.
—Vanessa Williams

You have reached the pinnacle of success as soon as you become uninterested in money, compliments, or publicity.   —Thomas Wolfe

A woman who is loved always has success.   —Vicki Baum

Success is not a doorway, it's a staircase.   —Dottie Walters

General Quotations about Success

There is no scientific answer for success. You can't define it. You've simply got to live it and do it.
—Anita Roddick

Marconi invented radio, but Ted Husing knew what to do with it.
—Ralph Edwards

The ultimate of being successful is the luxury of giving yourself the time to do what you want to do.
—Leontyne Price

I don't think success is harmful, as so many people say. Rather I believe it indispensible to talent: if for nothing else than to increase the talent.
—Jeanne Moreau

Success produces success, just as money produces money.
—Nicolas de Chamfort

If I do have some success, I'd like to enjoy it, for heaven's sake! What is the point of having it otherwise?
—Leontyne Price

God may allow His servant to succeed when He has disciplined him to a point where he does not need to succeed to be happy. The man who is elated by success and is cast down by failure is still a carnal man. At best his fruit will have a worm in it.
—A.W. Tozer

There is no business in the world so troublesome as the pursuit of fame: life is over before you have hardly begun your work.
—Jean de La Bruyère

Nothing fails like success because we don't learn from it. We learn only from failure.   —Kenneth Boudling

The insight to see possible new paths, the courage to try them, the judgment to measure results—these are the qualities of a leader.
—Mary Parker Follett

Success makes men rigid and they tend to exalt stability over all the other virtues; tired of the effort of willing, they become fanatics about conservatism.   —Walter Lippman

Success is a great healer.
—Gertrude Atherton

All outward success, when it has value, is but the inevitable result of an inward success of full living, full play and enjoyment of one's faculties.
—Robert Henri

There are three types of baseball players—those who make it happen, those who watch it happen, and those who wonder what happened.
—Tommy Lasorda

The exclusive worship of the bitch-goddess Success is our national disease.
—William James

Success causes us to be more praised than known. —Joseph Roux

Along with success comes a reputation for wisdom. —Euripides

Fame has only the span of the day, they say. But to live in the hearts of people—that is worth something.
—Ouida

Great men have not been concerned with fame. The joy of achievement that comes from finding something new in the universe is by far their greatest joy. —William P. King

Out of the strain of the Doing, into the peace of the Done.
—Julia Louise Woodruff

Success is like a liberation, or the first phase of a love affair.
—Jeanne Moreau

There is always room at the top.
—Daniel Webster

An act of love that fails is just as much a part of the divine life as an act of love that succeeds, for love is measured by its own fullness, not by its reception. —Harold Loukes

The best place to succeed is where you are with what you have.
—Charles M. Schwab

Success covers a multitude of blunders.
—George Bernard Shaw

How to succeed: try hard enough. How to fail: Try too hard.
—Malcolm Forbes

I have found that it is much easier to make a success in life than to make a success of one's life. —G.W. Follin

There could be no honor in a sure success, but much might be wrested from a sure defeat.
—T.E. Lawrence
(Lawrence of Arabia)

Bad will be the day for every man when he becomes absolutely contented with the life he is living, when there is not forever beating at the doors of his soul some great desire to do something larger.
—Phillips Brooks

When there is no feeling of accomplishment, children fail to develop properly and old people rapidly decline. —Joseph Whitney

Those who have easy, cheerful attitudes tend to be happier than those with less pleasant temperaments, regardless of money, "making it," or success. —Dr. Joyce Brothers

Theirs is not to reason why, theirs is
but to do or die.
                    —Alfred, Lord Tennyson

Victory at all costs, victory in spite of
all terror, victory however long and
hard the hard may be; for without
victory there is no survival.
                    —Sir Winston Churchill

In war there is no second prize for
the runner-up.
                    —General Omar N. Bradley

Luck

LUCK CAN BE VERY IMPORTANT

Luck is everything. . . . My good luck in life was to be a really frightened person. I'm fortunate to be a coward, to have a low threshold of fear, because a hero couldn't make a good suspense film.   —Alfred Hitchcock

Most of life is choices, and the rest is pure dumb luck.   —Marian Erickson

Exceptional talent does not always win its reward unless favoured by exceptional circumstances.
     —Mary Elizabeth Braddon

I would rather have a lucky general than a smart general. . . . They win battles, and they make me lucky.
     —Dwight D. Eisenhower

There is a spirit and a need and a man at the beginning of every great human advance. Every one of these must be right for that particular moment of history, or nothing happens.
     —Coretta Scott King

Everything in life is luck.
     —Donald Trump

'Tis man's to fight, but Heaven's to give success.   —Homer

I am persuaded that luck and timing have, in my case, been very important.
     —Mike Wallace

I have been extraordinarily lucky. Anyone who pretends that some kind of luck isn't involved in his success is deluding himself.   —Arthur Hailey

'Tis better to be fortunate than wise.
     —John Webster

I wish I could tell you that the Children's Television Workshop and Sesame Street were thanks to my genius, but it really was a lucky break.
     —Joan Ganz Cooney

In the queer mess of human destiny, the determining factor is luck.
     —William E. Woodward

Much of my good fortune was a matter of nothing more clever on my part than luck.   —James Fixx

Name the greatest of all inventors: Accident.   —Mark Twain

Though men pride themselves on their great actions, often they are not the result of any great design, but of chance.
—Francois de La Rochefoucauld

No writer should minimize the factor that affects everyone, but is beyond control: luck. —John Jakes

Everything that happened to me happened by mistake. I don't believe in fate. It's luck, timing and accident.
—Merv Griffin

STILL, WE CAN'T DEPEND TOO HEAVILY ON LUCK

Luck always seems to be against the man who depends on it. —Anon.

The doors we open and close each day decide the lives we live.
—Flora Whittemore

Good luck is often with the man who doesn't include it in his plans.
—Anon.

Depend on the rabbit's foot if you will, but it didn't work for the rabbit!
—Anon.

Destiny is the invention of the cowardly, and the resigned.
—Ignazio Silone

This world is run with far too tight a rein for luck to interfere. Fortune sells her wares; she never gives them. In some form or other, we pay for her favors; or we go empty away.
—Amelia Barr

Foolish indeed are those who trust to fortune. —Lady Murasaki

Luck enters into every contingency. You are a fool if you forget it—and a greater fool if you count upon it.
—Phyllis Bottome

They who await no gifts from chance have conquered fate.
—Matthew Arnold

The worst cynicism, a belief in luck.
—Joyce Carol Oates

To believe in luck . . . is skepticism.
—Ralph Waldo Emerson

Shallow men believe in luck, wise and strong men in cause and effect.
—Ralph Waldo Emerson

Those who trust to chance must abide by the results of chance.
—Calvin Coolidge

Luck is what a capricious man believes in. —Benjamin Disraeli

Luck serves . . . as rationalization for every people that is not master of its own destiny. —Hannah Arendt

It is a madness to make fortune the mistress of events, because in herself she is nothing, but is ruled by prudence. —John Dryden

Luck is a word devoid of sense; nothing can exist without a cause.
—Voltaire

Woe to him who would ascribe something like reason to Chance, and make a religion of surrendering to it.
—Johann von Goethe

Fortune is the rod of the weak, and the staff of the brave.
—James Russell Lowell

The man who is intent on making the most of his opportunities is too busy to bother about luck.   —B.C. Forbes

Luck implies an absolute absence of any principle.   —Chuang-tzu

WE MUST CREATE OUR OWN LUCK

I'm hardnosed about luck. I think it sucks. Yeah, if you spend seven years looking for a job as a copywriter, and then one day somebody gives you a job, you can say, "Gee, I was lucky I happened to go up there today." But dammit, I was going to go up there sooner or later in the next seventy years. . . . If you're persistent in trying and doing and working, you almost make your own fortune.
—Jerry Della Femina

I resolved to take Fate by the throat and shake the living out of her.
—Louisa May Alcott

I must have something to engross my thoughts, some object in life which will fill this vacuum and prevent this sad wearing away of the heart.
—Elizabeth Blackwell

To wait for someone else, or to expect someone else to make my life richer, or fuller, or more satisfying, puts me in a constant state of suspension.
—Kathleen Tierney Andrus

The champion makes his own luck.
—Red Blaik

It is a great piece of skill to know how to guide your luck, even while waiting for it.   —Baltasar Gracian

I was thinking of my patients, and how the worst moment for them was when they discovered they were masters of bad or good luck. When they could no longer blame fate, they were in despair.   —Anaïs Nin

Some are satisfied to stand politely before the portals of Fortune and to await her bidding; better those who push forward, who employ their enterprise, who on the wings of their worth and valor seek to embrace luck, and to effectively gain her favor.
—Baltasar Gracian

He alone is great
Who by a life heroic conquers fate.
—Sarah Knowles Bolton

Chance never helps those who do not help themselves.   —Sophocles

Failure and success seem to have been allotted to men by their stars. But they retain the power of wriggling, of fighting with their star or against it, and in the whole universe the only really interesting movement is this wriggle.   —E.M. Forster

Go and wake up your luck.
—Persian proverb

People make their own luck.
—David Liederman

When it comes time to do your own life, you either perpetuate your childhood or you stand on it and finally kick it out from under.
—Rosellen Brown

If fate means you to lose, give him a good fight anyhow. —William McFee

I was forced to live far beyond my years when just a child, now I have reversed the order and I intend to remain young indefinitely.
—Mary Pickford

We create our fate every day ... most of the ills we suffer from are directly traceable to our own behavior.
—Henry Miller

Of course, fortune has its part in human affairs, but conduct is really much more important.
—Jeanne Detourbey

You don't just luck into things. ... You build step by step, whether it's friendships or opportunities.
—Barbara Bush

I got well by talking. Death could not get a word in edgewise, grew discouraged, and traveled on.
—Louise Erdrich

You are in the driver's seat of your life and can point your life down any road you want to travel. You can go as fast or as slow as you want to go ... and you can change the road you're on at any time. —Jinger Heath

We must master our good fortune, or it will master us.   —Publilius Syrus

GOOD LUCK COMES FROM HARD WORK

I'm a great believer in luck, and I find the harder I work, the more I have of it.   —Thomas Jefferson

Good luck needs no explanation.
—Shirley Temple Black

Luck means the hardships and privations which you have not hesitated to endure, the long nights you have devoted to work. Luck means the appointments you have never failed to keep, the trains you have never failed to catch.   —Max O'Relling

Luck is what you have left over after you give 100 percent.
—Langston Coleman

Luck is not chance, it's toil; fortune's expensive smile is earned.
—Emily Dickinson

The lucky fellow is the plucky fellow who has been burning midnight oil and taking defeat after defeat with a smile.   —James B. Hill

There is no such thing as making the miracle happen spontaneously and on the spot. You've got to work.
—Martina Arroyo

I don't know anything about luck. I've never banked on it, and I'm afraid of people who do. Luck to me is something else; hard work and realizing what is opportunity and what isn't.   —Lucille Ball

Men who have attained things worth having in this world have worked while others idled, have persevered when others gave up in despair, have practiced early in life the valuable habits of self-denial, industry, and singleness of purpose. As a result, they enjoy in later life the success so often erroneously attributed to good luck.
—Grenville Kleiser

I don't believe in luck. We make our own good fortune.
—Dr. Joyce Brothers

You have to learn the rules of the game. And then you have to play better than anyone else.
—Dianne Feinstein

Luck is the by-product of busting your fanny.
—Don Sutton

When you work seven days a week, fourteen hours a day, you get lucky.
—Armand Hammer

The more you invest in a marriage, the more valuable it becomes.
—Amy Grant

Love doesn't just sit there, like a stone, it has to be made, like bread; remade all the time, made new.
—Ursula K. LeGuin

No man ever wetted clay and then left it, as if there would be bricks by chance and fortune.
—Plutarch

Some people go through life trying to find out what the world holds for them only to find out too late that it's what they bring to the world that really counts.
—L.M. Montgomery

Pennies do not come from heaven—they have to be earned here on earth.
—Margaret Thatcher

It's hard to detect good luck—it looks so much like something you've earned.
—Frank A. Clark

Chance favors those in motion.
—Dr. James H. Austin

Work and acquire, and thou hast chained the wheel of Chance.
—Ralph Waldo Emerson

Superiority to fate is difficult to gain, 'tis not conferred of any, but possible to earn.
—Emily Dickinson

Some folk want their luck buttered.
—Thomas Hardy

Diligence is the mother of good luck, and God gives all things to industry.
—Benjamin Franklin

Fortune is ever seen accompanying industry.
—Oliver Goldsmith

I find I'm luckier when I work harder.
—Dr. Denton Cooley

BOLDNESS AND COURAGE CAN HELP CREATE LUCK

Fortune favours the bold.   —Terence

A stout heart breaks bad luck.
—Miguel de Cervantes

All good fortune is a gift of the gods, and . . . you don't win the favor of the ancient gods by being good, but by being bold.
—Anita Brookner

Fortune reveres the brave, and overwhelms the cowardly.
—Marcus Annaeus Seneca

Fortune sides with him who dares.
—Virgil

We Must Prepare to Receive Our Luck

Chance favors the prepared mind.
—Louis Pasteur

You have to be eligible for luck to strike, and I think that's a matter of education and preparation, and character and all the other solid attributes that sometimes people laugh at.
—James A. Michener

Get as much experience as you can, so that you're ready when luck works. That's the luck.
—Henry Fonda

You've got to be in a position for luck to happen. Luck doesn't go around looking for a stumblebum.
—Darrell Royal

Luck is the residue of design.
—Branch Rickey

Luck affects everything. Let your hook be always cast. In the stream where you least expect it, there will be fish.
—Ovid

Chance does nothing that has not been prepared beforehand.
—Alexis de Tocqueville

Luck is being ready for the chance.
—J. Frank Dobie

Chance usually favors the prudent man.
—Joseph Joubert

Combine common sense and the Golden Rule, and you will have very little bad luck.
—Anon.

Thorough preparation makes its own luck.
—Joe Poyer

Luck is a matter of preparation meeting opportunity.
—Oprah Winfrey

We Must Recognize and Maximize Our Luck

There are so many people with all kinds of lucky things happening to them, and they don't know how to use it.
—Rocky Aoki

Probably any successful career has "X" number of breaks in it, and maybe the difference between successful people and those who aren't superachievers is taking advantage of those breaks.
—Joan Ganz Cooney

To get it right, be born with luck or else make it.
—Ruth Gordon

You must always be open to your luck. You cannot force it, but you can recognize it.
—Henry Moore

Genius is the gold in the mine; talent is the miner that works and brings it out.
—Lady Marguerite Blessington

It is one thing to be gifted and quite another thing to be worthy of one's own gift.
—Nadia Boulanger

Talent on its own sat gracefully only on the very young. After a certain age it was what you did with it that counted.
—Liza Cody

A wise man turns chance into good fortune.
—Thomas Fuller

Luck . . . taps, once in a lifetime, at everybody's door, but if industry does not open it, luck goes away.
—Charles Haddon Spurgeon

When something bad happens to me, I think I'm able to deal with it in a pretty good way. That makes me lucky. Some people fall apart at the first little thing that happens.
—Christie Brinkley

It's funny, but . . . you're sort of a moving target for fortune, and you never know when it will befall you.
—Thomas McGuane

Other Sources of Luck

Lady Luck generally woos those who earnestly, enthusiastically, unremittingly woo her.   —B.C. Forbes

Luck is good planning, carefully executed.   —Anon.

What helps luck is a habit of watching for opportunities, of having a patient, but restless mind, of sacrificing one's ease or vanity, of uniting a love of detail to foresight, and of passing through hard times bravely and cheerfully.
—Charles Victor Cherbuliez

Luck is believing you're lucky.
—Tennessee Williams

I think that one can have luck if one tries to create an atmosphere of spontaneity.   —Federico Fellini

Each man's character shapes his fortunes.   —Latin proverb

Chance works for us when we are good captains.   —George Meredith

Motivation triggers luck.
—Mike Wallace

Good and bad luck is a synonym, in the great majority of instances, for good and bad judgment.
—John Chatfield

Luck is a combination of confidence and getting the breaks.
—Christy Mathewson

I was born lucky, and I have lived lucky. What I had was used. What I still have is being used. Lucky.
—Katharine Hepburn

Luck is largely a matter of paying attention.   —Susan M. Dodd

Your luck is how you treat people.
—Bridget O'Donnell

Luck Changes

The only sure thing about luck is that it will change.   —Bret Harte

The man who glories in his luck may be overthrown by destiny.
—Euripides

There is in the worst of fortune the best of chances for a happy change.
—Euripides

It is more easy to get a favor from fortune than to keep it.
—Publilius Syrus

Since luck's a nine days' wonder, wait their end.   —Euripides

Fortune is with you for an hour, and
against you for ten!   —Arab proverb

Breaks balance out. The sun don't
shine on the same old dog's rear end
every day.   —Darrell Royal

What the reason of the ant labori-
ously drags into a heap, the wind of
accident will collect in one breath.
                 —J.C.F. von Schiller

Fortune is like the market, where
many times, if you can stay a little,
the price will fall.   —Francis Bacon

The profits of good luck are perish-
able; if you build on fortune, you build
on sand; the more advancement you
achieve, the more dangers you run.
                 —Marquis de Racan

Every possession and every happiness
is but lent by chance for an uncertain
time, and may therefore be demanded
back the next hour.
                 —Arthur Schopenhauer

Life is full of chances and changes,
and the most prosperous of men may
. . . meet with great misfortunes.
                    —Aristotle

Opportunity

Life Is Full of Opportunities, but We Often Miss Them

To see a shadow and think it is a tree—that is a pity; but to see a tree and to think it a shadow can be fatal.
—Phyllis Bottome

Great opportunities come to all, but many do not know they have met them. The only preparation to take advantage of them is simple fidelity to watch what each day brings.
—Albert E. Dunning

Opportunities are everywhere.
—Lucy Benington

Opportunities are usually disguised as hard work, so most people don't recognize them. —Ann Landers

The world is all gates, all opportunities, strings of tension waiting to be struck. —Ralph Waldo Emerson

No great man ever complains of want of opportunity.
—Ralph Waldo Emerson

Great opportunities to help others seldom come, but small ones come daily. —Ivy Baker Priest

Men do with opportunities as children do at the seashore; they fill their little hands with sand, and then let the grains fall through, one by one, till all are gone. —T. Jones

Do not wait for ideal circumstances, nor for the best opportunities; they will never come.
—Janet Erskine Stuart

Nothing is so often irretrievably missed as a daily opportunity.
—Marie von Ebner-Eschenbach

If a man looks sharply and attentively, he shall see fortune; for though she be blind, yet she is not invisible.
—Francis Bacon

Know thine opportunity. —Pittacus

In great affairs we ought to apply ourselves less to creating chances than to profiting from those that are offered.
—Francois de La Rochefoucauld

Opportunity is as scarce as oxygen; men fairly breathe it and do not know it. —Doc Sane

Opportunities do not come with their values stamped upon them. . . . To face every opportunity of life thoughtfully, and ask its meaning bravely and earnestly, is the only way to meet supreme opportunities when they come, whether open-faced or disguised. —Maltbie D. Babcock

We are told that talent creates its own opportunities. But it sometimes seems that intense desire creates not only its own opportunities, but its own talents. —Eric Hoffer

How many opportunities present themselves to a man without his noticing them? —Arab proverb

Luck affects everything. Let your hook be always cast. In the stream where you least expect it, there will be a fish. —Ovid

The opportunity that God sends does not wake up him who is asleep. —Senegalese proverb

Present opportunities are neglected, and attainable good is slighted, by minds busied in extensive ranges and intent upon future advantages. —Samuel Johnson

Opportunities multiply as they are seized; they die when neglected. Life is a long line of opportunities. —John Wicker

It is often hard to distinguish between the hard knocks in life and those of opportunity. —Frederick Phillips

I think luck is the sense to recognize an opportunity and the ability to take advantage of it. Everyone has bad breaks, but everyone also has opportunities. The man who can smile at his breaks and grab his chances gets on. —Samuel Goldwyn

To improve the golden moment of opportunity, and catch the good that is within our reach, is the great art of life. —Samuel Johnson

The greatest achievement of the human spirit is to live up to one's opportunities, and make the most of one's resources. —Vauvenargues

When one door closes, another opens. But we often look so long and so regretfully upon the closed door that we do not see the one which has opened for us. —Helen Keller

The opportunities for enjoyment in your life are limitless. If you feel you are not experiencing enough joy, you have only yourself to blame. —David E. Bresler

Opportunities are often things you haven't noticed the first time around. —Catherine Deneuve

The successful man is one who had the chance and took it. —Roger Babson

Vigilance in watching opportunity; tact and daring in seizing upon opportunity; force and persistence in crowding opportunity to its utmost possible achievement—these are the martial virtues which must command success. —Austin Phelps

To avoid an occasion for our virtues is a worse degree of failure than to push forward pluckily and make a fall.
—Robert Louis Stevenson

Opportunity knocks but once.
—Anon.

I was seldom able to see an opportunity until it had ceased to be one.
—Mark Twain

If Fortune calls, offer him a seat.
—Yiddish proverb

What the student calls a tragedy, the master calls a butterfly.
—Richard Bach

Opportunity is missed by most people because it is dressed in overalls, and looks like work.
—Thomas A. Edison

OPPORTUNITIES ARE OFTEN FOUND IN TOUGH SITUATIONS

Times of stress and difficulty are seasons of opportunity when the seeds of progress are sown.
—Thomas F. Woodlock

We must look for the opportunity in every difficulty instead of being paralyzed at the thought of the difficulty in every opportunity.
—Walter E. Cole

WE MUST PREPARE FOR OUR OPPORTUNITIES

The best impromptu speeches are the ones written well in advance.
—Ruth Gordon

Opportunity can benefit no man who has not fitted himself to seize it and use it. Opportunity woos the worthy, shuns the unworthy. Prepare yourself to grasp opportunity, and opportunity is likely to come your way. It is not so fickle, capricious and unreasoning as some complain.   —B.C. Forbes

Opportunity rarely knocks until you are ready. And few people have ever been really ready without receiving opportunity's call.
—Channing Pollock

The secret to success in life is for a man to be ready for his opportunity when it comes.   —Benjamin Disraeli

I always keep myself in a position of being a student.
—Jackie Joyner-Kersee

I think the young actor who really wants to act will find a way . . . to keep at it and seize every opportunity that comes along.
—Sir John Gielgud

If you want greater prosperity in your life, start forming a vacuum to receive it.   —Catherine Ponder

Unless a man has trained himself for his chance, the chance will only make him ridiculous.   —William Matthews

WE MUST ALSO CREATE OUR OWN OPPORTUNITIES

Capacity never lacks opportunity. It cannot remain undiscovered because it is sought by too many anxious to use it.   —Cochran

You create your opportunities by asking for them.   —Patty Hansen

A wise man will make more opportunities than he finds.   —Francis Bacon

Look for opportunity. You can't wait
for it to knock on the door. . . . You
might not be home.   —Jinger Heath

If you want to succeed in the
world, you must make your own
opportunities.   —John B. Gough

Life is a narrative that you have a
hand in writing.
       —Henriette Anne Klauser

Mediocre men wait for opportunity
to come to them. Strong, able, alert
men go after opportunity.
         —B.C. Forbes

A filly who wants to run will always
find a rider.   —Jacques Audiberti

Life is what we make it; always has
been, always will be.
       —Grandma Moses

God forgives those who invent what
they need.   —Ayn Rand

Many things are lost for want of
asking.   —English proverb

You don't just luck into things . . .
you build step by step, whether it's
friendships or opportunities.
       —Barbara Bush

Every man is the architect of his own
fortune.   —Sallust

He that waits upon fortune is never
sure of a dinner. —Benjamin Franklin

OPPORTUNITY AND SECURITY

There is no security on this earth.
Only opportunity.
    —General Douglas MacArthur

Too many people are thinking of
security instead of opportunity; they
seem more afraid of life than of
death.   —James F. Byrnes

Freedom is nothing else but a chance
to be better, whereas enslavement is a
certainty of the worst.
    —Albert Camus

WE OFTEN LOSE OPPORTUNITIES BY OVERDELIBERATION

The opportunity is often lost by
deliberating.   —Publilius Syrus

I have always been waiting for something better—sometimes to see the
best I had snatched from me.
    —Dorothy Reed Mendenhall

The sad truth is that opportunity
doesn't knock twice. You can put
things off until tomorrow but tomorrow may never come. Where will you
be a few years down the line? Will
it be everything you dreamed of?
We seal our fate with the choices we
take, but don't give a second thought
to the chances we take.
    —Gloria Estefan

You decide you'll wait for your pitch.
Then as the ball starts toward the
plate, you think about your stance.
And then you think about your
swing. And then you realize that the
ball that went past you for a strike
was your pitch.   —Bobby Murcer

General Quotations about Opportunity

Small opportunities are often the beginning of great enterprises.
—Demosthenes

Any ritual is an opportunity for transformation. —Starhawk

Ability is of little account without opportunity. —Napoleon Bonaparte

Our opportunities to do good are our talents. —Cotton Mather

Opportunity knocks at every man's door once. On some men's door it hammers till it breaks down the door and then it goes in and wakes him up if he's asleep, and ever afterward it works for him as a night watchman.
—Finley Peter Dunne

It is less important to redistribute wealth than it is to redistribute opportunity. —Arthur Vandenberg

You can't make soufflé rise twice.
—Alice Roosevelt Longworth

A door that seems to stand open must be a man's size, or it is not the door that Providence means for him.
—Henry Ward Beecher

Next to knowing when to seize an opportunity, the most important thing in life is to know when to forgo an advantage. —Benjamin Disraeli

The follies which a man regrets most in his life are those which he didn't commit when he had the opportunity.
—Helen Rowland

It is not manly to turn one's back on fortune. —Marcus Annaeus Seneca

Commitment

To Live Fully and Successfully, We Must Commit to Something

If you don't make a total commitment to whatever you're doing, then you start looking to bail out the first time the boat starts leaking. It's tough enough getting that boat to shore with everybody rowing, let alone when a guy stands up and starts putting his life jacket on.   —Lou Holtz

When I stand before God at the end of my life, I would hope that I would not have a single bit of talent left, and could say, "I used everything you gave me."   —Erma Bombeck

It seems safe to say that significant discovery, really creative thinking, does not occur with regard to problems about which the thinker is lukewarm.   —Mary Henle

If a man hasn't discovered something that he will die for, he isn't fit to live.
                —Martin Luther King, Jr.

Moderation in war is imbecility.
                —Admiral John Fisher

Let my name stand among those who are willing to bear ridicule and reproach for the truth's sake, and so earn some right to rejoice when the victory is won.   —Louisa May Alcott

Getting ahead in a difficult profession requires avid faith in yourself. You must be able to sustain yourself against staggering blows. There is no code of conduct to help beginners. That is why some people with mediocre talent, but with great inner drive, go much further than people with vastly superior talent.
                —Sophia Loren

The wonderful thing about saints is that they were human. They lost their tempers, got hungry, scolded God, were egotistical or impatient in their turns, made mistakes and regretted them. Still they went on doggedly blundering toward heaven.
                —Phyllis McGinley

A successful marriage requires falling in love many times, always with the same person.   —Mignon McLaughlin

Winners are men who have dedicated their whole lives to winning.
—Woody Hayes

Those who love a cause are those who love the life which has to be led in order to serve it.   —Simone Weil

Unless you can find some sort of loyalty, you cannot find unity and peace in your active living.   —Josiah Royce

Sometimes success is due less to ability than zeal. The winner is he who gives himself to his work body and soul.   —Charles Buxton

Now I am steel-set: I follow the call to the clear radiance and glow of the heights.   —Henrik Ibsen

Love me, please, I love you; I can bear to be your friend. So ask of me anything . . . I am not a tentative person. Whatever I do, I give up my whole self to it.
—Edna Saint Vincent Millay

I don't care a damn for your loyal service when you think I am right; when I really want it most is when you think I am wrong.
—General Sir John Monash

One's lifework, I have learned, grows with the working and the living. Do it as if your life depended on it, and first thing you know, you'll have made a life out of it. A good life, too
—Theresa Helburn

If you don't stand for something, you'll fall for anything.
—Michael Evans

If you deny yourself commitment, what can you do with your life?
—Harvey Fierstein

The person who makes a success of living is the one who sees his goal steadily and aims for it unswervingly. That is dedication.
—Cecil B. DeMille

Theirs is not to reason why, theirs is but to do or die.
—Alfred, Lord Tennyson

Either do not attempt at all, or go through with it.   —Ovid

If you start to take Vienna, take Vienna.   —Napoleon Bonaparte

If you aren't going all the way, why go at all?   —Joe Namath

You can be an ordinary athlete by getting away with less than your best. But if you want to be a great, you have to give it all you've got—your everything.   —Duke P. Kahanamoku

Put your heart, mind, intellect and soul even to your smallest acts. This is the secret of success.
—Swami Sivananda

It is fatal to enter any war without the will to win it.
—General Douglas MacArthur

Men, like snails, lose their usefulness when they lose direction and begin to bend.   —Walter Savage Landor

It is by losing himself in the objective, in inquiry, creation, and craft, that a man becomes something.
—Paul Goodman

The height of your accomplishments will equal the depth of your convictions.　　—William F. Scolavino

The dedicated life is the life worth living.　　—Annie Dillard

The secret of living is to find a pivot, the pivot of a concept on which you can make your stand.
　　—Luigi Pirandello

THE PERILS OF THE MIDDLE OF THE ROAD

There's nothing in the middle of the road but yellow stripes and dead armadillos.　　—Jim Hightower

Standing in the middle of the road is very dangerous; you get knocked down by traffic from both sides.
　　—Margaret Thatcher

He who walks in the middle of the road gets hit from both sides.
　　—George P. Schultz

I never liked the middle ground—the most boring place in the world.
　　—Louise Nevelson

The hottest places in hell are reserved for those who, in a period of moral crisis, maintain their neutrality.
　　—Dante Alighieri

The man who sees both sides of an issue is very likely on the fence or up a tree.　　—Anon.

The middle of the road is where the white line is, and that's the worst place to drive.　　—Robert Frost

The principle of neutrality . . . has increasingly become an obsolete conception, and, except under very special circumstances, it is an immoral and shortsighted conception.
　　—John Foster Dulles

We know what happens to people who stay in the middle of the road. They get run over.　　—Aneurin Bevan

Show me a person who is not an extremist about some things, who is a "middle-of-the-roader" in everything, and I will show you someone who is insecure.　　—G. Aiken Taylor

APATHY AND INDIFFERENCE

We should not permit tolerance to degenerate into indifference.
　　—Margaret Chase Smith

Most people are not for or against anything; the first object of getting people together is to make them respond somehow, to overcome inertia.　　—Mary Parker Follett

There is nothing harder than the softness of indifference.
　　—Juan Montalvo

I could not, at any age, be content to take my place by the fireside and simply look on. Life was meant to be lived. Curiosity must be kept alive. One must never, for whatever reason, turn his back on life.
　　—Eleanor Roosevelt

The accomplice to the crime of corruption is frequently our own indifference.　　—Bess Myerson

The opposite of love is not hate, it's indifference.
The opposite of art is not ugliness, it's indifference.
The opposite of faith is not heresy, it's indifference.
And the opposite of life is not death, it's indifference.   —Elie Wiesel

Science may have found a cure for most evils; but it has found no remedy for the worst of them all—the apathy of human beings.
                        —Helen Keller

The only difference between a rut and a grave is their dimensions.
                        —Ellen Glasgow

We're swallowed up only when we are willing for it to happen.
                        —Nathalie Sarraute

COMMITMENT AND THE HEART

The only place you can win a football game is on the field. The only place you can lose it is in your heart.
                        —Darrell Royal

I am seeking, I am striving, I am in it with all my heart.
                        —Vincent van Gogh

He did it with all his heart, and prospered.   —2 Chronicles 31:21

Wars may be fought with weapons, but they are won by men. It is the spirit of the men who follow, and of the man who leads, that gains the victory.   —General George S. Patton

It was my tongue that swore; my heart is unsworn.   —Euripides

Morale is the greatest single factor in successful wars.
                        —Dwight D. Eisenhower

COMMITMENT AND WILLPOWER

Nothing can resist a will which will stake even existence upon its fulfillment.   —Benjamin Disraeli

Nothing is difficult to those who have the will.
        —Motto of the Dutch Poets' Society

Our future and our fate lie in our wills more than in our hands, for our hands are but the instruments of our wills.   —B.C. Forbes

Nothing is so common as unsuccessful men with talent. They lack only determination.   —Charles Swindoll

The will to conquer is the first condition of victory.
                        —Marshal Ferdinand Foch

Strength is a matter of the made-up mind.   —John Beecher

Your own resolution to success is more important than any other one thing.   —Abraham Lincoln

COMMITMENT AND BELIEF

What distinguishes the majority of men from the few is their ability to act accordingly to their beliefs.
                        —Henry Miller

What a man believes, he will die for. What a man merely thinks, he will change his mind about.   —Anon.

When you have decided what you believe, what you feel must be done, have the courage to stand alone and be counted.   —Eleanor Roosevelt

The eloquent man is he who is no beautiful speaker, but who is inwardly and desperately drunk with a certain belief.   —Ralph Waldo Emerson

A belief which does not spring from a conviction in the emotions is no belief at all.   —Evelyn Scott

Whether you are really right or not doesn't matter, it's the belief that counts.   —Robertson Davies

Sometimes We Must Burn Our Bridges behind Us

Many a man has walked up to the opportunity for which he has long been preparing himself, looked it full in the face, and then begun to get cold feet . . . when it comes to betting on yourself and your power to do the thing you know you must do or write yourself down a failure, you're a chicken-livered coward if you hesitate.   —B.C. Forbes

The wise man puts all his eggs in one basket and watches the basket.
    —Andrew Carnegie

Poverty is uncomfortable, as I can testify: but nine times out of ten the best thing that can happen to a young man is to be tossed overboard and compelled to sink or swim for himself.   —James A. Garfield

Anytime you play golf for whatever you've got, that's pressure. I'd like to see H.L. Hunt go out there and play for $3 billion.   —Lee Trevino

There is a point at which everything becomes simple and there is no longer any question of choice, because all you have staked will be lost if you look back. Life's point of no return.
    —Dag Hammarskjold

Even now we can draw back. But once we cross that little bridge, we must settle things by the sword.
    —Julius Caesar,
    to his troops
    as they prepared to
    cross the Rubicon River

So will I go in unto the king . . . and if I perish, I perish.   —Esther 4:16

You don't know what pressure is until you play for $5 with only $2 in your pocket.   —Lee Trevino

The fixed determination to have acquired the warrior soul, to either conquer or perish with honor, is the secret of victory.
    —General George S. Patton

Commitment and Warfare

In war there is no substitute for victory.   —Dwight D. Eisenhower

Victory at all costs, victory in spite of all terror, victory however long and hard the road may be; for without victory there is no survival.
    —Sir Winston Churchill

601

Better that we should die fighting
than be outraged and dishonored.
Better to die than to live in slavery.
　　　　　—Emmeline Pankhurst

I sincerely wish war was a pleasanter
and easier business than it is, but it
does not admit of holidays.
　　　　　—Abraham Lincoln

Every attempt to make war easy and
safe will result in humiliation and
disaster.
　　—General William T. Sherman

If you start to take Vienna, take
Vienna.　　　—Napoleon Bonaparte

GENERAL QUOTATIONS
ABOUT COMMITMENT

The worth of every conviction consists precisely in the steadfastness
with which it is held.　—Jane Adams

The moment one definitely commits
oneself, the Providence moves, too.
All sorts of things occur to help that
would never otherwise have occurred.
A stream of events issues from the
decision, raising unforeseen incidents
and meetings and material assistance,
which no man could have dreamt
would have come his way.
　　　　　—W.H. Murray

There is no strong performance
without a little fanaticism in the
performer.　—Ralph Waldo Emerson

If you don't wake up with something in your stomach every day that
makes you think, "I want to make
this movie," it'll never get made.
　　　　　—Sherry Lansing

We can do whatever we wish to do
provided our wish is strong enough.
But the tremendous effort needed—
one doesn't always want to make
it—does one? . . . But what else can be
done? What's the alternative? What
do you want most to do? That's what
I have to keep asking myself, in the
face of difficulties.
　　　　　—Katherine Mansfield

I am a stranger to half measures.
　　　　　—Marita Golden

Perform without fail what you
resolve.　　　—Benjamin Franklin

To say yes, you have to sweat and
roll up your sleeves and plunge both
hands into life up to the elbows. It
is easy to say no, even if saying no
means death.　　　—Jean Anouilh

What one has, one ought to use; and
whatever he does, he should do with
all his might.　　　　　—Cicero

Nothing's far when one wants to get
there.　—Queen Marie of Rumania

Whatsoever thy hand findeth to do,
do it with thy might.
　　　　　—Ecclesiastes 9:10

He that rides his hobby gently must
always give way to him that rides his
hobby hard. —Ralph Waldo Emerson

Stay up and really burn the midnight
oil. There are no compromises.
　　　　　—Leontyne Price

Nothing of worthy or weight can be
achieved with half a mind, with a
faint heart, and with a lame endeavor.
　　　　　—Isaac Barrow

Don't ask me to give in to this body of mine. I can't afford it. Between me and my body there must be a struggle until death.
—Saint Margaret of Cortona

Morality, like physical cleanliness, is not acquired once and for all: it can only be kept and renewed by a habit of constant watchfulness and discipline. —Victoria Ocampo

Firmness of purpose is one of the most necessary sinews of character, and one of the best instruments of success. Without it, genius wastes its efforts in a maze of inconsistencies.
—Lord Chesterfield

My face is set, my gait is fast, my goal is Heaven, my road is narrow, my way is rough, my companions are few, my guide is reliable, my mission is clear. I cannot be bought, compromised, detoured, lured away, turned back, diluted, or delayed. I will not flinch in the face of sacrifice, hesitate in the presence of adversity, negotiate ... at the table of the enemy, ponder at the pool of popularity, or meander in a maze of mediocrity. I won't give up, shut up, let up, or slow up.
—Robert Moorehead

To have no loyalty is to have no dignity, and in the end, no manhood.
—Peter Taylor Forsyth

If you are ashamed to stand by your colors, you had better seek another flag. —Anon.

Great minds have purposes, others have wishes. —Washington Irving

I don't want people who want to dance, I want people who have to dance. —George Balanchine

What a man wants to do he generally can do, if he wants to badly enough.
—Louis L'Amour

Never grow a wishbone, daughter, where your backbone ought to be.
—Clementine Paddleford

Happy are those who dream dreams and are ready to pay the price to make them come true.
—L.J. Cardinal Suenens

He turns not back who is bound to a star. —Leonardo da Vinci

One advantage of marriage, it seems to me, is that when you fall out of love with him, or he falls out of love with you, it keeps you together until you maybe fall in love again.
—Judith Viorst

You can't try to do things; you simply must do them. —Ray Bradbury

I am in earnest; I will not equivocate; I will not excuse; I will not retreat a single inch; and I will be heard.
—William Lloyd Garrison

Concentration

The Importance of Concentration

The ability to concentrate and to use your time well is everything.
—Lee Iacocca

It is only when I dally with what I am about, look back and aside, instead of keeping my eyes straight forward, that I feel these cold sinkings of the heart. —Sir Walter Scott

A straight path never leads anywhere except to the objective. —André Gide

Nothing interferes with my concentration. You could put on an orgy in my office and I wouldn't look up. Well, maybe once. —Isaac Asimov

To be able to concentrate for a considerable time is essential to difficult achievement. —Bertrand Russell

If there is anything that can be called genius, it consists chiefly in the ability to give that attention to a subject which keeps it steadily in the mind, till we have surveyed it accurately on all sides. —Thomas Reid

If you don't concentrate, you'll end up on your rear. —Tai Babilonia

If I have ever made any valuable discoveries, it has been owing more to patient attention than to any other talent. —Isaac Newton

For him who has no concentration, there is no tranquility.
—Bhagaved Gita

The secret to success in any human endeavor is total concentration.
—Kurt Vonnegut

The secret of concentration is the secret of self-discovery. You reach inside yourself to discover your personal resources, and what it takes to match them to the challenge.
—Arnold Palmer

Don't Try to Do Too Many Things

Beware of dissipating your powers; strive constantly to concentrate them.
—Johann von Goethe

604

One arrow does not bring down two birds. —Turkish proverb

No horse gets anywhere until he is harnessed. No steam or gas ever drives anything until it is confined. No Niagara is ever turned into light and power until it is tunneled. No life ever grows great until it is focused, dedicated, disciplined.
—Harry Emerson Fosdick

A man may be so much of everything that he is nothing of everything.
—Samuel Johnson

Concentrate your energies, your thoughts and your capital. . . . The wise man puts all his eggs in one basket and watches the basket.
—Andrew Carnegie

One man; two loves. No good ever comes of that. —Euripides

One cannot both feast and become rich. —Ashanti proverb

The perplexity of life arises from there being too many interesting things in it for us to be interested properly in any of them.
—G.K. Chesterton

No country can act wisely simultaneously in every part of the globe at every moment of time.
—Henry Kissinger

CONCENTRATE ON ONE THING

The field of consciousness is tiny. It accepts only one problem at a time.
—Antoine de Saint-Exupery

To do two things at once is to do neither. —Publilius Syrus

I like to laugh, but on the court, it is my work. I try to smile, but it is so difficult. I concentrate on the ball, not on my face. —Steffi Graf

Successful minds work like a gimlet, to a single point. —Christian Bovee

A bird can roost but on one branch. A mouse can drink no more than its fill from a river. —Chinese proverb

Each man is capable of doing one thing well. If he attempts several, he will fail to achieve distinction in any.
—Plato

This one thing I do . . . I press toward the mark. —Philippians 3:13–14

All good is gained by those whose thought and life are kept pointed close to one main thing, not scattered abroad upon a thousand.
—Stephen McKenna

The first law of success . . . is concentration: to bend all the energies to one point, and to go directly to that point, looking neither to the right nor the left. —William Matthews

Give me a man who says this one thing I do, and not these fifty things I dabble in. —Dwight L. Moody

A single idea, if it is right, saves us the labor of an infinity of experiences.
—Jacques Maritain

One thought driven home is better than three left on base. —James Liter

605

Purity of heart is to will one thing.
—Søren Kierkegaard

ELIMINATE THE NON-ESSENTIAL

A man should remove not only unnecessary acts, but also unnecessary thoughts, for then superfluous activity will not follow.
—Marcus Aurelius

No man will swim ashore and take his baggage with him.
—Marcus Annaeus Seneca

Many people who wonder why they don't amount to more than they do have good stuff in them, and are energetic, persevering, and have ample opportunities. It is all a case of trimming the useless branches and throwing the whole force of power into the development of something that counts.   —Walter J. Johnston

A great man is one who seizes the vital issue in a complex question, what we might call the jugular vein of the whole organism, and spends his energies upon that.
—Joseph Rickaby

ALWAYS FOCUS ON THE IMMEDIATE TASK

While the work or play is on . . . don't constantly feel you ought to be doing the other.   —Franklin P. Adams

When one is learning, one should not think of play; and when one is at play, one should not think of learning.   —Lord Chesterfield

The immature mind hops from one thing to another; the mature mind seeks to follow through.
—Harry A. Overstreet

If you want to hit a bird on the wing you must have all your will in focus, you must not be thinking about yourself and, equally, you must not be thinking about your neighbor: you must be living in your eye on that bird. Every achievement is a bird on the wing.
—Oliver Wendell Holmes, Jr.

When walking, walk.
When eating, eat.   —Zen maxim

The difference in men does not lie in the size of their hands, nor in the perfection of their bodies, but in this one sublime ability of concentration: to throw the weight with the blow, to live an eternity in an hour.
—Elbert Hubbard

I go at what I am about as if there was nothing else in the world for the time being.   —Charles Lingsley

Choice of attention, to pay attention to this and ignore that, is to the inner life what choice of action is to the outer.   —W.H. Auden

Concentration is everything. On the day I'm performing, I don't hear anything anyone says to me.
—Luciano Pavarotti

The real essence of work is concentrated energy.   —Walter Begehot

You can't ring the bells and, at the same time, walk in the procession.
—Spanish proverb

I've learned ruthless concentration.
I can write under any circumstances
... street noises, loud talk, music, you
name it.   —Sylvia Porter

Do whatever you do intensely.
                    —Robert Henri

The effectiveness of work increases
according to geometrical progression
if there are no interruptions.
                    —André Maurois

Other people's interruptions of your
work are relatively insignificant compared with the countless times you
interrupt yourself.   —Brendan Francis

If you direct your whole thought to
work itself, none of the things which
invade eyes or ears will reach the
mind.   —Quintilian

A full mind is an empty baseball bat.
                    —Branch Rickey

There is time enough for everything
in the course of the day if you do but
one thing at once; but there is not
time enough in the year if you will do
two things at a time.
                    —Lord Chesterfield

OTHER SOURCES OF
CONCENTRATION

If you direct your whole thought to
work itself, none of the things which
invade eyes or ears will reach the
mind.   —Quintilian

Become so wrapped up in something
that you forget to be afraid.
                    —Lady Bird Johnson

Attention to a subject depends upon
our interest in it.   —Tyron Edwards

I can't concentrate on golf or bowling.
Those bowling pins aren't going to
hurt me. I can concentrate in the ring
because someone is trying to kill me.
                    —Carmen Basilio

When I come into a game in the bottom of the ninth, bases loaded, no
one out and a one-run lead ... it takes
people off my mind.   —Tug McGraw

Concentrate on finding your goal,
then concentrate on reaching it.
                    —Colonel Michael Friedsman

Those who set out to serve both God
and Mammon soon discover that
there is no God.
                    —Logan Pearsall Smith

When a man knows he is to be
hanged in a fortnight, it concentrates
his mind wonderfully.
                    —Samuel Johnson

Work

Work Is Essential to Most People's Happiness

The road to happiness lies in two simple principles: find what it is that interests you and that you can do well, and when you find it, put your whole soul into it—every bit of energy and ambition and natural ability you have.   —John D. Rockefeller III

Every woman is a human being—one cannot repeat that too often—and a human being must have occupation if he or she is not to become a nuisance to the world.   —Dorothy L. Sayers

The happy people are those who are producing something.
—William Ralph Inge

Congenial labor is essence of happiness.
—Arthur Christopher Benson

Work is a substitute "religious" experience for many workaholics.
—Mary Daly

When I can no longer create anything, I'll be done for. —Coco Chanel

Employment is nature's physician, and is essential to human happiness.
—Galen

No thoroughly occupied man was ever yet very miserable.
—Letitia Landon

When I stop [working], the rest of the day is posthumous. I'm only really alive when I'm working.
—Tennessee Williams

Continuity of purpose is one of the most essential ingredients of happiness in the long run, and for most men this comes chiefly through their work.   —Bertrand Russell

It is only when I am doing my work that I feel truly alive. It is like having sex.   —Federico Fellini

After fifty years of living, it occurs to me that the most significant thing that people do is go to work, whether it is to go to work on their novel or at the assembly plant or fixing somebody's teeth.   —Thomas McGuane

608

He who labors diligently need never despair, for all things are accomplished by diligence and labor.
—Menander

The fun of being alive is realizing that you have a talent and you can use it every day, so it grows stronger. . . . And if you're in an atmosphere where this talent is appreciated instead of just tolerated, why, it's just as good as sex. —Lou Centlivre

Work! Thank God for the swing of it, for the clamoring, hammering ring of it. —Anon.

There are certain natures to whom work is nothing, the act of work everything. —Arthur Symons

I am fierce for work. Without work I am nothing. —Winifred Holtby

ALL WORK HAS DIGNITY

Like plowing, housework makes the ground ready for the germination of family life. The kids will not invite a teacher home if beer cans litter the living room. The family isn't likely to have breakfast together if somebody didn't remember to buy eggs, milk, or muffins. Housework maintains an orderly setting in which family life can flourish.
—Letty Cottin Pogrebin

When I die, my epitaph should read: She Paid the Bills. —Gloria Swanson

There's no labor a man can do that's undignified, if he does it right.
—Bill Cosby

Never turn down a job because you think it's too small; you never know where it may lead. —Julia Morgan

If a man is called to be a streetsweeper, he should sweep streets even as Michelangelo painted, or Beethoven composed music or Shakespeare wrote poetry. He should sweep streets so well that all the hosts of heaven and earth will pause to say, here lived a great streetsweeper who did his job well. —Martin Luther King, Jr.

Don't be afraid of hard work.
—Marian Wright Edelman

The work praises the man.
—Irish proverb

Originality and the feeling of one's own dignity are achieved only through work and struggle.
—Fyodor Dostoyevsky

There is a kind of victory in good work, no matter how humble.
—Jack Kemp

Labor disgraces no man; unfortunately, you occasionally find men who disgrace labor. —Ulysses S. Grant

Honest labor bears a lovely face.
—Thomas Dekker

I have friends in overalls whose friendship I would not swap for the favor of the kings of the world.
—Thomas A. Edison

The world is moved not only by the mighty shoves of the heroes, but also by the aggregate of the tiny pushes of each honest worker. —Helen Keller

A professional is someone who can do his best work when he doesn't feel like it. —Alistair Cooke

The highest reward for man's toil is not what he gets for it, but what he becomes by it. —John Ruskin

THE IMPORTANCE OF FINDING THE WORK WE WERE MEANT TO DO

Starting out to make money is the greatest mistake in life. Do what you feel you have a flair for doing, and if you are good enough at it, the money will come. —Greer Garson

Ambition is destruction, only competence matters. —Jill Robinson

I was brought up to believe that the only thing worth doing was to add to the sum of accurate information in the world. —Margaret Mead

Never desert your own line of talent. Be what nature intended you for, and you will succeed. —Sydney Smith

Here I am, where I ought to be. —Louise Erdrich

To find in ourselves what makes life worth living is risky business, for it means that once we know we must seek it. It also means that without it life will be valueless. —Marsha Sinetar

Everybody undertakes what he sees another successful in, whether he has the aptitude for it or not. —Johann von Goethe

You have to do what you love to do, not get stuck in that comfort zone of a regular job. Life is not a dress rehearsal. This is it. —Lucinda Basset

Men take only their needs into consideration, never their abilities. —Napoleon Bonaparte

If you're in a good profession, it's hard to get bored, because you're never finished—there will always be work you haven't done. —Julia Child

Work means so many things! So many! Among other things, work also means freedom. . . . Without it even the miracle of love is only a cruel deception. —Eleanora Duse

One should stick to the sort of thing for which one was made; I tried to be an herbalist, whereas I should keep to the butcher's trade. —Jean de La Fontaine

One's lifework, I have learned, grows with the working and the living. Do it as if your life depended on it, and first thing you know, you'll have made a life out of it. A good life, too. —Theresa Helburn

One principal reason why men are so often useless is that they neglect their own profession or calling, and divide and shift their attention among a multitude of objects and pursuits. —Nathaniel Emmons

Men whose trade is rat-catching love to catch rats; the bug destroyer seizes on his bug with delight; the suppressor is gratified by finding his vice. —Sydney Smith

Work is creativity accompanied by the comforting realization that one is bringing forth something really good and necessary, with a conviction that a sudden, arbitrary cessation would cause a sensitive void, produce a loss.
—Jenny Heynrichs

Some people are born to lift heavy weights, some are born to juggle golden balls.　　—Max Beerbohm

Life is to be lived. If you have to support yourself, you had bloody well better find some way that is going to be interesting. And you don't do that by sitting around wondering about yourself.　　—Katharine Hepburn

To find out what one is fitted to do, and to secure an opportunity to do it, is the key to happiness.
—John Dewey

The high prize of life, the crowning fortune of man, is to be born with a bias to some pursuit which finds him in employment and happiness.
—Ralph Waldo Emerson

They are happy men whose natures sort with their vocations.
—Francis Bacon

WORK YOU LOVE ISN'T WORK

I know a lot of people think it's monotonous, down the black lines over and over, but it's not if you're enjoying what you're doing. I love to swim and I love to train.
—Tracy Caulkins

Do your duty until it becomes your joy.　—Marie von Ebner-Eschenbach

Duty is an icy shadow. It will freeze you. It cannot fill the heart's sanctuary.
—Augusta Evans

What a richly colored strong warm coat is woven when love is the warp and work is the woof.
—Marge Piercy

Whenever it is possible, a boy should choose some occupation which he should do even if he did not need the money.　　—William Lyon Phelps

Some people regard discipline as a chore. For me, it is a kind of order that sets me free to fly.
—Julie Andrews

Find something you're passionate about and keep tremendously interested in it.　　—Julia Child

There must be bands of enthusiasts for everything on earth—fanatics who shared a vocabulary, a batch of technical skills and equipment, and, perhaps, a vision of some single slice of the beauty and mystery of things, of their complexity, fascination, and unexpectedness.　　—Annie Dillard

I love Mickey Mouse more than any woman I've ever known.
—Walt Disney

The test of a vocation is the love of the drudgery it involves.
—Logan Pearsall Smith

Only he is successful in his business who makes that pursuit which affords him the highest pleasure sustain him.　　—Henry David Thoreau

Work is a world apart from jobs. Work is the way you occupy your mind and hand and eye and whole body when they're informed by your imagination. —Alice Koller

I believe in my work and in the joy of it. You have to be with the work and the work has to be with you. It absorbs you totally and you absorb it totally. —Louise Nevelson

Cooking is like love. It should be entered into with abandon or not at all. —Harriet Van Horne

Give me a man who sings at his work. —Thomas Carlyle

To love what you do and feel that it matters—how could anything be more fun? —Katherine Graham

When men are rightly occupied, their amusement grows out of their work, as the color-petals out of a fruitful flower. —John Ruskin

When love and skill work together, expect a masterpiece. —John Ruskin

Work consists of whatever a body is obliged to do, and play consists of whatever a body is not obliged to do. —Mark Twain

Winning the [Nobel] prize wasn't half as exciting as doing the work itself. —Maria Goeppert Mayer

Work and play are words used to describe the same thing under differing conditions. —Mark Twain

When people go to work, they shouldn't have to leave their hearts at home. —Betty Bender

Workaholics are energized rather than enervated by their work—their energy paradoxically expands as it is expended. —Marilyn Machlowitz

The more I want to get something done, the less I call it work. —Richard Bach

WORK AND SUCCESS

To deny we need and want power is to deny that we hope to be effective. —Liz Smith

Success depends in a very large measure upon individual initiative and exertion, and cannot be achieved except by a dint of hard work. —Anna Pavlova

Nothing worthwhile comes easily. Half effort does not produce half results, it produces no results. Work, continuous work and hard work, is the only way to accomplish results that last. —Hamilton Holt

If a man wakes up famous, he hasn't been sleeping. —Wes Izzard

Striving for success without hard work is like trying to harvest where you haven't planted. —David Bly

If your dream is a big dream, and if you want your life to work on the high level that you say you do, there's no way around doing the work it takes to get you there. —Joyce Chapman

Success is dependent on effort.
　　　　　　　　　—Sophocles

Hard work has made it easy. That is
my secret. That is why I win.
　　　　　　　　—Nadia Comaneci

Success comes before work only in
the dictionary.　　　　　—Anon.

Sweat plus sacrifice equals success.
　　　　　　　—Charles O. Finley

The only thing that separates successful people from the ones who aren't
is the willingness to work very, very
hard.　　　—Helen Gurley Brown

You can have unbelievable intelligence, you can have connections, you
can have opportunities fall out of the
sky. But in the end, hard work is the
true, enduring characteristic of successful people.　　　—Marsha Evans

Success usually comes to those who
are too busy to be looking for it.
　　　　　　—Henry David Thoreau

In all human affairs there are efforts,
there are results, and the strength of
the effort is the measure of the result.
　　　　　　　　—James Lane Allen

WORK HARD, BUT REMEMBER TO
PLAY, TOO

Busy work brings after ease;
Ease brings sport and sport brings
　　rest;
For young and old, of all degrees,
The mingled lot is best.
　　　　　　　　　—Joanna Baillie

Work, alternated with needful rest, is
the salvation of man or woman.
　　　—Antoinette Brown Blackwell

There is a time for work. And a time
for love. That leaves no other time.
　　　　　　　　　—Coco Chanel

Neither woman nor man lives by
work, or love, alone. . . . The human
self defines itself and grows through
love and work: All psychology before
and after Freud boils down to that.
　　　　　　　　　—Betty Friedan

Maintain a good balance. A personal
life adds dimensions to your professional life and vice versa. It helps
nurture creativity through a deeper
understanding of yourself.
　　　　　　　　—Kathy Ireland

For the happiest life, days should be
rigorously planned, nights left open
to chance.　　—Mignon McLaughlin

Work is the province of cattle.
　　　　　　　　—Dorothy Parker

The only sin passion can commit is to
be joyless.　　　—Dorothy L. Sayers

WORK PAYS DIVIDENDS

Skilled labor teaches something not
to be found in books or in colleges.
　　　　　　　　　—Laura Towne

Diligence is the mother of good luck,
and God gives all things to industry.
　　　　　　　—Benjamin Franklin

To industry, nothing is impossible.
　　　　　　　　　—Latin proverb

I believe in hard work. It keeps the wrinkles out of the mind and spirit.
—Helena Rubinstein

God sells us all things at the price of labor. —Leonardo da Vinci

The sport I love has taken me around the world and shown me many things. —Bonnie Blair

I realized that with hard work, the world was your oyster. You could do anything you wanted to do. I learned that at a young age. —Chris Evert

Fortune is ever seen accompanying industry. —Oliver Goldsmith

Manual labor to my father was not only good and decent for its own sake, but as he was given to saying, it straightened out one's thoughts.
—Mary Ellen Chase

I get satisfaction of three kinds. One is creating something, one is being paid for it and one is the feeling that I haven't just been sitting on my ass all afternoon. —William F. Buckley

The sentimentalist ages far more quickly than the person who loves his work and enjoys new challenges.
—Lillie Langtry

Busy people are never busybodies.
—Ethel Watts Mumford

What a man sows, that shall he and his relations reap. —Clarissa Graves

General Quotations about Work

The only way to enjoy anything in this life is to earn it first.
—Ginger Rogers

I have worked all my life, wanted to work all my life, needed to work all my life. —Liz Carpenter

The simple idea that everyone needs a reasonable amount of challenging work in his or her life, and also a personal life, complete with noncompetitive leisure, has never really taken hold.
—Judith Martin (Miss Manners)

There is no more dreadful punishment than futile and hopeless labor.
—Albert Camus

Whether we call it a job or a career, work is more than just something we do. It is a part of who we are.
—Anita Hill

If I could I would always work in silence and obscurity, and let my efforts be known by their results.
—Emily Brontë

Nobody ever drowned in his own sweat. —Ann Landers

The heights by great men reached
　and kept
Were not attained by sudden flight,
But they, while their companions
　slept,
Were toiling upward in the night.
—Henry Wadsworth Longfellow

Work in some form or other is the appointed lot of all. —Anna Jameson

Any man who has had the job I've had and didn't have a sense of humor wouldn't still be here.
—Harry S. Truman

Whatever the job you are asked to do at whatever level, do a good job because your reputation is your resume.   —Madeleine Albright

People should tell their children what life is all about—it's about work.
—Lauren Bacall

Marriage ain't easy but nothing that's worth much ever is.   —Lillian Carter

I don't think that work ever really destroyed anybody. I think that lack of work destroys them a hell of a lot more.   —Katharine Hepburn

For the last third of life there remains only work. It alone is always stimulating, rejuvenating, exciting and satisfying.   —Kathe Kollwitz

I slept, and dreamed that life was Beauty;
I woke, and found that life was Duty.
—Ellen Sturgis Hooper

Passion is never enough; neither is skill.
—Toni Morrison

It's not the having, it's the getting.
—Elizabeth Taylor

Opportunity is missed by most people because it is dressed in overalls, and looks like work.
—Thomas A. Edison

A man's work is from sun to sun, but a mother's work is never done.
—Anon.

Be strong!
We are not here to play, to dream, to drift;
We have hard work to do and loads to lift;
Shun not the struggle—face it; 'tis God's gift.
—Maltbie D. Babcock

If you could once make up your mind never to undertake more work . . . than you can carry on calmly, quietly, without hurry or flurry . . . and if the instant you feel yourself growing nervous and . . . out of breath, you would stop and take a breath, you would find this simple common-sense rule doing for you what no prayers or tears could ever accomplish.
—Elizabeth Prentiss

It is better to have no emotion when it is work. Do what needs to be done, and do it coolly.   —Louis L'Amour

What a man accomplishes in a day depends upon the way in which he approaches his tasks. When we accept tough jobs as a challenge to our ability and wade into them with joy and enthusiasm, miracles can happen. When we do our work with a dynamic, conquering spirit, we get things done.   —Arland Gilbert

The one important thing I have learned over the years is the difference between taking one's work seriously, and taking one's self seriously. The first is imperative, and the second is disastrous. —Margot Fonteyn

Work is the best method devised for killing time.   —William Feather

Industry is a better horse to ride than genius. —Walter Lippman

There are two kinds of talents, man-made talent and God-given talent. With man-made talent you have to work very hard. With God-given talent, you just touch it up once in a while. —Pearl Bailey

If you want something done, ask a busy person to do it. The more things you do, the more you can do. —Lucille Ball

With the power of conviction, there is no sacrifice. —Pat Benatar

I believe you are your work. Don't trade the stuff of your life, time, for nothing more than dollars. That's a rotten bargain —Rita Mae Brown

When you're following your energy and doing what you want all the time, the distinction between work and play dissolves. —Shakti Gawain

Work is the thing that stays. Work is the thing that sees us through. —Ellen Gilchrist

Energy is the power that drives every human being. It is not lost by exertion but maintained by it, for it is a faculty of the psyche. —Germaine Greer

It is not hard work that is dreary; it is superficial work —Edith Hamilton

As for me, prizes mean nothing. My prize is my work. —Katharine Hepburn

There can be no substitute for work, neither affection nor physical well-being can replace it. —Maria Montessori

Work is its own cure. You have to like it better than being loved. —Marge Piercy

Work . . . has always been my favorite form of recreation. —Anna Howard Shaw

A job is not a career. I think I started out with a job. It turned into a career and changed my life. —Barbara Walters

The only genius that's worth anything is the genius for hard work. —Kathleen Winsor

Elbow grease is the best polish. —English proverb

Never despair, but if you do, work on in despair. —Edmund Burke

Laziness is a secret ingredient that goes into failure. But it's only kept a secret from the person who fails. —Robert Half

WORKING ALONE—AND IN
CONCERT WITH OTHERS

Pears cannot ripen alone. So we ripened together. —Meridel Le Sueur

Ideally, couples need three lives; one for him, one for her, and one for them together. —Jacqueline Bisset

Exchange is creation. —Muriel Rukeyser

Whatever my individual desires were to be free, I was not alone. There were others who felt the same way.
—Rosa Parks

Now men and women are separate and unequal. We should be hand in hand; in fact, we should have our arms around one another.
—Cloris Leachman

Men and women are like right and left hands: it doesn't make sense not to use both.
—Jeannette Rankin

There are three ways of dealing with difference: domination, compromise, and integration. By domination only one side gets what it wants; by compromise neither side gets what it wants; by integration we find a way by which both sides may get what they wish.
—Mary Parker Follett

Women and men have to fight together to change society—and both will benefit.
—Muriel Fox

Every time a man unburdens his heart to a stranger he reaffirms the love that unites humanity.
—Germaine Greer

Good communication is as stimulating as black coffee, and just as hard to sleep after.
—Anne Morrow Lindbergh

Cooperation is an intelligent functioning of the concept of laissez faire—a thorough conviction that nobody can get there unless everybody gets there.
—Virginia Burden Tower

Most leaders are indispensable, but to produce a major social change, many ordinary people must also be involved.
—Anne Firor Scott

Communication is a continual balancing act, juggling the conflicting needs for intimacy and independence. To survive in the world, we have to act in concert with others, but to survive as ourselves, rather than simply as cogs in a wheel, we have to act alone.
—Deborah Tannen

My whole life, whether it be long or short, shall be devoted to your service and the service of our great imperial family to which we all belong. But I shall not have the strength to carry out this resolution alone unless you join in it with me.
—Queen Elizabeth II

A person who believes . . . that there is a whole of which one is a part, and that in being a part one is whole: such a person has no desire whatever, at any time, to play God. Only those who have denied their being yearn to play at it.
—Ursula K. LeGuin

Unless I am a part of everything I am nothing.
—Penelope Lively

For what is done or learned by one class of women becomes, by virtue of their common womanhood, the property of all women.
—Elizabeth Blackwell

We learn best to listen to our own voices if we are listening at the same time to other women—whose stories, for all our differences, turn out, if we listen well, to be our stories also.
—Barbara Deming

Remember the dignity of your womanhood. Do not appeal, do not beg, do not grovel. Take courage, join hands, stand beside us, fight with us.
—Christabel Pankhurst

Today whenever women gather together it is not necessarily nurturing. It is coalition building. And if you feel the strain, you may be doing some good work.
—Bernice Johnson Reagon

Women's art, though created in solitude, wells up out of community. There is, clearly, both enormous hunger for the work thus being diffused, and an explosion of creative energy, bursting through the coercive choicelessness of the system on whose boundaries we are working.
—Adrienne Rich

You've got to be willing to stay committed to someone over the long run, and sometimes it doesn't work out. But often if you become real honest with yourself and honest with each other, and put aside whatever personal hurt and disappointment you have to really understand yourself and your spouse, it can be the most wonderful experience you've ever had.
—Hillary Rodham Clinton

We must stand together; if we don't, there will be no victory for any one of us.
—Mother Jones

I've always believed that one woman's success can only help another woman's success.
—Gloria Vanderbilt

Alone we can do so little; together we can do so much.
—Helen Keller

I always feel the movement is a sort of mosaic. Each of us puts in one little stone, and then you get a great mosaic at the end.
—Alice Paul

We all act as hinges—fortuitous links between other people.
—Penelope Lively

We seldom stop to think how many people's lives are entwined with our own. It is a form of selfishness to imagine that every individual can operate on his own or can pull out of the general stream and not be missed.
—Ivy Baker Priest

Perfection

NOTHING IS PERFECT

Perfection does not exist. To understand this is the triumph of human intelligence; to expect to possess it is the most dangerous kind of madness.
—Alfred de Musset

So much perfection argues rottenness somewhere.   —Beatrice Potter Webb

The essence of man is imperfection.
—Norman Cousins

A new idea is rarely born like Venus attended by graces. More commonly it's modeled of baling wire and acne. More commonly it wheezes and tips over.   —Marge Piercy

The essence of being human is that one does not seek perfection.
—George Orwell

There is no perfection in humanity.
—Samuel Montagne

Perfection never exists in reality, but only in our dreams.
—Dr. Rudolf Dreikurs

He is lifeless that is faultless.
—English proverb

Perfection is out of the question.
—Anne Archer

His only fault is that he has no fault.
—Pliny, the Younger

If you're looking for perfection, look in the mirror. If you find it there, expect it elsewhere.
—Malcolm Forbes

A perfect poem is impossible. Once it has been written, the world would end.   —Robert Graves

It is the function of perfection to make one know one's imperfection.
—Saint Augustine

The man with insight enough to admit his limitations comes nearest to perfection.   —Johann von Goethe

A man would do nothing if he waited until he could do it so well that no one could find fault.
—John Henry Cardinal Newman

Nothing you write, if you hope to be any good, will ever come out as you first hoped. —Lillian Hellman

All of us failed to match our dreams of perfection. —William Faulkner

What, after all, is a halo? It's only one more thing to keep clean.
—Christopher Fry

Angels can do no better.
—K. Panuthos

We Don't Need to Be Perfect

To talk about the need for perfection in man is to talk about the need for another species. —Norman Cousins

Striving for perfection is the greatest stopper there is. You'll be afraid you can't achieve it. . . . It's your excuse to yourself for not doing anything. Instead, strive for excellence, doing your best. —Sir Laurence Olivier

The "C" students run the world.
—Harry S. Truman

You know what they call the guy who finishes last in medical school? They call him Doctor!
—Abe Lemons

A good garden may have some weeds. —Thomas Fuller

At times failure is very necessary for the artist. It reminds him that failure is not the ultimate disaster. And this reminder liberates him from the mean fussing of perfectionism.
—John Berger

Perfection is no more a requisite to art than to heroes. —Ned Rorem

People Don't Expect or Want Perfection

Living with a saint is more grueling than being one. —Robert Neville

A finished person is a boring person.
—Anna Quindlen

He is all fault who hath no fault at all. For who loves me must have a touch of earth.
—Alfred, Lord Tennyson

You're only human, you're supposed to make mistakes. —Billy Joel

Truth is immortal; error is mortal.
—Mary Baker Eddy

I don't like a man to be too efficient. He's likely to be not human enough.
—Felix Frankfurter

Sainthood is acceptable only in saints.
—Pamela Hansford Johnson

I like a man with faults, especially when he knows it. To err is human— I'm uncomfortable around gods.
—Hugh Prather

If the best man's faults were written on his forehead, it would make him pull his hat over his eyes.
—Gaelic proverb

Friendships aren't perfect, and yet they are very precious. For me, not expecting perfection all in one place was a great release.
—Letty Cottin Pogrebin

It Isn't Healthy to Seek Perfection

Almost anything carried to its logical extreme becomes depressing, if not carcinogenic. —Ursula K. LeGuin

A concern with the perfectibility of mankind is always a symptom of thwarted or perverted development. —Hugh Kingsmill

Perfectionism is self-abuse of the highest order. —Anne Wilson Schaef

When everything has to be right, something isn't. —Stanislaw Lec

The maxim "Nothing avails but perfection" may be spelled "Paralysis." —Sir Winston Churchill

Perfectionism is a dangerous state of mind in an imperfect world. —Robert Hillyer

Perfectionism is slow death. —Hugh Prather

Perfect order is the forerunner of perfect horror. —Carlos Fuentes

The more a human being feels himself a self, tries to intensify this self and reach a never-attainable perfection, the more drastically he steps out of the center of being. —Eugene Herrigel

The man who makes no mistakes lacks boldness and the spirit of adventure. He never tries anything new. He is a brake on the wheels of progress. —M.W. Larmour

We Just Need to Do the Best We Can

I only have to stop the puck, not beat it to death. —Don Beaupre, hockey goalie

To try to be better is to be better. —Charlotte Cushman

Even a clock that is not going is right twice a day. —Polish proverb

Have patience with all things, but chiefly have patience with yourself. Do not lose courage in considering your own imperfections, but instantly set about remedying them—every day begin the task anew. —Saint Francis de Sales

When we do the best that we can, we never know what miracle is wrought in our life, or in the life of another. —Helen Keller

We're the best team in baseball. But not by much. —Sparky Anderson, after winning the World Series

We fought hard. We gave it our best. We did what was right and we made a difference. —Geraldine Ferraro

Use what talents you have; the woods would have little music if no birds sang their song except those who sang best. —Reverend Oliver G. Wilson

I'll take any way to get into the Hall of Fame. If they want a batboy, I'll go in as a batboy. —Phil Rizzuto

General Quotations about Perfection

Perfection consists not in doing
extraordinary things, but in doing
ordinary things extraordinarily well.
——Angelique Arnauld

One must not hold one's self so
divine as to be unwilling occasionally
to make improvements in one's cre-
ations.   ——Ludwig van Beethoven

If I'd been a housemaid, I'd have been
the best in Australia—I couldn't help
it. It's got to be perfection for me.
——Nellie Melba

When something has been perfect,
there is a tendency to try hard to
repeat it.   ——Edna O'Brien

The artist who aims at perfection in
everything achieves it in nothing.
——Eugene Delacroix

You just have to learn not to care
about the dust mites under the beds.
——Margaret Mead

The secret of joy in work is contained in one word—excellence. To
know how to do something well is
to enjoy it.   ——Pearl S. Buck

Excellence encourages one about
life generally; it shows the spiritual
wealth of the world.   ——George Eliot

Excellence is not an act but a habit.
The things you do the most are the
things you will do the best.
——Marva Collins

Just Do the Footwork,
Then Let It Go

ACTION

Having the world's best idea will do you no good unless you act on it. People who want milk shouldn't sit on a stool in the middle of a field in hopes that a cow will back up to them. —Curtis Grant

Ideas are powerful things, requiring not a studious contemplation but an action, even if it is only an inner action. —Midge Dector

The only way to get positive feelings about yourself is to take positive actions. Man does not live as he thinks, he thinks as he lives.
 —Reverend Vaughan Quinn, O.M.I.

The only measure of what you believe is what you do. If you want to know what people believe, don't read what they write, don't ask them what they believe, just observe what they do. —Ashley Montagu

Our nature consists in motion; complete rest is death. —Blaise Pascal

Who can separate his faith from his actions, or his belief from his occupations? —Kahlil Gibran

The prayer of the chicken hawk does not get him the chicken.
 —Swahili proverb

The superior man is modest in his speech, but excels in his actions.
 —Confucius

There is no genius in life like the genius of energy and activity.
 —Donald G. Mitchell

An ounce of action is worth a ton of theory. —Friedrich Engels

Action is the only reality, not only reality but morality, as well.
 —Abbie Hoffman

Life happens at the level of events, not words. —Alfred Adler

623

Let us work as if success depended upon ourselves alone, but with heartfelt conviction that we are doing nothing, and God everything.
—Saint Ignatius of Loyola

Right action is the key to good living.
—*Twelve Steps and Twelve Traditions*

Even if you're on the right track, you'll get run over if you just sit there.
—Will Rogers

If faith without works is dead, willingness without action is fantasy.
—Anon.

Inspirations never go in for long engagements; they demand immediate marriage to action.
—Brendan Francis

The door of opportunity won't open unless you do some pushing.
—Anon.

The life of the spirit is centrally and essentially a life of action. Spirituality is something done, not merely something believed, or known or experienced.
—Mary McDermott Shideler

It is a great piece of skill to know how to guide your luck, even while waiting for it. —Baltasar Gracian

The man who has done nothing but wait for his ship to come in has already missed the boat. —Anon.

God doesn't make orange juice, God makes oranges. —Jesse Jackson

WE'RE RESPONSIBLE FOR THE EFFORT—NOT THE OUTCOME

Learn to do thy part and leave the rest to Heaven.
—John Henry Cardinal Newman

Trust in God and do something.
—Mary Lyon

God helps them that helps themselves.
—Benjamin Franklin

The true secret of giving advice is, after you have honestly given it, to be perfectly indifferent whether it is taken or not and never persist in trying to set people right.
—Hannah Whitall Smith

The success of your presentation will be judged not by the knowledge you send but by what the listener receives.
—Lily Walters

He will hew the line of right, let the chips fall where they may.
—Roscoe Conklin

You take people as far as they will go, not as far as you would like them to go. —Jeannette Rankin

Let me win, but if I cannot win, let me be brave in the attempt.
—Motto of the Special Olympics

We cannot merely pray to You,
O God, to end war;
For we know that You have made the world in a way
That man must find his own path to peace
Within himself, and with his neighbor.
—Jack Riemer

Oh Lord, thou givest us everything,
at the price of an effort.
                —Leonardo da Vinci

It's astonishing in this world how
things don't turn out at all the way
you expect them to.
                —Agatha Christie

On God for all events depend;
You cannot want when God's your
    friend.
Weigh well your part and do your
    best;
Leave to your Maker all the rest.
                —Nathaniel Cotton

You, yourself, must make the effort.
The buddhas are only teachers.
                —Buddhist proverb

There is a time for all things; a time
to preach and a time to pray, but
those times have passed away; there
is a time to fight, and that time has
come!   —General Peter Muhlenberg

Doing what's right is no guarantee
against misfortune. —William McFee

It is not yours to finish the task, but
neither are you free to take no part in
it.   —Anon.

Life has . . . taught me not to expect
success to be the inevitable result of
my endeavors. She taught me to seek
sustenance from the endeavor itself,
but to leave the result to God.
                —Alan Paton

That man is blest who does his best
and leaves the rest; do not worry.
                —Charles F. Deems

'Tis man's to fight, but Heaven's to
give success.   —Homer

If people are suffering, then they
must look within themselves. . . .
Happiness is not something ready-
made [Buddha] can give you. It
comes from your own actions.
                —The Dalai Lama

I am not bound to win, but
I am bound to be true.
I am not bound to succeed, but
I am bound to live up to what light I
    have.   —Abraham Lincoln

No way exists in the present to accurately determine the future effect of
the least of our actions.
                —Gerald Jampolsky

In vain our labours are, whatsoe'er
they be, unless God gives the
Benediction.   —Robert Herrick

God alone can finish.   —John Ruskin

In all human affairs there are efforts,
and there are results, and the strength
of the effort is the measure of the
result.   —James Lane Allen

God hasn't called me to be successful.
He's called me to be faithful.
                —Mother Teresa

An act of love that fails is just as
much a part of the divine life as an
act of love that succeeds, for love is
measured by its own fullness, not by
its reception.   —Harold Loukes

Happy people plan actions, they
don't plan results. —Dennis Wholey

On earth we have nothing to do with success or results, but only with being true to God, and for God. Defeat in doing right is nevertheless victory.
—Frederick W. Robertson

The man who has done his level best, and who is conscious that he has done his best, is a success, even though the world may write him down a failure. —B.C. Forbes

To create is to boggle the mind and alter the mood. Once the urge has surged, it maintains its own momentum. We may go along for the ride, but when we attempt to steer the course, the momentum dies.
—Sue Atchley Ebaugh

Try first thyself, and after call in
    God,
For to the worker God himself lends
    aid. —Euripides

If thou workest at that which is before thee ... expecting nothing, fearing nothing, but satisfied with thy present activity according to Nature, and with heroic truth in every word and sound which thou utterest, thou wilt live happy. And there is no man who is able to prevent this.
—Marcus Aurelius

We Can't—and Don't Need to—Control Things

It is the mark of great people to treat trifles as trifles and important matters as important. —Doris Lessing

If it is your time, love will track you down like a cruise missile.
—Lynda Barry

You always feel when you look it straight in the eye that you could have put more into it, could have let yourself go and dug harder.
—Emily Carr

If you can react the same way to winning and losing, that's a big accomplishment. That quality is important because it stays with you the rest of your life. —Chris Evert

You have striven so hard, and so long, to compel life. Can't you now slowly change, and let life slowly drift into you ... let the invisible life steal into you and slowly possess you.
—D.H. Lawrence

Coercive power is the curse of the universe; coactive power, the enrichment and advancement of every human soul. —Mary Parker Follett

I began to have an idea of my life, not as the slow shaping of achievement to fit my preconceived purposes, but as the gradual discovery and growth of a purpose which I did not know. —Joanna Field

A guru might say that spiritual deepening involves a journey toward the unselfconscious living of life as it unfolds, rather than toward a willful determination to make it happen.
—John Fortunato

Events that are predestined require but little management. They manage themselves. They slip into place while we sleep, and suddenly we are aware that the thing we fear to attempt, is already accomplished. —Amelia Barr

O golden Silence, bid our souls be
still, and on the foolish fretting of
our care lay thy soft touch of healing
unaware!   —Julia Dorr

Stress is basically a disconnection
from the earth, a forgetting of the
breath. Stress is an ignorant state. It
believes that everything is an emergency. Nothing is that important. Just
lie down.   —Natalie Goldberg

When you learn not to want things
so badly, life comes to you.
                   —Jessica Lange

No day is so bad it can't be fixed
with a nap.   —Carrie Snow

Much growth is stunted by too careful prodding,
Too eager tenderness.
The things we love we have to learn
   to leave alone.
       —Naomi Long Madgett

Believe there is a great power silently
working all things for good, behave
yourself and never mind the rest.
             —Beatrix Potter

One by one the sands are flowing,
One by one the moments fall;
Some are coming, some are going;
Do not strive to grasp them all.
           —Adelaide Proctor

Somehow, when we no longer feel
in control, we become available to
deeper aliveness.   —Richard Moss

Nothing fruitful ever comes when
plants are forced to flower in the
wrong season.   —Bette Bao Lord

The best direction is the least possible
direction.   —Joan Manley

Coercion. The unpardonable crime.
        —Dorothy Miller Richardson

People who make some other person
part of their job are dangerous.
          —Dorothy L. Sayers

We cannot alter facts, but we can
alter our ways of looking at them.
           —Phyllis Bottome

It had been my repeated experience
that when you said to life calmly and
firmly (but very firmly!) "I trust you,
do what you must," life had an uncan-
ny way of responding to your need.
               —Olga Ilyin

It is easy and dismally enervating
to think of opposition as merely
perverse or actually evil—far more
invigorating to see it as essential for
honing the mind, and as a positive
good in itself. For the day that moral
issues cease to be fought over is the
day the word "human" disappears
from the race.   —Jill Tweedie

Living upon a basis of unsatisfied
demands, we were in a state of continual disturbance and frustration.
Therefore, no peace was to be had
unless we could find a means of
reducing these demands.
             —*Twelve Steps and*
               Twelve Traditions

You have freedom when you're easy
in your harness.   —Robert Frost

The bird of paradise alights only
upon the hand that does not grasp.
               —John Berry

Life is made up of desires that seem big and vital one minute, and little and absurd the next. I guess we get what's best for us in the end.
—Alice Caldwell Rice

As the soft yield of water cleaves obstinate stone,
So to yield with life solves the insolv-able:
To yield, I have learned, is to come back again.   —Lao-tzu

As your faith is strengthened, you will find that there is no longer the need to have a sense of control, that things will flow as they will, and that you will flow with them, to your great delight and benefit.
—Emmanuel

For peace of mind, resign as general manager of the universe.   —Anon.

Eventually I lost interest in trying to control my life, to make things hap-pen in a way that I thought I wanted them to be. I began to practice sur-rendering to the universe and finding out what "it" wanted me to do.
—Shakti Gawain

It had been my repeated experience that when you said to life calmly and firmly (but very firmly!), "I trust you; do what you must," life had an uncan-ny way of responding to your need.
—Olga Ilyin

Men never cling to their dreams with such tenacity as at the moment when they are losing faith in them, and know it, but do not dare yet to con-fess it to themselves.
—William Graham Sumner

So often we try to alter circumstances to suit ourselves, instead of letting them alter us.   —Mother Maribel

Relinquishing control is the ultimate challenge of the Spiritual Warrior.
—*The Book of Runes*

Willfulness must give way to willing-ness and surrender. Mastery must yield to mystery.   —Gerald G. May

The worst thing you can do is to try to cling to something that's gone, or to recreate it.
—Johnette Napolitano

I claim not to have controlled events, but confess plainly that events have controlled me.   —Abraham Lincoln

Letting people be okay without us is how we get to be okay without them.
—Merrit Malloy

WE ARE INSTRUMENTS OF GOD

We are the wire, God is the current. Our only power is to let the current pass through us.   —Carlo Carretto

There are two kinds of people: those who say to God, "Thy will be done," and those to whom God says, "All right, then, have it your way."
—C.S. Lewis

Here am I; send me.   —Isaiah 6:8

'Tis God gives skill, but not with-out men's hands: he could not make Antonio Stradivarius violins without Antonio.   —George Eliot

I am like a little pencil in God's hand. He does the writing. The pencil has nothing to do with it.
—Mother Teresa

WE MUST TRUST OUR HIGHER POWER

Life is God's novel. Let him write it.
—Isaac Bashevis Singer

I see not a step before me as I tread
  on another year;
But I've left the Past in God's keep-
  ing, the Future
His mercy shall clear;
And what looks dark in the distance
  may brighten as I draw near.
—Mary Gardiner Brainard

To character and success, two things, contradictory as they may seem, must go together—humble dependence and manly independence: humble dependence on God, and manly reliance on self.
—William Wordsworth

Whate'er we leave to God, God does and blesses us.
—Henry David Thoreau

God will help you if you try, and you can if you think you can.
—Anna Delaney Peale

Doing what is right isn't the problem; it's knowing what is right.
—Lyndon B. Johnson

Let each look to himself and see what God wants of him and attend to this, leaving all else alone.
—Henry Suso

If you can't help it, don't think about it.
—Carmel Myers

God tests His real friends more severely than the lukewarm ones.
—Katheryn Hulme

In vain our labours are, whatsoe'er they be, unless God gives the Benediction.
—Robert Herrick

Much that I sought, I could not find;
much that I found, I could not bind;
much that I bound, I could not free;
much that I freed, returned to me.
—Lee Wilson Dodd

Wanna fly, you got to give up the shit that weighs you down.
—Toni Morrison

Do not inflict your will.
Just give love.
The soul will take that love and put it
  where it can best be used.
—Emmanuel

God alone can finish. —John Ruskin

Be God or let God.   —Anon.

With us is the Lord our God, to help us and to fight our battles.
—2 Chronicles 32:8

It is better to trust in the Lord than to put confidence in man.
—Psalms 118:8

Cast thy burden on the Lord, and he shall sustain thee. —Psalms 55:22

But I trusted in thee, O Lord; I said, Thou art my God. My times are in thy hand. —Psalms 141:8

God's will is not an itinerary, but an attitude. —Andrew Dhuse

Trust in the Lord with all thine heart,
and lean not unto thine own understanding; in all thy ways acknowledge
Him, and He shall direct thy paths.
                    —Proverbs 3:5

Casting all your care upon Him, for
He careth for you.   —1 Peter 5:7

My life is . . . a mystery which I do
not attempt to really understand, as
though I were led by the hand in a
night where I see nothing, but can
fully depend on the love and protection of Him who guides me.
                    —Thomas Merton

Be like the bird that, passing on her
flight awhile on boughs too slight,
feels them give way beneath her, and
yet sings, knowing that she hath
wings.   —Victor Hugo

I come to the office each morning
and stay for long hours doing what
has to be done to the best of my ability. And when you've done the best
you can, you can't do any better. So
when I go to sleep I turn everything
over to the Lord and forget it.
                    —Harry S. Truman

Even now I am full of hope, but the
end lies in God.   —Pindar

Take One Step at a Time

BIG THINGS ARE ACCOMPLISHED ONE STEP AT A TIME

When you have a great and difficult task, something perhaps almost impossible, if you only work a little at a time, every day a little, suddenly the work will finish itself.

—Isak Dinesen

Champions know there are no shortcuts to the top. They climb the mountain one step at a time. They have no use for helicopters!

—Judi Adler

The world doesn't come to the clever folks, it comes to the stubborn, obstinate, one-idea-at-a-time people.

—Mary Roberts Rinehart

One of the greatest evils of the day among those outside of prison is their sense of futility. Young people say, What is the sense of our small effort? They cannot see that we must lay one brick at a time, take one step at a time; we can be responsible only for the one action of the present moment.

—Dorothy Day

One only gets to the top rung of the ladder by steadily climbing up one at a time, and suddenly all sorts of powers, all sorts of abilities which you thought never belonged to you—suddenly become within your own possibility and you think, "Well, I'll have a go, too." —Margaret Thatcher

Nothing is particularly hard if you divide it into small jobs.

—Henry Ford

Let no one be deluded that a knowledge of the path can substitute for putting one foot in front of the other.

—Mary Caroline Richards

Look at a stone cutter hammering away at his rock, perhaps a hundred times without as much as a crack showing in it. Yet at the hundred-and-first blow it will split in two, and I know it was not the last blow that did it, but all that had gone before.

—Jacob A. Riis

Home wasn't built in a day.

—Jane Ace

Happiness is a tide: it carries you only a little way at a time; but you have covered a vast space before you know that you are moving at all.
—Mary Adams

Not to go back is somewhat to advance. And men must walk, at least, before they dance.
—Alexander Pope

Great things are not done by impulse, but by a series of small things brought together.
—Vincent van Gogh

Well-being is attained little by little, and is no little thing itself.
—Zeno

Bigness comes from doing many small things well. . . . Individually, they are not very dramatic transactions. Together, though, they add up.
—Edward S. Finkelstein

If you only keep adding little by little, it will soon become a big heap.
—Hesiod

He who would learn to fly one day must first learn to stand and walk and run and climb and dance; one cannot fly into flying.
—Friedrich Nietzsche

All that I have accomplished . . . has been by that plodding, patient, persevering process of accretion which builds the ant heap particle by particle, thought by thought, fact by fact.
—Elihu Burritt

If we take care of the moments, the years will take care of themselves.
—Maria Edgeworth

Many things which cannot be overcome when they are together, yield themselves up when taken little by little.
—Plutarch

True worth is doing each day some little good, not dreaming of great things to do by and by.
—Anon.

Little by little does the trick. —Aesop

It is by attempting to reach the top at a single leap that so much misery is caused in the world.
—William Cobbett

Yesterday I dared to struggle. Today I dare to win.
—Bernadette Devlin

I think and think for months, for years. Ninety-nine times the conclusion is false. The hundredth time I am right.
—Albert Einstein

Many strokes overthrow the tallest oaks.
—John Luly

Much rain wears the marble.
—William Shakespeare

Little drops of water, little grains of
    sand,
Make the mighty ocean, and the
    pleasant land:
So the little minutes, humble though
    they be,
Make the mighty ages of eternity.
Little deeds of kindness, little words
    of love,
Help to make earth happy, like
    Heaven up above. —Julia Carney

It is a mistake to look too far ahead. Only one link in the chain of destiny can be handled at a time.
—Sir Winston Churchill

One thing at a time, all things in succession. That which grows slowly endures.　　　　—J.G. Hubbard

A successful individual typically sets his next goal somewhat, but not too much, above his last achievement.
　　　　—Kurt Lewin

SMALL STEPS ARE BIG DEALS

One sits down first; one thinks afterwards.　　　　—Jean Cocteau

We can do no great things—only small things with great love.
　　　　—Mother Teresa

Many strokes, though with a little axe, hew down and fell the hardest-timber'd oak. —William Shakespeare

Progress is the sum of small victories won by individual human beings.
　　　　—Bruce Catton

What saves a man is to take a step. Then another step.
　　　　—Antoine de Saint-Exupery

A soul occupied with great ideas performs small duties.
　　　　—Harriet Martineau

The waters wear the stones.
　　　　—Job 14:19

One step and then another, and the
　　longest walk is ended.
One stitch and then another, and the
　　longest rent is mended.
One brick upon another, and the tallest wall is made.
One flake and then another, and the
　　deepest snow is laid.　　—Anon.

You don't just luck into things. . . . You build step by step, whether it's friendships or opportunities.
　　　　—Barbara Bush

The way a chihuahua goes about eating a dead elephant is to take a bite and be very present with that bite. In spiritual growth, the definitive act is to take one step and let tomorrow's step take care of itself!
　　　　—William H. Houff

INCHES ADD UP

Victory is won not in miles, but in inches. Win a little now, hold your ground, and later win a little more.
　　　　—Louis L'Amour

It is astonishing how short a time it takes for very wonderful things to happen.　　—Frances Hodgson Burnett

Inches make a champion.
　　　　—Vince Lombardi

Yard by yard, it's very hard. But inch by inch, it's a cinch.　　　　—Anon.

If we take care of the inches, we will not have to worry about the miles.
　　　　—Hartley Coleridge

When Ty Cobb got on first base he had an apparently nervous habit of kicking the bag. . . . By kicking the bag hard enough Cobb could move it a full two inches closer to second base. He figured that this improved his chances for a steal, or for reaching second base safely on a hit.
　　　　—Norman Vincent Peale

Yard by yard, it's very hard. But inch by inch, it's a cinch. —Anon.

Little Things Are Big Things

Most people would succeed in small things if they were not troubled with great ambitions.
—Henry Wadsworth Longfellow

A harbor, even if it is a little harbor, is a good thing. . . . It takes something from the world, and has something to give in return. —Sarah Orne Jewett

One can get just as much exultation in losing oneself in a little thing as in a big thing. It is nice to think how one can be recklessly lost in a daisy.
—Anne Morrow Lindbergh

Life is made up of little things. It is very rarely that an occasion is offered for doing a great deal at once. True greatness consists in being great in little things. —Charles Simmons

Life is a great bundle of little things.
—Oliver Wendell Holmes

Nothing can be done except little by little. —Charles Baudelaire

Practice yourself in little things, and thence proceed to greater.
—Epictetus

Those people work more wisely who seek to achieve good in their own small corner of the world . . . than those who are forever thinking that life is in vain, unless one can . . . do big things. —Herbert Butterfield

I recommend you to take care of the minutes, for the hours will take care of themselves. —Lord Chesterfield

You've got to think about "big things" while you're doing small things, so that all the small things go in the right direction. —Alvin Toffler

Little strokes fell great oaks.
—Benjamin Franklin

Take your needle, my child, and work at your pattern; it will come out a rose by and by. Life is like that; one stitch at a time taken patiently, and the pattern will come out all right, like embroidery.
—Oliver Wendell Holmes

Most of us miss out on life's big prizes. The Pulitzer. The Nobel. Oscars. Tonys. Emmys. But we're all eligible for life's small pleasures. A pat on the back. A kiss behind the ear. A four-pound bass. A full moon. An empty parking space. A crackling fire. A great meal. A glorious sunset. Hot Soup. Cold beer. Don't fret about copping life's grand awards. Enjoy its tiny delights. There are plenty for all of us.
—United Technologies Corporation advertisement

Why not learn to enjoy the little things—there are so many of them.
—Anon.

Human felicity is produced not so much by great pieces of good fortune that seldom happen as by little advantages that occur every day.
—Benjamin Franklin

The mere sense of living is joy
enough.   —Emily Dickinson

Trifles make up the happiness or the
misery of mortal life.
                    —Alexander Smith

Even a small star shines in the darkness.   —Finnish proverb

How far that little candle throws his
beams! So shines a good deed in a
naughty world.
                    —William Shakespeare

It is better to light a candle than to
curse the darkness.
                    —Chinese proverb

If you don't enjoy getting up and
working and finishing your work and
sitting down to a meal with family or
friends, then the chances are you're
not going to be happy. If someone
bases his happiness or unhappiness
on major events like a great new job,
huge amounts of money, a flawlessly
happy marriage or a trip to Paris,
that person isn't going to be happy
much of the time. If, on the other
hand, happiness depends on a good
breakfast, flowers in the yard, a drink
or a nap, then we are more likely to
live with quite a bit of happiness.
                    —Andy Rooney

The big things that come our way are
. . . the fruit of seeds planted in the
daily routine of our work.
                    —William Feather

The little things are infinitely the
most important.
                    —Sir Arthur Conan Doyle

Enjoy the little things, for one day
you may look back and realize they
were the big things.   —Robert Brault

It is in trifles, and when he is off his
guard, that a man best shows his
character.   —Arthur Schopenhauer

Life is denied by lack of attention,
whether it be to cleaning windows or
trying to write a masterpiece.
                    —Nadia Boulanger

It was only a sunny smile,
But it scattered the night
And little it cost in the giving;
Like morning light,
And made the day worth living.
                    —Anon.

Sometimes the littlest things in life
are the hardest to take. You can sit
on a mountain more comfortably
than on a tack.   —Anon.

Put your heart, mind, intellect, and
soul even to your smallest acts. This
is the secret of success.
                    —Swami Sivananda

The smallest effort is not lost,
Each wavelet on the ocean tost
Aids in the ebb-tide or the flow;
Each rain-drop makes some floweret
    blow;
Each struggle lessens human woe.
                    —Charles Mackay

In life's small things be resolute and
    great
To keep thy muscle trained;
Know'st thou when Fate
Thy measure takes, or when she'll say
    to thee,
"I find thee worthy; do this deed for
    me?"   —James Russell Lowell

He that is faithful in that which is least is faithful also in much; and he that is unjust in the least is unjust also in much. —Luke 16:10

We think in generalities, but we live in detail. —Alfred North Whitehead

JUST DOING WHATEVER WE CAN IS ENOUGH

I cannot do everything, but still I can do something; and because I cannot do everything, I will not refuse to do something that I can do.
—Edward Everett Hale

I am convinced that there are times in everybody's experience when there is so much to be done, that the only way to do it is to sit down and do nothing. —Fanny Fern

We cannot do everything at once, but we can do something at once.
—Calvin Coolidge

You have to accept whatever comes and the only important thing is that you meet it with the best you have to give. —Eleanor Roosevelt

Nobody makes a greater mistake than he who did nothing because he could only do a little.
—Edmund Burke

We must not . . . ignore the small daily differences we can make which, over time, add up to big differences that we often cannot foresee.
—Marian Wright Edelman

A terrace nine stories high begins with a pile of earth. —Lao-tzu

Not all things are blest, but the seeds of all things are blest.
—Muriel Rukeyser

God requires a faithful fulfillment of the merest trifle given us to do, rather than the most ardent aspiration to things to which we are not called.
—Saint Francis de Sales

MODEST BEGINNINGS CAN LEAD TO GREAT RESULTS

Large streams from little mountains flow, tall oaks from little acorns grow.
—David Everett

Instead of thinking about where you are, think about where you want to be. It takes twenty years of hard work to become an overnight success.
—Diana Rankin

The man who removes a mountain begins by carrying away small stones.
—Chinese proverb

The distance doesn't matter; only the first step is difficult.
—Madame Marquise du Deffand

Cultural transformation announces itself in sputtering fits and starts, sparked here and there by minor incidents, warmed by new ideas that may smolder for decades. In many different places, at different times, the kindling is laid for the real conflagration—the one that will consume the old landmarks and alter the landscape forever. —Marilyn Ferguson

The greatest masterpieces were once only pigments on a palette.
—Henry S. Haskins

It is not the straining for great things that is most effective; it is the doing the little things, the common duties, a little better and better.
—Elizabeth Stuart Phelps

It's a simple formula: do your best and somebody might like it.
—Dorothy Baker

A journey of a thousand miles must begin with a single step.
—Chinese proverb

Though thy beginning was small, yet thy latter end should greatly increase.
—Job 8:7

Almost everything comes from almost nothing.   —Henri Frederic Amiel

From a little spark may burst a mighty flame.   —Dante Alighieri

Start by doing what's necessary, then what's possible, and suddenly you are doing the impossible.
—Saint Francis of Assisi

If you wish to reach the highest, begin at the lowest. —Publilius Syrus

Great issues develop from small beginnings. —Norman Vincent Peale

Events of great consequence often spring from trifling circumstances.
—Livy

No matter how big and tough a problem may be, get rid of confusion by taking one little step toward solution. Do something.
—George F. Nordenholt

Most of the critical things in life, which become the starting points of human destiny, are little things.
—R. Smith

Sow an act, reap a habit; sow a habit, reap a character; sow a character, reap a destiny.   —G.D. Boardman

The way to succeed is never quit. That's it. But really be humble about it. . . . You start out lowly and humble and you carefully try to learn an accretion of little things that help you get there.   —Alex Hailey

GENERAL QUOTATIONS ABOUT
TAKING ONE STEP AT A TIME

A little neglect may breed great mischief. . . . For want of a nail, the shoe was lost; for want of a shoe, the horse was lost; for want of a horse, the battle was lost; for want of the battle, the war was lost.
—Benjamin Franklin

Inspiration does not come like a blot, nor is it kinetic energy striving, but it comes to us slowly and quietly all the time.   —Brenda Euland

There is time enough for everything in the course of the day if you do but one thing once; but there is not time enough in the year if you will do two things at a time. —Lord Chesterfield

Incident piled on incident no more makes life than brick piled on brick makes a house.
—Edith Ronald Mirrielees

It's a long old road, but I know I'm gonna find the end.   —Bessie Smith

Think not because no man sees, such things will remain unseen.
—Henry Wadsworth Longfellow

Connections are made slowly, sometimes they grow underground.
—Marge Piercy

I never stop to plan. I take things step-by-step.
—Mary McLeod Bethune

There are very few human beings who receive the truth, complete and staggering, by instant illumination. Most of them acquire it fragment by fragment, on a small scale, by successive developments, cellularly, like a laborious mosaic.
—Anaïs Nin

Connections are made slowly, sometimes they grow underground.
—Marge Piercy

Human successes, like human failures, are composed of one action at a time and achieved by one person at a time.
—Patty H. Sampson

The growth of understanding follows an ascending spiral rather than a straight line.
—Joanna Field

I look at victory as milestones on a very long highway.
—Joan Benoit Samuelson

No first step can be really great; it must of necessity possess more of prophecy than of achievement; nevertheless it is by the first step that a man marks the value, not only of his cause, but of himself.
—Katherine Cecil Thurston

I long to accomplish a great and noble task, but it is my chief duty to accomplish small tasks as if they were great and noble.
—Helen Keller

Let us then be up and doing,
With a heart for any fate,
Still achieving, still pursuing,
Learn to labor and to wait.
—Henry Wadsworth Longfellow

If, after all, men cannot always make history have a meaning, they can always act so that their own lives have one.
—Albert Camus

Every worthwhile accomplishment, big or little, has its stages of drudgery and triumph; a beginning, a struggle, and a victory.
—Anon.

The world is moved not only by the mighty shoves of the heroes, but also by the aggregate of the tiny pushes of each honest worker.
—Helen Keller

In great matters men show themselves as they wish to be seen; in small matters, as they are.
—Gamaliel Bradford

Perseverance

THE IMPORTANCE AND VALUE OF PERSEVERANCE

Grudge no expense—yield to no opposition—forget fatigue—till, by the strength of prayer and sacrifice, the spirit of love shall have overcome.
—Maria Weston Chapman

There is an incredible amount of magic and feistiness in black men that nobody has been able to wipe out. But everybody has tried.
—Toni Morrison

To look back is to relax one's vigil.
—Bette Davis

There's nothing in this world that comes easy. There are a lot of people who aren't going to bother to win. We learn in football to get up and go once more.
—Woody Hayes

Life is not easy for any of us. But what of that? We must have perseverance and above all confidence in ourselves. We must believe that we are gifted for something, and that this thing, at whatever cost, must be attained.
—Marie Curie

You can do what you want to do, accomplish what you want to accomplish, attain any reasonable objective . . . if you want it, if you will to do it, if you work to do it, over a sufficiently long period of time.
—William E. Holler

To persevere, trusting in what hopes he has, is courage in a man. The coward despairs.
—Euripides

If you don't wake up with something in your stomach every day that makes you think, "I want to make this movie," it'll never get made.
—Sherry Lansing

There are but two roads that lead to an important goal and to the doing of great things: strength and perseverance. Strength is the lot of but a few privileged men; but austere perseverance, harsh and continuous, may be employed by the smallest of us and rarely fails of its purpose, for its silent power grows irresistibly greater with time.
—Johann von Goethe

We conquer by continuing.
—George Matheson

639

When you stop talking, you've lost
your customer.　　　—Estee Lauder

When it goes wrong, you feel like
cutting your throat, but you go on.
You don't let anything get you down
so much that it beats you or stops
you.　　　—George Cukor

To tend, unfailingly, unflinchingly,
towards a goal, is the secret of success.
　　　　　—Anna Pavlova

Great works are performed not by
strength, but by perseverance.
　　　　　—Samuel Johnson

Any man can work when every
stroke of his hands brings down the
fruit rattling from the tree . . . but to
labor in season and out of season,
under every discouragement . . . that
requires a heroism which is transcendent.　　　—Henry Ward Beecher

Until I die, I'm going to keep doing.
My people need me. They need somebody that's not taking from them and
is giving them something.
　　　　　—Clara McBride Hale

Be like a postage stamp—stick to one
thing until you get there.
　　　　　—Josh Billings

Keep on going, and the chances are
that you will stumble on something,
perhaps when you are least expecting
it. I never heard of anyone ever stumbling on something sitting down.
　　　　　—Charles F. Kettering

With ordinary talent and extraordinary perseverance, all things are
attainable.
　　　　　—Sir Thomas Foxwell Buxton

For me, at least, there came moments
when faith wavered. But there is the
great lesson and the great triumph:
keep the fire burning until, by and by,
out of the mass of sordid details there
comes some result.
　　　　　—Oliver Wendell Holmes, Jr.

Nothing in the world can take place
of persistence. Talent will not; nothing is more common than unsuccessful individuals with talent. Genius
will not; unrewarded genius is almost
a proverb. Education will not; the
world is full of educated derelicts.
Persistence and determination alone
are omnipotent.　　　—Calvin Coolidge

Let me tell you the secret that has led
me to my goal: my strength lies solely
in my tenacity.　　　—Louis Pasteur

In the game of life nothing is less
important than the score at half time.
　　　　　—Anon.

In the realm of ideas everything
depends on enthusiasm; in the real
world, all rests on perseverance.
　　　　　—Johann von Goethe

Without perseverance talent is a barren bed.　　　—Welsh proverb

Don't be discouraged. It's often the
last key in the bunch that opens the
lock.　　　—Anon.

No pressure, no diamonds.
　　　　　—Mary Case

Diamonds are only lumps of coal that
stuck to their jobs.　　　—B.C. Forbes

Persistence is the master virtue.
Without it, there is no other. —Anon.

We Must Persevere to Be Successful

I am not the smartest or most talented person in the world, but I succeeded because I keep going, and going, and going. —Sylvester Stallone

I know the price of success: dedication, hard work and an unremitting devotion to the things you want to see happen. —Frank Lloyd Wright

Victory belongs to the most persevering. —Napoleon Bonaparte

Success generally depends upon knowing how long it takes to succeed. —Charles de Montesquieu

Success seems to be largely a matter of hanging on after others have let go. —William Feather

If you wish success in life, make perseverance your bosom friend. —Joseph Addison

They who are the most persistent, and work in the true spirit, will invariably be the most successful. —Samuel Smiles

If at first you don't succeed, try, try, try again. —W.E. Hickson

If at first you don't succeed, you're running about average. —M.H. Alderson

The secret of success is constancy of purpose. —Benjamin Disraeli

The only way to the top is by persistent, intelligent, hard work. —A.T. Mercier

The heights by great men reached
    and kept
Were not attained by sudden flight,
But they, while their companions
    slept
Were toiling upward in the night.
    —Henry Wadsworth Longfellow

I realized early on that success was tied to not giving up. Most people in this business gave up and went on to other things. If you simply didn't give up, you would outlast the people who came in on the bus with you. —Harrison Ford

Call the roll in your memory of conspicuously successful [business] giants and, if you know anything about their careers, you will be struck by the fact that almost every one of them encountered inordinate difficulties sufficient to crush all but the gamest of spirits. Edison went hungry many times before he became famous. —B.C. Forbes

Perseverance is a great element of success. If you only knock long enough and loud enough at the gate, you are sure to wake up somebody. —Henry Wadsworth Longfellow

Four steps to achievement: plan purposefully, prepare prayerfully, proceed positively, pursue persistently. —William A. Ward

Flaming enthusiasm, backed up by horse sense and persistence, is the quality that most frequently makes for success. —Dale Carnegie

It isn't hard to be good from time to time. . . . What's tough is being good every day. —Willie Mays

I'm hardnosed about luck. I think it sucks. Yeah, if you spend seven years looking for a job as a copywriter, and then one day somebody gives you a job, you can say, "Gee, I was lucky I happened to go up there today." But dammit, I was going to go up there sooner or later in the next seventy years. . . . If you're persistent in trying and doing and working, you almost make your own fortune.
    —Jerry Della Femina

It's the plugging away that will win
    you the day
So don't be a piker old pard!
Just draw on your grit; it's so easy to
    quit—
It's the keeping your chin up that's
    hard.   —Robert W. Service

No one succeeds without effort. . . . Those who succeed owe their success to their perseverance.
    —Ramana Maharshi

Big shots are only little shots who keep shooting.   —Christopher Morley

Be of good cheer. Do not think of today's failures, but of the success that may come tomorrow. You have set yourselves a difficult task, but you will succeed if you persevere; and you will find a joy in overcoming obstacles. Remember, no effort that we make to attain something beautiful is ever lost.   —Helen Keller

The way to succeed is never quit. That's it. But really be humble about it. . . . You start out lowly and humble and you carefully try to learn an accretion of little things that help you get there.   —Alex Haley

There are no shortcuts to any place worth going.   —Beverly Sills

Continuous efforts—not strength or intelligence—is the key to unlocking our potential.
    —Sir Winston Churchill

Plodding wins the race.   —Aesop

The difficulties and struggles of today are but the price we must pay for the accomplishments and victories of tomorrow.   —William J.H. Boetcker

Let me tell you the secret that has led me to my goal: my strength lies solely in my tenacity.   —Louis Pasteur

A winner never quits and a quitter never wins.   —Anon.

Men who have attained things worth having in this world have worked while others idled, have persevered when others gave up in despair, have practiced early in life the valuable habits of self-denial, industry, and singleness of purpose. As a result, they enjoy in later life the success so often erroneously attributed to good luck.
    —Grenville Kleiser

In the realm of ideas, everything depends on enthusiasm; in the real world, all rests on perseverance.
    —Johann von Goethe

There's such a thin line between winning and losing.   —John R. Tunis

WE MUST FINISH WHAT WE START

It is easier to begin well than to finish well.   —Plautus

The great majority of men are bundles of beginnings.
—Ralph Waldo Emerson

I hope I shall have ambition until the day I die.   —Clare Boothe Luce

When you put your hand to the plow, you can't put it down until you get to the end of the row.   —Alice Paul

Out of the strain of the Doing,
Into the peace of the Done.
—Julia Louise Woodruff

Great is the art of beginning, but greater is the art of ending.
—Henry Wadsworth Longfellow

There are two parts to the creative endeavor: making something, then disseminating it.   —Jane Alexander

We rate ability in men by what they finish, not by what they begin.
—Anon.

A chicken doesn't stop scratching just because worms are scarce.
—Grandma Axiom

Everyone has his superstitions. One of mine has always been when I started to go anywhere, or to do anything, never to turn back or to stop until the thing intended was accomplished.   —Ulysses S. Grant

I just kept on doing what everyone starts out doing. The real question is, why did other people stop?
—William Stafford

Men perish because they cannot join the beginning with the end.
—Alcmaeon

Business is full of brilliant men who started out with a spurt and lacked the stamina to finish. Their places were taken by patient and unshowy plodders who never knew when to quit.
—J.R. Todd

I can remember walking as a child. It was not customary to say you were fatigued. It was customary to complete the goal of the expedition.
—Katharine Hepburn

He that has cut the claws of the lion will not feel quite secure until he has also drawn his teeth.
—Charles Caleb Colton

Courage to start and willingness to keep everlasting at it are the requisites for success.
—Alonzo Newton Benn

I went for years not finishing anything. Because, of course, when you finish something you can be judged.... I had poems which were rewritten so many times I suspect it was just a way of avoiding sending them out.
—Erica Jong

Let no one 'til his death be called
   unhappy.
Measure not the work
Until the day's out, and the labor
   done:
Then bring your gauges.
—Elizabeth Barrett Browning

All is well that ends well.
—John Heywood

Either do not attempt at all, or go through with it.   —Ovid

In soloing—as in other activities—it
is far easier to start something than it
is to finish it.   —Amelia Earhart

It is a matter first of beginning—and
then following through.
                    —Richard L. Evans

Genius begins great works, labor
alone finishes it.   —Joseph Joubert

There is but an inch of difference
between the cushioned chamber and
the padded cell.   —G.K. Chesterton

SMALL, CONSTANT EFFORTS
PAY OFF

The only way to find out if you can
write is to set aside a certain period
every day and try. Save enough
money to give yourself six months to
be a full-time writer. Work every day
and the pages will pile up.
                    —Judith Krantz

I work every day—or at least I force
myself into my office or room. I may
get nothing done, but you don't earn
bonuses without putting in time.
Nothing may come for three months,
but you don't earn the fourth without it.   —Mordecai Richler

When nothing seems to help, I go
and look at a stonecutter hammering
away at his rock perhaps a hundred
times without as much as a crack
showing in it. Yet at the hundred and
first blow it will split in two, and I
know it was not that blow that did it,
but all that had gone before.
                    —Jacob A. Riis

The drops of rain make a hole in
the stone not by violence, but by oft
falling.   —Lucretius

PERSEVERANCE IS MORE
IMPORTANT THAN SPEED

It does not matter how slowly you
go, so long as you do not stop.
                    —Confucius

Live with no time out.
              —Simone de Beauvoir

The great thing in this world is not
so much where we are, but in what
direction we are moving.
              —Oliver Wendell Holmes

The race is not always to the swift,
but to those who keep on running.
                    —Anon.

My parents told me that people will
never know how long it takes you to
do something. They will only know
how well it is done.   —Nancy Hanks

By perseverance the snail reached the
Ark.   —Charles Haddon Spurgeon

Our desire must be like a slow and
stately ship, sailing across endless oceans, never in search of safe
anchorage. Then suddenly, unex-
pectedly, it will find mooring for a
moment.   —Etty Hillesum

The race is not to the swift, nor the
battle to the strong. —Ecclesiastes 9:11

If we are facing in the right direction,
all we have to do is keep on walking.
              —Ancient Buddhist proverb

It's the steady, constant driving to the goal for which you're striving, not the speed with which you travel, that will make your victory sure. —Anon.

I'm a slow walker, but I never walk back. —Abraham Lincoln

Slow and steady wins the race.
—Robert Lloyd

Character is built into the spiritual fabric of personality hour by hour, day by day, year by year in much the same deliberate way that physical health is built into the body.
—E. Lamar Kincaid

No great thing is created suddenly.
—Epictetus

Be content to grow a little each day. If the improvement is the sort of thing which is very slow, do not measure it too often. Do a self-comparison every two weeks, or every six months, whatever is appropriate.
—Lewis F. Presnall

Pray that success will not come any faster than you are able to endure it.
—Elbert Hubbard

Wisely and slow. They stumble that run fast. —William Shakespeare

Plodding wins the race. —Aesop

The way of progress is neither swift nor easy. —Marie Curie

One thing at a time, all things in succession. That which grows slowly endures. —J.G. Hubbard

Make haste slowly. —Augustus

Slow motion gets you there faster.
—Hoagy Carmichael

I'm not there yet, but I'm closer than I was yesterday. —Anon.

SOMETIMES WE JUST HAVE TO
GET OVER THE HUMP

Life begins on the other side of despair. —Jean-Paul Sartre

I am suffocated and lost when I have not the bright feeling of progression.
—Margaret Fuller

The lowest ebb is the turn of the tide.
—Henry Wadsworth Longfellow

You give 100 percent in the first half of the game, and if that isn't enough, in the second half you give what's left. —Yogi Berra

Don't get hung up on a snag in the stream, my dear. Snags are not so dangerous—it's the debris that clings to them that makes the trouble. Pull yourself loose and go on.
—Anne Shannon Monroe

One can go a long way after one is tired. —French proverb

The great thing, and the hard thing, is to stick to things when you have outlived the first interest, and not yet got the second, which comes with a sort of mastery.
—Janet Erskine Stuart

Effort only fully releases its reward after a person refuses to quit.
—Napoleon Hill

645

If something is boring after two minutes, try it for four. If still boring, try for eight, sixteen, thirty-two, and so on. Eventually, one discovers that it is not boring, but very interesting.
—Anon.

No one ever did anything worth doing unless he was prepared to go on with it long after it became something of a bore.   —Douglas V. Steere

I've been failing for like, ten or eleven years. When it turns, it'll turn. Right now I'm just tryin' to squeeze through a very tight financial period, get the movie out, and put my things in order.   —Francis Ford Coppola

In our day, when a pitcher got into trouble in a game, instead of taking him out, our manager would leave him in and tell him to pitch his way out of trouble.   —Cy Young

KEEP GOING, JUST A LITTLE LONGER

I'm a little wounded, but I am not slain; I will lay me down to bleed a while. Then I'll rise and fight again.
—John Dryden

The tragedy of life is not that man loses, but that he almost wins.
—Heywood Broun

Where I am today has everything to do with the years I spent hanging on to a career by my fingernails.
—Barbara Aronstein Black

Courage is fear holding on a minute longer.   —General George S. Patton

A hero is no braver than an ordinary man, but he is brave five minutes longer.   —Ralph Waldo Emerson

Hope says to us constantly, "go on, go on," and leads us to the grave.
—Francoise d'Aubigne marquisa de Maintenon

Every great work, every big accomplishment, has been brought into manifestation through holding to the vision, and often just before the big achievement, comes apparent failure and discouragement.
—Florence Scovel Shinn

The line between failure and success is so fine that we ... are often on the line and do not know it. How many a man has thrown up his hands at a time when a little more effort, a little more patience, would have achieved success. A little more persistence, a little more effort, and what seemed hopeless failure may turn to glorious success.   —Elbert Hubbard

When you get to the end of your rope, tie a knot and hang on.
—Franklin Delano Roosevelt

It is with enterprises as with striking fire; we do not meet with success except with reiterated efforts, and often at the instant when we despaired of success.
—Francoise d'Aubigne marquisa de Maintenon

Saints are sinners who kept on going.
—Robert Louis Stevenson

We can do anything we want to do if we stick to it long enough.
—Helen Keller

When you get into a tight place and everything goes against you, 'til it seems as though you could not hold on a minute longer, never give up then, for that is just the place and time that the tide will turn.

—Harriet Beecher Stowe

Men do not fail, they stop trying.

—Elihu Root

It ain't over 'til it's over. —Yogi Berra

Triumph often is nearest when defeat seems inescapable.   —B.C. Forbes

Don't bother about genius. Don't worry about being clever. Trust to hard work, perseverance and determination. And the best motto for a long march is, "Don't grumble. Plug on!"

—Sir Frederick Treves

Some men give up their designs when they have almost reached the goal; while others, on the contrary, obtain a victory by exerting, at the last moment, more vigorous efforts than before.   —Polybius

Never stop. One always stops as soon as something is about to happen.

—Peter Brook

Many of life's failures are men who did not realize how close they were to success when they gave up.

—Thomas A. Edison

Fight one more round. When your feet are so tired you have to shuffle back to the center of the ring, fight one more round.   —James J. Corbett

Don't leave before the miracle happens!   —Anon.

If something doesn't come up the way you want, you have to forge ahead.

—Clint Eastwood

Fortune is like the market, where many times, if you can stay a little, the price will fall.   —Francis Bacon

SOMETIMES IT PAYS NOT TO KNOW WE'RE "BEATEN"

This man Wellington is so stupid he does not know when he is beaten, and goes on fighting.

—Napoleon Bonaparte

He never knew when he was whipped ...so he never was. —Louis L'Amour

NEVER ADMIT DEFEAT

Entrepreneurs average 3.8 failures before a final success. What sets the successful ones apart is their amazing persistence. There are a lot of people out there with good and marketable ideas, but pure entrepreneurial types almost never accept defeat.

—Lisa M. Amos

As long as a person doesn't admit he is defeated, he is not defeated—he's just a little behind, and isn't through fighting.   —Darrell Royal

Only yield when you must, never "give up the ship," but fight on to the last "with a stiff upper lip!"

—Phoebe Cary

Defeat never comes to any man until he admits it.   —Josephus Daniels

There is something in me—I just can't stand to admit defeat.   —Beverly Sills

There was no such thing as defeat if you didn't accept it.   —Fay Weldon

Never give in! Never give in! Never, never, never, never. . . . In nothing great or small, large or petty, never give in except to convictions or honor and good sense!
—Sir Winston Churchill

First there are those who are winners, and know they are winners. Then there are the losers who know they are losers. Then there are those who are not winners, but don't know it. They're the ones for me. They never quit trying. They're the soul of our game.   —Paul William "Bear" Bryant

It's not worthy of human beings to give up.   —Alva Reimer Myrdal

Never admit defeat!
—Arthur Rimbaud

We shall go on to the end. We shall fight in France, we shall fight with growing confidence and growing strength in the air, we shall defend our island, whatever the cost may be. We shall fight on the beaches, we shall fight on the landing grounds, we shall fight in the fields, and in the streets, we shall fight in the halls. We shall never surrender.
—Sir Winston Churchill

ENDURANCE IS CRITICAL

Patient endurance attends to all things.   —Teresa of Avila

To be somebody you must last.
—Ruth Gordon

He conquers who endures.   —Anon.

Emotional maturity is the ability to stick to a job and to struggle through until it is finished, to endure unpleasantness, discomfort and frustration.
—Edward A. Strecker

To bear is to conquer our fate.
—Thomas Campbell

Keep breathing.   —Sophie Tucker

It helps, I think, to consider ourselves on a very long journey: the main thing is to keep to the faith, to endure, to help each other when we stumble or tire, to weep and press on.
—Mary Caroline Richards

The first and final thing you have to do in this world is to last in it, and not be smashed by it.
—Ernest Hemingway

The first need of being is endurance; to endure with gladness if we can, with fortitude in any event.
—Bliss Carman

I bend, but I do not break.
—Jean de La Fontaine

He that endureth to the end shall be saved.   —Matthew 10:22

Whatever necessity lays upon thee, endure; whatever she commands, do.
—Johann von Goethe

To be somebody you must last.
—Ruth Gordon

In the clutch of circumstance, I have not winced or cried aloud;
Under the bludgeoning of chance, my head is bloody, but unbowed.
—William E. Henley

We shall live to fight again, and to strike another blow.
—Alfred, Lord Tennyson

Giving up is the ultimate tragedy.
—Robert J. Donovan

God Almighty hates a quitter.
—Samuel Fessenden

Endurance is one of the most difficult disciplines, but it is to the one who endures that the final victory comes.
—Buddha

Endure, and preserve yourselves for better things.
—Virgil

Every kind of fortune is to be overcome by bearing it.
—Virgil

When we see ourselves in a situation which must be endured and gone through, it is best to make up our minds to meet it with firmness, and accommodate everything to it in the best way practical. This lessons the evil, while fretting and fuming only serve to increase your own torments.
—Thomas Jefferson

If you want to see the sun shine, you have to weather the storm.
—Frank Lane

If you want the rainbow, you gotta put up with the rain. —Dolly Parton

What cannot be altered must be borne, not blamed. —Thomas Fuller

He that can't endure the bad will not live to see the good.
—Yiddish proverb

To struggle when hope is banished.
To live when life's salt is gone!
To dwell in a dream that's vanished—
To endure, and go calmly on!
—Ben Johnson

A high heart ought to bear calamities and not flee them, since in bearing them appears the grandeur of the mind, and in fleeing them the cowardice of the heart. —Pietro Aretino

Endurance is nobler than strength, and patience than beauty.
—John Ruskin

They merit more praise who know how to suffer misery than those who temper themselves with contentment.
—Pietro Aretino

We must endure what fortune sends.
—Greek proverb

People can bear anything.
—Philip Slater

We must learn from life how to suffer it. —French proverb

This is courage in a man: to bear unflinchingly what heaven sends.
—Euripides

To be unable to bear an ill is itself a great ill. —Bion

Man never made any material as resilient as the human spirit.
—Bern Williams

Obstacles cannot crush me, every obstacle yields to stern resolve.
—Leonardo da Vinci

And let us not be weary in well doing; for in due season we shall reap, if we faint not. —Galatians 6:9

Hold on with a bulldog grip, and chew and choke as much as possible.
—Abraham Lincoln

There remain times when one can only endure. One lives on, one doesn't die, and the only thing that one can do is to fill one's mind and time as far as possible with the concerns of other people. It doesn't bring immediate peace, but it brings the dawn nearer.
—Arthur Christopher Benson

We Must Keep Getting Up

When I look at the kids training today . . . I can tell which ones are going to do well. It's not necessarily the ones who have the most natural talent or who fall the least. Sometimes it's the kids who fall the most, and keep pulling themselves up and trying again. —Michelle Kwan

Our greatest glory consists not in never falling, but in rising every time we fall. —Ralph Waldo Emerson

It takes far less courage to kill yourself than it takes to make yourself wake up one more time.
—Judith Rossner

Success consists of getting up just one more time than you fall.
—Oliver Goldsmith

If I don't get off the mat, I'll lose the fight. —Archie Moore

For a just man falleth seven times, and riseth up again. —Proverbs 24:16

We Must Keep Starting Over

Persistent people begin their success where others end in failure.
—Edward Eggleston

Think of a fine painter attempting to capture an inner vision, beginning with one corner of the canvas, painting what he thinks should be there, not quite pulling it off, covering it over with white paint, and trying again, each time finding out what his painting isn't, until he finally finds out what it is. And when you finally do find out what one corner of your vision is, you're off and running.
—Anne Lamott

Vitality shows not only in the ability to persist, but in the ability to start over. —F. Scott Fitzgerald

Regression in grief must be seen and supported as a means toward adaptation and health. —Lily Pincus

To be happy, drop the words "if only" and substitute instead the words "next time."
—Smiley Blanton, M.D.

We Must Keep at It Until We Learn What We Need to Know

Life is a maze in which we take the wrong turning before we learn to walk. —Cyril Connolly

Education is hanging around until you've caught on. —Robert Frost

Never go to bed mad. Stay up and fight. —Phyllis Diller

You go back to the gym and you just do it again and again until you get it right. —Arnold Schwarzenegger

As long as one keeps searching, the answers come. —Joan Baez

How many years you have to keep on doing, until you know what to do and how to do! —Johann von Goethe

There is no wisdom equal to that which comes after the event. —Geraldine Jewsbury

Tolerate the . . . process of coming to knowledge or certainty or clarity through sometimes apparently hopeless thickets of confusion or bewilderment. Learn not to be surprised or disheartened by the muddle you inhabit, and not to press too soon for a superficial reprieve. —Joe David Bellamy

Learn to self-conquest, persevere thus for a time, and you will perceive very clearly the advantage which you gain from it. —Teresa of Avila

What can any of us do with his talent but try to develop his vision, so that through frequent failures we may learn better what we have missed in the past. —William Carlos Williams

SOME THINGS THAT STIMULATE AND SUSTAIN PERSEVERANCE

All effort is in the last analysis sustained by faith that it is worth making. —Ordway Tead

Competition is easier to accept if you realize it is not an act of oppression or abrasion. . . . I've worked with my best friends in direct competition. —Diane Sawyer

Life has no smooth road for any of us; and in the bracing atmosphere of a high aim the very roughness stimulates the climber to steadier steps till the legend, "over steep ways to the stars," fulfills itself. —W.C. Doane

The one who cares the most wins. . . . That's how I knew I'd end up with everyone else waving the white flags and not me. That's how I knew I'd be the last person standing when it was all over. . . . I cared the most. —Roseanne

If I had refused to institute a negotiation or had not persevered in it, I would have been degraded in my own estimation as a man of honor. —John Adams

I read my own books sometimes to cheer me when it is hard to write, and then I remember that it was always difficult, and how nearly impossible it was sometimes. —Ernest Hemingway

The difference between perseverance and obstinacy is that one comes from a strong will, and the other from a strong won't. —Henry Ward Beecher

When you're a professional, you come back no matter what happened the day before.　　—Billy Martin

We can do whatever we wish to do provided our wish is strong enough. . . . What do you want most to do? That's what I have to keep asking myself, in the face of difficulties.
　　—Katherine Mansfield

Desire and hope will push us on toward the future.
　　—Michel de Montaigne

The champ may have lost his stuff temporarily or permanently, he can't be sure. When he can no longer throw his high hard one, he throws his heart instead. He throws something. He just doesn't walk off the mound and weep.
　　—Raymond Chandler

We attempt nothing great but from a sense of the difficulties we have to encounter; we persevere in nothing great but from a pride in overcoming them.　　—William Hazlitt

He turns not back who is bound to a star.　　—Leonardo da Vinci

What helps me go forward is that I stay receptive, I feel that anything can happen.　　—Anouk Aimee

There was a Texas Ranger one time who said that there's no stopping a man who knows he's in the right and keeps a-coming.　　—Louis L'Amour

GENERAL QUOTATIONS ABOUT PERSEVERANCE

When you get to the end of your rope, tie a knot in it and hang on.
　　—Eleanor Roosevelt

Whatever course you decide upon, there is always someone to tell you that you are wrong. There are always difficulties arising which tempt you to believe that your critics are right. To map out a course of action and follow it to an end requires . . . courage.
　　—Ralph Waldo Emerson

People with good intentions never give up!　　—Jane Smiley

If I see a door comin' my way, I'm knockin' it down. And if I can't knock down the door, I'm sliding through the window.　　—Rosie Perez

All my life I've been competing—and competing to win. I came to realize that in this way, this cancer was the toughest competition I had faced yet. I made up my mind that I was going to lick it all the way. I not only wasn't going to let it kill me, I wasn't even going to let it put me on the shelf.
　　—Babe Didrikson Zaharias

I have accepted fear as a part of life—specifically the fear of change. . . . I have gone ahead despite the pounding in the heart that says: turn back. . . .　　—Erica Jong

Tribulation produces perseverance; and perseverance, character; and character, hope.　　—Romans 5:3–4

The unifying of opposites is the eternal process.　　—Mary Parker Follett

"Brave admiral, say but one good
    word:
What shall we do when hope is
    gone?"
The words leapt like a leaping sword:
"Sail on! sail on! and on!"
                    —Joaquin Miller

In Hollywood, all marriages are
happy. It's trying to live together
afterwards that causes problems.
                    —Shelley Winters

We must dare, and dare again, and
go on daring.
                    —Georges Jacques Danton

Austere perseverance, harsh and
continuous, may be employed by
the least of us and rarely fails of its
purpose, for its silent power grows
irresistibly greater with time.
                    —Johann von Goethe

Grant me the courage not to give up,
even though I think it is hopeless.
                    —Admiral Chester W. Nimitz

I try. I am trying. I was trying. I will
try. I shall in the meantime try. I
sometimes have tried. I shall still by
that time be trying.   —Diane Glancy

Hard times ain't quit and we ain't
quit.   —Meridel Le Sueur

All the sugar was in the bottom of
the cup.   —Julia Ward Howe

I have often been adrift, but I have
always stayed afloat.   —David Berry

God helps those who persevere.
                    —Koran

Gnaw your own bone; gnaw at it,
bury it, unearth it, gnaw it still.
                    —Henry David Thoreau

Like ships, men flounder time and
time again.   —Henry Miller

To strive, to seek, to find, and not to
yield.   —Alfred, Lord Tennyson

To keep a lamp burning we have to
keep putting oil in it.
                    —Mother Teresa

If you stop struggling, then you stop
life.   —Huey Newton

One thing we learned. To make a
start and keep plugging. When I had
fights at school, the little while I
went, I just bowed my neck and kept
swinging until something hit the dirt.
Sometimes it was me, but I always
got up.   —Louis L'Amour

Jesus taught that perseverance is
the essential element of prayer. Men
must be in earnest when they kneel
at God's footstool. Too often we get
faint-hearted and quit praying at the
point when we ought to begin. We let
go at the very point where we should
hold on strongest. Our prayers are
weak because they are not impassioned by an unfailing and resistless
will.   —E.M. Bounds

Be strong!
It matters not how deep entrenched
    the wrong
How hard the battle goes, the day
    how long
Faint not—fight on!
Tomorrow comes the song.
                    —Maltbie D. Babcock

Never grow a wishbone, daughter,
where your backbone ought to be.
                    —Clementine Paddleford

Good people are good because
they've come to wisdom through failure.   —William Saroyan

You may have to fight a battle more
than once to win it.
                    —Margaret Thatcher

Problems

Everyone Has Problems

None of us can be free of conflict and woe. Even the greatest men have had to accept disappointments as their daily bread.   —Bernard M. Baruch

There is no man in any rank who is always at liberty to act as he would incline. In some quarter or other he is limited by circumstances.
                    —Bonnie Blair

Life has no smooth road for any of us; and in the bracing atmosphere of a high aim the very roughness stimulates the climber to steadier steps till the legend, "over steep ways to the stars," fulfills itself.   —W.C. Doane

When life's problems seem overwhelming, look around and see what other people are coping with. You may consider yourself fortunate.
                    —Ann Landers

If all our misfortunes were laid in one common heap, whence everyone must take an equal portion, most people would be content to take their own and depart.   —Socrates

Identifying Real Problems

A problem well stated is a problem half solved.   —Charles F. Kettering

It isn't that they can't see the solution, it's that they can't see the problem.
                    —G.K. Chesterton

If we can really understand the problem, the answer will come out of it, because the answer is not separate from the problem.
                    —Jiddu Krishnamurti

The man who most vividly realizes a difficulty is the man most likely to overcome it.   —Joseph Farrell

A good problem statement often includes: (a) what is known, (b) what is unknown, and (c) what is sought.
                    —Edward Hodnett

Every path has its puddle.
                    —English proverb

Several Ways to Solve Problems

You often get a better hold upon a problem by going away from it for a time and dismissing it from your mind altogether.   —Dr. Frank Crane

What one decides to do in crisis depends on one's philosophy of life, and that philosophy cannot be changed by an incident. If one hasn't any philosophy in crises, others make the decision.   —Jeannette Rankin

When I feel difficulty coming on, I switch to another book I'm writing. When I get back to the problem, my unconscious has solved it.
—Isaac Asimov

You can surmount the obstacles in your path if you are determined, courageous and hard-working. Never be fainthearted. Be resolute, but never bitter. . . . Permit no one to dissuade you from pursuing the goals you set for yourselves. Do not fear to pioneer, to venture down new paths of endeavor.   —Ralph J. Bunche

Any concern too small to be turned into a prayer is too small to be made into a burden.   —Corrie ten Boom

When you approach a problem, strip yourself of preconceived opinions and prejudice, assemble and learn the facts of the situation, make the decision which seems to you to be the most honest, and then stick to it.
—Chester Bowles

The art of living lies less in eliminating our troubles than in growing with them.   —Bernard M. Baruch

No matter how big and tough a problem may be, get rid of confusion by taking one little step towards solution. Do something. Then try again. At the worst, so long as you don't do it the same way twice, you will eventually use up all the wrong ways of doing it and thus the next try will be the right one.
—George F. Nordenholt

The greatest and most important problems of life are all in a certain sense insoluble. They can never be solved, but only outgrown.
—Carl Jung

You can overcome anything if you don't bellyache.
—Bernard M. Baruch

There is no other solution to a man's problems but the day's honest work, the day's honest decisions, the day's generous utterance, and the day's good deed.   —Clare Boothe Luce

Every problem contains the seeds of its own solution.   —Stanley Arnold

When you can't solve the problem, manage it.   —Dr. Robert H. Schuller

When Trying to Solve a Problem, Focus on Its Positive Aspects

The block of granite, which was an obstacle in the path of the weak, becomes a stepping stone in the path of the strong.   —Thomas Carlyle

Real difficulties can be overcome, it is only the imaginary ones that are unconquerable.   —Theodore N. Vail

Many a man curses the rain that falls upon his head, and knows not that it brings abundance to drive away hunger. —Saint Basil

Times of general calamity and confusion have ever been productive of the greatest minds. The purest ore is produced from the hottest furnace, and the brightest thunderbolt is elicited from the darkest storms.
—Charles Caleb Colton

What is difficulty? Only a word indicating the degree of strength requisite for accomplishing particular objects; a mere notice of the necessity for exertion . . . a mere stimulus to men.
—Samuel Warren

Problems are only opportunities in work clothes. —Henry J. Kaiser

We must look for the opportunity in every difficulty, instead of being paralyzed at the thought of the difficulty in every opportunity.
—Walter E. Cole

It's Usually Best to Face Problems Directly

I wish I were with some of the wild people that run in the woods, and know nothing about accomplishments! —Joanna Baillie

I used to believe that marriage would diminish me, reduce my options. That you had to be someone less to live with someone else when, of course, you have to be someone more.
—Candice Bergen

The human mind prefers to be spoon-fed with the thoughts of others, but deprived of such nourishment it will, reluctantly, begin to think for itself—and such thinking, remember, is original thinking and may have valuable results. —Agatha Christie

I'll have to, as you say, take a stand, do something toward shaking up that system. . . . Despair . . . is too easy an out. —Paule Marshall

Half the unhappiness in life comes from people being afraid to go straight at things. —William J. Lock

All work of man is as the swimmer's: a vast ocean threatens to devour him; if he front it not bravely, it will keep its word. —Thomas Carlyle

Hiding leads nowhere except to more hiding. —Margaret A. Robinson

There is no movement without our own resistance.
—Dr. Laura Schlessinger

All problems become smaller if you don't dodge them, but confront them.
—William F. Halsey

The best way out of a problem is through it. —Anon.

A great man is one who seizes the vital issue in a complex question, what we might call the jugular vein of the whole organism, and spends his energies upon that.
—Joseph Rickaby

Fear not those who argue but those who dodge.
—Marie von Ebner-Eschenbach

If the first woman God ever made was strong enough to turn the world upside down, these women together ought to be able to turn it right side up again. —Sojourner Truth

It is a fact of history that those who seek to withdraw from its great experiments usually end up being overwhelmed by them.
—Barbara Ward

Only one feat is possible: not to have run away. —Dag Hammarskjold

We must prepare and study truth under every aspect, endeavoring to ignore nothing, if we do not wish to fall into the abyss of the unknown when the hour shall strike.
—Marie von Ebner-Eschenbach

We only really face up to ourselves when we are afraid.
—Thomas Bernhard

Life is the acceptance of responsibilities or their evasion; it is a business of meeting obligations or avoiding them. To every man the choice is continually being offered, and by the manner of his choosing you may fairly measure him.
—Ben Ames Williams

The superior man makes the difficulty to be overcome his first interest; success comes only later. —Confucius

No man will succeed unless he is ready to face and overcome difficulties and is prepared to assume responsibilities.
—William J.H. Boetcker

IT'S A WONDERFUL THING TO OVERCOME PROBLEMS

The harder the conflict, the more glorious the triumph. What we obtain too cheap, we esteem too lightly; 'tis dearness only that gives everything it's value. —Thomas Paine

The greater the difficulty, the more glory in surmounting it. —Epicurus

Life affords no higher pleasure than that of surmounting difficulties.
—Samuel Johnson

Can it be that man is essentially a being who loves to conquer difficulties, a creature whose function is to solve problems? —Gorham Munson

Conquering any difficulty always gives one a secret joy, for it means pushing back a boundary-line and adding to one's liberty.
—Henri Frederic Amiel

To overcome difficulties is to experience the full delight of existence.
—Arthur Schopenhauer

Success is to be measured not so much by the position that one has reached in life as by the obstacles he has overcome trying to succeed.
—Booker T. Washington

Happiness is the overcoming of not unknown obstacles toward a known goal. —L. Ron Hubbard

Difficulties exist to be surmounted.
—Ralph Waldo Emerson

Failures and Mistakes

Everyone Makes Mistakes and Has Failures

Imagine a congress of eminent celebrities such as More, Bacon, Grotius, Pascal, Cromwell, Bossuet, Montesquieu, Jefferson, Napoleon, Pitt, etc. They would be an Encyclopedia of Errors.
—Lord Acton

Flops are a part of life's menu, and I've never been a girl to miss out on any of the courses.
—Rosalind Russell

Every man's got to figure to get beat sometime.   —Joe Louis

Who thinks it just to be judged by a single error?   —Beryl Markham

Man errs as long as he struggles.
—Johann von Goethe

Mistakes are part of the dues one pays for a full life.   —Sophia Loren

Mistakes are the usual bridge between inexperience and wisdom.
—Phyllis Therous

Be aware that young people have to be able to make their own mistakes and that times change.
—Gina Shapira

The best brewer sometimes makes bad beer.   —German proverb

We must somehow get comfortable with the reality of periodic failure. . . . Like a trip to the dentist, the thought of occasional reverses may not make us tingle with joyful anticipation, but then again, it's not the end of the world.   —Sam Collins

The progress of rivers to the ocean is not so rapid as that of man to error.
—Voltaire

All men are liable to error; and most men are . . . by passion or interest, under temptation to it. —John Locke

To err is human, to forgive divine.
—Alexander Pope

Show me a person who has never made a mistake and I'll show you somebody who has never achieved much.   —Joan Collins

659

He only is exempt from failures who makes no effort.   —Richard Whately

Only he who does nothing makes no mistakes.   —French proverb

The only man who makes no mistakes is the man who never does anything.   —Eleanor Roosevelt

Life is not life unless you make mistakes.   —Joan Collins

We all choke, and the man who says he doesn't choke is lying like hell. We all leak oil.   —Lee Trevino

He who has never failed somewhere, that man cannot be great.   —Herman Melville

He is always right who suspects that he makes mistakes.   —Spanish proverb

The man who makes no mistakes does not usually make anything.   —Bishop W.C. Magee

A good marksman may miss.   —Thomas Fuller

He that has much to do will do something wrong.   —Samuel Johnson

For a just man falleth seven times, and riseth up again.   —Proverbs 24:16

To make no mistake is not in the power of man; but from their errors and mistakes the wise and good learn wisdom for the future.   —Plutarch

All of us failed to match our dreams of perfection.   —William Faulkner

The greatest mistake you can make in life is to be continually fearing you will make one.   —Elbert Hubbard

The fellow who never makes a mistake takes his orders from one who does.   —Herbert B. Prochnow

Accept that all of us can be hurt, that all of us can—and surely will at times—fail. Other vulnerabilities, like being embarrassed or risking love, can be terrifying, too. I think we should follow a simple rule: if we can take the worst, take the risk.
   —Dr. Joyce Brothers

WINNERS JUST MAKE THE FEWEST MISTAKES

The greatest general is he who makes the fewest mistakes.
   —Napoleon Bonaparte

War is a series of catastrophes that results in victory.
   —Georges Clemenceau

Victory goes to the player who makes the next-to-last mistake.
   —Savielly Grigorievitch Tartakower

A man finds he has been wrong at every stage of his career, only to deduce the astonishing conclusion that he is at last entirely right.
   —Robert Louis Stevenson

One loss is good for the soul. Too many losses are not good for the coach.   —Knute Rockne

In all science, error precedes the truth, and it is better it should go first than last.   —Hugh Walpole

In the game of life it's a good idea to have a few early losses, which relieves you of the pressure of trying to maintain an undefeated season.
—Bill Vaughan

Virtually nothing comes out right the first time. Failures, repeated failures, are finger posts on the road to achievement. The only time you don't want to fail is the last time you try something. . . . One fails forward toward success.
—Charles F. Kettering

Big Mistakes

A clever man commits no minor blunders.　—Johann von Goethe

Sometimes a noble failure serves the world as faithfully as a distinguished success.　—Edward Dowden

No man ever progressed to greatness and goodness but through great mistakes.　—Frederick W. Robertson

The credit belongs to the man who is actually in the arena; whose face is marred by dust and sweat and blood; who strives valiantly; who errs and comes short again and again; who knows the great enthusiasms, the great devotions, and spends himself in a worthy cause; who, at the best, knows in the end the triumph of high achievement; and who, at the worst, if he fails, at least fails while daring greatly, so that his place shall never be with those cold and timid souls who know neither victory nor defeat.
—Theodore Roosevelt

The errors of great men are venerable because they are more fruitful than the truths of little men.
—Friedrich Nietzsche

There is something distinguished about even his failures; they sink not trivially, but with a certain air of majesty, like a great ship, its flags flying, full of holes.　—George Jean Nathan

If all else fails, immortality can always be assured by spectacular error.　—John Kenneth Galbraith

There is a glory
In a great mistake.　—Nathalia Crane

Any man whose errors take ten years to correct is quite a man.
—J. Robert Oppenheimer, speaking of Albert Einstein

If you have made mistakes, even serious mistakes, there is always another chance for you.　—Mary Pickford

Correcting Mistakes

Life, like war, is a series of mistakes, and he is best who wins the most splendid victories by the retrieval of mistakes.　—Frederick W. Robertson

A man who has committed a mistake and doesn't correct it is committing another mistake.　—Confucius

The great virtue of man lies in his ability to correct his mistakes and to continually make a new man of himself.　—Wang Yang-Ming

It is only error in judgement to make a mistake, but it shows infirmity of character to adhere to it when discovered.   —Christian Bovee

It is human to err, but it is devilish to remain willfully in error.
                        —Saint Augustine

Intelligence is not to make no mistakes, but quickly to see how to make them good.   —Bertolt Brecht

Our mistakes won't irreparably damage our lives unless we let them.
                        —James E. Sweaney

We Must Accept Responsibility for Our Errors and Mistakes

Peole do think that if they avoid the truth, it might change to something better before they have to hear it.
                        —Marsha Norman

We have not passed that subtle line between childhood and adulthood until . . . we have stopped saying "It got lost," and say, "I lost it."
                        —Sydney J. Harris

Ah, how steadily do they who are guilty shrink from reproof!
                        —Amelia Jenks Bloomer

I've arrived at this outermost edge of my life by my own actions. Where I am is thoroughly unacceptable. Therefore, I must stop doing what I have been doing.   —Alice Koller

Do not blame anybody for your mistakes and failures.
                        —Bernard M. Baruch

I believe we are solely responsible for our choices, and we have to accept the consequences of every deed, word, and thought throughout our lifetime.   —Elisabeth Kubler-Ross

A chief is a man who assumes responsibility. He does not say "My men were beaten," he says, "I was beaten."   —Antoine de Saint-Exupery

The most considerable difference I note among men is not in their readiness to fall into error, but in their readiness to acknowledge these inevitable lapses.
                        —Thomas Henry Huxley

It is very easy to forgive others their mistakes. It takes more grit and gumption to forgive them for having witnessed your own.
                        —Jessamyn West

Whenever at an accusation blind rage burns up within us, the reason is that some arrow has pierced the joints of our harness. Behind our shining armour of righteous indignation lurks a convicted and only half-repentant sinner . . . [and] we may be almost sure some sharp and bitter grain of truth lurks within it, and the wound is best probed.   —Jane Harrison

The fault, dear Brutus, is not in our stars, but in ourselves.
                        —William Shakespeare

There's folks 'ud stand on their heads and then say the fault was i' their boots.   —George Eliot

Admitting error clears the score, and proves you wiser than before.
                        —Arthur Guiterman

Mistakes fail in their mission of helping the person who blames them on the other fellow. —Henry S. Haskins

I have known men who could see through the motivations of others with the skill of a clairvoyant; only to prove blind to their own mistakes. I have been one of those men.
—Bernard M. Baruch

I have made mistakes, but I have never made the mistake of claiming that I never made one.
—James Gordon Bennett

The man who can own up to his error is greater than he who merely knows how to avoid making it.
—Cardinal de Retz

A man may fall many times, but he won't be a failure until he says that someone pushed him.
—Elmer G. Letterman

JUST DON'T MAKE THE SAME MISTAKE TWICE

Do not be afraid of mistakes, providing you do not make the same one twice.   —Eleanor Roosevelt

To stumble twice against the same stone is a proverbial disgrace.
—Cicero

Fool me once, shame on you; fool me twice, shame on me.
—Chinese proverb

There is no reason to repeat bad history.   —Eleanor Holmes Norton

I try to extract something positive from [every] situation, even if it's just learning not to make the same mistake twice.   —Claudia Schiffer

He who is shipwrecked twice is foolish to blame the sea.
—Publilius Syrus

He who is shipwrecked the second time cannot lay the blame on Neptune.
—English proverb

He that's cheated twice by the same man is an accomplice with the cheater.
—Thomas Fuller

If you would not have affliction visit you twice, listen at once to what it teaches.   —James Burgh

You can beat the Bear once, but never the same way twice.
—John McKay

Any man can make mistakes, but only an idiot persists in his error.
—Cicero

There is nothing wrong with making mistakes. Just don't respond with encores.   —Anon.

The road to wisdom? Well, it's plain and simple to express: Err, and err, and err again. But less, and less, and less.   —Piet Hein

NEVER BE NEGATIVE ABOUT MISTAKES AND FAILURES

I made a mistake today, I made a mistake yesterday. I think it's . . . very important to ignore the negative.
—Jerry Rubin

The biggest quality in successful people I think is an impatience with negative thinking. . . . How many opportunities come along? If you wait for the right one, that's wrong, because it may never be right, and what have you got to lose? Even if it's a disaster, you've tried, you've learned something, you've had an adventure. And that doesn't mean you can't do it again.
—Edward McCabe

A peacefulness follows any decision, even the wrong one.
—Rita Mae Brown

If you don't accept failure as a possibility, you don't set high goals, you don't branch out, you don't try—you don't take the risk.
—Rosalynn Carter

When we can begin to take our failures non-seriously, it means we are ceasing to be afraid of them. It is of immense importance to learn to laugh at ourselves.
—Katherine Mansfield

If I lose, I'll walk away and never feel bad. . . . Because I did all I could, there was nothing more to do.
—Joe Frazier

A man must learn to forgive himself.
—Arthur Davison Ficke

You must accept that you might fail; then, if you do your best and still don't win, at least you can be satisfied that you've tried.
—Rosalynn Carter

Who would not rather trust and be deceived?
—Eliza Cook

Forget mistakes. Forget failure. Forget everything except what you're going to do now and do it. Today is your lucky day.
—Will Durant

There is a way to look at the past. Don't hide from it. It will not catch you if you don't repeat it.
—Pearl Bailey

Forget your mistakes, but remember what they taught you.
—Dorothy Galyean

Supposing you have tried and failed again and again. You may have a fresh start any moment you choose, for this thing that we call "failure" is not the falling down, but the staying down.
—Mary Pickford

Failure is a disappointment but not defeat.
—Jeanne Robertson

Memories are the key not to the past, but to the future. —Corrie ten Boom

"FAILURE" IS JUST A DETOUR, A DELAY

Failure is delay, but not defeat. It is a temporary detour, not a dead-end street.
—William A. Ward

Finite to fail, but infinite to venture.
—Emily Dickinson

When in doubt, make a fool of yourself. There is a microscopically thin line between being brilliantly creative and acting like the most gigantic idiot on earth. So what the hell, leap.
—Cynthia Heimel

Failure really isn't terrible if you can say to yourself, hey, I know I'm gonna be successful at what I want to do someday. Failure doesn't become a big hangup then because it's only temporary. If failure is absolute, then it would be a disaster, but as long as it's only temporary you can just go and achieve almost anything.
—Jerry Della Femina

Failure is an event, never a person.
—William D. Brown

It is better to be boldly decisive and risk being wrong than to agonize at length and be right too late.
—Marilyn Moats Kennedy

I've never met a person, I don't care what his condition, in whom I could not see possibilities. I don't care how much a man may consider himself a failure, I believe in him, for he can change the thing that is wrong in his life anytime he is prepared and ready to do it. Whenever he develops the desire, he can take away from his life the thing that is defeating it. The capacity for reformation and change lies within.   —Preston Bradley

I think and think for months, for years. Ninety-nine times the conclusion is false. The hundredth time I am right.   —Albert Einstein

Take chances, make mistakes. That's how you grow. Pain nourishes your courage. You have to fail in order to practice being brave.
—Mary Tyler Moore

Take risks. You can't fall off the bottom.   —Barbara Proctor

When it goes wrong, you feel like cutting your throat, but you go on. You don't let anything get you down so much that it beats you or stops you.
—George Cukor

You must have long-range goals to keep you from being frustrated by short-range failures.
—Charles C. Noble

Life is a series of relapses and recoveries.   —George Ade

We learn courageous action by going forward whenever fear urges us back. A little boy was asked how he learned to skate. "By getting up every time I fell down," he answered.
—David Seabury

If I had to live my life over again, I'd dare to make more mistakes next time.   —Nadine Stair

Failure is only postponed success as long as courage 'coaches' ambition. The habit of persistence is the habit of victory.   —Herbert Kaufman

Entrepreneurs average 3.8 failures before final success. What sets the successful ones apart is their amazing persistence. There are a lot of people out there with good and marketable ideas, but pure entrepreneurial types almost never accept defeat.
—Lisa M. Amos

Success is going from failure to failure without loss of enthusiasm.
—Sir Winston Churchill

I don't accept defeat as final. Only death is final—and even then I hope for a reprieve.   —Phil Gramm

Never confuse a single defeat with a final defeat.   —F. Scott Fitzgerald

Men's best successes come after their disappointments.
                    —Henry Ward Beecher

I've been failing for, like, ten or eleven years. When it turns, it'll turn. Right now I'm just tryin' to squeeze through a very tight financial period, get the movie out, and put my things in order.   —Francis Ford Coppola

Don't let a kick in the ass stop you. It's how you cope that says what you are.   —George Cukor

What is to be got at to make the air sweet, the ground good under the feet, can only be got at by failure, trial, again and again and again failure.
                    —Sherwood Anderson

They say President Wilson has blundered. Perhaps he has, but I notice he usually blunders forward.
                    —Thomas A. Edison

SOME "FAILURES" AREN'T FAILURES

Some of the biggest failures I ever had were successes.   —Pearl S. Buck

Not all who seem to fail have failed indeed. Not all who fail have therefore worked in vain. There is no failure for the good and brave.
                    —Archbishop Trench

No honest work of man or woman "fails"; it feeds the sum of all human action.   —Michelene Wandor

Defeat in doing right is nevertheless victory.   —Frederick W. Robertson

The only failure a man ought to fear is failure in cleaving to the purpose he sees to be best.   —George Eliot

Sometimes what you want to do has to fail so you won't.
                    —Margueritte Harmon Bro

There are defeats more triumphant than victories.
                    —Michel de Montaigne

An error gracefully acknowledged is a victory won.
                    —Caroline L. Gascoigne

Nothing succeeds like failure.
                    —Rebecca West

WE'RE NOT A FAILURE UNTIL . . .

Because a fellow has failed once or twice, or a dozen times, you don't want to set him down as a failure until he's dead or loses his courage— and that's the same thing.
                    —George Horace Lorimer

What we have most to fear is failure of the heart.   —Sonia Johnson

No man is a failure who is enjoying life.   —William Feather

You are beaten to earth? Well, well, what's that? Come up with a smiling face, it's nothing against you to fall down flat, but to lie there—that's disgrace.   —Edmund Vance Cooke

He alone fails who gives up and lies down.   —Ralph Waldo Trine

Never give a man up until he has failed at something he likes.
—Lewis E. Lawes

They were never defeated, they were only killed.
—Said of the French Foreign Legion

Failure is not in losing, but in no longer believing that winning is worthwhile.
—Anon.

He's no failure. He's not dead yet.
—W.L. George

Inside of a ring or out, ain't nothing wrong with going down. It's staying down that's wrong.
—Muhammad Ali

It ain't no disgrace for a man to fall, but to lie there and grunt is.
—Josh Billings

If you have made mistakes, even serious ones, there is always another chance for you. What we call failure is not the falling down, but the staying down.
—Mary Pickford

SOME OF THE MOST IMPORTANT KINDS OF "FAILURE"

If a man has a talent and cannot use it, he has failed. If he has a talent and uses only half of it, he has partly failed. If he has a talent and learns somehow to use the whole of it, he has gloriously succeeded, and won a satisfaction and a triumph few men ever know.
—Thomas Wolfe

Not failure, but low aim, is a crime.
—Ernest Holmes

There is only one real failure in life that is possible, and that is not to be true to the best one knows.
—Frederic W. Farrar

Perhaps the only real failure is that implying waste, a conscious and flagrant non-use or misuse of ability.
—Joseph H. Odell

There are two kinds of failures: The man who will do nothing he is told, and the man who will do nothing else.
—Dr. Perle Thompson

The only failure a man ought to fear is failure in cleaving to the purpose he sees to be best.
—George Eliot

TRUE FAILURE IS IN NOT TRYING

There is no failure except in no longer trying.
—Elbert Hubbard

Men do not fail; they stop trying.
—Elihu Root

Most people live and die with their music still unplayed. They never dare to try.
—Mary Kay Ash

It is a very dangerous thing to have an idea that you will not practice.
—Phyllis Bottome

If you risk nothing, then you risk everything.
—Geena Davis

Men must try and try again.
—Lawson Purdy

In the past, few women have tried and even fewer have succeeded.
—Rosalyn Sussman Yalow

667

A mistake is not a failure, but evidence that someone tried to do something. —Anon.

Man must strive, and in striving, he must err. —Johann von Goethe

The person interested in success has to learn to view failure as a healthy, inevitable part of the process of getting to the top. —Dr. Joyce Brothers

Failure after long perseverance is much grander than never to have a striving good enough to be called a failure. —George Eliot

The sight of a cage is only frightening to the bird that has once been caught. —Rachel Field

Your success depends on your ability to dream and follow through on those dreams. —Jinger Heath

Keep trying. Take care of the small circle around you. When you have succeeded with them, then move outwards, one small step at a time. —Audrey Hepburn

It is better to be young in your failures than old in your successes. —Flannery O'Connor

There might be false starts and do-overs. You are entitled to experiment before you find your calling. —Jane Pauley

Life is the only real counselor. Wisdom unfiltered through personal experience does not become a part of the moral tissue. —Edith Wharton

The only failure which lacks dignity is the failure to try. —Malcolm F. MacNeil

To know that one has never really tried—that is the only death. —Marie Dressler

We have to keep trying things we're not sure we can pull off. If we just do the things we know we can do . . . you don't grow as much. You gotta take those chances on making those big mistakes. —Cybil Shepherd

If you're not failing, you're not trying anything. —Woody Allen

If you play it safe in life, you've decided that you don't want to grow anymore. —Shirley Hufstedler

Those who try and fail are much wiser than those who never try for fear of failure. —André Bustanoby

A man's life is interesting primarily when he has failed—I well know. For it's a sign that he tried to surpass himself. —Georges Clemenceau

To avoid an occasion for our virtues is a worse degree of failure than to push forward pluckily and fall. —Robert Louis Stevenson

The fearful are caught as often as the bold. —Helen Keller

Inaction, contrary to its reputation for being a refuge, is neither safe nor comfortable. —Madeleine Kunin

They fail, and they alone, who have not striven. —Thomas Bailey Aldrich

You may be disappointed if you fail, but you are doomed if you don't try.
—Beverly Sills

It takes as much courage to have tried and failed as it does to have tried and succeeded.
—Anne Morrow Lindbergh

Failure is something made only by those who fail to dare, not by those who dare to fail.   —Louis Binstock

You don't always win your battles, but it's good to know you fought.
—Marjorie Holmes

The man who has done his level best, and who is conscious that he has done his best, is a success, even though the world may write him down a failure.   —B.C. Forbes

Many a man never fails because he never tries.   —Norman MacEwan

MISTAKES CAN BE ENORMOUSLY VALUABLE

Good judgment comes from experience, and experience comes from poor judgment.   —Anon.

Life is very interesting, if you make mistakes.   —Georges Carpentier

When I have listened to my mistakes, I have grown.   —Hugh Prather

Mistakes and errors are the discipline through which we advance.
—William Ellery Channing

A stumble may prevent a fall.
—Thomas Fuller

A life spent making mistakes is not only more honorable but more useful than a life spent doing nothing.
—George Bernard Shaw

VALUABLE THINGS WE CAN GET FROM DEFEAT

It is defeat that turns bone to flint; it is defeat that turns gristle to muscle; it is defeat that makes men invincible. Do not then be afraid of defeat. You are never so near to victory as when defeated in a good cause.
—Henry Ward Beecher

Defeat should never be a source of discouragement, but rather a fresh stimulus.   —South

Besides the practical knowledge which defeat offers, there are important personality profits to be taken. Defeat strips away false values and makes you realize what you really want. It stops you from chasing butterflies and puts you to work digging gold.
—William M. Marston

No experiment is ever a complete failure. It can always be used as a bad example.   —Paul Dickson

Failure is the foundation of success, and the means by which it is achieved.   —Lao-tzu

There is much to be said for failure. It is more interesting than success.
—Max Beerbohm

Failure sometimes enlarges the spirit. You have to fall back upon humanity and God.   —Charles Horton Cooley

It is often the failure who is the pioneer in new lands, new undertakings, and new forms of expression.
—Eric Hoffer

Let us not be needlessly bitter; certain failures are sometimes fruitful.
—E.M. Cioran

If I win several tournaments in a row, I get so confident I'm in a cloud. A loss gets me eager again.
—Chris Evert Lloyd

There's nothing that cleanses your soul like getting the hell kicked out of you.
—Woody Hayes

Failure is only an opportunity to begin again more intelligently.
—Henry Ford

Disappointments are to the soul what the thunder-storm is to the air.
—J.C.F. von Schiller

The wisest person is not the one who has the fewest failures, but the one who turns failures to best account.
—Richard R. Grant

One of the advantages of defeat in life—maybe the main advantage—is that it provides an excuse for change. Defeat . . . invariably leads to new adventures.
—James Reston

Failure is God's own tool for carving some of the finest outlines in the character of his children.
—Thomas Hodgkin

I quit being afraid when my first venture failed and the sky didn't fall down.
—Allen H. Neuharth

FAILURE IS EDUCATIONAL

What is defeat? Nothing but education, nothing but the first step to something better.   —Wendell Phillips

From their errors and mistakes the wise and good learn wisdom for the future.
—Plutarch

Having harvested all the knowledge and wisdom we can from our mistakes and failures, we should put them behind us and go ahead.
—Edith Johnson

I think success has no rules, but you can learn a great deal from failure.
—Jean Kerr

Failure is just another way to learn how to do something right.
—Marian Wright Edelman

There are no mistakes, no coincidences. All events are blessings given to us to learn from.
—Elisabeth Kubler-Ross

We will be victorious if we have not forgotten how to learn.
—Rosa Luxemburg

It is the true nature of mankind to learn from mistakes, not from example.
—Fred Hoyle

The psychotherapist learns little or nothing from his successes. They mainly confirm him in his mistakes, while his failures, on the other hand, are priceless experiences in that they not only open up the way to a deeper truth, but force him to change his views and methods.   —Carl Jung

670

Failure . . . is, in a sense, the highway to success, inasmuch as every discovery of what is false leads us to seek earnestly after what is true, and every fresh experience points out some form of error which we shall afterward carefully avoid.   —John Keats

We need to teach a highly educated person that it is not a disgrace to fail and that he must analyze every failure to find its cause. He must learn how to fail intelligently, for failing is one of the greatest arts of the world.
        —Charles F. Kettering

When a man is pushed, tormented, defeated, he has a chance to learn something; he has been put on his wits; on his manhood; he has gained the facts; learned his ignorance; is cured of the insanity of conceit; has got moderation and real skill.
        —Ralph Waldo Emerson

There are no mistakes. The events we bring upon ourselves, no matter how unpleasant, are necessary in order to learn what we need to learn; whatever steps we take, they're necessary to reach the places we've chosen to go.
        —Richard Bach

Failure is instructive. The person who really thinks learns quite as much from his failures as from his successes.   —John Dewey

Failure is a school in which the truth always grows strong.
        —Henry Ward Beecher

The important thing is to learn a lesson every time you lose.
        —John McEnroe

It's good to fail now and again—you learn a lot more out of failure than you do out of success.   —Ian Hunter

One of the reasons mature people stop learning is that they become less and less willing to risk failure.
        —John W. Gardner

Through failure, we learn a lesson in humility which is probably needed, painful though it is.   —Bill W.

A failure is a man who has blundered, but is not able to cash in the experience.   —Elbert Hubbard

Like success, failure is many things to many people. With Positive Mental Attitude, failure is a learning experience, a rung on the ladder, a plateau at which to get your thoughts in order and prepare to try again.
        —W. Clement Stone

Disappointment is the nurse of wisdom.   —Sir Bayle Roche

When you make a mistake, don't look back at it long. Take the reason of the thing into your mind, and then look forward. Mistakes are lessons of wisdom. The past cannot be changed. The future is yet in your power.
        —Hugh White

What can any of us do with his talent but try to develop his vision, so that through frequent failures we may learn better what we have missed in the past.   —William Carlos Williams

Nothing is a waste of time if you use the experience wisely.
        —Auguste Rodin

To lose is to learn.   —Anon.

From the errors of others, a wise man
corrects his own.   —Publilius Syrus

Learn from the mistakes of others—
you can't live long enough to make
them all yourself.   —Martin Vanbee

The entire history of science is a progression of exploded fallacies.
                      —Ayn Rand

Don't use the conduct of a fool as a
precedent.   —Talmud

Wise men learn by other men's mistakes, fools by their own.
                      —H.G. Bohn

Learn to see in another's calamity the
ills which you should avoid.
                      —Publilius Syrus

A man is fortunate if he encounters
living examples of vice, as well as of
virtue, to inspire him.
                      —Brendan Francis

WE'RE OFTEN CLOSER TO
SUCCESS THAN WE THINK

The line between failure and success
is so fine that we scarcely know when
we pass it; so fine that we are often
on the line and do not know it.
                      —Elbert Hubbard

A series of failures may culminate in
the best possible result.
                      —Gisela Richter

Failure is that early morning hour of
darkness which precedes the dawning
of the day of success.
                      —Leigh Mitchell Hodges

People fail forward to success.
                      —Mary Kay Ash

Apparent failure may hold in its
rough shell the germs of a success
that will blossom in time, and bear
fruit throughout eternity.
                      —Frances Ellen Watkins Harper

SOME REASONS PEOPLE FAIL

The causes of mistakes are "I didn't
know"; "I didn't think"; and "I
didn't care."   —Henry H. Buckley

Failures are divided into two class-
es: those who thought and never
did, and those who did and never
thought.   —John Charles Salak

A failure establishes only this, that
our determination to succeed was not
strong enough.   —Christian Bovee

Self-distrust is the cause of most of
our failures. They are the weakest,
however strong, who have no faith in
themselves or their own powers.
                      —Christian Bovee

Defeat is a thing of weariness, of
incoherence, of boredom.
                      —Antoine de Saint-Exupery

Failure at a task may be the result of
having tackled it at the wrong time.
                      —Brendan Francis

We fail more often by timidity than
by over-daring.   —David Grayson

Failure is more frequently from want of energy than want of capital.
—Daniel Webster

Losers have tons of variety. Champions take pride in just learning to hit the same old boring winners.
—Vic Braden

Lack of will power has caused more failures than lack of intelligence or ability.   —Flower A. Newhouse

The word fate . . . is the refuge of every self-confessed failure.
—Andrew Soutar

Half the things that people do not succeed in are through fear of making the attempt.   —James Northcote

The man who fails because he aims astray, or because he does not aim at all, is to be found everywhere.
—Frank Swinnerton

Half the failures in life come from pulling one's horse in when he is leaping.   —A.W. Hare

I cannot give you the formula for success, but I can give you the formula for failure: try to please everybody.
—Herbert Bayard Swope

If your project doesn't work, look for the part that you didn't think was important.   —Arther Bloch

Ninety-nine percent of the failures come from people who have the habit of making excuses.
—George Washington Carver

One who fears failure limits his activities.   —Henry Ford

The difference between failure and success is doing a thing nearly right and doing a thing exactly right.
—Edward Simmons

We have forty million reasons for failure, but not a single excuse.
—Rudyard Kipling

The greatest mistake you can make in life is to be continually fearing you will make one.   —Elbert Hubbard

How to succeed: Try hard enough. How to fail: Try too hard.
—Malcolm Forbes

Most men fail, not through lack of education, but from lack of dogged determination, from lack of dauntless will.   —Orison Swett Marden

Failure comes only when we forget our ideals and objects and principles.
—Jawaharlal Nehru

An error is simply a failure to adjust immediately from a preconception to an actuality.   —John Cage

We are less likely to fail if we measure with judgement our chances and our capabilities.   —Agnes Repplier

Laziness is a secret ingredient that goes into failure. But it's only kept a secret from the person who fails.
—Robert Half

Failure is usually the line of least persistence.   —Wilfred Beaver

You can't expect to win unless you know why you lose.
—Benjamin Lipson

Most people don't plan to fail, they fail to plan.   —John L. Beckley

General Quotations about Mistakes and Failures

Failure is not sweet, but it need not be bitter.   —Anon.

The ultimate umpire of all things in life is—fact.   —Agnes C. Laut

Losses are comparative, imagination only makes them of any moment.
    —Blaise Pascal

I would prefer even to fail with honor than win by cheating.
    —Sophocles

Disillusion is a natural stage that follows the holding of an illusion.
    —Susan Shaughnessy

If any good results to a man from believing a lie, it certainly comes from the honesty of his belief.
    —Margaret Collier Graham

And what if I did run my ship aground; oh, still it was splendid to sail it!   —Henrik Ibsen

Success is a public affair. Failure is a private funeral.   —Rosalind Russell

It is not easy, but you have to be willing to make mistakes. And the earlier you make those mistakes, the better.
    —Jane Cahill Pfeiffer

If you're gonna be a failure, at least be one at something you enjoy.
    —Sylvester Stallone

Who would not rather flounder in the fight than not have known the glory of the fray?   —Richard Hovey

Better a false belief than no belief at all.   —George Eliot

A mistake is simply another way of doing things.   —Katherine Graham

The probability that we may fail in the struggle ought not to deter us from the support of a cause we believe to be just.
    —Abraham Lincoln

Three failures denotes uncommon strength. A weakling had not enough grit to fail thrice.   —Minna Antrim

The Advantages of Adversity

DIFFICULTIES CAN STIMULATE US TO OUR GREATEST ACHIEVEMENTS

A wounded deer leaps the highest.
—Emily Dickinson

The difficulties which I meet with in order to realize my existence are precisely what awaken and mobilize my activities, my capacities.
—José Ortega y Gasset

Whenever there is chaos, it creates wonderful thinking. I consider chaos a gift. —Septima Poinsette Clark

I have always been pushed by the negative. . . . The apparent failure of a play sends me back to my typewriter that very night, before the reviews are out. I am more compelled to get back to work than if I had a success.
—Tennessee Williams

What we want is never simple.
—Linda Pastan

For me life is a challenge. And it will be a challenge if I live to be a hundred or if I get to be a trillionaire.
—Beah Richards

To be thrown upon one's own resources is to be cast into the very lap of fortune, for our faculties then undergo a development and display an energy of which they were previously unsusceptible.
—Benjamin Franklin

Every failure made me more confident. Because I wanted even more to achieve things, as revenge. To show that I could. —Roman Polanski

Adversity is, to me at least, a tonic and a bracer. —Sir Walter Scott

Difficulties should act as a tonic. They should spur us to greater exertion. —B.C. Forbes

There are times in everyone's life when something constructive is born out of adversity . . . when things seem so bad that you've got to grab your fate by the shoulders and shake it.
—Anon.

Brave men rejoice in adversity, just as brave soldiers triumph in war.
—Marcus Annaeus Seneca

Some minds seem almost to create themselves, springing up under every disadvantage and working their solitary but irresistible way through a thousand obstacles.
—Washington Irving

Every calamity is a spur and valuable hint.   —Ralph Waldo Emerson

Treasure the memories of past misfortunes; they constitute our bank of fortitude.   —Eric Hoffer

If you will call your troubles experiences, and remember that every experience develops some latent force within you, you will grow vigorous and happy, however adverse your circumstances may seem to be.
—John Heywood

Necessity is often the spur to genius.
—Honore de Balzac

Necessity is the mother of "taking chances."   —Mark Twain

Necessity makes even the timid brave.
—Sallust

People wish to be settled; only as far as they are unsettled is there any hope for them.
—Ralph Waldo Emerson

Difficulties are meant to rouse, not discourage. The human spirit is to grow strong by conflict.
—William Ellery Channing

Adversity causes some men to break, others to break records.
—William A. Ward

I think there is this about the great troubles—they teach us the art of cheerfulness; whereas the small ones cultivate the industry of discontent.
—Mary Adams

OPPOSITION CAN INSPIRE AND IMPROVE US

Opposition inflames the enthusiast, never converts him.
—J.C.F. von Schiller

The thought that we are enduring the unendurable is one of the things that keeps us going.   —Molly Haskell

If you do things well, do them better. Be daring, be first, be different, be just.   —Anita Roddick

A certain amount of opposition is a great help to a man; it is what he wants and must have to be good for anything. Hardship and opposition are the native soil of manhood and self-reliance.   —John Neal

Difficulties, opposition, criticism— these things are meant to be overcome, and there is a special joy in facing them and in coming out on top. It is only when there is nothing but praise that life loses its charm and I begin to wonder what I should do about it.
—Vijaya Lakshmi Pandit

They sicken of calm, who know the storm.   —Dorothy Parker

Without the burden of afflictions it is impossible to reach the height of grace. The gift of grace increases as the struggles increase.
—Saint Rose of Lima

676

When the going gets tough, the tough get going.   —Frank Leahy

The effects of opposition are wonderful. There are men who rise refreshed on hearing of a threat, men to whom a crises, which intimidates and paralyzes the majority, comes as graceful and beloved as a bride!
    —Ralph Waldo Emerson

Remember that the Devil doesn't sleep, but seeks our ruin in a thousand different ways   —Angela Merici

Down you mongrel, Death! Back into your kennel!
    —Edna Saint Vincent Millay

He that wrestles with us strengthens our nerves and sharpens our skills. Our antagonist is our helper.
    —Edmund Burke

The block of granite which was an obstacle in the path of the weak becomes a steppingstone in the path of the strong.   —Thomas Carlyle

Strong people are made by opposition, like kites that go up against the wind.   —Frank Harris

Men strive for peace, but it is their enemies that give them strength, and I think if man no longer had enemies, he would have to invent them, for his strength only grows from struggle.
    —Louis L'Amour

You'll never find a better sparring partner than adversity.
    —Walt Schmidt

The English nation is never so great as in adversity.   —Benjamin Disraeli

Enemies can be an incentive to survive and become someone in spite of them. Enemies can keep you alert and aware.   —Louis L'Amour

Problems are the cutting edge that distinguishes between success and failure. Problems . . . create our courage and wisdom.   —M. Scott Peck

THERE'S TREMENDOUS VALUE IN HITTING BOTTOM

It is often better to have a great deal of harm happen to one than a little; a great deal may rouse you to remove what a little will only accustom you to endure.   —Grenville Kleiser

When things come to the worse, they generally mend.   —Susanna Moodie

Things have got to be wrong in order that they may be deplored.
    —Whitney Griswold

Remorse begets reform.
    —William Cowper

"The world is a wheel always turning," philosophized Mrs. Pelz. "Those who were high go down low, and those who've been low go up higher."   —Anzia Yezierska

Life begins on the other side of despair.   —Jean-Paul Sartre

It constantly happens that the Lord permits a soul to fall so that it may grow humbler.   —Teresa of Avila

In order to change, we must be sick and tired of being sick and tired.
    —Anon.

I have been in sorrow's kitchen
and licked out all the pots. Then I
have stood on the peaky mountain
wrapped in rainbows, with a harp
and sword in my hands.
 —Zora Neale Hurston

There is often in people to whom
"the worst" has happened an almost
transcendent freedom, for they have
faced "the worst" and survived it.
 —Carol Pearson

I didn't know I'd have to be torn
down before I could be built up.
 —Anon.

Suffering Also Has Its Benefits

Suffering! . . . We owe to it all that is
good in us, all that gives value to life;
we owe to it pity, we owe to it courage, we owe to it all the virtues.
 —Anatole France

It is only the women whose eyes have
been washed clear with tears who
get the broad vision that makes them
little sisters to all the world.
 —Dorothy Dix

Much of your pain is the bitter
potion by which the physician within
you heals your sick self.
 —Kahlil Gibran

Man cannot remake himself without
suffering, for he is both the marble
and the sculptor. —Dr. Alexis Carrel

Out of suffering have emerged the
strongest souls; the most massive
characters are seared with scars.
 —Edwin H. Chapin

The pain of love is the pain of being
alive. It is a perpetual wound.
 —Maureen Duffy

There is no coming to consciousness
without pain. —Carl Jung

Everybody's heart is open, you know,
when they have recently escaped
from severe pain, or are recovering
the blessing of health. —Jane Austen

Suffering is the sole origin of consciousness. —Fyodor Dostoyevsky

Pain makes man think. Thought
makes man wise. Wisdom makes life
endurable. —John Patrick

Time engraves our faces with all the
tears we have not shed.
 —Natalie Clifford Barney

Suffering raises up those souls that
are truly great; it is only small souls
that are made mean-spirited by it.
 —Alexandra David-Néel

To live is to suffer, to survive is to
find some meaning in the suffering.
 —Roberta Flack

If you suffer, thank God! It is a sure
sign that you are alive.
 —Elbert Hubbard

Suffering is also one of the ways of
knowing you're alive.
 —Jessamyn West

Don't look forward to the day when
you stop suffering. Because when it
comes, you'll know you're dead.
 —Tennessee Williams

How sublime a thing it is to suffer
and be strong.
—Henry Wadsworth Longfellow

He disposes Doom who hath suffered
him.   —Emily Dickinson

They merit more praise who know
how to suffer misery than those who
temper themselves in contentment.
—Pietro Aretino

Character cannot be developed in
ease and quiet. Only through experience of trial and suffering can the
soul be strengthened, vision cleared,
ambition inspired, and success
achieved.   —Helen Keller

Never to suffer would have been
never to have been blessed.
—Edgar Allan Poe

It is somehow reassuring to discover
that the word "travel" is derived
from "travail," denoting the pains of
childbirth.   —Jessica Mitford

True knowledge comes only through
suffering.
—Elizabeth Barrett Browning

Suffering raises up those souls that
are truly great; it is only small souls
that are made mean-spirited by it.
—Alexandra David-Néel

He disposes Doom who hath suffered
him.   —Emily Dickinson

Suffering has always been with us,
does it really matter in what form it
comes? All that matters is how we
bear it and how we fit it into our
lives.   —Etty Hillesum

We are healed of a suffering only by
experiencing it to the full.
—Marcel Proust

Those who have suffered understand
suffering and therefore extend their
hand.   —Patti Smith

The saints rejoiced at injuries and
persecutions, because in forgiving
them they had something to present
to God when they prayed to Him.
—Teresa of Avila

TOUGH TIMES AND ADVERSITY CAN GENERATE OPPORTUNITY AND PROGRESS

From the discontent of man, the
world's best progress springs.
—Ella Wheeler Wilcox

The difficulties and struggles of today
are but the price we must pay for
the accomplishments and victories of
tomorrow.   —William J.H. Boetcker

Experience may be hard but we claim
its gifts because they are real, even
though our feet bleed on its stones.
—Mary Parker Follett

And I think that's important, to
know how the water's gone over the
dam before you start to describe it.
It helps to have been over the dam
yourself.   —E. Annie Proulx

I think these difficult times have helped
me to understand better than before
how infinitely rich and beautiful life is
in every way that so many things that
one goes around worrying about are
of no importance whatsoever.
—Isak Dinesen

Problems are the price of progress. Don't bring me anything but trouble.
—Charles F. Kettering

Trouble is the thing that strong men grow by. Met in the right way, it is a sure-fire means of putting iron into the victim's will and making him a tougher man to down forever after.
—H. Bertram Lewis

Every time you meet a situation, though you think at the time it is an impossibility and you go through the torture of the damned, once you have met it and lived through it, you find that forever after you are freer than you were before.
—Eleanor Roosevelt

I have always fought for ideas—until I learned that it isn't ideas but grief, struggle, and flashes of vision which enlighten.   —Margaret Anderson

I have learned in the great University of Hard Knocks a philosophy that no woman who has had an easy life ever acquires. I have learned to live each day as it comes, and not to borrow trouble by dreading tomorrow. It is the dark menace of the future that makes cowards of us. —Dorothy Dix

Discontent and disorder were signs of energy and hope, not of despair.
—C. V. Wedgwood

We say: mad with joy. We should say: wise with grief.
—Marguerite Yourcenar

There are some things you learn best in calm, and some in storm.
—Willa Cather

Discontent is the first step in the progress of a man or a nation.
—Oscar Wilde

Were there none who were discontented with what they have, the world would never reach anything better.
—Florence Nightingale

Woman's discontent increases in exact proportion to her development.
—Elizabeth Cady Stanton

Restlessness is discontent, and discontent is the first necessity of progress.
—Thomas A. Edison

Noble discontent is the path to heaven.
—Thomas W. Higginson

No pain, no palm; no thorns, no throne; no gall, no glory; no cross, no crown.   —William Penn

Times of stress and difficulty are seasons of opportunity when the seeds of progress are sown.
—Thomas F. Woodlock

The gem cannot be polished without friction, nor man perfected without trials.   —Confucius

As there is no worldly gain without some loss, so there is no worldly loss without some gain. . . . Set the allowance against the loss, and thou shalt find no loss great.   —Francis Quarles

Never complain about your troubles; they are responsible for more than half of your income.
—Robert R. Updegraff

A problem is a chance for you to do your best.   —Duke Ellington

Emergencies have always been necessary to progress. It was darkness which produced the lamp. It was fog that produced the compass. It was hunger that drove us to exploration. And it took a depression to teach us the real value of a job.
—Victor Hugo

Many men owe the grandeur of their lives to their tremendous difficulties.
—Charles Haddon Spurgeon

It is often hard to distinguish between the hard knocks in life and those of opportunity.   —Frederick Phillips

Adversity As a Test

Fire is the test of gold, adversity of strong men.
—Marcus Annaeus Seneca

I think my biggest achievement is that after going through a rather difficult time, I consider myself comparatively sane. I'm proud of that.
—Jacqueline Kennedy Onassis

To be tested is good. The challenged life may be the best therapist.
—Gail Sheehy

I think hearts are very much like glasses—if they do not break with the first ring, they usually last a considerable time.   —L.E. Landon

Your first big trouble can be a bonanza if you live through it. Get through the first trouble, and you'll probably make it through the next one.
—Ruth Gordon

Calamity is the test of integrity.
—Richardson

The secret of a leader lies in the tests he has faced over the whole course of his life and the habit of action he develops in meeting those tests.
—Gail Sheehy

The fiery trials through which we pass will light us down in honor or dishonor to the last generation.
—Abraham Lincoln

Our trials are tests; our sorrows pave the way for a fuller life when we have earned it.   —Jerome P. Fleishman

Like Other Elements, People Develop through Pressure

Times of general calamity and confusion have ever been productive of the greatest minds. The purist ore is produced from the hottest furnace, and the brightest thunderbolt is elicited from the darkest storms.
—Charles Caleb Colton

The habits of a vigorous mind are formed in contending with difficulties.
—Abigail Adams

A diamond is a chunk of coal that made good under pressure.   —Anon.

A clay pot sitting in the sun will always be a clay pot. It has to go through the white heat of the furnace to become porcelain.
—Mildred W. Struven

It is the surmounting of difficulties that makes heroes.   —Kossuth

Men habitually use only a small part of the powers which they possess and which they might use under appropriate circumstances. —William James

It is the north wind that lashes men into Vikings; it is the soft, luscious south wind which lulls them to lotus dreams. —Ouida

It is grief that develops the powers of the mind. —Marcel Proust

Unless a man has been kicked around a little, you can't really depend upon him to amount to anything. —William Feather

Troubles cured you salty as a country ham, smoky to the taste, thick-skinned and tender inside. —Marge Piercy

If you have to be careful because of oppression and censorship, this pressure produces diamonds. —Tatyana Tolstaya

Adversity is another way to measure the greatness of individuals. I never had a crisis that didn't make me stronger. —Lou Holtz

It is not in the still calm of life, or the repose of a pacific station, that great characters are formed. . . . Great necessities call out great virtues. —Abigail Adams

The Value of Adversity in Youth

Of all the advantages which come to any young man . . . poverty is the greatest. —Josiah G. Holland

My luck was my father not striking oil . . . we'd have been rich. I'd never have set out for Hollywood with my camera, and I'd have had a lot less interesting life. —King Vidor

[A difficult childhood gave me] a kind of cocky confidence. . . . I could never have so little that I hadn't had less. It took away my fear. —Jacqueline Cochran

If you have been sunned through and through like an apricot on a wall from your earliest days, you are over-sensitive to any withdrawal of heat. —Margot Asquith

I was lucky I wasn't a better boxer, or that's what I'd be now—a punchy ex-pug. —Bob Hope

At every step the child should be allowed to meet the real experience of life; the thorns should never be plucked from his roses. —Ellen Key

Hot water is my native element. I was in it as a baby, and I have never seemed to get out of it ever since. —Edith Sitwell

When I was very young, I tried selling used cars. It didn't last long. I guess that was my good luck too, that I didn't show more promise at it, or I might have been an automobile dealer. —King Vidor

Supporting myself at an early age was the best training for life I could have possibly received. —Lea Thompson

In my youth, poverty enriched me, but now I can afford wealth. —Marc Chagall

I'm very grateful that I was too poor to get to art school until I was 21. . . . I was old enough when I got there to know how to get something out of it.
—Henry Moore

The most valuable gift I ever received was . . . the gift of insecurity . . . my father left us. My mother's love might not have prepared me for life the way my father's departure did. He forced us out on the road, where we had to earn our bread.   —Lillian Gish

Americans are like a rich father who wishes he knew how to give his sons the hardships that made him rich.
—Robert Frost

I would never have amounted to anything were it not for adversity. I was forced to come up the hard way.
—J.C. Penney

ADVERSITY HELPS US LEARN ABOUT OURSELVES

Adversity introduces a man to himself.
—Anon.

I thank God for my handicaps for, through them, I have found myself, my work, and my God.
—Helen Keller

When one's own problems are unsolvable and all best efforts are frustrated, it is lifesaving to listen to other people's problems.
—Suzanne Massie

This struggle of people against their conditions, this is where you find the meaning in life.   —Rose Chernin

Adversity has ever been considered as the state in which a man most easily becomes acquainted with himself, being free from flatterers.
—Samuel Johnson

In all things preserve integrity; and the consciousness of thine own uprightness will alleviate the toil of business, soften the hardness of ill-success and disappointments, and give thee an humble confidence before God, when the ingratitude of man, or the iniquity of the times may rob thee of other rewards.
—Barbara Paley

He knows not his own strength who hath not met adversity.
—Samuel Johnson

Adversity leads us to think properly of our state, and so is most beneficial to us.   —Samuel Johnson

In the depth of winter, I finally learned that there was in me an invincible summer.   —Albert Camus

Who hath not known ill fortune, never knew himself, or his own virtue.
—David Mallett

Adversity is the trial of principle. Without it a man hardly knows whether he is honest or not.
—Henry Fielding

I think the years I have spent in prison have been the most formative and important in my life because of the discipline, the sensations, but chiefly the opportunity to think clearly, to try to understand things.
—Jawaharlal Nehru

We only really face up to ourselves
when we are afraid.
—Thomas Bernhard

Difficulties are things that show what
men are.   —Epictetus

Even if misfortune is only good for
bringing a fool to his senses, it would
still be just to deem it good for something.   —Jean de La Fontaine

Never does a man know the force
that is in him till some mighty affection or grief has humanized the soul.
—Frederick W. Robertson

Disappointment is the nurse of
wisdom.   —Sir Bayle Roche

Challenges make you discover things
about yourself that you never really
knew. They're what make the instrument stretch, what make you go
beyond the norm.   —Cicely Tyson

A woman is like a tea bag: you never
know her strength until you drop her
in hot water.   —Nancy Reagan

TOUGH TIMES ARE
GREAT TEACHERS

Trouble brings experience, and experience brings wisdom.   —Anon.

A woman has got to love a bad man
once or twice in her life to be thankful for a good one.
—Marjorie Kinnan Rawlings

Adversity has the effect of eliciting
talents, which, in prosperous circumstances, would have lain dormant.
—Horace

Adversity is a severe instructor. . . . He
that wrestles with us strengthens our
nerves and sharpens our skill. Our
antagonist is our helper.
—Edmund Burke

Experience is a good teacher, but she
sends in terrific bills.
—Minna Antrim

Forget the times of your distress, but
never forget what they taught you.
—Herbert Gasser

You can learn little from victory. You
can learn everything from defeat.
—Christy Mathewson

A smooth sea never made a skillful
mariner.   —English proverb

When a man is pushed, tormented,
defeated, he has a chance to learn
something; he has been put on his
wits . . . he has gained facts, learned
his ignorance, is cured of the insanity
of conceit, has got moderation and
real skill.   —Ralph Waldo Emerson

From their errors and mistakes, the
wise and good learn wisdom for the
future.   —Plutarch

By becoming more unhappy, we
sometimes learn how to be less so.
—Madame Swetchine

Every experience, however bitter, has
its lesson, and to focus one's attention on the lesson helps one overcome the bitterness.
—Edward Howard Griggs

A good scare is worth more to a man
than good advice.
—Edgar Watson Howe

It is from the level of calamities . . . that we learn impressive and useful lessons.
—William Makepeace Thackeray

When I have listened to my mistakes, I have grown.　　—Hugh Prather

We only think when we are confronted with a problem.　—John Dewey

Adversity comes with instruction in its hand.　　　　　　—Anon.

There is no education like adversity.
—Benjamin Disraeli

Mistakes are often the best teachers.
—James A. Froude

Pain, indolence, sterility, endless ennui have also their lesson for you.
—Ralph Waldo Emerson

Prosperity is a great teacher; adversity is a greater. Possession pampers the mind; privation trains and strengthens it.　　—William Hazlitt

Wisdom comes by disillusionment.
—George Santayana

You have learned something. That always feels at first as if you had lost something.　—George Bernard Shaw

I have always grown from my problems and challenges, from the things that don't work out. That's when I've really learned.　　—Carol Burnett

Those things that hurt, instruct.
—Benjamin Franklin

Pain is the root of knowledge.
—Simone Weil

Life can be real tough . . . you can either learn from your problems, or keep repeating them over and over.
—Marie Osmond

Bad times have a scientific value. These are occasions a good learner would not miss.
—Ralph Waldo Emerson

Adversity and Prosperity

Prosperity is not without many fears and distastes, and adversity is not without comforts and hopes.
—Francis Bacon

If we had no winter, the spring would not be so pleasant; if we did not sometimes taste of adversity, prosperity would not be so welcome.
—Anne Bradstreet

The good things that belong to prosperity are to be wished, but the good things that belong to adversity are to be admired.
—Marcus Annaeus Seneca

One who was adored by all in prosperity is abhorred by all in adversity.
—Baltasar Gracian

Prosperity provideth, but adversity proveth friends.　—Queen Elizabeth I

The human race has had long experience and a fine tradition in surviving adversity. But we now face a task for which we have little experience, the task of surviving prosperity.
—Alan Gregg

Adversity reveals genius, prosperity conceals it.　　　　　　—Horace

The virtue of prosperity is temperance; the virtue of adversity is fortitude.
—Francis Bacon

In the day of prosperity be joyful, but in the day of adversity consider.
—Ecclesiastes 9:11

In victory even the cowardly like to boast, while in adverse times even the brave are discredited.   —Sallust

Adversity is sometimes hard upon a man; but for one man who can stand prosperity, there are a hundred that will stand adversity.
—Thomas Carlyle

Darkness and Light

Some knowledge and some song and some beauty must be kept for those days before the world again plunges into darkness.
—Marion Zimmer Bradley

Though outwardly a gloomy shroud,
The inner half of every cloud
Is bright and shining:
I therefore turn my clouds about
And always wear them inside out
To show the lining.
—Ellen Thorneycroft Fowler

There is not enough darkness in all the world to put out the light of even one small candle.   —Robert Alden

Hope begins in the dark, the stubborn hope that if you just show up and try to do the right thing, the dawn will come. You wait and watch and work: you don't give up.
—Anne Lamott

Truth, like the burgeoning of a bulb under the soil, however deeply sown, will make its way to the light.
—Ellis Peters

Flowers grow out of dark moments.
—Corita Kent

I have brightness in my soul, which strains toward Heaven. I am like a bird!   —Jenny Lind

When it is dark enough, you can see the stars.   —Charles A. Beard

Some Spiritual Advantages and Aspects of Adversity

All sorts of spiritual gifts come through privations, if they are accepted.
—Janet Erskine Stuart

There is nothing the body suffers which the soul may not profit by.
—George Meredith

Often God has to shut a door in our face, so that He can subsequently open the door through which He wants us to go. —Catharine Marshall

God will not look you over for medals, degrees or diplomas, but for scars.
—Anon.

He who serves God with what costs him nothing, will do very little service, you may depend on it.
—Susan Warner

There are three modes of bearing the ills of life: by indifference, by philosophy, and by religion.
—Charles Caleb Colton

Sorrow has its reward. It never leaves us where it found us.
—Mary Baker Eddy

The same reason makes a man a religious enthusiast that makes a man an enthusiast in any other way: an uncomfortable mind in an uncomfortable body.   —William Hazlitt

WORTHY VICTORIES

Victories that are cheap are cheap. Those only are worth having which come as the result of hard fighting.
—Henry Ward Beecher

The greater the difficulty, the more glory in surmounting it.   —Epicurus

But the fruit that can fall without shaking indeed is too mellow for me.
—Lady Mary Wortley Montagu

The greater the obstacle, the more glory in overcoming it.   —Moliere

The harder the conflict, the more glorious the triumph. What we obtain too cheaply, we esteem too lightly; 'tis dearness only that gives everything its value.   —Thomas Paine

The fiery trials through which we pass will light us down in honor or dishonor to the last generation.
—Abraham Lincoln

To conquer without risk is to triumph without glory.   —Pierre Corneille

There could be no honor in a sure success, but much might be wrested from a sure defeat.   —T.E. Lawrence
(Lawrence of Arabia)

TO REALLY APPRECIATE GOOD THINGS, WE MUST KNOW THE NOT-SO-GOOD THINGS

In order to have great happiness, you have to have great pain and unhappiness—otherwise how would you know when you're happy?
—Leslie Caron

To really enjoy the better things in life, one must first have experienced the things they are better than.
—Oscar Homoka

There is no victory without pain.
—Lolita Lebron

Those who don't know how to weep with their whole heart don't know how to laugh either.   —Golda Meir

Excellence costs a great deal.
—May Sarton

If you want a place in the sun, you've got to put up with a few blisters.
—Abigail Van Buren

Misfortunes tell us what fortune is.
—Thomas Fuller

A man is insensible to the relish of prosperity till he has tasted adversity.
—Sa'di

Who has never tasted what is bitter does not know what is sweet.
—German proverb

Victory is sweetest when you've known defeat.   —Malcolm Forbes

No man better knows what good is than he who has endured evil.
—Anon.

He that has never suffered extreme adversity knows not the full extent of his own depravation.
—Charles Caleb Colton

Sleep, riches and health, to be truly enjoyed, must be interrupted.
—Jean Paul Fichter

You can't be brave if you've only had wonderful things happen to you.
—Mary Tyler Moore

If there were no tribulation, there would be no rest; if there were no winter, there would be no summer.
—Saint John Chrysostom

If you want the rainbow, you gotta put up with the rain. —Dolly Parton

If you want to see the sun shine, you have to weather the storm.
—Frank Lane

He that can't endure the bad will not live to see the good.
—Yiddish proverb

I have lived long enough to be battered by the realities of life, and not too long to be downed by them.
—John Mason Brown

EVERY SITUATION HAS POSITIVE ASPECTS; WE MUST FIND AND FOCUS ON THEM

If you will call your troubles experiences, and remember that every experience develops some latent force within you, you will grow vigorous and happy, however adverse your circumstances may seem to be.
—John Heywoodr

If your house is on fire, warm yourself by it. —Spanish proverb

A broken heart is what makes life so wonderful five years later, when you see the guy in an elevator and he is fat and smoking a cigar and saying "long-time-no-see." If he hadn't broken your heart, you couldn't have that glorious feeling of relief!
—Phyllis Battelle

Anything other than death is a minor injury. —Bill Muncey

The most valuable gift I ever received was the gift of insecurity my father left us. My mother's love might not have prepared me for life the way my father's departure did. He forced us out on the road, where we had to earn our bread. —Lillian Gish

Being disabled gave me an immense advantage. People are kinder to you. It puts you on a different level than if you go into a situation whole and secure. —Dorothea Lange

When written in Chinese, the word "crisis" is composed of two characters. One represents danger, and the other represents opportunity.
—John F. Kennedy

From a fallen tree, make kindling.
—Spanish proverb

Our real blessings often appear to us in the shape of pains, losses and disappointments; but let us have patience, and we soon shall see them in their proper figures.
—Joseph Addison

688

To every disadvantage there is a corresponding advantage.
—W. Clement Stone

The same wind that extinguishes a light can set a brazier on fire.
—Pierre de Beaumarchais

Other Definitions of Adversity
Adversity is the touchstone of virtue.
—Anon.

Adversity is the first path to truth.
—Lord Byron

GENERAL QUOTATIONS ABOUT ADVERSITY

Glee! The great storm is over!
—Emily Dickinson

Diseases can be our spiritual flat tires—disruptions in our lives that seem to be disasters at the time, but end by redirecting our lives in a meaningful way.
—Bernie S. Siegel, M.D.

To say that my grief will be eternal would be ridiculous—nothing is eternal.
—Marie Bashkirtseff

What the student calls a tragedy, the master calls a butterfly.
—Richard Bach

Our way is not soft grass, it's a mountain path with lots of rocks. But it goes upwards, forward, toward the sun.
—Dr. Ruth Westheimer

Until you've lost your reputation, you never realize what a burden it was or what freedom really is.
—Margaret Mitchell

Failure is, in a sense, the highway to success, inasmuch as every discovery of what is false leads us to seek earnestly after what is true, and very fresh experience points out some form of error which we shall afterward carefully avoid.
—John Keats

Although the world is full of suffering, it is also full of the overcoming of it.
—Helen Keller

There is in the worst of fortune the best of chances for a happy change.
—Euripides

Let us not be needlessly bitter: certain failures are sometimes fruitful.
—E.M. Cioran

It is only after an unknown number of unrecorded labors, after a host of noble hearts have succumbed in discouragement, convinced that their cause is lost; it is only then that cause triumphs.
—Madame Guizot

When you can't remember why you're hurt, that's when you're healed. When you have to work real hard to re-create the pain, and you can't quite get there, that's when you're better.
—Jane Fonda

Sweet are the uses of adversity.
—William Shakespeare

However confused the scene of our life appears, however torn we may be who now do face that scene, it can be faced, and we can go on to be whole.
—Muriel Rukeyser

In adversity, remember to keep an even mind.
—Horace

Strength does not come from winning. Your struggles develop your strengths. When you go through hardships and decide not to surrender, that is strength.
   —Arnold Schwarzenegger

The ultimate measure of a man is not where he stands in moments of comfort and convenience, but where he stands at times of challenge and controversy.
   —Martin Luther King, Jr.

Do not free a camel of the burden of his hump; you may be freeing him from being a camel.
   —G.K. Chesterton

I walk firmer and more secure up hill than down.   —Michel de Montaigne

Adversity is like the period of the rain . . . cold, comfortless, unfriendly to man and to animal; yet from that season have their birth the flower, the fruit, the date, the rose and the pomegranate.   —Sir Walter Scott

If we survive danger, it steels our courage more than anything else.
   —Reinhold Niebuhr

The virtue of adversity is fortitude, which in mortals is the heroical virtue.   —Francis Bacon

To turn an obstacle to one's advantage is a great step towards victory.
   —French proverb

Great occasions do not make heroes or cowards; they simply unveil them to the eyes of men . . . crisis shows us what we have become.
   —Bishop Westcott

Strong men greet war, tempest, hard times. They wish, as Pindar said, to tread the floors of hell, with necessities as hard as iron.
   —Ralph Waldo Emerson

Reacting to Events

How We React to Events Is Very Important

All that is necessary is to accept the unacceptable, do without the indispensable, and bear the unbearable.
—Kathleen Norris

We don't strain at a gnat and swallow a camel, nor swim in an ocean and drown in a puddle.
—Taylor Caldwell

The great difference between one person and another is how he takes hold and uses his first chance, and how he takes his fall if it scored against him
—Thomas Hughes

You don't get ulcers from what you eat. You get them from what's eating you.
—Vicki Baum

There is no sin nor wrong that gives a man such a foretaste of hell in this life as anger and impatience.
—Saint Catherine of Siena

Wise men ne'er sit and wail their loss, but cheerily seek how to redress their harms.
—William Shakespeare

The prizes go to those who meet emergencies successfully. And the way to meet emergencies is to do each daily task the best we can.
—William Feather

Mishaps are like knives that either serve us or cut us as we grasp them by the blade or the handle.
—James Russell Lowell

Fortune does not change men; it unmasks them.
—Madame Necker

I love the man that can smile in trouble, that can gather strength from distress, and grow brave by reflection.
—Thomas Paine

Trouble has no necessary connection with discouragement; discouragement has a germ of its own, as different from trouble as arthritis is different from a stiff joint.
—F. Scott Fitzgerald

Life is a grindstone, and whether it grinds a man down or polishes him up depends on the stuff he's made of.
—Josh Billings

When we accept tough jobs as a challenge and wade into them with joy and enthusiasm, miracles can happen.
—Arland Gilbert

He who, having lost one ideal, refuses to give his heart and soul to another and nobler, is like a man who declines to build a house on rock because the wind and rain ruined his house on the sand.
—Constance Naden

Whenever you fall, pick something up.
—Oswald Avery

I have seen boys on my baseball team go into slumps and never come out of them, and I have seen others snap right out and come back better than ever. I guess more players lick themselves than are ever licked by an opposing team. The first thing any man has to know is how to handle himself.
—Connie Mack

Consider how much more you often suffer from your anger and grief than from those very things for which you are angry and grieved.
—Marcus Aurelius

We must never despair; our situation has been compromising before, and it has changed for the better; so I trust it will again. If difficulties arise, we must put forth new exertion and proportion our efforts to the exigencies of the times. —George Washington

What counts in making a happy marriage is not so much how compatible you are, but how you deal with incompatibility. —George Levinger

Noble souls, through dust and heat, rise from disaster and defeat the stronger.
—Henry Wadsworth Longfellow

Let no feeling of discouragement prey upon you, and in the end you are sure to succeed. —Abraham Lincoln

I'm not happy, I'm cheerful. There's a difference. A happy woman has no cares at all. A cheerful woman has cares but has learned how to deal with them. —Beverly Sills

Our mistakes won't irreparably damage our lives unless we let them.
—James E. Sweaney

Oh, a trouble's a ton, or a trouble's
    an ounce,
Or a trouble is what you make it,
And it isn't the fact that you're hurt
    that counts,
But only how you take it.
—Edmund Vance Cooke

When the rock is hard, we get harder than the rock. When the job is tough, we get tougher than the job.
—George Cullum, Sr.

To be happy, drop the words "if only" and substitute instead the words "next time."
—Smiley Blanton, M.D.

Always take an emergency leisurely.
—Chinese proverb

Keep strong if possible; in any case, keep cool. —Sir Basil Liddell Hart

Happiness is not the absence of conflict, but the ability to cope with it.
—Anon.

When something bad happens to me, I think I'm able to deal with it in a pretty good way. That makes me lucky. Some people fall apart at the first little thing that happens.
—Christie Brinkley

Concern should drive us into action, not into a depression.
—Karen Horney

A man has no more character than he can command in a time of crisis.
—Ralph W. Sockman

Results? Why, man, I have gotten a lot of results. I know several thousand things that won't work.
—Thomas A. Edison

The tragedy is not that things are broken. The tragedy is that they are not mended again.   —Anon.

Don't curse the darkness—light a candle.   —Chinese proverb

Any man can shoot a gun, and with practice he can draw fast and shoot accurately, but that makes no difference. What counts is how you stand up when somebody is shooting back at you.   —Louis L'Amour

We are troubled on every side, yet not distressed; we are perplexed, but not in despair.   —2 Corinthians 4:8

Anyone can hold the helm when the sea is calm.   —Publilius Syrus

An error is simply a failure to adjust immediately from a preconception to an actuality.   —John Cage

What the caterpillar calls a tragedy, the Master calls a butterfly.
—Richard Bach

You are beaten to earth? Well, well, what's that?
Come up with a smiling face,
It's nothing against you to fall down flat
But to lie there—that's a disgrace.
—Edmund Vance Cooke

The longer we dwell on our misfortunes, the greater is their power to harm us.   —Voltaire

When the going gets tough, the tough get going.   —Frank Leahy

The difficulties of life are intended to make us better, not bitter.   —Anon.

Acceptance of what has happened is the first step to overcoming the consequences of any misfortune.
—William James

We can either change the complexities of life . . . or develop ways that enable us to cope more effectively.
—Herbert Benson

It is arrogance to expect that life will always be music. . . . Harmony, like a following breeze at sea, is the exception. In a world where most things wind up broken or lost, our lot is to tack and tune.   —Harvey Oxenhorn

The winds and waves are always on the side of the ablest navigators.
—Edward Gibbon

REACTING TO DIFFICULT SITUATIONS

No matter what has happened, always behave as if nothing had happened.
—Arnold Bennett

Tears mess up your makeup.
—Julia Child

When things go wrong, don't go with them.
—Anon.

Nothing is so bad that you have to sit down and go crazy.
—John Telgen

When you make a world tolerable for yourself, you make a world tolerable for others.
—Anaïs Nin

In adversity, remember to keep an even mind.
—Horace

Do not lose your inward peace for anything whatsoever, even if your whole world seems upset.
—Saint Francis de Sales

OUR PERCEPTIONS AND THOUGHTS ABOUT WHAT HAPPENS ARE WHAT COUNT

All that is really necessary for survival of the fittest, it seems, is an interest in life, good, bad, or peculiar.
—Grace Paley

We are not troubled by things, but by the opinion which we have of things.
—Epictetus

Things are in their essence what we choose to make them. A thing is, according to the mode in which one looks at it.
—Oscar Wilde

We are never so happy or so unhappy as we think.
—Francois de La Rochefoucauld

We exaggerate misfortune and happiness alike. We are never either so wretched or so happy as we say we are.
—Honore de Balzac

The most unhappy of all men is he who believes himself to be so.
—David Hume

Happiness does not depend on outward things, but on the way we see them.
—Leo Tolstoy

The mind is its own place, and in itself can make a heaven of hell, a hell of heaven.
—John Milton

Almost all our misfortunes in life come from the wrong notions we have about the things that happen to us.
—Stendhal

Riches, like glory or health, have no more beauty or pleasure than their possessor is pleased to lend them.
—Michel de Montaigne

Losses are comparative, imagination only makes them of any moment.
—Blaise Pascal

Man is only miserable so far as he thinks himself so.
—Jacopo Sannazaro

The art of life consists in taking each event which befalls us with a contented mind, confident of good. . . . With this method . . . rejoice always, though in the midst of sorrows, and possess all things, though destitute of everything. —James Freeman Clarke

So long as one does not despair, so long as one doesn't look upon life bitterly, things work out fairly well in the end. —George Moore

The meaning of things lies not in the things themselves, but in our attitude towards them.
—Antoine de Saint-Exupery

Pain is inevitable. Suffering is optional.
—Anon.

If you are distressed by anything external, the pain is not due to the thing itself but to your own estimate of it; and this you have the power to revoke at any moment.
—Marcus Aurelius

Little things affect little minds.
—Benjamin Disraeli

Do not weep; do not wax indignant. Understand. —Baruch Spinoza

No emotional crisis is wholly the product of outward circumstances. These may precipitate it. But what turns an objective situation into a subjectively critical one is the interpretation the individual puts upon it—the meaning it has in his emotional economy; the way it affects his self-image. —Bonaro Overstreet

There is nothing either good or bad, but thinking makes it so.
—William Shakespeare

Men are not influenced by things, but by their thoughts about things.
—Epictetus

Nothing is miserable unless you think it so. —Boethius

I can complain because rose bushes have thorns, or rejoice because thorn bushes have roses. It's all how you look at it. —J. Kenfield Morley

MAKE THE BEST OF WHATEVER HAPPENS

I make the most of all that comes and the least of all that goes.
—Sara Teasdale

A great wind is blowing, and that gives you either imagination or a headache. —Catherine the Great

Though his beginnings be but poor and low,
Thank God a man can grow!
—Florence Earle Coates

It seems that we learn lessons when we least expect them but always when we need them the most, and, the true "gift" in these lessons always lies in the learning process itself.
—Cathy Lee Crosby

Boys, this is only a game. But it's like life in that you will be dealt some bad hands. Take each hand, good or bad, and don't whine and complain, but play it out. If you're men enough to do that, God will help you and you will come out well.
—Ida Eisenhower

Sometimes only a change of viewpoint is needed to convert a tiresome duty into an interesting opportunity.
—Alberta Flanders

Nothing in life is so hard that you can't make it easier by the way you take it. —Ellen Glasgow

We must make the best of those ills which cannot be avoided.
—Alexander Hamilton

If you have to be in a soap opera, try not to get the worst role.
—Boy George

Never regret. If it's good, it's wonderful. If it's bad, it's experience.
—Victoria Holt

I think we should look forward to death more than we do. Of course everybody hates to go to bed or miss anything but dying is really the only chance we'll get to rest.
—Florynce Kennedy

What you can't get out of, get into wholeheartedly.
—Mignon McLaughlin

True contentment is the power of getting of any situation all that there is in it.
—G.K. Chesterton

On the occasion of every accident that befalls you . . . inquire what power you have for turning it to use.
—Epictetus

All that is necessary is to accept the impossible, do without the indispensable, and bear the intolerable.
—Kathleen Norris

When all that hate energy was focused on me, it was transformed into a fantastic energy. It was supporting me. If you are centered and you can transform all this energy that comes in, it will help you. If you believe it is going to kill you, it will kill you.
—Yoko Ono

If you are being run out of town, get in front of the crowd and make it look like a parade.
—Sally Stanford

Things turn out best for people who make the best of the way things turn out.
—Anon.

Experience is not what happens to you; it is what you do with what happens to you.
—Aldous Huxley

Whatever evil befalls us, we ought to ask ourselves . . . how we can turn it into good. So shall we take occasion, from one bitter root, to raise perhaps many flowers.
—Leigh Hunt

There are no accidents so unlucky from which clever people are not able to reap some advantage, and none so lucky that the foolish are not able to turn them to their own disadvantage.
—Francois de La Rochefoucauld

A wise man turns chance into good fortune.
—Thomas Fuller

Losses are comparative, only imagination makes them of any moment.
—Blaise Pascal

Your living is determined not so much by what life brings to you as by the attitude you bring to life; not so much by what happens to you as by the way your mind looks at what happens.
—John Homer Miller

Riches, like glory or health, have no more beauty or pleasure than their possessor is pleased to lend them.
—Michel de Montaigne

When fate hands you a lemon, make lemonade.
—Dale Carnegie

Trouble is the thing that strong men grow by. Met in the right way, it is a sure-fire means of putting iron into the victim's will and making him a tougher man to down forever after.
—H. Bertram Lewis

To a brave man, good and bad luck are like his right and left hand. He uses both. —Saint Catherine of Siena

There are two ways of meeting difficulties. You alter the difficulties or you alter yourself to meet them.
—Phyllis Bottome

Turn your stumbling blocks into stepping stones. —Anon.

One cannot get through life without pain. . . . What we can do is choose how to use the pain life presents to us.
—Bernie S. Siegel, M.D.

Never despair, but if you do, work on in despair. —Edmund Burke

Groan and forget it. —Jessamyn West

Let us not be needlessly bitter: certain failures are sometimes fruitful.
—E.M. Cioran

The most important thing in life is not to capitalize on your gains. Any fool can do that. The really important thing is to profit from your losses. —William Bolitho

Disease can be seen as a call for personal transformation through metamorphosis. It is a transition from the death of your old self into the birth of your new. —Tom O'Connor, person with ARC

Find the grain of truth in criticism—chew it and swallow it. —Don Sutton

LIFE IS LIKE A GAME OF CARDS

You gotta play the hand that's dealt you. There may be pain in that hand, but you play it. —James Brady

Boys, this is only game. But it's like life in that you will be dealt some bad hands. Take each hand, good or bad, and don't whine and complain, but play it out. If you're men enough to do that, God will help and you will come out well.
—Dwight D. Eisenhower's mother

Life is like a game of cards. The hand that is dealt you represents determination; the way you play it is free will.
—Jawaharlal Nehru

Life consists not in holding good cards, but in playing those you do hold well. —Josh Billings

The game of life is not so much in holding a good hand as playing a poor hand well. —H.T. Leslie

All I can do is play the game the way the cards fall. —James A. Michener

True luck consists not in holding the best cards at the table; luckiest he who knows just when to rise and go home. —John Hay

COURAGE IS CRITICAL

The greatest test of courage on earth is to bear defeat without losing heart.
—Robert G. Ingersoll

Courage is to take hard knocks like a man when occasion calls.   —Plautus

This is courage . . . to bear unflinchingly what heaven sends. —Euripides

To accept whatever comes, regardless of the consequences, is to be unafraid.   —John Cage

Let us be brave in the face of adversity.
          —Marcus Annaeus Seneca

Courage, in the final analysis, is nothing but an affirmative answer to the shocks of existence.
                    —Dr. Kurt Goldstein

Courage is a perfect sensibility of the measure of danger, and a mental willingness to endure it.
          —General William T. Sherman

To have courage for whatever comes in life—everything lies in that.
                    —Teresa of Avila

Humor Helps

Humor is an antidote to isolation.
                    —Elizabeth Janeway

Learn to laugh at your troubles and you'll never run out of things to laugh at.   —Lyn Karol

Warning: Humor may be hazardous to your illness.   —Ellie Katz

There is no defense against adverse fortune which is so effectual as an habitual sense of humor.
                    —Thomas W. Higginson

When we begin to take our failures non-seriously, it means we are ceasing to be afraid of them. It is of immense importance to learn to laugh at ourselves.   —Katherine Mansfield

Humor prevents one from becoming a tragic figure even though he/she is involved in tragic events.
                    —E.T. "Cy" Eberhart

I think laughter may be a form of courage. . . . As humans we sometimes stand tall and look into the sun and laugh, and I think we are never more brave than when we do that.
                    —Linda Ellerbee

Keep your sense of humor. There's enough stress in the rest of your life to let bad shots ruin a game you're supposed to enjoy.   —Amy Alcott

Delicate humor is the crowning virtue of the saints.   —Evelyn Underhill

Humor is my sword and my shield. It protects me. You can open a door with humor and drive a truck right through.   —Alan Simpson

Laughter can be more satisfying than honor; more precious than money; more heart-cleansing than prayer.
                    —Harriet Rochlin

Laughter is ever young, whereas tragedy, except the very highest of all, quickly becomes haggard.
                    —Margaret Sackville

A chuckle a day may not keep the doctor away, but it sure does make those times in life's waiting room a little more bearable.
                    —Anne Wilson Schaef

Humor brings insight and tolerance.
—Agnes Repplier

A sense of humor can help you overlook the unattractive, tolerate the unpleasant, cope with the unexpected, and smile through the unbearable.
—Moshe Waldoks

One loses many laughs by not laughing at oneself.
—Sara Jeannette Duncan

To jealousy, nothing is more frightful than laughter.   —Françoise Sagan

Humor is an affirmation of dignity, a declaration of man's superiority to all that befalls him.   —Roman Gary

Humor is the instinct for taking pain playfully.   —Max Eastman

Laugh and the world laughs with
     you;
Weep and you weep alone;
For the sad old earth must borrow its
     mirth,
But has trouble enough of its own.
—Ella Wheeler Wilcox

Wrinkles should only indicate where smiles have been.   —Ethel Barrymore

Humor is a means of obtaining pleasure in spite of the distressing effects that interface with it.
—Sigmund Freud

If you're going to be able to look back on something and laugh about it, you might as well laugh about it now.
—Marie Osmond

Humor is just another defense against the universe.   —Mel Brooks

Humor is the healthy way of feeling "distance" between one's self and the problem, a way of standing off and looking at one's problems with perspective.   —Rollo May

A person without a sense of humor is like a wagon without springs, jolted by every pebble in the road.
—Henry Ward Beecher

Total absence of humor renders life impossible.   —Colette

If I had no sense of humor, I should long ago have committed suicide.
—Mahatma Gandhi

A sense of humor judges one's actions and the actions of others from a wider reference . . . it pardons shortcomings; it consoles failure. It recommends moderation.
—Thornton Wilder

Were it not for my little jokes, I could not bear the burdens of this office.
—Abraham Lincoln

Any man who has had the job I've had and didn't have a sense of humor wouldn't still be here.
—Harry S. Truman

Humor is an attitude. It's a way of looking at life and of telling others how you feel about what's happening around you.   —Gene Perret

Optimism and humor are the grease and glue of life. Without both of them we would never have survived our captivity.   —Philip Butler,
Vietnam POW

Comedy is tragedy plus time.
—Carol Burnett

GENERAL QUOTATIONS ABOUT REACTING TO EVENTS

Good people are good because
they've come to wisdom through
failure.   —William Saroyan

Everyday . . . life confronts us with
new problems to be solved which
force us to adjust our old programs
accordingly.   —Dr. Ann Faraday

What can any of us do with his talent
but try to develop his vision, so that
through frequent failures we may
learn better what we have missed in
the past. —William Carlos Williams

There are more serious problems in
life than financial ones, and I've had
a lot of those. I've been broke before,
and will be again. Heartbroke? That's
serious. Lose a few bucks? That's not.
—Willie Nelson

A life of reaction is a life of slavery,
intellectually and spiritually. One
must fight for a life of action, not
reaction.   —Rita Mae Brown

Self-Pity

It's Human to Be Tempted by Self-Pity

Self-pity comes so naturally to all of us. —André Maurois

Every man supposes himself not to be fully understood or appreciated. —Ralph Waldo Emerson

Some Disastrous Effects of Self-Pity

Self-pity is our worst enemy and if we yield to it, we can never do anything wise in this world. —Helen Keller

What poison is to food, self-pity is to life. —Oliver C. Wilson

It's odd that you can get so anesthetized by your own pain or your own problem that you don't quite fully share the hell of someone close to you. —Lady Bird Johnson

Grumbling is the death of love. —Marlene Dietrich

Being sorry for myself is a luxury I can't afford. —Stephen King and Peter Straub

To feel sorry for oneself is one of the most disintegrating things the individual can do to himself. —Winifred Rhoades

Self-pity is one of the most dangerous forms of self-centeredness. It fogs our vision. —Anon.

Self-pity is one of the most unhappy and consuming defects that we know. It is a bar to all spiritual progress and can cut off all effective communication with our fellows because of its inordinate demands for attention and sympathy. It is a maudlin form of martyrdom, which we can ill afford. —As Bill Sees It

To hear complaints is wearisome to the wretched and the happy alike. —Samuel Johnson

We Must Banish Self-Pity

Sympathy is never wasted except when you give it to yourself.
—John W. Raper

The opposite of having faith is having self-pity.
—Og Guinness

Optimism and self-pity are the positive and negative poles of modern cowardice.
—Cyril Connolly

He who complains, sins.
—Saint Francis de Sales

This life is not for complaint, but for satisfaction.
—Henry David Thoreau

How to Get Past Self-Pity

Is life so wretched? Isn't it rather your hands which are too small, your vision which is muddled? You are the one who must grow up.
—Dag Hammarskjold

There is only one way to end a self-pity cycle: stop comparing yourself to others, and simply follow Christ.
—Linda Harry

Suffering isn't ennobling, recovery is.
—Christian N. Barnard

You can overcome anything if you don't bellyache.
—Bernard M. Baruch

There is only one way to end a self-pity cycle: stop comparing yourself to others, and simply follow Christ.
—Linda Harry

Do not weep; do not wax indignant. Understand.
—Baruch Spinoza

When any fit of gloominess, or perversion of mind, lays hold upon you, make it a rule not to publish it by complaints.
—Samuel Johnson

Taking Action Is a Great Way to Overcome Self-Pity

The secret of being miserable is to have leisure to bother about whether you are happy or not. The cure for it is occupation.
—George Bernard Shaw

The cure for grief is motion.
—Elbert Hubbard

I got the blues thinking of the future, so I left off and made some marmalade. It's amazing how it cheers one up to shred oranges or scrub the floor.
—D.H. Lawrence

When you find yourself overpowered, as it were, by melancholy, the best way is to go out and do something.
—John Keble

The best mask for demoralization is daring.
—Lucan

We Choose to Indulge in Self-Pity

Self-pity is a death that has no resurrection, a sinkhole from which no rescuing hand can drag you because you have chosen to sink.
—Elizabeth Elliot

Pain is inevitable. Suffering is optional.
—Anon.

I am convinced, the longer I live, that life and its blessings are not so entirely unjustly distributed as when we are suffering greatly we are inclined to suppose.   —Mary Todd Lincoln

Despair is the absolute extreme of self-love. It is reached when a man deliberately turns his back on all help from anyone else in order to taste the rotten luxury of knowing himself to be lost.   —Thomas Merton

GENERAL QUOTATIONS ABOUT SELF-PITY

Our family never had any hard luck, because nothing seemed hard luck to it, nor was it ever disgraced for there was nothing which it would acknowledge as disgrace.   —Boxcar Bertha

Sometimes I go about pitying myself, and all the time I am being carried on great winds across the sky.
—Ojibway dream song

Others may argue about whether the world ends with a bang or a whimper. I just want to make sure mine doesn't end with a whine.
—Barbara Gordon

I never saw a wild thing sorry for
    itself.
A small bird will drop frozen dead
    from a bough
Without ever having felt sorry for
    itself.   —D.H. Lawrence

Old age is no place for sissies.
—Bette Davis

Every message of despair is the statement of a situation from which everybody must freely try to find a way out.
—Eugene Ionesco

Pain is inevitable, suffering is optional.
—M. Kathleen Casey

Opposition may become sweet to a man when he has christened it persecution.   —George Eliot

A man's as miserable as he thinks he is.
—Marcus Annaeus Seneca

Your distress about life might mean you have been living for the wrong reason, not that you have no reason for living.   —Tom O'Connor,
person with ARC

Children seldom have a proper sense of their own tragedy, discounting and keeping hidden the true horrors of their short lives, humbly imagining real calamity to be some prestigious drama of the grown-up world.
—Shirley Hazzard

It's not the load that breaks you down, it's the way you carry it.
—Lena Horne

I'm not overweight, I'm just nine inches too short.   —Shelley Winters

Sadness is almost never anything but a form of fatigue.   —André Gide

The human mind can bear plenty of reality, but not too much unintermittent gloom.   —Margaret Drabble

Misery is a communicable disease.
—Martha Graham

If you believe, then you hang on.
If you believe, it means you've got
imagination, you don't need stuff
thrown out on a blueprint, and don't
face facts—what can stop you? If
I don't make it today, I'll come in
tomorrow.   —Ruth Gordon

He's simply got the instinct for being
unhappy highly developed.
                    —Saki (H.H. Munro)

Never give way to melancholy; resist
it steadily, for the habit will encroach.
                    —Sydney Smith

Despair is criminal.
                    —Samuel Johnson

Even the cry from the depths is an
affirmation: Why cry if there is no
hint or hope of hearing?
                    —Martin Marty

Index

1 John 5:14 196
1 Kings 14:6 431
1 Peter 5:7 198, 630
1 Samuel 20:3 271
1 Thessalonians 5:17 191
2 Chronicles 31:21 369, 565, 600
2 Chronicles 32:8 629
2 Corinthians 4:8 693
2 Corinthians 5:7 162
2 Corinthians 9:7 113
2 Corinthians 12:9 184
2 Corinthians 12:10 183
2 Timothy 4:7 168, 285, 575

A

Abbott, Berenice 391
Abbott, Shirley 32
Abd al-Rahman 33, 91
Abrams, General Creighton W. 361
Ace, Jane 631
Acheson, Dean 323
Ackerman, Diane 6, 251, 379
Acton, Lord 659
Acts 20:35 113
Adams, Abigail 552, 681, 682
Adams, Franklin P. 606
Adams, George Matthew 117, 141,
    274, 281, 284, 317, 347, 368, 460,
    489, 497, 564
Adams, Henry 144, 148
Adams, Jane 351, 602
Adams, John 651
Adams, John Quincy 531, 568
Adams, Mary 632
Adams, Maude 226, 469
Adams, Sheryl 365
Adams, Thomas 484, 514, 566
Adams, William 165
Addams, Jane 569
Addison, Joseph 12, 14, 39, 69, 73,
    124, 160, 172, 271, 536, 572, 641,
    688
Ade, George 665
Adenauer, Konrad 379
Adfani, Isabelle 551

Adler, Alfred 121, 623
Adler, Felix 359
Adler, Judi 631
Adler, Polly 519
Aeschylus 45, 46, 80, 190, 200, 261,
    335, 478, 490, 492, 547
Aesop 52, 84, 89, 104, 199, 525, 573,
    579, 632, 642, 645
African proverb 555
Agnes, Saint 159
Aguilar, Grace 103, 526
Aide, Charles Hamilton 195
Aimee, Anouk 652
Aird, Catherine 386, 388
Aitken, W.H. 194
Aitken, William Maxwell 562
Akins, Zoë 59
Al-Bistami, Bayazid 160
Alacoque, Saint Margaret Mary 158,
    160
Albright, Madeleine 427, 615
Alcmaeon 643
Alcoholics Anonymous 55, 61, 160
Alcott, Amy 107, 236, 698
Alcott, Louisa May 7, 9, 130, 234,
    240, 251, 264, 274, 341, 351, 466,
    469, 482, 545, 586, 597
Alden, Robert 686
Alderson, M.H. 572, 641
Aldrich, Thomas Bailey 668
Alexander, Jane 643
Alfieri, Conte Vittorio 530
Alfredsson, Helen 62
Alfred of Rievaulx, Saint 123, 148
Ali, Muhammad 667
Alighieri, Dante 2, 105, 293, 473, 599,
    637
Allen, Charles L. 176, 200, 375
Allen, Dick 267
Allen, Earl 119
Allen, Florence Ellinwood 20, 354
Allen, Fred 544
Allen, George Matthew 12
Allen, James Lane 261, 342, 346, 406,
    531, 568, 569, 613, 625

Allen, Woody 75, 92, 282, 547, 668
Alley, Kirstie 393
Alliluyeva, Svetlana 101, 409
Allingham, Margery 236, 351, 354, 367, 405
Allison, Mary Ann 26, 441
Almanac, Mary S. 233
Alt, Carol 95
Alther, Lisa 18, 137, 571
Altman, Robert 518
Ambrose, David V.A. 368, 564
Amiel, Henri Frederic 36, 47, 55, 170, 172, 229, 262, 268, 276, 286, 367, 415, 418, 419, 422, 451, 502, 529, 536, 637, 658
Amory, Cleveland 229, 451
Amos, Lisa M. 573, 647, 665
Amos, Wally "Famous" 246
Ancient Buddhist proverb 644
Ancis, Foe 90
Anderson, H. Van 412
Anderson, Laurie 41
Anderson, Lorraine 141
Anderson, Margaret 115, 225, 424, 680
Anderson, Marian 115, 183
Anderson, Sherwood 231, 240, 263, 304, 312, 488, 666
Anderson, Sparky 266, 621
Andrada, Fernandez de 24
Andrews, H.W. 408
Andrews, Julie 395, 572, 611
Andrews, Lynn V. 162
Andrus, Ethel Percy 26, 115, 116, 242
Andrus, Kathleen Tierney 257, 258, 586
Angela of Foligno, Saint 156, 162
Angelou, Maya 130, 521
Anne of England, Princess 92
Anon. 3, 11, 15, 21, 25, 26, 27, 28, 29, 32, 33, 35, 36, 37, 38, 40, 45, 48, 50, 55, 56, 61, 64, 65, 70, 71, 73, 75, 78, 79, 83, 84, 85, 86, 89, 90, 104, 107, 112, 118, 120, 123, 124, 125, 130, 131, 132, 134, 136, 137, 140, 143, 145, 146, 147, 149, 150, 151, 152, 155, 158, 161, 165, 166, 167, 169, 171, 173, 174, 178, 179, 180, 181, 182, 184, 185, 186, 187, 188, 189, 192, 194, 196, 197, 198, 199, 200, 202, 203, 204, 208, 209, 211, 212, 213, 224, 229, 231, 235, 249, 251, 257, 259, 260, 263, 264, 266, 271, 274, 277, 279, 280, 282, 285, 287, 288, 289, 293, 295, 297, 299, 300, 301, 302, 303, 306, 307, 308, 313, 315, 317, 319, 320, 322, 326, 330, 331, 332, 333, 336, 347, 348, 354, 358, 360, 362, 363, 371, 372, 374, 376, 378, 379, 383, 386, 393, 396, 408, 413, 414, 423, 425, 429, 438, 439, 450, 451, 453, 454, 455, 460, 461, 479, 485, 486, 488, 491, 492, 494, 495, 496, 497, 499, 503, 508, 512, 513, 514, 515, 518, 522, 524, 525, 526, 527, 528, 530, 532, 533, 535, 536, 539, 544, 547, 548, 550, 551, 554, 556, 557, 560, 566, 567, 568, 573, 574, 578, 579, 580, 585, 589, 590, 594, 599, 600, 603, 609, 613, 615, 624, 625, 628, 629, 632, 634, 635, 638, 640, 642, 643, 644, 645, 646, 647, 648, 657, 663, 667, 668, 669, 672, 674, 675, 677, 678, 681, 683, 684, 685, 686, 687, 689, 692, 693, 694, 695, 696, 697, 701, 703
Anouilh, Jean 228, 233, 477, 487, 498, 523, 530, 538, 602
Anspacher, Louis 303
Anthony, Dr. Robert 62, 480, 483
Anthony, Susan B. 24, 222, 242, 251, 341, 362
Anthony of Padua, Saint 179
Antisthenes 135
Antrim, Minna 109, 278, 674, 684
Anzaldua, Gloria Evangelina 250
Aoki, Rocky 589
Apocrypha 144, 149, 290
Apostolius, Michael 87
Appalachian folk song 431
Applebroog, Ida 110
Appleton, George 209
Appleton, Sir Edward 369, 565
Appollonius of Tyana 198
Aquinas, Saint Thomas 123, 162, 170,

171, 478
Aquino, Corazan 461
Arab proverb 80, 147, 200, 210, 261,
  556, 591, 593
Aragon, Vicky 568
Arbus, Diane 498, 516
Archer, Anne 619
Arden, Elizabeth 26, 243
Arendt, Hannah 7, 59, 64, 447, 490,
  491, 526, 585
Aretino, Pietro 143, 235, 649, 679
Aristotle 5, 9, 10, 21, 34, 47, 54, 122,
  124, 131, 133, 146, 148, 149, 154,
  235, 239, 258, 286, 361, 374, 431,
  491, 549, 591
Armstrong, John 373, 374
Arnauld, Angelique 622
Arnold, Matthew 20, 71, 214, 227,
  292, 431, 557, 585
Arnold, Stanley 656
Arnold, Thomas 370
Arnow, Harriette 168
Arrington, Eva 350
Arroyo, Martina 587
As Bill Sees It 56, 208, 216, 307, 701
Asch, Sholem 60, 295
Ascher, Barbara Lazear 424
Ash, Mary Kay 109, 110, 341, 442,
  445, 470, 543, 667, 672
Ashanti proverb 605
Ashe, Arthur 383
Ashley, Elizabeth 102
Ashley, Laura 236
Ashton-Warner, Sylvia 108, 413, 518
Asimov, Isaac 604, 656
Asquith, Margot 46, 447, 541, 682
Assaglioli, Robert 61
Astaire, Fred 443, 462
Astley, Jacob 180
Astor, Brooke 117
Astor, Lady 398
Astor, Mary 543, 577
Astor, Nancy 89, 244, 354, 476, 493
Atherton, Gertrude 234, 582
Atkinson, Brooks 400, 449, 511
Atkinson, Ti-Grace 526
Attlee, Clement R. 34
Atwood, Margaret 7, 41, 111, 244,

356, 379, 482, 538
Auchincloss, Louis 370
Auden, W.H. 37, 167, 255, 406, 547,
  606
Audiberti, Jacques 256, 595
Auerbach, Berthold 225
Auerbach, Red 469
Aughey 69
Augustine, Jerry 348
Augustine, Saint 2, 14, 64, 111, 129,
  162, 164, 165, 198, 255, 264, 281,
  287, 326, 353, 444, 526, 619, 662
Augustus 645
Aurelius, Marcus 3, 13, 16, 23, 28, 47,
  52, 75, 85, 154, 252, 253, 256, 283,
  290, 305, 312, 314, 335, 394, 395,
  425, 449, 458, 469, 472, 473, 484,
  525, 540, 606, 626, 692, 695
Ausonius 88
Austen, Jane 24, 38, 42, 178, 238,
  308, 356, 408, 678
Austin, Dr. James H. 588
Auvil, Myrtle 7
Avery, Oswald 692
Axiom, Grandma 643

B

Bâ, Mariama 137
Babcock, Maltbie D. 67, 186, 282,
  318, 593, 615, 653
Babilonia, Tai 604
Babson, Roger 593
Bacall, Lauren 18, 84, 139, 244, 382,
  496, 506, 615
Bach, Jean 361
Bach, Richard 438, 576, 594, 612,
  671, 689, 693
Bachmann, Ingeborg 161
Bachrach, Burt 454
Bacon, Francis 30, 56, 125, 135, 138,
  151, 255, 259, 289, 290, 337, 391,
  394, 415, 477, 504, 565, 591, 592,
  595, 611, 647, 685, 686, 690
Bacon, Martha 228
Baeck, Leo 162
Baez, Joan 105, 150, 245, 364, 407,
  424, 556, 651
Bailey, Henry Christopher 165

Bailey, Pearl 17, 40, 86, 102, 163, 217, 221, 222, 227, 311, 392, 427, 616, 664
Bailey, Philip James 157, 210, 221
Baillie, James 458
Baillie, Joanna 18, 276, 311, 364, 366, 489, 613, 657
Baillie, John 170
Bain, Alexander 417
Baker, Anita 31, 139, 217
Baker, Dorothy 268, 637
Baker, Ella 41, 112, 245
Baker, Josephine 467
Baker, Russell 10
Balanchine, George 603
Baldwin, Christina 59, 60, 105, 162, 356, 404
Baldwin, Faith 146, 289, 395, 548
Baldwin, James 97
Baldwin, Monica 240, 313
Baldwin, Roger 255
Balfour, J. 365
Ball, George W. 291
Ball, Ivern 369
Ball, Lucille 16, 228, 341, 521, 587, 616
Ballantyne, Sheila 379, 466, 540, 543
Ballou, Hosea 10, 80, 172, 370
Balzac, Honore de 30, 68, 69, 98, 137, 153, 247, 347, 377, 387, 498, 529, 676, 694
Bambara, Toni Cade 88, 305, 356, 548
Bamber, Helen 219
Bancroft, Ann 111
Bankhead, Tallulah 88, 224, 293, 413, 417
Banning, Margaret Culkin 140, 409
Banville, Theodore de 12
Ban Breathnach, Sarah 342
Barber, Margaret Fairless 294
Barbey d'Aurevilly, Jules 331
Barclay, William 3, 33, 101, 165, 534
Barcus, Nancy 579
Bardot, Brigitte 91, 92, 242, 243, 251, 313
Barker, Raymond Charles 354
Barnard, Christian N. 702
Barnes, Sondra Anice 446

Barney, Natalie Clifford 93, 539, 678
Barnhouse, Dr. Ruth Tiffany 243
Barr, Amelia 17, 20, 23, 101, 110, 272, 311, 342, 364, 542, 585, 626
Barrett, Alfred 179
Barrett, Colleen C. 552
Barrett, Ethel 223
Barrett, Rona 120, 535
Barrie, Sir James M. 22, 104, 119, 183, 291, 531, 537
Barrow, Isaac 602
Barrows, Sydney Biddle 349
Barry, Lynda 626
Barrymore, Ethel 144, 183, 232, 470, 699
Barrymore, John 19, 308
Barrymore, Lionel 27
Bartek, E.J. 23, 459, 472
Barth, Karl 78
Barthel, Mildred 257
Barthelemy, Auguste 396
Bartholomew, Saint 208, 216, 363, 419
Bartlett, Allen E. 180
Bartol, C.A. 374
Barton, Bruce 245, 391, 448, 548
Barton, Clara 113, 234, 266, 424, 467, 485
Baruch, Bernard M. 50, 92, 224, 260, 285, 453, 456, 655, 656, 662, 663, 702
Baseball scout (quoted by Tom Wolfe) 266
Bashkirtseff, Marie 229, 468, 498, 689
Basil, Saint 69, 356, 657
Basilio, Carmen 444, 607
Basinger, Kim 417, 418
Basset, Lucinda 610
Bate, Julius 465
Bates, Elmer E. 69
Bateson, Gregory 362
Bateson, Mary 110, 111, 393, 492
Battelle, Phyllis 6, 688
Baudelaire, Charles 24, 54, 90, 182, 288, 331, 486, 546, 557, 634
Baudouin, Charles 358, 483, 506, 561
Baugh, Laura 95
Baum, Vicki 105, 494, 578, 581, 691
Bauman, Clarence 196

Baxter, J. Sidlow 180
Baxter, Richard 113
Beard, Charles A. 686
Beard, Mary Ritter 110
Beard, Miriam 113, 280
Beard, Rebecca 293
Beaton, Cecil 330
Beattie, Melody 41, 78, 277
Beaumarchais, Pierre de 6, 689
Beaumont, Francis 81
Beausacq, Maria de 516
Beauvoir, Simone de 44, 49, 103, 110, 112, 162, 252, 253, 304, 353, 398, 462, 525, 548, 580, 644
Beaver, Wilfred 673
Beck, Fred 183
Becker, Margaret 112
Becker, Verne 166
Beckett, Mary 324
Beckley, John L. 674
Beecher, Henry Ward 27, 42, 46, 59, 67, 78, 117, 118, 120, 169, 174, 176, 186, 197, 285, 304, 310, 325, 329, 365, 390, 433, 443, 470, 490, 491, 517, 596, 640, 651, 666, 669, 671, 687, 699
Beecher, John 600
Beeken, Gilbert M. 376
Beerbohm, Max 92, 113, 299, 611, 669
Beethoven, Ludwig van 622
Begbie, Janet 355
Begehot, Walter 606
Begley, Sharon 225
Behn, Aphra 392
Bejar, Heda 112
Belasco, David 268, 289
Belenky, Mary Field 105, 110, 563
Bell, Alexander Graham 292
Bell, James F. 353, 478, 489
Bellamy, Joe David 651
Belloc, Hilaire 124
Bellow, Saul 413
Belmont, Eleanor R. 49
Ben-Gurion, David 173, 300, 533
Benatar, Pat 616
Benavente, Jacinto 265
Bench inscription 333

Bendele, Lewis K. 318
Bender, Betty 513, 612
Bender, George H. 433
Bendry, Paula A. 3, 258
Benedict, Ruth 23, 145, 172, 312, 324, 325, 471
Benet, Stephen Vincent 311
Bengermino, Ted 285
Bengis, Ingrid 383
Benham, Sir William Gurney 175, 200
Benington, Lucy 592
Benn, Alonzo Newton 319, 531, 557, 568, 643
Bennett, Arnold 132, 247, 272, 277, 403, 495, 694
Bennett, James Gordon 571, 663
Bennett, William 19, 224
Benson, Arthur Christopher 30, 119, 143, 396, 408, 429, 477, 524, 608, 650
Benson, Herbert 693
Benson, Robert Hugh 353
Benson, Stella 32
Benton, William 538, 547
Berberova, Nina 52
Bercovitz, Zachary T. 348
Berdyaev, Nicholas 287, 482
Berenson, Bernard 275, 401
Beresford, Elizabeth 255
Bergen, Candice 95, 657
Berger, John 620
Berger, Sally 548
Berggrav, Eivind Josef 4
Bergman, Ingmar 420
Bergman, Ingrid 32, 228, 423, 563
Bergson, Henri 363, 392, 421
Berkus, Rusty 224
Berlin, Irving 47, 579
Bernanos, Georges 211, 376, 476, 552
Bernard, Dorothy 533
Bernard, Saint 260
Bernard of Clairvaux 199, 363
Bernhard, Thomas 490, 526, 658, 684
Bernhardt, Sarah 24
Bernikow, Louise 111, 150
Berra, Yogi 347, 544, 645, 647
Berridge, John 175
Berrigan, Daniel 378

Berry, David 653
Berry, John 18, 627
Besant, Annie 523
Bestavros, Adel 162
Bethune, Ada 18, 29
Bethune, Mary McLeod 24, 26, 163, 171, 219, 220, 224, 351, 461, 538, 638
Bettelheim, Bruno 416
Better, Cathy 255, 341
Betti, Ugo 227, 276, 304, 427, 431
Bevan, Aneurin 599
Bhagaved Gita 604
Bhutto, Benazir 571
Bibesco, Elizabeth Asquith 68, 74, 259, 405, 543
Bieber, Margarete 284
Bierce, Ambrose 377, 578
Bierig, Sandra 224
Bigelow, Hilde 385
Bilkey, Dr. James G. 69
Billings, Josh 10, 19, 65, 69, 76, 108, 167, 169, 217, 260, 355, 498, 499, 640, 667, 691, 697
Bill W. 189, 204, 409, 476, 671
Binchy, Maeve 98
Binstock, Louis 669
Bion 649
Biount, George W. 551
Bird, Caroline 214
Birrell, Augustine 150
Bishop, Jim 306
Bisset, Jacqueline 94, 215, 243, 616
Bisson, Alexandre Charles Auguste 299
Black, Barbara Aronstein 646
Black, Diana 240
Black, Hugh 18, 470
Black, Shirley Temple 93, 259, 383, 510, 587
Blacker, Valentine 261
Blackwell, Antoinette Brown 110, 219, 421, 462, 613
Blackwell, Elizabeth 222, 586, 617
Blackwell, Emily 420
Blaik, Red 586
Blair, Bonnie 92, 655
Blair, Bonnie 462, 614
Blair, Paxton 495
Blake, William 10, 43, 46, 65, 79, 101, 124, 252, 364, 379, 402, 555
Blanchard, John 201
Blandford, Linda 549
Blanton, Smiley 15, 58, 433, 499, 650, 692
Blessington, Lady Marguerite 9, 16, 23, 41, 83, 228, 409, 445, 488, 589
Bloch, Arther 673
Bloch, Ivan 414
Bloomer, Amelia Jenks 662
Bloomfield, Harold H. 119
Blough, Roger M. 411
Bloy, Leon 185
Blum, Arlene 452
Blum, Leon 527
Blum, Ralph 296
Blume, Judy 120
Bly, David 568, 612
Bly, Mary 275
Boardman, G.D. 637
Bodett, Tom 372
Bodhidharma 557
Boehm, Helen 309
Boetcker, William J.H. 116, 222, 242, 259, 356, 524, 549, 565, 573, 642, 658, 679
Boethe 312
Boethius 56, 57, 221, 695
Bogan, Louise 351
Bogomoletz, Alexander A. 440
Bohn, H.G. 65, 302, 388, 539, 554, 672
Boileau, Nicolas 84
Boiste 241
Bolen, Jean Shinoda 219, 563
Bolitho, William 697
Böll, Heinrich 546
Bolton, Sarah Knowles 282, 295, 304, 560, 586
Bombeck, Erma 98, 126, 220, 235, 526, 556, 597
Bonaparte, Napoleon 164, 230, 239, 254, 273, 288, 358, 361, 373, 397, 415, 441, 446, 451, 482, 513, 522, 536, 571, 573, 596, 598, 602, 610, 641, 647, 660
Bonar, Andrew 174

Bonaventura, Saint 285

Bond, Carrie Jacobs 106, 122

Bonhoeffer, Dietrich 182, 187, 194, 210, 276, 397, 413, 444, 556

Boniface VIII 117

Bonnano, Margaret 278

Bonnell, John Sutherland 9

Booher, Dianna 235

Book of Common Prayer 170

Book of Runes, The 297, 628

Boone, Daniel 361

Boorstin, Daniel 545

Boosler, Elayne 220

Booth, Evangeline Cory 274

Booth, William 199

Boothroyd, Betty 237

Borges, Jorge Luis 75

Borland, Hal 333, 392

Borsi, Giosue 551

Bosco, Antoinette 273

Boseley, Sarah 225

Boswell, James 129

Bottome, Phyllis 32, 47, 166, 335, 585, 592, 627, 667, 697

Boucicault, Dion 276

Boudling, Kenneth 581

Boulanger, Nadia 422, 589, 635

Bouleau-Despreaux, Nicolas 482

Bounds, E.M. 174, 175, 176, 178, 179, 181, 182, 184, 186, 187, 190, 193, 194, 196, 198, 201, 204, 205, 209, 210, 653

Bourge, Paul 29, 39, 348

Bourgeois, Louise 225

Bourke-White, Margaret 110, 485

Bourne, Randolph 125, 127, 141, 422, 516, 533

Bouton, E.S. 271

Bovee, Christian 41, 80, 245, 255, 324, 369, 386, 397, 487, 505, 506, 514, 565, 566, 605, 662, 672

Bowen, Catherine Drinker 141

Bowen, Elizabeth 76, 97, 152, 216, 286, 341, 358, 441, 448, 455, 481, 504, 555

Bower, B.M. 6

Bower, Sharon Anthony 239

Bowles, Chester 656

Bowles, Paul 507

Boxcar Bertha 703

Boyd, Malcolm 186, 212

Boy George 696

Boyle, Hal 292

Boyle, Kay 20, 222

Bradburn, Norman 35, 85

Bradbury, Ray 519, 603

Braddon, Mary Elizabeth 584

Braden, Vic 267, 382, 673

Bradford, Gamaliel 84, 638

Bradley, Amanda 5

Bradley, F.H. 34

Bradley, General Omar N. 160, 583

Bradley, Marion Zimmer 60, 373, 577, 686

Bradley, Preston 253, 354, 355, 395, 523, 665

Bradstreet, Anne 126, 165, 235, 305, 409, 685

Brady, James 697

Bragan, Bobby 411

Brahmananda, Swami 3

Braiker, Dr. Harriet 230, 452

Brainard, Mary Gardiner 156, 158, 629

Brande, Dorothea 351, 359, 379, 381, 403, 407, 539, 542

Brandeis, Louis 250

Branden, Nathaniel 232, 246

Brando, Marlon 225

Brannon, Joan L. 426

Brault, Robert 25, 104, 635

Braverman, Kate 114

Bray, Billy 182

Breathnach, Sarah Ban 342

Brecht, Bertolt 9, 18, 73, 86, 100, 227, 230, 390, 404, 425, 452, 662

Brenan, Gerald 363

Brent, Madeleine 62

Bresler, David E. 258, 593

Brice, Fanny 8, 430

Bridges, Madeline 357

Bridges, William 170

Bridget of Sweden, Saint 100, 189

Briffault, R. 23, 457, 472

Brilliant, Ashleigh 121, 211

Brinkley, Christie 590, 693

Brisbane, Arthur 134, 275
Briskin, Jacqueline 91, 92, 333, 439, 576
Bristow, Gwen 60
Brittain, Vera 141
Bro, Margueritte Harmon 666
Brodie, Gene 267
Brodie, John 312
Brontë, Anne 413
Brontë, Charlotte 28, 59, 63, 99, 148, 410, 455
Brontë, Emily 122, 241, 342, 383, 426, 557, 614
Brook, Peter 647
Brooke, Rupert 123
Brookner, Anita 40, 525, 588
Brooks, Gwendolyn 532
Brooks, Mel 699
Brooks, Phillips 23, 109, 197, 209, 210, 309, 434, 463, 471, 582
Brooks, Thomas B. 176, 185, 193
Brother Lawrence 178, 188, 189
Brothers, Dr. Joyce 8, 34, 41, 58, 59, 63, 109, 246, 407, 408, 419, 423, 449, 450, 486, 498, 515, 582, 588, 660, 668
Broumas, Olga 504
Broun, Heywood 646
Brown, Charles R. 431
Brown, David 175
Brown, Gene 327, 542
Brown, Helen Gurley 236, 348, 398, 462, 467, 481, 613
Brown, John Mason 302, 470, 688
Brown, Les 469
Brown, Rita Mae 134, 243, 255, 266, 285, 354, 466, 545, 616, 664, 700
Brown, Rosellen 586
Brown, Trisha 510
Brown, William D. 665
Browne, Harry 250
Browne, Merry 82, 125, 525
Browne, Sir Thomas 84, 114, 145, 252, 530
Browning, Elizabeth Barrett 203, 228, 243, 282, 306, 309, 569, 643, 679
Browning, Robert 5, 89, 225, 234, 310, 326, 327, 469

Brummett, Nancy Parker 156
Bruner, Jerome S. 420
Brunner, Emil 170, 375
Brussell, Eugene E. 537
Bryan, William Jennings 247, 259, 416, 460, 485, 566
Bryant, Paul William "Bear" 648
Bryant, William Cullen 393
Bryson, Lyman Lloyd 405
Buchanan, Edna 126, 137
Buchman, Frank N.D. 539
Buchrose, J.E. 7
Buchwald, Art 304
Buck, Pearl S. 37, 136, 260, 352, 363, 373, 408, 409, 445, 467, 471, 525, 527, 539, 541, 542, 553, 622, 666
Buckham, A.G. 329
Buckley, Henry H. 347, 672
Buckley, William F. 614
Buckner, Thomas A. 349, 368, 564
Buddha 62, 64, 306, 346, 369, 649
Buddhist proverb 263, 625
Budgell, Eustace 130
Buffon, Georges de 336
Bulgarian proverb 557
Bulwer-Lytton, Edward 50, 107, 172, 305, 365, 434, 453, 472
Bunch, Charlotte 221, 467
Bunche, Ralph J. 532, 656
Bunyan, John 186, 188, 192, 209, 210
Burbank, Luther 118, 280, 400
Burchill, Julie 403
Burckhardt, Jakob 323
Burdette, Robert Jones 297, 496
Burgess, Gelett 30, 142, 402
Burgh, James 663
Burke 387
Burke, Edmund 326, 358, 477, 479, 493, 496, 616, 636, 677, 684, 697
Burke, Kenneth 413
Burke, Michael 421
Burmese proverb 77
Burnett, Carol 685, 700
Burnett, Frances Hodgson 171, 543, 633
Burnett, Leo 467
Burney, Fanny 411
Burnham, William 486

Burns, Carl 90
Burns, George 436
Burns, Robert 404
Burr, Amelia 122, 125
Burr, Charles H. 115
Burritt, Elihu 632
Burroughs, John 19, 277, 336
Burrows, Eva 155
Burton, Henry 104
Burton, Lady Isabel 34
Burton, Marion L. 223
Burton, Robert 30, 97, 337, 373, 375
Burton, Sir Richard 429
Buscaglia, Leo 68, 430, 480
Bush, Barbara 5, 102, 126, 140, 219, 234, 467, 587, 595, 633
Bushnell, Horace 65
Bussy-Rabutin 49, 453
Bustanoby, André 668
Butler, Edward B. 369, 565
Butler, Nicholas Murray 277, 352, 368, 535, 536, 564
Butler, Philip 352, 699
Butler, Samuel 6, 49, 133, 136, 171, 245, 252, 266, 288, 312, 397, 400, 407, 410, 411, 422, 428, 442, 453, 465, 491, 503, 570, 579
Butterfield, Herbert 634
Buttrick, George A. 170, 550
Butts, Mary Frances 12
Buxton, Charles 277, 369, 564, 565, 598
Buxton, Sir Thomas Foxwell 640
Byatt, A.S. 88
Bynion, Bernard 248
Byrhhe, Anne 555
Byrne, James F. 484
Byrne, Robert 461
Byrnes, James F. 148, 509, 595
Byron, George Gordon (Lord) 28, 150, 292, 294, 343, 689

C

Caan, James 368, 564
Cabell, James Branch 517
Cade, Toni 92
Caesar, Julius 524, 601
Cage, John 89, 270, 528, 552, 673, 693, 698
Cahn, Peggy 335
Caird, Mona 383
Calavera, Ferrant Sanchez 501
Calcagnini, Celio 7
Calderón de la Barca, Pedro 422
Caldwell, Taylor 236, 691
Calhoun, John C. 401
Calisher, Hortense 106
Calvin, John 164, 170, 202
Cameron, Julie 539
Campbell, Bebe Moore 364
Campbell, Joseph 426, 462
Campbell, Thomas 648
Campton, Arthur H. 300
Camus, Albert 20, 76, 135, 220, 229, 259, 273, 308, 407, 451, 476, 501, 506, 549, 565, 595, 614, 638, 683
Camus, Jean Pierre 493
Canning, George 134
Cantor, Eddie 574
Capote, Truman 241
Capriati, Jennifer 563
Capshaw, Kate 441, 516
Cardone, Michael 539
Cardozo, Benjamin N. 340
Carlson, Jo Ann 181
Carlyle, Jane Welsh 94
Carlyle, Thomas 30, 104, 170, 209, 265, 280, 289, 303, 317, 352, 367, 399, 411, 415, 422, 425, 436, 461, 512, 530, 550, 580, 612, 656, 657, 677, 686
Carman, Bliss 368, 563, 648
Carmichael, Amy 112
Carmichael, Hoagy 645
Carnegie, Andrew 246, 342, 561, 601, 605
Carnegie, Dale 72, 119, 279, 301, 360, 368, 487, 497, 511, 563, 573, 641, 696
Carney, Julia 632
Carney, Julia A. Fletcher 26
Caron, Leslie 687
Carpenter, Liz 107, 539, 614
Carpentier, Georges 669
Carr, Emily 292, 626
Carr, Owen 180

Carrel, Dr. Alexis 56, 60, 105, 164, 177, 204, 207, 210, 253, 282, 418, 678
Carretto, Carlo 178, 628
Carroll, Lewis 293, 319
Carroll, Pat 357
Carroll, Ramona C. 171
Carruther, Thomas N. 368, 564
Carson, Rachel 93, 107, 156, 226, 385, 468, 518, 548
Carter, Elizabeth 78
Carter, Jimmy 64
Carter, Lillian 93, 457, 504, 515, 567, 615
Carter, Rosalynn 126, 381, 437, 557, 664
Carter-Scott, Cherie 543
Carty, Margaret 26, 99
Carver, George Washington 437, 673
Cary, Joyce 391
Cary, Phoebe 278, 647
Casarjean, Robin 281
Case, Mary 640
Casey, M. Kathleen 703
Cash, Rosanne 403
Cashman, Nellie 252
Casson, Herbert N. 512
Castaneda, Carlos 254, 398, 430
Castillego, Irene Claremont de 17, 315
Castle, Barbara 522
Castro, Rosalia 16, 257
Cathedral inscription 57
Cather, Willa 8, 21, 53, 61, 122, 268, 298, 364, 456, 467, 471, 508, 680
Catherine II 445
Catherine the Great 24, 217, 357, 441, 695
Catherine of Genoa, Saint 313
Catherine of Siena, Saint 155, 398, 691, 697
Catherwood, Mary 311
Cato "the Elder," Marcus Porcius 65
Catt, Carrie Chapman 427
Catton, Bruce 633
Catullus 292
Caulkins, Tracy 611
Cavell, Edith 59
Cecil, Richard 181

Centlivre, Lou 435, 609
Centlivre, Susannah 149
Ceram, C.W. 268
Cerami, Charles A. 365
Cerf, Bennett 188
Cervantes, Miguel de 66, 145, 146, 259, 296, 321, 323, 440, 444, 478, 492, 515, 523, 529, 533, 546, 565, 588
Chadwick, Samuel 175, 210
Chagall, Marc 289, 682
Chamberlain, Wilt 91
Chambers, Oswald 176, 179, 181, 182, 184, 185, 186, 187, 190, 191, 195, 200, 201, 204, 207, 208, 210, 211, 213, 366
Chamfort, Nicolas de 225, 229, 284, 363, 366, 450, 552, 581
Chamorro, Violeta Barrios de 59
Chance, Pauline Rose 409, 489
Chandler, Mitzi 495
Chandler, Raymond 652
Chanel, Coco 83, 93, 217, 227, 277, 341, 398, 543, 563, 608, 613
Channing, William Ellery 14, 118, 169, 278, 428, 552, 669, 676
Chapian, Marie 234
Chapin, Edwin H. 232, 536, 678
Chapman, George 135
Chapman, John Jay 167, 330
Chapman, Joyce 612
Chapman, Maria Weston 334, 639
Chardin, Pierre Teilhard de 27
Charles, Elizabeth 356
Charnock, Stephen 178
Chase, Alexander 60, 65, 215, 393
Chase, Ilka 564
Chase, Mary 383, 395
Chase, Mary Ellen 614
Chatfield, John 590
Chaucer, Geoffrey 48
Cheek, Alison 333
Cheever, Susan 466
Chekhov, Anton 6, 292, 329, 340, 458
Cher 25, 150, 284, 422, 465
Cherbuliez, Charles Victor 590
Chernin, Rose 298, 683
Chesnut, Mary Bokin 480

Chester, Henry 371
Chesterfield, Lord 27, 117, 145, 272, 277, 287, 465, 469, 603, 606, 607, 634, 637
Chesterton, G.K. 7, 36, 37, 57, 66, 71, 76, 77, 85, 172, 217, 262, 326, 377, 378, 458, 466, 537, 551, 605, 644, 655, 690, 696
Chevalier, Maurice 554
Chewning, Richard C. 120
Chiat, Jay 432, 513
Child, Julia 7, 17, 24, 25, 32, 234, 284, 285, 312, 341, 367, 568, 610, 611, 694
Child, Lydia M. 8, 32, 80, 93, 117, 129, 419
Childress, Alice 102, 110, 171, 292
Chinese proverb 19, 27, 28, 35, 45, 89, 91, 131, 134, 258, 336, 357, 362, 405, 439, 464, 486, 547, 548, 551, 553, 605, 635, 636, 637, 663, 692, 693
Chinese rhyme 547
Chinese woman, Anonymous 194
Chisholm, Shirley 120, 515
Cholmondeley, Mary 275
Chopin, Frédéric 524
Chosa, Heart Warrior 334, 541
Christie, Agatha 70, 216, 294, 392, 625, 657
Christina Augusta 468
Christy, Howard Chandler 160, 497
Chrysler, Walter 368, 564
Chrysostom, Saint John 98, 180, 206, 210, 211, 688
Chuang-tzu 18, 40, 48, 214, 586
Chung, Connie 96, 485
Churchill, Jennie Jerome 22, 51, 53, 126, 133, 146, 510, 519
Churchill, Sir Winston 51, 52, 268, 276, 306, 323, 368, 399, 402, 456, 486, 498, 521, 541, 564, 569, 573, 579, 583, 601, 621, 632, 642, 648, 665
Cicero 29, 50, 78, 83, 97, 123, 128, 138, 139, 142, 147, 149, 218, 245, 292, 348, 365, 445, 453, 479, 537, 602, 663

Cioran, E.M. 365, 446, 513, 670, 689, 697
Claplers, Luc de 268
Clarendon, Lord 273
Clare of Assisi, Saint 164
Clark, Alexander 548
Clark, Frank A. 108, 588
Clark, John 432
Clark, Karen Kaiser 391
Clark, Kenneth 350
Clark, R.W. 252
Clark, Ramsay 393
Clark, Septima Poinsette 675
Clark, Susanna 367
Clark, William Newton 161
Clarke, Adam 188
Clarke, James Freeman 18, 694
Clarke, Jean Illsley 31
Claudel, Paul 21
Claudian 82, 114
Clay, Henry 411, 419
Clemenceau, Georges 660, 668
Clement of Alexandria 209
Clemmer, Mary 7
Clendening, Dr. Logain 411
Clinton, Hillary Rodham 37, 107, 222, 394, 618
Cloete, Stuart 28, 116
Cloud of Unknowing, The 189
Coates, Florence Earle 7, 476, 695
Coats, Carolyn 386
Cobb, Ty 487
Cobbett, William 353, 632
Cochran 594
Cochran, Jacqueline 468, 488, 511, 682
Cockle Bur, The 18
Cocteau, Jean 633
Cody, Liza 589
Cody, Robert 530
Coeur, Du 114
Coffin, Henry Sloane 154
Coffin, William Sloane 227, 374, 506
Cohen, Mark N. 483
Colborn, Theo E. 223
Cole, Johnnetta Betsch 394
Cole, Larry 362
Cole, Walter E. 594, 657

Coleman, Bessie 468
Coleman, Langston 587
Coleridge, Hartley 633
Coleridge, Samuel Taylor 24, 179, 419, 478, 491
Colette 33, 35, 41, 86, 99, 366, 438, 575, 699
Colgrove, Dr. Melba 16, 119
Collier, Jeremy 374, 532, 557
Collins, Dr. Joseph 388
Collins, Joan 96, 659, 660
Collins, John Churton 98, 128, 138, 487
Collins, Judy 63
Collins, Marva 622
Collins, Sam 659
Collins, Vincent 302
Collyer, Robert 173
Colossians 3:23 366
Colton, Charles Caleb 9, 11, 18, 85, 113, 116, 136, 143, 151, 257, 277, 309, 329, 360, 403, 408, 429, 431, 445, 464, 527, 534, 537, 570, 643, 657, 681, 686, 688
Comaneci, Nadia 613
Compton-Burnett, Ivy 16, 113, 116
Conant, James Bryant 515, 567
Condie, Sheryl 137
Condorcet, The 97
Confucius 15, 52, 60, 147, 263, 523, 531, 534, 567, 623, 644, 658, 661, 680
Congolese proverb 58
Congreve, William 308, 480, 506, 509
Conklin, Roscoe 624
Conley, Philip 351
Connery, Sean 230, 452
Connolly, Cyril 12, 21, 53, 80, 148, 534, 650, 702
Connor, Ralph 536
Conrad, Charles 48
Conrad, James 2, 466
Conrad, Joseph 11, 66, 217, 257, 291, 443, 486, 489, 523, 529, 555
Cook, Eliza 16, 80, 123, 137, 311, 576, 664
Cook, Mary Lou 16, 519
Cooke, Alistair 610

Cooke, Edmund Vance 321, 666, 692, 693
Cookson, Catherine 20
Cooley, Charles Horton 163, 407, 669
Cooley, Dr. Denton 588
Coolidge, Calvin 285, 499, 585, 636, 640
Coolidge, Susan 293
Cooney, Joan Ganz 584, 589
Cooper, Anna Julia 106
Cooper, Diana 262
Cooper, Peter 411, 421
Coppola, Francis Ford 334, 646, 666
Corbett, James J. 647
Cordes, Liane 347
Corea, Chick 264, 432
Corelli, Marie 59, 354
Corneille, Pierre 42, 93, 289, 456, 517, 538, 687
Corson, Fred 252
Cosby, Bill 609
Cotton, Nathaniel 32, 90, 625
Councilman, Emily Sargent 525
Course in Miracles, A 15, 66, 160, 302, 480
Cousins, Norman 44, 65, 277, 343, 348, 353, 484, 619, 620
Cousins, Park 363
Cousteau, Jacques 165, 375
Coward, Noel 223, 267, 443
Cowley, Abraham 79, 145, 303, 373, 401
Cowper, William 23, 34, 51, 212, 305, 314, 471, 508, 677
Cox, Coleman 367
Cox, Harvey 414
Cox, Marcelene 21, 99, 234, 449, 541
Cox, Raymond L. 570
Cozzens, James Gould 302
Craig, John 563
Craik, Dinah Maria Mulock 99, 115, 135, 314
Crampton, Bruce 454
Crane, Dr. Frank 49, 90, 105, 286, 346, 452, 481, 656
Crane, Frederick E. 13, 30
Crane, Nathalia 661
Crashaw, Richard 185

Crawford, Cindy 94, 96
Crawford, Francis Marion 142, 346
Crawford, V.L. 210
Crebillion, Prosper Jolyot de 522
Crews, Harry 574
Croce, Arlene 225
Croce, Benedetto 552
Crockett, Davy 247
Cronin, A.J. 141, 159, 376, 496
Crook, Jayne 192
Cropp, Frederick W. 488
Crosby, Cathy Lee 695
Crothers, Samuel McChord 228, 450
Crotts, Stephen 201
Crowley, Mary 250
Cudahy, John 508
Cukor, George 571, 640, 665, 666
Culbertson, William 206
Cullum, George 692
Cumberland 118
cummings, e.e. 68, 316, 428
Cummins, Maria S. 171
Cunningham, Sir Andrew 361
Cunningham, Tom 301
Cuomo, Mario 423
Curie, Marie 482, 639, 645
Curtis, Edward L. 352, 367, 550
Curtis, George William 73
Curtis, Jamie Lee 95
Curtiz, Michael 517, 550
Cushman, Charlotte 621
Cutler, Laurel 323, 410
Cuyler, T.L. 202, 203
Czech proverb 151

D

D'Aubigne, Francoise 646
D'Hericourt, Jenny P. 382
D'Youville, Saint Mary Margaret 32
Dac, Pierre 325
Daishonen, Nichiren 449
Dalai Lama, The 36, 258, 625
Daly, Mary 521, 608
Daly, Tyne 349
Dametz, Maurice 78
Damon, Bertha 34
Danforth, William H. 359
Dangerfield, Rodney 332

Daniels, Josephus 647
Danish proverb 98
Danton, Georges Jacques 520, 522, 653
Darwin, Charles 276
Dass, Ram 50, 233, 453
Daugherty, Duffy 184
Davenport, Russell W. 542
David-Néel, Alexandra 678, 679
Davies, Maty Caroline 295
Davies, Robert H. 50
Davies, Robertson 430, 477, 601
Davis, Belva 504
Davis, Bette 18, 33, 114, 326, 349, 462, 513, 639, 703
Davis, Elmer 493
Davis, Geena 667
Davis, Kenneth S. 510
Davis, Mildred 348
Davis, Mrs. Hubbard 250
Davis, Rebecca Harding 106
Day, Clarence 45
Day, Doris 496
Day, Dorothy 549, 631
Debs, Eugene V. 459
DeCaussade, J.P. 158, 312
Dector, Midge 623
Dee, Ruby 522
Deems, Charles F. 284, 499, 625
Deffand, Madame Marquise du 557, 636
DeFloris, Marie 155
DeFrantz, Anita 466
Degas, Edgar 543
Dekker, Thomas 322, 496, 609
Delacroix, Eugene 272, 456, 622
Deland, Margaret 105, 336, 348, 381, 403, 448
Delille, Jacques 140, 377
Delp, Alexis 441
Deluzy, Madame Dorothee 66, 132, 150
Demetrius 138
DeMille, Cecil B. 598
Deming, Barbara 617
Demosthenes 217, 596
Deneuve, Catherine 593
Denham, Sir John 558

Dennis, Nigel 537
Denton, Jeremiah A. 209
DePasquale, John 349, 351
DeRohan, Ceanne 65
Descartes, Rene 360
Deschamps, Eustache 140
Desert Fathers, The 178, 180, 198, 212
Deshimaru, Taisen 279, 288
Deshouliere, Antoinette 87
Deterding, Henri 266
Detourbey, Jeanne 587
Devlin, Bernadette 518, 530, 632
Dewey, John 30, 170, 247, 325, 392, 403, 435, 523, 577, 611, 671, 685
Dewey, Thomas E. 324, 481
Dewhurst, Colleen 231
De Angelis, Barbara 8, 20, 163, 231, 250, 301, 446, 513, 528
De Bono, Dr. Edward 39, 51
De Chantal, Jane Frances 168, 185, 188
De Gaulle, Charles 252
De Gaulle, Yvonne 140
De Girardin, Delphine 418
De Lenclos, Anne 319
De Maintenon, Madame 26
De Mille, Agnes 167, 415, 545
De Pottiers, Diane 536
De Rougemont, Denis 22, 53
De Sales, Saint Francis 282
De Waal, Esther 266
Wolfe, Elsie de 112
Dhuse, Andrew 629
Diana, Princess of Wales 32, 103, 106, 110, 214, 424
Diane, Comtesse 78, 105, 126, 166, 364
Dickens, Charles 86, 289, 293, 549
Dickey, James 319
Dickinson, Emily 6, 25, 31, 40, 41, 59, 62, 71, 77, 83, 92, 93, 102, 119, 120, 123, 223, 319, 377, 468, 516, 587, 588, 635, 664, 675, 679, 689
Dickson, Paul 669
Diderot, Denis 114, 366, 421, 510
Didion, Joan 98, 221, 239, 241, 299, 355, 427
Dienert, B. Graham 184

Dietrich, Marlene 59, 60, 82, 103, 136, 137, 165, 248, 357, 471, 701
DiGiovanna, Kara 233
Dillard, Annie 461, 599, 611
Diller, Phyllis 93, 651
Dimnet, Ernest 25
Dinesen, Isak 17, 218, 323, 333, 495, 631, 679
Ding Ling 486
Diogenes, Laertius 273
Dion, Celine 505
Dior, Christian 365
Dirksen, Everett M. 402
Disney, Walt 611
Disraeli, Benjamin 109, 142, 144, 173, 254, 312, 324, 336, 367, 394, 481, 490, 494, 518, 537, 561, 572, 585, 594, 596, 600, 641, 677, 685, 695
Ditz, Nancy 265, 461
Dix, Dorothy 678, 680
Di Cavour, Camillo 132
Doane, W.C. 45, 90, 651, 655
Dobie, J. Frank 589
Dobrin, Arthur 247
Dobson, Rosemary 372
Dodd, C.H. 113
Dodd, Lee Wilson 629
Dodd, Susan M. 590
Dodds, Dr. Harold W. 509
Dodgson, Charles Lutwidge 514, 566
Dogen 57
Doherty, Catherine de Hueck 374
Doherty, Sarah 511, 516
Dole, Charles F. 104
Dole, Elizabeth 16, 250, 351
Donleavy, J.P. 88
Donne, John 165, 211, 256, 534
Donnell, John 363
Donovan, Robert J. 649
Dorr, Julia 357, 375, 377, 627
Dostoevsky, Anna 505
Dostoyevsky, Fyodor 41, 57, 85, 186, 231, 404, 609, 678
Douchan, Gersi 279
Doudney, Sarah 342
Douglas, I.D. 108
Douglas, James 77
Douglas, LeRoy 373

Douglas, Lloyd C. 479
Douglas, Norman 132, 466, 547
Douglas, Sandra L. 175, 177
Douglas, William O. 399, 508
Douglass, Frederick 298
Dowd, Maureen 44
Dowden, Edward 661
Dowes, Donald 493
Downing, Christine 152, 237
Doyle, Sir Arthur Conan 24, 635
Drabble, Margaret 93, 342, 503, 506, 703
Draper, John 287
Dreier, Thomas 302, 308
Dreikurs, Dr. Rudolf 619
Dresselhaus, Mildred Spiewak 215
Dresser, Horatio W. 271, 283
Dressler, Marie 94, 668
Driscoll, Louise 383
Drucker, Peter 406, 531, 568
Drummond, Henry 27, 28, 104, 117, 119
Drummond, William 321
Dryden, John 42, 137, 245, 279, 324, 481, 522, 529, 585, 646
Dubuffet, Jean 397
Dudevant, Madame 407
Duffy, Maureen 8, 678
Dugan, Dennis 513
Duhamel, Georges 71
Duke, Patty 8
Dulles, John Foster 538, 599
Dumas, Alexandre 336, 358, 375, 505
Dunaway, Faye 95
Duncan, David Douglas 279
Duncan, Isadora 106, 238, 468, 512
Duncan, Sara Jeannette 228, 699
Dunham, Katherine 571
Dunn, Elizabeth Clarke 43
Dunne, Finley Peter 596
Dunning, Albert E. 318, 592
Dunsany, Lord 326
DuPont IV, Pierre S. 361
Durant, Will 22, 51, 302, 472, 664
Durocher, Leo 267, 309
Duse, Eleonora 83, 610
Dutch Poets' Society 600
Dutch proverb 151, 416, 548

Du Autermont, Harriet 383
Du Bos, Charles 397, 519
Du Marier, George 258
Du Maurier, Daphne 4, 17, 294
Dwight, Timothy 81
Dwight D. Eisenhower's mother 58
Dyer, Wayne 303, 306
Dyke, Henry Van 14
Dykstra, C.A. 458

E

Eakins, Thomas 369, 463, 564
Earhart, Amelia 249, 294, 413, 424, 442, 497, 516, 537, 644
Eastman, Dick 211
Eastman, Max 699
Eastwood, Clint 346, 350, 647
Ebaugh, Sue Atchley 231, 626
Eberhardt, Isabelle 19, 484
Eberhart, E.T. "Cy" 698
Eberhart, Mignon G. 499
Ebner-Eschenbach, Marie von 34, 66, 113, 151, 236, 242, 244, 245, 318, 540, 542, 592, 611, 657, 658
Ecclesiastes 3:1 332
Ecclesiastes 5:2 188
Ecclesiastes 7:8 337
Ecclesiastes 7:10 299
Ecclesiastes 9:4 372
Ecclesiastes 9:10 602
Ecclesiastes 9:11 336, 644, 686
Ecclesiastes 9:14 143
Ecker, Frederick H. 30
Eckhart, Meister 78, 153, 191, 208
Eddington, Sir Arthur 422
Eddy, Mary Baker 15, 61, 153, 154, 156, 158, 161, 162, 169, 297, 302, 513, 620, 687
Eddy, Sherwood 165
Edelgard 57
Edelman, Marian Wright 100, 102, 120, 133, 228, 355, 609, 636, 670
Edgeworth, Maria 28, 151, 546, 632
Edison, Thomas A. 148, 277, 336, 497, 532, 594, 609, 615, 647, 666, 680, 693
Edman, Irwin 391
Edwards, Bryon 206

Edwards, Flora 116
Edwards, Jonathan 158, 185
Edwards, Ralph 581
Edwards, Tyron 22, 274, 286, 347,
  385, 401, 471, 607
Eggleston, Edward 650
Ehrenreich, Barbara 106, 569
Ehrlich, Gretel 352
Ehrmann, Max 15, 97, 479
Einstein, Albert 62, 118, 154, 159,
  262, 263, 287, 326, 421, 570, 575,
  632, 665
Einstein, Elsa 164
Eisenhower, Dwight D. 198, 349, 365,
  368, 370, 500, 507, 564, 584, 600,
  601, 697
Eisenhower, Ida 695
Eisler, Riane 356
Elders, Joycelyn 154
Eldridges, Paul 98
Elfman, Jenna 284
Elgin, Suzette Haden 525
Eliashev, Isidor 299
Eliot, Charles W. 117, 256, 278, 502
Eliot, George 9, 62, 89, 97, 99, 101,
  110, 115, 125, 129, 137, 151, 158,
  163, 237, 245, 272, 283, 296, 299,
  342, 349, 360, 362, 382, 391, 407,
  408, 409, 440, 448, 449, 454, 455,
  462, 501, 503, 534, 549, 555, 622,
  628, 662, 666, 667, 668, 674, 703
Eliot, Robert 48, 497
Eliot, T.S. 14, 53, 281, 334, 390, 443,
  513, 525, 556, 574
Elizabeth I, Queen 272, 539, 685
Elizabeth II, Queen 215, 617
Elizabeth of Hungary, Saint 159
Ellerbee, Linda 126, 698
Ellington, Duke 680
Elliot, Elizabeth 702
Elliott, Charlotte 211
Elliott, L.G. 560
Elliott, Thelma 316
Ellis, Alice Thomas 484
Ellis, Havelock 98, 168, 401, 430, 510
Ellis, Henry Havelock 93
Ellis, Sarah 150
Ellman, Lucy 172

Emerson, Ralph Waldo 3, 10, 11, 14,
  21, 29, 30, 36, 39, 47, 50, 53, 68,
  74, 81, 90, 105, 114, 115, 121, 124,
  127, 129, 130, 131, 135, 142, 144,
  145, 149, 155, 161, 162, 172, 197,
  202, 210, 221, 232, 234, 245, 257,
  262, 268, 270, 271, 272, 278, 279,
  280, 287, 289, 297, 299, 303, 304,
  306, 309, 312, 315, 321, 327, 328,
  329, 332, 336, 346, 347, 350, 353,
  357, 363, 367, 368, 369, 371, 379,
  390, 400, 401, 407, 414, 419, 423,
  435, 436, 438, 444, 453, 469, 479,
  480, 485, 487, 490, 491, 498, 499,
  510, 511, 528, 530, 533, 537, 538,
  541, 547, 552, 558, 561, 562, 563,
  565, 567, 575, 576, 577, 580, 585,
  588, 592, 601, 602, 611, 643, 646,
  650, 652, 658, 671, 676, 677, 684,
  685, 690, 701
Emmanuel 53, 115, 153, 172, 233,
  325, 628, 629
Emmons, Nathaniel 464, 610
Engels, Friedrich 623
English proverb 28, 77, 114, 266, 289,
  516, 550, 554, 557, 595, 616, 619,
  655, 663, 684
Ennius, Quintus 128, 249
Ephesians 4:31–32 64
Ephesians 14:26 321
Ephron, Delia 354
Ephron, Nora 395
Epictetus 11, 22, 34, 47, 53, 74, 81,
  238, 252, 257, 261, 265, 281, 282,
  336, 360, 426, 463, 484, 539, 634,
  645, 684, 694, 695, 696
Epicurus 74, 76, 79, 81, 124, 125,
  200, 260, 305, 309, 489, 499, 517,
  658, 687
Epitaph of Alexander the Great 230,
  452
Erasmus 20, 128, 227, 430, 522
Erdrich, Louise 9, 237, 399, 587, 610
Erhard, Werner 52, 54
Erickson, Marian 584
Erikson, Erik H. 424, 484
Ertz, Susan 274
Ervin, Sam J. 171

Eskimo proverb 14
Estefan, Gloria 595
Esther 4:16 601
Estonian proverb 78, 545
Euland, Brenda 637
Euripides 43, 46, 58, 75, 79, 92, 136, 138, 139, 140, 146, 270, 278, 283, 302, 328, 333, 352, 377, 391, 425, 433, 449, 507, 528, 530, 534, 567, 582, 590, 600, 605, 626, 639, 649, 689, 698
Evans, Augusta 611
Evans, Colleen Townsend 178, 209
Evans, J.H. 178
Evans, Marsha 613
Evans, Michael 598
Evans, Richard L. 74, 532, 558, 644
Everett, David 636
Evert, Chris 245, 366, 614, 626
Exodus 5:13 282

F

Faber, Frederick W. 144
Fabre, Jean-Henri 147
Fairbrother, Nan 130
Fairless, Benjamin F. 560
Fallaci, Oriana 40, 217, 384, 578
Falls, Rebecca 103
Faludi, Susan 215
Faraday, Dr. Ann 700
Farber, Leslie H. 51
Farley, James A. 347
Farmer, Frances 148
Farrall, Joseph 38
Farrar, Frederic W. 667
Farrell, Joseph 270, 454, 524, 655
Faulkner, William 267, 287, 294, 436, 478, 482, 540, 620, 660
Feather, William 18, 21, 130, 229, 277, 283, 308, 412, 451, 547, 551, 553, 572, 615, 635, 641, 666, 682, 691
Feinstein, Dianne 588
Fellini, Federico 252, 370, 419, 435, 489, 590, 608
Femina, Jerry Della 573, 586, 642, 665
Fenelon, Francois de 3, 76, 175, 181, 196, 499, 537
Fenwick, Millicent 237

Ferber, Edna 224, 240, 295
Ferguson, Marilyn 395, 487, 490, 518, 636
Fergusson, Harvey 65
Fern, Fanny 636
Ferraro, Geraldine 102, 237, 256, 621
Ferrier, Susan 136
Fessenden, Samuel 649
Fichter, Jean Paul 688
Ficke, Arthur Davison 664
Field, Joanna 335, 470, 477, 479, 532, 557, 568, 626, 638
Field, John Hancock 552
Field, Rachel 668
Field, Sally 251, 430
Fielding, Henry 283, 302, 683
Fields, Debbi 44, 114, 437, 520
Fields, Dorothy 427
Fierstein, Harvey 512, 598
Filson, Floyd V. 247
Fine, Robert M. 275
Fink, David Harold 427
Finkelstein, Edward S. 632
Finley, Charles O. 568, 613
Finley, John H. 315, 504
Finney, Charles G. 174
Finnish proverb 635
Firkins, Oscar W. 151
Fischer's Law 402
Fishel, Elizabeth 126
Fisher, Admiral John 456, 597
Fisher, Carrie 63, 571
Fisher, Dorothy Canfield 94, 109, 458, 461
Fisher, Geoffrey 429
Fisher, M.F.K. 308
Fiske, John 325
Fitz-Gibbon, Bernice 342
Fitzgerald, Ella 446
Fitzgerald, F. Scott 362, 376, 650, 666, 691
Fitzgerald, Gerald B. 117
Fitzgerald, Zelda 8
Fitzhenry, R.I. 330, 505, 506
Fitzosborne, Thomas 26, 118
Fixx, James 584
Flack, Roberta 678
Flagg, Fannie 462

Flanders, Alberta 695
Flandrau, Charles Macomb 272
Flanner, Janet 224
Flaubert, Gustave 292, 297
Fleishman, Jerome P. 536, 681
Fleming, Peggy 425
Flemming, Paul 28, 121
Fletcher, Admiral Frank Jack 415
Fletcher, Horace 478
Flint, Annie Johnson 160
Florus 525
Foch, Marshal Ferdinand 361, 368, 370, 564, 600
Foley, Elizabeth 131, 138
Foley, Rae 63
Follett, Mary Parker 106, 109, 162, 236, 251, 364, 387, 464, 581, 599, 617, 626, 652, 679
Follin, G.W. 582
Fonda, Henry 589
Fonda, Jane 100, 250, 432, 542, 689
Fontane, Theodore 278
Fontenelle, Bernard de 29, 42, 230, 323, 348, 451
Fontey, Margaret 230, 451
Fonteyn, Margot 615
Forbes, B.C. 33, 34, 91, 98, 117, 130, 150, 172, 246, 260, 264, 368, 386, 387, 406, 435, 459, 463, 497, 513, 532, 557, 563, 566, 572, 574, 586, 590, 594, 595, 600, 601, 626, 640, 641, 647, 669, 675
Forbes, Malcolm 54, 60, 84, 233, 343, 355, 367, 484, 562, 575, 582, 619, 673, 687
Forbus, Lady Willie 94
Ford, Harrison 11, 438, 444, 572, 575, 641
Ford, Henry 23, 109, 301, 346, 352, 409, 436, 460, 472, 508, 561, 562, 631, 670, 673
Ford II, Henry 504
Fornés, Maria Irene 520
Forrest, Nathan Bedford 267
Forster, E.M. 169, 586
Forsyth, Peter Taylor 603
Fortunato, John 626
Fosdick, Harry Emerson 62, 120, 166,

171, 201, 220, 396, 488, 511, 605
Foster, Bill 362, 371
Foster, Jodie 7, 20, 462
Foster, John 302, 414
Fowler, Charles H. 386
Fowler, Ellen Thorneycroft 686
Fowler, Gene 447
Fox, Matthew 204
Fox, Muriel 357, 617
France, Anatole 36, 74, 268, 293, 323, 336, 367, 370, 391, 403, 412, 543, 678
France, Marie de 237
Francis, Arlene 138, 146
Francis, Brendan 178, 298, 324, 388, 412, 481, 486, 547, 580, 607, 624, 672
Francis de Sales, Saint 228, 229
Francis of Assisi, Saint 64, 195, 265, 637
Francke, Katherine 102
Frank, Anne 9, 77, 157, 254, 342, 347, 443, 462, 546
Frankel, Viktor 19
Frankfurter, Felix 620
Frankl, Viktor 354, 406
Franklin, Benjamin 10, 25, 76, 79, 81, 101, 146, 165, 199, 251, 257, 273, 275, 276, 278, 281, 301, 307, 321, 335, 336, 358, 370, 387, 414, 472, 508, 552, 562, 578, 588, 595, 602, 613, 624, 634, 637, 675, 685
Franklin, Jon 268
Franklin, Miles 462
Franzblau, Rose N. 106
Frazer, Sir James 390
Frazier, Joe 664
Frederick, Robert E. 142
Frederick the Great 426
Free, Spencer M. 125
Freedman, Ruth P. 228, 511
Freehill, Maurice 493
French, Marilyn 103, 139, 326
French Foreign Legion 667
French proverb 56, 75, 82, 88, 146, 166, 230, 390, 413, 421, 441, 443, 451, 645, 649, 660, 690
Freud, Anna 231

Freud, Sigmund 37, 227, 334, 408, 418, 424, 699
Friday, Nancy 218
Friedan, Betty 251, 424, 544, 556, 613
Friedman, Colonel Michael 463
Friedman, Cynthia 268
Friedman, Dr. Martha 438, 575
Friedmann, Isaac 63
Friedsman, Colonel Michael 607
Fripp, Patricia 214, 215, 274
Frohman, Daniel 128
From a fortune cookie 335
Fromm, Erich 46, 80, 101, 163, 247, 263, 276, 329, 331, 429, 450, 466, 502, 506
Frost, Paul 154
Frost, Robert 48, 132, 329, 378, 477, 496, 599, 627, 651, 683
Froud, J.A. 230, 452
Froude, James A. 549, 685
Fry, Christopher 48, 442, 620
Fry, Dr. William F. 490
Fuentes, Carlos 621
Fulbright, James W. 350
Fuldheim, Dorothy 94, 237
Fulghum, Robert 580
Fuller, Elizabeth 100
Fuller, Margaret 32, 241, 645
Fuller, Margaret Witter 244
Fuller, R. Buckminster 154, 410, 520, 545
Fuller, Thomas 29, 49, 57, 65, 73, 76, 81, 82, 83, 97, 113, 132, 136, 138, 140, 146, 147, 149, 168, 180, 186, 251, 292, 316, 324, 348, 368, 372, 373, 374, 452, 455, 464, 469, 480, 484, 490, 493, 511, 514, 518, 523, 536, 564, 566, 589, 620, 649, 660, 663, 669, 687, 696
Fuller, Timothy 406

G

Gabirol, Solomon Ibn 170
Gaelic proverb 620
Gaines, Frank 460
Gaines, William 69
Gaither, Ralph 72
Galagani, Gemma 156

Galatians 6:7 357
Galatians 6:9 650
Galbraith, John Kenneth 402, 661
Gale, Zona 33
Galen 608
Galgani, Gemma 157
Galyean, Dorothy 664
Gambrell, J.B. 534
Gandhi, Indira 62, 234, 468, 547
Gandhi, Mahatma 20, 168, 170, 177, 190, 699
Gann, Keith 120
Garagiola, Joe 279
Garcia, Will 56, 361, 404
Garden, Mary 245
Gardening headline 264
Gardiner, Lisa 448
Gardner, Ava 218
Gardner, Herb 271
Gardner, John W. 270, 671
Garfield, James A. 255, 518, 524, 550, 601
Garrison, William Lloyd 603
Garson, Greer 435, 439, 576, 610
Gary, Roman 699
Gascoigne, Caroline L. 571, 666
Gaskell, Elizabeth 109
Gassen, Ira 347
Gasser, Herbert 684
Gatty, Margaret 63, 243
Gawain, Elizabeth 479, 481
Gawain, Shakti 46, 55, 155, 156, 227, 340, 366, 418, 436, 616, 628
Gay, John 98, 146, 250
Gayler, T.L. 285
Gellert, Christian Furchtegott 23, 424, 472
Gelman-Waxner, Libby 107
Gendler, J. Ruth 160, 212, 493
Genesis 42:21 121
Genesis Rabbah 44:15 53
Gentry, Dave Tyson 128
George, David Lloyd 515, 567
George, Henry 405
George, Jean Craighead 489
George, W.L. 667
George V of England 57
Gerhart, Susan 404

German proverb 84, 98, 113, 119, 199, 260, 261, 319, 335, 391, 398, 464, 478, 492, 531, 567, 659, 687

Gertrude the Great 241

Geyer, Georgie Anne 254, 430

Ghandi, Mahatma 61

Gibb, Margaret 163, 194

Gibbon, Edward 255, 544, 693

Gibbons, Cardinal James 531, 567

Gibbs, Nancy 166

Gibbs, Willard 264

Gibran, Kahlil 24, 68, 115, 149, 166, 184, 268, 271, 272, 296, 316, 354, 420, 505, 623, 678

Gibson, Althea 100, 150, 483

Gibson, Josh 281, 442

Gide, André 11, 13, 39, 55, 75, 76, 211, 228, 279, 304, 307, 352, 400, 425, 429, 459, 465, 487, 503, 604, 703

Gideon, Lillian 102

Gielgud, Sir John 245, 594

Gilbert, Arland 52, 283, 369, 565, 615, 692

Gilbert, W.S. 89

Gilchrist, Ellen 295, 616

Gilder, George 393, 516

Giles, Henry 173

Gilman, Charlotte P. 21, 216, 232, 401, 439, 550

Gilman, Dorothy 106

Gilmore, Dame Mary 270

Ginott, Haim 359

Ginsberg, Ruth Bader 344

Giono, Jean 329

Giovanni, Nikki 100, 248, 423, 511

Giraudoux, Jean 314

Gish, Lillian 683, 688

Gissing, George R. 54, 225, 311, 356, 531, 567

Given, William B. 412

Gladstone, William 275

Glancy, Diane 653

Glasgow, Ellen 55, 115, 399, 468, 600, 695

Glasow, Arnold 130, 152, 250, 266, 491, 497

Glenconner, Pamela 115

Godden, Rumer 35

Godin, André 346, 363

Godwin, Gail 125, 218, 382

Goethe, Johann von 9, 12, 31, 35, 42, 49, 103, 121, 132, 146, 169, 223, 226, 229, 241, 252, 264, 270, 272, 277, 280, 289, 311, 312, 319, 328, 359, 370, 374, 392, 395, 435, 436, 451, 452, 458, 464, 465, 473, 480, 501, 526, 532, 541, 543, 547, 548, 552, 556, 574, 579, 585, 604, 610, 619, 639, 640, 642, 648, 651, 653, 659, 661, 668

Golas, Thaddeus 498

Goldberg, Herb 418

Goldberg, Natalie 507, 627

Goldberg, Whoopi 224

Golden, Marita 602

Golding, Henry J. 470

Goldman, Emma 102, 107, 110, 382, 425

Goldsmith, Oliver 80, 223, 377, 386, 455, 588, 614, 650

Goldstein, Dr. Kurt 528, 698

Goldwyn, Samuel 28, 593

Gomez, Lefty 266

Goode, Kenneth 318

Goodier, Alban 279

Goodman, Ellen 63, 233

Goodman, Paul 19, 470, 598

Gorbachev, Raisa M. 296, 382

Gordimer, Nadine 381

Gordon, A.J. 200

Gordon, Arthur 44

Gordon, Barbara 94, 703

Gordon, Julian Weber 528

Gordon, Ruth 120, 349, 538, 589, 594, 648, 681, 704

Gordon, Winifred 67, 529

Goretti, Maria 156

Gorky, Maxim 41, 77

Gorman, Paul 50, 453

Gospel According to Zen, The 19, 333

Gosse, Edmund 296

Gottlieb, Annie 150, 152

Goudge, Elizabeth 163, 492, 540, 542

Gough, John B. 259, 565, 595

Goulburn, Edward M. 179

Gouthey, A.P. 514, 566
Gracian, Baltasar 54, 74, 85, 98, 123, 131, 149, 360, 385, 522, 531, 543, 546, 586, 624, 685
Graf, Steffi 605
Grafton, Sue 251, 571
Graham 406
Graham, Gordon 414
Graham, Katherine 221, 612, 674
Graham, Margaret Collier 20, 394, 674
Graham, Martha 226, 349, 703
Graham, Ruth 188, 196
Graham, Sheila 366
Gramm, Phil 665
Grant, Amy 588
Grant, Cary 263, 280
Grant, Curtis 623
Grant, Richard R. 670
Grant, Robert 406
Grant, Ulysses S. 138, 609, 643
Granville, George 117
Graves, Clarissa 614
Graves, Richard 137
Graves, Robert 619
Gray, Francine Du Plessix 135
Graydon, David 430
Grayson, David 2, 30, 53, 81, 129, 149, 227, 303, 392, 518, 672
Greek proverb 32, 84, 89, 90, 136, 137, 206, 548, 551, 649
Greeley, Horace 292
Green, Russell 499
Greene, Graham 230, 258, 451, 506, 544
Greene, Vivian 355
Greenfield, Jeff 268
Greenfield, Meg 237
Greer, Germaine 96, 292, 616, 617
Greer, Jackie 404
Gregg, Alan 685
Gregory, Augusta 79, 249
Gregory, Dick 27
Grenfell, Wilfred 101, 538
Gribble, Phillip 307
Grieg, Edvard 142
Griffin, Merv 585
Griffin, Susan 100, 127, 134, 237

Griggs, Edward Howard 684
Grillparzer, Franz 358, 505
Grimes, Martha 439
Griswold, Whitney 677
Grou, Jean Nicholas 50, 453
Grumbach, Doris 237
Guest, Judith 459
Guicciardini, Francesco 144, 324, 386, 487
Guideposts 162
Guiney, Louise Imogen 28
Guinness, Og 171, 702
Guiterman, Arthur 526, 662
Guizot, Elizabeth de Meulan 100, 121
Guizot, Madame 689
Gunther, John 37
Gurdjieff, Georges 216, 526
Gurnall, William 203

H

Haddow, Sir Henry 278
Haecker, Theodore 287, 330
Hafez 84, 378
Hagen, Walter 500
Haggard, Merle 11
Hagman, Larry 318
Hailey, Alex 227, 431, 573, 637, 642
Hailey, Arthur 584
Halberstam, David 319
Hale, Clara McBride 107, 251, 640
Hale, Edward Everett 230, 282, 436, 439, 452, 576, 636
Hale, Nancy 77, 241, 381
Hale, Sarah Josepha 83, 225
Half, Robert 616, 673
Haliburton, Thomas C. 320
Halifax, Lord 133, 294
Hall, Jerry 96
Hall, Joseph 283
Hall, Manly 508
Hall, Monty 574
Hall, Robert 207, 209, 210
Hall, Tom T. 560
Hallesby, O. 174, 179, 180, 181, 183, 185, 187, 188, 189, 190, 191, 192, 195, 196, 198, 199, 204, 205, 206, 208, 211
Halloway, Richard 14, 264

Halsey, Margaret 218, 551
Halsey, William F. 524, 657
Halverson, Richard 490
Hamilton, Alexander 48, 411, 696
Hamilton, Edith 168, 410, 616
Hamilton, Frank 554
Hamilton, Gail 226, 436
Hamilton, Sir Ian 267, 502
Hammarskjold, Dag 51, 64, 69, 149, 255, 265, 301, 383, 415, 426, 461, 508, 523, 540, 601, 658, 702
Hammer, Armand 588
Hammerstein II, Oscar 357
Hammond, John Hays 570
Hampl, Patricia 295
Hand, Learned 399
Haney, Carol 572
Hanks, Marion D. 110
Hanks, Nancy 644
Hannibal 255
Hansbury, Lorraine 11, 226, 318, 323, 427
Hansen, Grace 484
Hansen, Patty 595
Han Suyin 32
Hardwick, Elizabeth 107
Hardy, Thomas 588
Hare, A.W. 673
Hare, Julius Charles 81, 135, 166, 427
Harjo, Joy 127
Harper, Frances Ellen Watkins 672
Harper, Lucille S. 240
Harriman, E.H. 324, 481
Harriman, Florence Hurst 237
Harris, Barbara 555
Harris, Corra May 83
Harris, Frank 677
Harris, Sydney J. 60, 105, 214, 259, 293, 411, 662
Harrison, Barbara Grizzuti 111, 253, 313, 380, 507
Harrison, Elizabeth 442
Harrison, George 255
Harrison, Harry 20
Harrison, Jane 94, 662
Harry, Linda 702
Hart, Sir Basil Liddell 692
Harte, Bret 590

Hartley, Leslie Poles 299
Hartog, Jan de 456
Harvey, Joan C. 483
Harvey, Paul 297
Harwood, Gwen 410
Haskins, Henry S. 55, 58, 259, 388, 402, 423, 536, 543, 636, 663
Hastings, James 491
Hathaway, Katharine Butler 54, 125, 137, 394, 396, 414, 417, 418, 479
Havel, Vaclav 377
Havergal, Frances Ridley 27, 120, 197, 238, 244, 358, 505
Havighurst, Robert J. 31, 127
Havner, Vance 164, 179
Havoc, June 502, 508
Hawes, J. 467
Hawkes, Elizabeth 430
Hawking, Stephen 456
Hawley, Charles A. 228
Hawn, Goldie 94, 228
Hawthorne, Nathaniel 17, 19
Hay, John 125, 145, 697
Hay, Louise L. 33, 343
Hayakawa, S.I. 215
Hayes, Helen 166, 220, 505, 562, 572
Hayes, Woody 598, 639, 670
Hayford, Jack W. 209
Hazlitt, William 21, 50, 84, 98, 115, 132, 139, 143, 145, 150, 171, 222, 231, 242, 268, 286, 310, 363, 369, 371, 372, 411, 412, 428, 453, 487, 541, 565, 652, 685, 687
Hazzard, Shirley 703
Heath, Jinger 241, 439, 587, 595, 668
Hebrews 10:36 337
Hebrews 11:1 161
Hebrews 11:6 207
Hebrews 13:5 85
Hecht, Ben 289
Hedge, H.F. 253
Hegel, George 366, 459
Height, Dorothy 100, 106
Heilbrun, Carolyn 538
Heimel, Cynthia 664
Hein, Piet 663
Heine, Heinrich 6, 64, 166
Helburn, Theresa 598, 610

Heller, Elizabeth 94
Heller, Joseph 456, 579
Hellman, Lillian 20, 51, 86, 238, 241,
   291, 299, 360, 395, 411, 415, 420,
   430, 620
Helps, Sir Arthur 104, 415
Helvetius, Claude 366
Hemingway, Ernest 263, 386, 481,
   534, 537, 547, 557, 648, 651
Hemingway, Mary 495
Henderson, Hazel 55, 432
Henker, Dr. Fred O. 376
Henle, Mary 597
Henley, Linda 83
Henley, William E. 261, 649
Henri, Robert 5, 36, 423, 582, 607
Henry, Matthew 73, 175, 180, 181,
   187, 195
Henry, O. 77, 449
Henry, Patrick 294
Henry, Philip 180, 185
Hepburn, Audrey 16, 472, 668
Hepburn, Katharine 42, 96, 236, 257,
   281, 365, 426, 427, 435, 512, 524,
   535, 590, 611, 615, 616, 643
Heraclitus 295, 319, 391, 393, 405
Herbert, A.P. 158
Herbert, Edward 320
Herbert, Gary 376
Herbert, George 179, 191, 194, 248,
   289, 495
Herodotus 252, 477, 514, 522, 566
Herold, Don 39, 460
Herrick, Robert 81, 114, 186, 272,
   625, 629
Herrigel, Eugene 621
Hersey, John 396
Hershey, Barbara 395, 483
Heschel, Abraham 70, 160, 209
Hesiod 632
Hesse, Herman 62, 253
Hewett, Phillip 159, 288
Heynrichs, Jenny 611
Heyward, Carter 116
Heywood, John 79, 558, 643, 676,
   688
Hickok, Eliza M. 198, 202
Hicks, R.D. 130

Hickson, W.E. 572, 641
Higginson, Thomas W. 72, 680, 698
Hightower, Cullen 170, 497
Hightower, Jim 599
Hildebrand, Kenneth 460
Hildegard of Bingen 156
Hill, Anita 614
Hill, James B. 587
Hill, Napoleon 449, 461, 496, 645
Hillel 233
Hillesum, Etty 83, 156, 482, 496, 644,
   679
Hilliard, Nicholas 351
Hillis, Burton 297
Hillyer, Robert 496, 621
Hindu proverb 28, 117, 119, 147, 173
Hine, Lorraine 197
Hippocrates 199
Hippolytus 135
Hirohito, Emperor 416
Hirsch, Michael 349, 356
Hiscox, E.T. 167
Hitchcock, Alfred 267, 584
Hite, Shere 32, 126, 355
Hobbes, John Oliver 75, 92, 293
Hobbes, Thomas 170, 376
Hodges, Leigh Mitchell 315, 672
Hodgkin, Thomas 670
Hodgson, Ralph 161
Hodnett, Edward 655
Hoffer, Eric 57, 104, 170, 257, 260,
   309, 330, 353, 359, 374, 387, 403,
   444, 446, 491, 502, 593, 670, 676
Hoffman, Abbie 301, 556, 623
Hoffman, Barbara 499
Hoffman, Dustin 91
Hofmann, Hans 265
Holdcroft, L. Thomas 3, 298, 322
Holderlin, Friedrich 49, 452
Holiday, Billie 123, 462
Holland, Isabelle 60
Holland, Josiah G. 199, 260, 682
Holler, William E. 123, 639
Holmes 418
Holmes, Carol 24, 103
Holmes, Dr. J.A. 543
Holmes, Ernest 154, 159, 667
Holmes, John Andrew 100, 117

Holmes, Marjorie 669
Holmes, Oliver Wendell 11, 67, 71,
    130, 133, 142, 158, 169, 170, 228,
    271, 272, 280, 282, 294, 387, 401,
    410, 420, 450, 465, 501, 502, 505,
    541, 577, 606, 634, 640, 644
Holmes Jr., Oliver Wendell 549
Holt, Hamilton 568, 612
Holt, John 545
Holt, Victoria 696
Holtby, Winifred 195, 439, 609
Holtz, Lou 597, 682
Holtzman, Fanny Ellen 249
Holz, Julie 143
Homer 79, 139, 149, 405, 522, 584,
    625
Homoka, Oscar 687
Honda, Soichire 444
Hood, Thomas 321
Hooker, Richard 403
Hooper, Ellen Sturgis 615
Hoover, Herbert 54, 68, 449, 551
Hoover, J. Edgar 209
Hope, Bob 682
Hope, Laurence 54
Hopf, Harry A. 412, 550
Hopi Indian saying 162
Hopper, Grace Murray 394, 432
Horace 35, 55, 57, 62, 71, 79, 80, 86,
    88, 89, 92, 229, 271, 301, 308, 323,
    333, 376, 413, 437, 450, 522, 524,
    525, 532, 553, 557, 684, 685, 689,
    694
Horban, Donald 81
Horne, Lena 703
Horne, Marilyn 348, 446
Horney, Karen 215, 473, 693
Houff, William H. 633
Housman, A.E. 115, 316, 492
Houston, Libby 381
Hovey, Richard 674
Howard, Jane 31, 127, 138, 405
Howe, Edgar Watson 84, 128, 132,
    133, 140, 259, 316, 321, 434, 444,
    454, 488, 490, 498, 502, 534, 555,
    565, 684
Howe, John 270
Howe, Julia Ward 238, 653

Howe, Louise Kapp 96
Howells, W.D. 552
Howland, Bette 38
Hoyle, Fred 670
Huang Po 501
Hubbard, Elbert 31, 63, 71, 113, 120,
    148, 149, 163, 256, 265, 281, 289,
    299, 309, 317, 357, 358, 359, 477,
    482, 491, 552, 558, 570, 580, 606,
    645, 646, 660, 667, 671, 672, 673,
    678, 702
Hubbard, J.G. 633, 645
Hubbard, Kin 33, 59, 81, 362
Hubbard, L. Ron 23, 460, 472, 658
Huber, R.M. 92
Huerta, Dolores 65, 107, 349
Hufstedler, Shirley 514, 668
Hughes, Frank 362
Hughes, Henry Ward 496
Hughes, Langston 382
Hughes, Thomas 128, 691
Hugo, Victor 36, 118, 166, 181, 274,
    318, 377, 461, 509, 539, 630, 681
Hulbert, William A. 438, 575, 576
Hulme, Katheryn 163, 200, 629
Hulst, Maurice 119
Humboldt, Wilhelm von 22, 47, 471
Hume, David 22, 47, 347, 694
Hummell, Charles 305
Humphrey, Hubert H. 77, 297, 422
Humphrey, Muriel 262
Humphreys, Harry E. 128
Hungarian proverb 97
Hungerford, Margaret Wolfe 94
Hunt, Diana Scharf 461
Hunt, Earl G. 180, 204
Hunt, Leigh 321, 696
Hunter, Catfish 365, 441
Hunter, Ian 671
Hunter, Kristin 120, 395
Hurd, Pearl Strachan 238
Hurdle, Clint 434
Hurston, Zora Neale 5, 7, 21, 109,
    116, 122, 252, 489, 504, 678
Hutton, Bettina von 90
Hutton, Lauren 102
Huvelin, Abbé Henri 170
Huxley, Aldous 19, 68, 86, 147, 172,

236, 254, 264, 292, 321, 401, 402, 420, 696
Huxley, Thomas Henry 546, 549, 571, 662

I

Iacocca, Lee 274, 412, 503, 554, 604
Iannelli, Richard 419
Ibarruri, Delores 514
Ibsen, Henrik 6, 430, 458, 575, 598, 674
I Ching 337
Ignatius of Loyola, Saint 624
Iles, George 374
Ilyin, Olga 627, 628
Inchbald, Elizabeth 441
Independent, The 548
Indian proverb 200
Indigo Girls 116
Inge, William Ralph 17, 30, 79, 158, 170, 329, 330, 499, 608
Ingelow, Jean 206
Ingenieros, José 298
Ingersoll, Robert G. 34, 306, 378, 450, 528, 697
International Standard Bible Encyclopedia 210
Ionesco, Eugene 414, 703
Ireland, Kathy 374, 427, 468, 613
Irion, Mary Jean 164
Irish proverb 114, 225, 251, 490, 609
Iron, Mary Jean 67, 328
Irving, John 267, 473
Irving, Washington 392, 457, 603, 676
Irwin, Ben 271
Irwin, William A. 277
Isaiah 6:8 628
Iswolsky, Helene 139
Italian proverb 373, 448, 464
Ivener, Goldie 307
Izzard, Wes 568, 612

J

Jacks, L.P. 350
Jackson, Andrew 529
Jackson, Delma 175
Jackson, Dr. Bill 228
Jackson, Glenda 94

Jackson, Helen Hunt 142, 240, 299, 315, 335, 445, 554
Jackson, Holbrook 9, 18, 432
Jackson, Jesse 314, 378, 624
Jackson, LaToya 95
Jackson, Mahalia 319, 428
Jackson, Reggie 359
Jackson, Robert H. 442
Jacobi, Friedrich 159
Jacobs, Joseph 66
Jakes, John 585
James 4:2 189
James 4:3 189
James, Alice 94, 219, 382, 507
James, Bessie Rowland 100
James, Henry 6, 23, 102, 437, 471, 575
James, P.D. 366
James, Paul Moon 377
James, Sally 31
James, William 21, 55, 127, 129, 150, 154, 172, 204, 232, 329, 340, 342, 359, 387, 400, 414, 418, 420, 422, 426, 473, 482, 484, 511, 549, 550, 555, 578, 582, 682, 693
Jameson, Anna 7, 463, 614
Jameson, Storm 12, 15, 266, 302, 312, 452
Jampolsky, Gerald 59, 64, 317, 400, 421, 625
Janeway, Elizabeth 698
Janis, Byron 358, 481
Japanese proverb 82, 84, 430, 465, 512
Japanese saying 295
Jarvik, Dr. Robert 384, 493
James 1:6 190
James 2:26 168
James 5:11 35
James 5:16 179, 191, 193
Jasefowitz, Natash 577
Javits, Jacob K. 554
Jaworski, Ron 352
Jay, W.M.L. 569
Jayasi, Malik Muhammad 137
Jefferson, Thomas 13, 33, 37, 48, 74, 202, 276, 296, 326, 375, 439, 489, 498, 526, 587, 649

Jenkins, David 153
Jenkyn, William 193
Jennings, Gary 273
Jepson, J.W. 249
Jeremiah 13:23 58
Jeremiah 48:44 485
Jerome, Jerome K. 14
Jerrold, Douglas 32, 90, 136
Jessye, Eva 293
Jewett, Sarah Orne 138, 144, 298, 496, 634
Jewish proverb 535
Jewsbury, Geraldine 651
Ji Kang 293
Jimenel, Juan Ramon 271
Joan of Arc 492, 539
Job 5:7 45
Job 8:7 637
Job 10:21–22 303
Job 11:18 373
Job 14:19 633
Joel, Billy 232, 620
John 14:13 190
John 15:13 151
John, Henry Saint 499
Johnson, Ben 275, 386, 388, 563, 649
Johnson, Edith 670
Johnson, Georgia Douglas 469
Johnson, Lady Bird 355, 359, 486, 607, 701
Johnson, Lyndon B. 320, 326, 539, 629
Johnson, Osa 235
Johnson, Pamela Hansford 620
Johnson, Robert 247
Johnson, Samuel 18, 20, 24, 30, 43, 49, 74, 76, 79, 90, 104, 124, 129, 130, 142, 144, 145, 147, 148, 150, 239, 245, 265, 275, 305, 306, 309, 310, 362, 372, 373, 376, 388, 399, 405, 413, 478, 495, 509, 517, 521, 537, 554, 579, 593, 605, 607, 640, 658, 660, 683, 701, 702, 704
Johnson, Sonia 167, 394, 427, 512, 519, 543, 666
Johnson, Steward B. 574
Johnston, Walter J. 570, 606
Johnston, William J. 400

Johnstone, Margaret B. 277
Jolus, Eugene 274
Joly, Eugene 169
Jonah 2:7 184
Jones, Charles 144
Jones, E. Stanley 491, 504
Jones, Franklin P. 535
Jones, James 455
Jones, John Paul 353, 488
Jones, Margo 351
Jones, Mother 618
Jones, Rufus M. 154
Jones, T. 592
Jong, Erica 58, 98, 121, 183, 260, 283, 405, 423, 434, 485, 486, 511, 516, 531, 539, 643, 652
Joplin, Janis 429, 578
Jordan, David Starr 366, 458, 459
Jordan, Sara 282
Jordaon, Barbara 468
Jordon, Sara 279
Jouber, Joseph 402
Joubert, Joseph 23, 29, 35, 73, 74, 84, 112, 131, 253, 282, 284, 348, 365, 404, 472, 589, 644
Joyce, James 307
Joyner, Florence Griffith 168, 467
Joyner-Kersee, Jackie 29, 42, 462, 594
Judson, Adoniram 201, 203
Julian of Norwich 375
Jung, Carl 39, 40, 50, 55, 56, 173, 214, 453, 480, 509, 656, 670, 678
Jung, Emma 292
Jusserano, Jules 251
Juvenal 22, 194, 444, 479

K

Kaat, Jim 412
Kafka, Franz 9, 433
Kahanamoku, Duke P. 598
Kaiser, Henry J. 69, 657
Kall, Bob 379
Kant, Immanuel 399
Kanteletar, The 135
Kapp, Joe 575
Karol, Lyn 698
Karon, Jan 220
Karr, Alphonse 73, 404

Karras, Alex 527
Kassorla, Irene 549
Kastner, Erich 460
Katz, Ellie 698
Kaufman, Herbert 531, 567, 665
Kaufman, Lois L. 125
Kaufman, Susan 25
Kazan, Elia 511
Keats, John 671, 689
Keble, John 186, 702
Keith, Edwin 210
Keith, Penelope 245
Keller, Helen 4, 22, 35, 37, 38, 41, 51,
    53, 85, 96, 101, 102, 111, 121, 125,
    159, 168, 171, 227, 230, 237, 246,
    248, 281, 324, 334, 343, 350, 352,
    359, 361, 373, 405, 427, 437, 438,
    452, 470, 471, 503, 505, 507, 512,
    514, 516, 518, 538, 570, 573, 576,
    593, 600, 609, 618, 621, 638, 642,
    646, 668, 679, 683, 689, 701
Kelley, Emma Dunham 427
Kelley, Kitty 571
Kelly, Larry 369, 565
Kelty, Mary Ann 25
Kemp, Harry 457
Kemp, Jack 609
Kendall, Donald M. 369, 565
Kenmore, Carolyn 418, 441
Kennedy, Charles 533, 538
Kennedy, Eugene 65
Kennedy, Florynce 276, 549, 696
Kennedy, John F. 275, 372, 376, 390,
    391, 469, 483, 503, 521, 530, 550,
    688
Kennedy, Marilyn Moats 665
Kennedy, Robert F. 514, 566
Kennedy, Rose Fitzgerald 77, 243, 313,
    471
Kenny, Elizabeth 62
Kenny, Sister Elizabeth 271
Kenshin, Uyesugi 516
Kent, Corita 311, 313, 371, 580, 686
Kent, Dorothea 500
Kenyon, E.W. 210
Kerr, Jean 224, 490, 670
Kerrigan, Nancy 482, 506
Ketchel, Holly 116

Kettering, Charles F. 326, 352, 394,
    513, 518, 640, 655, 661, 671, 680
Key, Ellen 35, 467, 682
Keyes, Ken 22, 38, 42, 57, 75, 86, 279,
    307
Kezer, Pauline R. 393
Kiam, Victor 546
Kiemel, Ann 167
Kieran, John 331
Kierkegaard, Søren 16, 19, 137, 167,
    174, 192, 207, 294, 351, 422, 454,
    513, 541, 606
Killebrew, Harmon 458
Kincaid, E. Lamar 645
Kiner, Ralph 515, 566
King, A. Jackson 560
King, Admiral Ernest J. 57
King, Basil 512
King, Billie Jean 215, 261, 483
King, Coretta Scott 584
King, Elizabeth T. 47
King, Guy H. 175
King, Harriet 112
King, Martin Luther 44, 303, 434,
    533, 597, 609, 690
King, Stephen 219, 436, 701
King, William P. 582
Kingsley, Charles 36, 68, 105, 309,
    365, 460, 549
Kingsmill, Hugh 621
Kingsolver, Barbara 17, 31, 382
Kingston, Maxine Hong 580
King Vidor 682
Kipling, Rudyard 158, 312, 673
Kirk, Lisa 238
Kirkland, Gelsey 327
Kirkpatrick, George R. 560
Kirkpatrick, Jeane 110, 509
Kissinger, Henry 93, 413, 416, 454,
    487, 574, 605
Kitselman, A.L. 343, 356
Kitt, Eartha 232
Klassen, William 231
Klauser, Henriette Anne 595
Klein, Allen 489
Kleiser, Grenville 27, 115, 256, 280,
    317, 318, 360, 384, 574, 587, 642,
    677

Klemme, E.J. 504
Klopstock, Friedrich 256
Knapp, Joe 365
Knowlton, Judith M. 540
Knox, E.V. 331
Koashoggi, Adnan 361
Koestler, Arthur 533
Koller, Alice 217, 612, 662
Kollwitz, Kathe 615
Konner, Dr. Melvin 263
Koran 653
Korda, Michael 574
Korey, Lois 490, 535
Kossuth 681
Koufax, Sandy 493
Kozel, Jonathan 408
Kraft, J.L. 201
Krantz, Judith 366, 644
Kraus, Karl 409, 505
Krishnamurti, Jiddu 454, 494, 655
Kristol, Irving 579
Kroc, Ray 436
Krone, Julie 280
Kronenberger, Louis 56, 221
Krutch, Joseph Wood 79, 85, 411, 508
Kubler-Ross, Elisabeth 252, 353, 387, 432, 662, 670
Kubrick, Stanley 419, 552
Kuhlman, Kathryn 171
Kuhn, Maggie 94
Kunin, Madeleine 668
Kupferberg, Tuli 397
Kushner, Rabbi Harold 27, 154, 333
Kwan, Michelle 650

L

L'Amour, Louis 45, 47, 48, 49, 50, 61, 62, 63, 81, 168, 225, 252, 254, 259, 306, 311, 324, 327, 332, 363, 378, 444, 453, 460, 476, 490, 498, 566, 603, 615, 633, 647, 652, 653, 677, 693
L'Engle, Madeleine 215, 243, 449
L'Estrange 412
LaCordaire, Jean Baptiste 129
LaFollette, Suzannea 107
Lagerfeld, Karl 461
Lagerlöf, Selma 445

Lahti, Christine 96
Laidlaw, John 177
Lamartine, Alphonse de 278
Lamb, Charles 136, 272, 534
Lamb, Mary 108
Lamott, Anne 71, 650, 686
Lamport, Felicia 569
Lancaster 195
Landers, Ann 33, 139, 247, 293, 348, 526, 580, 581, 592, 614, 655
Landon, L.E. 111, 293, 365, 544, 681
Landon, Letitia 295, 608
Landor, Walter Savage 45, 52, 81, 135, 145, 306, 446, 459, 598
Landry, Tom 447
Lane, Frank 649, 688
Lane, Rose Wilder 18
Lange, Dorothea 688
Lange, Jessica 627
Langtry, Lillie 296, 614
Lanier, Sidney 266
Lansing, Sherry 602, 639
Lao-tzu 15, 18, 55, 83, 103, 163, 215, 235, 264, 357, 555, 628, 636, 669
Larcom, Lucy 294
Larmour, M.W. 621
Larson, Doug 41, 85, 291
Lasorda, Tommy 251, 582
Latin proverb 74, 80, 89, 147, 252, 272, 370, 399, 412, 421, 516, 590, 613
Laubach, Frank C. 195
Lauder, Estee 640
Lavagetto, Cookie 531, 568
Lavater, Johann Kaspar 273, 281, 312, 533
Lavin, Christine 462
Law, Donald 33
Law, William 78, 155, 176, 199
Lawes, Lewis E. 667
Lawlor, Burt 406
Lawrence, D.H. 123, 271, 303, 327, 330, 366, 418, 421, 422, 525, 527, 626, 702, 703
Lawrence, Hilda 555
Lawrence, T.E. 517, 582, 687
Lawton, C.R. 275
Layne, Bobby 361

La Bruyère, Jean de 26, 118, 132, 270, 277, 304, 358, 360, 581
La Fontaine, Jean de 73, 80, 85, 101, 135, 199, 217, 261, 301, 333, 334, 435, 459, 486, 489, 610, 648, 684
La Rochefoucauld, Francois de 3, 17, 29, 63, 81, 90, 98, 132, 144, 145, 147, 240, 246, 249, 268, 310, 312, 329, 331, 347, 358, 360, 362, 366, 367, 371, 373, 387, 421, 422, 442, 446, 479, 535, 578, 585, 592, 694, 696
Leach, Penelope 486, 535
Leachman, Cloris 617
Leacock, Stephen 270, 383
Leahy, Frank 677, 693
Leavell, Landrum P. 570
Leblanc, Georgette 26, 405
Lebowitz, Fran 99
Lebron, Lolita 687
Lec, Stanislaw 73, 621
Leduc, Violette 428
Lee, Hannah Farnham 79
Lee, Harper 426, 483
Lee, Robert E. 56, 65, 571
Lefevre, Georges 174
LeGuin, Ursula K. 55, 61, 219, 231, 281, 379, 409, 477, 506, 577, 588, 617, 621
Leighton, Robert 198
Lemley, Bill 449
Lemon, Bob 123
Lemons, Abe 620
Lenéru, Marie 231, 238
Lennon, John 57, 479, 503, 544
Lennox, Charlotte 238
Lenzkes, Susan L. 77
Leonardo da Vinci 262, 321, 459, 490, 603, 614, 625, 650, 652
Leopardi, Giacomo 74, 89, 218, 316, 425, 530
Lerner, Harriet 250
Lerner, Max 154, 577
LeRow, Caroline Begelow 235
Lesage, Alain-Rene 28, 85, 348
Leslie, H.T. 697
Lessing, Doris 33, 35, 134, 256, 468, 626

Lessing, Gotthold Ephraim 146, 298
Letterman, Elmer G. 143, 663
Levenson, Sam 276
Leverson, Ada 445
Levi, Peter 374
Levias, Jerry 533
Levinger, George 692
Levinson, Leonard L. 299
Lewin, Kurt 633
Lewis, Anne 200
Lewis, C.S. 148, 165, 186, 190, 197, 203, 315, 325, 335, 392, 469, 521, 628
Lewis, Carol 461
Lewis, H. Bertram 45, 680, 697
Lewisohn, Ludwig 449
Le Corbusier 312
Le Gallienne, Eva 432, 461, 465, 517
Le Sueur, Meridel 65, 297, 440, 470, 616, 653
Lichtenberg, Georg Christoph 54, 79, 253, 286, 398, 399, 473, 524
Liddon, H.P. 235
Liebman, Joshua L. 45, 218, 493
Liederman, David 586
Lilly, John 340
Lima, Lucimar Santos de 352
Lincoln, Abraham 10, 12, 48, 149, 156, 183, 257, 296, 323, 361, 368, 386, 400, 441, 455, 461, 517, 564, 578, 600, 602, 625, 628, 645, 650, 674, 681, 687, 692, 699
Lincoln, Mary Todd 86, 375, 553, 703
Lincoln, Victoria 527
Lind, Jenny 356, 686
Lindberg, Carter 173
Lindbergh, Anne Morrow 79, 112, 131, 215, 243, 276, 394, 397, 409, 428, 508, 527, 531, 568, 617, 634, 669
Lindbergh, Charles 371
Lindquist, Raymond 528
Lindsay, Gordon 207
Lindsay, Vachel 396
Lindsey, Hal 373
Lingsley, Charles 606
Link, Henry 491
Lin Yutang 3, 22, 54, 217, 230, 265,

353, 363, 376, 451, 497

Linz, Phil 556

Lippman, Walter 581, 616

Lipson, Benjamin 525, 673

Litchfield, Paul W. 272

Liter, James 605

Littre, Emile 275

Lively, Penelope 617, 618

Livingstone, Belle 232

Livingstone, Sir Richard 413

Livy 522, 637

Lloyd, Chris Evert 670

Lloyd, Marie 235

Lloyd, Robert 645

Lock, William J. 464, 524, 657

Locke, John 73, 400, 491, 659

Locke, William J. 23, 472

Lockyer, Herbert 185, 193

Loeb, Sophie Irene 132

Logan, Joshua 267

Lomask, Milton 426

Lombardi, Vince 248, 266, 350, 367, 571, 633

London, Jack 271, 473

Long, Nancy 167

Long, Shelley 572

Longfellow, Henry Wadsworth 45, 114, 143, 166, 225, 289, 293, 296, 303, 305, 307, 316, 320, 321, 325, 332, 336, 337, 377, 386, 390, 467, 485, 529, 533, 550, 555, 572, 614, 634, 638, 641, 643, 645, 679, 692

Longworth, Alice Roosevelt 262, 263, 596

Lopez, Nancy 520

Lord, Bette Bao 627

Lord, Shirley 243, 436

Lorde, Audre 61, 223, 381, 488, 492, 535, 553

Loren, Sophia 243, 252, 387, 597, 659

Lorimer, George Claude 546

Lorimer, George Horace 530, 567, 666

Loughrane, John P. 233, 544

Louis, Joe 659

Louis XIV 234

Loukes, Harold 582, 625

Lover, Samuel 254

Lowe, Watterson 370

Lowell, Amy 9

Lowell, James Russell 52, 67, 158, 160, 169, 173, 207, 287, 313, 314, 391, 393, 402, 415, 428, 469, 498, 533, 549, 578, 586, 635, 691

Lubbock, John 134, 496, 513

Lucan 324, 346, 482, 702

Lucas, E.V. 38

Lucas, F.L. 367

Luce, Clare Boothe 17, 101, 280, 375, 521, 643, 656

Luchies, Vernon 76

Luckman, Charles 561

Lucretius 81, 644

Ludwig, Emil 141

Luke 16:10 636

Luke 17:21 155

Luke 18:27 157

Luke 22:44 183

Luly, John 632

Lund, Doris 433

Lunden, Joan 254, 342

Lupton, D. 136

Lush, Jean 218

Luther, Martin 64, 155, 158, 168, 178, 181, 182, 188, 209, 333, 428, 442

Luxemburg, Rosa 226, 670

Luzzatto, Moses 63

Lye, Thomas 212

Lynch, John W. 289

Lynd, Helen Merrell 429, 460

Lynd, Robert 134

Lyon, Mary 480, 624

Lyons, Jimmy 325

Lyons, Kay 305

M

Mabie, Hamilton Wright 420

MacArthur, General Douglas 369, 370, 507, 518, 530, 564, 595, 598

Macaulay, Rose 263, 501

MacDonald, Betty 235

MacDonald, George 3, 66, 155, 168, 202, 270, 275, 325, 326, 488

MacDonald, John D. 127

MacEwan, Norman 28, 118, 669

Machado, Antonio 89, 396, 506

Machiavelli, Niccolo 251, 405, 407,

408, 440, 480, 509, 512, 543
Machlowitz, Marilyn 612
MacInness, Helen 330
MacIver, Robert 392
Mack, Connie 692
Mackay, Charles 635
Mackintosh 84
MacLaine, Shirley 61, 159, 167, 349,
360, 392, 395, 402, 425, 478, 508
Maclean, J.K. 179, 204, 205
MacMillan, Harold 511
MacMurray, John 169
MacNaughton, John 102
MacNeil, Malcolm F. 668
MacPhail, Agnes 251
Macquarrie, John 169
Madame Chiang Kai-Shek 17, 196,
208, 294
Madgett, Naomi Long 627
Madonna 247, 469, 470
Maeterlinck, Maurice 29, 42, 116,
229, 300, 309, 325, 346, 347, 348,
450, 498, 529
Magee, Bishop W.C. 660
Magoon, Elias L. 107
Mahan, Henry T. 175
Maharshi, Ramana 573, 642
Mailer, Norman 329, 479
Maintenon, Madame Dde 117
Makeba, Miriam 111
Malamud, Bernard 268, 386
Malay proverb 358, 482
Malesherbez, C. 368, 564
Mallet-Joris, Françoise 168, 526
Mallett, David 683
Malloch, Douglas 340, 537
Mallory, G.H.L. 447
Malloy, Merrit 628
Malraux, André 519
Maltz, Maxwell 233, 343, 355, 359,
529
Mandel, Evelyn 426, 431
Manilius 309
Mankiller, Wilma Pearl 231, 468
Manley, Joan 627
Manley, Mary Delarivière 60
Mann, Horace 23, 275, 281, 284, 411,
471

Mann, Phillip 492
Mann, Thomas 216, 335
Mannes, Marya 63, 76, 102, 113, 240,
313, 353, 419
Mansfield, Katherine 48, 56, 135, 138,
221, 293, 334, 343, 405, 441, 463,
519, 525, 602, 652, 664, 698
Mansfield, Mike 499
Manton, Thomas 191, 202, 207
Mao Tse-Tung 267
Marbury, Elizabeth 8, 136
Marden, Orison Swett 46, 108, 346,
375, 378, 673
Margareth II 365
Margaret of Cortona, Saint 603
Maribel, Mother 628
Marie of Rumania, Queen 602
Marion, Frances 462
Maritain, Jacques 605
Mark 1:35 182
Mark 11:24 202
Markham, Beryl 217, 659
Markham, Edwin 157, 319, 407
Markoe, Merrill 223
Marquez, Gabriel Garcia 291, 454
Marquis, Don 6, 39, 40, 70, 128, 284,
294, 331, 421, 466
Marryat, Frederick 251
Marshall, Catharine 44, 57, 65, 349,
562, 686
Marshall, Paule 216, 657
Marshall, Rosamond 32
Marshall, S.L.A. 483
Marston, William M. 669
Martial 87, 227, 228, 278, 301, 305,
306, 429
Martin, Billy 652
Martin, C.D. 176
Martin, Judith 241, 614
Martin, Labiche et 129
Martin, Martha 139
Martin, Sir Theodore 21, 30
Martineau, Harriet 30, 235, 302, 372,
633
Martineau, James 175
Marty, Martin 378, 704
Marx, Karl 396
Mary Paul, Sister 278

Masefield, John 35
Maskin, J. Robert 78
Maslow, Abraham 307, 435, 438, 483, 576
Mason, Jackie 96
Mason, John 273
Mason, Martha 136
Massie, Suzanne 119, 683
Massieu, Jean Baptiste 78
Massinger, Philip 138, 237
Masson, Thomas L. 253
Mather, Cotton 596
Mather, Increase 476
Matheson, George 639
Matthew 6:6 185
Matthew 6:11–12 65
Matthew 6:24 413, 464
Matthew 6:27 495
Matthew 6:34 496
Matthew 7:1 64
Matthew 7:7 189
Matthew 10:22 648
Matthew 14:31 166
Matthew 25:4 434
Mathewson, Christy 590, 684
Matthews, William 69, 83, 594, 605
Maturin, Basil W. 442
Maugham, W. Somerset 50, 84, 262, 313, 402, 435, 453, 502, 570
Maupassant, Guy de 268
Maurice, Frederick Denison 185
Maurois, André 11, 35, 296, 463, 487, 513, 607, 701
Maxwell, Elaine 261
Maxwell, Elsa 102
Maxwell, Gilbert 333
Maxwell, Lady 175
May, Gerald G. 628
May, Rollo 62, 309, 395, 419, 425, 521, 528, 534, 537, 699
Mayer, Maria Goeppert 468, 612
Mayo, Charles W. 494
Mays, Benjamin 457, 467
Mays, Willie 280, 573, 641
McBride, Angela Barron 406
McCabe, Edward 352, 554, 664
McCant, Jerry W. 3
McCarthy, Mary 377

McCartney, Paul 363
McCormick, Anne O'Hare 412
McCracken, Robert J. 19, 116, 531
McCullough, Colleen 94
McDonald, Claude 514, 566
McEnroe, John 671
McFee, William 367, 453, 480, 587, 625
McGill, William 177
McGinley, Phyllis 108, 220, 236, 397, 578, 597
McGinnis, Allen Reid 55
McGinnis, Mack 232
McGranahan, Norvin G. 216
McGraw, John 525
McGraw, Tug 271, 332, 607
McGuane, Thomas 590, 608
McGuirk, John J. 562
McHugh, Neal 359
McIndoe, Sir Archibald 563
McIntosh, Joan 15
McIntosh, M.C. 30, 54
McIntyre, D.M. 179
McKay, John 663
McKenna, Stephen 426, 460, 468, 605
McLaughlin, Mignon 36, 52, 76, 133, 218, 254, 313, 402, 448, 538, 539, 597, 613, 696
McLuhan, Marshall 134
McRarie family 551
McSorely, Joseph 303
McWilliams, Peter 119
Meacock, Norma 335
Mead, Margaret 98, 237, 355, 580, 610, 622
Meador, Douglas 203
Meir, Golda 69, 92, 94, 216, 220, 274, 349, 397, 463, 687
Melanchthon, Philipp 169, 175, 184
Melba, Nellie 622
Melchart, Harold B. 279
Mellencamp, John 493, 498
Melville, Herman 101, 186, 660
Menander 261, 609
Mencius 365
Mencken, H.L. 39, 42, 303, 493, 509
Menclus 149
Mendel, Menachem 212

Mendelssohn, Moses 288
Mendenhall, Dorothy Reed 309, 595
Menninger, Dr. Karl 231, 373, 376, 482
Menninger, Dr. William 258, 330
Menuhin, Hephzibah 255
Mercer, Bobby 412, 544
Mercier, A.T. 572, 641
Meredith, George 186, 195, 201, 350, 429, 502, 590, 686
Meredith, Owen 464, 502
Merici, Angela 113, 447, 677
Merrick, James 194
Merrill, Bradford 444
Merrill, William P. 457
Merton, Thomas 157, 247, 407, 488, 541, 630, 703
Metastasio, Pietro 91, 514, 566
Metchnikoff, Elie 482, 487, 498
Meyer, Agnes 298, 387
Meyer, F.B. 202, 204
Meyer, Ron 476
Meynell, Alice 29, 347, 395, 399
Michelangelo 163, 245, 336
Michener, James A. 48, 524, 535, 589, 697
Midler, Bette 226, 436
Mikulski, Barbara 469
Milburn, John F. 446, 478
Milk, Harvey 373
Mill, John Stuart 38, 40, 81
Millay, Edna Saint Vincent 151, 155, 171, 520, 526, 598, 677
Miller, Alice Duer 99, 102, 135
Miller, Arthur 303
Miller, Bud 434
Miller, Denny 26
Miller, Donald A. 579
Miller, Henry 3, 46, 255, 270, 353, 386, 418, 424, 507, 508, 523, 550, 555, 587, 600, 653
Miller, Joaquin 378, 653
Miller, John Homer 696
Miller, Olin 502
Millhuff, Charles 407
Millman, Dan 75
Milnes, Richard M. 174
Milton, John 239, 246, 247, 289, 347,

375, 551, 694
Minab, Sandor 281
Mindess, Harvey 58
Mingus, Charles 264
Minna Antrim 109
Miro, Joan 268
Mirrielees, Edith Ronald 540, 637
Miss Piggy 235
Mistletoe, John 423
Mitchell, Donald G. 326, 623
Mitchell, Margaret 51, 88, 253, 258, 276, 689
Mitchell, Maria 219, 233, 283, 387
Mitchell, S. Weir 144
Mitchison, Naomi 569
Mitford, Jessica 679
Mitford, Mary Russell 122
Mizner, Wilson 143, 199
Moliere 134, 360, 401, 425, 517, 525, 552, 687
Molly Yard 244
Monaghan, Tom 495
Monash, General Sir John 140, 598
Monroe, Anne Shannon 526, 645
Monroe, Marilyn 33
Montagne, Samuel 619
Montagu, Ashley 437, 623
Montagu, Lady Mary Wortley 417, 687
Montaigne, Michel de 39, 46, 54, 86, 89, 116, 148, 200, 222, 228, 236, 261, 288, 335, 358, 376, 402, 429, 443, 455, 457, 459, 460, 477, 480, 499, 528, 534, 652, 666, 690, 694, 696
Montalvo, Juan 599
Montesquieu, Charles de 10, 97, 571, 574, 641
Montessori, Maria 108, 109, 616
Montgomery, James 178, 187, 209, 288
Montgomery, L.M. 235, 362, 448, 495, 563, 588
Moodie, Susanna 677
Moody, Dwight L. 186, 196, 198, 199, 202, 211, 223, 605
Moore, Archie 650
Moore, George 285, 407, 695

Moore, Hannah 142, 238, 368, 512, 547
Moore, Henry 317, 318, 320, 364, 425, 547, 589, 683
Moore, Marianne 61, 115, 163, 166, 218, 235, 236
Moore, Mary Tyler 665, 688
Moore, Olive 61
Moorehead, Robert 603
Moorish proverb 479
More, Hannah 187, 459
Moreau, Jeanne 6, 63, 581, 582
Moreland, John Richard 188
Morely, Christopher 458
Morgan, Charles L. 37, 392
Morgan, Julia 609
Morgan, Marlo 397
Morgan, Robin 141
Morgenstern, Christian 364
Morley, Christopher 13, 289, 408, 437, 573, 575, 642
Morley, J. Kenfield 13, 695
Morley, John 229, 268, 451, 473
Morley, Viscount 263, 281, 393
Moroccan proverb 133
Morrison, Jim 56
Morrison, Toni 438, 615, 629, 639
Morrow, Elizabeth Cutter 131
Mortman, Doris 85, 233
Moses, Grandma 21, 103, 285, 299, 595
Moses, Robert 398
Moses, Yula 548
Mosheim, Johann L. von 92
Moskos, Charles E. 267, 455
Moss, Richard 627
Moss, Stirling 511
Mother Jones 571
Motto of the Benedictine Order 211
Motto of the United States 157
Mueller, George 207
Mueller, Walter A. 184
Muhlenberg, General Peter 200, 625
Muir, John 131
Mulford, Prentice 118
Muller, Robert 64
Mumford, Ethel Watts 140, 275, 614
Mumford, Lewis 410

Muncey, Bill 688
Munro, Alice 103
Munson, Gorham 658
Munthe, Axel 228
Murasaki, Lady 585
Murcer, Bobby 554, 595
Murdoch, Iris 336
Muresell, James L. 500
Murphy, Thomas P. 273
Murray, Andrew 178, 181, 182, 183, 184, 192, 198, 203, 205
Murray, Gilbert 316
Murray, Kathryn 229, 284
Murray, Pauli 377
Murray, W.H. 541, 602
Murrow, Edward R. 489
Musial, Stan 361
Musset, Alfred de 619
Muzzey, David S. 170
Myers, Isabel Briggs 111
Myers, Joyce A. 83
Myerson, Bess 599
Myrdal, Alva Reimer 648

N

Naden, Constance 692
Namath, Joe 266, 598
Nansen, Firdtjof 295
Napolitano, Johnette 296, 628
Nash, Constantine 555
Nash, N. Richard 169
Nash, Ogden 91, 139, 295
Nathan, George Jean 150, 363, 661
Nathan, Robert 70
Navratilova, Martina 466, 564
Naylor, Gloria 127, 141
NcNabb, Vincent 375
Necker, Madame 158, 691
Nee, Watchman 176
Needham, Richard J. 206
Neel, Alice 163
Nehru, Jawaharlal 392, 407, 446, 476, 478, 525, 552, 673, 683, 697
Neicoll, W. Robertson 298
Neihardt, John G. 534
Neilen, A. 27, 118
Nelms, Cynthia 377
Nelson, Donald M. 403

Nelson, Harriet Uts 64
Nelson, Horatio 502, 519
Nelson, Mariah Burton 56, 514
Nelson, Richard H. 296
Nelson, Willie 700
Nerval, Gerard de 148
Nerys, Major Kira 164
Neuharth, Allen H. 491, 670
Nevelson, Louise 55, 433, 454, 540, 599, 612
Neville, Robert 620
Newbern, John W. 304
Newcomb, Charles B. 167, 256, 350, 492
Newell, Arlo F. 190
New England Sampler 191
Newhart, Bob 6
Newhouse, Flower A. 673
Newman, Ernest 371
Newman, John Henry Cardinal 165, 167, 391, 410, 420, 484, 501, 503, 511, 517, 537, 558, 619, 624
Newman, Mildred 355
Newton, A. Edward 21, 31
Newton, Frances 480
Newton, Huey 653
Newton, Isaac 604
Newton, John 176, 189, 202, 211, 305
Newton, Joseph Fort 75
Nicholas, Ben 286, 413, 554
Nichols, Dudley 491
Nichols, Mike 491, 509
Nicklaus, Jack 442
Niebuhr, Reinhold 44, 63, 169, 405, 536, 690
Nielsen, Helen 241, 494
Nietzsche, Friedrich 69, 130, 134, 147, 284, 291, 328, 330, 373, 400, 415, 441, 457, 458, 482, 522, 532, 632, 661
Nigerian proverb 143
Nightingale, Florence 355, 404, 477, 479, 551, 680
Nimitz, Admiral Chester W. 195, 527, 653
Nin, Anaïs 5, 115, 124, 127, 133, 142, 220, 224, 232, 238, 296, 403, 405, 425, 430, 484, 511, 523, 530, 586, 638, 694
Nixon, Patricia 446
Noble, Charles C. 458, 459, 665
Noll, Chuck 34, 51, 577
Nordenholt, George F. 637, 656
Norman, Jessye 572
Norman, Marsha 662
Norris, Kathleen 45, 60, 62, 127, 150, 381, 392, 470, 691, 696
Northcote, James 483, 673
Norto, Isabelle 149
Norton, Eleanor Holmes 663
Norwegian proverb 535
Novak, Michael 421
Nyad, Diana 514

O

O'Brien, Edna 405, 622
O'Connor, Flannery 53, 219, 243, 286, 417, 433, 449, 668
O'Connor, Sandra Day 127, 557
O'Connor, Tom 361, 362, 441, 697, 703
O'Donnell, Bridget 590
O'Donnell, Rosie 220, 463
O'Hara, Mary 516
O'Hara, Scarlett 324
O'Keefe, Georgia 298, 531
O'Malley, Austin 144, 183
O'Neil, Nena 431
O'Neil, Rose 514
O'Neill, Eugene 6, 305, 307
O'Neill, William L. 514, 566
O'Reilly, Jane 241
O'Relling, Max 587
O'Shaughnessy, Arthur 440
Oakley, Virginia 555
Oates, Joyce Carol 94, 312, 379, 473, 555, 585
Ocampo, Victoria 603
Odell, Joseph H. 527, 667
Ogburn, Charlton 36, 49, 89, 450, 502, 553
Ohba, Minako 61
Ojibway dream song 703
Okakura Kakuzo 47
Old Eskimo proverb 302
Old German proverb 44, 255, 522

Olford, Stephen 539
Oliphant, Margaret 234
Olivier, Sir Laurence 264, 364, 544, 620
Olmedo, José Joaquin 372
Olsen, Merlin 441
Olsen, Tillie 133, 436
On an old inn 195
Onassis, Jacqueline Kennedy 101, 140, 238, 457, 681
On Hope 119
Ono, Yoko 696
Oppenheimer, J. Robert 661
Optimist, The 149
Orben, Robert 375
Orczy, Baroness 314
Ortega y Gasset, José 49, 228, 294, 308, 399, 407, 430, 438, 458, 469, 575, 675
Ortese, Anna Maria 490
Orwell, George 306, 439, 535, 540, 619
Osborne, Joan 163
Osler, Sir William 321, 406, 546, 561
Osmond, Marie 685, 699
Otto, Herbert 255
Otto, Louise 382
Ouida 8, 32, 133, 134, 235, 373, 443, 582, 682
Oursler, Fulton 297, 422
Overstreet, Bonaro 115, 223, 489, 695
Overstreet, Harry A. 478, 606
Ovid 20, 57, 73, 74, 137, 286, 289, 290, 291, 322, 391, 454, 499, 512, 522, 529, 589, 593, 598, 643
Owen, John 186
Oxenham, John 322
Oxenhorn, Harvey 45, 450, 693
Ozick, Cynthia 68, 71, 95, 108, 221, 380, 425, 518

P

Packe, Paul C. 562
Packwood, Robert 295
Paddleford, Clementine 261, 603, 654
Page, Geraldine 544
Paige, Satchel 184, 296, 443
Paine, Thomas 20, 428, 517, 658, 687, 691

Pakuda, Joseph Ibn 288
Palatine of Posnan, The 519
Paley, Barbara 683
Paley, Grace 108, 362, 694
Palladas 450
Pallotti, Saint Vincent 439
Palmer, Arnold 436, 604
Palmer, Charles 307
Palmer, Clara 204
Palmer, Gretta Brooker 118
Palmer, Laura 295, 306
Paltrow, Gwyneth 340, 385
Panchatantra, The 83, 146, 570
Pandit, Vijaya Lakshmi 538
Panin, Nikita Ivanovich 94
Pankhurst, Christabel 219, 618
Pankhurst, Emmeline 105, 519, 602
Pankhurst, Sylvia 219
Panuthos, K. 620
Parent, Gail 34
Park, Eva Rose 101
Parker, Dorothy 138, 141, 519, 545, 613
Parker, Helen Barker 123, 124
Parker, Ida White 569
Parker, Maude 61
Parker, Paul 477
Parker, Robert B. 232
Parker, S.N. 359
Parker, Seth 118
Parkhurst, C.H. 457, 460
Parks, Rosa 617
Parmenter, Ross 379
Parr, Ellen 330
Parton, Dolly 432, 649, 688
Partridge, Frances 218
Pascal, Blaise 5, 9, 27, 39, 91, 134, 154, 162, 165, 166, 172, 207, 208, 281, 308, 310, 393, 401, 408, 420, 422, 431, 443, 445, 502, 577, 623, 674, 694, 696
Pastan, Linda 675
Pasteur, Louis 423, 573, 589, 640, 642
Pastrano, Willie 433
Pater, Walter 369, 564
Paterno, Joe 579
Paterson, Katherine 341, 377, 485

Paterson, Sir Alexander 440
Paton, Alan 454, 472, 478, 625
Patri, Angelo 428
Patrick, John 678
Patterson, John H. 272, 402
Patton, General George S. 247, 267,
    370, 408, 473, 476, 492, 515, 519,
    533, 537, 541, 600, 601, 646
Paul, Alice 618, 643
Pauley, Jane 668
Paulus, Trina 397
Pavarotti, Luciano 606
Pavese, Cesare 227, 311, 431, 558
Pavlova, Anna 7, 463, 612, 640
Paz, Octavio 288
Peabody, Josephine Preston 105
Peale, Anna Delaney 205, 346, 629
Peale, Charles Clifford 46
Peale, Norman Vincent 43, 57, 66,
    177, 199, 347, 357, 633, 637
Peale, Robert C. 261
Peale, Ruth Stafford 200, 560, 562
Pearson, Carol 398, 678
Pearson, Roy M. 203
Peck, M. Scott 263, 524, 677
Peck, William M. 316
Peebles, Melvin 494
Peguy, Charles 268, 492
Peirce, Charles Sanders 51, 176, 419,
    553
Pendergrass, Teddy 456
Penn, William 85, 98, 103, 128, 129,
    194, 284, 289, 346, 680
Penn-Lewis, Jessie 175
Penney, J.C. 683
Pepys, Samuel 183
Perelman, S.J. 266, 466
Peretz, Isaac L. 289
Perez, Rosie 652
Pericles 288
Perlman, Alfred Edward 396
Perón, Eva 113, 417
Perret, Gene 699
Perry, Anne 410
Perry, Gaylord 250
Perse, Saint John 331, 550
Persian proverb 97, 149, 431, 586
Peter, Irene 399, 542, 544

Peter, Laurence J. 132, 411
Peters, Ellis 526, 686
Petersen, James 324, 480
Peterson, Tom 227, 431
Pethick-Lawrence, Emmeline 540
Petit-Senn, J. 75, 151
Petro, Mary-Ann 78
Petronius 377
Pfeiffer, Jane Cahill 674
Phean, Luella F. 244
Phelps, Austin 211, 593
Phelps, Elizabeth Stuart 250, 256, 457,
    637
Phelps, William Lyon 29, 40, 42, 68,
    328, 348, 435, 484, 611
Phil, Sidney J. 251
Philippians 3:13–14 605
Philippians 4:6 189
Philips, Wendell 541
Phillippus 534
Phillips, Bum 251, 252
Phillips, Frederick 593, 681
Phillips, Wally 360
Phillips, Wendell 412, 549, 553, 670
Picard, Max 208
Picasso, Pablo 142, 438, 575
Pickford, Mary 295, 317, 587, 661,
    664, 667
Pierce, Frederick 383
Pierce, John 443
Piercy, Marge 8, 71, 130, 360, 410,
    446, 611, 616, 619, 638, 682
Pike, James A. 231
Pilgrim, Peace 17, 109, 116, 343, 351,
    569
Pincus, Lily 650
Pindar 51, 75, 217, 227, 230, 332,
    335, 391, 429, 434, 451, 555, 630
Pinero, Arthur Wing 325
Pink, A.W. 189
Pirandello, Luigi 23, 232, 401, 423,
    439, 440, 458, 471, 599
Pirsig, Robert M. 253, 310, 433, 577
Pittacus 274, 592
Platford, Lois 513
Plato 11, 103, 215, 256, 288, 434,
    443, 444, 533, 537, 555, 605
Plato, Ann 103, 108

Plautus 74, 123, 151, 234, 337, 473, 528, 529, 537, 538, 546, 642, 698
Pletcher, Barbara 29
Plies, Dan 184
Pliny 287, 374, 481, 503, 619
Plumer, William S. 185, 193, 200, 203
Plutarch 56, 137, 286, 288, 303, 386, 456, 523, 588, 632, 660, 670, 684
Poe, Edgar Allan 41, 343, 437, 679
Pogrebin, Letty Cottin 133, 141, 448, 609, 620
Polanski, Roman 675
Poling, Daniel A. 184
Polish proverb 621
Polite, Carlene Hatcher 391
Pollock, Channing 37, 80, 240, 594
Polybius 647
Ponder, Catherine 60, 64, 445, 594
Poole, Mary Pettibone 105, 143, 243
Poole, William 203
Popcorn, Faith 576
Pope, Alexander 10, 66, 91, 113, 124, 377, 632, 659
Pope, Candice M. 341
Pope Leo X 52
Pope Pius XI 404
Porizkova, Paulina 95
Porteous, Beilby 324, 480
Porter, Catherine 60
Porter, Eleanor H. 109, 127, 445
Porter, Jane 28
Porter, Katherine Anne 335, 468, 482
Porter, Sylvia 443, 607
Portuguese proverb 291, 465
Post, Emily 15, 246, 286, 388
Potter, Alice 343
Potter, Beatrix 355, 627
Powell, General Colin L. 561
Powell, John 381, 470, 526
Powell, Sidney 117
Powell, Vavasor 207
Power, Thomas S. 267
Powers, David Guy 315
Powers, Jessica 318
Powers, Llewelyn 6, 420
Powter, Susan 356
Poyer, Joe 589
Prather, Hugh 121, 190, 230, 233,
301, 308, 312, 331, 390, 452, 620, 621, 669, 685
Prayer Card 155
Prayer from the North Woods 192
Prazlin, Duchess 126
Prejean, Helen 60
Preminger, Otto 516
Prentice, George 104
Prentiss, Elizabeth 437, 615
Presley, Priscilla 93
Presnall, Lewis F. 645
Preston, Margaret Junkin 74, 577
Pretty-Shield 521
Price, Leontyne 227, 317, 432, 581, 602
Priest, Ivy Baker 25, 32, 334, 503, 592, 618
Priestly, J.B. 315
Prince 34, 580
Prince Phillip of England 393
Prior, Matthew 374
Priscian 135
Prochnow, Herbert B. 414, 660
Proctor, Adelaide 236, 296, 325, 380, 627
Proctor, Barbara 665
Propertius 469
Proulx, E. Annie 679
Proust, Marcel 274, 287, 299, 396, 399, 411, 464, 679, 682
Proverbs 3:5 630
Proverbs 3:5–6 157
Proverbs 10:27 5
Proverbs 14:21 27, 118
Proverbs 17:4 136
Proverbs 24:16 650, 660
Proverbs 25:28 235
Proverbs 26:27 355
Proverbs 27:6 140
Proverbs 27:10 143
Proverbs 27:17 150
Proverbs 29:18 384
Psalms 5:3 182
Psalms 20:1–2 203
Psalms 21:1–2 203
Psalms 25:4–5 196
Psalms 30:5 314
Psalms 34:4 489
Psalms 36:1–2 488

Psalms 39:7 303, 554
Psalms 51:10 197
Psalms 55:17 180
Psalms 55:22 198, 629
Psalms 61:1 190
Psalms 90:12 271
Psalms 95:2 192
Psalms 102:17 184
Psalms 104:23 282
Psalms 118:8 629
Psalms 118:24 302, 328
Psalms 139:23–24 187
Psalms 143:8 182
Puller, General Lewis "Chesty" 267
Punshion, William M. 465, 472, 561
Purana, Garuda 11, 258
Purdy, Lawson 667
Purkiser, W.T. 78
Pusey, E.B. 203
Pushkin, Aleksandr 48
Putnam, Vi 27, 121
Putney, Mary Jo 297
Pyle, Ernie 58
Pyrrhus 580
Pythagoras 286, 407, 429

Q

Quarles, Francis 148, 185, 320, 556, 680
Queen Latifah 536
Quindlen, Anna 31, 620
Quinn, Jane Bryant 501
Quinn, Reverend Vaughan 623
Quintilian 607
Quisenberry, Dan 326

R

Raabe, Amy R. 26
Rabelais, Francois 89
Rabutin-Chantal, Marie de 125, 136, 151Sevigne, Marquise de
Racan, Marquis de 591
Racine, Jean 168
Rader, Doug 410
Radford, Arthur 410
Radiguet, Raymond 286
Radner, Gilda 501
Raine, Kathleen 413

Raleigh, Sir Walter 229, 450
Rambert, Marie 120
Ramsey, Arthur M. 169
Ramuz, C.F. 54, 81
Rand, Ayn 20, 42, 347, 351, 386, 595, 672
Rangell, Leo 494
Rank, Beata 385
Rankin, Diana 382, 636
Rankin, Jeannette 466, 516, 617, 624, 656
Raper, John W. 702
Raquel Welch 244
Rathbone, Josephine 14
Rattlesnake 333
Raven, Arlene 246, 347
Rawlings, Marjorie Kinnan 684
Rawls, Robert 508, 516
Ray, Marie Beynon 313, 370, 547
Ray, Sondra 233
Reading, Lady Stella 450
Reagan, Nancy 684
Reagan, Ronald 317
Reagon, Bernice Johnson 398, 618
Reardon, Daniel L. 352, 577
Redpath, Alan 199
Reece, Gabrielle 150
Reed, Charles 270
Reed, Myrtle 234, 238, 392
Reed, Scott 460
Rees, George E. 211
Rees, Paul 178
Reese, Charley 98
Reeves, George 362
Register, Dean 207
Regnard, Jean Francois 80
Rehrat, Arthur J. 61
Reid, Thomas 153, 604
Reik, Theodor 13
Reiland, Karl 26, 118
Renan, Ernest 165
Renard, Jules 258, 330
Renault, Mary 61
Reno, Janet 355, 569
Repplier, Agnes 6, 8, 16, 28, 42, 50, 258, 350, 434, 437, 561, 673, 699
Reston, James 464, 498, 670
Retton, Mary Lou 215

Retz, Cardinal de 477, 513, 571, 663
Revelation 2:10 172
Reynolds, Sir Joshua 262
Rhoades, Winifred 701
Rhodesian proverb 464
Rhys, Jean 225
Ribble, Margaret A. 423
Rice, Alice Caldwell 495, 628
Rice, Anne 42, 479
Rich, Adrienne 106, 216, 219, 313, 405, 618
Richards, Ann 108, 295, 385
Richards, Beah 675
Richards, Charles 273
Richards, Mary Caroline 417, 631, 648
Richardson 681
Richardson, Dorothy Miller 627
Richelsen, John 128, 357
Richler, Mordecai 281, 644
Richter, Gisela 672
Richter, Jean Paul 64, 154
Rickaby, Joseph 265, 524, 606, 657
Rickenbacker, Eddie 346, 352, 534
Rickey, Branch 589, 607
Ridler, Anne 31
Rieger, W.N. 70
Riemer, Jack 624
Riesman, David 425
Riggs, Donald 560
Riis, Jacob A. 359, 631, 644
Riley, James Whitcomb 52, 336, 337, 357
Riley, Pat 407, 442
Rilke, Rainer Maria 93, 247, 258, 271, 329, 334, 396, 487, 545, 549
Rimbaud, Arthur 171, 648
Rinehart, Mary Roberts 27, 631
Ripley, Alexandra 293
Ristad, Eloise 483
Rittenhouse, Jessie 158
Rivers, Joan 244, 245
Rizzuto, Phil 621
Road sign in upstate New York 416
RoAne, Susan 357, 516, 563
Robbins, Howard Chandler 211
Robbins, Tom 38
Robert Louis Stevenson 69

Roberts, Bernadette 37
Roberts, Cokie 139
Roberts, Jane 232
Robertson, Frederick W. 242, 575, 626, 661, 666, 684
Robertson, Jeanne 664
Robinson, Corinne Roosevelt 6, 123
Robinson, Diana 208
Robinson, Edwin Arlington 172, 399
Robinson, Haddon W. 500
Robinson, James Harvey 527
Robinson, Jill 468, 610
Robinson, Margaret A. 657
Robinson, Marilynne 127
Robinson, Mary F. 237
Robson, Dame Flora 199, 260
Robson, George 266
Roche, Arthur Somers 481, 496
Roche, Sir Bayle 671, 684
Rochlin, Harriet 698
Rockefeller III, John D. 29, 435, 608
Rockne, Knute 660
Roddick, Anita 581
Rodin, Auguste 671
Rodman, Frances 536
Roethke, Theodore 410, 544
Rogers, Carl 396
Rogers, Gary 37
Rogers, Ginger 614
Rogers, Will 101, 284, 438, 544, 547, 576, 624
Rolland, Romain 51, 230, 451, 453
Romans 5:3–4 652
Romans 8:26 195
Romans 15:13 374
Rommel, Field Marshal Erwin 444, 464, 530, 540
Romulo, Carlos P. 123
Ronsard, Pierre de 302
Ronstadt, Linda 470
Rood, Ronald 482
Rooney, Andy 25, 635
Roosevelt, Eleanor 6, 12, 19, 88, 119, 149, 217, 222, 225, 230, 241, 250, 253, 326, 341, 382, 404, 407, 417, 426, 430, 432, 447, 448, 449, 473, 485, 540, 550, 551, 599, 601, 636, 652, 660, 663, 680

Roosevelt, Franklin Delano 23, 166, 197, 265, 325, 472, 477, 505, 551, 646

Roosevelt, Theodore 197, 225, 265, 280, 484, 515, 553, 562, 567, 661

Roosman, Colonel John S. 331, 528

Root, E. Merrill 31

Root, Elihu 647, 667

Rorem, Ned 132, 620

Rose, Pete 267, 367, 579

Roseanne 249, 489, 651

Rosenstock-Huessy, Eugene 331

Rosetti, Christina 295

Rose of Lima, Saint 676

Rosmanith, Olga 173

Ross, Joseph 336, 574

Ross, Ruth 283, 381

Rossetti, Christina 550, 558

Rossner, Judith 650

Rostand, Jean 154

Rosten, Leo C. 30, 473

Rothchild, John 73

Rothschild, Madame de 95, 454

Rousseau, Jean-Jacques 74, 84, 104, 275, 396, 515, 544

Roux, Joseph 42, 43, 75, 85, 97, 122, 132, 372, 582

Rowan, Carl T. 393

Rowland, Gena 350

Rowland, Helen 514, 517, 596

Roy, Gabrielle 42

Royal, Darrell 589, 591, 600, 647

Royce, Josiah 173, 253, 256, 261, 598

Rubenstein, Arthur 53

Rubin, Jerry 350, 663

Rubinstein, Arthur 38, 70, 353

Rubinstein, Helena 614

Ruckelshaus, Jill 127

Ruddick, Sara 117

Rudhyar, Dane 380

Rudolph, Wilma 217, 245

Ruffini, Giovanni 495

Rukeyser, Muriel 219, 300, 342, 382, 480, 540, 577, 616, 636, 689

Rule, Jane 9, 68, 261

Rumi, Jelaluddin 350

Runbeck, Margaret Lee 37, 152, 278, 526, 578

Runes, Dagobert D. 129

Ruskin, John 10, 24, 31, 39, 70, 71, 257, 328, 340, 361, 382, 435, 436, 445, 539, 610, 612, 625, 629, 649

Russell, Bertrand 26, 30, 35, 36, 39, 49, 85, 93, 128, 242, 309, 329, 365, 372, 376, 393, 414, 452, 477, 478, 484, 493, 497, 503, 579, 604, 608

Russell, Bertrand A. 491, 496

Russell, Bill 441

Russell, Lady R. 17

Russell, Rosalind 9, 659, 674

Russian proverb 46, 58, 104, 200, 288, 314

Rutherford, Mark 132, 308, 489, 500, 503

Rutherford, Samuel 191

Rutledge, Horace 341

Ryan, Meg 218, 227

Ryle, J.C. 175, 181, 193, 199

Ryuh, Jim 286

S

Sa'di 80, 84, 96, 108, 200, 492, 687

Sacher, Dr. Abram 299

Sackville, Margaret 698

Sackville-West, Vita 232, 237, 503

Sacred ritual chant 86

Sadat, Anwar 400

Sadler, Lena K. 169

Sagan, Françoise 219, 349, 699

Sager, Carole Bayer 454

Sahler, Leslie Jeanne 398

Saint-Exupery, Antoine de 122, 124, 221, 249, 260, 273, 369, 379, 421, 422, 425, 455, 459, 554, 605, 633, 662, 672, 695

Saki 704

Salak, John Charles 672

Sales, Saint Francis de 129, 130, 315, 337, 428, 437, 452, 621, 636, 694, 702

Sallust 147, 259, 535, 552, 566, 595, 676, 686

Sampson, Patricia 261

Sampson, Patty H. 638

Samuelson, Joan Benoit 638

Sanchez, Cristina 492

Sand, George 8, 10, 13, 40, 88, 95, 164, 241, 396

Sandburg, Carl 273, 288, 305, 382, 464, 538

Sane, Doc 593

Sanger, Margaret 56, 261

Sangster, Margaret Elizabeth 44, 95, 171, 286

Sannazaro, Jacopo 347, 694

Sanskrit, The 304

Sanskrit proverb 284

Santayana, George 5, 6, 22, 46, 76, 112, 135, 141, 144, 148, 199, 263, 266, 286, 291, 294, 394, 421, 449, 454, 465, 685

Santmyer, Helen Hoover 94

Sapirstein, Milton R. 96

Sarandon, Susan 95, 441

Sarault, Deidra 3

Sarnoff, David 371, 461, 469, 509

Saroyan, William 40, 70, 654, 700

Sarraute, Nathalie 600

Sarton, May 5, 99, 131, 230, 243, 284, 333, 341, 448, 452, 687

Sartre, Jean-Paul 40, 645, 677

Satir, Virginia 354

Saturday Night and Sunday Morning 466

Saunders, Jeraldine 493

Savant, Marilyn vos 111, 218

Sawyer, Charles 372

Sawyer, Diane 428, 569, 651

Sayers, Dorothy L. 39, 139, 365, 463, 555, 608, 613, 627

Scarf, Maggie 50, 453

Schabacker, Ruth Ann 68

Schaef, Anne Wilson 237, 417, 430, 621, 698

Schaeffer, Francis 78

Schiapirelli, Elsa 25

Schiff, Jacqueline 114

Schiff, Miriam 352, 395, 469

Schiffer, Claudia 663

Schiller, J.C.F. von 10, 22, 35, 53, 222, 250, 258, 297, 304, 314, 371, 378, 387, 412, 421, 431, 466, 470, 484, 493, 512, 513, 515, 522, 530, 532, 540, 543, 550, 566, 567, 591, 670

Schinz, Maria 504

Schlessinger, Dr. Laura 286, 454, 463, 549, 657

Schmidt, Walt 677

Schneider, Diana 350, 415

Schoeder, Caroline 446

Schopenhauer, Arthur 10, 34, 40, 73, 105, 151, 241, 257, 271, 288, 315, 316, 449, 524, 591, 635, 658

Schouler, James 165

Schreiner, Olive 8, 35, 54, 101, 104, 219, 220, 454, 496, 576

Schuller, Dr. Robert H. 167, 656

Schultz, George P. 599

Schulz, Charles M. 38

Schumacher, E.F. 264

Schumann-Heink, Ernestine 461

Schwab, Charles M. 129, 367, 532, 554, 556, 563, 582

Schwarzenegger, Arnold 651, 690

Schweitzer, Albert 23, 27, 46, 101, 114, 119, 260, 285, 387, 439, 471, 576

Schweitzer, Gertrude 103

Scofield, Paul 364

Scolavino, William F. 599

Scott, Anne Firor 617

Scott, Dr. Loretta 120

Scott, Evelyn 111, 454, 601

Scott, George. C. 540

Scott, Hazel 139, 249

Scott, Sir Walter 121, 131, 140, 273, 376, 533, 556, 557, 604, 675, 690

Scott-Maxwell, Florida 139, 233, 243, 254

Scottish proverb 53, 129, 131, 322

Scriven, Joseph 197

Scully, Frank 518, 522

Seabury, David 536, 665

Segall, Lee 80

Seitz, Nick 444

Selden, John 188

Sendak, Maurice 76, 580

Seneca 2, 11, 195

Seneca, Lucius Annaeus 448

Seneca, Marcus Annaeus 17, 26, 29, 52, 54, 57, 61, 62, 68, 69, 70, 72, 75, 78, 79, 80, 81, 85, 93, 103, 117,

145, 148, 223, 235, 242, 250, 272, 280, 283, 316, 320, 337, 347, 396, 416, 429, 431, 442, 443, 458, 459, 478, 479, 480, 481, 484, 485, 488, 494, 508, 512, 513, 522, 523, 525, 529, 530, 533, 561, 578, 588, 596, 606, 675, 681, 685, 698, 703

Senegalese proverb 593

Senzaki, Nyogen 208, 505

Seredy, Kate 244

Sertillanges, A.G. 535

Service, Robert W. 217, 277, 573, 642

Setanti, Joaquin 519

Seton, Anya 323

Seton, Cynthia Propper 214, 329

Seton, Elizabeth Ann 40, 139, 157, 159, 160

Seton, Julia 136

Setter, Maurice 70, 455

Severance, Joan 95

Seville, Saint Isidore of 308

Seward, William H. 402

Sewell, Anna 480, 542

Sexton, Anne 226, 427

Seymour, Jane 10, 283

Shabazz, Betty 394

Shackelford, Ted 263

Shafer, Paul D. 386

Shakespeare, William 55, 57, 70, 75, 83, 84, 85, 92, 108, 130, 143, 183, 186, 194, 205, 229, 240, 244, 251, 259, 260, 275, 276, 287, 289, 291, 297, 305, 321, 324, 331, 332, 335, 336, 337, 359, 374, 377, 429, 451, 481, 487, 497, 505, 534, 535, 538, 550, 566, 632, 633, 635, 645, 662, 689, 691, 695

Shalala, Donna E. 490, 515

Shange, Ntozake 8

Shannon, R. 275

Shapira, Gina 659

Shaprut, Hasdai Ibn 231

Shaughnessy, Susan 674

Shaw, Ann 131

Shaw, Anna Howard 616

Shaw, Artie 298

Shaw, George Bernard 19, 21, 22, 23, 28, 38, 46, 60, 97, 101, 130, 190,

236, 255, 259, 280, 285, 293, 329, 392, 394, 400, 418, 426, 440, 459, 466, 471, 472, 522, 566, 578, 582, 669, 685, 702

Sheehan, Patty 74

Sheehy, Gail 221, 236, 393, 397, 433, 445, 681

Sheen, Fulton J. 158, 256, 341

Sheerin, John B. 16, 257

Sheffield, John 63

Shekerjian, Denise 226

Sheldon, Charles M. 319

Sheldon, William H. 23, 472

Shelley, Mary Wollstonecraft 138, 249, 457

Shelley, Percy Bysshe 235, 297, 333, 375

Shenstone, William 81, 90

Shepard, Odell 396

Shepherd, Cybil 95, 96, 514, 668

Sher, Barbara 62, 226, 307, 330, 512, 517, 552, 553

Sherfey, Mary Jane 79

Sherman, Frank Dempster 314

Sherman, General William T. 455, 528, 602, 698

Sherman, Harold 488

Sherwood, Margaret 22

Shideler, Mary McDermott 624

Shields, Brooke 96

Shields, Carol 217

Shih King, The 481

Shinn, Florence Scovel 116, 355, 358, 381, 423, 470, 523, 646

Shirer, W.L. 17

Shirley, James 45, 92

Shoemaker, Samuel M. 177, 196

Shoffstal, Veronica 327

Shore, Dinah 120

Sibbes, Richard 188

Sidney, Sir Philip 117, 321

Siegel, Bernie S. 4, 45, 233, 373, 504, 506, 689, 697

Sigourney, Lydia H. 342

Sills, Beverly 39, 222, 226, 366, 573, 642, 648, 669, 692

Silone, Ignazio 585

Simmons, Charles 634

Simmons, Edward 673
Simms, Nancy 486
Simms, William Gilmore 549
Simon, Julian 72
Simon, Neil 511
Simons, Minot 458
Simonton, O. Carl 376, 378
Simpson, A.B. 176, 181, 194, 195,
    209, 210
Simpson, Alan 698
Simpson, E.L. 546
Simpson, Louis 370
Simpson, O.J. 260, 446, 491
Simpson, Wallis 395
Sinetar, Marsha 433, 438, 610
Singer, Isaac Bashevis 50, 104, 340,
    356, 453, 629
Sirtis, Marina 96
Sisson, Art 350
Sitwell, Edith 361, 426, 682
Sivananda, Swami 562, 598, 635
Skelton, Philip 21
Slack, W.B. 192
Slaney, Mary Decker 466
Slater, Philip 649
Slick, Grace 315
Slim, W.J. 413
Small Change 70
Smalley, Dave E. 47
Smart, Elizabeth 387
Smedley, Ralph C. 563
Smeltzer, Ruth 284
Smiles, Samuel 370, 572, 641
Smiley, Jane 442, 652
Smith, Adam 14
Smith, Alexander 152, 273, 516, 532,
    635
Smith, Anna Deavere 410
Smith, Belle Eugenia 66
Smith, Bessie 637
Smith, Betty 283
Smith, Dodie 393, 570
Smith, Elizabeth O. 169
Smith, General Oliver Prince 361
Smith, Hannah Whitall 161, 624
Smith, Horace 536
Smith, Horatio 401
Smith, Huston 540

Smith, Jack 271
Smith, Joseph 6
Smith, Julie O. 330
Smith, Lillian 170, 330, 505
Smith, Liz 16, 554, 555, 612
Smith, Logan Pearsall 10, 34, 71, 133,
    144, 319, 331, 434, 473, 508, 530,
    567, 574, 607, 611
Smith, Margaret Chase 214, 599
Smith, Mortimer 47
Smith, Patti 440, 679
Smith, R. 637
Smith, Roy L. 77, 242, 320
Smith, Stan 242
Smith, Sydney 74, 281, 284, 299, 308,
    317, 374, 419, 434, 435, 438, 485,
    546, 576, 610, 704
Snead, Audrey 291, 343
Snow, C.P. 18
Snow, Carrie 627
Snowden, Roscoe 534
Sockman, Ralph W. 286, 529, 693
Socrates 6, 145, 194, 292, 439, 460,
    555, 557, 655
Sokoloff, Dr. Boris 11
Sölle, Dorothy 111, 112
Solomon 147, 379
Solon 80, 97
Solzhenitsyn, Aleksandr 11, 512
Somerset, Lady Henry 124
Sondheim, Stephen 86
Sondreal, Palmer 18
Song of Solomon 2:11–12 333
Sontag, Susan 45, 80, 216, 233, 298,
    304, 545
Soong Mei-Ling 191
Sophocles 5, 35, 38, 128, 130, 143,
    200, 258, 260, 272, 354, 411, 429,
    489, 544, 568, 586, 613, 674
Sorel, Julia 490, 513
Soubirous, Bernadette 157
Soutar, Andrew 673
South 669
Spahn, Warren 266
Spalding, George Lancaster 173
Spalding, John Lancaster 41, 164, 277,
    429, 481, 527
Spangler, David 547

Spanish proverb 28, 75, 122, 134, 143, 147, 152, 159, 202, 216, 464, 465, 473, 484, 515, 551, 567, 606, 660, 688

Spark, Muriel 108, 238, 243

Speakman, Frederick 407

Special Olympics 624

Speers, Theodore C. 114

Spellman, Archbishop Francis J. 199

Spencer, Herbert 276, 391

Spender, J.A. 308

Spender, Stephen 246

Spinks, Michael 511

Spinoza, Baruch 58, 169, 375, 441, 463, 493, 497, 695, 702

Spock, Dr. Benjamin 19

Spolin, Viola 106

Sprat, Thomas 75

Spurgeon, Charles Haddon 177, 181, 186, 187, 189, 202, 207, 208, 213, 590, 644, 681

Spyri, Johanna 93

Sri Krishna 332

St. Johns, Adela Rogers 334

Staël, Madame de 60, 113, 119, 211, 299, 331, 364, 569, 718

Stafford, William 643

Stainback, Arthur H. 125

Stair, Nadine 281, 285, 665

Stallone, Sasha 316

Stallone, Sylvester 91, 424, 428, 432, 571, 641, 674

Stanford, Sally 696

Stanislaus I, King 166, 504, 524

Stanislaw, Jerzy Lec 164

Stanley, Bessie A. 580

Stanley, Mrs. Herman 548

Stanton, Elizabeth Cady 108, 220, 233, 508, 538, 680

Starhawk 161, 336, 548, 596

Stark, Admiral Harold R. 272

Stark, Freya 7, 20, 163, 233, 238, 290, 390, 404, 545

Starr, Pamela Vaull 382, 473

Statius 478, 505

Stead, Christina 366

Stebbing, L. Susan 88

Steere, Douglas V. 62, 646

Steichen, Edward 263

Steichen, Joanna T. 225

Steifel, Herbert J. 411

Stein, Gertrude 2, 102, 220, 238, 241, 243, 256, 407, 426, 430, 492, 494, 499

Steinbaum, Rosemary Konner 254

Steinbeck, John 76, 288, 315, 322, 359, 478, 509, 578

Steinem, Gloria 241, 244, 378, 438, 527, 570, 575

Steiner, Rudolph 212, 295

Stekhel, Dr. Wilhelm 151

Stendhal 38, 331, 694

Stengel, Casey 577

Stephanie of Monaco, Princess 91

Stephen, Caroline 426

Sterling, John 420

Stern, Ellen Sue 225, 455

Stern, Gladys Browyn 79

Sterne, Laurence 61, 303, 557

Stettinius, E.R. 36

Stevens, Abel 351

Stevenson, Anne 138

Stevenson, John 236, 560

Stevenson, Robert Louis 9, 25, 35, 37, 69, 134, 149, 202, 258, 280, 287, 318, 390, 402, 415, 426, 429, 459, 486, 493, 519, 533, 537, 548, 551, 577, 578, 594, 646, 660, 668

Stewart, George David 175

Stewart, Martha 315

Stewart, Mary W. 523

Stilkind, Marie 48

Stimson, Henry L. 353, 359, 377

Stingray 456

Stock, Eleanor B. 104

Stoddard, R.H. 88

Stokes, Rose Pastor 116, 211

Stone, Elizabeth 151

Stone, Lucy 113, 223, 343, 428, 463

Stone, W. Clement 70, 362, 487, 671, 689

Storey, David 132

Storm, Hyemeyohsts 397, 405

Stowe, Harriet Beecher 133, 157, 244, 254, 304, 550, 647

Stratford, Bishop John de 195

Straub, Peter 701
Stravinsky, Igor 303
Strecker, Edward A. 648
Streep, Meryl 250
Street, D.M. 155, 158
Streisand, Barbra 92, 218, 418
Strindberg, August 21
Strode, Muriel 519
Strug, Kerri 270
Struthers, Sally 103
Struven, Mildred W. 681
Stryon, William 431
Stuart, General J.E.B. 242
Stuart, Janet Erskine 412, 428, 553,
    592, 645, 686
Stuart, Mary 297
Stukane, Eileen 71
Styron, William 230, 451
Sucking, Sir John 455
Suenens, L.J. Cardinal 374, 603
Suetonius 322
Sullivan, William L. 524
Summerskill, Baroness Edith 107
Sumner, William Graham 249, 355,
    416, 628
Sunde, Karen 8
Suso, Henry 629
Suttner, Bertha von 104, 252
Sutton, Don 588, 697
Swahili proverb 623
Swanson, Gloria 609
Sweaney, James E. 662, 692
Swedish proverb 15, 251, 264, 494
Sweeney, James E. 349
Sweeney, Paul 483
Sweetland, Ben 27, 116, 577
Swetchine, Anne-Sophie 12, 60, 111,
    241, 244, 386, 514
Swetchine, Madame 39, 104, 684
Swift, Jonathan 147, 212, 270, 308,
    379, 400, 401, 434, 526
Swinburne, Algernon 288, 404
Swindoll, Charles 600
Swinnerton, Frank 76, 472, 673
Switzer, Maurice 460
Swope, Herbert Bayard 561, 673
Sylva, Carmen 242
Symonds, John Addington 125

Symons, Arthur 609
Syrus, Publilius 11, 42, 46, 65, 80,
    101, 105, 132, 137, 143, 147, 282,
    388, 404, 412, 415, 482, 483, 515,
    522, 544, 553, 566, 587, 590, 595,
    605, 637, 663, 672, 693
Szasz, Thomas 59, 89, 255, 432

T

Taber, Gladys 168, 242, 465
Tabito, Otoma no 465
Tagore, Rabindranath 278, 289, 315,
    393, 421, 429
Takeda, Kiyoko 294
Talmage, T. DeWitt 465
Talmud 120, 191, 307, 388, 391, 450,
    540, 672
Tan, Amy 218, 252
Tangye, Sir Richard 274
Tannen, Deborah 617
Tanqueray, Adolphe 169
Tarbell, Ida 234
Tarkington, Booth 77
Tartakower, Savielly Grigorievitch 660
Tate, Allen 456, 550
Tatelbaum, Judy 42
Tawney, R.H. 12
Taylor, Ann 273
Taylor, Bayard 157
Taylor, Elizabeth 95, 223, 516, 615
Taylor, G. Aiken 599
Taylor, Harold 118
Taylor, Ida Scott 557
Taylor, J. Hudson 194
Taylor, Jane 127, 159, 336
Taylor, Jeremy 78, 124, 180
Taylor, Lisa 397
Taylor, Susan 351
Tead, Ordway 651
Teale, Edwin Way 264, 308, 314, 369,
    564
Teasdale, Sara 51, 82, 362, 695
Teekens, Inga 398
Tehyi Hsieh 147, 504, 553
Teilhard de Chardin, Pierre 543
Teixeira, Ada 572
Telgen, John 694
Temple, William 191, 201

Tennyson, Lord 36, 87, 165, 169, 201, 238, 246, 404, 549, 583, 598, 620, 649, 653

Ten Boom, Corrie 60, 160, 161, 213, 471, 495, 656, 664

Terence 49, 89, 149, 376, 452, 539, 552, 588

Teresa, Mother 105, 114, 141, 204, 238, 264, 276, 306, 373, 387, 625, 629, 653

Teresa of Avila 111, 153, 155, 159, 164, 166, 168, 169, 193, 206, 207, 215, 230, 235, 332, 333, 348, 452, 484, 528, 648, 651, 677, 679, 698

Terrell, Mary Church 382

Tersteegen, Gerhard 153

Tertullian 375

Texas Guinan 578

Thackeray, William Makepeace 522, 685

Thalberg, Irving 97

Thales 217

Thatcher, Margaret 236, 242, 283, 398, 463, 468, 568, 588, 599, 631, 654

Thaxter, Celia 319

Thayer, Nancy 378, 398

Theisen, Kathleen Casey 44

Theophrastus 273, 288

Thérèse of Lisieux 99, 104, 157, 162, 164, 529, 550

Therous, Phyllis 659

Thirkell, Angela 526

Thoele, Sue Patton 33

Thomain, Puzant 151

Thomas, Danny 105, 581

Thomas, David 21

Thomas, Dylan 258, 329

Thomas, Edith M. 505

Thomas, Gwyn 77

Thomas, Louisa 366

Thomas, Marlo 326, 501, 577

Thomas, Rosie 263

Thomas à Kempis 45, 47, 55, 60, 91, 155, 157, 196, 198, 216, 223, 227, 579

Thompson, Dorothy 62, 477, 527

Thompson, Dr. Perle 667

Thompson, Emma 570

Thompson, Francis 393, 552

Thompson, Kay 331

Thompson, Lea 682

Thomson, James 73

Thomson, Linda 215

Thoreau, Henry David 11, 45, 52, 71, 82, 83, 117, 124, 134, 145, 150, 155, 163, 215, 223, 229, 246, 257, 265, 276, 289, 313, 318, 346, 353, 360, 370, 396, 428, 450, 451, 454, 459, 467, 472, 524, 525, 531, 561, 568, 569, 611, 613, 629, 653, 702

Thornton, Agnes 503

Thucydides 131, 512

Thurber, James 518, 524

Thurston, Katherine Cecil 638

Tibetan master, A 49

Tibolt, Frank 554

Tillich, Paul 159, 171, 227, 329, 488

Tillotson 548

Tilton, Theodore 333

Tingley, Katherine 492

Tinker, Grant 579

Titzel, Margaret 456

Tocqueville, Alexis de 434, 438, 532, 576, 589

Todd, J.R. 643

Todd, Mike 334, 361

Toffler, Alvin 634

Tolstaya, Tatyana 682

Tolstoy, Leo 24, 29, 49, 171, 212, 265, 331, 337, 348, 404, 694

Tomlin, Lily 207, 236, 250, 544, 579

Tongan proverb 149

Tooke, Horne 359

Torre, Joe 535

Tossetti, Christina Georgina 41

Tower, Virginia Burden 518, 617

Towne, Laura 613

Toynbee, Arnold J. 371, 443

Tozer, A.W. 186, 191, 581

Tracy, Spencer 267

Trapp, John 190

Trappist monk 202

Trenary, Jill 504

Trench, Archbishop 666

Trench, Richard C. 112
Treves, Sir Frederick 647
Trevino, Lee 476, 601, 660
Tricky, Sister Mary 488
Trine, Ralph Waldo 317, 666
Triolet, Elsa 276
Trollope, Anthony 231, 247
Trueblood, Elton 18
Truman, Harry S. 284, 285, 385, 410, 416, 561, 615, 620, 630, 699
Truman, Margaret 515, 533
Trump, Donald 305, 443, 584
Truth, Sojourner 191, 551, 658
Tsvetaeva, Marina 261
Tucker, Abraham 51, 68
Tucker, Sophie 13, 262, 570, 648
Tunis, John R. 573, 642
Tunnell, Sophie 491
Turkish proverb 132, 143, 147, 310, 397, 605
Turmell, Kitte 21
Turnbull, Agnes 48, 279
Turner, Kathleen 245
Turner, Tina 216
Twain, Mark 12, 21, 28, 41, 66, 83, 103, 119, 124, 137, 140, 185, 223, 242, 256, 280, 321, 372, 379, 386, 399, 401, 409, 445, 466, 499, 519, 533, 547, 584, 594, 612, 676
Tweed, Ordway 168
Tweedie, Jill 627
Tweedy, Henry H. 491
Twelve Steps and Twelve Traditions 178, 195, 196, 624, 627
Tyger, Frank 98, 115, 249, 273
Tyler, Anne 140
Tyson, Cicely 387, 684

U
Ueland, Brenda 6, 107, 226, 423, 445, 479, 538
Uhnak, Dorothy 111, 551
Ukrainian proverb 447
Ullman, James Ramsey 420
Ullmann, Liv 134, 249, 354, 579
Ulmer, Ernestine 501
Unamuno, Miguel de 55, 166, 168, 360, 491

Underhill, Evelyn 16, 698
Undset, Sigrid 293
United Technologies Corporation 72, 634
Updegraff, Robert R. 37, 278, 578, 680
Uris, Leon 440, 459
Ustinov, Peter 63

V
Vail, Theodore N. 500, 656
Valery 543
Valois, Marguerite de 100
Valois, Ninette de 107
Vanbee, Martin 388, 672
Vandenberg, Arthur 596
Vanderbilt, Gloria 123, 618
Vanderlip, Frank A. 144
Vanier, Jean 98, 229, 451
Vann, Gerald 119, 200
Van Buren, Abigail 56, 62, 103, 447, 449, 510, 687
Van Der Post, Laurens 486
Van Dooren, L.A.T. 178
Van Doren, Mark 302
Van Dyke, Henry 2, 70, 287, 484
Van Gogh, Vincent 54, 122, 351, 423, 485, 511, 532, 600, 632
Van Horne, Harriet 612
Van Horne, William 207
Van Rensselaer, Mariana Griswold 67
Van Slyke, Helen 242
Van Zeller, Hubert 178
Van Zeller, Hubert 2
Vare, Daniele 447
Varro, Marcus Terentius 260
Vaughan, Bill 661
Vaughan, Roger 519
Vauvenargues 40, 50, 86, 107, 136, 268, 369, 374, 375, 400, 410, 414, 421, 422, 434, 441, 467, 479, 483, 521, 536, 553, 556, 565, 593
Veeck, Bill 69
Vega, Lope de 98
Verdi 434
Vernon, Lillian 356
Victoria, Queen 343
Villanueva, Alma 254

Viorst, Judith 7, 8, 343, 603
Virgil 36, 70, 105, 245, 334, 335, 344, 347, 365, 476, 478, 492, 522, 547, 588, 649
Viscot, David 511
Viscount Cecil 532
Voltaire 9, 50, 55, 154, 165, 187, 388, 453, 466, 480, 492, 502, 551, 585, 659, 693
Vonnegut, Kurt 89, 360, 604
Von Braun, Wernher 352, 544
Von Clausewitz, Karl 455
Von Furstenberg, Diane 511, 514
Voronel, Nina 167
Vorse, Mary Heaton 547
Vreeland, Diana 95

W

Waddles, Charleszetta 156, 380
Wade, Joseph Marshall 146
Wade, Virginia 444
Wagner, Jane 229, 535
Wainwright, John 533
Waitely, Denis 274
Waldoks, Moshe 699
Walesa, Lech 166, 488
Walford, W.W. 198, 203
Walker, Alice 126, 151, 160, 259, 387, 432, 536
Walker, Harold B. 495
Walker, Lou Ann 106
Walker, Madame C.J. 549
Walker, Philipa 285
Walker, Stuart 531, 533, 567
Wallace, John Aikman 174
Wallace, Mike 584, 590
Walpole, Horace 13, 47, 142, 480
Walpole, Hugh 22, 24, 53, 660
Walsh, Basil S. 460
Walsh, Tom 38
Walters, Barbara 5, 229, 238, 242, 417, 432, 442, 452, 616
Walters, Dottie 581
Walters, Lily 624
Walters, Reverend R. 337
Walton, Izaak 72, 125
Walton, Sir John 362
Walton, William H. 61

Wandor, Michelene 666
Wang Yang-Ming 661
Ward, Artemus 52
Ward, Barbara 502, 658
Ward, C.M. 58
Ward, Mary Augusta 111
Ward, William A. 77, 562, 572, 641, 664, 676
Warner, Charles Dudley 26, 47, 141, 230, 451
Warner, Susan 686
Warner, Sylvia Townsend 343, 428
Warren, Robert Penn 366
Warren, Samuel 657
Washington, Booker T. 283, 574, 658
Washington, George 22, 128, 145, 146, 471, 551, 692
Washington, Martha 29, 39, 348
Wasserstein, Wendy 224
Waterman, Nixon 302, 499
Watkins, Susan M. 577
Watson, Lillian Eichler 88, 291
Watson, Thomas 186, 207, 209, 210, 360
Watson, Thomas J. 509, 541
Wattleton, Faye 101
Watts, Alan 51, 262, 265, 304, 307
Watts, Isaac 61, 256
Waugh, Alec 89, 323
Waugh, Evelyn 129, 391
Wavell, Sir Archibald 437
Wayne, John 294, 360, 534
Weatherford, Cathy Warner 385
Weatherly, G. 2, 64
Weaver, Sigourney 220
Webb, Beatrice Potter 504, 619
Webb, Mary 86, 108, 141
Webster, Daniel 582, 673
Webster, John 584
Wedgwood, C.V. 680
Weeks, Claire 335
Weeks, Edward 485
Weidman, Jerome 423
Weil, Simone 39, 60, 62, 70, 113, 115, 152, 242, 304, 326, 426, 598, 685
Weinberg, George 376
Weiner, Norbert 415
Weissmuller, John 267

Weitzman, Geri 254
Welby, Amelia C. 298
Welch, Raquel 220, 224, 246, 419
Weldon, Fay 46, 220, 233, 354, 500, 648
Weller, Frances Ward 150
Wellesley, Arthur 477, 579
Wells, Albert M. 112, 414
Wells, Carolyn 343, 414
Wells, H.G. 53, 296, 325, 334, 402
Welsh proverb 640
Welty, Eudora 298, 507, 519, 577
Wesley, Charles 180, 194
Wesley, John 169, 194, 422, 502
West, Dame Rebecca 262, 358
West, E.N. 112
West, Jessamyn 66, 106, 109, 531, 662, 678, 697
West, Mae 74, 86, 95, 365, 460, 509, 517, 553
West, Meredith 398
West, Morris 308
West, Rebecca 128, 134, 433, 465, 666
Westcott, Bishop 690
Westcott, Edward Noyes 402
Westermayer, H.U. 78
Westheimer, Dr. Ruth 349, 689
Westmoreland, General William 529
Wharton, Edith 19, 150, 414, 517, 668
Whately, Richard 101, 660
Wheatley, Margaret J. 393
Whistling Elk, Agnes 432, 518
White, Betty 135
White, E.B. 495
White, Hugh 671
White, Stewart E. 222
White, William Allen 304, 309, 324, 401, 442, 481
Whitehead, Alfred North 142, 295, 296, 304, 363, 394, 417, 511, 527, 636
Whitehorn, Katharine 434
Whitman, Marina von Neumann 390
Whitman, Walt 79, 114, 155, 224, 268, 400, 504, 579
Whitney, Joseph 582
Whitney, Phyllis 444
Whittemore, Flora 585

Whittier, John Greenleaf 86, 153, 159, 160, 165, 172, 174, 189, 299, 305, 329, 334, 479, 517
Whittlesey, Faith 219
Wholey, Dennis 36, 449, 625
Whyte, Alexander 210
Whyte, Edna Gardner 109
Wicker, John 353, 593
Widdemer, Margaret 550
Wiebe, Bernie 298
Wieder, Marcia 119, 383, 427, 470, 556
Wiederkehr, Macrina 253, 562
Wiesel, Elie 600
Wigmore, Ann 190, 365
Wilberforce, William 185
Wilcox, Colleen 109
Wilcox, Ella Wheeler 7, 36, 46, 86, 107, 127, 136, 140, 187, 225, 319, 360, 394, 415, 427, 679, 699
Wilcox, Frederick B. 515, 567
Wilde, Oscar 34, 57, 65, 69, 89, 206, 264, 297, 390, 395, 401, 422, 444, 463, 466, 469, 509, 517, 680, 694
Wilder, Billy 294, 417, 457
Wilder, Laura Ingalls 25
Wilder, Thornton 38, 53, 54, 97, 278, 314, 325, 335, 545, 699
Wilkinson, Marguerite 32
Willey, Charley 27
William, Charles 65
Williams, Ben Ames 523, 658
Williams, Bern 649
Williams, Frank Curtis 259, 565
Williams, Heather 357
Williams, Robin 421
Williams, Ted 441
Williams, Tennessee 290, 312, 324, 364, 398, 434, 481, 503, 509, 513, 562, 578, 590, 608, 675, 678
Williams, Terry Tempest 164
Williams, Vanessa 581
Williams, William Carlos 288, 651, 671, 700
Williamson, Marianne 67, 116, 117, 403, 482
Wilmot, John 534
Wilson, Angus 97

Wilson, Ethel 331
Wilson, Flip 515, 567
Wilson, Frederick B. 549
Wilson, Geoffrey B. 185
Wilson, Henry B. 346, 399, 400
Wilson, John M. 442, 446, 478
Wilson, Oliver C. 701
Wilson, Reverend Oliver G. 621
Wilson, Woodrow 101, 124, 147, 337, 403, 405
Wiman, Erastus 133
Winder, Barbara W. 40
Winfrey, Oprah 62, 70, 109, 138, 140, 235, 326, 420, 483, 492, 589
Winnemucca, Sarah 111, 343, 351
Winsor, Kathleen 357, 616
Winterburn, Florence H. 143
Winters, Jonathan 261
Winters, Shelley 362, 653, 703
Winterson, Jeanette 385
Wise, Stephen S. 112
Witherspoon, John 490
Wittgenstein, Ludwig 41, 303, 411
Wolf, Naomi 428
Wolfe, Thomas 349, 435, 439, 576, 581, 667
Wolfe, W. Beran 21, 279
Wolff, Ruth 20
Wolff, Victoria 62
Wonder, Stevie 379
Woodberry, George E. 104, 131, 299, 315, 418, 425
Wooden, John 574
Woodhull, Nancy 504
Woodhull, Victoria Claffin 551
Woodlock, Thomas F. 594, 680
Woodman, Marion 62, 526
Woodruff, Julia Louise 582, 643
Woods, Harriet 80
Woods, Ralph L. 391
Woodward, Joanne 392
Woodward, William E. 584
Woolf, Virginia 48, 126, 138, 152, 215, 298, 381, 463
Woolson, Constance Fenimore 429
Woosnam, Phil 266
Wordsworth, William 169, 261, 491, 629

Work of the Chariot, The 155
World War II refugee 161
Worsham, James A. 259, 531, 532, 565, 568
Wozniak, Angela L. 479
Wright, Frank Lloyd 340, 561, 571, 641
Wright, Gordon 297
Wright, Richard 424
Wrigley, William 244, 477, 505
Wylie, Elinor 350
Wyse, Lois 404

Y

Yakima Indian Nation 287
Yalow, Rosalyn Sussman 667
Yard, Molly 244
Yasunari Kawabata 155, 162
Yeager, Chuck 287
Yeats, William Butler 31, 311, 421
Yevtushenko, Yevgeny 97
Yezierska, Anzia 677
Yiddish proverb 57, 334, 539, 594, 649, 688
Yogananda, Paramahansa 63, 118, 128
Yost, Fielding 577
Young, Cy 646
Young, Edward 13, 39, 91, 169, 325, 468, 557
Young, Eva 553
Young, Leontine 223
Young, Owen D. 530, 567
Young, Robert M. 300
Yourcenar, Marguerite 403, 680
Ywahoo, Dhyani 306

Z

Zaharias, Babe Didrikson 467, 652
Zangwill, Israel 294
Zen maxim 606
Zeno 36, 632
Zen saying 330, 437
Ziege, W.W. 343
Zinn, Howard 548
Zolde, Henrietta 296
Zusya of Hanipoli 430
Zworykin, Vladimir 224, 253, 532, 557